Studia Fennica
Historica 21

The Finnish Literature Society (SKS) was founded in 1831 and has, from the very beginning, engaged in publishing operations. It nowadays publishes literature in the fields of ethnology and folkloristics, linguistics, literary research and cultural history.

The first volume of the Studia Fennica series appeared in 1933. Since 1992, the series has been divided into three thematic subseries: Ethnologica, Folkloristica and Linguistica. Two additional subseries were formed in 2002, Historica and Litteraria. The subseries Anthropologica was formed in 2007.

In addition to its publishing activities, the Finnish Literature Society maintains research activities and infrastructures, an archive containing folklore and literary collections, a research library and promotes Finnish literature abroad.

Studia Fennica Editorial board
Editors-in-chief
Pasi Ihalainen, Professor, University of Jyväskylä, Finland
Timo Kaartinen, Title of Docent, University Lecturer, University of Helsinki, Finland
Taru Nordlund, Professor, University of Helsinki, Finland
Riikka Rossi, Title of Docent, University Researcher, University of Helsinki, Finland
Katriina Siivonen, Title of Docent, University Teacher, University of Turku, Finland
Lotte Tarkka, Professor, University of Helsinki, Finland

Deputy editors-in-chief
Eeva Berglund, Title of Docent, University of Helsinki, Finland
Anne Heimo, Title of Docent, University of Turku, Finland
Saija Isomaa, Professor, University of Tampere, Finland
Sari Katajala-Peltomaa, Title of Docent, Researcher, University of Tampere, Finland
Eerika Koskinen-Koivisto, Postdoctoral Researcher, Dr. Phil., University of Helsinki, Finland
Laura Visapää, Title of Docent, University Lecturer, University of Helsinki, Finland

Tuomas M. S. Lehtonen, Secretary General, Dr. Phil., Finnish Literature Society, Finland
Tero Norkola, Publishing Director, Finnish Literature Society
Kati Romppanen, Secretary of the Board, Finnish Literature Society, Finland

oa.finlit.fi

Editorial Office
SKS
P.O. Box 259
FI-00171 Helsinki
www.finlit.fi

Sofia Kotilainen

Literacy Skills as Local Intangible Capital

The History of a Rural Lending Library
c. 1860–1920

Finnish Literature Society · SKS · Helsinki

Studia Fennica Historica 21

The publication has undergone a peer review.

The open access publication of this volume has received part funding via
a Jane and Aatos Erkko Foundation grant.

© 2016 Sofia Kotilainen and SKS
License CC-BY-NC-ND 4.0. International

A digital edition of a printed book first published in 2016 by the Finnish Literature Society.
Cover Design: Timo Numminen
EPUB: Tero Salmén

ISBN 978-952-222-739-3 (Print)
ISBN 978-952-222-796-6 (PDF)
ISBN 978-952-222-797-3 (EPUB)

ISSN 0085-6835 (Studia Fennica)
ISSN 1458-526X (Studia Fennica Historica)

DOI: https://doi.org/10.21435/sfh.21

This work is licensed under a Creative Commons CC-BY-NC-ND 4.0. International License.
To view a copy of the license, please visit http://creativecommons.org/licenses/by-nc-nd/4.0/

A free open access version of the book is available at https://doi.org/10.21435/sfh.21
or by scanning this QR code with your mobile device.

Contents

Preface 8

1. **Introduction: A Library for the People? 9**
   Have the books on popular lending libraries already been written and read? 9
   Previous research on rural literacy and the significance of libraries in the countryside 20
   Why libraries influenced the common people's reading skills 31
   Less known library archives and the methods utilised in researching them 41

2. **The Foundation of a Local Lending Library 59**
   What kind of world were the people's libraries born into? 59
   The slow shift towards functional reading skills 59
   A revolution in ideals: popular education as part of the Fennoman ideology 68
   The slow modernization of the society of the estates under the scourge of a natural catastrophe 74
   Why were the lending libraries established? 80
   The early history of Finnish libraries 80
   The foundation for lending libraries created by reading societies and fee-charging libraries 84
   The birth of Finnish people's libraries, initially in the urban centres 88
   The enlightening and educative background to the birth of popular libraries in the countryside 92
   The book collections of the church parish: the early years of Kivijärvi library 99
   The establishment of Kivijärvi lending library 99
   The re-establishment of Kivijärvi lending library 107
   A closely-knit sawmill community as a centre of informational capital 113
   Sawmilling in the middle of the wilds 113
   The birth of the library in the Tichanoff era 116

      The traditions of the sawmill library continued by Leppälänkylä lending library 123
      The Evangelical movement flourishes in northern Central Finland 127

3. **The Founders and the Care of the Collection** 132
   The founders, the operational principles and the Fennoman ideology 132
      The operational principles of Kivijärvi lending library 132
      The founders and members of the board of governors of Kivijärvi lending library 139
   The librarians and the premises 146
      Librarianship: a supplementary duty for elementary school teachers, members of the clergy and cantors 146
      The gradual professionalization of librarianship 151
      Rural libraries without their own premises 156
      Opening times of libraries 160
   The funding and acquisition of the collections 167
      The financial position of the library 167
      The acquisition of books by Kivijärvi lending library 175
   The organization of the library and practical lending activities 184
      The ideal of precise order and regulated operations 184
      The lending and care of books and the imposition of fines 190

4. **The Book Collections** 197
   The extent and the contents of the collections 197
      The value of the collections and the genres of literature in them 197
      Loans statistics of the Kivijärvi lending library 201
   The oldest collection of the church parish library 206
      The most borrowed works in the period 1877–1897 206
      The influence of traditional Pietist literature on the Evangelical revival 212
   The collection of the privately founded library 216
      The rise of the novel 216
      Works of popular enlightenment 225
   New acquisitions at the turn of the century 231
      Realist literature in people's libraries 231
      Translated and Finnish literature 236

5. **The Rural People as Readers** 240
   The rural population's opportunities for reading 240
      The weak reading and writing skills of the people of Kivijärvi 240
      The roots of the Finnish school system in Lutheran popular education 244
   The ownership of books and private collections 247
      The clergy and revivalist movements as disseminators of Finnish-language literature 247

The acquisition of books on trips to town 252
　　　The ownership of books on the basis of the evidence of deeds
　　　　of estate 257
　　The customers of Kivijärvi lending library 265
　　　The age and gender of the borrowers 265
　　　The social groups and places of abode of the borrowers 269
　　　The most assiduous users of the library 274
　　　The reading and writing abilities of the library's customers 276
　　'Borrower profiles', short biographies of readers 279
　　　Different rural readers 279
　　　A portrait of the Kivijärvi reader 287

6. **Readership and Reader Response: Why the library failed to attract readers and ensure its survival 291**
　　The end of Kivijärvi lending library 291
　　Achieving the founders' goals and satisfying the readers' needs 298

Appendix 1: Index of persons involved with the libraries of Kivijärvi and members of their families 310
Appendix 2: The populations of the church and civic parishes of Kivijärvi, Kinnula and Kannonkoski by decade 1730–1960 316
Appendix 3: The ministers of Kivijärvi up till 1959 318
Appendix 4: History of the Finnish-Language Publishing Business 320

Bibliography 326
Abstract 352
Index of Names 353
Index of Place Names 360

Preface

People's libraries constituted an essential element in popular enlightenment work carried out by supporters of the Finnish national ideal in the countryside in the nineteenth century together with the establishment of elementary schools and the activities of organizations and associations that promoted national values. Since there was no universal compulsory education in Finland at the time, all voluntary and even charitable activities aimed at educating the common people were held in high esteem by members of the higher social groups. But what did the poorer elements of the agricultural population think of all this, and how did they receive these endeavours? To what extent did the enlightenment work produce results that led to an increase in functional reading and writings skills in the remote countryside? In this book I address these questions and others by examining the birth and life of a people's library in rural Central Finland.

This research was carried out as part of a Finnish Academy doctoral research project (The Benefits of Literacy in Everyday Life: The impacts of improved literacy on the opportunities for social advancement in remote local communities [c. 1800–1930], 2011–2014). I am grateful for the funding I received and for the working space provided for me for the duration of the project by the Department of History and Ethnology of the University of Jyväskylä. I further thank the Publishing Committee of the Finnish Literature Society for finally approving the book for publication. Many thanks are likewise due to the editor-in-chief of the Studia Fennica Historica series, Professor Pasi Ihalainen. I also thank the publishing coordinator Kati Romppanen and the publishing editor Eija Hukka for their seamless cooperation in preparing the work for publication. In addition, I owe a debt of gratitude to all the archives and libraries that I have visited during my research work. I further thank Jari Järvinen, who drew the maps 1–2 for the book. My warm thanks also go to Gerard McAlester for his expert language editing of the research.

Rauhala, Kivijärvi 1/4/ 2016
Sofia Kotilainen

1. Introduction: A Library for the People?

Have the books on popular lending libraries already been written and read?

The birth of the Finnish lending libraries examined in this book is connected with a long-term Western European trend that had been continuing ever since the time of the Renaissance. It was this trend, which saw the creation and reinforcement of the rural population's enthusiasm for reading[1] (and the desire of people of the higher classes to strengthen it for popular educational or nationalist reasons) that made the lending libraries necessary.[2] The European libraries of the eighteenth century were typically subscription libraries. In Europe, the ideal of public libraries that were freely available to all sections of the population gradually spread from Britain to other countries.[3] In France, municipal libraries had been established in the aftermath of the Revolution and were part of its heritage.[4] Although the history of libraries goes back well into the Middle Ages in Britain and Ireland, there too public lending libraries intended for all social classes only became common in the course of the nineteenth century. In Britain, municipal libraries funded by local taxation were established after the Public Libraries Act (1850). In the Nordic countries (Denmark, Finland, Iceland, Norway and Sweden), legislation on public libraries was enacted considerably later, in the twentieth century, although these countries had begun to provide financial support for libraries before the laws were passed.[5]

Public libraries were created in all the Nordic countries at about the same time, at the turn of the nineteenth and twentieth centuries. They were modelled on the public libraries in North America, for which the development of libraries in Britain had in turn served as a model. In the mid-nineteenth century, the libraries in the United States, too, were still 'social libraries',[6] until the first municipal libraries supported by tax revenues were founded in the late 1870s. On the other hand, the libraries intended for the

---

1   Lyons 2010, 119; Mäkinen 1997, 15–19.
2   Black 1996, 45–46; Karjalainen 1977; Mäkinen 1997.
3   Chartier 1987, 215; Martino 1990, 854–859; Skouvig 2007, 224; Torstensson 1996, 12, 22.
4   Barnett 1973; Markiewicz 2000, 17.
5   Black 2006b, 25–26; Leedham-Green & Webber 2006; Table 1.
6   Crawford 2007; Shera 1949, 51–126.

common people gradually changed from charitable works into institutions for self-improvement.[7] The Public Library Movement came into being in the mid-nineteenth century in Boston, where public ownership and free use of the library for all were implemented for the first time.[8]

Training in librarianship commenced in America in the course of the nineteenth century, and Melvil Dewey developed an American cataloguing and a classification system, thereby advancing the profession of librarian in a more scientific and professional direction from the 1870s on.[9] The American public libraries were open free of charge to everyone and were maintained by public funding. Usually their operations were also regulated by legislation. These same principles were adopted in the Nordic countries, where public libraries were born out the traditions established by church libraries (going back to the seventeenth century), reading societies (beginning in the eighteenth century), people's libraries (the forerunners of public libraries, established from the beginning of the nineteenth century on) and elementary school libraries (established in Finland usually in the latter half of the nineteenth century), and they continued the activities of these earlier local libraries, which were generally intended for the use of the common people.[10]

There are many rural public libraries in Finland which, after the First, or at the latest, the Second World War, became libraries owned and funded exclusively by the municipalities and intended for the use of all their inhabitants. However, many of them still preserve books from the end of the nineteenth century, although they perhaps show a little wear and tear and the patina of time. Some of them are from even earlier decades. Why have these older collections survived in the modern libraries? Because the history of Finnish public libraries is usually considered to have begun already in the latter half of the nineteenth century in the days when the first lending libraries, or people's libraries, were founded in the countryside, the modern public libraries have considered it to be totally natural that these old collections, which are often separately located from the library's main collection of books as an 'older layer', should be preserved. And although the operations of some of the old popular libraries did not necessarily continue without a break into the middle of the twentieth century, the collections of these old libraries are usually reverently conserved as a reminder of the continuum of the library's activities into modern times.

When working at a summer job in my home parish library about fifteen years ago, I came across such a collection of old books. Its existence was not exactly 'news' to me because at that time I already knew something about the history of libraries in Finland. But when I examined the collection more closely, it brought in a concrete form a fresh perspective on the history of the library of my home community. At the same time, it shattered the simple

---

7   Held 1963; Rubin 2004, 273–274.
8   Vatanen 2002, 12; Shera 1949, 157–181.
9   Garrison 1979, 5, 106; Rubin 2004, 439–443. In the nineteenth century, the practices of German scholarly libraries provided a model for libraries in the USA too. Vatanen 2002, 27.
10 Eide 2010; Byberg 2009; Mäkinen 2009g, 109–114; Rubin 2004, 284–285; Torstensson 2009.

and consistent picture of the development of the library institution that I had previously formed from general historical descriptions: the view that Finnish libraries were founded towards the end of the nineteenth century and that they now exist as the product of a triumphal progress that lasted almost 150 years. An examination of the library in question[11] and a closer scrutiny of earlier research literature on the history of libraries in Finland showed that many such projects in fact failed: libraries fell into disuse and were founded again; collections were lost; and dreams of educating the people were shattered.

In retrospect, the creation and development of Finnish lending libraries would on the surface seem to have been a great success. After the latter half of the nineteenth century, books written in the vernacular language (Finnish) in an endeavour to promote a national awakening and to encourage an enthusiasm for reading were made available in increasing numbers to the Finnish-speaking people, to whom the Lutheran Church had for centuries taught the rudiments of reading literacy in their own mother tongue. At least one library was soon founded in every parish. As predecessors of the national public library institution, the parish popular libraries gradually paved the way for a dense and uniform network of libraries,[12] which by the end of the twentieth century covered the whole country and whose services were free to all citizens.[13] Education progressed concomitantly with the founding of libraries and promoted the aims of popular enlightenment. In any case, the tale of the birth of the lending libraries, which was initially the product of free improvisation, was moulded by the educators of the people in the nineteenth century into a success story. Their objective was to create a real mass product: 'A library for every village!' was the slogan.[14] Particularly earlier historical research largely, and a little uncritically, repeated the national myth with its slightly fictitious elements, that the would-be enlighteners of the people created.[15]

---

11 I became interested in the history of this lending library already at the turn of the millennium. This work is based on my proseminar thesis in Information Studies (2005) and my presentation at the SHARP conference 'Book Culture from Below – The Eighteenth Annual Conference of the Society for the History of Authorship, Reading and Publishing' in Helsinki, Finland, 17–21 August 2010. This book is part of my postdoctoral researcher's project funded by the Academy of Finland, 2011–2014: *The Benefits of Literacy in Everyday Life: The impacts of improved literacy on the opportunities for social advancement in remote local communities (c. 1800–1930)*, which I started to plan already in 2008, when I wrote the first versions of my research plan.
12 Mäkinen 2009f, 426–430, 432.
13 Subsequently, of course, the virtual data networks of the Internet have annihilated the idea of a library bound to a built concrete space and geographical location. The development of the Internet has been compared with the revolution caused by the development of printing in the fifteenth century. Darnton 2009, xiv.
14 Werkko 1879, 246.
15 On the other hand, a positive development in recent years has been the examination of the history of lending and parish libraries also from more microhistorical perspectives than was previously the case and also the problematization of the historical development in academic theses, studies of local history and other works. See for example Määttä 2014; Ojanen 2011.

But was everything really that easy and simple in the middle of the nineteenth century and the decades that followed? The old book collection of my municipal library only served to arouse more thoughts and questions in me. Where ultimately did the books come from, and what does their existence actually tell us? Many general historical representations simplistically describe a straightforward continuum between the development of the libraries of the late nineteenth century and those of the twentieth century without taking into consideration that perhaps we do not yet possess all the information about the lending libraries that might be available. Were all the small libraries that were established in rural villages towards the end of the nineteenth century identical to each other and equally successful, in the same way as the later public libraries founded after the passing of the Act on People's Libraries (1928), which created a unified national library institution with guaranteed funding from the state? And what about the founders of the lending libraries? Did they all hold convergent opinions about the function of the libraries? And what were the attitudes of the users to the libraries? After all, it was for them that the libraries were founded and maintained.

I claim that there are innumerable important details which we still do not know about the success story of lending libraries in the Nordic countries. There was also a 'grey area', an examination of which may uncover numerous reasons why literacy skills did not always automatically expand rural people's informational capital or enhance their social status. These details may help us to question earlier assumptions, open up new viewpoints and inspire interpretations of various phenomena connected with library history, offer more specific explanations for them and provide an opportunity for conducting more international and transnational (considering interaction between individuals, groups, organizations and states across national borders) comparisons in this field. To these ends, I take a local community as a case study in an examination of the early history of the lending library institution in northern Europe and particularly in the Nordic countries. In other words, I examine how the first lending libraries were founded in outlying rural parishes, why they were founded and why they did not always initially succeed in their aims. This story forms a kind of counter narrative to the traditional view of research on people's libraries, which believes in a fairly linear progression with diligent popular educational efforts automatically producing a better educated and better behaved common people, who would be able not only to utilize their new knowledge in their own lives but also to serve their nation with devotion and obedience.

The history of literacy has been widely and internationally studied for several decades, but only lately has the significance of these skills for people's everyday life been the object of increased attention in microhistory and the history of mentalities.[16] There were considerable differences in the individual readers' levels of literacy and their opportunities to exploit their reading skills in practical life. These differences partly arose from the different ways in which reading literacy was defined in different times and the level of skills

---

16 Blommaert 2004; Jarlbrink 2010; Lyons 2013; Sulkunen 1999.

that those who taught the rural people to read expected them to attain in any particular age. Rather than accepting the idea of a 'triumphal progress', the success of the library institution in its task of popular enlightenment should be called into question and problematized more often, for example with regard to the quality of the people's reading and writing skills or their opportunities for using a library.

The birth and development of reading in Finland and of the concomitant public library institution during the nineteenth and twentieth centuries was certainly successful when viewed in retrospect.[17] The Finns have become accustomed to the fact that since the 1970s the comprehensive school has guaranteed a general and universal basic education. Since the beginning of the 1920s, the elementary school, which preceded it, also offered almost every child a compulsory general education which ensured that pupils were at least literate and possessed all the other basic skills that were regarded as important in those days. But, in practice, the opportunities for rural people to obtain further education in the middle of the twentieth century were not yet as good as they came to be at the end of the century. In earlier decades and centuries, the differences between the classes (estates), the sexes, and the different areas of the country were considerable in terms of literacy skills and indeed of education generally.[18] However, from the point of view of the study of library history, we need to examine the less successful aspects of the past in order that our overall view of it should not remain too narrow.

Consequently, it is necessary to explicate the story of the birth of the lending library studied here using the methods of microhistory. It constitutes only a minute part of the history of the Finnish and European library institution together with those of thousands of other popular libraries, but it still opens up a perspective that allows for the framing of wider questions and global comparisons. The history of the life of the lending library studied here includes stories about the belief in the future of a farmer's orphaned son, the enthusiasm for reading of a crofter's wife, a young rural police chief[19] who was born in the parish and had received a little more education and was encouraged by his family to take up library work, the municipal leaders' efforts to take care of the community's affairs when the culture of local administration became more written, and of a noblewoman who was familiar with world literature and her daughter, who brought enlightenment to the common people in a region where traditionally members of the upper classes had not lived. But why should others than enthusiasts of local history

---

17 One reflection of its continued achievements is the brilliant results of Finnish students in the PISA studies of the OECD in the early 2000s. Linnakylä & Arffman 2007; Sahlberg 2011. Consequently, the news that the literacy of the whole population is very young in Finland may come as a considerable surprise in view of the excellent success it has produced in the PISA rankings and especially in the students' native language skills.
18 Heikkinen & Leino-Kaukiainen 2011; Kettunen & Simola 2012.
19 This term is used in this work to represent the post of *nimismies*, for which there is no exact equivalent in English. The duties of the *nimismies* included not only those of a law enforcement officer but also those of a bailiff and public prosecutor as well as other administrative functions.

be interested in details of this kind? What significance do they have for the history of the library institution?

As will become apparent later in this book, all these details are connected to the more general history of lending libraries because in the nineteenth century all over Europe nationalist ideology created an important foundation for popular education. The higher social classes and groups emphasized the importance of education (at least of a kind that was suitable for the common people) and of training together with the official use of the vernacular language as prerequisites of citizenship. In Western Europe and North America, 'ordinary people', in other words the majority of the population, began to acquire functional literacy skills in the nineteenth century, often only in conjunction with the advent of compulsory education. In earlier twentieth-century research, libraries were often regarded as institutions that promoted popular education and as a form of charitable work whose aim was to enhance people's quality of life and increase their intellectual capital. In national historiography, this has been associated with pride in the nation's skills and its ability to educate itself. But what if these goals were not achieved? Is there room in research on library history for findings that contradict the old paradigm? And is it even possible to consider the failure of the endeavours for popular enlightenment?

What is exceptionally and extremely interesting about the library chosen as the subject of this research is that in practically no way did it represent the 'success story' but was rather an example of a glitch in the endeavours to enlighten the people. In this work, in which I study the development of one Nordic popular library into a modern public library and the way it was received by the local population, I compare its operations and fate by the means of literature with those of other libraries of the same kind elsewhere in Europe. A comparative approach is very necessary in library research because it helps us to discern statistical similarities in some phenomena and cultural or historical differences in others. Comparisons between several areas can reveal significant differences between local communities and force us to question previous generalizations made on the basis of research limited to just one country or nation.[20] In this study, I therefore combine global aspects of the history of libraries with local history because the comparative method is generally best suited to interrelating the micro- and macro levels.

An historical study of the activities of a local library offers a unique view of the effect that the usage of the collection had in increasing the functional reading skills of the local population. By functional literacy skills I mean that the inhabitant of the countryside in the nineteenth century was able to read and write and possibly also possessed the basic arithmetical skills (adding and subtracting) in order to perform the requirements that society and everyday life imposed on him or her as a seeker and interpreter of information. Functional reading skills means that a person can understand, interpret and assess what he or she reads, and reading is not limited to

---

20 Haupt 2007, 709; Melin 2005, 55.

the rote learning of written texts, as was often the case when the Lutheran Church required that the parishioners should know at least the main articles of faith (by heart).[21]

The history of the Finnish people's literacy skills is a fascinating story set in a period that saw a transition from a mainly oral culture into a written one. This took place at a time (the nineteenth century and especially its last decades) when other great economic, political and ideological changes were taking place. During that period, various nationalist and popular educational aspirations were intertwined with factors connected with the nationhood of the Finnish people. In 1809 Finland, which had earlier been a part of the Kingdom of Sweden, was annexed into the Russian Empire as a consequence of the Napoleonic wars. The political and geographical position of Finland between Sweden and Russia created a unique situation, which, among other things, affected legislative matters, popular education and the development of the Finnish language during the nineteenth century.[22] The promotion of literacy became one of the major factors in the formation of the nation.

The position of the peasants in the Nordic countries had traditionally been very independent, and ever since the Reformation the Lutheran Church had encouraged them and their family members to acquire reading skills and also supervised their ability to read. Lutheranism brought with it a new attitude to popular literacy because it regarded it as doctrinally important that the people should be able to peruse the teachings of the Bible and other important religious texts in their own mother tongue.[23] In the Nordic countries, the Lutheran Church had taken responsibility for teaching the common people to read ever since the time of the Reformation, and this had led to the existence of small local collections of devotional literature for the people to read. In practice, however, the task of teaching small children to read fell to the families at home.[24]

However, literacy as defined by the church was mainly limited to learning the most important articles of faith by heart, and few possessed the ability to write before the end of the nineteenth century. While the church regarded this level of literacy skills as sufficient, it does not correspond with the conception of functional literacy as defined by later scholars.[25] The Nordic concept of literacy was also different from the main European one, for example, in that reading and writing skills were distinguished from each other right up to the late nineteenth century in the popular education provided by the church. This had a significant impact, making the development of functional reading

---

21 Leino-Kaukiainen 2007a, 420–423. See below for a more detailed discussion of the concept of functional reading skills.
22 Häkkinen 1994, 47–55; Jussila 1999; S. Kotilainen 2015a. For English research on the development of the Finnish written language in the 19th century, see also e.g. Lauerma 2013; Saari 2012.
23 Appel & Fink-Jensen 2011; Häggman 2001, 2. The following sections deal with the concept of literacy in greater detail.
24 Hyyrö 2011, 327; Mäkinen 2009b, 31–33.
25 Häggman 2001, 6; Leino-Kaukiainen 2007a, 422.

literacy slow and causing the expansion of the ability to write to come late. These were not seen as particularly necessary skills for the rural people.[26]

There was more work for educators in some parts of Northern Europe because there was little active literacy for example among the majority of the Finnish population before the middle of the nineteenth century. It should be noted that Finland's administrative language was Swedish, an inheritance from the country's former dependence on Sweden, and although the most important legal documents and religious works were translated into Finnish, the amount of literature available in the vernacular was scant.[27] The people's libraries became important instruments for the dissemination of literature in the countryside as well, where the acquisition of new literature and reading matter was more difficult.

In the Nordic countries, the people's libraries of the nineteenth century and the later public libraries were preceded by local collections of books and parish libraries, which were taken care of by the church parishes and other local agents. There were also some subscription libraries, especially in the towns. A similar development was also typical elsewhere in Europe. For example, in German-speaking regions, fee-charging libraries (*Leihbibliotheken*) had played a significant role in disseminating literature.[28] For example, in France, too, traditional religious and ecclesiastical book collections later formed the basis of the collections of public libraries.[29] The advent of public libraries often came about in conjunction with elementary education and popular enlightenment.[30] However, Finland differed from many other countries of Western Europe and United States in that popular education, universal compulsory education and also public libraries and the legislation regulating them had all been realized several decades later there than in those countries.[31]

In Finland the popular libraries acquired a special position as part of the national awakening, which was inspired by nationalism and Finland's position as an autonomous part of the Russian Empire. The language question became a crucial issue in popular educational endeavours since the reformers wished to replace the traditional language of administration, Swedish, with the people's own language, Finnish. Initially, the Russian authorities looked on the renunciation of the language of their former enemy (Sweden) with favour because it separated the Finns from their former mother country and bound them more closely to the empire. In the mid-nineteenth century, there was still very little literature written in the vernacular in Finland, although the majority of the population spoke and read only Finnish, which is quite different from the Scandinavian languages. However, some typical Enlightenment literature such as agricultural and

---

26 Matti Peltonen 1992, 93.
27 Häkkinen 1994, 79–102, 146.
28 Martino 1990.
29 Barnett 1973, 100–101.
30 Chartier 1987, 209–210; Manley 2003; Mäkinen 2009g, 111–115.
31 Hanska & Vainio-Korhonen 2010; Heikkinen & Leino-Kaukiainen 2011; Hoare 2006.

natural scientific guidebooks, had certainly been published in Finnish already in the eighteenth century. The articles concerning the same themes were also published in Finnish in newspapers and almanacs. Finnish-language literature grew powerfully at the end of the century, at the same time as popular libraries were developed, and thus the libraries to some extent represent the (language-)political dimensions of literacy at the micro-level. Later, at the turn of the century, the Finns also opposed the Russification of the administration and its language, and the Finnish language became a tool for emphasizing their own existence as a nation.[32]

Influences regarding the significance of first people's libraries and later public libraries for the enlightenment of the people were gradually imported into Finland, initially from German, then from Anglo-American culture and subsequently also from the other Nordic countries and especially Sweden. Seen from the broader European perspective, the Finnish countryside was a backward area in this development, although the ideal of the lending library spread fairly rapidly all over Finland during the last few decades of the nineteenth century once it had been absorbed. A comparison between the Nordic and Baltic countries shows that the development in these areas was fairly simultaneous in many respects.[33] Moreover, the sources relating to the opportunities and facilities for reading are very similar, which allows for transnational comparisons between the Nordic countries, for example. This is especially true because the ideas and ideologies that influenced the establishment of lending libraries tended to coalesce and spread from one country to another.[34] On the other hand, significant differences between the practices in the Nordic countries can be observed since local conditions varied linguistically, administratively and geographically.

There was a widespread transition in the Nordic countries from Continental European and particularly German influences on public libraries based on the American model at the turn of the century. Norway was the first of the Nordic countries to be influenced by the American way of organizing public library services at the end of the nineteenth century. At that time, it was believed in the United States that reading and learning had no intrinsic value in themselves but should be usefully applicable in practical life. In Europe, on the other hand, books were regarded as being objects of value in themselves whether they were read or not. The works in the collections of German libraries, whose purpose was mainly educative, were predominantly informative, while the American library system was based on the needs of the 'public at large' and the fact that the libraries were open to everyone. In addition to the United States, Britain also served as a model for the new libraries in the Nordic countries. The first influences of the Public Library Movement arrived in Finland, to begin with in the towns, in the 1870s. However, it was not until the turn of the century that this ideology began to influence Finnish library activities more extensively.[35]

---

32 Häkkinen 2002, 34–38; S. Kotilainen 2015a; T. Laine 2013, 32–35.
33 Dyrbye et al. 2009; Garrison 1979, 42; Vatanen 2002, 40.
34 Mäkinen 2009c, 74–98, 105.
35 Byberg 1993, 22; Byberg 2009, 44–45; Kelly 1977; Vatanen 2002, 34.

Table 1. The development of people's libraries in the Nordic countries into modern public libraries.

	Finland	Sweden	Norway	Denmark	Iceland
First popular libraries	1802	1799	c. 1830	c. 1800*	1830**
First library law	1928	1997	1935	1920	1955
Establishment of a library authority	1921	–	1902	1902	1978
State financial support	1921	1905	1876***	1920	–
Foundation of a national library association	1910	1915	1913	1919	1960
Compulsory (school) education	1921	1842 (1882)	1889	1814	1907****

* Public book collections
** Branch libraries (quarter libraries)
*** Subsidized by the parliament (Storting)
**** Education was compulsory for all children between the ages of 11 and 14. School attendance was not compulsory, and the educational level of all children was assessed by means of a placement examination.
Sources: Byberg 2009, 42–46; Dyrbye 2009, 52, Hannesdóttir 1993, 16, 18–19; Mäkinen 2009a; Stenquist 2004; Torstensson 2009, 86, 90–91.

Until the late nineteenth century, Finnish cultural links were in many respects much closer to German than to Anglo-American ones, and in consequence the American library movement only became properly established as a model for the activities of Finnish libraries from the end of that century on. Popular education played a greater role in the traditional German philosophy on libraries, and the collections there were smaller and comprised works that strove to provide more 'enlightenment' and to mould the readers' *Weltanschauung*, while the American models took a less paternalistic attitude to their customers and allowed them greater choice in what they read. The German approach necessarily influenced the activities of libraries in Finland, particularly in the countryside, where the librarians were often teachers and pedagogical ideas were also influenced by the German tradition.[36]

The development of libraries in the Nordic countries was almost without exception connected with popular enlightenment work, which in the latter half of the nineteenth century saw a defining of boundaries between obligatory schooling and free educational endeavours. The fundamental conditions for the functioning of the libraries, such as relevant legislation and state (or municipal) financial support for their activities were not implemented until the beginning of the twentieth century. Although in Norway, for example, the parliament had begun to support the libraries earlier, they became regulated by law considerably later than the enactment of legislation on education. By creating a foundation for the administrative and financial conditions for library activities, the various states supported the transition to a modern library philosophy and a nationally comprehensive

---

36 Vatanen 2002, 184–188.

library system, although these measures were not implemented until a later date. The debates on libraries, their objectives and the direction in which they were to be developed were similar in the different the Nordic countries from the end of the nineteenth century on.[37]

In the best cases, the task assigned to the popular and public libraries was accomplished, and they undoubtedly promoted the acquisition of functional literacy and were a significant tool in the implementation of literacy education. In this book, I consider why the newly learned functional literacy skills so significantly changed the formation of intangible capital in nineteenth century and early-twentieth-century local relations. The history of literacy and written culture has been well researched internationally, but only in the last few decades has attention been paid to how literacy skills affected the life, the public communal activities and the ways of thinking of the lower social groups. Compared with the longer Anglo-American tradition, Nordic research on library history has not yet been so specific in its theoretical analysis.

In earlier research on library history, there has been some dispute about the significance of the fact that libraries were often founded and maintained by more educated persons who came from the highest social ranks. Thus the people's libraries have been seen as part of the work of an elite to educate the lower classes and in doing so to exert a form of social control. On the other hand, many other public institutions of the late nineteenth century are regarded as having been authoritarian in nature, which does not mean that the popular libraries of the time did not provide a useful service for the lower ranks of society too.[38] In spite of all this, the people of the countryside were themselves sometimes actively involved in establishing the libraries if the circumstances were favourable.

Because research of this kind based on the collective biographical method has not previously been carried out in Finnish historical studies, or indeed to any great extent in research elsewhere in Europe either[39], this book will produce new and more profound information about the significance that the acquisition of functional literacy skills had for peasants and local communities. The results of the research will explain what factors enhanced or impeded the learning of literacy skills, how these skills could be utilized in the local community and what gender and generational differences there were.

The present study emphasizes the readers' response to the books. Many of the examples that I have studied 'from below' in the traditional area of

---

37 Table 1; Dyrbye et al. 2009. On the planning and establishment stages of the Finnish elementary school system, see also Jalava 2011; S. Kotilainen 2016; Nurmi 1964; Nurmi 1988.
38 Rubin 2004, 289.
39 I shall return in greater detail in the following section to research that has been conducted in Finnish and European historiography on the functioning of libraries and their users in local communities.

slash-and-burn agriculture[40] shared common features with contemporary phenomena in the Nordic and other Western European countries, even though little historical research has been carried out on these from the viewpoint of the rural libraries. On the other hand, the way in which the phenomena of the times were manifested in the sparsely populated countryside in a border region between western and eastern cultural influences, are explained by special Finnish characteristics. As a case example, Finland can help us to understand a more general phenomenon, in which the lower social groups were offered education from above but were not necessarily always 'ready' to receive it gratefully. And what did the people of the very remote countryside, to which literacy came late, themselves think of these efforts, and what does their behaviour reveal about these mentalities even though they have not been recorded in written form anywhere?

Previous research on rural literacy and the significance of libraries in the countryside

Research in book history has blossomed in an unprecedented way in the last few decades. In Finland, as also in other parts of Europe and North America, the history of libraries and the production, acquisition and reading of books have been studied from new perspectives.[41] In the early 2000s, the historical study of books and libraries has expanded internationally to engage with new themes, and the multiplicity of local studies makes possible an international and also transnational[42] comparison between different local communities, for example between those in Finland and the other Nordic countries or Western Europe.[43] Research on the history of literacy is

---

40 Slash-and-burn agriculture was an eastern Finnish practice of creating land for cultivation by felling and cutting back the trees, drying them and finally burning them. The slash-and-burn technique, the use of which went back to the sixteenth century, was still common in the studied area in the 1860s, and it continued, albeit on a very small scale, until the end of the century. Korhonen 2003, 405–408; Markkanen 1988, 145–148.
41 Ahokas 2011a; Armstrong 2003; Casper et al. 2002; Cressy 1980; Crawford 2007; Cullen 2007; Darnton 1997[1996]; Darnton 2000; Duckett 2003; Dyrbye et al. 2009; Engelsing 1974; Engelsing 1976; Ginzburg 2007; Hakapää 2008; Hoare 2006; Häggman 2001; Häggman 2008; Jarlbrink 2010; T. Laine 2006; Leffler 1999; Manley 2003; Minter 2009; Mäkinen 1997; Mäkinen 2009a; Peatling 2004; Skouvig 2007; Smith-Peter 2005; Towsey 2010; Book History Journal, The Johns Hopkins University Press 1998–.
42 See the following section for a more detailed discussion of the concept of transnational comparison.
43 See for example Black & Hoare 2006a; Dyrbye et al. 2009.

a highly multidisciplinary area of study, combining as it does various fields of historical research and several other disciplines.[44]

In 2010 Martyn Lyons produced a comprehensive overview of the history of reading and writing in the Western world.[45] Library history has also recently been studied more comprehensively and from comparative perspectives in the Nordic countries.[46] These studies constitute a contrast to the present work in the sense that they examine the development in the Western world from a macro-perspective. For example, some fresh comparative northern European research on library and book history was carried out within the HIBOLIRE network[47] in the early 21st century, and to some extent it elucidated the reading habits of the rural population elsewhere in the Nordic countries than in Finland, but it focused mainly on the eighteenth century. This book, on the other hand, has yielded more exact and detailed information about differences in local conditions at a time when a 'mass reading public' came into being in the nineteenth century and particularly its latter half, which saw a strong expansion of functional literacy in the Nordic countries[48].

Below, I present the major recent research literature according to topic in slightly greater detail. The selection is based on the principle of choosing those works that present the most interesting questions with regard to this book. The topics are: 1) definitions of functional literacy; 2) reading and writing literacy as a social and cultural practice; 3) the influence of books on people's thinking and actions; 4) the influence of the tradition of earlier research with its nationalistic features and its exaggerated belief in the progressive nature of the development of literacy; and 5) recent Finnish research on the history of the library institution, which focuses on the macro level and the history of large urban centres.

Recent international research has adopted a multidisciplinary approach to the examination of functional literacy and specifically to the development of the writing skills associated with it particularly in the Early Modern Age.[49] This research trend is also closely connected with research on the history of education. For example, Daniel Lindmark (2004) has examined the development of the Swedish school system from the mid-seventeenth century to the beginning of the nineteenth century. At that time, education

---

44 For research on this subject in Finland, see Kauranen 2009; Leino-Kaukiainen 2007a; Myllyntaus 1990; Mäkinen 2007. For recent research in ethnology and Finnish literature, see e.g. Makkonen 2005; Stark 2011. For linguistic research, see e.g. Nordlund 2007.
45 Lyons 2010.
46 Hoare 2006; Navickienė, Mäkinen, Torstensson, Dyrbye & Reimo 2013.
47 The Nordic-Baltic-Russian Network on the History of Books, Libraries and Reading, http://www.helsinki.fi/historia/hibolire/.
48 See also Edlund 2012; Edlund & Haugen 2013; Edlund, Edlund & Haugen 2014.
49 E.g. Barton, Hamilton & Ivanic 2000; Edlund & Haugen 2013; Lorenzen-Schmidt & Poulsen 2002; Lyons 2013; Magnússon 2010; 'Vardagligt skriftbruk' network, http://www.sprak.umu.se/forskning/vardagligt-skriftbruk/.

in Sweden, as everywhere else in Europe in the Early Modern Age, was divided along two main strands: the Latin School system with its classical curriculum for pupils, generally males from the higher estates, aiming to enter into the services of the state and the church, while for others the rudiments of Christian doctrine constituted the major part of their schooling. It only became possible for the commons to acquire functional reading skills midway through the nineteenth century. Moreover, the differences in the amount of education available between rural and urban dwellers and males and females were considerable.[50] The majority of the population of Finland lived in the countryside, where the development of the school system came even later in the nineteenth century than in the former mother country, Sweden.[51] This book shows how closely entwined the early history of popular libraries was with the development of the elementary school system. At the same time, however, it questions the assumptions of earlier research not only in history but in other disciplines too concerning the extent to which the common people were willing to be educated 'from above' and to accept the enlightenment they received as such. I also examine what kind of literature the people of the countryside themselves preferred and why.

In the 1950s Richard D. Altick wrote what was, from the perspective of the history of popular literacy, a highly significant work: *The English Common Reader*, which dealt with the reading habits and experiences of ordinary British people and the rise of mass literacy in the nineteenth century.[52] Robert Darnton, for his part, has examined the history of reading and literacy in numerous studies in which he places particular emphasis on the written culture of the eighteenth century and the Enlightenment.[53] One of the methodologically most exciting histories of vernacular literacy is Carlo Ginzburg's *Il formaggio e i vermi* (1976), [English translation: *The Cheese and the Worms* (1982)], in which he studies the world view of an Italian miller in the sixteenth century. Menocchio the miller formed an original and strange vision of the creation of the world from the literature he had read, and as a result was sentenced for heresy by the Inquisition. Ginzburg's study shows how the reading of literature in the vernacular language raised the conceptual faculty of the common people to a quite new level.[54]

In Finland, the amount of literature in the vernacular was still very meagre at that time. Most of it was religious. The administrative language was that of the mother country, Sweden, even though the majority of the population, and especially the inhabitants of the countryside, were Finnish-speaking. It is also important to remember that administrative texts concerning the Finnish-speaking subjects had begun to be translated in Finnish much earlier. And even if there were no written texts in Finnish, nearly all the subjects heard such administrative announcements when they were read out in translation on Sunday in church, a factor that has been shown to have had a significant effect

---

50 Altick 1967[1957], 42; Lindmark 2004, 15–44.
51 Jalava 2011, 75; Nurmi 1988, 94; Westberg 2014.
52 Altick 1967[1957].
53 E.g. Darnton 1982b; Darnton 1984; Darnton 1997[1996]; Darnton 2010.
54 Ginzburg 2007.

on ordinary people's sense of linguistic correctness.[55] The first book published in Finnish was an ABC primer written by Michael Agricola in 1543, who later became the Bishop of Turku (Åbo, in south-western Finland).[56] Agricola was also a learned humanist and theologian who had studied under Martin Luther and Philip Melanchthon in Wittenberg in the 1530s and had also been a student of Erasmus of Rotterdam. Agricola played an important role in developing a written Finnish idiom. His translation of the New Testament into Finnish, which was published in 1548, created the foundation for the Finnish written language in much the same way as the German translation of Martin Luther established a standard German language.[57]

Ginzburg's *The Cheese and the Worms* is one of the most important works not only in the study of literacy but also of the 'new history' movement, which has been gaining in strength ever since the 1970s. As a representative of the microhistorical school, his research method consists in an exact analysis of the surprising or exceptional event. The atypical can also tell us about ordinary life, about folk culture and about popular everyday thinking, for which no sources have usually been left for researchers to study. Ginzburg considers the extent to which the reading habits of the rural population were affected by the fact that their culture was mainly oral. Was the content of the texts that they read therefore adapted and even perhaps (unconsciously) distorted? Their relationship to the texts may have been completely different from those of readers belonging to the higher social groups and estates.[58]

We can conclude with Ginzburg that in research on popular libraries it is important to distinguish between the mentalities and attitudes of the founders of the libraries on the one hand and those of the users on the other and to take into account the effect of these differences on the preconditions for the operation and survival of the libraries. No sources corresponding to Ginzburg's concerning the differences between the reading habits of different local social groups were available for this study, but his work still offers a discussion of the subject that gives food for thought. It shows how important it is to be able to evaluate the phenomena of the past from the point of view of the actors themselves. Ginzburg also criticizes the idea of the collectivity of mentalities and points out how important it is to perceive the differences in individual and group mentalities, in other words the stable and unconscious factors in people's ways of thinking.[59] Therefore, it is important to study, as a kind of a counter narrative to the general macro-level view of history, people's actions and thinking on the micro level as well,

---

55 Laitinen & Nordlund 2012, 67; Pajula 1960.
56 For localities with significant Swedish-speaking populations, the place names are given in Finnish followed by the Swedish names in parenthesis on their first appearance in the text. Thereafter they are indicated only by their Finnish names. The only exception to this is Vyborg (Finnish: Viipuri; Swedish: Viborg), which is conventionally referred to by its transcribed Russian name.
57 Heininen 1999, 37–39, 42; Häkkinen 1994, 43–44, 79–86; Häkkinen 2015. On the influence of printing and the Reformation on the development of European vernacular languages, see also Febvre & Martin 1998[1958], 319.
58 Ginzburg 2007, 37.
59 Ginzburg 2007, 38–39.

because otherwise these may remain without representation.[60] While it may also be that this counter narrative of the mentalities of the common people does not constitute a complete antithesis to studies of readers from the upper strata of society, at least it supplements them from a different perspective.

Like Ginzburg and Darnton, many other researchers have approached reading primarily as a social and cultural practice.[61] In Sweden, both Egil Johansson and Daniel Lindmark (Umeå History of Education Research Group) have developed an important research methodology for the study of vernacular literacy.[62] Because of Sweden's and Finland's long common history, it is relatively easy to compare Finnish and Swedish sources relating to the ability to read, and significant results can be produced thereby. Among other relevant research contributions, Martyn Lyons has made some interesting comparisons and syntheses concerning literacy and written culture covering the whole of Europe,[63] while David Barton, for his part, has developed a theory of the concept of literacy in many of his works and has carried out ethnographic studies of popular reading and writing practices in local communities.[64]

The historiography of the Nordic library institution and research on literacy skills deviates from similar Western European and American studies in that in the English-speaking world, for example, research on public libraries and literacy is based on a longer tradition and a wider-ranging body of research literature than in the Nordic countries. There has been a strong trend in recent research everywhere to focus on the formation of theory at the expense of empirical studies. However, a society like that of Finland, to which a vernacular written culture came relatively late, calls for empirical research so that all of its particular features may be revealed. Moreover, the conditions under which libraries operated especially in remote areas of the countryside in other parts of the world may well have resembled those that existed in Finland as late as the mid-nineteenth century. Furthermore, nationalist issues became important themes in the literature of that age everywhere in Europe. Therefore an empirical examination and a micro-level approach facilitate comparison with the situation in countries with a longer tradition of popular libraries.[65]

In Finland, a considerable amount of research 'from below' has been conducted in several other disciplines than in history. In them, however, it is based on source materials of a very different kind. Within other disciplines, such as literary studies, linguistics and ethnology, recent Finnish research on the subject has been to a great extent based on autobiographical sources

---

60 For example, in Finland Kaisa Kauranen has studied the literary output of a particular 'common man'. Kauranen 2013a. However, in this volume I study persons who may not even have been able to write or who, even if they could, have left no written records.
61 See also Lyons, Kotilainen & Mäkinen 2015, 283–286.
62 Graff et al. 2009; Johansson 1972; Johansson 1977; Johansson 2002; Lindmark 2003; Lindmark 2004.
63 Lyons 2010; Lyons 2012; Lyons 2013.
64 E.g. Barton & Hamilton 1998; Barton & Papen 2010.
65 Eide 2010; Peatling 2004; Skouvig 2007.

that have already been published or at least on databases collected by other researchers,[66] but there has been less empirical historical research utilizing as a main source the combination of those traditional original sources, in which the authorities or other people than themselves described the life of rural persons studied. This is pertinent, when the persons studied here did not produce any autobiographical sources by themselves, because otherwise we would know hardly anything about their relationship to the literacy skills and the significance they, i.e. the majority of the Finnish-speaking population, gave to these skills. Of course oral memories can give us a lot of useful information of popular mentalities, but they and other sources should more often complete each other, so that their weight as evidence would be even more credible.[67]

However, this research which has already been done in other disciplines concerns mostly the wealthier areas of Finland, where the economic, social or educational circumstances were very different kind of than in the northern Central Finland. Or then these researchers have studied working class, but there was never such industrial workforce or very strong working class culture in area studied in this book, because the workers were mainly agricultural workers, whose living was dependent on the local farmers.

In the field of history, there has not yet been sufficient empirical research on lending libraries at the micro level, although this would be important for the sake of international comparison. Here, however, I wish to make a clear distinction between these works and microhistorical research proper: theologians, linguists and folklorists do not necessarily follow the same methods of historical research that historians do. I study the subject specifically from the point of view of historical research, which means that historical methods, source criticism and the analysis of written (also official, not only or primarily unofficial and personal) documents take precedence over these other disciplines. In this sense, we have different viewpoints on the same set of problems and the results of our research are therefore not fully comparable. The scholars with whom I principally interact and discuss in this book are historians because we operate according to the same scholarly principles and research paradigm. Since the present research situation is

---

66 Kauranen 2009; Makkonen 2005; Stark 2011.
67 The influence of the advance of book culture on the mentalities of different strata of the population has been studied (for example by Kati Mikkola and Laura Stark), and on social mobility (by Anna Kuismin for instance). The boundary between the written and oral traditions and its influence on people's noetic world has also been studied by Kirsti Salmi-Niklander, Lea Laitinen and Taru Nordlund, among others. Laitinen & Mikkola 2013. This valuable research has been highly international: it has been carried out in the other Nordic countries and Western Europe as well, and the results have been published in English and thereby aroused the interest of readers in other countries. E.g. Elspaß 2007; Fairman 2007; Laitinen & Mikkola 2013; Lyons 2015; Nordlund 2007; Sandersen 2007; Vandenbussche 2007. The above mentioned scholars have been pioneers in the study of popular literacy in their own disciplines, as have others who have carried out research in the fields of folkloristics and theology in Finland and the Scandinavian countries.

examined within the discipline of (Finnish) historical research, I believe that the source material should extend beyond autobiographical sources[68], because there are many other archival sources than directly narrative ones that shed light on the reading and writing skills of the common people.

An absolute classic in the modern study of the history of books is *L'Apparition du livre* (1958), (English translation: *The Coming of the Book* (1976)][69] by Lucien Febvre and Henri-Jean Martin, which examines the effect of written culture and the printed word on the surrounding society.[70] Book history is a field of research which has long multidisciplinary traditions and utilizes the methods of historical research, sociology, information studies and literary studies, among other disciplines. The study of book history can be divided into analytical and historical bibliography. Analytical, or descriptive, bibliography is an Anglo-American research tradition[71] that emphasizes the significance of the book as an object and man-made artefact; it takes books as printed entities and preferably deals with originals. Historical bibliography, for its part, studies everything connected with the history of books which cannot be elucidated from the works themselves or their production process. It is rather a matter of studying the history of the influence of books, of how information has been spread and attempts have been made to affect people's thinking and actions through books. Other important objects of this research orientation include the kind of reactions and consequences that the reading or writing of books has had on different persons and groups in past centuries and in different social situations. The study of the social and cultural history of books using a methodology focussing on the influence that they have had requires not only more versatile methods than before but also sources external to the books themselves; these can include records of various organizations and other archive sources, private records such as diaries and letters that discuss reading and writing, catalogues of book auctions, estate inventory deeds and library catalogues. In this sub-branch of book history, what is most important is not studying the originals of works and fine special editions but investigating the reading experiences of ordinary people. This approach has traditionally been strong in German and Nordic research on book history,[72] and it is also emphasized in this book.

Robert Darnton is one of the best known researchers on the history of the influence of books. Based on his study of French book history, he has developed a concept called 'the communications circuit', which describes

---

68 See also Vauhkonen 2016.
69 In this book all works are referred to by their titles in their original languages. If a work has been translated into English, the title of the published translation is given in brackets. For works not translated into English, ad hoc English translations of their original titles are appended in brackets following the convention that capitalization follows normal textual usage not that of titles. This practice is particularly relevant to the titles of works in the libraries discussed, which were naturally nearly all read in Finnish translations.
70 Febvre & Martin 1998 [1958].
71 See e.g. Adams & Barker 2001; Dane 2012; Darnton 1982a, 65.
72 Darnton 1982a, 66; T. Laine 2011a, 341.

the circuit of the book from the author to the reader and back (in terms of the influence of the latter on the former) via those who participate in its production and dissemination. At the same time, his model shows that, in addition to publicity, numerous social, ideological, economic, legislative and political factors simultaneously affect this communication and that all these factors are inevitably in interaction with each other. At the centre of the research in Darnton's model are, however, those people who have affected the circulation of the book.[73] Book history in this sense is above all cultural and social history, and it can focus on the following subjects: the production, manufacture, dissemination, selling, buying and reading of books; genres, writers, readers, buyers, owners, borrowers and their motives; various institutions (the channels of the acquisition and transmission of literature, such as reading societies, printers, bookshops, libraries, the press, public discussion, social behaviour); reception (reading experiences, reading habits); political and juridical limitations (preventive censorship, residual censorship and self-censorship, possible restrictions on the book trade and book production and avoidance of them); ideological influences (philosophy, theology, politics, nationalism, revolutionism or reactionism); book collections (school libraries, public lending libraries or private libraries).

However, Darnton has emphasized that even though the availability and circulation of books can be studied with great precision, one cannot know merely on the basis of what books were bought and disseminated how they were read or how they affected the thinking of contemporaries.[74] In Finnish research on public libraries, too, it has been noted that not much is known about the libraries' customers (for example during the period c. 1920–1940).[75] But, in fact, it is possible to obtain information about the borrowers' activities in even earlier times than this if the sources which have been preserved are utilised in more versatile ways, as in the present research. I examine here the cultural history of the books and reading, in other words the reception and use of books and the effects of the ability to read and write on communal networks and social relations, especially from the perspective of microhistory and the history of mentalities. Studies of the reception of literature usually concentrate on the reader's experiences, his or her cultural understanding of the world – which in turn determines the reception of the text – and on the reader's values, feelings and other subjective factors.[76] Nor does this study, either, indicate comprehensively how the common people received the libraries or how the readers', who could not write diary or autobiographical texts, thinking was affected by the works they read because the lack of sources (in the period studied there was naturally no such thing as a customer satisfaction survey) makes this impossible to carry out fully by merely studying the reading experiences of the population. Nevertheless, it reveals many details which have hitherto received little attention about how the common people reacted to the popular education mediated by the libraries and what kind of library books they were interested in. These issues

73 Darnton 1982a, 67–69.
74 Darnton 2005, 21–22.
75 Eskola 2001, 80.
76 Kovala 1997, 145–147.

are examined here using empirical sources as one example of how a library was received by the readers.

The historical study of books has also become a more multidisciplinary field and one that favours new approaches. During the last few decades, new ways of examining sources and creating extensive databases have been introduced. In Finland, scholars have been interested particularly in the distribution of books and the influences they brought with them. An object of particular interest has been the stocks of books in Finland's towns in the eighteenth century; initially this concerned mainly Helsinki, which has been studied using estate inventory deeds and auction catalogues.[77] Henrik Grönroos's and Ann-Charlotte Nyman's book *Boken i Finland* [The book in Finland], published in 1996, has been an important aid to many researchers because it compiles the data which Grönroos had collected mainly in the 1930s; these data consisted of mentions of books as property in estate inventory deeds in Finnish towns dating from the times when Finland was part of the realm of Sweden (1656–1809). Later some of the data have also been published on the Internet in the HENRIK database maintained by the Finnish Literature Society.[78] In addition, other ready compiled databases and collections (for example, the autobiographies and other texts of popular writers stored in the Literary Archives of the Finnish Literature Society and the digital newspaper archives of the Finnish National Library[79]) have also been frequently used to study literacy skills and the reception of books in Finland.[80] Less often have the researchers themselves compiled databases of the original sources that they have used in their historical research, as Grönroos did.

Earlier Finnish, and partly also Scandinavian, studies as well as many non-academic histories of local libraries have traditionally regarded the advancement in reading literacy created by the development of the libraries as a very straightforward and progressive process with few interruptions or halts. Rather, they have attempted to show that Finland was in the front line of development in Europe and that active popular enlightenment led exclusively to the inclusion of a broader section of the population within the sphere of education.[81] The majority of Finnish local histories of libraries, especially non-scholarly ones, continued right up to the late twentieth century and the turn of the millennium to treat the oldest libraries, in other words, the lending libraries, only as forerunners of the present-day municipal public libraries. The past was to some extent examined from the perspective of the present. Many of these works follow much the same chronological

---

77 af Forselles & Laine 2011, 6–7.
78 Grönroos & Nyman 1996; HENRIK Database, Books and their owners in Finland up to 1809, http://dbgw.finlit.fi/henrik/.
79 Selected list of folk writers in the Literature Archives of the Finnish Literature Society, http://www.finlit.fi/kia/kansankirjoittajat.htm; the digital newspaper archives of the Finnish National Library, http://digi.kansalliskirjasto.fi.
80 Several articles in Laitinen & Mikkola 2013; Stark 2011.
81 E.g. Werkko 1879. See also several non-academic histories of libraries. On the educational ideas of the Public Library Movement in Finland, see Vatanen 2002, 11–14, 23.

line: the library is founded in connection with popular education in the nineteenth century, it grows and its activities continue to expand until it progresses into the age of the Internet at the end of the twentieth century. This picture portrays a rather linear development in which the information society was gradually established in the countryside in spite of the challenges it faced there. But what if the rural people did not in the first place want to be educated by reading the works of their local library? A microhistorical approach can show more detailed reasons why the work of lending libraries in the Finnish countryside did not always succeed. Such a study can also serve as a useful example for wider comparisons of situations in which all does not go according to plan.

Earlier Finnish historical research, with its nationalist emphasis, based its findings on entries in the church records and considered that the degree of literacy among the Finnish rural population was exceptional and that they became literate at an unusually early time. However, several more recent European comparisons have shown that, in terms of active literacy, Finland was a quite backward region up to the end of the nineteenth century.[82] The reason for the big divergence between these results lies in the different ways in which researchers have defined the concept of literacy over the decades.[83]

The earlier research on the Finnish library institution was mainly quantitative and nationalistic in character. The study of local popular and lending libraries in Finland began in the 1870s with the work of Kaarle Werkko.[84] His interest in libraries was born in the teacher training seminary in Jyväskylä, where he studied to be an elementary school teacher, and he actively tried to promote the establishment of popular libraries. Werkko familiarized himself with the origins and working conditions of the libraries and compiled a parish-specific report covering the whole country on the early stages and current state of the libraries entitled *Tietoja ja mietteitä Suomen kansa- ja lasten-kirjastoista ynnä luku-yhdistyksistä ja luennoista vuoteen 1875* [Information and reflections on the people's and children's libraries and reading societies of Finland] (1879). He obtained his information mainly by correspondence with the informants of each locality, who were often elementary school teachers and clergymen. This was the first attempt to compile a general overview of the existing state of Finland's lending libraries. He himself admitted that there were certain shortcomings in the completeness and comparability of these statistics. Although the collected information had to be published nearly in its original form despite its lack of cohesion and internal contradictions, the source value of Werkko's work from the point of view of the history of the Finnish library institution is considerable because it describes in detail the working conditions that prevailed in the early days of each local library. Thus this material is still an important source of information about the operations of the earliest libraries, especially since not even the persons who were active at that time

---

82 Häggman 2008, 38.
83 E.g. Alamäki 1996; Kauranen 2013b, 29–38, Leino-Kaukiainen 2007a; Mäkinen 2007; Vauhkonen 2016, 34–39.
84 Kaarle Werkko's (1850–1926) original name was Karl Johan Wickström before he Finnicized it.

in local administration always knew about the library which had been opened in their parish. Moreover, there are not necessarily other documents dating from the nineteenth century that contain corresponding information concerning these libraries. Werkko published another book in 1892 titled *Tutkimuksia kansankirjaston asiassa* [Studies concerning the people's lending library].[85]

Later on, in the early twentieth century, Leo Schadewitz edited a book of statistical data on Finnish lending libraries collected parish by parish by *Kansanvalistusseura* (The Society for Popular Enlightenment [today called The Finnish Lifelong Learning Foundation]), which supplemented Werkko's work. In the foreword of the book, he regretted the fact that the collecting of the material had not been planned nor the collectors instructed so as to make the data as mutually comparable as possible. Indeed, the data did not completely satisfy this condition in that they were for different years between 1895 and 1903, although the majority were for the years 1900 and 1901. Furthermore, Schadewitz noted that in the popular libraries of the beginning of the century the bookkeeping was often deficient with regard to the kind of information solicited so that in many cases the figures might have even been based on estimates rather than exact statistics.[86] In eastern Finland, where the poorest parts of the countryside were situated, the information was gathered by recipients of special bursaries, but for the rest of the country there were no funds for this kind of collecting work. Eventually, some secondary school graduates and other enthusiasts collected some of the data from their home areas in different parts of the country, and the rest was collected by postal correspondence.[87]

More recent Finnish research on the history of the library institution mainly focuses on the macro level or on the history of libraries in the large urban centres, and there is still a lack of more precise research on communal history concerning the birth and early growth of popular libraries in the countryside. Much more of this would need to be carried out, especially from a comparative perspective. *Suomen yleisten kirjastojen historia* [The history of Finland's public libraries] (2009, 880 pages), edited by Ilkka Mäkinen, is a fundamental work of library history which collects together existing research on the history of Finnish public and lending libraries. However, the book concentrates more on lending libraries in towns. Moreover, it is not possible for a general work like this to bring out the very considerable differences between the conditions of rural and urban libraries using detailed microhistorical studies of communities. It is quite natural that the whole Finnish library field should first be studied on the macro level in order to clarify the main outlines, and in this Mäkinen has been a pioneer. The micro-level, on the other hand, offers opportunities for more exact qualitative analyses, of the kind that Mäkinen himself has also made, for example in his study of notable Finns who influenced the development of the library institution.[88] For the most part, the history of rural libraries

85 Karjalainen 1977, 4; Mäkinen 2000a; Werkko 1879.
86 Schadewitz 1903, 3, 17.
87 Inkilä 1960, 173; S. Kuusi 1946, 404–405; Schadewitz 1903, 15–16.
88 Mäkinen 2000a; Mäkinen 2000b.

has for a long time only been dealt with in numerous historical accounts of local libraries, many of which have also been published.[89] Naturally, not all of them are of a scholarly quality, but even so they do reveal important facts about the history of local libraries, and for the present work they constitute an extremely useful supplement to the research literature.

Why libraries influenced the common people's reading skills

In this work, I examine how the ideas of the Public Library Movement were received in Northern Europe and the ways in which they were implemented locally at the micro-level in a country like Finland (which was then part of the Russian Empire), where the reading skills of the rural people were rather low compared with those of the populations of Western Europe. I present the point of view of the people of the countryside on the development of libraries from below and discuss the extent to which their reading experiences influenced the development and continuity of the libraries' activities. I further continuously consider what the community that I study and the activities of its libraries indicate more generally about the significance of people's libraries. I shall now present, delimit and justify my research questions more specifically.

In Europe, too, previous historical research concerning whole communities has mainly examined the literacy and libraries of town dwellers and those belonging to the higher classes, or of those literate inhabitants of the countryside who had an opportunity to absorb influences from nearby towns. The early history of a large number of public libraries in towns has been thoroughly studied.[90] Recent Finnish research on library history has focused on the social elite and the intelligentsia.[91] Rural lending libraries have also been studied, but from the point of view of the founders (the clergy, elementary school teachers and other functionaries).[92] In contrast, the microhistory of the poorest population and their rural libraries has not been really studied from below by historians. The history of literacy in Finland is basically familiar to Finnish scholars. However, it is very often a history dealing only with the most talented, eminent and privileged readers and writers. That is the case even when it studies the rural population, or at least those members of it who were able to express themselves by writing to the newspapers or authoring autobiographies, and who thus were able to tell about their relationship to books and reading.[93]

---

89 E.g. Ellä 1994; Elonheimo 1996; Mantovaara 2001; Niiranen 1999; Penttilä 1986, 14–20; Rainio 1988; Ruoho 2013; Samppala 2010; Tarikka 2002.
90 af Forselles & Laine 2008; Hietala 2001; Hirn 1998; Huttunen 1981; Hypén, Koivunen & Tunturi 2015; Kanerva & Peltonen 1961; Kaukiainen 2005; Kauranen 200; Leffler 1999; Lehtikanto 1964; Makkonen 2005; Mäkinen 1997; Mäkinen 2000b; Niskala 2007; Närhi 1963; E. Seppälä 1963; Wacklin 2011.
91 Degerman 2008; Forssell 2010; Havu 2008; Knapas 2012; H. Kuusi 2011; Åström 2012.
92 E.g. Mäkinen 2009a.
93 E.g. Ivendorff 2006.

However, the stories of the birth and development of the small rural lending libraries with their modest origins are to some extent more fascinating than those of the public libraries, which have continued to flourish throughout their existence. What can the occasional falling-off in the borrowing of books at the same time as the influence of the national awakening was increasing in the countryside tell about the circumstances in which the libraries operated? My objective is to find out what the first stumbling steps of the lending library studied here tell about the small community it sought to serve and the possibilities that existed for popular education in the outlying countryside, where there was certainly plenty of work for educators to do, and where a vernacular written culture arrived quite late, in the latter half of the nineteenth century. A study of the poorest areas of the countryside (such as northern Central Finland), which were the last to adopt a written culture[94], can supplement previous research and set the general view that it presents in a wider perspective.

For a long time Finnish research on literacy conducted from below has lacked an exploitation of several other historical sources than oral history, autobiographical and direct narrative material in studying the effects of literacy (mainly because the researchers have often come from other disciplines and paradigms than historians). Combining these other archival sources with narrative sources can offer us a more precise and multifaceted view of what reading and writing skills meant for the common people. Certainly autobiographical and more ethnological material can supplement the research in an important way, but from the point of view of historical research the basis of the research still resides in the use and critical interpretation of also other documentary sources. In this work, therefore, I intentionally refrain from using autobiographical material to study popular literacy and the advance of book culture among the people because this approach is already common in other disciplines in Finland. I wish to see to what extent research based on different kind of archival documents and sources (produced by the authorities or others than the local common people themselves) and interpreted from a new perspective yields results. An even more important reason for my approach is the fact that in the remote area that is the object of my research less such material has been preserved, which means that from the start the research must be based on other kinds of source material. This lack does not mean that literacy cannot be studied when autobiographical material has not survived in the same way as in more prosperous localities.

My study differs from earlier research in that the history of Nordic lending libraries has not previously been studied by connecting the sources describing their operations with an extensive long-term collective biographical (prosopographical) database. The use of this method is crucial for obtaining new findings because it makes an examination of the use of literature much richer and also provides more details about the readers' background. The actors in microhistories are often strong persons, who as individuals are taken to represent the whole phenomenon being examined.

---

94 Haapala 2007, 91, 107, 144, 152, 155, 160, 183.

However, in Finland library history has not previously been studied by using biographical information about the inhabitants of a local rural community; rather, the main focus of the numerous non-academic histories of libraries, for example, has been on how the library was organized as an institution that was separate from the local people.[95] In this research, connecting a collective-biographical method together with population, family and settlement history to the study of literacy skills means that I study literacy primarily as part of the concrete activities of a human community and the human capital of its daily life. This approach helps us to understand the cause-and-effect relations and the influence of the factors that promoted literacy and to relate them to a wider entity. It is important to be familiar with the real living conditions and family backgrounds of the founders and users of the library because such factors often explain the development of literacy and of libraries and may complete a mere approach of the history of ideas, which rather examines what the development of literacy meant at the level of proclamations and manifestos particularly in the debates carried on at the highest levels of society[96].

The 1860s were characterized by the active establishment of people's libraries all over Finland. In contrast, the first decades of the twentieth century saw changes in the functions of popular libraries. The Public Library Movement in North America had begun to have a stronger influence on the activities of Finnish libraries from the 1890s on, but it was only in the first decades of the following century that there was a movement towards modern public libraries and more professional librarianship.[97] The library activities in the local community that I study offer a good example of this broader development in Finland. The first popular lending library in this community was founded in the early 1860s, which is why I limit this study to extend from that decade to the beginning of the 1910s, when the library's activities languished. During that period, the community examined was going through a huge transitional stage as a result of numerous social, cultural and economic changes. It is interesting that the development of a vernacular literature and the number of publications in Finnish increased considerably in the years 1870–1920; in other words they coincided chronologically with the time frame of this study.

I omit from my examination the years of the First World War, Finland's independence and the birth of the Republic of Finland in 1917 because my example library had by then ceased to function. Probably, there were many other important matters in society that occupied the attention of the higher social groups (and indeed of the lower ones, too) in those years. It was a challenging time for the people of the age with regard to national politics because after the parliamentary reform of 1906, the Finns considered that the Tsar's Russification policy, which aimed at the unification of the Russian Empire, began to exert a tighter hold on the country from 1909 on. The

---

95 E.g. Ahlstedt 1987; Teuvo Heikkilä 1987; Toivola 1995.
96 On the concepts 'the people' and 'the common people', see also Laitinen & Mikkola 2013: Liikanen 2003.
97 Mäkinen 2009d, 145; Vatanen 2002, 131–141, 189.

years of the First World War were anyway an exceptional time, and from 1917 on the political atmosphere began to grow tenser at the local level, eventually leading to the Finnish Civil War in 1918. Admittedly, that war was not waged in the area of the community studied in this book, although at least over 150 parishioners did take part in the hostilities[98] in more southern parts of Finland.

On the other hand, from the point of view of popular education, the number of those who went to elementary school increased slowly but surely, and universal compulsory education came into force in the early 1920s, when the textbooks and libraries of elementary schools inevitably made the younger generation literate from an early age. They, therefore, had a much better opportunity to become acquainted with literature in Finnish and develop their literacy 'as a civic skill' than the young children of the 1870s had had. I follow the development of people's libraries, which along with the birth of the modern library movement in Finland became public libraries either side of the turn of the century, but the established operations of public libraries around the mid-twentieth century are excluded from this research, and my examination concentrates above all on an analysis of the conditions for, and the results of, early voluntary library work.

Why write about the library of a small rural parish in Central Finland, unknown to the majority of historians in the world? Writing about the lives of persons who have already been studied elsewhere does not yield the same joy of discovery as giving a place in history to less notable or unknown people of the past and thereby demonstrating the significance of their existence. They, too, performed interesting and important deeds, for which they should be remembered. Often their lives tell a very different story about the past than those of persons who spent their days at the centre of events or were otherwise prominent in times of great changes. Of course, it is easier to write about the latter since necessarily more sources about them have survived, but still it is always more fascinating to chart the unknown in the manner of an explorer.

In this book, I study the early history of those lending libraries, which adopted the principles of the Public Library Movement at the turn of the century: in other words, I examine how the first popular libraries were founded in outlying country parishes since the 1860s, why they were established and why in most cases they did not succeed in the first stages of their operations. I use a microhistorical approach in studying 'from the bottom up' the history of a less successful library in the late nineteenth century in the rural parish of Kivijärvi, which is located in Central Finland. By the terms 'popular library' or 'lending library', I mean the Finnish lending libraries, parish libraries[99], village libraries and church libraries of the nineteenth century that were mainly intended for the use of the lower social classes.[100]

---

98   Manninen 1986, 479.
99   The terms 'lending library' and 'parish library' are used synonymously in this work to describe the popular and parish libraries of the Finnish countryside in the period studied.
100 Lehtinen 1988, 41; Mäkinen 1997, 50.

My main research task has thus been to answer the following questions: What were the 'biography' of a lending library in a remote rural area and the collective biography[101] of the actors involved with it like? And why did this people's library live the life that it did? How did the course of its life turn out? I examine its birth, the factors which had led to its establishment, and its viability. However, my objective is not to produce a mere chronology of the different stages of the organization but rather to examine the work of the people who participated in its activities and the background ideas and practices which affected its operation, in other words, the products of the actions of several persons and the impact of the lending library on them. At the same time, I discuss the methodological means by which this kind of history of a popular lending library can be written by comparing the activities of this library with those of others of the same period. However, my aim is not to write a collective history of several different libraries; rather at the core of the examination and the comparison lies the question of why the lending library's activities were not as well received in the local community examined here as in some other places, and the part played by the culture of the local community in its success or failure.

The story of the library is divided into three sub-topics. They are needed to explain the main topic, and they help in ascertaining more exact details about the operation of the library.

The first sub-topic concerns the acquisition, reception and use of the book collections of a lending library in the outlying countryside of Central Finland at the end of the nineteenth century. What makes the examination fruitful is the fact that it focuses on the everyday history of the rural population who lived in a very remote area and whose literacy skills were still weak even after the mid-nineteenth century. This focus distinguishes it from recent Finnish research on the history of literacy, which has concentrated mainly on able rural readers and writers of the past. Thus it is interesting to clarify what kind of persons the lending library's activities in the first stage of its life attracted in a community where there were very few able readers and writers. At the same time, this collective biographical research on a remote area challenges the general view that predominates in Finnish historiography. According to that view, the establishment of cultural institutions like popular libraries led almost inevitably to an improvement both in literacy and in opportunities for social advancement.

In **the second major sub-topic**, the elucidation of these points helps us to ascertain what kind of people were involved in the activities of the libraries, in other words, not only the founders but also the readers and their motives, needs and opportunities for participating in the work of the library. The study thus focuses on the resources and operational prerequisites of the institution for the transmission of information as well as on the people's informational needs, their ability to receive the information the library offered and the ways in which they did so. The subject of this study is above all the level and quality of the functional literacy skills of the Finnish-speaking population and how people felt they could utilize the knowledge and informational capital that the libraries provided.

---

101 For the concept of a 'biography' of a town, see Montefiore 2012.

I examine why the operations of the library began falteringly and what this generally tells about the informational capital of the people of the countryside, about the interface between the oral and written cultures[102] and the significance of education and learning in the transition into a modern civil society. I also study how the development of literacy[103] and the use of the library possibly increased mental and immaterial capital or opportunities for social advancement in communal relations. Furthermore, I analyse how this capital was distributed according to age, gender and social status. The study concentrates particularly on the perspective of the agricultural readers and on what kind of opportunities they had for reading, creating and consuming written culture in the local environment.

At the same time, I use this research to conduct a methodological experiment in order to ascertain the extent to which it is possible to study the reading habits and the use of the library by the people of the outlying countryside. How did they read books, what did they think about them, and how did their behaviour differ from the habits of town-dwellers? Information about how they acted and why also indirectly reveals how they thought. Hardly any study of this kind has so far been carried out in the context of Finland or the Nordic countries. This research shows that it is possible to examine what the poorest section of the population read and how they experienced what they read, even though this information cannot be ascertained directly from collections of letters or diaries (because the majority of the population were still unable to write at that time and would have been incapable of recording to their experiences in writing). It is however possible to study the reception of literature from their point of view as well, although it is an extremely demanding task. Among other sources, library catalogues have been used for this purpose, and for example Jonathan Rose has examined the reading habits of the British working class by studying their autobiographical memoirs.[104] Because I do not have such sources produced by the readers themselves at my disposal, I must mainly settle for sources that describe their behaviour. At the same time, however, my research can complement and challenge the traditional 'national' study of library history by approaching the subject from below. The history of reading should be above all the history of the readers. The best way to study the significance of the ability to read and write is to analyse the readers' life stories because they related everything they read to their experience of life.

The third major research sub-topic concerns the question of whether the whole concept of a people's library (and especially the corresponding terms in Finnish and Swedish[105]) should be split into finer strands. Can one talk about a *people's* library? The first public lending libraries had been

102 See Goody 1987; Vansina 1985.
103 I examine the development of literacy as a skill and its communal use more widely elsewhere (see also e.g. Kotilainen 2013a; Kotilainen 2013c; Kotilainen 2015b). In this study I am interested in literacy mainly with regard to the level of skills that made it possible for people to use the lending library, and how these skills enhanced their intangible capital.
104 Rose 2001, 1–2. See also Dolatkhah 2008.
105 Sw. *Folksbibliotek*, Fin. *kansankirjasto*.

founded for the people, but how much did the people really use them, for example in the region examined in this book? It is important to note that by no means all the members of the local community necessarily availed themselves of the services of the library. That being the case, one can well ask why they failed to use them. Did education not have the desired effect on people? Was it was too ineffective or boring? Or did the peasants not realize the existence of the library or know how to utilise it as an opportunity to become more educated? What kind of attitudes were associated with the lending libraries in the people's minds?

In a broader framework, the object of my research represents a peripheral area, but it is exactly the point of view of the people of the periphery that this study is based on, and thus their local community lies at the heart of it. From the point of view of the operation of the lending libraries, there lies an extensive and complex range of background factors behind the peripheralization of an area, which my study also elucidates; in other words it seeks to explain why this region never became a pioneer in the field of library activity at the turn of the nineteenth and twentieth centuries. Here, I utilize a comparative approach. The comparative method, involving the comparison of histories of the library institution in Finland (based on original sources and research literature) and in different countries (based on research literature), helps to relate the findings connected with this particular library to a broader field than the local community and reveals the existence of similarities between different cultures.

The functional ability to read and write is one of the key concepts of this study. It can refer to literacy skills that can be actively used to achieve objectives and even social advancement in the local community. In that sense, the ability to read is a social practice.[106] Reading and writing skills are used differently in different areas of life and in different cultures. The literacy practices associated with them are part of broader social relations that affect the everyday lives of members of the community. These skills form part of the communication between people by means of which they describe the world and situations to themselves and others. Moreover, different communal institutions direct people's reading and writings towards what they consider to be desirable goals.[107] For example, the Lutheran Church aimed at a different kind of reading and writing literacy for the people from that which the rural elementary schools that were established after the enactment of the Decree on Elementary Education in 1866 sought to achieve.

However, it is not just a question of what literacy does for people but rather what people do with it. In itself, it does not necessarily produce a completely new way of thinking in people, but the writing down of things may, for example, help them to perform things they had not been able to do

---

106 Barton & Hamilton 1998, 6–13.
107 Barton 2007, 34–35. For example the historian Nils Erik Villstrand (2008, 2011) has used a concept 'political writing skills' (*politisk skrivkunnighet*) to describe how the Finnish common people (often with the assistance of a scribe) managed to further their interests and endeavours by sending written communications to the judiciary and political decision-makers.

before: to return to earlier matters, to study or to interpret and think about texts more deeply.[108] In the society of the nineteenth century, improved literacy skills also increased people's possibilities for social advancement. It was possible to consider literacy and the education acquired by means of it as mental capital in a situation where few people in the countryside had an opportunity to learn to read and write and to continue their studies by going to school and thereby acquire more informational capital.[109] The significance of education and school attendance lay in the opportunity for the social advancement it offered especially from the late 19th century and early 20th century on, at a time when there was less inherited wealth for each of those who seeked better future. (although people needed to have some financial resources in order to be able to get to the nearest school, which was often situated far from a rural pupil's home).[110] Here I mean with the concept 'social advancement' also the social position, respect and a good name a person could achieve in his or her own local community at the countryside, not necessarily moving from one social class to another or economic benefits. Informational capital is one of the types of immaterial social capital that the individual uses in reciprocal communal relations. Literacy skills could be used in communal networks to promote an individual's own objectives or those of a certain social group. Informational and cultural capital also consisted in the ability to follow the practices that each community adhered to.[111]

The idea of education and literacy as mental capital has been criticized because their mere existence does not show what the overall significance of education has been for the development of the economy and society in general. The methods used for measuring literacy in different periods are in part mutually incommensurable. It is thus important to consider what people have read and learnt in different eras and how this has taken place.[112] However, the regional and chronological comparison of literacy is problematic because the ability to read meant different things at different times and in different cultures[113]. A person who signed documents with his or her signature was not necessarily literate. On the other hand, a person who was able to write may have made a mark instead of writing his or her signature.[114] The mere ability to read does not reveal the nature and quality of the literature that a person read: Was it literature recommended by the church or popular song sheets? Furthermore, the possession of books and literacy skills by some individuals does not tell everything about the literacy of the whole community; books may have been borrowed from their owners, or they may have been read aloud to one or more persons gathered

108 Olson 1985, 15.
109 Bourdieu 1985b, 148; Huuhka 1955.
110 E.g. Häkli 1991, 39; S. Kotilainen 2015b. E.g. in Spain, see Lyons 2013, 170–200. Cf. however Kauranen (2007), who has studied less than ten life histories and received different results.
111 Bourdieu 1986[1983], 242–255; Coleman 1988, S98, S101–105; Lin 2003[2001], 14–15, 191–192; Putnam 2000, 19–22.
112 Matti Peltonen 1992, 88–89. See also Ginzburg 2007.
113 See also Ekko 2002; Street 1994, 11.
114 E.g. S. Kotilainen 2013b.

together.[115] In order to estimate the quality of literacy skills, I combine as many different original sources as possible in my analysis in order to be able to obtain the most thorough view of its character at the local rural level.

The efforts to enhance the people's education and literacy from the nineteenth century on were not just about promoting written culture or enabling people to speak for themselves in a public discussion, and in fact the enhancement of popular literacy was very strictly controlled by the upper classes.[116] For example, attempts were made to influence the contents of the libraries' book collections so that they would provide 'suitable' reading for the people, in other words moral, socially moderate and ideologically fairly conservative literature. The development of popular education and libraries played a significant role in Finland, too, in the early years of the process that has been called 'modernization', i.e. from the about mid-nineteenth century on[117]. However, the modernization process was by no means straightforward but rather a complex development that took place at different times in different regions and in different spheres of life.[118] Theories of modernization have often emphasized the significance of education and literacy. However, they are frequently premised on a belief in progress for which the traditional values constituted an impediment and on a model of development that was one and the same for all Western nation states.[119] In Finland, too, it was still thought at the end of the nineteenth century that the common people should be educated by the upper estates so that they might become literate and catch up with the 'civilized nations' of Western Europe, which they lagged behind. On the other hand, the people's oral culture was also elevated into an ideal of nationalist ideology, and literature and the arts time and again returned to the traditional landscapes and verses of the *Kalevala* (the national epic). The controlled transcription of the oral tradition into written form was the most important project in this process. For example, Elias Lönnrot planned and rewrote the folk poems he had collected for the *Kalevala* into a more 'readable' form, correcting the language and revising the stories in order to give the epic a more coherent plot. In the nineteenth century, the oral tradition was valued by the upper estates according to how well it served the aspirations of nationhood.[120]

Against this background, the fact that recent Finnish research on vernacular literacy has dealt with the 'unschooled' or 'self-taught' elements of the common people raises certain questions. In principle, in the nineteenth century there were no longer any young Finns who had not been to school, if 'school' is understood in the broad sense that the different forms of educational institution in the Finnish countryside represented. Often this schooling took the form of confirmation classes, which were usually

---

115 Matti Peltonen 1992, 77–78.
116 M. Lehtonen 2001, 53.
117 For a corresponding development in France, see Barnett 1973, 292.
118 For the local community examined here, see also S. Kotilainen 2008a, 68–69, 110–112. In the United States, as well, there was a debate at the end of the nineteenth century about the suitability for public libraries of fiction that was considered immoral. Garrison 1979, 67–75.
119 Matti Peltonen 1992, 86.
120 K. Laitinen 1997, 174, 176–184.

attended at the age of 15 or at the latest when a young person wanted to get married, as confirmation was a precondition of marriage.[121]

Every year the whole population had to attend parish catechetical meetings, in which the clergy examined the people's knowledge of Christian teaching, and at least in principle people prepared for these occasions. In the countryside, curates or cantors[122] taught the young people to read in special 'cantor's schools' and also tested people in the parish catechetical meetings. On Sundays, the parishes arranged Sunday school teaching for the children of the area of each village. Moreover, parents were obligated by the Swedish Church Law of 1686 to provide their children with elementary instruction[123], a task that often fell to the mother. Home teaching played an extremely significant role in the countryside, where there were no actual schools in the first part of the nineteenth century.[124] Up to the end of the nineteenth century, the teaching of elementary reading skills was carried out at home in Finland, and the official requirement for admission to a school was a command of the rudiments of reading skills. In 1723, a fine was imposed on those parents who neglected to provide their children with active reading skills and a knowledge of the scriptures.[125]

Even though it was usually only a question of learning the main elements of Christian teaching by rote and the amount of knowledge offered by the schools was restricted, the whole population perforce received some kind of schooling in the rudiments of literacy. The rural population gradually became aware of the different types of institutions that offered elementary instruction. The conditions under which these operated varied greatly in different areas, but even so no totally "schoolless' areas existed; it was just that the teaching in the countryside was arranged differently from that in the towns. Therefore, the word 'school' should be defined in this context more precisely, and it should be understood more broadly than the modern concept of the word since there were really no elementary schools with permanent buildings in the countryside before the 1860s.

At the same time, one can ask whether a completely 'self-taught' reader or writer actually existed. The ability to read is not created out of nothing, and someone who has taught him- or herself to write has first had to have some kind of instruction in the identification of letters in order to be able to read and write or must have learnt using some kind of model or example provided by other people.[126]

---

121 Laine & Laine 2010, 280–281.
122 The word 'cantor' is used here to translate the Finnish word *lukkari* (Swedish: *klockare*). However, in addition to leading the singing in church services, the *lukkari* had educational and other duties. He also assisted the vicar in many ways in the local administration. See also S. Kotilainen 2015b.
123 Hellemaa et al. 1986[1686]: The Swedish Church Law of 1686, XXIV, XI §.
124 Jalkanen 1976, 103, 151–157; Jalkanen 1986, 39–59. About similarities in home teaching in other Nordic countries: see Garðarsdóttir 2013, 140–141. See also S. Kotilainen 2013d.
125 Matti Peltonen 1992, 95.
126 On the ability to distinguish between written and spoken language and the adoption of formulaic expression: Elspaß 2012; Laitinen & Nordlund 2012; Laitinen & Nordlund 2013.

Learning to read is always linked to the culture in which the person lives and to his or her experiences of the collective culture. The inhabitants of the countryside were traditionally surrounded by numerous manifestations of the written culture, such as religious texts, sermons in services and written texts that were heard (or read) in other congregational meetings and, at the latest from the 1850s on, in newspapers in Finnish. Even though most people were not literate themselves, they came into contact with written texts and the written instruction provided by the church; in other words they did not live in a purely oral culture. In the community studied in this book, there were already a few able readers in the mid-nineteenth century who could read newspapers or calendars and knew how to tell others about the information contained in them. Just like 'self-taught' readers, 'self-taught' writers, too, constituted a minority. Most people learned to read and write only when somebody else who possessed these skills taught them. Similarly, the notion presented in some earlier Finnish research about readers and writers being "self-taught" may lead to wrong assumptions if this concept is not defined properly. The conception of the unschooled or uneducated commons suddenly learning to read and write in the late nineteenth century is literally problematic, and it reflects the same attitude that the educators of the time had towards the rural people. The development of reading and writing skills is generally the result of a longer history, often going back several generations. Previous research also considered that reading increased and that the general education of the people was enhanced as a fairly automatic consequence of popular education. Was this true in all cases? What do the sources which describe the reading habits of the common people have to say about this?

Less known library archives and the methods utilised in researching them

The history of reading can be studied only from the traces it has left in the sources. Traditionally these have taken the form of information about subscriptions to newspapers and magazines, diary entries, autobiographies or letters to the editor.[127] Even as late as the mid-nineteenth century, the examination of the level of the reading skills of wider sections of the population and above all of lower social groups was considered to be difficult, if not impossible, to execute because the level of people's functional reading and writing ability was not necessarily recorded in the documents drawn up by the authorities or other public instances, let alone the purposes and ways in which these skills were exploited in everyday life.[128]

However, the improvement in the reading and writing skills of the common people at the micro-level can be studied even with regard to those people who did not leave autobiographical records: for example, it is possible to ascertain their reading practices from sources produced by

---

127 Jarlbrink 2010, 43; McDowell 2009, 240.
128 Burch 2006, 372–373.

others, as I do in this study. A microhistorical analysis and close reading of the sources reveals traces of information about functional literacy as well. Microhistory often studies either exceptional individuals or a very limited group of people, event or area. In the former case, the exceptional person may also reveal something about more 'normal', ordinary life in functioning as a contrast to it, and in the latter case concentrating on a limited subject enables a more profound and wider-ranging analysis of the phenomenon under investigation. By 'microhistorical analysis' I do not here mean the study of exceptional persons; rather, I study in greater detail a few hundred individuals as representative of the whole local community in which they lived. At the same time, the study produces more profound information on the history of libraries with regard to the stage when they were founded in the Nordic countries and their first customers as seekers of information.

In order to be able to examine Finnish rural lending libraries, it is necessary to peruse a very scattered, fragmented and multifarious range of source material because only small scattered scraps of information about the libraries have been preserved. Those documents that were produced in connection with the operation of the library studied here, of course, form the most important source, insofar as they have survived. The source material concerning the libraries of the rural interior of Finland is sometimes very fragmentary, but that only makes it a more inspiring object of research, because by combining small observations it is possible to build piece by piece an overall picture of what the library activities once meant for the actors themselves. I use as my sources the archives of local public libraries that have been preserved up to the 2000s. Such sources are rather rare and have hardly been used in previous research. Their preservation has not been a matter of course that can be taken for granted, because the libraries were managed by companies, associations and private persons in addition to their other duties and thus, the creation of archives was not as carefully planned as the conservation of other documents by the congregational and municipal authorities.

Because an examination of all the Finnish rural libraries would be too large an undertaking (they were founded in every parish of the countryside towards the end of the nineteenth century), the approach I adopt in this book is a microhistorical one. I chose as the location of my study one of the remotest rural areas of the country, northern Central Finland. This region lay at a distance of more than a hundred kilometres from the nearest towns; there was no railway connection; nor was there any significant industry[129] or other sources of economic wealth, unless one takes into account the fact that many of the peasants owned forest, the value of which began to rise in the 1870s. Further educational institutions were located far away. So I did not choose this library because its archive sources were particularly well preserved or because it otherwise offered an insight into progressive library activities, but rather because its location was as humble as possible.

---

129 Apart from Kannonsaha Saw Mill. See the following section for further details.

MAP 1: The location of Kivijärvi and neighbouring parishes in Central Finland. Drawn by Jari Järvinen.

Vaasa (Vasa) was the capital of the province, Helsinki (Helsingfors) the capital of the whole country and Jyväskylä the most important town in Central Finland.

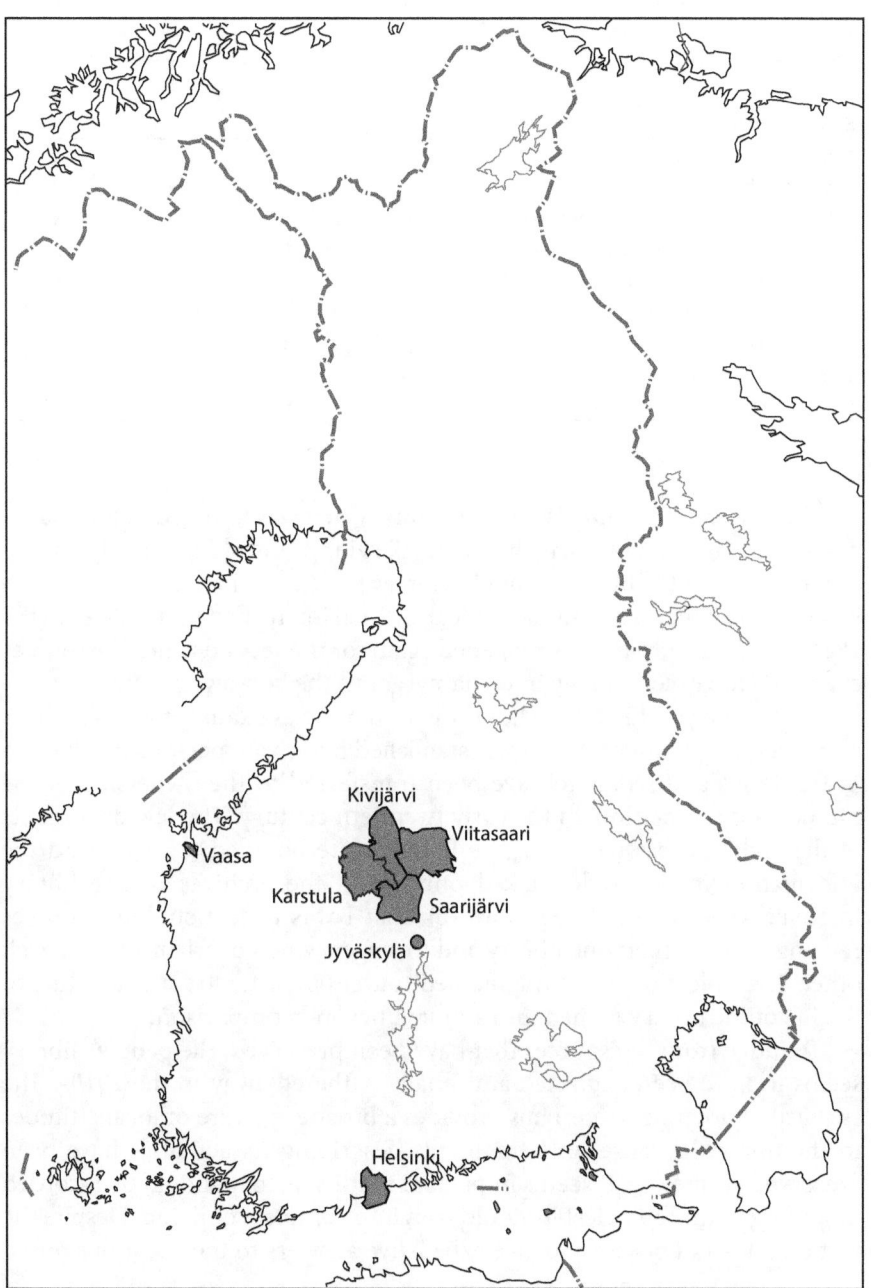

Table 2. *The main and supplementary sources for the research and the chronological periods covered by them.*

Sources	1800–1849	1850–1879	1880–1899	1900–1940
Main sources				
Kivijärvi library archives		x	x	x
Kivijärvi church parish archives	x	x	x	x
Kivijärvi library collection of old books	x	x	x	x
Collective biographical database	x	x	x	x
Bibliographical database	x	x	x	x
Supplementary sources				
Leppälänkylä library archives			x	x
Saarijärvi library archives	x	x	x	x
Saarijärvi library collection of old books	x	x	x	x
Leppälänkylä library collection of old books	x	x	x	x
Karstula library collection of old books	x	x	x	x
Kivijärvi municipal archives			x	x
Newspapers	x	x	x	x
Estate inventory deeds	x	x	x	x
Oral history		x	x	x

The object of the study is a lending library that was founded in the church parish and later the municipality of Kivijärvi in Central Finland. The study concentrates on the life of the public library which was located in the church village[130] of Kivijärvi and the activities of which intensified particularly in the 1880s, when the library was reopened again for the second time. The sources examined are exceptionally informative about the borrowers' activities.

When I began this research, I thought that I was examining the archives of one lending library which was established by private persons in Kivijärvi in the 1880s and seems to have been transferred to the ownership of the municipality some time in the early twentieth century. The few documents of the archives that tell about the library were bundled together, and the information in the folder talked only about the archives of one library in Kivijärvi. Later I noticed, however, that I was in fact studying sources relating to more than one library and to stages which overlapped with each other. The collection of the fragmented sources in order to form a picture of the life of the library turned into a drama beyond comparison.

To judge from the sources that have been preserved, the people's library seems to have been neglected and finally withered away in the 1910s. The survival of documents perhaps provides a broader picture of local attitudes to the library, because only fragments describing its activities have been preserved. Therefore, it seems important that its history should be recorded in writing in this book lest it should pass into complete oblivion. Despite the fact that it is not possible to give exhaustive answers to the questions posed

---

130 A church village is the principal village of a parish and the site of the main parish church.

for my research, the endeavour to do so remains a challenge and a journey of exploration into the history of libraries. I have supplemented the sparse surviving sources which tell directly about the library with other sources and databases relating to them that I have compiled.

The archive sources for the library examined in this study show what kind of phenomenon the ability to read was in a remote area. The most important source consists of the few documents preserved of the archives of the library of Kivijärvi dating from the 1870s up to the 1910s and some even up to the 1940s.[131] All in all, the number of surviving archival sources that relate to the story of the lending library of Kivijärvi up to the present day is fairly small. The records are mostly the minutes of annual general meetings of the library, but there are only a few records of the meetings of the board of governors, and probably they were never documented in any detail. No records were kept at all during the quietest years of the library's operation, so it is sometimes difficult to ascertain exactly when the library operated and when it ceased to function. In addition to the records, some accounts, a list of borrowers and catalogues of the book collection have been preserved.[132]

Similar sources and registers of loans kept by Kangasala parish library over a period of about 20 years, 1874–1895, have also been studied.[133] The parish of Kangasala, which lies near the city of Tampere, was the home of Agathon Meurman, a noble-born non-fiction author and supporter of the Finnish cause and of the writer Jalmari Finne. There were several manor houses in the area, and the owners of the largest agricultural estates were considerably more prosperous than the peasant farmers of Kivijärvi. In its cultural life, Kangasala was in other respects, too, a much more vital and economically developed area than a backwoods parish like Kivijärvi. It contained altogether 70 villages, several dozen more than Kivijärvi, although the populations of the two parishes were approximately the same at the beginning of the nineteenth century.[134]

The surviving source material covering the early stages of the library of Kivijärvi is sparse, at least if one wants to analyze the attitude of the peasants to public libraries. Furthermore, the sources were mostly drawn up by the few educated people in the community, but the very fact that they remain silent about some matter can in itself be significant. The second main source is the library's collection of old books. However, only slightly over 170 of the books belonging to the old library have been preserved. The books in the collection were published mainly between the 1840s and the 1920s. Strictly speaking, it is a question of several different book collections which were merged together in the course of time. It is possible to identify altogether

---

131 See Table 2.
132 The archives of the library of Kivijärvi (KKA).
133 Ojanen 2011, 5.
134 Ojanen 2011, 6, 15–16. Similar minutes of the meetings of the board of governors have been preserved from the 1870s for example in the archives of the Nivala lending library and a list of borrowers 1885–1895 from the library of Rovaniemi. H. Mäkelä 1991, 22; Vuontisjärvi 2010, 15–16.

about 470 books that belonged to the collection[135] so the analysis mainly depends on the surviving catalogues of the library.

The third main source is the archives of the church parish of Kivijärvi. In the minutes of the church meetings of Kivijärvi there is a small entry that throws light on the activities of the library in the 1870s. I also use the parish registers of Kivijärvi in compiling biographical information about the persons who were mainly concerned with the library. Furthermore, the records of the parishioners' literacy skills in the confirmation records show how the clergy assessed their ability to read in the nineteenth century.[136] The minutes of the meetings of the board of governors of the library indicate that announcements concerning the library were made by the clergy during church services,[137] but in the parish archives of Kivijärvi there are hardly any church announcements concerning the library dating from those times, even though the church announcements from that period have otherwise been preserved. This would indicate that the library did not see a need to broadcast its activities very often. The choice to have announcements made in church is an indication that in that way they would reach the parishioners better (or at any rate) more cheaply than for example by publishing them in newspapers; in other words, it was probably thought that the information would get through better if the parishioners heard and passed it on by word of mouth to others than if they read it in a newspaper.

With the help of the registers of baptisms, marriages and funerals and the confirmation records of the church parish, I have been able to gather biographical information about the persons who participated in the operation of the library: the founders and members of the board of governors and the borrowers. The identification of some borrowers has been made more difficult by the fact that the same families had lived in the small locality for centuries and consequently there were several persons of the same name living there. This was a result of the fact that hereditary surnames had been in use ever since the 1500s, and forenames were also hereditary. Because more exact information about the place of residence or the social status of all the borrowers was not marked in the loans registers, it is impossible to identify some of them with certainty.[138]

For the purposes of comparison, I use the archives and collections of old books from the lending libraries of Saarijärvi, Karstula and the village

---

135 It is impossible to estimate the exact number because no comprehensive list exists, and it is possible that some of the books of a suitable age may have been added to the collection afterwards, but this cannot be verified any more through any of the written sources.
136 The archives of the parish of Kivijärvi (KSA), records of baptisms, marriages and funerals 1800–1939, confirmation records 1802–1939; Minutes of meetings of the church and parish councils 1816–1913.
137 KKA, minutes of the annual general meeting held on1 9/2/1891, minutes of the board governors of the library held on 20/1/1911.
138 KSA, records of baptisms, marriages and funerals 1800–1939, confirmation records 1802–1939. For more detailed source criticism relating to the compilation of the church records, see S. Kotilainen 2008a, 28–34.

of Leppälänkylä (in the municipality of Kivijärvi) to the extent that they have survived down the present day. Some of the documents relating to the libraries are privately owned, so they have been omitted from this study. Only after the research had been completed and this book had already been written did it come to light that the loans registers of Karstula library have apparently been preserved, at least for the years 1884–1894, in the archives of the Municipality of Karstula.[139] However, despite my request I was not given access to the oldest archival sources concerning the activities of the library when I visited Karstula Municipal Archives in autumn 2011, although I would have wished to peruse all possible archival material concerning the library. The oldest archives of these libraries, too, would appear to have been preserved in a very fragmentary form, but numerous old books have nevertheless been preserved in the collections of the later municipal libraries, although these collections, too, are no more complete than those of any other older lending libraries, from which some of the works have disappeared in the lending process over the course of time.[140]

Other supplementary sources that I use include estate inventory deeds appended to the records of court sessions (or alternatively contained in the parish archives) and oral accounts recalling reading activities. The material of a general survey of church folklore that has been stored in the Folklore Archives of the Finnish Literature Society was collected from three rural parishes in the area of the former mother parish of Kivijärvi in Central Finland in the 1970s.[141] Originally this material was collected by the Department of Church History of the University of Helsinki. Since the survey used the same list of questions for every parish, the material is extremely suitable for the purposes of comparison and gives a representative overview of the people's attitudes to reading in the whole area around Kivijärvi.[142] I use also oral memories of the local population from the mid-nineteenth to the early twentieth century, preserved in the Folklore Archives of the Finnish Literature Society and the Institute for the Languages of Finland.

Furthermore, in this book the Finnish-language press of the time is used in order to find possible discussions and expressions of public opinion concerning the necessity or uselessness of the local library, matters which are not conveyed in the pages of the documents produced by the library itself. The newspaper articles constitute source material that reveals how the popular library operated in the local community, how it was discussed and who were concerned with it.[143] In the light of my earlier research on the same

---

139 Luukkanen 2013.
140 The archives of the lending library of Leppälänkylä village; the archives of the lending library of Saarijärvi.
141 Church folklore has been recorded and stored in the form of transcripts and partly as tape recordings in the Recorded Archives of the Finnish Literature Society's Folklore Archives (SKSÄ). Archives of Ecclesiastical Folklore, general survey of church folklore (survey nr 1): Kannonkoski (1975), Kinnula (1974) and Kivijärvi (1975).
142 Murtorinne 1986. On the use of sources in other research on these local communities, see S. Kotilainen 2008a; S. Kotilainen 2013c; S. Kotilainen 2013d.
143 Mäkinen (2007) has also used newspapers as a source in studying the writing skills of the peasants.

local community, it is only to be expected that little source material written by the users of the library concerning their own motives has survived in its original form, so their own voices are not heard directly in the sources. The available source material inevitably emphasizes the founders' point of view. On the other hand, information about the activities of the users such as the number of loans and other data on borrowing can be regarded as indirect indicators of their attitudes and their reception of the library. For the earlier years studied here, the minutes of the Municipality of Kivijärvi offer no assistance because it seems that they have not been preserved for that period. The records of the meetings of the municipal assembly of Kivijärvi have as far as can be ascertained only been preserved since 1895 and the records of the municipal board since 1899.[144] Unfortunately, the oldest documents relating to the elementary school of Kivijärvi, which date from the end of the nineteenth century, have not been made available to me. The minutes of the board of governors of the school have been preserved from that time, but in spite of my numerous requests, I have not got to see them for this study. However, Saara Tuomaala used the oldest records as source material for her doctoral dissertation, which was published in 2004.[145]

In the analysis of the sources, a combination of three approaches has been used. I examine the object of my study from the perspective of microhistory and the history of mentalities[146]; I base my analysis on a collective biographical method;[147] and I employ a comparative approach, based on both original sources and literature. These three methods complement each other and have made possible a voyage of exploration that has yielded more information about the history of the lending library studied here than has been available hitherto.

In this research I have used extensive systematically compiled databases which are founded on the empirical study of original sources and the collation of the information yielded by them. On the basis of the sources used for this study, I have first compiled two extensive databases: a bibliographic database (Kivijärvi BOOKS) and a collective biographical database of the borrowers of the library (Kivijärvi READERS). In the bibliographic database I have combined information about the works in the collection of old books in the library of Kivijärvi up to 1915 (I have gone through these books and recorded their bibliographic data in my database) with the information contained in the catalogues of the library's collections (the only documents that exist for some of the books). However, the bibliographic information about the books has been entered in the handwritten lists of loans and books

---

144 Archives of the Municipality of Kivijärvi.
145 S. Tuomaala 2004.
146 'The method of clues' developed by Ginzburg consists in the interpretation of insignificant, even unconscious, marginal and routine activity as a clue to the existence of some wider phenomenon. The information it yields is not in fact hidden but visible; it just needs to be recognized by the researcher. Davis 2001; Ginzburg 1996, 48, 74; Ginzburg 2007; Matti Peltonen 1992, 29, 33, 45; Matti Peltonen 2012, 45.
147 On the viewpoint of the local community studied here, see also S. Kotilainen 2011.

in a much abbreviated form, often containing only the title of the book or the beginning of it, and perhaps also the author's surname.

When I was compiling the database, I noticed that some of the works that were listed in the catalogues also still existed in the collection of old books, so in such cases, after verifying that it was in fact the same book, I combined the information about it from the two sources as one entry in the database. For example, there are marks in the books indicating their classification or order of arrival, and when I found a similar number or mark in a book catalogue, I was able to conclude that it was a question of the same book. I have supplemented the information missing from the lists, such as publication years, authors and numbers of pages, with the help of published (national) bibliographies. It is not always possible to ascertain the exact year of publication and hence the edition of the work in question, if the book has not anymore existed in the collection of old books. This has also affected the collection of other bibliographical information. In such cases, I have entered in the database a mention of the possible years between which a work may have been published.

The same books are sometimes mentioned several times in different book catalogues of the library and even by different titles, so the identification of the books has been quite a detective work. For example, a translation of a work by Walter Scott with the exceptional title *Romaneja ja kertomuksia* [Novels and stories] did not seem to be in any of the bibliographies that I was using until, getting to the end of the library catalogues of Kivijärvi, I noticed that the same work had been recorded almost at the end of the catalogue under the title *Perthin kaupungin kaunotar* [The Fair Maid of Perth]. When I looked for a book with this title, I found out that the work in question had been published in Finnish as the fifth volume in a series called *Romaneja ja kertomuksia*. To be sure whether one is dealing with the same or a different book, one must first of all collate all the information and notes made at different times in the library catalogues and after that use as corroboration totally different kind of bibliographies, from the national bibliographies published in book form in the nineteenth century to the sales catalogues of second-hand book shops and bibliographies on the Internet. The most important source, of course, is the national Finnish bibliography, *Fennica*, maintained by the National Library, although surprisingly many of the works which were preserved in the library are missing from *Fennica*'s digital bibliography and from the internet database of the Library of the University of Jyväskylä (which is one of the libraries entitled to a free copy of all works published in Finland since 1919 and thus includes a fairly comprehensive collection of the oldest Finnish literature).[148] For the sake of comparison, I also compiled the databases of the old book collections of Saarijärvi and Leppälänkylä libraries.[149]

---

148 Antikvaari, the Internet antiquarian bookshop, www.antikvaari.fi; Fennica, http://fennica.linneanet.fi; Kirjasampo, the web service of works of fiction, www.kirjasampo.fi; the Internet database of the collections of Kuopio City Library, http://kirjasto.kuopio.fi; T. Laine 2000b; Pipping 1856–1857; Suomalainen kirjallisuus: aakkosellinen ja aineenmukainen luettelo 1878–1938; Vasenius 1878.
149 Saarijärvi BOOKS; Leppälänkylä BOOKS.

Only one list of borrowers of the library of Kivijärvi for the period 1877–1897 has been preserved; it refers to 129 books. So I have compiled a second database which includes information about the approximately 364[150] borrowers of these books and which books each of them has borrowed. The hardest work has been to identify these borrowers more precisely because the register of borrowers often only mentions a person's forename and surname and possibly also his or her place of abode. The persons in the list were also sometimes designated in the following ways: "'Mistress of Saramäki' (the name of a farm), 'Wife of Juho Hänninen' or 'Maidservant at the vicarage'.[151] A more sensible researcher would save him- or herself the bother of examining the borrowers any further at this stage and be content with stating that it was not possible to identify them more specifically with the help of the lists. On the other hand, there are small scraps of biographical information about the parishioners in plenty in the church records: details of their birth, attendance at confirmation classes and confirmation, followed by information about their ability to read in the annual parish catechetical meetings, their place of abode, their social positions and occupations, marriages, the birth of children, illnesses and their deaths. By collating these data with the information in the catalogue of borrowers, a more curious researcher can find out at least something about their lives. Because, in any case, in this study I examine literacy as a social activity or practice, I decided that 'with the same trouble' I might as well also examine the borrowers' biographical data so that I could find out who they were and discover their mutual networks and the relationships on which their everyday life was based. The collation of personal data with the borrower register can reveal surprisingly multifarious information about the enthusiasm of the rural population for reading and about their informational needs and how these were satisfied.[152]

In practice, of course, the compilation of a collective biography of the borrowers is a laborious and challenging task. This method, which is based on genealogical research, has been widely used in historical research in the most varied connections.[153] In the research of literacy skills, Christine Pawley has used the term 'reading community' to refer to the collective study of readers as part of the community in which they practise reading. Generally, these reading communities shared common customs, values and opinions.[154] In just the same way, it is necessary to employ a collective biographical method when little information about the readers as individuals and their reading habits has survived.

---

150 This number contains also some 'units' of borrowers, i.e. entities such as elementary schools, local courts and households that were designated only by the place of residence or the surname of the family. This is why in some of the tables in this book the total number of borrowers is 360 instead of 364, because these units have been excluded in examining the gender of borrowers for example.
151 KKA, register of borrowers 1877–1897.
152 Kivijärvi READERS.
153 Keskinen 2012; Levi 1992; Piilahti 2007; Sabean 1998; Salomies 2001, 73–91; Stone 1971. For a definition and critique of the concept 'prosopography', see Keats-Rohan 2007, 140–145.
154 Pawley 2002, 144–146.

When one seeks a particular individual among a large crowd or collates biographical data from several different sources into one biography, it is easy to make small mistakes in numerical data and the identification of persons even when one takes particular care. On the other hand, the method also is self-correcting because it is possible by employing a collective biographical or prosopographical method to find out what the members of the local community as borrowers were like as a group even when defective sources do not allow us to ascertain all the biographical facts connected with an individual borrower. This is an advantage in the study of social lower groups in particular because fewer biographical sources relating to them have usually been preserved. Collective biography can be used to study community structures more profoundly than individual biographies, and it also produces denser microhistorical information. The use of a collective biographical method typically allows one to study, for example, the interaction between the members of a particular group of people and its outcomes, i.e. common experiences that are shared by the whole group.[155]

The most important innovative idea behind this research has thus been to collate a collective biographical database with the information provided by the list of the borrowers of the library. This has yielded an informationally rich database, which also contains information about the readers' families. However, the identification of persons for the borrower database from the other parishioners has taken considerable time. In fact, the identification of the less affluent members of the rural population from the archives is in itself challenging because they were not always individualized very carefully in the lists of the popular libraries. Sometimes their place of abode was entered in the parish registers at the turn of the century only with a mention that they lived on the lands of a certain house or farm, and one farm could have numerous crofts and cots spread over a wide area. No comprehensive lists of crofts and cots in those days was compiled by the clergy in the registers of Kivijärvi church parish, and in the catechetical records, in which the other personal information about persons belonging to the landless populations has been marked, they are mentioned only randomly together with the names of the landless families.

As stated above, in a small countryside parish, different persons often had the same personal names, and there were several full namesakes as a result of the tight-knit kinship ties. Unless they were identified in the lists of borrowers by their place of abode (for landless persons often only the village[156] where they lived was mentioned, or the fact that they were cottars, but with no mention of the name of the cot), the researcher must be able to decide who out of the several namesakes among the cottars or their children might be the one who borrowed books from the library. Sometimes it is not possible to ascertain this from any source, although on some rare occasions

---

155 Caine 2010, 48.
156 The Finnish word *kylä* (village) indicates a geographically limited administrative area. However, these villages of northern Central Finland were often little more than hamlets containing a few farms.

the parish records offer surprising information which can be used to narrow down the number of possible candidates. When, for example, one has to decide whether the person who borrowed a book was an old grandfather living on a farm on a life-annuity or the master of another household living on the same estate, information about the grandfather's blindness can at least rule him out of the number of possible borrowers.[157] But then again, it is, of course, also possible that the grandfather did borrow the book from the library and somebody else read it aloud to him. The sources do not permit us to verify this in retrospect.

An examination of the archive material of a local library employing a microhistorical approach also reveals broader phenomena and processes, such as the development of literacy, the significance of elementary education for the common people themselves, opportunities for social advancement and the increase in people's informational capital and its exploitation in communal relations. At the micro-level, it is also possible to discern new explanations for already familiar phenomena. Microhistory has typically studied exceptional individuals or unusual situations[158] and details. A change in the perspective of the research to focus, for example, on the clash between exceptional events with long-term societal and cultural structures reveals the longer historical development. It would not be possible otherwise to discern this long-term process from the existing sources.[159] In the same way, the documents of the lending library describe above all the activities of the higher social strata in the parish, but at the same time they also provide new information about the lower groups that would not otherwise be available.

Sometimes in historical research surprising information is revealed when the researcher creatively combines sources that are not usually connected with one another. That is also the case with the collation of the library archive material with the biographical data about the borrowers in this study: by using these two sources we can obtain extremely detailed information that enables us to examine the reading activities of the whole local community and the influence that these activities had on it. A precise study of one local community can serve as a useful example and provide material for the formation of hypotheses in the study of other similar cases. The microhistorical method consists in combining the local and the global and relating them to each other. A microhistorical approach to global history means starting the analysis with an actor-centered approach on a local level. It is said that we can only understand the global while studying the local. The local stands in relation to other localities, and it is defined by and through these relations. This is why the concept of locality should be broadened by the concept of translocality.[160]

For example, in the study of lending libraries, the perspective from below can offer a lot of new information about the rural population especially if the examination of the social group also intersects with information about

---

157 Kivijärvi READERS.
158 See e.g. Davis 2001; Ginzburg 2007.
159 Ginzburg 2007.
160 Epple 2012, 169–170.

gender, age and worldview. At the same time, it is possible to conceptualize the differences as well as the interaction between the founders and administrators on the one hand and the users of the library on the other. The history of mentalities is often combined with microhistory in an endeavour to study the ways of thinking of people of the past from their behaviour. Broadly defined, mentalities embrace worldviews, norms, habits and traditions; in other words, factors that are related not only to people's thinking but also to their actions. According to Matti Peltonen, the study of mentalities has, in fact, called into question the relationship between thought and action. At the centre of the research on mentalities are crystallized forms of human behaviour; in other words, practices which are the focus of interest in studying the relationship between thinking and behaviour.[161] In this study, too, I examine people's own ways of thinking insofar as their behaviour reveals them. At the same time, one can examine the difference between the culture 'produced' by the people and the culture 'thrust upon' them.[162]

Microhistory has a lot in common with comparative research. In order to be able to make comparisons, one must be familiar with the details. Correspondingly, comparative research of local communities enables generalization and contextualization, which are essential elements of microhistory.[163] The advantage of a comparative approach at both the micro- and the macro-levels is that it makes for broader interpretations, the construction of theories and the further development of the research method. By examining in detail the significance of the activity of a local library in a single community, this study will provide material and a basis for later comparative historical research.

Over a long period, and especially in the latter half of the twentieth century, a lot of local historical research has been carried out in Finland and published in the form of parish histories. Before long, however, this research began to follow the same kind of fixed pattern, in which the local histories of different parishes were fitted into a mould created and formed by earlier researchers. The tables of contents of these works were often nearly identical and consisted of headings referring to different aspects of parish life, such as the history of settlement, economic life, local government, parochial history and the wartime situation. Only the local events particular to each parish changed under the same headings, but the overall structure remained the same. From the 1960s and 1970s on, many leading historians began to criticize the fixed structure of local parish histories. However, it was not until the 1980s that the first works challenging the traditional study of local history were written. At the same time, academic historical research began to be influenced by the so-called 'new histories': microhistory, the history of mentalities and oral history.[164] Thus one should not force all the

---

161 Matti Peltonen 1992, 8, 15–16.
162 Ginzburg 2007, 28–29.
163 Alapuro 2012, 141–142; Bloch 1928, 16–23. Among others, Giovanni Levi has pointed out that in studying microhistory, one should attempt to understand the differences that lie behind superficially similar cases. Alapuro 2004, 58.
164 Ahtiainen et al. 2010, 7–14.

histories of local libraries into the same mould as has been traditionally done in research, but rather base one's study on an empirical examination of the sources for each local library in order to discern the differences between them and to reveal the existence of less successful libraries like the one that is the subject of this book. However, it is beyond the scope of this study to draw up a comprehensive comparison of all Finnish libraries;[165] that would be the subject of another study.

Previous microhistorical research on lending libraries has usually concentrated on just one local community. This microhistory, too, focuses on a single community. However, I also continually compare my results with other local communities and micro-level library studies in order to bring out the larger picture that my case exemplifies and relate it to the whole Nordic or European library field with regard to its exceptional and common features. An internal comparison within the local community examined, for example in terms of differences between gender, social group and the level of literacy, would also be important, but further extensive comparison is required to address these matters.

Not only the mere comparison of national histories, but especially transnational historical research has produced new outlooks for research, particularly in the field of gender history, for example.[166] Therefore, the focus of my international comparisons consists of lending libraries in the other Nordic countries and elsewhere in Europe. In the comparative method, the comparability and the commensurability of the objects of research can be weakened by the fact that certain concepts that are crucial for the research are defined differently at different times and in different places.[167] The circumstances of the objects of comparison can also differ crucially. The findings of studies on the history of libraries conducted in other countries are not always directly applicable to conditions in Finland or Sweden. Already in the seventeenth and eighteenth centuries, the amount of published material and literature available to readers in more southern parts of Europe was considerably greater than it was in the Nordic countries. There were also many more publishers, printers, book merchants, libraries and readers in the rest of Europe in those days.[168]

In spite of this, I am interested in ascertaining as far as possible how typical or exceptional the object of my research actually was by comparison for example with Swedish, English, Irish, Scottish or American libraries. I am interested in learning whether there were similar library activities in any other places. Such a comparison makes it easier to see how the library of the local community studied compares with European ideas of popular lending libraries and how typical a representative of the libraries of its time it was. The comparison also indicates what phenomena require further investigation when they are examined in a larger context and when, for example, the

165 See Mäkinen 2009a; Schadewitz 1903; Werkko 1879.
166 Jonsson & Neusinger 2007, 258–259.
167 Melin 2005, 60.
168 T. Laine 2006, 19.

reasons for and origins of a particular phenomenon are compared at the international level.[169] For such a comparison to be significant, there must be, above all, diverse interaction between the communities involved, i.e. the movement and exchange of influences.[170] For this reason, popular education and literacy make for excellent objects of international comparison; the development of these was a project shared by all Western countries in the nineteenth century, and influences spread for example through personal contacts and via literature and the press from one country to another.

The transnational approach is positively distinguished from the international in that, rather than making a mere international comparison (which basically consists in the discovery of differences between intra-European cultural fields or between those of Europe and other parts of the world and in this way strengthening the national borders), it strives to discover and express phenomena and factors that transcend the borders of several nations, in the present case mutually similar endeavours to educate the common people and to develop national educational systems. The foundation of libraries accelerated along with the active debate relating to them and the influx of popular educational ideals from one Nordic country to another at that time.[171] For example, despite local differences, the basic principles of popular enlightenment were very similar in all the Nordic countries in the nineteenth century. Consequently, I choose to examine the birth and development of libraries from a transnational perspective since it better permits a comparative study of similarities, interactions and generally the spread of influences.

At the same time, it complements the comparative approach by bringing to it the possible influences of cross-border interaction as an explanatory factor. This extends the traditional approach of international comparison, which focuses on nation states, because cultural and social phenomena are not limited by the boundaries of nation states in the same way as state administrative and legal systems, for example, but naturally spread across national frontiers. Furthermore, it does not mean analyzing the interactions between nation-states as sole agents – mostly with an emphasis on diplomatic and economic relations (this is how the concept 'international' can be defined in historical research), but transcending and comparing politically defined and geographically fixed territories.[172]

My comparison between the libraries is conducted on several levels. The objects of the most precise comparison are as follows: in addition to international comparison, I compare the practices of local library operations nationally and regionally in order that the direction and significance of the influences on them should be more clearly apparent:

---

169 Alapuro 2004, 56.
170 Haupt 2007, 711.
171 Jonsson & Neusinger 2007, 260; Mäkinen 2009c; Vatanen 2002.
172 Epple 2012, 162.

MAP 2: The location of Kannonkoski, Kinnula and Kivijärvi. Drawn by Jari Järvinen.

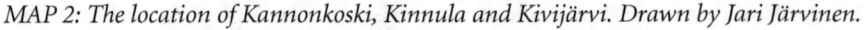

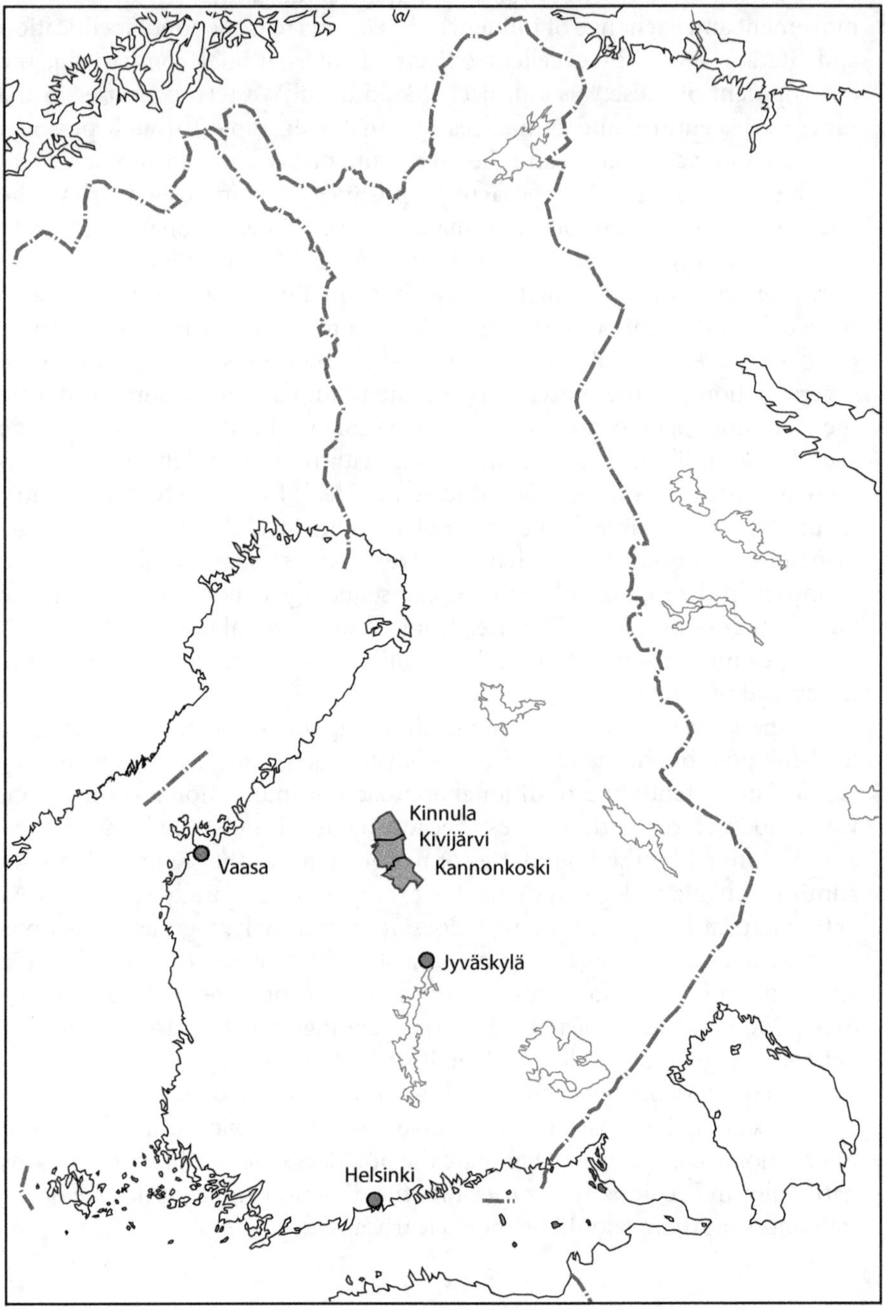

First, libraries in the neighbouring area of Kivijärvi in northern Central Finland, such as those in Saarijärvi and Kannonkoski (Leppälänkylä),[173] which I examine partly on the basis of original sources. It is my hypothesis that these libraries most resembled that of the local community examined in this study. I first of all examine the conditions that existed when the first library in Kivijärvi was founded and study which members of the local community were involved and what kind of prerequisites existed for its operation. At the same time, I compare the time of the establishment of the small rural library and the early days of its operation with the beginning of library activities in neighbouring parishes in order to find out how progressive or backward it was in relation to them. Two important objects of comparison are the library of Saarijärvi, a neighbouring parish, which was well established and in whose establishment and operation the local peasant population was actively involved, and then the library of Leppälänkylä, formerly the library of the Kannonsaha Sawmill community, which represents the reading activities of the population of an early rural factory community.

Other comparable parishes in the vicinity were Karstula and its chapelry Kyyjärvi (which later became an independent parish in the twentieth century), Saarijärvi together with its chapelry Pylkönmäki (which likewise later became an independent parish) and Viitasaari which was originally the old mother parish of Kivijärvi. From the last mentioned parish, Kivijärvi and Pihtipudas seceded to become parishes in their own right in the mid-nineteenth century. Moreover, Kinnula, in the northern part of Kivijärvi – which in the last decades of the nineteenth century was an even smaller mother parish than Viitasaari – and later Kannonkoski in the south split off to become independent parishes, the former in 1914 and the latter in 1934. I also make some further comparisons with the neighbouring Southern Ostrobothnian Lake District, which lay to the west of northern Central Finland, and particularly with the Alajärvi region, as it makes for an interesting object of comparison. The northern part of Central Finland belonged administratively to the Province of Vaasa in the late nineteenth century, as did the region of Ostrobothnia. The traditional routes for transportation and trips to town and market led into Ostrobothnia, and usually to the town of Kokkola (Gamla Karleby) in Central Ostrobothnia.

I compare my primary object of study with the Lake District because culturally they resemble one another in many ways. Like northern Central Finland, the Lake District belongs to what is called the 'Savonian Wedge', into which settlers began to migrate from the Savonia region in eastern Finland in the early years of the Modern Age. Moreover, the Lake District is geographically closer to Karstula and Saarijärvi than it is to Central

---

173 Leppälänkylä was previously one of the villages in the parish of Kivijärvi before it became the church village of the new municipality of Kannonkoski, which has existed since 1934, when "Kannonkoski" was adopted as the name of the municipality. The municipality was formed by uniting areas that had previously belonged to Kivijärvi and Viitasaari into one parish. Kannonsaha, too, was one of the villages of Kivijärvi and was also incorporated into Kannonkoski.

Ostrobothnia (which in turn is more comparable to Kinnula, which was connected to it by road). An old road connection (the Kuopio-Vaasa highway) ran from Saarijärvi in the direction of the Lake District in Ostrobothnia. This makes it more sensible to compare Kivijärvi with the environs of Karstula since a new highway built in the famine years of the 1860s and completed in 1872 soon became established as the main route for trips to town, which in this case was Jyväskylä. The distance of the journey was halved, and the postal service began to run along this road from Karstula to Kivijärvi. When the railway was built, the major transport node from 1882 on became Myllymäki station in the municipality of Ähtäri in Southern Ostrobothnia, and from there transportation continued by horse and cart (or sleigh in winter) to Kivijärvi until the early twentieth century. A regular bus service along this route was not established until 1925.[174]

However, mere national and regional comparison is not sufficient in this context. Therefore, the **second object of comparison,** which I use to a lesser extent is the libraries of the largest towns and cities in Finland and (Northern) Europe. This I do in order to reveal the real differences that existed between urban and rural libraries all over Finland and also in Western Europe. These comparisons probably show the greatest differences because one can assume that the popular libraries of the larger towns were among the most progressive lending libraries of the time, and many new practices connected with library activities reached them first. In addition to the international comparison, an interesting regional object of study is the lending library of Jyväskylä, the principal town of Central Finland, and also the site of the first Finnish-language teacher training institution in the country. Other Finnish reference points include the lending libraries of Helsinki, Turku, Tampere, Kuopio and Vaasa. **Thirdly,** I make some rather more random comparisons with popular libraries in other parts of the remote countryside in Finland and the other Nordic countries. I compare these libraries with that of Kivijärvi with a view to revealing similarities and differences between different parts of these countries. This also indicates where the library that is my principal object of study is located on the map of library activity in Europe, and whether it was perhaps less successful than most in its operation.

174 Lampinen 1986, 263, 265.

2. The Foundation of a Local Lending Library

What kind of world were the people's libraries born into?

THE SLOW SHIFT TOWARDS FUNCTIONAL READING SKILLS

> The newspaper *Suomalainen*[175] has now been coming out here too for over a year, and hardly a letter from Kivijärvi has appeared in the columns of *Suomalainen*. Here, too, we're steadily carrying on. However, education is on the rise, and it is best furthered by elementary schools, of which there are two in our parish. Nor is there any lack of enthusiasm for reading here, for we have a lending library in our municipality, which greatly enhances people's desire to read, and also numerous newspapers are ordered here. During this winter, we have been busy repairing the highway bridges. They have been raised and broadened and lined with stone parapets. Fodder is likely to be expensive here this spring because there are men buying straw and hay around here almost every day. Twenty two marks have been paid for a barrel of rye here[176]. Since the weather has recently been calm, the farmer has had a good opportunity to do his winter chores.[177]

In the same edition of this paper, the foreign news section reported that a new government (de Freycinet's cabinet) had been formed in France, that Reichskanzler Bismarck had resigned from his post in Germany and been succeeded by Leo von Caprivi and that the Mississippi river was flooding so heavily that it was threatening to inundate several towns on its banks.

---

175 *Suomalainen*, which began to come out in Central Finland in early 1889, was the organ of the Old Finns Party. The paper was founded as a rival to the *Keski-Suomi* paper of the Young Finns Party, and it was published by Jaako Länkelä, a lecturer at Jyväskylä Teacher Training Seminar. It defined itself as 'a religious, national and economic paper for the people'. Landgren 1988, 399. These two Jyväskylä newspapers were amalgamated in 1918 into a new paper called *Keskisuomalainen*, which is still published.
176 The average tax price of a hectolitre of rye in 1890 for the whole country was 11 marks 49 pence and in the Province of Vaasa (to which Central Finland belonged) 10 marks 49 pence. At the same time, a man's day wage excluding meals was 1 mark 32 pence in winter and 2 marks 7 pence in summer. Vattula 1983, 407, 437.
177 W. L., Kivijärveltä. Maaliskuulla. [W. L., from Kivijärvi, in March] Suomalainen No 24, 24. March 1890.

2. The Foundation of a Local Lending Library

In Louisiana, cattle had drowned, and the cotton crop had been destroyed. The paper also advertised a fast mail boat steamer connection to the United States from the coastal city of Vaasa. The Vaasa agent (V. K. Hultin), who sold tickets to emigrants, also had a branch office in Karstula run by shopkeeper Johan Rosenlund. There was a situation vacant for a new midwife in the parish of Saarijärvi, and there was a furnished room to let in the building of Weilin & Göös's publishing house in the town of Jyväskylä. Furthermore, a raffle was to be held in the Taulumäki district of Jyväskylä for the benefit of the local elementary school.[178] There seemed to be a lot going on in the small rural parish that was the subject of the letter quoted above, and information about events in the big wide world also reached it.

The development of literacy among the people of Kivijärvi must be set in a larger framework in order that their actions may be understood in relation to the existing circumstances. In this chapter their opportunities for developing their reading skills will be examined first against the main lines of the development of literacy in Europe and then against the gradual modernization process in the Finnish countryside at the end of the nineteenth century. The individual societal and cultural factors that promoted reading and writing skills included revivalist movements and reforms in local government and elementary education. Among other reasons, the early Evangelical revival in Kivijärvi deserves a longer treatment in this book because previous local historical research has ignored it, and for example the official history of the parish does not address its significance in the early period of Evangelism in its Nordic form in Central Finland. I also compare the developments in local society with regard to the birth of popular libraries with those in the rest of Europe.

Microhistory does not exist without details: indeed, the study of details is a *sine qua non* of its existence. Only from an examination of apparently insignificant details can one glean something new, for one never knows just what will lead one to new revelations. I have therefore included more details in this chapter than might appear to be necessary. As an inevitable consequence of a sufficiently broad extension of the micro-level analysis, they provide the basis for the major findings of the research. Moreover, the comparative approach presupposes the presentation of a certain amount of reference points in order that the reader might be able to discern the similarities and differences between them. Another of the purposes of this chapter is to provide foreign readers with sufficient background information on Finnish history, which they may not be so thoroughly familiar with, in a compact form. Transnational comparison reveals both the non-coincident nature of events and also similarities and common background influences in the development of libraries and book culture in Finland as compared with that in the rest of Europe.

---

178 'W. L., Kivijärveltä. Maaliskuulla' [W. L., from Kivijärvi, in March]. *Suomalainen* No 24, 24. March 1890. The number of Finnish emigrants had grown considerably during the 1880s, and the sale of tickets in Finland commenced in 1886, which further facilitated their departure. V. K. Hultin from Vaasa had established his network of agents by 1890, the same year when this letter was written. Kero 1986, 25, 103–105.

The letter to the newspaper mentioned a lending library. This library, which was run by an association, was founded in 1888, and it was the third lending library to be founded in the church village of Kivijärvi. It had been established by private persons for the advancement of popular enlightenment. The target of the enlightenment was the local common people, whose active reading ability had generally still been very low when the first lending library was founded in the 1860s. The first elementary school did not begin to function in the parish until a decade later: it was opened on 1 September 1873. The church village of Kivijärvi was situated about midway up the long and narrow Lake Kivijärvi. The School District of Kinnula was established at the northern end of the lake in the following year, and a school opened there on 1 October. Like the school in the church village, it was for both girls and boys.[179]

The children of Kinnula got their own school for two reasons. One was that the journey from this well populated village to the school in Kivijärvi was long and, if it had to be made over the lake, bad weather conditions could sometimes make it difficult or even impossible. For the same reason, the people of Kinnula had obtained their own chapelry about ten years previously and had built their own church. During the time when water traffic was the main form of communication, the lake served as a waterway which connected the parishioners better, and their journeys over the water were shorter than by land. Indeed, the clergy of Kivijärvi still made some of their official journeys by boat right up to the 1950s. However, the demise of the transportation of whole villages to church in single long rowing boats and the concomitant expansion of the road network led to a situation in which those who were able to travelled by horse and cart (or sleigh) while the rest made the journey on foot or later by bicycle; this was before motor vehicles were acquired by broader sections of the rural population, which generally happened only after the Second World War. In addition to a rapid growth in the local population, this was one of the factors that encouraged the remotest village communities to found their own parishes.[180] In any case, in the matter of the school, the farmers of Kinnula also employed a degree of legitimate guile: the recently enacted Elementary Education Decree of 1866 made it possible for them to get a permanent preacher for their church by employing a schoolteacher who was also qualified to preach, and the state paid his wages. Otherwise the clergy of Kivijärvi would have come to hold religious services in the chapelry only four times a year, which the people of Kinnula considered far too infrequently.[181]

---

179 KSA, Minutes of the church parish assembly meeting 13/9/1874; Berner 1878, 94.
180 See also S. Tuomaala 1986, 338–339.
181 A similar practice was adopted in Central Finland by the chapelries of Pylkönmäki and Konginkangas, both of which belonged to the parish of Saarijärvi. It is possible that the idea of combining the duties of the teacher with those of a preacher originally came from the Vicar of Saarijärvi, Karl Stenius. Mönkkönen 1988a, 563–564. For further details, see S. Kotilainen 2013d.

The initials of the newspaper correspondent from Kivijärvi very probably refer to one Wille Lyytinen, who is known to have written letters to the press about rural matters in Kivijärvi.[182] In his letter, he too uses a contemporary catchphrase that was current in the public debate in Finland: 'desire to read'.[183] This and similar expressions (such as 'lust for reading', 'passion for reading', 'reading frenzy') signifying a hunger for reading refer to a phenomenon that started during the Enlightenment in the eighteenth century and which, according to contemporary educated observers, seemed to be spreading like wildfire from one social group to another; even women were devoured by its all-consuming power. A person who possessed the desire to read turned to literature primarily for the pure pleasure of reading. Previously, only a small minority who had received a classical education had been able to read what little literature was available, and they had usually read it for vocational reasons. The practice of reading was part of the professional exercise of the lettered classes and resembled a form of craftsmanship. However, the increase in the amount of printed material in the eighteenth century aroused a fear that the judgement of ordinary people might not be sufficient to discriminate what was necessary for them from what constituted unsuitable reading.[184]

The discussion about the reading mania began at the same time as the genre of the novel became popular. In Sweden (and Finland, which had belonged to it), the whole population had been taught to read by the church from early on, but, despite their mechanical reading ability, the common people of the remote countryside in Finland lived in a culture that was more oral than written right up to the mid-nineteenth century. This was a result not only of the lack of reading material in Finnish but also of the fact that reading did not constitute a part of ordinary people's daily life, nor for that matter was it necessarily among the activities practised by the higher estates either. Moreover, the reading of a fictional text was a new experience that required a certain amount of training. The growth in the desire to read was accompanied by an increase in the establishment of institutions that purveyed literature (for example reading societies, bookshops and libraries), the birth of new literary genres and reforms in publishing.[185]

Elsewhere in Europe, too, the ability to read was initially the exclusive property of the highest classes and only later spread to the commons. From the mid-eighteenth century on, new Frenchified customs began to spread into Finland via Sweden, bringing novel fashions in leisure time activities; these were adopted particularly by members of the military officer class. At the same time, the number of clerics and functionaries increased, and their incomes rose. This development further emphasized the distinction between the ways of life of the higher estates and the peasants. The former now spent their time and means on new cultural activities like reading.

---

182 Tommila 1973, 246. About the rural newspaper correspondents in ethnological research, cf. Stark 2011; Stark 2013.
183 Mäkinen 2009c, 130–132.
184 Littau 2006, 4–5, 39–40; Mäkinen 1999, 163; Mäkinen 2015, 288–289; 292–294.
185 Mäkinen 1999, 164, 166.

Previously, even among members of the upper classes, reading had been a ritual activity, bound to certain situations and events. The aims of the new reading culture were partly to satisfy the individual's desire for information but above all to provide entertainment.[186] The upper estates began increasingly to own books, and this together with the new literary culture led to the establishment of libraries in the manor houses of the gentry. The nobility possessed extensive collections, which above all were intended to demonstrate the social status of the owners. These libraries contained a wide variety of literature in several languages; in the age of the Enlightenment, French literature was particularly favoured.[187]

Novels in foreign languages began reach the countryside, too, from the 1780s on. The practice of reading was at first a fashionable fad, and it was even condemned as such. It became a common activity only slowly, not until the inception of the nineteenth century. At the turn of the eighteenth and nineteenth centuries, it was still common for members of a family or a group to read aloud to one another. This kind of communal reading was particularly practised by women and children. One person read aloud, while the others did handicraft work.[188] In France, too, reading spread slowly among the rural population. In the late eighteenth century, despite the wishes of the clergy, it was still not particularly common even for someone to read aloud from some religious work to the rest of the household on long winter evenings.[189]

It is considered that a 'reading revolution' took place from the mid-eighteenth century on concomitantly with an increase in the consumption of books. To put it briefly and simply, according to this view, reading in previous centuries had been 'intensive', but from then on it became more 'extensive'. However, the stages were not chronologically distinct but to some extent overlapped. Extensive reading rapidly began to predominate from the late eighteenth century on. 'Intensive' means the repeated reading of a few works, often aloud either to a group of people, or then alone to oneself. Typically, it was devotional works and above all the Bible that were read intensively, and they were not just read but also experienced or 'lived' through. These works were considered 'sacred' and treated with reverence; they were used in ritual connections and were instruments of communal religious life. Often an individual could not even afford to acquire more books, and anyway there were few persons who were capable of reading them. By contrast, extensive, one-off, reading made the reading experience private. At the same time, the amount of the available literature grew, and the readers with their increased wealth and ability to acquire more literature constantly craved for more reading matter. Books generally were no longer regarded as sacred to the same extent as before, and the ways in which they were read became freer with attention being focused less strictly on the actual words of the text. Typically, the material consisted of newspapers and

186 Mäkinen 1999, 165.
187 Ahokas 2011a, 182–194; Åström 2012.
188 Mäkinen 1999, 166.
189 Chartier 1987, 226.

periodicals, travel literature and prose fiction, especially novels. By the turn of the eighteenth and nineteenth centuries, the proportion of fiction among all published works had become greater than that of devotional literature. However, this change affected only a small section of the population. It is really only in the second half of the nineteenth century that one can speak of the rural masses in Northern Europe possessing active reading skills. The change in reading culture happened at the same time as the Industrial Revolution and various political changes took society into the Late Modern Age.[190]

However, Robert Darnton has criticized this dichotomous characterization of reading, claiming that it was by no means always so clear-cut. The repetitive reading of a book did not necessarily have anything to do with the wealth of the reader, and it was also very typical for the Bible and other devotional literature to be read mainly ritually and mechanically while the new novels were read very intensively and repeatedly.[191] Thus the extensive way of reading did not automatically follow the intensive one chronologically; rather both may have co-existed at certain times. Furthermore, Giovanni Levi has pointed out that seeing the reader in the Early Modern Age as an individual who is singled out from the other members of his or her family distorts the true picture. At that time, society was still constructed in such a way that the members of the family functioned as a single unit or 'household' in the performance of many activities, with their duties shared out so as to complement each other. In Levi's opinion, illiteracy should not be measured by the percentage of individuals who could not read or write, but rather examined in the light of the number of families in which at least one person was literate.[192] One could pursue this notion and consider that in practice these co-operative networks might have been even more complex, and that neighbours or close relatives other than those living in the same household could provide support in matters that required literacy.

According to previous research, about 20–30 percent of the Finnish peasantry were literate in the 1720s and 1730s. On the basis of sources reporting the literacy of the members of church parishes, it has been estimated that by the 1750s half of the population even in remote areas could read.[193] However, the definition of literacy is a crucial factor in research on illiteracy. Transnational comparison is made difficult by the fact that reading skills became common among the people in Finland and Sweden much earlier than writing skills.[194] Thus the latter were rarer

---

190 The differences between intensive and extensive reading have been discussed in greater detail and more broadly by Rolf Engelsing (1970, 958–960, 966–990, and 1974, 182–183). The notion of a change in reading habits is also dealt with in Finnish research on the history of reading at the turn of the nineteenth and twentieth centuries. Mäkinen 1997, 29. See also Chartier 1987, 222, 224; Darnton 1997[1996], 218; Mäkinen 1999, 163–164; Tatlock 2010, 6.
191 Darnton 1997[1996], 218.
192 Levi 1992, 98, 240.
193 Tommila 1986, 178.
194 E.g. Johansson 1977.

than the former; moreover, the majority of the population did not attend a regular school, and it was the church that took care of popular education, mainly through the annual catechetical meetings that were held to test the people's knowledge of the scriptures. Children were also taught in classes given by the cantors and Sunday schools, and their abilities were further tested in confirmation classes, the ability to read being a precondition of confirmation.[195] The history of writing in Finland is a short one, especially if we think of everyday life. At least from the Middle Ages on, a few people in Finland did write, but the majority of the population did not learn to write until the latter half of the nineteenth century. In the 21st century, writing is considered a natural human skill in the Western world, but its history is a complicated one, and its development has been a slow process.

The increase in the number of printing presses together with the Reformation and the Enlightenment gradually expanded the number of readers, but the old reading habits endured for a long time.[196] In the first half of the seventeenth century, the Bishop of Turku, Isaac Rothovius, wished to promote the learning of the catechism and began to further the education of the people more vigorously. Using his work as a basis, Bishop Johannes Gezelius the Elder developed some forms of popular education in Finland and improved the teaching of the catechism and the instruction of the people generally. However, even in the 1680s, he still emphasized the importance of rote learning. In the seventeenth century, reading skills mainly meant learning the main articles of Christian scripture by heart. The ordinary people were not usually able to obtain even a religious postil to read.[197]

Thus the reading skills of the ordinary Finns were traditionally nominal and based on a mechanical mastery of the religious texts taught by the church. Reading often consisted in the passive learning of a familiar text by heart. It was by no means guaranteed that people would be able to understand the content of more secular texts even if they were nominally designated as 'able to read'. And they would not necessarily be able to comprehend anything at all of a text that they were less familiar with. Reading was equated by most people with a devotional exercise. Moreover, the common Finnish people faced the problem that there was very little literature written in plain Finnish available in the countryside. In the first half of the nineteenth century, the word 'book' for them meant not necessarily even the Bible, but more likely and mainly a hymnbook, a catechism, an ABC primer and some kind of devotional text like a postil. The reading of secular literature was often thought to be sinful.[198] The most important secular text was for a long time an almanac, which served ordinary people as an important source of information.[199]

In earlier times, communication between members of the commons was generally oral. Information based on traditional lore was passed down by

---

195 Häkli 1991, 38; Laine & Laine 2010, 267–271, 277–282.
196 Mäkinen 1999, 163.
197 Häkli 1991, 34–36, Laasonen 1977, 260–261.
198 Häggman 2001, 2; Karjalainen 1977, 21–22.
199 Häkli 1991, 38.

members of the older generation, while news about what was happening in the world outside the local community was brought by travellers. District court sessions, church services and other social gatherings brought people together, and in them announcements were read out and items of news were heard. Well into the nineteenth century, the spoken word was the most significant source of information among the common people, and for example official announcements were made in connection with church services.[200] Thus, in terms of written culture, the people of the countryside in the first half of the nineteenth century were still 'semiliterate'.[201] It has been estimated that in the 1830s only five percent of the rural male population possessed reading and writing skills, and the level of literacy did not spread very rapidly.[202] However the local communities of the countryside were not exclusively based on an oral culture, nor were their members totally illiterate; rather there existed semi-literacies, in which the basic practices and skills of reading and writing were suited to various purposes.[203]

Moreover, there was a certain amount of bilingualism in the countryside of the interior, including Kivijärvi, since, although the rural population did not speak it themselves, Swedish was not entirely unfamiliar to them as it was the language of administration and was used by members of the higher estates. For example, members of the Swedish-speaking gentry spoke a form of Finnish to their servants that contained a large number of Swedish loanwords connected with household matters – for example, the word *hantuuki* (meaning a towel) was borrowed from the Swedish *handduk*, and *vörkkeli* (apron) from the Swedish *förkläde*.[204] From here they spread into the everyday speech of the rest of the rural population.

In Germany, for example, about 30 percent of all people over six years of age were literate in 1830. Thereafter, literacy increased at the rate of approximately ten percent a decade until in practice the whole population could read.[205] According to the 1850 census, 90 percent of the adult white population of the United States were literate, while in Britain the literacy rate among adults was about 60 percent.[206]

The reading skills of the Finns had for a long time been a matter of rote learning, and few people really understood what they read. In 1880, about three quarters of the population possessed at least passive reading skills, but only one in ten knew how to write. The inability to write in Finland was exceptionally widespread by European standards. On the other hand, this is understandable when we take into account the fact that in the mid-nineteenth century almost all administrative matters, for example in the

---

200 Tommila 1980, 255.
201 Häggman 2001, 2.
202 Tommila 1988, 111–116.
203 Announcements in church occupied an important position between oral and written communication. For more on this subject, see also Laitinen & Nordlund 2012; Laitinen & Nordlund 2013; Lyons 2013, 181–82; Reutersward 2001; Street, 1984, 129.
204 S. Kotilainen 2001, 512.
205 Tatlock 2010, 6.
206 Brown 2004, 10.

lower courts, had been handled in Swedish,[207] which was a foreign language for the common people of the interior. Thus there was not much to be gained from writing in Finnish, unless one was writing for one's own amusement or sending letters to other people who understood Finnish. Nevertheless, a few documents of an official nature (such as agreements between individual members of the population and letters addressed to the authorities) were sometimes written in Finnish.[208] Nor were there many people to buy books in Finnish, apart from religious literature, since lettered Finns (members of the higher estates) generally read books in other languages than Finnish.[209] Functional reading and writing skills had not yet come to constitute forms of immaterial capital for most of the rural population since they could rarely use them for any useful purpose in their daily lives. This would have required a change in socio-economic conditions so as to permit literacy skills to serve the persons who possessed them in a practical way.[210] In Kivijärvi, as elsewhere in the rural interior of Finland, the amount of literature available for reading was still very meagre in the mid-nineteenth century.

Literature in foreign languages (German, Russian, French and English) had been read in Finland since the Early Modern Age, and in Latin and Greek ever since the Middle Ages. Although in the seventeenth and eighteenth centuries German was understood better than English,[211] English literature was also read in Finland if only in Swedish, Finnish and German translations. Generally people who knew foreign languages belonged to the educated or the upper classes.[212] Naturally, people also read a lot of literature in Swedish, which was the mother tongue of most of the readers, although at least in its written form it was a foreign and to a great extent incomprehensible language for the population of the Finnish-speaking countryside. It has been estimated that in the 1860s the number of potential readers of Finnish-language books and newspapers, i.e. persons who possessed active reading skills, amounted to about 25,000 out of a total population of around 1.8 million.[213] The appreciation of the Finnish language increased in the latter half of the nineteenth century, and its development was promoted for political reasons. Traditionally, Swedish had been the language used in public affairs, although some religious and legal texts had been translated into Finnish to serve the needs of the Finnish-speaking people. Even so, the documents of local government were to a great extent written in Swedish before the middle of the century.

207 On the other hand, administrative and religious texts had been translated into Finnish for centuries, ever since pre-modern times, for example, to be read aloud as announcements in church. See Pajula 1960.
208 E.g. Villstrand 2011, 220–222.
209 Häggman 2001, 6. See also Table 3.
210 Leino-Kaukiainen 2007a, 434–435.
211 This was a result of the influence of the Lutheran religion and the fact that from the beginning of the Modern Age Finns had primarily gone to study at German universities, in which orthodox Lutheran theology was taught.
212 T. Laine 2000; T. Laine 2003.
213 Häggman 2001, 6–7.

Table 3. The development of literacy in Finland 1880–1900.

Year	Only reading skills	Reading and writing skills %	Total population (N)
1880	85.0	12.6	1,625,574
1890	76.9	21.1	1,902,635
1900	58.1	40.8	2,220,690

The figures for 1880 and 1890 are for persons over 10 years of age and for 1900 for persons over 15. Source: Leino-Kaukiainen 1990, 8.

In fact the local communities of the countryside could have functioned perfectly well using the existing mainly oral forms of communication. On the other hand, the organized development of literacy among the Finnish-speaking common people by means of schools and libraries provided the educated estates with the opportunity to 'feed' them ideas that they wished to inculcate in them. The popular enlightenment programme of the Fennomans was based on the idea that they needed the political support of the peasant population in order to get their own nationalist policies through.[214] In the latter half of the nineteenth century, the clergy, in particular, played a significant role as conveyors of written culture in the countryside. The writing, reading and dissemination (as purveyors of books) of literature as well as the teaching of reading skills had traditionally been the remit of the clergy,[215] and many clerics were also active supporters of Fennoman ideals.

A REVOLUTION IN IDEALS: POPULAR EDUCATION AS PART OF THE FENNOMAN IDEOLOGY

At the beginning of the nineteenth century and up to the Finnish War in 1809, Finland had constituted the eastern part of the realm of Sweden. Thereafter it became an autonomous grand duchy in the Russian Empire. Helsinki was made the capital of autonomous Finland in 1812, and the university was moved there from Turku in 1828. Industrialization got under way in Finland in the 1830s and 1840s thanks to steam power. The first Finnish-language secondary school in Finland began to operate in Jyväskylä in 1858. The first railway was built between Helsinki and Hämeenlinna in 1862, and the line from Helsinki to Saint Petersburg was completed in 1870.[216]

The expansion of the railway network in Europe led to the practice of reading on longer rail journeys, and this further increased the consumption of literature. It was more difficult for passengers to hold conversations and admire the scenery in trains than in the old horse-drawn carriages, but the journey by rail was so smooth that reading and even writing became perfectly possible. In Britain, bookshops and places where books could be borrowed began to be established at railway stations from the 1850s on, and similar practices spread to other European countries in the course of the following decades. However, this was above all a pastime of the middle and

---

214 Matti Peltonen 1992, 86–87.
215 T. Laine 2011b, 31, 33.
216 K. Laitinen 1997, 144–145.

upper classes.[217] In Finland, the rail network was still sparse, and distances in the interior long, which had the effect of slowing down the sale of books and the propagation of literature to the countryside.

Finnish society also underwent a radical upheaval as a result of demographic changes. The population of Finland nearly quadrupled from half a million to almost two million between the 1750 and the 1860s, an exceptionally rapid population growth by European standards – indeed in the latter half of the eighteenth century there was a record increase: in 1750 the population of Finland was about 421,500, and by 1800 it had risen to around 832,700 inhabitants.[218] The writer and reporter Zacharias Topelius[219] estimated that in 1852 there were at most 30,000 potential customers of bookshops in Finland. However, he did not include the common people who read religious literature in this figure. Around 1858, the reading skills of people in the countryside were to a great extent limited to learning texts by rote. If a certain parish adopted the use of a new slightly differently worded catechism, these persons who were 'able to read' encountered difficulties when they were tested on their knowledge of the scriptures. There were instances of this all over the country.[220]

The significant prerequisites for reading were sufficient free time, the wherewithal to purchase books and the amount of light available for reading after the working day or before it in the morning.[221] As early as 1686, the Church Law in Sweden had drawn attention to this as an important factor limiting the spread of reading among the common people: in the winter, when the amount of daylight was minimal, reading was difficult in the dim cabins and other rural dwellings, especially before the advent of glass windows. In the summer, on the other hand, when the light lasted longer, the agricultural population had to direct their efforts to more useful and necessary tasks. The working day during the week was long, and there was little time left over for 'leisure activities'. This the church law accepted as a given fact.[222] The climatic conditions in the Nordic countries were severe, and for example in Central Finland, where the peasants still lived in chimneyless cabins even in the 1860s, the lighting was particularly bad for a very long time.[223]

Revivalist movements within the Evangelical-Lutheran Church brought the concept of individual independent thinking to the spiritual life of the common people. It became possible for lay persons to read and interpret the Bible differently from the church. On the other hand, many priests were

217 Altick 1967[1957], 89; Black & Hoare 2006b, 11; Heikkinen 2013, 228–229.
218 Koskinen 2007, 323.
219 Topelius (1818–1898) was later made a professor and appointed Rector of Helsinki University. He was given the honorific title of Councillor of State in 1878. Klinge 1997.
220 Häggman 2008, 27, 30–31, Pitkänen 2007, 59–60.
221 Heikkinen 2013, 226.
222 Häkli 1991, 37.
223 E.g. Kotus, Paikannimiarkisto, Pohjanmäki 1970, Hosia, 1971; SKS KRA. Rautiainen, Albert 4016. 1960. Still in the 1860s and 1870s northern Central Finland was typically area of chimneyless cabins, like Eastern Finland. In the dwelling houses, the main type of ovens was chimneyless. Hämäläinen 1930, 37–38.

also leading figures in the revivalist movements,[224] which arrived in Central Finland quite a lot later than in the rest of the country. In this respect, it is particularly noteworthy that the first information about the advent of Evangelism in Central Finland is from Kivijärvi, since the movement initially established itself in south-western and southern parts of the country, and the communications between Kivijärvi and the south were poor.[225] The spread of Evangelism, like that of many other phenomena in the nineteenth century, to remote rural areas was a result of the influential activities of a number of individual persons. The spiritual life of the people of Kivijärvi experienced some upheavals at the end of the 1850s when the Evangelical revival reached the parish along with the arrival of a new cantor, Ferdinand Konstantin Kjellman. The curate and the first vicar, Karl Gustaf Dahlgrén, also soon converted to Evangelism. [226]

At the turn of the century, there were also independent Evangelist preachers operating in the villages of the area of the later municipality of Kannonkoski. The most notable of them was Seve (or to give him his proper baptismal name, Sehvanias Heikki or Zefanias Henrik) Oikari(nen), an itinerant labourer who was born the son of a dependent lodger in Pudasjärvi, a village in the parish of Kivijärvi. Pudasjärvi was later to become part of the municipality of Kannonkoski. He sometimes held evangelical meetings for days on end in the local farms. Such meetings were also organized regularly elsewhere in the Kivijärvi area, where local Evangelical meetings, usually lasting one day, were held once a summer in the church village.[227] The Evangelical movement spread in the course of the 1860s. One of the early centres of the movement was Turku, where among others two master bookbinders called Anders Kuhlman and Tobias Hellsten were active lay preachers.[228] While there was an Evangelical community in many parishes in Central Finland at the end of the nineteenth century, a Finnish Pietist-inspired movement called *Herännäisyys* (The Awakening), which was influential in certain other parts of the country, was almost unknown there.[229] Evangelism was favoured by the clergy of Central Finland and obtained a stronger foothold there than other revivalist movements. It began to spread in the mid-nineteenth century, particularly through the towns. Craftsmen and teachers came to Jyväskylä from other parts of the country, and they brought with them new religious convictions. At the same time as a clockmaker called Otto Wilhelm Holmgren, who was one of the best colporteurs of the Evangelical Association, was promulgating the message of Evangelism in Jyväskylä and in the surrounding countryside around 1860, an ecstatic Evangelical wave reached Kivijärvi as well. Karl Gustaf Tötterman, a pastor in the neighbouring parish of Viitasaari, was disseminating the message of Evangelism in the years 1860–1864. He also served as a curate

224 Mönkkönen 1988b, 472.
225 Vesisenaho 1970, 98.
226 S. Tuomaala 1986, 351.
227 Kivijärvi READERS.
228 Koskenniemi 1967, 17.
229 Viljanen 1931, 1.

in Kivijärvi in 1864. In Saarijärvi, Evangelism was promoted by Karl Otto Holm, who was the cantor there from 1866 to 1903.[230]

The Conservative Laestadian movement, for its part, began to spread in the parish of Kivijärvi from the 1870s on, and the area became one of the two enduring centres of Laestadianism in Central Finland. However, at that time the movement never attained the same significance in the region as Evangelism, and its support in the parishes was limited to a few families, although initially the publicity it received had been considerable. At first, the message of Laestadianism, which at the time was a kind of social protest movement and was critical of the state church,[231] was aimed at the crofters and other poorer members of the community. In particular, log drivers and small tradesmen and craftsmen in the towns joined the movement. Initially, the clergy were generally hostile to it and sought to prevent it from spreading by means of tough measures if necessary. In the early twentieth century, there were very few Laestadian priests in Central Finland.[232]

The first person in Kivijärvi who is known to have been a Laestadian was a tanner called Juho Johansson (b. 25/6/1836), who had already converted to the sect when he moved into the parish from Korpilahti in Central Finland in 1878. Johansson came there to build a tannery for a shopkeeper called Johan Anjelin, whose store was in the church village. He then stayed on to work as a tanner for Anjelin. He had previously been a foreman at a logging site in Ostrobothnia, but apparently as a result of pangs of conscious over some double dealing he had decided to mend his ways and join the Laestadian revivalist movement. Johansson was himself a preacher, and he held religious meetings in his home at Pajamäki (very near the place where the elementary school of Kivijärvi later stood); he himself preached at these meetings, although sometimes there were also visiting preachers from Central and Northern Ostrobothnia. The Laestadian movement was initially spread by lay persons since the parish vicar of the time, Viktor Konsin, did not favour it, although he did not actually oppose it either.[233]

Frans Petter Krank, who had become the vicar of Kivijärvi in 1883, felt that he had achieved practically nothing in the area of spiritual work in his parish. All that changed in 1888, when he got a young assistant called Arthur Leopold Heideman (b. 8/3/1862), who was an enthusiastic Laestadian. The two clerics earnestly discussed religious matters, and one night the vicar decided to repent. The other members of his family soon followed his example.[234] Laestadianism grew up later than the other revivalist movements in Finland. It originated in an area of northern Sweden where there was a Finnish-speaking population. It took its name from its founder, Pastor Lars Levi Laestadius. Originally a Swedish movement that spread into northern Finland, its meetings were characterized by the participants' ecstatic violent

---

230 S. Kotilainen 2008a, 366; Mönkkönen 1988b, 473–474; Tommila 1972, 538; Tommila 1970, 319–320.
231 Murtorinne 1992, 186.
232 Mönkkönen 1988b, 473–476.
233 S. Tuomaala 1986, 351; Viljanen 1931, 1–2.
234 S. Tuomaala 1986, 322; Viljanen 1931, 6–8.

convulsions and loud cries.[235] Many felt that it was beyond the pale that the parish vicar should convert to Laestadianism and thereby become guilty of 'heresy', which is how the movement was regarded by some in those days. By no means all the parishioners liked Heideman, because he was zealous and intransigent in his beliefs, and he sometimes addressed the parishioners in a sharp tone of voice in an effort to awaken in them the same faith that he himself had found. He preached the message of repentance in the church and in the cabins where revivalist meetings were held. The movement found a lot of adherents in the local area, and even as far afield as Viitasaari, because Heideman eagerly travelled around the parish preaching among the people.[236] The Laestadian revival continued to establish itself among the parishioners thanks to the prestige of the vicar Frans Petter Krank. At the turn of the century, there was also a strong Free Church movement in the parish.[237]

The parishioners had already disapproved of the strict discriminatory dogma of Laestadianism at the time of the tanner Juho Johansson. A local wrote to the paper about this 'heresy which in recent years has appeared here in the church village and the forefather of which is the tanner Juho Johansson; they dare to say that they are the only Christian congregation in which sins are forgiven and that he who does not confess his sins to their congregation has lost his hope [of redemption].'[238] Those who did not belong to the movement felt that the Laestadians were preaching that they represented the only true faith. In a letter to the Cathedral Chapter in July 1888, two farmers called Antti Katajamäki and Matti Kotilainen reported that the vicar Krank and his assistant Heideman had caused much harm in the parish with the proclamation of their beliefs, which the correspondents regarded as being contrary to the church's articles of faith, and they therefore demanded that Krank and Heideman be removed from their posts. The Cathedral Chapter set up an investigation into the matter in Kivijärvi on 7 November in the same year. The result was that Heideman was suspended from his post for one year and Krank received a warning.[239]

The influence of the revivalist movements on the spiritual life of the people of Kivijärvi was considerable, and the religious upheavals created a fertile soil in which the desire to read flourished; in their search for a spiritual faith people experienced a powerful need to read for further enlightenment. This need had not previously been so significant. The local revivals in the 1850s and 1880s thus also left their marks on the activities of the lending library.

The 1860s saw a vigorous activation of political life in Finland. The philosopher Johan Vilhelm Snellman, who was the chief ideologist behind the national revival, became the leading figure in the Senate. In 1863, during the reign of Tsar Alexander II, the Diet of the Estates was convened for the first

---

235 Murtorinne 1992, 178–180, 185.
236 Viljanen 1931, 5, 8.
237 S. Tuomaala 1986, 351–352.
238 Nimimerkki Ensikertalainen (Signed: 'A first-timer'), *Keski-Suomi* 1/11/1879.
239 S. Tuomaala 1986, 323, 351; Viljanen 1931, 41–42, 54–57.

time since 1809, and this procedure became an established practice with the Diet Act in 1869. Although, as a result, Finland in practice had its own diet, it was directly responsible to the Tsar, and thus the system of administration in Finland was not a parliamentary one in the modern sense of the word. The Tsar summoned the Diet to pass legislation concerning internal affairs, but he alone held the supreme power of ratification.[240] Under the leadership of J. V. Snellman, a new Language Decree was enacted in 1863, stipulating that Finns should be able if they so wished to have official documents drawn up by the authorities in Finnish. Previously all such documents had been in Swedish. However, a transition period of twenty years was reserved for the implementation of this measure. The monetary reform of 1865 saw Finland get its own unit of currency, the mark (*markka*), which entered into force alongside the Russian rouble.[241] In 1869 a new Church Law creating the basis for confessional freedom was enacted, although the actual Freedom of Religion Act did not come into force until 1/11/1923.[242]

Local government was separated from parochial administration in the Municipal Decree of 1865, but the administrative autonomy of the local parishes had a long tradition, going back to the beginning of the Early Modern Age. In Finland the reform of local government to a great extent followed the lines of the corresponding municipal reform that was enacted in Sweden in 1862. The model for it was the Prussian Municipal Ordinance of 1808. It was thought that local administration could best be handled by leaving it in the hands of the local people. In order that the tasks of municipal administration be carried out, each member of the municipality was obligated to take up unpaid official duties when necessary. On the other hand, municipal administration was regulated and supervised by state officials.[243] Kivijärvi had seceded from the parish of Viitasaari in 1858 to become a parish in its own right. The Municipality of Kivijärvi was established and was administratively separated from the church parish in 1868.[244]

The nineteenth century in Finland saw the development of the educational system, but the proportion of readers among the whole population remained low.[245] Children in towns had had the opportunity to go to school before the middle of the eighteenth century,[246] and people learned to read earlier in urban and coastal areas than in the (inland) countryside.[247] Swedish-speaking persons generally became literate earlier than Finnish-speakers, and literacy skills spread more slowly among women than men. Literacy more than quadrupled during the last two decades of the nineteenth century, and by the beginning of the twentieth century there were almost a million

240 Haapala 1997[1995], 23–24; Ihalainen, Ilie & Palonen 2016, 1–14; Jakobsen & Kurunmäki 2016, 97–110.
241 Initially the mark was in practice only a nominal unit of currency.
242 K. Laitinen 1997, 145. See also S. Kotilainen 2015a.
243 Heuru, Mennola & Ryynänen 2011, 27–28.
244 Myllymäki 1986, 90.
245 Vartiainen 2009, 352.
246 Parland-von Essen 2011, 17.
247 See also Iisalo 1992.

potential readers in Finland, since the reading skills of the common people had improved considerably with the development of elementary education particularly in the 1890s. In the countryside, schools were established slowly because the Elementary School Decree of 1866 did not stipulate compulsory education, and the decision about whether or not to establish an elementary school was left to the discretion of the local municipality. It was not until the District Division Decree was enacted in 1898 that every municipality was obligated to arrange facilities for all children of school age to attend a school within a reasonable distance of their homes. All parishes were to be divided into districts in such a way that the distance between the nearest school and the child's home should not exceed five kilometres, except in sparsely populated areas.[248]

The Elementary School Decree of 1866 thus saw the establishment of Finnish-language elementary schools in Finland. However, because the establishment of these schools was initially voluntary, even in the 1870s there were still hundreds of rural municipalities in the Finnish countryside without a single elementary school.[249] The aim of Uno Cygnaeus, who had played a significant role in drafting the decree, was to provide elementary education for the whole nation. The premise of the final decree, however, was that, when they first came to school, children already knew how to read as a result of instruction given at home or the basic teaching provided by the church parishes. In practice, however, many elementary school teachers saw their time taken up with teaching the pupils the rudiments of reading literacy. In the remote countryside, elementary schools were established at a slow pace, and often the decision to establish a school was made only after strong pressure to do so had been exerted by the local pastor. The educational authorities of the grand duchy admitted that they had had too rosy a picture of the children's reading skills, and in consequence, measures were initiated to establish separate pre-schools and ambulatory schools (which children attended for only a few weeks in the year) to prepare pupils for the elementary schools proper.[250] The recently established elementary schools came to have an unexpectedly important role in the development of the people's libraries. However, the endeavours to promote elementary education soon encountered the harsh reality in a predominantly agricultural and sparsely populated country like Finland.

THE SLOW MODERNIZATION OF THE SOCIETY OF THE ESTATES
UNDER THE SCOURGE OF A NATURAL CATASTROPHE
Although the parish libraries in Finland initially received considerable support from the developing elementary education system, the progress was slow by comparison with the Anglo-Saxon countries. In Britain, the Public Libraries Act was passed in 1850. At first, it affected only England and Wales, but it was extended to include Ireland and Scotland in 1853.[251]

248 Häggman 2008, 32; Leino-Kaukiainen 1990, 8. Mönkkönen 1986, 447.
249 Häggman 2001, 6, 31. For Kivijärvi, see S. Kotilainen 2013d.
250 Häggman 2008, 31; Nurmi 1988.
251 Black 2006a, 21.

However, the foundation of libraries in Britain took off properly only in the 1870s and the last decades of the century after the passing of the Education Acts led to the establishment of 'free libraries' subsidized by local taxation in most of the larger towns.[252] Legislation governing libraries was enacted much later in the Nordic countries. In Finland, the first Library Act only came into force in 1928, while in Denmark the Act on Public Libraries was passed in 1920.[253] In Britain, the first Elementary Education Act,[254] which brought in compulsory education for all children in England and Wales, was ratified in 1870. In Sweden, the Elementary Education Statute had already been ratified in 1842.[255] There, too, educational legislation focused attention on the development of the library institution. In Finland, universal compulsory education did not come into force until 1921, after the country had obtained independence from Russia. Even so, as in the case of the Anglo-American and Nordic models, the development of lending libraries there followed the establishment and development of elementary schools, although the practical implementation of library activities varied from one parish to another owing to the lack of regulatory legislation.

The nation-wide famine in the 1860s constituted a sharply contrasting background to the batch of social reforms that were enacted in that decade. There was naturally nothing anybody could do about the natural conditions. In the Kivijärvi area, the size of the annual agricultural product had already been poor in the 1850s, and there were continual crop failures in the years 1862–1867. They took place in the aftermath of the so-called 'Little Ice Age', when for some years the seasonal temperatures were lower than normal. The crop in 1862 was estimated to be so poor that it was enough to provide nourishment for only one fifth of the parishioners. Poverty also increased since the inhabitants were unable to pay for the seed sold to them on credit by the Crown.[256] Obituaries that were recorded in the parish's register of death for the year show that about one seventh of the population of the parish perished in 1868. About a half of them were estimated to have died as a result of starvation, although the cause of death was officially registered as typhoid fever, a disease that more easily took the lives of persons who were already weakened by hunger. At that time, numerous whole families perished in the course of a few days. This happened especially among the poorer and landless sections of the population, whose mortality rate was anyway higher than that of other groups. Severe frosts in early September 1867 destroyed almost the entire crop, which had ripened late because the previous winter had lasted longer than usual, and even on 18 June Lake Kivijärvi was still covered with ice. Although the parishioners did manage to get to church for the Midsummer service a few days later by boat over the lake, there were still slabs of ice floating on it. Many people had nothing to eat but straw and tree bark.[257]

252 Ollé 1971, 32.
253 Dyrbye 2009, 52.
254 Altick 1967[1957], 171.
255 Torstensson 2009, 75–76.
256 Myllymäki 1986, 102.
257 KSA, registers of deaths and burials 1868.

What do the climate and weather conditions have to do with the operations of the lending library? A lot. The deterioration of the famine into a lethal catastrophe affected those who were involved with the running of the library and was reflected in many matters that inevitably impacted on the work of popular enlightenment. This work had got off to a good start in the early years of the decade, and, among other things, the parish library, the first lending library in Kivijärvi, was established then. However, the times were hard, and mortality began to rise in Kivijärvi from the beginning of the 1860s on. By 1868 it was higher there than the national average. In 1865 the population amounted to nearly 3500 persons, while three years later it had fallen to just over 3000. Kivijärvi lost over one tenth of its population in the famine years, and in 1868 it was the second worst-hit parish immediately after Jämsä in Central Finland. Mortality was at its highest in the spring and early summer. Over 500 people in the parish went down with typhoid fever, and 286 of them died, including 145 persons under the age of 25.[258]

Among others, the cantor Ferdinand Konstantin Kjellman died of what was classified at that time as typhoid fever in August 1868 at the age of 46. His death cut off his successful work in popular education and his career as an active and, in the context of Central Finland, a pioneering preacher in the Evangelical movement. In November, the vicar Johan Werner Limón (b. 1826) succumbed at the age of only 42. He was ordained as a minister in 1850, and he had previously worked as a curate assisting his father in Pälkäne in central southern Finland and after that in various clerical posts in different parts of the country until he was appointed vicar of the parish of Kivijärvi in 1867. The first years of his tenure turned out to be hard since he had to lay to rest all those who died of hunger and disease in the parish. He died on 25 November 1868, according to his family's oral account after contracting brain fever on one of his official tours in the parish.[259]

The harvests had also been bad ever since the mid-1850s elsewhere in northern Central Finland, so that people had had to survive on poor nourishment for several years, and the famine years were harder there than in other parts of the country. Viitasaari had already suffered from famine in 1857. As a result of the very cold winter, the soil frost was deep, and the strength of the ice on the lakes was so great that it was still possible to drive across them with a horse and sleigh in May (usually the lakes become free of ice in mid-May), and the snow blizzards never seemed to end. The cattle perished from starvation during the spring. The summer was short, and around mid-August ground frosts carried off the cereal crop.[260]

In those years, there was a general famine all over Finland. Moreover, diseases accompanied the beggars who travelled from one locality to another. In the course of the years 1866–1868, the population of Finland went down by over 100,000 persons. About 60,000 perished from typhoid fever and other typhoid diseases. The high mortality from disease was caused above all

---

258 E. Laitinen 1988, 80; Myllymäki 1986, 103–104.
259 Limón was usually known by his second name Werner. KSA, registers of deaths and burials 1868; Haahti 1945, 157; Haahti 1956, 74–75; Appendix 3.
260 Sarlin 1911, 71–72.

by hunger, but some of those who were less undernourished also succumbed to illness. In the early autumn of 1867, an advisory booklet was distributed to the representatives of every local village after services in Kivijärvi Church. The booklet gave advice about the preparation of emergency nourishment. As a precautionary measure, work was begun at the end of the year on repairing the road leading to Karstula and the bridges along it.[261] The distribution of the booklet indicates that among the representatives of the villages there was at least one or more persons among them who could read well enough to understand the instructions, or at least so it was assumed. With the parishioners dying in such large numbers, it was unreasonable to expect that they should pay any proper attention to the popular enlightenment efforts. A new vicar was not appointed to the parish until 1872. In his episcopal visitation in 1875, Bishop Frans Ludvig Schauman noted that the people of Kivijärvi were indeed sufficiently knowledgeable about the scriptures but that their reading skills were desperately poor.[262]

General freedom of trade in the countryside came into force in 1879, which made possible the establishment of new branches of industry there. After the Franco-Prussian war of 1870–1871, exports of Finnish sawn products to Europe increased, resulting in a momentary rise in the price of timber. This brought in ready cash for the farmers, who generally possessed some forest on their lands.[263] The saw-milling and timber-processing industries got under way, and soon the price of forest land rose in Central Finland, which increased the wealth of the local forest-owning peasants.[264] The population of Finland reached the three million mark in 1908, although the famine years and emigration to America had taken their toll.[265]

Despite the high mortality rate, the population of Kivijärvi, too, rose at the end of the century. In 1880, the parish had about 4000 inhabitants, while ten years later the figure was just under 4900. The population of Kivijärvi reached its peak in 1912, when it amounted to over 6000 inhabitants. Soon after this, however, the figure fell when the villages of the Kinnula area seceded to form an independent parish.[266] Most of the inhabitants of Kivijärvi gained their living from agriculture, but at the end of the nineteenth century the numbers of members of the "gentry", state officials and rural tradesmen – many of the last-mentioned group were themselves first-generation descendants of peasant families – also increased slightly. From the early 1870s on, an elementary school teacher and a series of new curates moved into the church village, and in the 1880s, a forestry officer of the Salamajärvi Forest Reserve, a local police chief, a postmaster, and in the 1890s a pharmacist and later a chemist shop proprietor were living in the village, most of them together with their families. Even so, the proportion of functionaries and independent professionals in the whole population was

261 Myllymäki 1986, 103–104.
262 Mönkkönen 1986, 437.
263 Kuisma 2006, 290–291.
264 Jokipii 1988, 21–22.
265 K. Laitinen 1997, 146.
266 Myllymäki 1986, 90.

small, and at the turn of the century about 80 percent of the inhabitants still got their living from agriculture.[267]

One of the nineteenth-century nationalist ideologists, the above mentioned statesman and philosopher J. V. Snellman, believed that Finland, which was part of the Russian Empire, now had better opportunities for acting independently as a nation, and that the process of becoming a nation state had to start with language and culture. He believed that the advancement of Finland into the family of civilized nations would be possible only after a Finnish-language press was established and a body of national literature created.[268] Snellman called for an improvement in the position of the people by educating it so as to create a national spirit and national consciousness.[269] Furthermore, in addition to educating the lower strata of the population, Snellman thought that the educated classes should change their language from Swedish to Finnish.[270]

Thus the task of the Finnish-language press that supported the nationalist cause was to arouse a national awareness not only among the Finnish-speaking common people but also in the educated classes. Finnish-language newspapers functioned in two different ways: on the one hand, the educated classes used them to disseminate popular enlightenment, while, on the other, the papers sought to teach the educated section of the population about the conditions and ways of thinking of the commons. The main organization of the Fennomans' political and organizational activities was *Kansanvalistusseura* (The Society for Popular Enlightenment), which was founded in 1874. The society was run by leading members of the Fennoman Party, and in terms of membership it soon became the largest civic association in the country.[271]

There was a social awakening in many spheres of life after the Crimean War. As elsewhere in the country, local civic associations began to spring up in Kivijärvi at the end of the nineteenth century: a youth association was founded in 1897 and a countryman's association in 1899.[272] Particularly in the latter half of the nineteenth century, civic associations began to direct the attention of the common people towards ideological and political activities, while at the same time access to membership of the societies and increased opportunities to influence matters lowered the existing rigid class barriers between the estates.[273] The foundation of lending libraries and making them accessible to all the people constituted a natural part of all this popular enlightenment work.

---

267 Myllymäki 1986, 118–120.
268 Häggman 2001, 4.
269 Kotkaheimo 2002, 58.
270 Häggman 2001, 4–5; Jalava 2006, 114–119.
271 Häggman 2001, 8. For a further discussion of the relationship between people and the Society for Popular Enlightenment, see Päivärinne 2010.
272 Mönkkönen 1986, 451; Numminen 2011, 18–30.
273 Alapuro & Stenius 1989[1987], 20–21, 31–35.

Table 4. The distribution of the population of Kivijärvi by social group in the period 1880–1900.

Social group	1880 N	1880 %	1890 N	1890 %	1900 N	1900 %	1910 N	1910 %
Educated	11	0.2	13	0.3	10	0.2	–	–
Landed farmers	1311	33.0	1257	25.8	1099	20.1	–	–
Leaseholders	801	23.2	940	20.9	–	–	881	19.3
Agricultural workers	1368	39.6	2199	49.0	–	–	2228	50.7

Source: Myllymäki 1986, 122–123. The statistics do not include data for all years, but even so they offer a picture of the situation at the turn of the century.

In 1860, the population of Finland was about 1,746,700 persons, in 1880 around 2,060,800 and in 1910 approximately 2,943,400.[274] Landed peasants had made up over half of the rural population of Finland in 1815, but by the beginning of the twentieth century their proportion had dropped to a little over a third. At the same time, the proportion of the landless population grew from under 15 percent to nearly 50 percent.[275] The population of Kivijärvi, where there had been permanent settlement only since the sixteenth century, grew from 3000 in the late 1850s to about 6000 in the early 1910s. The growth in the population there was relatively more rapid than in Finland generally in the last decades of the nineteenth century. The proportion of landless persons in the population of Kivijärvi was considerable. In 1910 only about 20 percent of families in Kivijärvi were land-owning farmers and about 19 percent tenant farmers, while the number of agricultural labourers, cottars and other members of the landless population amounted to approximately 56 percent. Of this last group, about 60 percent owned no abode of their own, and lived in cabins on land owned by others, in rented accommodation or in the homes of others (for example, in their sauna buildings).[276]

The shortage of land for people to own their own farms was one of reasons for the strong growth of emigration to North America at the turn of the century. The number of emigrants was high in Ostrobothnia, as it was in the bordering parishes of Karstula and Kivijärvi in Central Finland. Many of those who left were members of the landless population or the younger children of farmers, whose chances of gaining a living without land to till seemed weak. Emigration to America from Kivijärvi began in the 1870s, but the largest numbers of emigrants left in the years 1891–1900 (over 300) and 1901–1910 (nearly 900). Statistics based on travel documents indicate that between 1870 and 1914 over 1500 emigrants departed for America, but in reality there were probably more. Another reason that encouraged young men, in particular, to leave was the repressive policy of Russification imposed by the Tsar, which in the early years of the twentieth century could include aleatory enlistment in the Russian army.[277]

274 Koskinen 2007, 323.
275 K. Laitinen 1997, 147.
276 Myllymäki 1986, 90, 121, 123. See also Table 4.
277 Kero 1974, 230; Myllymäki 1986, 114–115.

An ability to read and write helped the emigrants to keep in contact with the relatives that they had left behind in Finland. The literacy of the emigrants from Kivijärvi in relation to that of the rest of the population has not been studied in any detail, but in any case the requirements of the Modern Age put the traditional notion of literacy to the test, and to an ever increasing extent the execution of important duties in the local community required fluent reading and writing skills. As elsewhere in Europe, efforts were also made to enhance these skills among the people of Kivijärvi through the establishment of lending libraries.

Particularly in the last decades of the nineteenth century, there was a boom in reading by the masses in Europe: the numbers of readers increased, and mass markets were created for newspapers, periodicals and books. In fact, the number of readers had risen at an enormous rate ever since the mid-eighteenth century. Many of the new readers at the end of the nineteenth century were women, and more books and periodicals began to be published for them.[278]

In Finland, literacy gradually improved towards the turn of the century. At the national level, the period was overshadowed by the so-called 'years of repression', during which the Grand Duchy of Finland was on the receiving end of numerous repressive Russification measures, a situation that finally came to an end with the outbreak of the First World War. In 1905, when there was a slight relaxation in the implementation of the Russification policy, there was a national strike, and in the following winter a decision was made to establish a Finnish parliament based on universal and equal suffrage, which at the time was one of the most progressive legislatures in Europe. This decision was influenced by Russia's defeat in its war against Japan and the need for domestic political measures to settle the social unrest. Finland became independent in 1917, and by 1919 as many as 122 newspapers and 295 periodicals were being published in the young independent republic. However, according to a census made in that year, only 56 percent of the population could both read and write.[279] Popular education had had an impact, but not everywhere, and further efforts were needed. What was the role of the rural parish libraries in this work?

Why were the lending libraries established?

THE EARLY HISTORY OF FINNISH LIBRARIES

When they founded the first libraries, the early educators of the people envisaged a network of libraries covering the whole country. This was anticipated in 1879 by Kaarle Werkko, who called it 'the university of the people'.[280] A corresponding epithet was used at that time to describe public libraries in the United States.[281] These ideas reveal a belief in the value of continuing the development of institutions that provided information for the

---

278 Tatlock 2010, 6–7.
279 Häggman 2001, 17.
280 Karjalainen 1977, 3.
281 Garrison 1979, 39.

people. Although the parish libraries did not actually turn into university-like institutions in miniature, libraries have always been important centres for learning[282] in their own communities.

The people's lending libraries in Finland were in principle available for all to use and accessible to members of every social class. In practice, the books had to be offered in both Finnish and Swedish in bilingual areas of the country. While the use of the libraries could not be expected to be totally free of charge, they did have social goals that aimed at the common good. Outside libraries of this kind lie the commercial subscription libraries which operated on business principles: the fees they charged were used to subsidize the upkeep of the collections, the running costs of the library and the income of the entrepreneur concerned.[283]

The popular lending libraries of the nineteenth century had deep roots going back beyond the time when Finland was an autonomous grand duchy in the Russian Empire. In this book the examination of the history of Finnish libraries sets out from the Middle Ages because this makes it possible to show the influence of the then pan-European Catholic Church on the establishment of a written culture in the area. However, for the most part this study remains within the limits of the so-called 'long nineteenth century', stretching from the Enlightenment and the upheaval of the French Revolution in the eighteenth century up to the outbreak of the First World War. An examination of this contextual background to the development of libraries is necessary in order to be able to compare the reasons that led to the establishment of popular libraries and to ascertain whether there was something special about the people's libraries of the Finnish countryside or whether the the motives for establishing libraries were common in different parts of Europe. In this section will be first discussed the early history of libraries, the influence of the tradition of Continental European reading societies and fee-charging libraries on people's libraries and the differences between the towns and the countryside in their activeness in establishing popular libraries at the time when the Public Library Movement, which was American in origin, finally modernized traditional practices and Finland, too, moved from libraries that were based on membership or charged fees to public libraries that were open to all free of charge.

Before the establishment of public libraries in the nineteenth century, the book collections were accessible to very few Finns. Nevertheless, the history of libraries stretches back thousands of years. The oldest known libraries came into being in the Middle East and Asia Minor. The most important of the ancient libraries was founded in Alexandria in Egypt in the fourth century BC.[284] In the Middle Ages and the Early Modern Age in Europe, monarchs and rulers, such as the popes of Rome, the kings of France and the Medici dynasty in Italy owned large private libraries.[285] Most libraries were owned by communities or institutions such as monasteries and dioceses.

---

282 Darnton 2009, xv.
283 Hirn 1998, 13.
284 Casson 2002; Goody 2010, 32, 34; Rubin 2004, 260–264; Vartiainen 2009, 38.
285 Casson 2002; Febvre & Martin 1998 [1958], 263–264; Merisalo 2003, 139, 141, 157–159.

Significant libraries were also built in conjunction with the universities that were then growing up. However, in terms of the number of works they contained, medieval libraries were fairly small. It was not until the advent of printing that it became possible for private persons as well as institutions to accumulate larger collections. The first library known to have existed in Finland dates back to the thirteenth century. It belonged to Thomas, the Bishop of Finland (d. 1248), and it is known to have contained 58 works, which constituted a fairly large collection in those days. Apparently, the manuscripts had been copied and acquired in Paris, where Thomas had studied in the early years of the century. Most of the collection later provided the basis for the library of the Diocese of Turku. In addition to commentaries on the Bible, it contained mainly works on theology and ecclesiastical law, liturgical works, lives of the saints and sermons. Unfortunately, the collection was later destroyed almost totally.[286]

In the late Middle Ages, only high-ranking clerics and the most powerful members of the secular aristocracy were able to collect private libraries, provided they had the inclination and means to do so. In fact, one of the functions of the libraries of the princes was to display the wealth and power of their owners. The collections of the burghers and members of the intelligentsia and of the towns, on the other hand, were in general accumulated exclusively for practical use. The meagre collections of Turku Cathedral and of individual rural parish churches in Finland grew in the course of time, but for a long time there was a dearth of manuscripts. Not all manuscripts were acquired from abroad, and at least from the latter half of the thirteenth century on they were copied within the confines of the Diocese of Turku.[287]

Turku Cathedral already had its own library of liturgical handbooks for the celebration of Mass in the thirteenth century. The Bishops of Turku and other clerics there also possessed books of their own. Bishop Hemming (d. 1366) donated 30 works to the cathedral in 1354. Outside Turku, the most important collection of books in Finland was possessed by the Brigittine Convent in Naantali. Its mother convent in Vadstena in Sweden owned the largest collection of books in the Nordic countries in the fifteenth and sixteenth centuries. Some parishes also maintained modest collections of books. There were very few library rooms, let alone library buildings, in the Middle Ages. The collections fitted onto a shelf or into a cupboard, and churches typically stored their collections in the sacristy. After the foundation of the Academy of Turku, the collection of Turku Cathedral lost its significance as a scholarly library. In 1681, it was partly deposited into the library of the Academy, into which it was gradually completely incorporated.[288]

The first presses in the Nordic countries were established in Denmark and Sweden in 1482 and 1483 respectively. With the advent of printing, books

---

286 Barnett 1973, 27; Goody 2010, 21; Tuomas Heikkilä 2009, 117–121, 126.
287 Tuomas Heikkilä 2009, 121, 124, 127–128; Rubin 2004, 270.
288 Tuomas Heikkilä 2009, 119, 129; E. Seppälä 1963, 9–10.

finally became accessible to members of all classes.[289] However, even in the sixteenth century, they were still owned mainly by clerics and teachers; this was the case for example in Italian village schools.[290] Monasteries had long had their own libraries, and after Lutheranism came to Finland, Johannes Gezelius, the Bishop of Turku gave detailed instructions in 1666 concerning the compilation and care of church libraries.[291] Academic libraries developed in connection with monasteries and universities all over Europe in the Middle Ages and the Early Modern Age.[292]

In addition to these scholarly libraries, privately maintained libraries were established in cities like London and Paris during the fifteenth, sixteenth and seventeenth centuries. Some other cities, particularly in Germany, had also possessed their own libraries ever since the Middle Ages.[293] The library of the Academy of Turku obtained the right to receive free copies of books printed by its press in 1651, and in 1707 this right was extended to include the production of all presses in the realm of Sweden. For example, when the librarian and later professor Henrik Gabriel Porthan (born in Viitasaari in Central Finland), died in 1804, the library possessed over 20,000 volumes, and by 1827 the number had risen to about 40,000. Porthan's ambition had been to acquire all works produced in Finland, written by Finns or dealing with Finland. The collection was mainly destroyed in the Fire of Turku in 1827. After the fire, the works that had been out on loan were called in, but the remaining collection only amounted to 827 books. The destruction of the library of the Academy of Turku was accounted to be a national catastrophe, and it has been compared to the loss of the ancient library of Alexandria in a fire. One person who was of great assistance to the university personnel in re-assembling the collection of Finnish books was a peasant bibliophile called Matti Pohto.[294] He was an exceptional common man since peasants at that time were generally not so well acquainted with the arcana of older literature, although the situation was changing.

---

289 In Europe, the technology of printing was invented and developed in Mainz in Germany in the 1450s. The use of moveable metal type for printing was influenced by the discovery in the thirteenth century of the use of block printing in China, which was based on the use of woodcuts. Around the same time, the Europeans learnt the techniques of processing paper from the Arabs. In the fifteenth century, the raw material used for the production of paper was still cloth. Paper was a significantly cheaper material for the printing presses than parchment. The implementation of the new printing technology also required the development of a new oil-based ink and the skill to cast metal type. A Latin Bible printed in the press of Johann Gutenberg in 1455 was the first work to be produced by means of the new technology. Vartiainen 2009, 205–206.
290 Ginzburg 2007, 84.
291 E. Seppälä 1963, 10.
292 Hietala 2001, 7–9.
293 Närhi 1963, 70.
294 Mäkinen 2009b, 29–30; E. Seppälä 1963, 12–13.

The foundation for lending libraries created by reading societies and fee-charging libraries

In order to understand the development of people's libraries it is also necessary to acquaint oneself more broadly with the operation of libraries and the circulation of books at the turn of the eighteenth and nineteenth centuries. In eighteenth-century society, reading was still an advantage possessed by only a few groups in society. The production and sale of books were protected by privileges and guilds and governed by whatever censorship regulations were in force at the time. Reading and literature were thus clearly linked to the use of power in society.[295]

In the eighteenth century, in addition to the churches and universities, some private persons also owned considerable collections of books, and that century also saw the development of lending libraries. In England, book lending had started in the seventeenth century, while in France lending libraries had become common by the eighteenth century. Lending libraries were also established in Sweden in the late eighteenth century, mainly in the major university cities.[296] At that time, libraries were typically commercial lending libraries (German: *Leihbibliothek*), which loaned books for a fee with the object of commercial profit and were often a side business for bookshops.[297] In Finland, too, ever since the seventeenth century members of the higher estates had sought to improve their facilities for obtaining information, for example, by means of joint subscriptions to newspapers.[298]

The first libraries in Finnish towns were generally established at the end of the eighteenth century in connection with reading societies founded by members of the upper classes. The model for them came from Germany via Sweden. Thus the establishment of the library of the oldest reading society in Finland,[299] which was founded in Vaasa in 1794, took as its main model the German reading society or reading library. The establishment of this library may also have been influenced by the American social or subscription libraries as distant, ideal models. The first of these subscription libraries, the Library Company of Philadelphia, was founded in 1731 on the initiative of a young printer called Benjamin Franklin.[300] From there, a new form of library activity based on subscriptions spread to other parts of North America and Europe such as France and Germany, where there were

---

295 Darnton 2009, 5–6.
296 Chartier 1987, 204–217; Närhi 1963, 12.
297 Martino 1990, 57–62.
298 Mäkinen 2009b, 35.
299 The history of public libraries in Finland is considered to have begun with the establishment of this library. Mäkinen 2009b, 46.
300 Martino 1990, 63; Mäkinen 2009b, 41–46; Prüsener 1973; Shera 1949, 31–33. At the end of the nineteenth century Kaarle Werkko considered the library founded by Benjamin Franklin to have been one of the models for the Finnish people's libraries. Werkko 1879, 269. Subsequently it has been established that it was rather a just distant model as similar endeavours had been going on previously or were being implemented at the same time in Europe. Mäkinen 1997, 117.

active reading societies in the late eighteenth century. The model for the American subscription libraries was provided by book clubs in Britain.[301] In Germany, the 'general desire to read' created more and more reading societies and lending libraries in the first half of the nineteenth century.[302] In Denmark, too, urban reading societies developed earlier than in Sweden, for example. From the 1770s on, the reading societies in Copenhagen and other Danish cities gradually became the major source of new reading matter for the burghers and particularly for civil officials. Similar reading societies were also established in Norwegian cities. In both Denmark and Norway, reading societies were also founded by the clergy for the peasantry at the turn of the eighteenth and nineteenth centuries.[303]

The lending library ideal came to Finland through the reading societies' libraries. In the eighteenth century, library activities were based on the operation of these reading societies, which were in a sense co-operative enterprises that were accessible mainly to the upper classes and the civil servants of the cities.[304] In the 1760s, there was at least one reading circle operating in Southern Ostrobothnia; it called itself a 'book society' (Sw. *Bok Societet*), and it had 12 members, most of them surveyors and clerics, who lived in the environs of Vaasa. Among them were Johan Aejmelaeus, the vicar of Isokyrö, Israel Reinius, the curate of Laihia, and Henrik Moliis, the curate of Närpiö (Närpes). Each member acquired a book, which was passed on to the other members before eventually returning to its original owner.[305] The next reading society was founded in Turku in 1798, and a third in 1800 in Kokkola.[306]

Several other reading societies, most of which had libraries, were established in Finnish towns in the early decades of the nineteenth century.[307] Members of the higher estates also frequently lent books to one another privately, outside the reading societies.[308] Some of the societies continued to operate for quite a long time. For example, the 11 shareholder members of the Vaasa reading society's library in the spring of 1830 included Pastor Johan Fredrik Reinius,[309] who served as an assistant to his father, Israel Reinius the Youngest, when the latter was the curate of Isokyrö. The educated classes thus became (over several generations) familiar with the opportunities offered by libraries and learned how to establish and maintain them. The kind of reading matter acquired by the reading societies for their members consisted mainly of political and historical literature in addition

---

301 Allan 2008, 24–57; Lehtikanto 1964, 7; Närhi 1963, 9, 14.
302 Martino 1990, 52–54; Tatlock 2010, 6.
303 Mäkinen 2009b, 43–44.
304 Toivanen 1985, 17.
305 Mäkinen 1999, 170; Mäkinen 2009b, 36–37.
306 Lehtikanto 1964, 7.
307 Mäkinen 2009b, 56–64; Närhi 1963, 10.
308 Mäkinen 1999, 172; Mäkinen 2009b, 42–43.
309 Lehtikanto 1964, 19–20. When the Vaasa reading society ceased to operate in the 1840s, its collection was donated to the local lyceum (senior secondary school). Hirn 1998, 14.

to newspapers, and periodicals. The activities of the reading societies had ceased almost entirely by the middle of the nineteenth century.[310] In Finland, as in Britain, too, reading societies in the early decades of the nineteenth century were mainly a pastime of the middle classes.[311]

In addition to the reading societies, commercial lending libraries began to be founded in Finland in the early nineteenth century. They were often commercial enterprises that operated in conjunction with bookshops. Similar lending libraries were already common in more southern parts of Europe in the late eighteenth century. They often went under the name of 'reading libraries' (German: *Lesebibliotek*), and this name was used for the libraries of the first reading societies in Finland at the turn of the eighteenth and nineteenth centuries (for example, Wasa Läse-Bibliothek). In Germany commercial lending libraries had begun to function at the end of the seventeenth century,[312] but the first commercial lending libraries in Finland were only founded in Helsinki in the early nineteenth century. Usually, however, such libraries were meant for the 'educated' and more affluent sections of the population.[313]

There were also several such commercial libraries operating in Turku in the nineteenth century[314] and a few in other towns.[315] Johan Wilhelm Lillja, a publisher, and Gustav Leopold Söderström, a book merchant who was the father of the publisher Werner Söderström (who was to be the founder of a leading Finnish publishing house), also established lending libraries in Turku in the second half of the nineteenth century.[316] Lillja began his publishing operations in the 1840s and created what was to be the most important publishing company of its time in Finland. Thanks to him, the number of works of Finnish literature that were published increased by about 500 titles. The lending library that Lillja opened in Turku in the early 1850s contained about 13,000 volumes.[317]

The foundation of public libraries began in the Anglo-American world. The first public libraries were established in England in the fifteenth century. The reading room of the British Museum Library, which had been accessible to scholars and researchers ever since the 1750s, was opened to the general public in 1867. In the United States, the first local school library began to operate in 1835 and the first public library in 1847. Most of the German public libraries were based on the American and British models. From the sixteenth century on, a large number of town libraries had also been established in Germany in traditional centres of commerce and administration such as the former Hanseatic towns. Municipal libraries and public reading rooms were

310 Karjalainen 1977, 12–15.
311 See Altick 1967[1957], 218.
312 Engelsing 1974, 274; Närhi 1963, 11; Prüsener 1973, 383.
313 Hirn 1998, 14; Närhi 1963, 19–30, 258–259.
314 E. Seppälä 1963, 56.
315 Mäkinen 1999, 172; Mäkinen 2009b, 68–71.
316 Närhi 1963, 14.
317 Hirn 1998, 14; Kovala 2013, 47, E. Seppälä 1963, 30–31.

also established in many industrial towns in the nineteenth century. The urban libraries also had separate reading rooms for children.[318]

Like the enthusiasm for reading societies, the popular lending library movement spread to Finland via Sweden, where several libraries intended for the use of the rural population had been established by the beginning of the nineteenth century. In Finland, as in its mother country Sweden, members of the higher estates and the educated classes held intensive discussions about popular education and the issue of the establishment of libraries in connection with it. For example, proposals were made for the establishment of parish reading societies intended for all classes. These proposals did not assume that the rural population would take the initiative in organizing such activities. According to the sources, the first people's library in Finland was founded by Baron Rabbe Gottlieb Wrede in conjunction with the Regina School in the parish of Anjala in 1802. He was a member of a society called *Pro fide et christianismo*.[319] Wrede's Scottish-born mother had been interested in charitable work, and in her will she bequeathed funds for the foundation of the school that later bore her name. Although at that time there were other schools in Finland that had been founded by the owners of manorial estates and factory and ironworks owners, the Regina School was exceptional in that, in addition to the offspring of the employees of the manor, the other children of the parish were also allowed to attend it. Wrede called it a 'parish school'. The library also received books from the *Pro fide et christianismo* society as donations. In the second half of the nineteenth century, Otto Rosvall was the long-serving schoolmaster and librarian of the school.[320]

In addition to the library of the Regina School, a library was established on the initiative of the headmaster of the Vyborg Lyceum (senior secondary school), to which the townsfolk donated books from their private libraries to be read by other inhabitants of the city. In 1807, the shareholders decided to renounce their right to get their books back if they so wished, and the library got the name *Die Wiburgische Stadtbibliothek* (Vyborg City Public Library). The collection consisted almost entirely of works in German, and Swedish-language literature was not even available in translation. On the other hand, it did contain a large number of works translated from English.[321] Vyborg was an important centre of trade between east and west, and its cultural life at that time was by Finnish standards extremely international and multilingual.

The oldest Finnish parish library can be considered to be that established in the parish of Pohja in 1837 by Mathias Weckström, a postal expeditor. According to the rules, members of both the higher estates and the common

---

318 Hietala 2001, 7–9, 14–16; Leapman 2012, 41.
319 This society was founded in 1771 and it operated under the auspices of the Swedish Evangelical Lutheran Church. Initially the society discussed matters relating to Christian education, missionary work and so on.
320 Karjalainen 1977, 23; Mäkinen 2009c, 74–88; Torstensson 2009, 76–78; Werkko 1879, 38.
321 Toivanen 1985, 17.

people, even from outside the parish, were entitled to borrow books from its fairly extensive Swedish-language collection. Under the influence of Swedish models and efforts to support popular enlightenment, in the parishes of Hammarland and Eckerö in the Åland Islands, a Swedish-language parish library was established by Dean Pehr Ulrik Ferdinand Sadelin at Hammarland in 1841, while in Karelia Pastor Johannes Hertz founded a library at Heinjoki. The Hammarland and Eckerö library was intended for all inhabitants of the parishes, but in practice the members of the higher estates were not expected to borrow books from it.[322] With the advent of continental European influences that arrived through Sweden, the usefulness of libraries for the purposes of popular enlightenment had been noticed. Thus there were more and more endeavours to establish them in different parts of the country.

The birth of Finnish people's libraries, initially in the urban centres

Helsinki became the literary centre of Finland in the 1830s. The city had been made the capital of the Grand Duchy of Finland in 1812, and after the Fire of Turku, the Academy (university) moved there together with its library.[323] Several presses had been established in the larger cities of Finland in the 1820s despite the fact that the demand for literature was still meagre at that time. Their establishment did, on the other hand, create a basis for the publication of local and national newspapers.[324] In the 1830s and 1840s, the educated members of the population conducted a discussion in the press about the importance and benefits of founding parish libraries based on the model of other countries in Finland too. The most assiduous of those correspondents who wrote to the papers pressing for the establishment of people's libraries was Johan (Juho) Pynninen from Vyborg,[325] who proposed in the Finnish-language newspaper *Kanava* in 1845 the establishment of a network of parish libraries covering the whole country. He also established a people's library in his home town. Pynninen's letters to the papers received more attention than earlier writings on the issue because they coincided with the rise of the movement for a national awakening, whose purposes the library project suited well.[326]

Juho Pynninen, a shop assistant, was inspired by the writer and philosopher J. V. Snellman, who later became a senator and a notable

---

322 Hirn 1998, 15; Mäkinen 2000b, 104–118; Mäkinen 2009b, 46, 99.
323 The Library of Helsinki University was re-named the National Library of Finland in 2006.
324 af Forselles-Riska 2006, 10–11.
325 Vyborg was the most international of all the cities in Finland from the Early Modern Age up to the Second World War, after which the conditions of the Paris Peace Treaty of 1948 compelled Finland to cede it along with other Finnish territory in the Karelian Isthmus to the Soviet Union, and the population of these areas was evacuated to other parts of Finland. The city had once before been ceded to Russia in the Treaty of Uusikaupunki (Nystad) in 1721, but during the time when Finland was an autonomous grand duchy in the Russian Empire it was reincorporated into Finland.
326 Karjalainen 1977, 24–32.

Finnish statesman. Snellman wrote articles promoting the nationalist movement in a newspaper called *Saima*, which he published in Kuopio in eastern Finland. Pynninen, for his part, wrote about the library issue in 1846 in *Kanava*, a newspaper that came out in Vyborg. In the same year, a decision was made to establish a Finnish-language library in Vyborg, but it was not immediately successful. Over a half of the libraries that began to operate in the 1840s were located in the Province of Vyborg. Another figure who played a leading role in promoting the establishment of libraries was Adam Wilke, a commercial accountant also from Vyborg, who worked in the merchant house of Hackman.[327]

Wilke was one of the founders of the Vyborg Finnish Literature Society in 1845, and a couple of years later he bequeathed a considerable portion of his wealth (11,000 silver roubles) to the society, stipulating that it should use the interest accruing from this capital to maintain a school for the common people of Vyborg or its neighbouring parishes. A people's library was also established in conjunction with the school. The Vyborg Finnish Literature Society continued to press for the establishment of popular lending libraries in the region, and in 1859, the society sent circular letters to the leading figures in the parishes around Vyborg concerning the establishment of libraries. At least in the parish of Lappee, they would seem to have had an effect. Moreover, the society sent to all the libraries that functioned in the province copies of the works it published as well as model sets of library regulations and loan catalogues, and it also initially acted as an agent for the libraries' book acquisitions and book binding orders.[328]

In other cities, the development was less vigorous. By the end of the 1850s, popular lending libraries had been established in seven Finnish cities. The Finnish-language libraries of Tornio and Vyborg were founded in the 1840s, and libraries were established in Rauma, Raahe, Oulu and Pori in the 1850s. Elsewhere in Europe, most of the popular libraries in the towns and cities were established from the beginning of the nineteenth century on. In fact, even before that century there had been numerous public libraries in towns, but in general they were used only by the educated and more affluent classes. The foundation of popular lending libraries from the early nineteenth century on was mainly connected with efforts to educate the common people.[329]

In the period from the 1830s to the 1850s, more conservative circles in Finland continued to look askance at inappropriate reading habits and reading in general among both the educated classes and the commons, even though they admitted that literacy was a useful skill. However, they thought that it might incite the rural population into taking part in political activities and increase their awareness and religious independence, all matters that they regarded with horror. The French Revolution and the Napoleonic Wars cast their shadow over these fears of popular unrest. There had also been warning examples of the connection between the mania for reading and

---

327 Toivanen 1985, 18.
328 Toivanen 1985, 19.
329 Hirn 1998, 16; Närhi 1963, 69–70.

political unrest in Sweden and Germany. In particular, it was feared that the influence of new theories in the natural sciences and ideas inspired by the reading of novels on the world view of the common people would cause too much unrest.[330]

For example, the censorship of newspapers and books in the reign (1825–1855) of Tsar Nicholas I, who sought in every possible way to suppress potential revolutionary movements, shackled the public debate in Finland, although the country did succeed in those decades in impressing the Tsar as being a kind of model pupil, at least by comparison with countries like Poland. The discussion about elementary education and the aspirations to establish libraries that followed in its wake saw little progress in these years, and in fact threatened to wither away altogether. For example, in Sweden a statute on elementary education was enacted a couple of decades earlier than corresponding legislation in Finland. Halfway through the century, opposition to elementary education lessened, and the attitudes to it all over Europe began to be more favourable.[331]

In Finland, the debate on literacy in the mid-nineteenth century saw the expression of varying views: people read too little or too much, or they read the wrong things in the wrong way. There had been corresponding debates in Sweden and Britain. In the former country, one suitable way of averting these threats was considered to be the establishment of parish libraries, which by selecting appropriate works for the collections would make it possible to control what the commons read.[332] In Helsinki, too, it was thought that in addition to the university and the student organizations, the ordinary townsfolk and particularly the working class needed their own libraries.[333]

The library ideal which had spread into Finland during the 1840s gave birth to numerous popular libraries in the following decade. Certainly, during the first half of the century there still prevailed views according to which it was enough to provide above all the rural population with devotional literature and practical works connected with their daily toil in Finnish. It was not until the late 1950s and early 1860s that there began a real boom in the establishment of people's libraries, but even in the 1870s it was still thought that the literature read by the common people should be mainly instructive. The same issue – that popular libraries should direct the reading habits of their customers towards literature of a more worthy nature – was also the subject of attention for example, in France in the mid-nineteenth century, and concern was expressed there that members of the working class borrowed so many novels from the libraries for the purpose of entertainment.[334] The establishment of an individual library was a slow process, and it could take years to amass enough money to purchase

---

330 Mäkinen 2009c, 117–118. For the situation in Britain in the eighteenth century, see Altick 1967 [1957], 72–74.
331 Mäkinen 2009c, 119–121; Westberg 2014, 20–23.
332 Jarlbrink 2010, 51.
333 Hirn 1998, 16.
334 Barnett 1973, 324–325.

the books and start lending them out in earnest. Another peak in the establishment of libraries in Finland came in the mid-1880s.[335] In Kivijärvi, too, the establishment and reorganization of popular libraries would seem to have taken place at just those times when the process was at its most vigorous in other parts of the country.

On the basis of the facts described above, we can state that the development of people's libraries was a global phenomenon that was influenced not only by national but also transnational factors. The establishment of many popular lending libraries in Europe was connected with urbanization and the birth of new political movements. New lending libraries for the common people were being founded in towns and cities everywhere. They were the forerunners of the modern public libraries.[336]

The use of public funds to establish public libraries in the cities of Britain only got under way after the Diet passed legislation stipulating that tax revenue could be used in determined amounts to fund the operation of libraries. The Public Library Act of 1850 allowed cities with populations of over 10,000 inhabitants to collect half a penny in the pound in local rates for the building of a public library on condition that two thirds of the electorate agreed to this. The funds collected on the basis of this law could be used only for the actual construction of the library building, but not for the maintenance of the library or the acquisition of books. In 1855, the rate was increased to one penny in the pound, and the funds could thenceforth also be used for the acquisition of books. By 1877, public libraries had been established in 77 towns and cities. In 1859, when the planning of a people's library in Helsinki began, there were already such libraries in 21 British towns. In Germany, municipal libraries began to be established from the mid-nineteenth century on alongside the existing more academically oriented city libraries.[337]

In the United States, too, some cities had begun to assist and maintain public libraries in the first half of the nineteenth century. Moreover, legislative efforts had been made in America to promote the activities of libraries at an early date: in the 1830s, the establishment of school libraries was approved in various states, and in the following decades further legislation was enacted concerning public libraries. By 1875, most states had a law on libraries. Over 250 public libraries were established in the United States between 1850 and 1875. By contrast, in the cities of the Nordic countries, people's libraries were generally not established until the last decades of the nineteenth century and the beginning of the twentieth, although in Sweden numerous valuable collections of books had existed for a long time, including some belonging to dioceses and grammar schools that dated back to medieval times.[338]

The idea of establishing a people's library in Helsinki was the brainchild of some young women of the higher estates. The founders of a people's library

---

335 Karjalainen 1977, 24–33, 35; Lehtinen 1988, 44–46, 49–53; Mäkinen 2009d, 145.
336 Haasio 2010, 8; Hietala 2001, 18; Mäkinen 2009c, 109; Torstensson 2009, 75; Vatanen 2002.
337 Kelly 1977, 20; Närhi 1963, 71.
338 Närhi 1963, 72.

in the town of Rauma in 1850 were likewise young upper-class women. In Pori, too, women were active in the establishment of a library in 1858.[339] The initiative for establishing a city library in the capital came from the Helsinki Ladies Society[340] in the autumn of 1859. The association, which was founded in 1848 to engage in socially beneficial activities, also occupied itself with the collection of funds to implement the project. In Rauma, too, the collections of funds for the library was carried out by upper-class women. However, according to the rules of these societies, their activities did not directly include endeavours to educate the common people. One of the members of the Helsinki Ladies Society was a teacher called Helene Simelius, the daughter of Jakob Simelius, who had established the first printing press in Helsinki. The society collected altogether 517 roubles and 63 kopeks for the library. The founding of the library was also inspired by the writer Zacharias Topelius and Professor Frans Ludvig Schauman,[341] who had both served as secretaries of the Ladies Society.[342]

In the early years of the 1860s, more people's libraries began to be built in other cities, too: for example, in Tampere in 1861, in Turku in 1862 and in Vaasa and Jyväskylä in 1863.[343] In Vaasa a library that had begun to operate in 1850 funded by annual subscription fees served the burghers and members of the upper class. It was descended from an eighteenth-century reading society library. The library that was established by the clergy in 1863, on the other hand, was intended for the common people. Later these two libraries were merged.[344] There was a fall-off in library activity in both Turku and Tampere in the 1860s; this was a result partly of inadequate funding and partly of the impact of the famine years.[345] Thus ladies of quality played a central role in the acquisition of funds for libraries and in promoting popular education. In a way it was part of their public duties. Later, in the countryside, too, female members of the upper classes and other women in prestigious positions were involved in the establishment of popular libraries and collecting funds for them.

THE ENLIGHTENING AND EDUCATIVE BACKGROUND
TO THE BIRTH OF POPULAR LIBRARIES IN THE COUNTRYSIDE

In 1903, Leo Schadewitz still defined a people's library as one which loaned books to the people, that is to all inhabitants of a locality and beyond. Such a library was intended above all for the enlightenment of 'people of the lower ranks' or 'the people proper'. Outside this definition lay academic libraries and city libraries (apart from those people's libraries established by different towns and cities) and the libraries of various official offices and public

---

339 Närhi 1963, 77.
340 *Helsingin Rouvasväen yhdistys/Fruntimmers föreningen i Helsingfors.*
341 The Finnish Church Law of 1869 was drafted under the direction of Frans Ludvig Schauman, who was later to serve as the Bishop of the Diocese of Porvoo. M. Heikkilä 2001.
342 Hirn 1998, 17, 19.
343 Kanerva & Peltonen 1961; Närhi 1963, 76; E. Seppälä 1963, 58.
344 Lehtikanto 1964, 8.
345 E. Seppälä 1963, 66.

institutions that were used by others than the organization's own officials. He also did not include in his definition the libraries of private societies whose books were loaned only to members. Nevertheless, his statistical list of people's libraries did comprise those run by private societies in the countryside because it was known that they generally lent their books to others than members. In only a few rare cases was this prohibited by the rules.[346] Thus for example, in Kivijärvi, the library maintained by a society could easily be regarded as a lending library for the common people.

However, it was in the countryside that the earliest people's libraries began to be built not only in Finland and the other Nordic countries but also in England and Scotland. In both Sweden and Finland there had been church libraries originally intended for the clergy, which from the seventeenth century on also lent books to the parishioners. They were the early forerunners of the rural lending libraries and public libraries.[347] The literature in the collections of the church libraries was mostly devotional, but their activities sometimes had features that resembled the operation of lending libraries, and sometimes they took part in wider educational activities. For example, circular letters sent out from certain dioceses in Sweden encouraged the parishes to establish libraries and lend out books for a small charge.[348]

Parish churches were also established in Scotland, England and the United States from the turn of the seventeenth and eighteenth centuries on. Instrumental in this activity were, for example, a Scotsman, Pastor James Kirkwood, and an Englishman, the Rev. Thomas Bray. By 1730 there were over sixty parish libraries in Britain and its colonies. In the early nineteenth century, many localities in England and Scotland had parish or village libraries that had been established by individuals, societies and church parishes, the maintenance of which was subsidized by the parishes. In the Nordic countries, there were popular libraries operating in the countryside in Norway and Denmark at the end of the eighteenth century, and from the turn of the century on they began to be established in Sweden as well.[349] Thus in principle there were libraries here and there, but in character they were much more humble institutions than the later public libraries, and their collections were more limited.

The major background factors that influenced the establishment of libraries in the Finnish countryside were the national awakening and the Lutheran religion. The Fennoman ideology was based among other things on the nationalist philosophy conceived by J. V. Snellman, who thought that the ordinary people should be taught to read and encouraged to study.[350] In Ostrobothnia, for example, people's libraries were established in the mid-nineteenth century in order to distract the people away from drinking and violence, which were manifested in the activities of the so-called

---

346 Schadewitz 1903, 22.
347 Närhi 1963, 69.
348 Hirn 1998, 14; Mäkinen 2009b, 31–33.
349 Allan 2008, 164–174; Närhi 1963, 69; Shera 1949, 26–28.
350 Ahonen 2003, 9; Mäkinen 2015, 294–295.

'knife-fighters',[351] and get them interested in reading. At the same time, The Awakening revivalist movement was strong in the region.[352] According to the Fennoman way of thinking, reading was not regarded as a dangerous activity, but as instructive and useful as long as the reading matter was not mere frivolous entertainment.[353] The need for libraries as a means of raising the educational level of the people was regarded as important by the university students, who participated in establishing numerous people's libraries in the nineteenth century. The student nations (organizations) began to support the establishment of parish libraries by donating books to them. Thus it was not always the locals who took the initiative in establishing the libraries; often they simply received small basic collections from elsewhere to start up their activities.[354]

Correspondingly, in the United States in the 1870s, public libraries were seen as promoting social stability and preventing crime and social rebellion, although their principal purpose was naturally educational.[355] In Britain, too, at the end of the century it was thought that libraries existed to provide not only opportunities for study and obtaining information but also a kind of training for proper citizenship. Right up to the First World War, public libraries were regarded as promoting social stability. It was hoped that they would help to solve socio-political problems at the same time as they supported the efforts of adults in particular to educate themselves.[356]

In Finland, the establishment of libraries for the common people proceeded apace from the 1840s on. At that time, however, the population of the countryside did not enjoy the same opportunities to form societies as the upper-class members of the reading societies in the towns because the countryside was sparsely settled and distances were long. Moreover, the local people were generally uneducated, and they did not have the same ready cash resources available for reading society activities as members of the higher estates.[357] By the turn of the 1850s, several dozen lending libraries had been founded thanks to the activities of the students and their nations. The establishment of libraries slowed down at the beginning of that decade only to pick up again towards the end. At the same time, correspondents began to write to the newspapers more actively on the issue of libraries. They drew attention to the fact that in the United States, for example, special school libraries had begun to be established.[358] From the end of the 1850s

---

351 The 'knife-fighters' were young hoodlums in Southern Ostrobothnia whose acts of violence and gang fights often led to killings. The reasons behind this delinquent activity were social and economic; for example, despite the fact that the young rowdies were from diverse social groups, their leaders usually had farming backgrounds, and the fact that there was not enough land for all the young men to farm caused their frustration to erupt in violence. Ylikangas 1998.
352 S. Seppälä 1954, 58.
353 Mäkinen 2009c, 118.
354 Hirn 1998, 14–15.
355 Garrison 1979, 36.
356 Black 2000, 4, 13.
357 Mäkinen 2009d, 138.
358 Mäkinen 2009d, 138–139; Närhi 1963, 74.

on, members of the clergy, in particular, began to promote the establishment of people's libraries in the countryside.[359]

The university students, who had cherished an ideal image of the common people from the 1840s on, also became active founders of people's libraries later on in their working lives. For example, those who had trained for the ministry had become familiar in their student years with the ideals of popular education and the activities of people's libraries, and they later promoted these in the parishes in which they served as clerics.[360] However, the libraries established by the upper classes for the common people tended to wither away after an enthusiastic start. It was also typical of the early popular libraries and those that were based on the endeavours of private persons that their activities were not continuous but were sometimes interrupted and even ceased altogether. Kansanvalistusseura (The Society for Popular Enlightenment) was founded in 1874 by educated members of the Fennoman movement to distribute inexpensive literature that was comprehensible to ordinary people and to educate the commons; this society helped to unify the people's libraries on a national basis, and it was only then that their activities began to be characterized by some kind of continuity.[361]

In Sweden, it had been proposed in the Diet as early as 1828 that state funding should be allocated for the establishment of parish libraries. Although the proposal was not passed, a number of parish libraries were established in the 1830s in Sweden, most of them in the Diocese of Karlstad in the County of Värmland, where by the 1840s there were libraries in 38 of the 42 parishes. A clause in the 1842 Swedish Elementary School Act, which sought to increase the number of parish libraries, stipulated that it was the duty of the clergy to promote the establishment of people's libraries.[362] The clergy were given the task of encouraging the people to establish them and suggesting literature that they considered to be suitable for them to acquire.[363]

In the 1850s, there was a discussion in the Swedish press about whether novels in the people's libraries were suitable reading for popular enlightenment. In some places, in fact, the local people themselves rejected lending libraries and considered that devotional literature sufficed for them. As in Finland, the establishment of libraries took off in the late 1850s. Some of the libraries were run by societies and were funded by donations and subscriptions. However, the majority were church and municipal institutions, whose librarians were often elementary school teachers. In 1871 there were over 1500 parish libraries operating in Sweden.[364]

In Finland, the Crimean War increased people's enthusiasm for reading enormously as they were eager to read the war news published

---

359 Järvelin 1966, 34; Närhi 1963, 76.
360 Karjalainen 1977, 34, 36–37.
361 Hirn 1998, 13–14; Karjalainen 1977, 34; see also e.g. Mantovaara 2001, 2–4; H. Mäkelä 1991, 13–17; Vatanen 2002, 46.
362 Närhi 1963, 69.
363 Jarlbrink 2010, 47.
364 Jarlbrink 2010, 47–48.

in the newspapers. There was a change of ruler in the later stages of the war, when Alexander II rose to the Russian throne in 1855. The earlier censorship regulations were gradually relaxed, and a new, more progressive administrative era ensued. For example, popular education and the establishment of elementary schools occupied a central place in the programme of reforms proposed by the new Tsar on his tour of Finland in 1856.[365] In the final stages of the war, other societally important actors, too, were able to sense a change in the political climate and began to support progressive projects in the field of popular enlightenment. For example, Archbishop Edvard Bergenheim began a campaign that aimed to support the foundation of libraries in church parishes. His endeavour was to go one step further than the university students' projects in the countryside to activate the desire for reading among the local people.[366]

The campaign for the establishment of lending libraries was in practice implemented at the local level by the young auxiliary clergy, curates and assistant vicars, who would in any case soon have carried out some corresponding measures to continue the earlier work of the students. An essential feature of the archbishop's project was the collection of financial support for the libraries from the people. This was the first time that a person of high authority gave his support to the establishment of people's libraries, and it meant that thereafter the clergy experienced at least a moral obligation to promote libraries. The foundation of libraries was also supported in the ministerial conventions of the time. The activeness of the archbishop was also inspired by the fear of the church that the secular authorities would in future assume the responsibility for the education of the people, which had up till then remained the remit of the church. The establishment of lending libraries was part of the church's plan for the reform of popular education, in which the responsibility for a child's education was to be shared between the family, the school and the church.[367]

An assessment of the total number of libraries in Finland is made difficult by the fact that in the early decades most of the local parish libraries failed and were re-established several times. As a result, different estimates of their number have been presented in earlier research. According to the diocesan records, over 300 local lending libraries were established between 1851 and 1865.[368] By 1860 there were already over 90 parish libraries operating in Finland.[369] The 1860s was the golden age of the foundation of lending libraries, but already in the following decades it became necessary to revive many of them and reinvigorate their operations, since they had not aroused the interest of the rank and file in the desired way. Moreover, the first elementary schools were opened in many rural parishes in the 1870s, and the end of that decade witnessed brisk activity in the foundation of

---

365 Häggman 2008, 13–14; Mäkinen 2009d, 136–137, 141.
366 Mäkinen 2009b, 137.
367 Mäkinen 2009b, 137, 140–144.
368 Mäkinen 2009d, 145–146. See also e.g. Karjalainen 1977; Schadewitz 1903.
369 Hirn 1998, 15.

civic societies, including reading societies, which were a popular activity among private persons.[370] Schadewitz estimated that at the beginning of the twentieth century there were there were between 1800 and 2000 people's libraries in Finland, although in half of them the collection contained 200 books at most, and a library of over 1000 volumes was a rarity in the countryside. At the beginning of the twentieth century, 99 percent of Finnish rural municipalities had lending libraries.[371]

At the turn of the nineteenth and twentieth centuries, there were fewer libraries in rural areas of England, for example, than in the cities, but circulating libraries, which offered their customers popular literature and subscription libraries, which favoured higher-brow literature, had begun to be established by private persons from the late eighteenth century on. The latter type of libraries were also used by women.[372] People's libraries in the Nordic countries were typically fixed parish libraries. For example, in Denmark these libraries were funded by donations and state subsidies, and the state also began to establish circulating libraries in the late nineteenth century. In Norway, too, libraries were subsidized by the state. In Sweden, at the turn of the century there were still numerous collections of books that went under the name of parish libraries, the contents of which mainly consisted of outdated devotional literature.[373]

There were also popular libraries funded by private individuals and associations in Sweden. Stockholm City Library only came into being in the 1920s when the collections of several libraries run by various associations and parishes were merged. In Norway, Oslo Public Library was founded in 1785 when an industrial magnate called Carl Deichman bequeathed his collection of books to it. In Copenhagen, too, there was a large library founded in 1775 by a private collector 'for the lettered and the unlettered'. It was later merged with the Royal Library in Copenhagen. The city's municipal library was established in 1885.[374] The libraries established in the countryside and cities of the Nordic countries were above all characterized by the strong ecclesiastical tradition of lending out mainly devotional literature. On the other hand, the late nineteenth century was also marked by the endeavours of individual actors to promote popular education. These endeavours were often charitable in nature and accompanied by considerable donations. In the background also lay the ideal of nationhood, to which a realization of the importance of elementary education and popular enlightenment for its attainment was particularly strongly connected in Finland.

One can conclude that the development of the people's libraries that had been established all over Finland into modern public libraries based on British and American models only began in the early twentieth century. Behind this, however, lay a long tradition that was based on the activities of

---

370 Werkko 1879, 287–288.
371 Schadewitz 1903, 18, 20–23.
372 Allan 2008, 63–82, 119–156; Eliot 2006; Forster & Bell 2006; Schadewitz 1903, 11; Shera 1949,127.
373 Schadewitz 1903, 13.
374 Närhi 1963, 73.

reading societies and commercial lending libraries and which along with the advent of Lutheranism had absorbed numerous German influences. The operational model for the public libraries that were then established in Finland came from the American Public Library Movement, whose ideas had spread into Finland and the other Nordic countries at the turn of the century. The principles of the movement included the notion that the same library services should be available to all classes of the population. It was originally an urban movement, and in Finland, too, the development of public libraries began in the cities. The Society for Popular Enlightenment had for a long time spoken out about the need for libraries and helped to organize the activities of the existing ones.[375]

The people's libraries were originally established expressly for the use of the lower classes, but in the early twentieth century an attempt was made to get away from the association of the popular libraries principally with charitable work and assistance for the poor.[376] In the introduction to his statistical work that was published in 1903, Schadewitz mentioned that there had been endeavours in all 'civilized countries' to achieve this goal. The whole people, he stated, regardless of class, age or gender should participate not only in obtaining their daily bread in agriculture but also in the cultivation of their minds and thereby 'partake of the ennobling influence of enlightenment'.[377]

In practice, however, the people's libraries continued to be stigmatized by their function as institutions intended for the lower strata of society. Although the so-called 'society of the estates' was gradually breaking down, and there was a transition to public libraries that were in principle open to everyone, the traditional library organizations continued their activities. For example, in 1879 the new City Library of Vyborg began to operate alongside the existing people's library. The situation was administratively confusing, and the libraries finally merged only in 1910.[378]

Turku Public Library was founded in 1891, but the existing people's library continued to operate inside the same building, and the activities of the two institutions remained separate for a long time. In Helsinki, on the other hand, the City Library managed to avoid this kind of dichotomous activity.[379] There was less need for such amalgamations in the countryside because the members of the upper classes living in the poorer parishes were few in number and they could often use the same lending library as the rest of the population.

In Finland, as in many other countries in Europe, the spread of libraries was affected by many different factors, such as increased interaction between communities, trade and travel, a fall in the costs of book production, the development of education, the growth of literacy, an increase in the amount of literature written in the vernacular language, charitable work and greater

375 Haasio 2010, 9; Mäkinen 1999, 38; Vatanen 2002, 39–41.
376 Karjalainen 1977, 6–7.
377 Schadewitz 1903, 7.
378 Hirn 1998, 76.
379 Hirn 1998, 75.

leisure time. Above all, nationalism and national aspirations provided the ideological background for the endeavours to promote the establishment of libraries for the people throughout the nineteenth century. These activities were often conducted by members of the educated classes in Helsinki, although in a few cases they also originated in regional centres like Jyväskylä; the activities included donations of books by students and writing letters to the newspapers.

An examination of the history of Finnish people's libraries shows that the operation of the libraries was initially regarded above all by the members of the higher estates as a form of charitable work, and most of the libraries operated under their direction. Moreover, my research reveals that a striking feature of the history of the library institution in Finland is the active role played by women in the establishment of libraries. This kind of popular enlightenment work was probably felt to be mainly the responsibility of women in the same way as other efforts to promote Christian morality and provide social assistance.[380] However, perhaps the most important factor in the development of popular libraries was constituted by the activities of those few educated supporters of popular enlightenment who achieved a lot in their small rural communities when for one reason or another they decided to cater for the people's desire to read. One of these persons was a cantor from Sumiainen in Central Finland. He arrived to take up his post in Kivijärvi at about the same time as its separation from its mother parish of Viitasaari in 1858. The newly independent parish needed someone to point the way in its spiritual life, and the cantor, who was strong in his faith, became just such an agent of change.

The book collections of the church parish: the early years of Kivijärvi library

THE ESTABLISHMENT OF KIVIJÄRVI LENDING LIBRARY

At the turn of the 1850s and the 1860s, the new cantor of Kivijärvi, Ferdinand Konstantin Kjellman, held long and deep discussions with the vicar about his own Evangelical religious convictions. These discussions played on the minds of both men. Kjellman's strong faith finally persuaded the vicar, Karl Gustaf Dahlgrén, to convert to Evangelism, and under the influence of these two the movement burgeoned among the parishioners too. There are memories of how whole villages 'confessed themselves blessed', as the typical expression of Evangelism in the nineteenth century put it. Dahlgrén had come to Kivijärvi as a curate in 1852. When Kivijärvi seceded from Viitasaari, he became the first vicar of the new parish.[381] The dynamism of the movement abated in 1866, when he moved away from the parish, but there were still adherents of Evangelism living there in the 1930s, when, however, many of them converted to Laestadianism.[382] The activeness of revivalist

---

380 See e.g. Markkola 2002.
381 Appendix 1.
382 S. Tuomaala 1986, 351.

movements in Kivijärvi typically depended on what movement the vicar adhered to at the time in question. From the point of view of the initiation of popular library activities, the revivalist movements and Evangelism in particular were of crucial significance. However, one can ask why a book collection promoting Evangelism was created specifically in Kivijärvi and what was the importance of individual actors or local conditions in the birth of the lending library there.

The first lending library in Kivijärvi was established in 1862 by Dahlgrén, who was also the first librarian, a task which he performed unpaid. After a few years, the operations of the library languished.[383] This was probably a result of the fact that Kivijärvi got a new vicar in 1868 and of the severe famine that afflicted that the region in the late 1860s, when the people were more concerned with finding something to eat than reading. The existence of lethal infections would anyway have made the operation of the library impossible, and this offers a natural explanation for its temporary demise.

Kivijärvi was the eighth parish in Central Finland to get a library.[384] The first people's library in the region was established in Saarijärvi in 1857. It was originally funded with donations,[385] and later it received further donations of money and books from time to time. According to the information obtained by Kaarle Werkko, the library was 'launched by gentlefolk who gave donations for the purpose'. Even the Finnish Imperial Society of Commerce donated a few books.[386]

However, according to an earlier study, it is highly probable that the establishment of the library had been planned by a farmer called Matti Taipale together with Karl Stenius, who was the vicar of Saarijärvi from 1853 to 1884. The parish chief of police, Wilhelm Gotthard von Hertzén, was also involved in the scheme. These three are regarded as having been the founders of the parish library in Saarijärvi. Taipale was responsible for the practical running of the library, and he was appointed to be the first librarian. Most of the donations came from members of the higher estates. To begin with, the funds were used for the purchase of 88 books, which were entered into the library catalogue on 12 May 1857, the birthday of J. V. Snellman. The fact that just that day was chosen to mark the official foundation of the library was doubtless inspired by Fennoman ideology. At the end of its first year of operation, Saarijärvi parish library possessed 168 volumes, and the number increased in the two following years by just under a hundred.[387]

Matti Taipale was an exceptional person to be a founder of a library in Finland in those days. He was born at Taipale Farm in the village of Hännilä in Saarijärvi parish on 13 October 1825. According to legend, he was by nature a calm, friendly, jovial and popular man. Unlike the well-known Finnish folk poet, Paavo Korhonen, who left the running of his farm to others and concentrated on writing poetry, Matti Taipale was handy in

---

383 Werkko 1879, 181.
384 Mönkkönen 1988a, 538.
385 Suomela 1963, 651–652; Werkko 1879, 192.
386 Werkko 1879, 192.
387 Suomela 1963, 651–652; Werkko 1879, 192.

many practical jobs on the farm: he was a skilful smith, he could if necessary mend his neighbours' clocks and he made all the wooden objects and tools that were needed in his household himself.[388] Taipale seems to have been a man of many talents and one who took a wide interest in social affairs.

Matti Taipale had not had any elementary schooling because when he was a boy there were no elementary schools in the parish, but through his own efforts he had acquired a great deal of learning. His library contained what was for the time a wide range of literature on different fields. Taipale was certainly better read and educated than the usual peasant farmer, and this encouraged him to take up numerous municipal and parochial duties when still a young man. He was also widely employed in the parish as a scribe for drawing up letters, promissory notes and other documents when the illiterate peasants could not do so themselves. In the 1850s and 1860s, Taipale actively participated in Saarijärvi parish meetings and in the activities of the parish assembly. He wrote numerous articles for the newspapers, and he was a local correspondent, a task that involved the regular reporting of affairs in Saarijärvi. Taipale also taught the members of his household to read and write. He played a role in getting Tarvaala Agricultural School established in Saarijärvi in 1867, and he was appointed to serve on its first board of governors.[389]

The second library to be established in Central Finland was in Keuruu in 1858, but it did not start to function until 1861. Where devotional literature had made up about one third of the books of Saarijärvi library, only secular Finnish-language literature was acquired for the new library in Keuruu, although the founders were also clerics and the first librarian was the daughter of the parish curate.[390]

The first library in the parish of Karstula was established in 1861. It was founded with voluntary donations, and initially it aroused considerable enthusiasm but subsequently it fell into disuse. However, it was decided to revive the library in 1876 with monetary donations amounting to 125 marks. Behind this effort were a farmer called Heikki Krook, the schoolteacher Juho Enqvist, the temporary curate Frans Karl Otto Vilhelm Winter and the cantor Erik Lindeqvist. At that time, the library's collection comprised about a hundred works, the borrowing of which was made free of charge the following year. In the late 1870s, it was proposed that regulations governing the operation of the library should be drawn up. Farmer Heikki Krook took up the running of the re-established library, again without payment, and he was followed in this task by a shop-owner called J. Backman and a teacher called Jaakko Ollila. Juho Enqvist, who was originally from Saarijärvi and who served as an ambulatory teacher in the parish of Karstula taking care of

---

388 Haavio 1952, 397.
389 Haavio 1952, 397–399. Taipale is mentioned also as an example of a peasant writer and newspaper correspondent in Laitinen & Mikkola 2013, 179–180, 202. For a further discussion of the importance of Taipale for library work and the advancement of Finnish-language culture at the local level, see Kotilainen 2013a.
390 Rainio 1988; Suomela 1963, 653.

the instruction of the illiterate section of the population, was appointed the chairman of the board of governors of the library.[391]

Viitasaari, too, had a library. It was established in 1861 by the dean and a few other enthusiasts of popular enlightenment in the parish. However, the activities of the library, to which they donated 66 volumes, languished until a group of parishioners began to revive it in 1868. The new founders were the deputy pastor, Karl Gustaf Tötterman, the cantor Konstantin Sarlin and two men called Sederholm and Lindholm. The first two also served as librarians before they were followed in this task by K. Kempas, an elementary school teacher, who performed this duty without pay. By 1875, the library collection had grown to around 150 volumes. The monetary value of the collection was about 250 marks. A satisfactory amount of books were loaned out for a fee, which for small books was two pence a month and 4 pence for bigger ones. The library's activities were not yet governed by any rules.[392] Thus all these libraries were founded before the first library in Kivijärvi, and they certainly offered at least a partial model for the organization of its activities.

In Central Finland, the libraries were mainly established by clerics. This applies to a third of the oldest popular libraries. In addition to the clergy, the local gentry were also active in establishing libraries in their parishes. Only a few of the founders were farmers, and Kaarle Arvelin from Jämsä, Elias Krook from Karstula, Kustaa Raitanen from Multia and Matti Taipale from Saarijärvi were exceptions among the peasant estate.[393] Only rarely were the members of the rural population themselves involved in planning and organizing the activities of the popular libraries. The participation of local farmers together with schoolteachers and members of the clergy in the foundation of libraries in Karstula and Saarijärvi was exceptional. And even in these localities, ministers, cantors and other clerics and local functionaries were heavily involved both in setting up the libraries and in reviving their activities. In Kivijärvi, the founders of the libraries all belonged to the educated classes and were members of the families of functionaries, merchants or clergymen who had moved to the parish from elsewhere and who only remained in Kivijärvi for as long as the head of the family was posted or operated there.[394]

From the communal point of view, the parish vicars held a key position in the establishment of the early people's libraries. By lending their authority to the activities of the libraries, they assured a certain continuity in their activities. By contrast, if there was no local person who could take charge of the library's activities, the use of the book collections donated by the students, for example, might sometimes be lower than expected.[395]

It has been estimated that of the Finnish popular libraries established before 1860, over 40 percent were founded by members of the clergy and in

---

391 Alamäki 1998, 458; Koski 1998, 584–585; Werkko 1879, 178.
392 Werkko 1879, 194–195.
393 Mönkkönen 1988a, 538–539.
394 Table 5. For further details on the backgrounds and places of birth of those involved in organizing the activities of the libraries, see Appendix 1.
395 Mäkinen 2009d, 139.

Table 5. The founders of people's libraries (Werkko's statistics 1874).

Library	Establishment			Re-establishment			
	Founder 1	Founder 2	Founder 3	Founder 1	Founder 2	Founder 3	Founder 4
Karstula	n/a			Farmer	Ambulatory teacher	Vicar	Cantor
Kivijärvi	Vicar	Cantor		Vicar			
Kannonsaha	Sawmill owner			–			
Perho	Juror, church warden			–			
Saarijärvi*	Farmer	Chief of police	Vicar	–			
Viitasaari	Dean	Other popular educators		Substitute pastor	Cantor	etc.	

* Information supplemented from other literature.
n/a = not available Source: Werkko 1879.

the years 1855–1865 the clergy were involved in establishing about 60 percent of the libraries.[396] Towards the end of the century, other local figures came to be more actively involved. Before the separation of parochial and secular administration, the parish vicars were in effect the local administrative leaders because they generally acted as chairmen (and often also as secretaries) in the church and parish assembly meetings. Even after the Decree on Municipal Government and the establishment of municipal assemblies (the forerunners of municipal councils), they often served actively on the boards of governors of elementary schools and as the chairmen of municipal meetings. There were practical reasons for this: in small rural parishes, the vicars or curates were often the only persons who possessed a higher education and were thus were best qualified to undertake these tasks.

The fact that in the nineteenth century the clergy played a significant role in the establishment of popular libraries and were active in library affairs primarily arose out of the ideological influences of educational and nationalist ideals and the above mentioned interest of the clergy in keeping popular education under the control of the church even after the mid-nineteenth century, a state of affairs that Archbishop Bergenheim sought to promote in practice by initiating a campaign to support the establishment and functioning of libraries in the unsettled years following the Crimean War. The activities of the church parish lending libraries were founded on the practice in the previous century of lending books from the churches' collections to the parishioners. The first book that was lent was usually the Bible, which many parishioners did not have the means to acquire for themselves. Gradually the lending expanded to include other books. More comprehensive information about the lending activities of church libraries has been preserved in Sweden than in Finland. The lending activities in Sweden were also enhanced by the fact that most of the books in the church libraries were in Swedish.[397]

396 Mäkinen 2009d, 139–140.
397 Karjalainen 1977, 10–11.

The significant role played by churchmen in the establishment of libraries is also explained by the fact that, up to the establishment of elementary schools, the education of the people was the responsibility of the church. On the other hand, the parish vicar is often mentioned as the founder of a library even though the actual initiative for its establishment may have come from elsewhere. This was because the support of the clergy was a prerequisite for the continuity of its activities. This again increased the importance and indispensability of the clergy in the eyes of the rulers, and consequently the Clerical Estate sought to cling on to its popular educational remit in order to increase its influence. Particularly in the countryside, the church was still in practice teaching the common people to read right up to the beginning of the twentieth century.[398]

According to Kaarle Werkko's information, people's libraries were generally established in Central Finland earlier than in the Lake District of Ostrobothnia. However, it should be noted that supplementing this relatively sparse information with the findings of later local historical research can yield a very different picture of the beginnings of popular libraries. For example, a library had already been established in Vimpeli in the Ostrobothnian Lake District in 1858.[399] According to the information obtained by Werkko, of the libraries in this region Viitasaari Library had the largest collection of books. Typically, and particularly in the 1870s, the lending libraries in the area studied charged no fee for borrowing books. Thus the loan fees exceptionally charged in the parish of Viitasaari most probably allowed for a greater expansion of the collection than elsewhere. In Kivijärvi, rules governing the operation of the library were adopted rather late compared with the other lending libraries in the region.[400]

Several libraries had been established in the region of Southern Ostrobothnia in the Province of Vaasa before Matti Taipale opened his lending library to the readers of Saarijärvi. For example, lending libraries in Ilmajoki, Jalasjärvi, Laihia, Munsala and Mustasaari (Svartholm) began to operate in the 1850s and in Isojoki one was founded already in 1848. According to Werkko, libraries were also established in Alavus, Isokyrö, Kauhajoki, and Keuruu and in the parish of Ruununkylä (today Kruunupyy [Kronoby]) in the 1850s, but their activities either ended or were languishing and in need of revitalization. Similar libraries had been established in Korsnäs, Lapväärtti (Lappfjärd) and Teuva in 1849. The first libraries were founded in most parishes in the 1860s. It is noteworthy that, apart from the library in Saarijärvi, the first libraries in the nineteenth century in the actual region of Central Finland (later to become a province in its own right) were not established until the 1860s, in other words slightly later than in the more prosperous country parishes of Southern Ostrobothnia.[401] By the end of 1874, there were, according to Werkko, 62 libraries and two reading societies operating in the rural parishes of the Province of Vaasa.[402]

398 Karjalainen 1977, 11–12, 99–100; Matti Peltonen 1992, 94–95.
399 Kivipelto 1966, 231.
400 Table 6.
401 Schadewitz 1903, 100–107.
402 Werkko 1879, 199.

Table 6. The establishment of people's libraries in the Province of Vaasa (Werkko's statistics).

Library	Established	Re-established	Books	Value (marks)	Loan fee	Rules
Karstula	1861	1876	100	380.00	free	in preparation 1877
Kivijärvi	1862	1872	80	n/a	free	n/a
Kannonsaha	1862	–	n/a	n/a	free	n/a
Perho	1862	–	105	121.08	free	yes
Pihtipudas	n/k					
Saarijärvi	1857	–	n/a	n/a	n/a	n/a
Pylkönmäki	n/k					
Viitasaari	1861	1868	150	250	2–4 pence per month	no
Alajärvi	n/k					
Evijärvi	–	–	–	–	–	–
Lappajärvi	–	–	–	–	–	–
Lehtimäki	1874	–	80	170.00	yes	yes
Soini	1874	1876	n/a	n/a	n/a	n/a
Vimpeli	n/k					

n/a = not available; n/k = not known
Source: Werkko 1879. Alajärvi Library was established in 1865, and initially charged a loan fee, but later borrowing was made free. Kivipelto 1966.

The national statistical data on libraries became a bit more exact with the advent of the twentieth century, and they supplement information concerning the existing situation of libraries in rural parishes. The libraries of Viitasaari and Pihtipudas, where there had clearly been continuity in the libraries' activities, continued to be the best stocked. Borrowing was most active in Perho, a neighbouring parish of Kivijärvi in Central Ostrobothnia. Southern Ostrobothnia (including the Lake District), Central Ostrobothnia, and the northern part of Central Finland all belonged to the Province of Vaasa. A comparison between the statistics for the different localities is, however, vitiated by the fact that the data are for different years, covering a period of eight years in all.[403]

There is one local example that is worth pointing out in this connection. A library was established in Alajärvi in the Ostrobothnian Lake District in 1865. A list of the donations of books made to the library by the founders dates from the following year. Among the donators, who belonged to all classes, were not only Pastor Johan Werner[404] Limón and local officials such as a forestry officer, the local chief of polices, a surveyor and the cantor but also farmers, crofters, hired hands and even a few married women. Limón, who later held the post of vicar in Kivijärvi, had moved to Alajärvi from Kokemäki, where there had earlier been a people's library, as there had been in the parishes where the other officials who had helped to found the library in Alajärvi had previously resided. A collection made in 1866 resulted in a donation of about 129 marks from 20 people. The largest contributions were made by Pastor Werner Limón and the chief of police Johan Granlund. These funds were used to purchase the first 74 books for the library. Lending

403 Table 7.
404 Limón was usually known by his second name.

2. The Foundation of a Local Lending Library

Table 7. The first parish libraries in the Province of Vaasa (Schadewitz's statistics).

Parish	Founded	Volumes	Value of collection (marks)	Loans (previous year)	Information from
CENTRAL FINLAND					
Karstula parish	1876	578	1440.90	411	1902
Kyyjärvi Elementary School district	1886	120	270.00	114	1902
Kivijärvi church village	1862	78	312.00	–	1895
Kivijärvi private	1888	145	399.00	–	1896
Leppälänkylä	1895	63	67.35	–	1896
Youth association	–	102	80.00	–	1903
Jauhoniemi village	1896	123	324.75	–	1899
Perho	1862	135	175.00	800	1901
Pihtipudas	1878	668	1000.00	–	1901
Saarijärvi	1857	197	324.25	117	1901
Pylkönmäki chapelry	1876	–	–	–	1895
Viitasaari	1861	–	–	–	1895
SOUTHERN OSTROBOTHNIA					
Alajärvi	1865	166	300.00	–	1901
Evijärvi	1866	200	600.00	–	1902
Kortesjärvi	1881	443	768.02	457	1903
Lappajärvi	1875	–	–	–	1895
Lehtimäki	1874	238	481.90	153	1903
Soini	1901	29	100.00	–	1900
Kivijärvi Village	1899	65	160.00	–	1901
Vimpeli (youth association)	1890	216	400.00	201	–

Source: Schadewitz 1903, 100–107. Schadewitz has seen that e.g. Karstula parish library was actually established only in 1876.

activities, however, did not begin in Alajärvi until 1868. The library was for a long time under the protection of the church parish, although it was not owned by it. Funds were collected at various parish events, and the clergy made donations to the library for the acquisition of books. In addition, a church warden served as the librarian. For a long time, the municipality failed to take care of the library, and as a result its activities suffered, and indeed it was inactive from the end of the 1870s until 1912. Another problem was that in 1880 only about one percent of the people of Alajärvi possessed the ability to write.[405]

This short digression into the local history of a parish in Southern Ostrobothnia shows that Limón, who was later to become the vicar of Kivijärvi was extremely enthusiastic about popular enlightenment. In Kivijärvi, however, he did not have much time to promote the activities of the people's library, although he had become acquainted with the work of lending libraries in the form of a military library when he was serving

405 Kivipelto 1966, 232–234.

as the padre of a battalion of the Finnish Grenadier Rifles[406] in Turku. The battalion's library was as far as we know the first lending library established in Finland for the use of the troops. August Edward Granfelt, Limón's predecessor as padre, had been the moving force behind the establishment of the library in an effort to improve the reading and writing skills of the soldiers. Limón had also been involved in establishing people's libraries at any rate in 1860 in Kokemäki and Harjavalta.[407]

Limón succeeded Karl Gustav Dahlgrén, who had taken an active part in local administrative planning, as vicar of Kivijärvi, and he was the first chairman of the municipal assembly. The cantor, F. K. Kjellman, was appointed to be the vice-chairman. The vicars of Kivijärvi served as the chairmen of the municipal assembly up till 1876. This was also the case with Viktor August Konsin, who served in this capacity from 1871 to 1876. In the years 1873–1886, the duties of the chairman of the Municipal Board were also combined with this post. To Limón also fell the task of recording the minutes of the meetings in 1868. He was assisted in this duty by the deputy cantor Antti Herranen.[408] However, the activities of the lending library in the parish suddenly waned when its major supporters died in the years of high mortality. The famine disaster took both the vicar and the cantor, who served as his assistant in local administrative duties, in the same year.

The re-establishment of Kivijärvi lending library

The Kivijärvi lending library did not remain unused for long before it found a new supporter. The lending library of Kivijärvi was re-established in 1872 by the Vicar Konsin with the support of the church assembly. Konsin also served unpaid as the librarian. The books that had survived from the earlier library were collected and new volumes were purchased with funds from voluntary donations. Altogether 69 works were obtained for the library. Halfway through the 1870s, the library possessed 80 volumes, and their value amounted to about 380 marks. According to information supplied to Werkko, at that time 'books [had been] borrowed satisfactorily'. No fees were charged for borrowing books, and the library had no set of rules.[409] This collection, which was based on the work done by Dahlgrén, contained only religious literature.[410]

Pastor Konsin took office as vicar of Kivijärvi in 1872. He was 36 years of age when he first attained this position and had served for thirteen years in lower-ranking clerical posts. He immediately took a strong grip on the administration of his parish. In a church assembly held in the vicarage on

---

406 In Finnish: *Suomen Krenatööri-tarkk'ampujapataljoona.*
407 Mäkinen 1990, 38–41; Werkko 1879, 58, 68. On military libraries, see also Murphy 2009.
408 Martti Peltonen 1986, 377, 380, 382–384.
409 KSA, Minutes of the church parish assembly meeting 25/5/1872; Werkko 1879, 181. In the same way the library was re-established e.g. in Lapua. See Ylitalo 2012, 28–29.
410 KKA, Collection catalogues of Kivijärvi lending library.

25 May, he brought up the question of establishing an elementary school, but his hopes were quashed. The church parish assembly did not consider that there were enough funds even for an ambulatory school. So the new vicar had to be satisfied with the appointment of Sunday school teachers to take care of the children's education in each of districts where catechetical meetings were held. He did, however, obtain one small concession: the congregation agreed to establish his proposed lending library and decided to collect voluntary monetary contributions at the catechetical meetings. The vicar promised to take care of the collection of donations himself. Konsin also announced that he had made an interesting discovery in his new home, the Lepistö vicarage. He had found a pile of brand new illustrated bibles that had lain forgotten there, and he therefore asked his flock who they belonged to. When he was told that they naturally did not belong to anyone, it was decided to add them to the collection of the lending library.[411]

Viktor Konsin used his negotiating skills to good effect, and in September the church parish assembly decided to establish the first elementary school in the parish and also to employ ambulatory teachers to give instruction to the children of the outlying villages.[412] Thus the first elementary school began to operate in the church village in 1873. To begin with, it was housed in the old vicarage building, in the same yard as Konsin's home. Because at that time the state funded only one elementary school teacher per parish, the small parishes of Central Finland like Kivijärvi headed the statistics for school attendance. When the limitations on state subsidies were removed in the following decade and more village elementary schools began to be established in the larger parishes, the proportion of elementary school pupils in the poorer outlying areas became smaller than elsewhere. Even as late as 1906, only a little over one tenth of the children of school age attended school in Kivijärvi.[413]

Pastor Konsin was an able administrator, and he tried to establish an ambulatory school for the villages of Kivijärvi on a permanent basis. While still the vicar of Kivijärvi he also held the post of Provincial Dean of Jyväskylä in the years 1877–1878. In 1878, Konsin applied for the post of vicar in Korpilahti in Central Finland. In the election in February he received the second highest number of votes and was not chosen for the post. Finally, he moved away to become vicar of Orimattila in central southern Finland in 1882, and he received the title 'Dean' in 1886. Viktor Konsin was extremely well versed in ecclesiastical law, and as a result he held numerous offices of trust in addition to his official post. When he was vicar of Orimattila, he was appointed as the representative of the Diocese of Porvoo (Borgå) in the Estate of the Clergy at the Diets of 1897, 1899 and 1900. He was also a member of the Legal and Economic Committee. Konsin is said to have been a good speaker and preacher.[414] He was fairly young when he took up his post in Kivijärvi, and his intention seems to have been to use it to

---

411 KSA, Minutes of the church parish assembly meeting 25/5/1872; Appendix 1.
412 KSA, Minutes of the parish assembly meeting 21/9/1872.
413 Mönkkönen 1986, 440–441, 446–448.
414 Konsin 2000, 4; Lahti 1991, 6–7; S. Tuomaala 1986, 320.

gain experience for more demanding positions. Despite this, he sought to promote popular education in Kivijärvi, and he pushed through his planned school and library projects.

The influence of other individual clerics on the educational conditions in the region was also considerable. For example, Karl Stenius, the vicar of Saarijärvi, was behind the establishment of elementary schools in Pylkönmäki and Konginkangas (both chapelries of the parish of Saarijärvi). Pylkönmäki lending library was founded by an elementary schoolteacher called Kaarlo Johannes Rahikainen, but in the literature there is conflicting information about the year when it was established: it was either 1873, 1876 or 1878. A municipal popular library was not established there until 1923, and in 1926 its stocks were transferred to the main library of the municipality, which was established in the same year, although, according to another source, it did not commence operating until 1930.[415]

Thus the libraries came under municipal administration fairly slowly. The number of schools and the libraries that operated in conjunction with them increased in the different parishes after the turn of the century. In Karstula at the beginning of the twentieth century, in addition to the one in the church village, there were libraries operating in the villages of Kiminki, Mulikka, Mötönkylä and Saunamäki and in the elementary school districts of Kyyjärvi and Raja-aho, and there was also a youth association library. In Viitasaari, in addition to the parish library there were libraries in the villages of Haapaniemi, Ilmolahti, Keiteleenpohja and Suovanlahti and a youth association library in the village of Huopana.[416]

A comparison of the early libraries in Central Finland reveals the surprising fact that the first people's libraries were established in the northern parts of the region.[417] Jyväskylä was the only large urban centre in the area, but libraries were founded not only in the old parishes of Viitasaari, Keuruu and Jämsä but also in Karstula, Kivijärvi, Korpilahti and Kuhmoinen before one was established in Jyväskylä. However, although the earliest libraries came into being in the countryside, Jyväskylä held a significant position as an educational centre with important schools and other educational institutions, and in this capacity it advanced popular enlightenment in numerous ways. While the people's library in Saarijärvi was the oldest in Central Finland, the first people's library in Jyväskylä was not founded until 1863, despite the fact that the city was the site of the country's first Finnish-language teacher training seminary.[418] It was established by a district doctor called Wolmar Schildt and was funded with private donations.[419]

The fact that a library was established in Kivijärvi in 1862 mainly stems from the discussions between the vicar and the cantor. The Evangelical revival that was dominant in the parish at the time was the factor that influenced the spiritual content of the library's collection. Through their

415 E.g. Schadewitz (1903) mentions the year 1876. Sinisalo 1984, 77, 83.
416 Schadewitz 1903, 102, 107.
417 Table 8.
418 Junnila 1995, 243.
419 Werkko 1879, 28.

Table 8. Years of the establishment of the first people's libraries in Central Finland.

YEAR OF ESTABLISHMENT		DISSEMINATION OF LENDING LIBRARIES		
Parish	Year	Parish	Year	Order of establishment
Hankasalmi	1864	Saarijärvi	1857	1st
Joutsa	1864	Keuruu, church village	1858	2nd
Jyväskylä	1863	Kuhmoinen	1858	2nd
Jämsä, church village	1861	Jämsä, church village	1861	4th
Koskenpää	1887	Karstula, church village	1861 (1876)	4th
Karstula, church village	1861 (1876)	Korpilahti, church village	1861	4th
Kyyjärvi	1886	Viitasaari	1861 (1868)	4th
Keuruu, church village	1858	Kannonsaha	1862	8th
Mänttä	1871	Kivijärvi, church village	1862 (1872)	8th
Kivijärvi, church village	1862 (1872)	Jyväskylä	1863	10th
Kannonsaha	1862	Hankasalmi	1864	11th
Konginkangas	1890	Joutsa	1864	11th
Korpilahti, church village	1861	Luhanka	1864	11th
Muurame	1884	Multia	1865 (1872)	14th
Kuhmoinen	1858	Uurainen	1868	15th
Laukaa, church village	1869	Laukaa, church village	1869	16th
Äänekoski	1884	Mänttä	1871	17th
Leivonmäki	1875	Pihlajavesi	1872	18th
Luhanka	1864	Leivonmäki	1875	19th
Multia	1865 (1872)	Petäjävesi	1876	20th
Petäjävesi	1876	Pylkönmäki	1876	20th
Pihlajavesi	1872	Pihtipudas	1878	22nd
Pihtipudas	1878	Muurame	1884	23rd
Pylkönmäki	1876	Äänekoski	1884	23rd
Saarijärvi	1857	Kyyjärvi	1886	25th
Sumiainen	1892	Koskenpää	1887	26th
Uurainen	1868	Konginkangas	1890	27th
Viitasaari	1861 (1868)	Sumiainen	1892	28th

Source: Mönkkönen 1988a. The years in parenthesis refer to the possible re-establishment of the libraries.

efforts, Dahlgrén and Kjellman had succeeded in creating an active revivalist movement in the parish, one of the first in the region. However, Evangelism did not spring out of nowhere in the former chapelry of Viitasaari; it had deeper roots.

The vicar of Viitasaari between 1794 and 1823 was Dean Johan Boxström (b. 1762 in Porvoo), who possessed a doctorate in theology. His wife, Eva (née Krogius) was the daughter of the vicar of Rautalampi, Gabriel Krogius. Boxström was selected as the new vicar of Rautalampi in 1822.[420] He was interested in educating the people and teaching them to read.[421] Johan

---

420 Kotivuori 2005. Ylioppilasmatrikkeli 1640–1852: Johan Boxström. Web publication 2005. Accessed 7/8/2012; Markkanen 1983, 530; Sarlin 1910, 23.
421 Sarlin 1910, 23. The Boxströms were an educated family, and Johan's elder brother, Anders (b. 1760), is an interesting person in connection with the history of medicine in Finland. He served as a physician in military hospitals in Turku and Loviisa (Lovisa) in the Russo-Swedish War (The Russo-Swedish War of 1788–1790

Boxtröm's term of office as vicar of Viitasaari lasted about 30 years. During that time Pietism was rampant in the parish, and its adherents actively practised their faith up to the middle of the century. For example, translations of Johan Gerhard's *Mediationes sacrae* [Sacred Meditations][422] and a book by Thomas à Kempis (probably *De imitatio Christi* [The Imitation of Christ]) were popular reading. Family devotions were held on Sundays in private homes at the time of the church service.[423]

Dean Alexander Dahlström (b. 1797) was vicar of Viitasaari from 1840 to 1862. The cantor, Konstantin Sarlin, described Dahlström as a good-natured man of the people. He had originally been educated at the home of his uncle and foster father, who was the curate of Laukaa. The uncle's wife and Dahlström's foster mother was Ingrid Cheilán, the daughter of Mikael Cheilanus (1707–1771), the curate of Keuruu.[424] Dahlström left his uncle's home and went to sea, sailing on merchant vessels for several years and gaining experience and information on many practical matters. In Viitasaari, Dahlström developed the poor relief of the parish, established a seed bank on a loan basis there, effected repairs to the church and the vicarage and promoted agriculture by introducing more productive strains of cereal seeds to the farmers. Dahlström was renowned nation-wide as a preacher, and according to Sarlin's (perhaps not particularly unbiased) estimate, he was one of the most successful sermonizers: he 'employed metaphors from the land and the sea most aptly'. He put himself at the disposal of the congregation and helped them. Dahlström took care of the instruction in reading of the young members of the congregation and in the confirmation class activities. A religious revival began to burgeon with the arrival of his young assistant, Karl Gustaf Tötterman.[425]

Dahlgrén and Kjellman thus in a way continued the work in Kivijärvi that Dahlström had commenced in the mother parish. Carl Gustaf Dahlgrén had become acquainted with The Awakening movement when he was a curate in Hirvensalmi in the years 1849–1852.[426] The Awakening, which was one of the four oldest and largest revivalist movements in Finland (the other three being the Prayer Movement, Evangelism and Laestadianism), sprang

---

is known as 'Gustav III's Russian War' in Sweden, 'Gustav III's War' in Finland and 'Catherine II's Swedish War' in Russia) of 1788–1780. Then he worked as a poor people's doctor in Stockholm from 1795 to 1797 until he moved to Turku to serve as the acting district doctor in the years 1797–1799. He completed a doctoral degree in medicine and worked from 1806 to 1849 as a temporary assistant in medicine at the Academy of Turku (which became the Alexander University in Helsinki in 1828). He was made a professor in 1812. Anders Boxtröm was a significant figure in Finnish medicine in that in 1802 he became the first Finnish doctor to use vaccination. Kotivuori 2005. Ylioppilasmatrikkeli 1640–1852: Johan Boxtröm. Web publication 2005. Accessed 7/8/2012.

422 Finnish title: *Pyhät tutkistelemukset*.
423 Sarlin 1910, 24.
424 Kotivuori 2005. Ylioppilasmatrikkeli 1640–1852: Mikael Cheilanus. Web publication 2005. Accessed 10/8/2012.
425 Sarlin 1910, 26–28.
426 Kivijärvi READERS; Rosendal 1915, 121.

like the others out of German seventeenth-century Pietism. Revivalist movements were a widespread phenomenon in nineteenth-century Europe, but their influence on Finnish society was particularly strong. The revivalist movements in a way corresponded to a romantic ideology that was typical of the literature read at least by the intelligentsia of the time. To some extent, it was an escape from the mundane, a search for a more profound conception of life, an emphasis on emotions and an idealization of what was considered to be a simple way of life.[427]

There began to be rifts within The Awakening movement towards the mid-nineteenth century, when a group led by Pastor Fredrik Gabriel Hedberg (1811–1893) broke away and formed what gradually came to be the core of the Finnish Evangelical movement. Early on, in the 1840s, his adherents received support from the Evangelical revivalist movements that were coming into being in Sweden at the same time.[428] Evangelism obtained a foothold in Kivijärvi in the mid-nineteenth century. The Vicar, Carl Gustaf Dahlgrén, preached outside his own parish as well: for example, in devotional meetings held in the chapelry of Sumiainen in the parish of Laukaa and in Evangelical meetings held at the home of Maria Willgren in Jyväskylä, where she had moved from Rautalampi. She was originally from Sumiainen. Dahlgrén later became the vicar of Rautalampi, and he still occupied this office when he died in 1896. The Evangelism of the above-mentioned persons was not in any way fanatical, and they also performed missionary work.[429] It should be noted that Sumiainen was the birthplace and former home of the cantor of Kivijärvi, F. K. Kjellman.

Thanks to the powerful sermons of Dahlgrén, who is said to have joined the Evangelical movement under the influence of Kjellman, many parishioners experienced a religious awakening.[430] Of the two, it was Kjellman who was initially more strongly involved in Evangelism in that he served as a lay preacher in the movement.[431] According to oral tradition, Kjellman even had contacts among the friends of Hedberg in Helsinki.[432] He delivered public instructional sermons to the congregation of Kivijärvi, which initially caused some differences of opinion between him and the vicar. Before he joined the Evangelical movement, the latter had not deemed it suitable for the cantor to appear in public as an exegesist of the Bible, especially as in his opinion the cantor's learning was 'not quite right'. However, Kjellman explained to Dahlgrén exactly why he felt this task to be indispensible. When the vicar, too, then realized that Evangelism was closer to his own way of thinking, they both began to organize devotional meetings in the vicarage and elsewhere in the parish.[433] During the time of Dahlgrén

427 Murtorinne 1992, 99–100.
428 Murtorinne 1992, 154–160.
429 Rosendal 1915, 424.
430 S. Tuomaala 1986, 320.
431 Koskenniemi 1967, 20.
432 The local heritage archive of the Municipality of Kannonkoski. The ecclesiastical folklore (oral history) of Kannonkoski].
433 Lyytinen 1904, 78–79.

and Kjellman, other Evangelists in Viitasaari included the curate Karl Gustaf Tötterman and the cantor Konstantin Sarlin.[434] Evangelism flourished elsewhere in Central Finland as well. In Jämsä, the Evangelical movement was promoted by Pastor Tötterman, who toured the neighbouring parishes and also preached there.[435]

The long-term presence of at least one official or other person who was actively interested in the activities of the libraries favoured the continuity of their activities. If one of the persons who were mainly involved in these activities fell ill, died or moved away, the operation of the library might cease, at least for the time being if not altogether. In Kivijärvi and its neighbouring parishes, the library institution was supported by the first vicars of the parish and other leading figures in parochial life. But there were also library activities outside the church village. Although Cantor Kjellman would seem to have played a rather minor role in the activities of the congregation after the early years of the 1860s, when his superior Vicar Dahlgrén joined the Evangelical movement, he definitely did not disappear entirely from the scene. However, the arena of his activities shifted a little further afield, to the sawmilling community of Kannonsaha in the southern parts of the parish of Kivijärvi. It is necessary to consider these activities in some detail here because, apart from some brief references in general parish histories, no detailed historical treatment of the sawmill as an industrial community has been written.

A closely-knit sawmill community as a centre of informational capital

SAWMILLING IN THE MIDDLE OF THE WILDS

> In Kannonkoski there used to be a big sawmill, from which large amounts of board were transported in winter by horse-drawn sleighs over the ice of Lake Kivijärvi and then on by road all the way to Pietarsaari [Jakobstad, on the Gulf of Bothnia]. From Pietarsaari, all kinds of wares were brought back.[436]

The area around Kannonsaha Sawmill became an exceptionally strong centre for the promotion of written culture and reading literacy around the mid-nineteenth century, which was the time when Cantor Kjellman lived there. In this section is examined why this all happened, the significance of the Evangelical revival and the rapid changes in economic life for the development of the informational capital of this rural community. I also study how at the end of the century various associations and popular movements began to play their own part in carrying out popular enlightenment duties and concomitantly in promoting the activities of the libraries.

The former Kannonsaha industrial community lived on for a long time, even down to the 1930s, in the memories of the local people because in the

---

434 The ecclesiastical folklore (oral history) of Kannonkoski.
435 Lahti 1991, 93.
436 SKS KRA. Kotilainen, Elsa PK 15: 2739. 1938.

mid-nineteenth century it had been the major industrial centre in the area. Northern Central Finland was heavily forested. For example, Karstula and Kannonkoski were said to have been among the most densely forested areas in the country in the 1830s. Previously, the value of the forests had been low there, as they had been all over Finland.[437]

The forests were cut down and burnt to create arable land, and timber was used as a household material for burning, building, making wooden implements, etc. The local farmers got extra income from tar burning and selling timber for masts to the coastal towns on the Gulf of Bothnia (e.g. Kokkola and Pietarsaari) – the forest reserves of Ostrobothnia had become so depleted that already in the late eighteenth century the shipowners had had to buy timber for masts and spars from as far afield as the Saarijärvi region[438] – but the long distances involved in transporting the timber made higher production volumes unprofitable. In the early nineteenth century, the demand for export lumber grew, which produced an increase in the number of sawmills that were established. The restrictions of the authorities and the long transportation distances meant that initially they tended to be established close to the coast. When the areas for the procurement of lumber were restricted by law, it soon became necessary to establish water-powered sawmills in the interior as well.[439]

In the 1830s, as the forests of Ostrobothnia became depleted and there was a dearth of large sawtimber trees, merchants from Kokkola (Karleby, formerly Gamlakarleby) began to arrive in Central Finland. They had heard the inhabitants of Viitasaari on their trips to town telling of suitable sites for a sawmill in their home parish. So they came with the intention of surveying possible locations for sawmills, and the area around Kivijärvi seemed to offer good possibilities. In 1835, the Crown Bailiff of the Eastern Bailiwick of Mustasaari (Korsholm), Daniel Philip Danielson[440] and a merchant from Kokkola called Carl Gustaf Favorin[441] applied to the Senate for a licence to establish a double-frame sawmill and also a grinding mill for the production of export lumber at Kannonkoski, which was located in the then chapelry of Kivijärvi. The Crown Bailiff had a year previously rented arable land and forest around the Kannonkoski Rapids for the sawmill and the lumber yard. In 1834, he had obtained ownership of the rapids together with a frieze stamp mill and two domestic flour mills beside them. He intended to obtain the timber for the sawmill not only from the Kivijärvi area but also from the forests of Salamajärvi (including parts of Perho) and

---

437 Hyytiäinen 1968, 134.
438 Hyytiäinen 1968, 133–134.
439 Kallio 1972 408–409; Lampinen 1986, 278.
440 The Crown Bailiff, who was born in Viitasaari, was the highest-ranking Crown official living in Saarijärvi. He was the grandfather of the historian Johan Richard Danielson-Kalmari, whose works were in the collection of Kivijärvi lending library. The national poet J. L. Runeberg lived at the home of Crown Bailiff Danielson when he worked as a family tutor in his student days. Kallio 1872, 316.
441 He was a merchant, shipowner and alderman in Kokkola.

Karstula. The Senate granted Danielson and Favorin privilege rights for this in April 1837. According to these privileges, the sawmill had the right to use 10,000 logs a year, which was the equivalent of an annual production of 2500 dozen boards. The size of the rights received by Kannonsaha sawmill was considerable. In the Province of Vaasa, only Inha Sawmill in Ähtäri, which was established in 1833 by a merchant called Peter Malm from Pietarsaari (Jakobstad), enjoyed such extensive rights. Malm's merchant house was the largest shipping agent for lumber exports in Ostrobothnia in the mid-nineteenth century.[442] In 1843, Favorin also became a shareholder of Kiminki Ironworks in Karstula.[443]

Sawmilling began at Kannonkoski, the first sawmill in northern Central Finland, in September 1836. The mill was a so-called fine-blade sawmill with two double frames and a double-bladed circular saw. The value of the first year's production exceeded 8000 silver roubles. The products of the sawmill were all for export, which was why the establishment had been granted the most extensive sawing rights in Central Finland. During the first year of operation, the mill employed 25 local people and a trained foreman. The mill operated for only five months of the year: it was at a standstill in the heart of winter and early spring (from January to April) and also for half of July and at harvest time in August and September. Sawing began in May and continued until the waters froze. Sometimes the sawing was hindered by a lack of water in the rapids. The average sawing rate was about 60 logs a day. Logging and sawing were done in the intervals between the tasks of the agricultural year, when there was plenty of work for everybody to do. The processed lumber was first freighted along Lake Kivijärvi by two large sailing vessels and barges, and in winter over the ice by horse and sleigh to Kinnulanlahti Bay at the northern end of the lake. From there the transportation continued overland by horse to the area of Lestijokivarsi, from where the lumber was floated along the river to the coast. The transportation, floating, logging and the actual sawmilling operations all brought some income to the people of Kannonsaha area. Apart from these activities, the main sources of income in the area were slash-and-burn agriculture and fishing.[444]

Initially, the problem with sawmilling was transportation because at that time the possibilities afforded by timber floating on the waters of the interior were not exploited sufficiently. In northern Central Finland, the waterways mostly consisted of chains of small lakes joined by rapids, which made log floating difficult.[445] For example, it was said that the transportation of lumber from Kannonkoski to the coast on the Gulf of Bothnia cost at least as much as the purchase of the raw timber.[446] In 1857, the Tichanoff merchant house of Vyborg planned to build a hydro-powered sawmill on the Myllykoski

---

442 Ahvenainen 1984, 175, 208; Hyytiäinen 1968, 148–149, 152, 223; Kallio 1972, 409.
443 Kallio 1972, 417.
444 Hyytiäinen 1968, 174–176; Kinnunen 1951, 13; Kokkinen 1994, 12; Lampinen 1986, 278; Markkanen 1983, 462–463.
445 Kallio 1972, 410.
446 Hyytiäinen 1968, 174.

Rapids along the River Kymijoki south of Lake Päijänne[447] and to get the timber for it from Viitasaari, Saarijärvi and Laukaa, which all lay north of Lake Päijänne. However, this project, which would have involved long floating distances, fell through as a result of opposition and also bureaucracy arising from the fact that the sawmill would have been situated in a different province from that where the raw material was located.[448] Many others, both before and after the Tichanoffs, had similar aspirations, but the floating of the forest resources of northern Central Finland down to the south of the country only got under way several decades later.

The birth of the library in the Tichanoff era

In 1857 it became permissible to establish steam-powered sawmills, and in 1861 the authorities strove to promote the industry by removing the last restrictions on sawmilling. At the same time, however, the state began to keep a strict account of the forest resources that it owned. A national forestry and parks service (the forerunner of today's Metsähallitus, the Finnish national forestry board) was established in 1864, and the Eastern Administrative District of Vaasa, to which the northern parts of Central Finland belonged, was divided into six areas. Forest wardens were assigned to the districts, and each area received its own senior forestry officer. There were widespread forest fires in northern Central Finland in 1858, in consequence of which 1.3 million tree trunks were damaged, and they had to be quickly felled and collected for sawmilling. This situation enhanced the local trade in timber.[449]

C. G. Favorin, a merchant who between 1824 and 1853 owned seven ships and had shares in numerous others, lost his largest vessels during the Crimean War, as did many other shipowners.[450] These losses were probably behind his decision to give up Kannonkoski Sawmill. In 1858 it was bought by the Vyborg merchant house of T. Tichanoff & Sons. At that time, some of the workers lived in their own cabins, and there was also a large barracks-like building constructed for the rest of the workers in the precincts of the sawmill. It had a corridor with rooms on each side, and it accommodated ten families. Another building was constructed to house the sawmill's office and its staff. The sawmill itself was a tall building; according to the recollections of the locals it had two storeys and was painted red. In the 1830s, on the other hand, according to documentary evidence it was originally a three-storey building 30 cubits long and 15 wide. The factory halls had glass windows. The building of the first industrial unit in the parish was an exceptional and imposing sight in the Viitasaari countryside at that time.[451]

By the turn of the 1850s and 1860s, a small village community had grown up around the sawmill. Among other things, it had a shop and a school that

---

447 Lake Päijänne is a large lake linking Jyväskylä with southern Finland. It is connected with the River Kymijoki, which runs into the Gulf of Finland.
448 Ahvenainen 1984, 207.
449 Hyytiäinen 1968, 135, 177–179; Kallio 1972, 412.
450 Hyytiäinen 1968, 152.
451 Ahvenainen 1984, 184; Hyytiäinen 1868, 149; Kokkinen 1994, 12; Markkanen 1983, 462.

had been established by the sawmill owner.[452] In 1862, the parish of Kivijärvi got a second library, a kind of village library, when the sawmill owner, Michael Tichanoff (1816–1891)[453] founded a lending library in connection with the sawmill at his own expense and donated a collection of books to it. Like the first lending library in the church village of Kivijärvi, this library was not governed by a set of regulations, and borrowing was free of charge. The library was run without pay by the cantor of Kivijärvi, F. K. Kjellman.[454] Kjellman was a schoolmaster in the sawmill school, which was open mainly to the children of the mill's employees. According to legend, he also held devotional prayer meetings in the area around Kannonkoski. He is said to have been a powerful preacher.[455]

From the eighteenth century the Finnish economy had inherited a structure that was typically based on close co-operation between merchant houses, shipping and sawmilling, and this continued up to halfway through the following century. The biggest merchant houses typically integrated their sawmilling activities with their export operations. The strength of their business lay in its diversity. The large concerns in Vyborg strengthened their position in the Finnish sawmilling industry in the mid-nineteenth century.[456]

Hackman & Co., the biggest merchant house in Vyborg and probably in the whole of Finland at that time, owned or had shares in about thirty sawmills in the mid-nineteenth century. Together with only a few other major merchant houses in Vyborg, it controlled about four fifths of the sawmilling industry in eastern Finland and half of this industry in the whole country. Among the concerns was the Tichanoff merchant house, which was led by Michael Tichanoff. Its original name was Timofei Tichanoff & Co. as it had been founded by Michael's father, Timofei Tichanoff, in the 1820s. He had arrived in Vyborg in the early 1810s and set up as a provisions merchant. He prospered so well that he was able to amass a significant amount of capital, which enabled him to take up more extensive business activities. Like the other Vyborg merchants, he owned several sawmills in eastern Finland (for example, in Enonkoski, Kuhakoski and Säynetkoski). Of these merchants, he was the one who was engaged in the sawmilling industry for the longest time. Tichanoff's operations were concentrated in Enonkoski in Savonia in eastern Finland.[457] By the 1840s, the Tichanoff merchant house already owned several sawmills and was engaged in extensive lumber exporting activities. Together with the other merchant houses, it owned a fleet of deep-sea vessels. After Timofei Tichanoff died in 1833, his widow Paraskovia Tichanova took over the management of the business until this task was

452 Lampinen 1986, 279.
453 Hämynen 2009.
454 Werkko 1879, 181. For the cantors serving the librarians of the local lending libraries, see also Mäkinen 2000b, 107.
455 Kinnunen 1951, 14; Kokkinen 1994, 12. For a more detailed discussion of the significance of the education provided in the sawmill community in the countryside at that time, see S. Kotilainen 2015c.
456 Kuisma 2006, 204–205.
457 Ahvenainen 1984, 184–185; Kuisma 2011, 44.

assumed by the oldest son, Michael, in 1852. He was awarded the honorific title of Councillor of Commerce in 1856.[458]

Michail Tichanoff has been described as an enlightened, educated and generous captain of industry, who spoke Russian, French and English. Under his direction, the concern really expanded from a wholesale business into a shipping and timber company with sawmills in different parts of Finland.[459] Michail Tichanoff had gone to school at Vyborg Lyceum and continued his studies in St. Petersburg. His brothers Wasili and Alexander also took part in running the business. After the father's death, the name of the firm was changed to T. Tichanoff & Sons. In the mid-nineteenth century, it was the fourth largest concern in Vyborg, and it owned a wholesale business, a glass factory, a shipping company and eight sawmills. Its five ships transported lumber to other parts of the world and brought back salt and barrels of herrings to Vyborg. The opening of the Saimaa Canal in 1856 also increased the number of vessels engaged in domestic trade that were owned by Vyborg merchants. In 1867 the Tichanoff merchant house already owned about thirty vessels. Michail Tichanoff also acquired ownership of a tobacco and cigar factory and a tile and faïence pottery.[460]

Thanks to his character, education, wide-ranging linguistic abilities and wealth, Michail Tichanoff was an important figure in social affairs in the Vyborg region. He was particularly interested in the development of popular education, not only in his home city but also in those localities where his industrial plants were situated. His work in popular education was most active in the 1860s, when, for example, he was a member of the boards of governors of the Vyborg Infant School and the Russian Elementary School. In the famine years, he provided assistance in the form of deliveries of cereals to the places where his factories were located. In addition, he founded Finnish-language schools and reading rooms in these parishes. He was also a strong supporter of the temperance movement.[461] In popular education, even small acts could have great significance: for example, in 1843, the owner of Säynetkoski Sawmill sent 80 Finnish-language ABC primers and devotional literature to the value of 20 roubles to the sawmill community; the books were distributed to the workers and their children free of charge.[462]

Several elementary schools were established in the early 1860s by the big German industrial magnates and merchant dynasties of Vyborg for the Finnish-speaking children of the workers in their industrial establishments. Employed in their concerns were a number of citizens of Vyborg like Johan Pynninen and Adam Wilke who were interested in Finnish-language popular education and particularly people's libraries. Woldemar Hackman, the son of Councillor of Commerce Johan Friedrich Hackman, the owner of the largest merchant house in Vyborg, was interested in these popular

---

458 Annala 1948, 295; Hämynen 2009; Lakio 1981, 391; Ruuth & Kuujo 1981, 63.
459 Annala 1948, 295.
460 Ahvenainen 1984, 242; Hämynen 2009, Lakio 1981, 370–372, 410, 417; Ruuth & Kuujo 1981, 68.
461 Aurola 1961, 84; Hämynen 2009; Nissilä 1981, 453.
462 Hämynen 1986, 263.

enlightenment schemes, and he was also a member of the Vyborg Finnish Literature Society. He favoured projects for the establishment of schools, not least because his brother-in-law was Julius Krohn, who was one of the most important researchers of Finnish folk poetry in the nineteenth century and later to be made Professor of Finnish Language and Literature at the University of Helsinki. Krohn was also a journalist, and he helped to develop the Finnish written language and its vocabulary. The other big merchant houses soon followed the example of Hackman in promoting Finnish-language culture and elementary education at the turn of the 1850s and 1860s.[463]

Tichanoff was a traditional patriarchal sawmill owner who strove in numerous ways to take care of the well-being of his workforce, and this also drew the attention of the press in the early 1860s. He is known to have founded at least three libraries for the workers of his industrial establishments, which were mainly located in Savonia and Karelia.[464] These were the library of Kannonsaha Sawmill in Kivijärvi, the library of Enonkoski Mill in Kerimäki (with a donation of 70 roubles) in 1860 and probably also the library of Utra Sawmill in Kontiolahti in the parish of Liperi.[465] Thus the establishment of the school and library of Kannonsaha Sawmill were the distant manifestations in Central Finland of a popular enlightenment campaign that had started far away in Vyborg.

In the school, Cantor Kjellman mainly gave religious instruction, but he also taught writing, arithmetic and Finnish history. At least in the schools of the Tichanoff industrial plants in eastern Finland, geography was also one of the subjects taught. It was part of the curriculum of the elementary schools that began to operate in the early 1860s.[466] Discipline was strict. Kjellman had a wicker cane, which he wielded on the fingers of the more recalcitrant pupils. The pupils used a feather quill for writing and dried the ink with sand. Kjellman was a good singer, and a number of young men who later became cantors studied under him. They included Antti Herranen, Matti Nykänen and Juho Leppänen. These pupils also received further instruction in Vaasa for a period lasting four weeks to equip them for their duties as cantors. Many other inhabitants of the surroundings also attended the 'University of Kannonkoski' as it was playfully called – after all, it was the first educational establishment in the area,[467] and it increased the informational capital of the youth of the area in a significant way. Study could lead to social advancement, particularly for men and boys.

Kjellman's educational and spiritual activities in Kannonkoski paved the way for the Evangelical revivalist movement in the 1860s.[468] But what kind of man was Kjellman really? And what kind of qualifications did he have for teaching in a school? The Kjellman family was of Swedish origin

---

463 Aurola 1961, 82–84.
464 Annala 1948, 296; Hämynen 1986, 84.
465 Aurola 1961, 84–85, 139; A. Kotilainen 1979, 2; Werkko 1879, 150, 181.
466 Aurola 1961, 149.
467 Kinnunen 1951, 14; Kokkinen 1994, 13.
468 The ecclesiastical folklore (oral history) of Kannonkoski.

and descended from Pehr Kjellman (b. 1719), who came from the county of Skaraborg. He was one of the young surveyors who moved from Sweden to Finland in the 1740s. He first made a survey of Sysmä and then in the years 1749–1754 of the parish of Rautalampi. Kjellman got married 1751 in Laukaa. Subsequently he was engaged in duties relating to the redistribution of land in Tavastia in the latter half of the eighteenth century, and he drafted the town plan of Kuopio in 1775. The generation of the family after his son moved to the remotest parishes of Central Finland, from where some of them moved on to Southern Ostrobothnia. In their early days in Finland, the Kjellmans were a very typical family of country functionaries. Other families and individuals with the name 'Kjellman' (also spelled Kellman or Kjällman) have also lived in Finland at various times.[469]

Ferdinand Konstantin Kjellman was born in Sumiainen in 1822. He was the youngest child of his father Magnus Kjellman and his mother Johanna (Jeanne) Schöneman. The father was a son of surveyor Pehr Kjellman and an independent surveyor working under the Provincial Surveyor of the Province of Vaasa. In practice, his field of operation was Central Finland. The family's children were born in the chapelry of Sumiainen. The father-in-law of Magnus Kjellman was Carl Gustaf Schöneman, a sergeant-major and later an ensign in the Rautalampi Company of the Tavastia Province Foot Regiment, which was stationed in Viitasaari. The eldest of the sons, Carl Magnus, was the vicar of Savitaipale.[470]

Cantor F. K. Kjellman married Anna Susanna Salin (b. 1822) in Sumiainen in 1847. They had altogether nine children. As far is known, he became the cantor of Kivijärvi in 1858, and at the same time he began to practise as a schoolteacher and lay preacher. Kjellman and his family first lived in Kannonkoski, moving there at the latest in 1862 on. His oldest children were born in Sumiainen. From the 1860s on, the Kjellman family owned part of Lauttamäki Farm in the village of Pääjärvi in Karstula and part of Ahola Farm in the village of Hännilänkylä in Saarijärvi (later part of Pylkönmäki). Kjellman's widow subsequently lived together with her children on Lauttamäki Farm.[471] Probably Matti Nykänen (b. 1839 in Kivijärvi), the son-in-law of Kjellman and later the cantor of Pihtipudas, also attended the Kannonsaha school. It might be mentioned as a curiosity that his mother was Maija Brita Kemppainen. Farmer Kustaa Orava together with Matti Rytkönen and the aforementioned Antti Herranen had married the three daughters of Antti Kemppainen from Kivijärvi. Maja Brita was Antti's sister, in other words, Nykänen was the cousin of the three Kemppainen girls.[472]

After Kjellman arrived in the parish of Kivijärvi, he initially settled with his family in Kannonkoski, and his pupil Anders Herranen lived in the same household with him.[473] The sources do not reveal just why he decided to settle in Kannonsaha; usually the cantor, like the vicar, moved into the church village, from where it was easier to carry out his duties. One

469 Berndtson 1983, 292; Wanne et al. 1943–1946, 353.
470 Berndtson 1986, 88–89; Wanne et al. 1943–1946, 354.
471 Wanne et al. 1943–1946, 356–357.
472 Kivijärvi READERS.
473 Appendix 1.

possible explanation may be that he first came to the sawmill community as a teacher and only later took up his post as cantor, but there is no certain information about this. Another explanation is that the cantor did not move to Kannonkoski from Kivijärvi until 1862, when it turned out that the school needed a teacher. There is no exact information about his training. However, he seems to have received sufficient education to be able to teach others. His calling as a preacher undoubtedly also helped in this. In any case, according to legend, Kjellman is traditionally regarded as the person who brought Evangelism to Kivijärvi. He is known to have experienced an Evangelical awakening on one of his trips to Helsinki, and when he returned he gradually converted the vicar K. G. Dahlgrén to his faith.[474] It is thus possible that he experienced this awakening when he was already living in Kivijärvi, but there is no certainty about this.

Previous research erroneously mentions that Kjellman was the cantor of Kivijärvi up till 1869 and that he ran the sawmill library until 1872. It is assumed that the school operated for the same period.[475] However, Kjellman died in 1868, so if the school continued to function after that, it was run by someone else. Moreover, in August 1867 he moved to live on Seppälä Farm in the village of Heinolahti, which was only a few kilometres away from the church of Kivijärvi. It may be that the move was in some way connected with the current crop failures and the fact that operations at the sawmill were concomitantly at a standstill. At the same time, Antti Herranen (b. 1840) and his family also moved to Seppälä Farm. The church records state that Herranen, who was the cantor from 1869 to 1913, is actually mentioned in them as having been temporary cantor already in 1866. After attending the sawmill school, he stayed on as a pupil and an assistant of Kjellman and served as his deputy when the need arose. Kjellman certainly needed a deputy when he fell seriously ill in 1868. After he died, his family moved to Saarijärvi in 1871. Herranen's temporary post as cantor of Kivijärvi was made into a permanent one in 1872.[476] Thus Kjellman raised and trained Herranen to be his assistant and successor. The job would later come to include duties connected with the administration of the library. The interest of the members of Kjellman's family in literature is indicated by the fact that his youngest son, Rafael Aleksander Kjellman, who was born in Kivijärvi in 1862, later kept a bookshop in Saarijärvi, where he worked as an agent and a representative of companies that sold machinery.[477]

The Tichanoff merchant house practised sawmilling in Kannonkoski up till 1872, when it went into liquidation as a result of the non-payment of debts by British merchant houses, this despite the fact that there was a current boom in the lumber trade. The debts of the bankrupt company exceeded three million marks, and it possessed less than half a million in assets. The largest creditor (who owed 2 million marks) was a British merchant house.

474 Recorded Archives of the Finnish Literature Society's Folklore Archives, Ecclesiastical folklore, Kannonkoski and Kivijärvi, Esa Tuomaala's fieldwork report, 1975.
475 Kokkinen 1994, 13.
476 Appendix 1. See also S. Kotilainen 2015b.
477 Wanne et al. 1943–1946, 357.

The final years of the 1860s were difficult for the Tichanoff concern because of the severe crop failures. For example, the Kannonsaha Sawmill operated only sporadically and finally shut down temporarily owing to difficulties in transporting its products during the famine years of the late 1860s. As a result of the poor harvests and wars in Western Europe, and particularly in Russia, and the threat of a Pan-European war paralyzed international trade and weakened the economic outlook. Investment and construction slowed down in Finland's major export countries and its export revenues collapsed.[478]

The unproductiveness of Kannonsaha Sawmill was also caused by the dredging operations that got under way in that decade along the Viitasaari and Saarijärvi waterways in order to make them suitable for log floating. The development of log floating in the 1870s sealed the fate of the sawmills of the interior. The logs began to be floated to the sawmills of the south, and the small rural sawmills were no longer competitive. It was cheaper to transport the raw timber to the coast than sawn lumber. This had been done previously when lumber had been floated by river to the coast on the Gulf of Bothnia. However, this was deleterious to the quality of the finished planks and boards, which were badly damaged by the water, and their value dropped. At the same time, the price of raw timber began to rise, and Kannonsaha Sawmill lost the profit margin that had previously enabled it to operate.[479] The activities of the sawmill library ceased with the bankruptcy of the mill owner, and the books in its collection were auctioned off as part of the bankrupt's estate.[480]

In its first issue in 1873, the newspaper *Keski-Suomi* published the following notice:

> 'In accordance with a decision made by the parties concerned, the double frame sawmill of Kannonkoski and the windmill belonging to the bankrupt estate of T. Tichanoff & Sons in the village of Pudasjärvi in Kivijärvi Parish in the Province of Vaasa together with two loading platforms and buildings at Kinnula loading station are to be sold by public auction in the City Hall of this city [Jyväskylä] on 24th day of this month at 11 a.m. In addition to that, the estate includes purchased forests comprising about 35,000 sawn logs as well as the buildings and structures at the Raumo loading site in the parish of Lohtaja.'[481]

The Vyborg merchant house sold the unproductive sawmill in 1872 to Johan Anjelin, a former clerk of the mill, who later became a country shopkeeper. Sawmilling ended altogether in 1885 owing to force of circumstances.[482] Although the sawmilling industry of the nineteenth century made the owners and the local inhabitants rich, it was typically the sawmill clerks who profited most of all from it. For example, the sawmill clerks in Heinävesi

478 Kuisma 2011, 166–168.
479 Ahvenainen 1984, 234, 276; Annala 1948, 299; Hyytiäinen 1968, 135, 156; Hämynen 2009; Markkanen 1988, 239; Tigerstedt 1952, 577, 626.
480 Lampinen 1986, 279; Werkko 1879, 181.
481 *Keski-Suomi* no. 1, 4. 1. 1873.
482 Lampinen 1986, 279; Markkanen 1988, 239.

owned reclaimed forests and shares in the sawmills, and Dalin, the clerk of Säynetkoski Sawmill, which was then owned by Michail Tichanoff, made himself a fortune that surpassed the value of the whole sawmill.[483]

Anjelin was remembered to have been a similarly able businessman, who in his duties as a clerk had spotted the opportunities for enrichment and become an entrepreneur himself.[484] His career as a businessman started off at what was for the sawmill an unfortunate time in that the European market for lumber had gradually started to decline in the summer of 1873 and there was a stock market collapse. Large companies fell into bankruptcy, and investors experienced large losses. The financial crisis, which had swollen to international proportions, soon affected European and Finnish economic life as well, albeit with some delay in the timber trade compared with other branches of the economy. Sales of timber to Great Britain fell sharply in 1875, and export prices fell considerably at the end of the decade.[485]

Gradually, the hustle and bustle that had grown up around the sawmill over the decades died down as the old building fell into disrepair. It was no longer profitable for a water-powered sawmill to saw timber for export, and it only operated to satisfy local demand. Locals remembered that on one fine, calm Saturday evening in the summer of 1896 a loud bang was heard in the area as the old two-storey sawmill collapsed.[486] In 1904, a farmer called Lauri Vesterinen built a new sawmill on the eastern bank of the rapids.

THE TRADITIONS OF THE SAWMILL LIBRARY CONTINUED BY LEPPÄLÄNKYLÄ LENDING LIBRARY

The 1890s saw the final 'break-through' of people's libraries, and in that decade a lending library was established in the village of Leppälänkylä in the parish of Kivijärvi. It began to operate on the site of the present church village of Kannonkoski, and in a way continued the tradition of the earlier sawmill library in the area. A source titled *Nimi ja Lainauskirja* [Name and loan register] from the library contains information about the time of its foundation, stating that it was established on 14 March 1895.[487] A lending library was also established in the village of Jauhoniemi in Kivijärvi in 1896, and in three years time it had 124 books amounting to 324 marks and 75 pence in value. One of the founders of the Leppälänkylä library is thought to have been a farmer called Johan (Juho) Lyytinen, who also served as its first librarian.[488] The library was housed in a room of his farmhouse, where the books initially fitted into a single bookcase with a glass door. The master of the household encouraged his servants to actively borrow books from the library. On the day when the Leppälänkylä library was founded, the only borrower was one Pauliina Hirvainen; she took out a work titled *Kuvauksia Itä-Suomesta* [Descriptions of Eastern Finland] for one week. The loan fee

---

483 Hämynen 1986, 260.
484 S. Kotilainen 2005.
485 Kuisma 2011, 188–191.
486 Kinnunen 1951, 14.
487 Names and loans register of Leppälänkylä lending library.
488 Schadewitz 1903, 102.

was five pence. The book had been donated to the library by who else than Juho Lyytinen.[489]

The activities of Leppälänkylä library began with a small collection of books. Sixty-two volumes were collected from the villagers as donations. In 1896 the collection contained altogether 63 books with a value amounting to 67 marks 35 pence.[490] Despite the smallness of the collection, the villagers used the library actively in its first year of operation. After this, however, enthusiasm waned, only to increase again in 1906. Records of loans have been preserved only up till 1910, and for some years they are missing altogether. In 1902 Kivijärvi Youth Association donated 20 volumes to the library, and by 1910 its collection had grown to 249 volumes. Leppälänkylä's own youth association[491] also acquired books for borrowing, and in the 1910s the books of Leppälänkylä lending library and the youth association were borrowed from the same bookcase, although each institution used its own funds to acquire the books.[492]

Juho Lyytinen ran the lending library for almost ten years. In 1903, he passed this duty on to his younger brother, Eevert Lyytinen (a farmer), who was still managing the library at the beginning of the 1920s. The last information about its activities is from 1921. Eevert Lyytinen took part in efforts to improve conditions in his home village in a variety of ways. Ever since he was a young boy his interests had included photography, painting, woodwork and even embroidery – in addition to his enthusiasm for literature. In its early years, the library does not appear to have had a board of governors, which was by no means unusual for popular libraries.[493] However, in December 1906, a board of governors was appointed to take care of the library, and they decided to obtain a set of approved regulations for it.[494] It would seem that the administration of Leppälänkylä library was re-organized at that time. Another motive for this was the fact that the municipality only subsidized an association if it possessed a set of rules.

The meeting of the board of governors of Leppälänkylä library held in the elementary school on 20 December 1906 was significant in that the district chief of police, Toivo Anjelin (later Anjala), the son of the clerk of Kannonsaha Sawmill, was authorized to obtain a set of approved rules for the library from the Office of the Provincial Governor, and these regulations were swiftly supplied. When he sent them to the library, the chief of police stated in his covering letter: 'Not even the Governor has had time to spend Christmas since he has had to study these and ratify them. So now all that's left, I suppose, is to start begging for books from the gentry.' The rules strictly defined the duties of the librarian, whose post was unpaid. According to

---

489 A. Kotilainen 1979, 2–3.
490 Schadewitz 1903, 102.
491 Leppälänkylä youth association was founded in 1902, whereas the youth association of the parish of Kivijärvi (in the church village) had already been established in 1897. Mönkkönen 1986, 451–452.
492 Names and loans register of Leppälänkylä lending library; A. Kotilainen 1979, 3.
493 Names and loans register of Leppälänkylä lending library; A. Kotilainen 1979, 4; Werkko 1879, 249.
494 A. Kotilainen 1979, 4.

them, the board of governors was elected either directly or by electors. It was composed of six members, men or women, who were to be versed in literature and culture. The board of governors was obligated to maintain the library in good order and to hold evening entertainments of a 'reinvigorating and pure nature' once or more a year in order to acquire funds to expand the collection. The rules required that the library be open every week at times stipulated by the board of governors. However, there were no official opening hours in the years 1908–1910. Books could be borrowed whenever the librarian, Eevert Lyytinen, was available. The borrowers used the library whenever they had other business at Leppälä Farm, since at that time one of its rooms also functioned as a post office, likewise run by Eevert Lyytinen.[495] Leppälänkylä postal coach halt was only established in 1900 after the road to Viitasaari was completed. The establishment of post offices at the turn of the century was closely connected with the development of the highway network.[496]

The youth association movement, which was intended to promote popular enlightenment among young people, began in Southern Ostrobothnia and spread all over Finland in the 1880s and 1890s. The founding of local youth associations was dependent on the ever more widespread network of elementary schools. In many rural parishes, the school and the teacher served as the basis for a wide variety of enlightenment activities. The youth associations often came into being in connection with some such activity as a local reading society or a choir, and subsequently promoted these pastimes. Initially, activity at the local level was vigorous, and it was not until after 1906 that a national central organization became an important body in the youth association movement.[497] In Leppälänkylä, the local youth association met in the elementary school of Leppälänkylä to read books and hold discussions. A score of members of the entertainments committee of the reading circle met in the school on 16 January 1921 to plan the organization of a grand evening gala for the benefit of the library in March. In a meeting a few days later, it was announced that the planning of the programme was ready. The programme was extensive and varied; it ended with the singing of the national anthem after the performance of a play titled *Syitten kirous* [The curse of causes][498]. Hardly any information about the practical activities of the library in the 1920s has survived. However, in 1921 it is known that the keenest enthusiasts for literature tried to boost the funds of the library by arranging evening entertainments.

Later, after the Second World War, a board of governors for the new municipal library in Kannonkoski was elected at a meeting of the Municipal Board of Kannonkoski on 26 January 1948. It found premises for the library, and procured the necessary equipment and bookcases as well as books.

---

495 Regulations of Leppälänkylä lending library; A. Kotilainen 1979, 5; Schadewitz 1903, 102.
496 Lampinen 1986, 265.
497 Numminen 2011, 200–201, 212–215.
498 This play was written by Evald Jakku, a writer of plays for amateur dramatic societies who was born in Laihia in Southern Ostrobothnia.

It was noted that there were many usable works among the books of the old Leppälänkylä library. They were sorted and checked, and some were transferred to the main library. A post for a librarian was also advertised. The actual day of the founding of the main municipal library in Kannonkoski was 15 December 1948.[499] Thus the library activity that had burgeoned when Kannonsaha Sawmill continued, despite some small interruptions, into the mid-twentieth century, when it was transferred from volunteer enthusiasts to the responsibility of the municipality.

Similar activities to those of Kannonkoski Youth Association can be found elsewhere in northern Central Finland. Pylkönmäki Youth Association, too, had its own library, which in the early twentieth century contained about 80 volumes. When the club's activities ceased in 1912, the books were transferred to the lending library maintained by the school. Pylkönmäki Countryman's Association also had its own library at least as early as 1905. It mostly contained works connected with agriculture. Up till the first decade of the twentieth century, it was located in Kuoppala elementary school. The local workers' association and the co-operative bank likewise maintained small collections of books around 1910.[500] Associations thus continued to be important important patrons of the libraries and literary culture in northern Central Finland.

The first reading room in Pylkönmäki began to function in a room of Mulikka Farmhouse in 1897, where it was open every Sunday evening. In it the annual volumes of the newspapers and periodicals *Pohjalainen, Suomalainen, Lasten Lehti* (a children's magazine), *Peltomies, Maanviljelyslehti* (both agricultural periodicals) and *Sanansaattaja* (the main organ of the Evangelical movement) were read. In 1901, a reading room was also established in the church village partly on the initiative of the youth association. The reading room was located in the school, and it was decided to order several papers for it, including *Suomalainen, Pohjalainen, Uusi Suometar* and *Pellervo*. In these reading rooms, the main reading matter consisted of newspapers and enlightened periodicals. In 1899 altogether 110 copies of annual volumes of newspapers and periodicals were ordered for Pylkönmäki.[501] In the small village societies of the countryside, the collections and borrowing facilities of local libraries were developed by a number of different actors. In the Kannonkoski area people had already become acquainted with using the earlier sawmill library. But there was also another and more fundamental explanation for the library taken root in the area, i.e. Evangelism.

---

499 Kotilainen 1979, 6–7.
500 Sinisalo 1984, 102.
501 Sinisalo 1984, 104.

The Evangelical movement flourishes in northern Central Finland

Thanks to the efforts of Kjellman and Dahlgrén, Evangelism in its Nordic form obtained a firm foothold in Kivijärvi in the 1860s, and later on particularly in the Kannonkoski area rather than in the church village proper. It would seem that after Dahlgrén moved away it was difficult to find someone who possessed the same authority to lead the revival. Laestadianism, which arrived in the parish later, came to challenge and partly oust Evangelism. Around the turn of the century, the message of Evangelism was mainly being spread by independent lay preachers, the best known of whom was a labourer called Seve Oikarinen.[502]

Part of the later Municipality of Kannonkoski belonged to Kivijärvi, while the Huopana side belonged to Viitasaari. The journey to the churches of both these parishes from Kannonkoski was about forty kilometres. Some persons went to church in Karstula or Saarijärvi, but most of them travelled to Kivijärvi, mainly because administratively they belonged to the congregation of Kivijärvi. They usually set off in summer, rowing along the lake in large communal 'church boats'. This continued even into the early years of the twentieth century. They departed on a Saturday in order to be able to do their trading and other business in the church village in the afternoon. Young people also eagerly took part in these journeys to church because they afforded an opportunity to meet the other young persons who congregated there. Numerous boats gathered on the shore by the church in Kivijärvi, and on the journey home the different boats often raced each other. Parishioners from the Hilmonkoski and Vuoskoski side of the parish travelled by boat in summer to the church in Viitasaari. The road to Viitasaari was also better than those leading to Saarijärvi or Karstula, so the trip was often made by horse and cart as well. After the church boats had fallen into disuse in the early twentieth century, church-goers often made the journey in summer in their own small boats. A steamboat connection for passengers and freight established by a farmer called Lauri Vesterinen ran on Lake Kivijärvi from 1904 to 1916.[503] In terms of its congregation, Kannonkoski was a remote peripheral area which developed a spiritual culture of its own owing to the long distances to the parish centres. Evangelism took a particularly firm hold there among the sawmill community in Kannonsaha.

In 1875 in northern Central Finland, there were adherents of Evangelism mainly in the parishes of Karstula, Pylkönmäki and Saarijärvi. By 1880 it had also obtained a foothold in Viitasaari and Pihtipudas. In the 1870s, the Evangelicals began to arrange big religious gatherings for the people, which was then something new. Later strongly revivalist 'Evangelical gatherings' were held in the areas where revivalism sprang up in the nineteenth century. At the same time, they helped to spread the revivalist message to neighbouring areas. In the 1870s, Central Finland and the Southern Ostrobothnian Lake

---

502 Recorded Archives of the Finnish Literature Society's Folklore Archives, Ecclesiastical folklore, Kannonkoski and Kivijärvi, Esa Tuomaala's fieldwork report, 1975.
503 Nokkala & Niskanen (nd), 1.

district became the main areas of Evangelical revivalism. The first annual gathering of the Evangelical Association was held in Soini in 1877, and in the following year a regional assembly was held in Karstula. It was attended by about 3000 followers and one in Saarijärvi in 1879 by 4000–5000.[504]

A significant religious awakening was created by the gathering in Karstula, and in a short time it spread as far afield as Kivijärvi and Alajärvi. The religious revival in northern Central Finland gave rise to a wide variety of activities. A four-voice choir was founded, and large numbers of books published by the Evangelical Association were sold. Kaarlo Rahikainen, a teacher in Pylkönmäki, estimated that between 1875 and 1879 books published by the association amounting in value to 15,000 marks were disseminated in the area. Evangelical gatherings were also arranged there in the following years, and even further east in Viitasaari in 1882. Two boats took the participants from the different parishes to Viitasaari, and the whole congregation could not fit into the church. Finally, a prayer meeting following the gathering was held at the home of the cantor, Konstantin Sarlin, in Kokkila.[505]

In 1875 the clerical members of the Evangelical Association included K. G. Dahlgrén, who subsequently held a central position in the movement. On 27 June 1883 a combined missionary and Evangelical gathering was held in Rautalampi. Among the speakers were the vicar, Dean K. G. Dahlgrén, the cantor Konstantin Sarlin and Jaakko Kolanen, a teacher. Johannes Bäck, who was to become the first head of the Evangelical Association in 1884, also attended. Of the vicars of Kivijärvi, both Dahlgrén and V. A. Konsin were members of the Evangelical Association, the former from 1876 to 1896 and the latter from 1885 to 1904.[506]

Among the most active rural congregations around 1895 were those of the parishes of Toholampi and, in Central Finland, Saarijärvi. Evangelical gatherings continued to be held actively in Saarijärvi, Karstula and Viitasaari into the early 1890s, and in Saarijärvi they became a regular event. The activities of the Evangelical movement were particularly lively in Viitasaari and Saarijärvi in the early 1890s. Kivijärvi, on the other hand, remained apart from this religious revival.[507] There the powerful spread of Laestadianism and the fact that the long-serving vicar, F. P. Krank, had experienced a Laestadian awakening, took the spiritual life of the parish in a different direction.

The books for the rural libraries were often selected by the clergy, teachers and local police chiefs. In the Evangelical movement, the sale and dissemination of publications and books that were of central importance to it was a significant feature of its activities.[508] A long-serving purveyor of the books of the Evangelical Association was a shopkeeper called Heikki Puranen from Karstula. In northern Central Finland, the elementary school

---

504 Koskenniemi 1967, 66, 84, 111–112.
505 Koskenniemi 1967, 85.
506 Koskenniemi 1967, 68, 115, 133, 291.
507 Koskenniemi 1967, 217–218, 237–239.
508 See also Brown 2004.

teachers served as Evangelist colporteurs. The most able of them in the late nineteenth century was perhaps Kaarlo Johannes Rahikainen (1848–1909). He eventually became one of the leading figures in the great popular Evangelist revival in Central Finland, in the late 1870s, but most of his work as a colporteur took place in the 1890s.[509]

Rahikainen was a supreme spiritual leader, who initiated the Evangelical revival in Pylkönmäki and at the same time in the whole of Central Finland. He had devoted himself to popular education, and he maintained a school partly at his own expense at Patama Farm in Kuoppala in the years 1873–1878. At the same time, he was involved in numerous different social activities: he founded the Saarijärvi Farmers' Association in 1885, was chairman of the Saarijärvi Temperance Association from 1885 to 1887, established a cooperative-style shop in Pylkönmäki in 1866, pushed for the establishment of Pylkönmäki as an independent church parish in its own right, applied in 1881 for the construction of a highway linking Saarijärvi, Pylkönmäki and Myllymäki railway station and also sought to implement various improvements in agriculture. In 1881, Rahikainen moved to take up a post as a teacher in Ylihärmä in Southern Ostrobothnia because he wished to concentrate on teaching proper instead of being distracted by all these sideline activities. He worked as an elementary teacher again in Pylkönmäki from 1885 to 1890. Here also the duties of a chapelry preacher were combined with this post.[510]

Jaakko Kolanen (1845–1897), a school teacher from Southern Ostrobothnia, also started to work as a colporteur in 1883. He came from Lappajärvi and was the son of a crofter. During the years of the Great Famine, he had travelled as a beggar as far as Sweden. However, thanks to the assistance of his home villagers and encouraged by the curate of Vimpeli he had got into the teacher training seminary in Jyväskylä and qualified as an elementary school teacher in 1872. It was envisaged that Kolanen would serve as a teacher in the chapelry of Kauhajärvi (established in 1871), where a church had just been built. It was the duty of the teacher also to serve as a preacher. Kolanen taught writing and arithmetic to the adults of the area in addition to his duties proper. In 1875 Kolanen moved to Saarijärvi to be a teacher there. He became one of the leaders of the Evangelical movement that began in the late 1870s in Central Finland, and every year he travelled from Saarijärvi to preach not only in Central Finland but also in the parishes of Central Ostrobothnia. Later, from 1886 to 1896, he worked as an elementary school teacher in Viitasaari and moved from there back to Kauhajärvi to be a teacher in the parish of Lappajärvi, where he died already in his middle age in 1897.[511] Kolanen was the head teacher of the elementary school in the church village of Saarijärvi from 1875 to 1886, librarian from 1875 to 1886 and chairman of the Saarijärvi Municipal Board between 1879 and

509 Koskenniemi 1964, 111; Koskenniemi 1967, 72, 145.
510 Koskenniemi 1964, 112; Sinisalo 1984, 89.
511 Alanen 1937, 12–13; Koskenniemi 1964, 126; Koskenniemi 1967, 143; V. Mäkelä 1963, 306–307.

1881.[512] In addition to colporteurs, the Evangelical Association used both men and women to go round selling its books, although it did not permit them to deliver religious sermons. Nevertheless, many of them did preach. In the 1880s, the number of women among the Evangelical purveyors of books grew, and indeed some of the longest serving colporteurs were women. By 1885 the activities of the Evangelical colporteurs had reached Kivijärvi too.[513] In this area, too, the revivalist movements had a significant influence on popular enlightenment work and the development of literacy. The dissemination of literature among the people was an integral part of the Evangelical movement's local activities.

Kannonsaha Sawmill, an industrial plant established 'in the middle of the wilderness', soon began both to promote literacy in its surroundings and to provide new reading material for the local inhabitants. The major figure in the sawmill society was the cantor, who not only took care of tasks connected with popular enlightenment but also served as a kind of spiritual leader for those inhabitants who belonged to the Evangelical movement. The goal of both Dahlgrén and Kjellman was clearly to advance reading and writing skills in the parish of Kivijärvi and, because of their religious convictions, to promote the Evangelical version of Christianity. Kjellman took care of teaching in Kannonkoski independently, and thus there was a clear division of tasks between the two men.

In the light of everything that has been mentioned above, the library that was established for the workers of Kannonsaha Sawmill and their children turns out not to be just any branch or village library in the remote wilderness but becomes part of what was the major phenomenon in Finnish economic and industrial history in the nineteenth century: the rise of the wood-processing industry. The foundation of the library was a result of broader developments such as the growth of sawmilling, the efforts to advance popular enlightenment that came with industrialization, social assistance and charitable work, and the social and communal impacts of the revivalist movements. Indeed, the library of Kannonsaha Sawmill was more important from the perspective of popular education than the library in the church village of Kivijärvi because it was closely connected with the sawmill school at a time when there was no elementary school in the church village. It is not certain which of these two libraries was established first, nor from which of them local ideas about popular enlightenment sprang. It may well also be the case that the library in the church village came into being as a kind of by-product of the sawmill school and library.

It is possible to summarize what has been stated above by concluding that the factors that most significantly influenced the foundation of Kivijärvi's libraries and promoted their activities were primarily the aims of developing popular education and enhancing the people's literacy. Secondly, the acquisition of religious literature by the revivalist movements and its dissemination among them also furthered the cause of popular libraries.

512 Suomela 1963, 660.
513 Koskenniemi 1967, 74, 146, 153–154.

Thirdly, the early industrial community of Kannonsaha Sawmill in the environs of Kivijärvi came to be a centre that was of considerable economic significance for the functioning of the library and thereby one that was also a hub of information. By contrast, the poverty and high mortality from disease in the years of famine and the distant location of towns slowed down the spread of literacy and the use of libraries and hindered the acquisition of literature. On a more general, the same interdependencies also affected level the viability of other similar popular libraries in remote areas, but in Kivijärvi the improvement of literacy skills of the local people was exceptionally slow compared with the rest of the Finnish countryside. Even so, the local elite tried to do all they could for enhancement of the popular education.

3. The Founders and the Care of the Collection

The founders, the operational principles and the Fennoman ideology

The operational principles of Kivijärvi lending library

> Albertina Zengerlein was bored in the heart of winter in the brand new rooms of Rauhala, whose many-paned windows looked onto a view of the church village enveloped in a thick covering of snow. Fortunately there was at least the large lake. Sometimes in summer when she was walking towards the shore and the waters were open, memories of the old days in Stockholm came to her in glimpses. But then she was brought back to reality by the stench of cow dung, the squeaking of the windmill and that incomprehensible Finnish yackety-yak of the farmers' and crofters' wives babbling among themselves. Fortunately, Albertina had her library. For days on end she would immerse herself in her books, and then the mistress of the house was not to be disturbed. Not even by the maid on household matters. Helga, on the other hand, was always talking with great enthusiasm about the local lending library and frequently visited the ladies in the church village on business connected with the board of governors. Albertina couldn't always quite understand why her daughter insisted on voluntarily trying to educate half the parish, the inhabitants of which couldn't even understand Swedish properly, although she realized just how useful a pastime reading was, if the reader really had time to get into it.

Or at least that is what one might imagine it was like. In fact we do not know with any certainly in the light of the available sources what Albertina thought about the matter. Perhaps, it was she who had encouraged her daughter to engage herself in the library work. The work of the members of the board of governors of the Kivijärvi library can later be examined with the help of the minutes of their meetings and other information about the organization of the library. They show how the acquisition, lending and maintenance of the books was organized. At the same time, they reveal the part played by Fennoman ideology in the organization of people's libraries and in the drafting of their rules.

In any case, Helga Hemmer was involved in the activities of a library established by private persons in Kivijärvi for only a couple of years. What is more significant is that she was a member of the first board of governors because of her family background, which was exceptional among the parishioners. Her mother, Albertina Mathilda Zengerlein (1828–1902) and her father, Eric Erland Hemmer (1823–1911), a forestry officer in the Salamajärvi Forestry Reserve together with their children constituted indeed an exceptional family in the church village in that they were the grandparents of the future Swedish-speaking Finnish poet and writer Jarl Hemmer (1893–1944), who was born in Vaasa and who became famous in the first part of the twentieth century. Jarl Hemmer began writing as a poet in 1914.[514] He was the son of Balder Hemmer (1864–1947), a lawyer, and his wife Emmy (1866–1943). He had two brothers: Professor Ragnar Hemmer and Fjalar Hemmer, a lawyer like his father. But how did his noble-born grandmother Albertina end up in the backwoods of Kivijärvi and Perho surrounded by the gloomy wilderness and the vast forests?

Birger (Börje) Hemmer, a forefather of Eric Hemmer, was appointed captain of a merchant vessel in Stockholm, the capital of the realm of Sweden, on 14 July 1778. He had moved to the capital from the town of Kungsbacka. He married into the de Broen family of industrialists, who were Dutch in origin but lived and ran their business in Stockholm. He died off the coast of Dover in 1798. His son, Johan Abraham Hemmer, became a silk and haberdashery merchant, who according to the census list 'drank wine and coffee and played cards'. Johan's son, Eric Erland Hemmer, was born in 1823, but he was soon orphaned.[515]

Eric Erland Hemmer studied forestry in Sweden, (at Brukssocietetens Forestry Institute in Sweden), and qualified in 1848, after which he moved to Finland to be the estate manager of the vast forest properties of the noble Armfelt family in Uskela and Halikko. Soon, however, he took up a post as a forestry officer (which was made permanent in 1866) in the Salamajärvi area[516] in the Province of Vaasa, and this became his real life's work. He had decided to move to Finland because there was a shortage of forestry officers there. Immediately after qualifying, Hemmer had looked after the forests belonging to an ironworks in Ockelbo in Sweden, and there he had met a poor young girl of noble birth from Stockholm called Albertina Zengerlein. Her family was of German origin but had been ennobled in Sweden in 1719. The family had never really prospered, and Albertina's father, Jakob, who was a chief accountant in the Swedish National Debt Office, was said to have been at one time a page boy at court, but after the coup of 1809, in which King Gustav IV Adolf was deposed, he paid dearly for his defiant devotion to the monarch. In any case, after his death his widow was left with no funds

514 In his early anthologies there are features than link him with the modernists, although he is not always regarded as having been one of them. K. Laitinen 1997, 317.
515 According to legend a kind-hearted friend of his mother took care of him and sent him to be raised in the home of Captain von Fieandt, a hero of the Finnish War, on the latter's farm at Kananoja in the parish of Vyborg in south-eastern Finland. Salminen 1955, 10.
516 The extensive Salamajärvi forestry reserve was situated on the borders of the parishes of Kivijärvi and Perho. A national park was established there in 1982 and is known particularly for the white-tailed deer that live in it.

at all to pay for the future education of their children. Thus Albertina's marriage in 1853 to a vigorous young forestry officer solved many of her problems.[517]

For a long time, the Hemmers owned a farm in Perho. Then they built a villa in the church village of Kivijärvi in the 1880s. Erik Hemmer was by nature a confidently calm person,[518] while Jarl Hemmer described his grandmother as 'strongly morose'. On the other hand, she was also considered to be energetic and determined. In any case, living in the Finnish-speaking interior meant for the Swedish-born and Swedish-speaking Albertina a melancholy feeling of foreignness, far from the life that she had been used to in Stockholm. She drew and read. She had a command of the major 'civilized' languages, and for her amusement she used to translate the works of Chateaubriand and Lamennais, among others. She also had an English-language edition of Shakespeare in her library at home.[519] Thus Helga Hemmer, too, had become acquainted at home with a much wider range of world literature than the collection of the Kivijärvi lending library, which was intended for the Finnish-speaking commons, ever had to offer and contained works in no other languages than Finnish.[520]

In this book the local cultural and educational work that was carried in connection with Kivijärvi lending library are examined through key agents like Helga Hemmer because this makes it possible to see what kind of persons were behind the operating principles of the library. A common denominator of the operational principles of all Finnish lending libraries was Fennomania, the promotion of a Finnish national culture. The growth in the number of people's libraries in Finland in the nineteenth century was connected with efforts to educate the common people. The establishment of the elementary school institution came into being at the same time, and in many places the activities of the local library took place in conjunction with a recently established elementary school.[521] In fact, the Fennomans' express policy, as outlined in the proposals of Yrjö Koskinen and Agathon Meurman, for example, was to integrate the activities of the elementary schools and the parish libraries. This policy was naturally inspired by the popular enlightenment philosophy of J. V. Snellman.[522]

The development was very similar elsewhere in Europe and in the United States. For example, in Sweden the establishment of people's libraries was closely connected with the idea of popular education and promoting the activities of the elementary schools.[523] In France, a determined effort was made through legislation to enhance the position of school libraries to cater not only for the needs of teachers and pupils but also for those of the general public from the end of the eighteenth century on, when the concept of

517 Salminen 1955, 10–11.
518 Salminen 1955, 11.
519 Salminen 1955, 12.
520 KKA, Collection catalogues of Kivijärvi lending library.
521 Mäkinen 1999, 37–38.
522 E.g. Mäkinen 1997, 381–383; Mäkinen 2009e, 152–169.
523 Leffner 1999, 94–96.

a dual role for these institutions as both school and public libraries came into being.[524]

Public libraries were generally regarded in France as institutions that supplemented the activities of the schools. They continued to offer opportunities for reading to those who had already finished school so that they might keep up their reading skills and their education might not be wasted. It was thought that the people could not reasonably be expected to read if no reading material was available to them after they left school. The hope was that young people would borrow books for the whole family and read aloud to their illiterate parents and relatives in the evening. Literate adults, for their part, could use the library for the purposes of self-education. Later on, in the mid-nineteenth century, the adult population of France naturally also had access to other reading material than library books.[525] In the United States, school libraries began to be established more actively at the end of the nineteenth century.[526] There, too, the activities of public libraries were typically integrated with those of schools.

In the 1870s Finland, the intellectuals in the Fennoman movement began to approach the common people of the countryside through various types of voluntary civic activities,[527] and in that decade, the number of associations, clubs and other organizations in the countryside grew at a dizzy speed. This development was an example of how the ways of thinking and acting that were characteristic of the 'society of the estates' began to give way and at the same time the basis for a new political culture came into being. However, the breaking-down of estate barriers was a slow process, and the establishment of a popular library for everybody did not necessarily mean a renunciation of the class mentality. For example, the aim of the joint activities of the educated classes and the common people to establish popular libraries in the 1870s was to level out class distinctions rather than to abolish them altogether.[528] The organizational activities in the countryside in the 1870s were characterized by a large number of associations and educational societies. This development was connected with the active engagement of the educated members of the Fennoman movement in work to promote popular enlightenment. Against this background, it is no wonder that the library project of the people of Kivijärvi was based on the activities of the upper-class members of an association.

The Fennoman ideology was an important factor that inspired and provided the principles and values of the organization of Kivijärvi library, too. The ideology had become more unificatory after the Diet began to convene regularly from the 1860s on. The movement was supported not only by the Clerical Estate but also by that of the Peasants, and it became

---

524 Barnett 1973, 113–114.
525 Barnett 1973, 307.
526 Rubin 2004, 281.
527 In the 1860s the participation of the Fennomans in civic activities had been limited to mutual association between members of the educated classes. Liikanen 1995, 112.
528 Liikanen 1995, 179–180, 185, 190–191, 211, 235.

ever more clearly ideologically oriented towards agrarian and religious values. The aim of the Fennomans was to create an upper class that was culturally connected with the common people. Snellman did not wish to create a new upper class by educating the Finnish-speaking common people into an elite, but rather to keep the old one, who, however, would adopt Finnish as their native language instead of (usually) Swedish. When the educated Fennomans defined themselves as 'Finnish', they felt close to the common people and regarded themselves as their spokesmen. They also considered themselves to be a kind of vanguard, who deserved the trust of the people, in contradistinction to those groups that were 'not of the people', in other words, Swedish-speakers and often persons of a liberal persuasion. The same factors were involved in the rapid rise of civic organizations such as temperance and youth associations from the 1880s on. The Fennomans thought that through participation in these activities it was possible to take a stand and adapt the higher estates' own position to those of other groups in society and thereby build a nation. Connected with this was also a new way of defining political activity, which required that the state, too, have the endorsement of the individual citizens for its actions. The activities of the civic organizations in a way sowed the seed for the gradual birth of a civil society.[529]

The oldest Finnish parish libraries, which contained mainly devotional literature, were usually established by the clergy. However, there were also other members of the educated classes, such as university students and elementary school teachers, who were active in establishing libraries, and sometimes members of the commons, too, took an interest in these projects. Usually the people's libraries were owned by a municipality, a village community or an elementary school district. Fewer than a fifth of all the popular libraries in Finland were owned by clubs or societies. Schadewitz described the interest in the issue of people's libraries in the 1880s as feeble until the establishment of village libraries revived in the following decade along with youth association activities.[530] However, in April 1888 it was decided to boost the activities of the old lending library in Kivijärvi by giving the responsibility for running it to a dedicated association.[531]

The re-organization of Kivijärvi lending library in 1888 was carried out by a few private persons. On 9 April they met in the elementary school[532] in the church village to consider the question of the state of the local library and to draft a proposal for a new set of rules for it. At least the following persons are known to have been present: Mrs Ida Anjelin (a shopkeeper's wife) and her son Axel, the above-mentioned Miss Helga Hemmer and the elementary school teacher Sakari Niemi. It was noted in the meeting that the lending library had fallen into such a miserable condition because of the

---

529 Alapuro & Stenius 1989[1987], 14, 17–18.
530 Schadewitz 1903, 28, 29, 31.
531 KKA, Minutes of the meeting of the board of governors of Kivijärvi lending library, 9/4/1888.
532 In Sweden, too, it was the custom to hold founding and other meetings connected with the library in the local school. Jarlbrink 2010, 43.

the library as being part of the duties of a teacher. As a result, this task was performed for decades by teachers (supposedly with enthusiasm), and it was unnecessary for the municipalities to employ librarians separately. Elsewhere, too, in the late nineteenth century librarianship was regarded as being naturally associated with other educational work. Of the over one thousand libraries that were operating in Finland in 1898, more than 600 were located in elementary schools and were generally tended by teachers.[593] In the United States, for example, the task of public libraries was considered to be not only to support the public school system but also to encourage those broad sections of the population who only possessed the rudiments of literacy to engage in continuous life-long learning and thereby enhance their own personal development. In this respect, the task of the librarian was regarded as resembling that of the teacher.[594]

There is only scattered information about the librarians of Kivijärvi lending library before 1888, which further obstructs our picture of the life of the library. The first two libraries, at least at the time of their foundation, had been run by the parish vicars. Since the entries in the register of borrowers of the privately founded library of Kivijärvi date right back to 1877, one can assume that the lending library established in 1872 by the church parish that functioned in the church village at that time was run by one of the parish officials. The vicar, Viktor Konsin, who initially served as the librarian, did not necessarily continue to perform that task after half-way through that decade. One possible librarian might have been the cantor, Antti Herranen, but there is no certain evidence of this. He was, however, a teacher in the first elementary school in 1873 and 1874 and again from 1877 to 1880 and in 1884. At that time, care of the library was part of the duties of the teacher, since a register of elementary schools in Finland published in 1878 relates that in the years 1874–1877 Daniel Liukkonen, a student of Jyväskylä Teacher Training Seminary, who held the post of teacher on a temporary basis, was the librarian of the school library. At that time it comprised 140 works. The chairperson of the board of governors was then a farmer called Kustaa Orava, who was also a juror of the jurisdictional district.[595]

The library of Kinnula Elementary School at the same time possessed 80 volumes. It was maintained by a teacher called Antti Räsänen, who in conjunction with this task also performed the duties of a preacher in Kinnula chapelry. He had studied in the Finnish Mission School and had previously worked as a preacher both in Viitasaari and in the city prison in Kuopio.[596] The chairman of the board of governors was the Crown Chief of Police, Nils Gustav Holmström.[597] For example, in the school library that had been opened in the autumn of 1869 in Saarijärvi, there were about 150

---

593 Järvelin 1966, 67. Elementary school teachers as librarians and developers of the lending libraries, see also e.g. Ellä 1994, 10–11; Penttilä 1986, 16–17.
594 Garrison 1979, 38.
595 Berner 1878, 94; Table 10.
596 See also S. Kotilainen 2013d, 123, 130.
597 Berner 1878, 94.

Table 10. *The headmasters and teachers of the elementary school in the church village of Kivijärvi 1873–1937.*

Years	Teacher
1873–1874	Antti Herranen (cantor)
1874–1877	Daniel Liukkonen (seminary student)
1877–1880	Antti Herranen (cantor)
1880–1884	Antti Tokkola (seminary student)
1884	Antti Herranen (cantor)
1885	K. F. Steenroos (Salo) (seminary student)
1885–1898	Sakari Niemi (seminary student and elementary school teacher)
1898–1899	O. A. Ylänkö (seminary student)
1899–1905	Heikki Lipponen (elementary school teacher)
1905–1909	Karl Järvinen (elementary school teacher)
1909–1912	Kalle Hänninen (elementary school teacher)
1912–1937	Juho Vihtori Salmi (elementary school teacher)

Source: Mönkkönen 1986, 441–442; Werkko 1893, 419.

volumes at that time.[598] Thus the book collection of Kivijärvi elementary school was quite considerable in size when one takes into account the fact that Saarijärvi was a more populous parish and that the reading culture there was stronger than in Kivijärvi.

Sakari Niemi was the teacher when the privately founded library was opened in 1888. The falling-off in the library's activities that had taken place at the turn of the 1870s and 1880s was possibly a result of the fact that in the years 1873–1885[599] the duties of the teacher at the elementary school were carried out by a number of students from Jyväskylä Teacher Training Seminary or, when no temporary trained teacher seems to have been available, by Cantor Antti Herranen in addition to his other duties. The practice of issuing a letter of confirmation of appointment to teachers of Kivijärvi elementary school was only officially adopted in 1888, when Niemi held the post.[600]

It was very common, and indeed recommended, for the clergy of the parish to belong to the board of governors of the local elementary school. For example, in 1872 the local vicar or curate was the chairperson of the board of governors of the elementary schools in all of the parishes of Central Finland, apart from those in chapelries, which did not have ministers of their own.[601] In addition to Vicar Konsin, the following persons were appointed as members of the first board of governors of the elementary school in Kivijärvi: Heikki Kotilainen (a lay assessor), Matti Rytkönen, Matti Kinnunen and Kustaa Orava (all farmers) and another Heikki Kotilainen (a church warden).[602]

598 Berner 1878, 101.
599 Mönkkönen 1986, 441–442; Werkko 1893, 418–419; Table 7.
600 Mönkkönen 1986, 441.
601 Mönkkönen 1988a, 567–568.
602 Mönkkönen 1986, 441.

From the time of V. A. Konsin on, the chairperson of the board of governors of the elementary school in the church village of Kivijärvi was usually the vicar, until in 1902 the cantor, Antti Herranen, was selected to replace the Vicar Frans Petter Krank in this post. Krank had punctiliously exploited the influence afforded by his authority, and in practice it was he who decided on the appointment of teachers. For example, he forced through the appointment of Niemi to the post of teacher in the 1880s, although the local common people did not like Niemi or his attitude to them. The appointment of Heikki Lipponen as teacher was also opposed because he was considered to be unnecessarily strict.[603]

When the activities of the church village library began to be revived after Niemi's position had been made permanent, it is in theory possible that Vicar Krank tried to promote the activities of the library, at least as some kind of éminence grise, especially since in earlier decades this had been the responsibility of the parish and the vicars. All in all, this examination of the family background of the members of the board of governors has permitted me to note that the clergy in Kivijärvi maintained their interest in the activities of the library and assumed responsibility for its continued operation for a fairly long time.

THE GRADUAL PROFESSIONALIZATION OF LIBRARIANSHIP

Libraries were for a long time run by clergymen and elementary school teachers who had no proper professional training in librarianship. How then did the situation change at the turn of the nineteenth and twentieth centuries, when more attention began to be paid in the Western world and gradually also in Finland, to the professional qualifications of librarians and the development of the field of librarianship? In this respect, the libraries of the Finnish countryside still continued to function to a great extent in conjunction with the elementary schools.

In 1875, all the pupils in the school were from the immediate environs of the Kivijärvi church village.[604] Regular elementary education did not come to the remote villages of the southern parts of the parish of Kivijärvi until about 30 years after the ratification of the Decree on Elementary Schools. For example, Leppälänkylä elementary school was founded in 1894. School attendance was at that time still voluntary, and only a small proportion of the children got to go to school because they were needed to work at home.[605] The dearth of elementary schools was supplemented with ambulatory schools, which it was cheaper for the parishes to arrange.

At first, the number of elementary schools increased in more southern parts of Finland. Further north, the lack of funds, the low population density and the absence of a local educated class slowed down the spread of elementary schools. Moreover, the ordinary people regarded them with suspicion. Thus in Central Finland, for example, it was the clergy who actively used their authority to get schools established in parishes which would

603 Mönkkönen 1986, 442.
604 Mönkkönen 1986, 441.
605 Kokkinen 1994, 11.

otherwise have postponed their establishment to an even later date. This reluctance arose not least from the fact that the construction of premises for the school alone meant a considerable outlay for the parishioners. In several parishes of Central Finland, it was planned to establish elementary schools in the late 1860s after the Decree on Elementary Schools was passed, but the implementation of the decision was postponed because of the outbreak of famine in that decade.[606]

In the countryside, attendance at an elementary school was fairly rare up to the beginning of the twentieth century. However, the number of elementary school pupils in Central Finland did grow, particularly in the 1870s and 1890s. In the former decade, many farmers had prospered as a result of the demand for timber and the rise in the value of forested land. From the 1890s on, by contrast, it was the landless population who began to grow richer. In many parishes, the children would have wished to go to school, but often families, particularly among the poorest crofters and other landless groups, could not afford to send them.[607]

The poor communications and the bad roads also worsened opportunities for going to school. The children of the remote villages in the sparsely populated countryside had to find lodgings in the church villages, which was where the first and, for a long time, the only elementary schools were usually located. In Kivijärvi, for example, irregular attendance at school was sometimes explained by bad weather conditions. This was also mentioned in the reports of the school inspectors as a reason for school absenteeism. One such case that was mentioned was a heavy snow storm in Kinnula.[608] Although schools were hardly ever closed completely in Finland because of bad weather, in Kivijärvi this could prevent the children from outlying villages from getting to school because the journey was sometimes made over the lake, and at times of the year when the ice was breaking up or when there were strong winds, the children could not travel across the water.

As mentioned above, the parish vicars acted as librarians of the early people's libraries in Kivijärvi without payment. Nor were the librarians in Viitasaari and Karstula paid a separate remuneration, at any rate not in the 1870s. The clergy, in particular the cantors, and the schoolteachers handled this task in addition to their other duties.[609] Likewise in other parts of in Finland – for example in Northern Karelia – the post of librarian was rarely occupied by a landed farmer or his children in the nineteenth century, and when it was, it was usually a question of a village library or the library of a particular association.[610] Werkko recommended that the librarian should be paid a small remuneration for his or her work, especially as he set, or at least hoped for, certain standards of competence in librarians.[611] There is no exact information about the remuneration paid to the teacher Sakari Niemi. On the other hand, it was decided to pay an annual sum of 10 marks

606 Mönkkönen 1988a, 562. See also S. Kotilainen 2013d.
607 Mönkkönen 1988a, 575.
608 Mönkkönen 1986, 446; Mönkkönen 1988a, 576–577.
609 Werkko 1879, 178, 181, 19; Table 11.
610 Järvelin 1966, 100.
611 Werkko 1879, 243.

on specified days and at specified times? The times at which books were really borrowed in practice have not previously been studied in such detail in Finnish, or for that matter in other Nordic, literature,[655] although they could yield a lot of new information about the borrowing practices and the conditions governing the visiting of libraries. The opening times crucially limited the extent to which books were borrowed, and this was ultimately manifested in how actively the library was used. Therefore, it is important to examine the subject in greater detail. In practice, a study of the times at which a library was used is hampered by the available sources. If the loans registers have been preserved, as in the case of Kivijärvi, this provides strong motivation for examining this rare source material dating back to the 1870s, 1880s and 1890s.

In examining the opening times of lending libraries, one must take into account the fact that the customers used them in their spare time, in the evening, at weekends or on holidays.[656] In fact, it was precisely the hours following Sunday services that Kaarle Werkko recommended for the library opening time. However, he thought that in the countryside the opening hours should be flexible, and that those who needed to should be able to borrow books on weekdays as well if they travelled to the church village on other business.[657] The traditional and most common time when lending libraries were open (in the Province of Oulu and the Province of Turku and Pori, for example) was Sunday after twelve o'clock[658], a time which served church-goers in particular. Even in the late 1920s, libraries were commonly open on Sundays. The first regulations concerning the opening hours of libraries were issued in the Library Act of 1928, which stipulated that libraries that received a state subsidy must be open at least twice a week in the countryside and four times a week in towns.[659]

In the countryside, these minimal opening times were generally adhered to, but sometimes libraries applied for exemption from them because of the lack of demand. On the other hand, when the librarian performed his or her duties as a kind of hobby and the library was located adjacent or close to the librarian's residence, it was possible to be flexible about opening times. If necessary, the library was 'always' open, or at least whenever the librarian or a member of his or her family was at home.[660]

For example, in the 1870s Karstula library was open on Sunday mornings between eight and ten o'clock, in other words, before the church service began. However, the municipal assembly had to prohibit the borrowing of books when the church service was in progress, which had evidently been the practice in the early years of the library's operation.[661] In Saarijärvi, too, it

655 For a seasonal borrowing in Kangasala lending library, see also Ojanen 2011, 57–58.
656 Kelly 1977, 71.
657 Werkko 1879, 245.
658 See also Samppala 2010, 6 (Jalasjärvi); Vuontisjärvi 2010, 14 (Rovaniemi).
659 Eskola 1999, 130–131; Eskola 2001, 79.
660 Eskola 1999, 131.
661 Koski 1998, 584–585.

was possible to borrow books every Sunday before or after the service.[662] The library of Jyväskylä Teacher Training Seminary was also open on Sunday mornings from 8:30 to 9:30.[663] In the set of rules drawn up for the library in Kivijärvi in 1888, it was decided that the library should be open on every Saturday (except religious holidays) from three to five in the afternoon. This was exceptional in Finland. Those who lived further away would be allowed to use the library at other times if circumstances permitted.[664] One can only hazard a guess as to why these opening times were chosen. Probably it was the teacher Sakari Niemi who chose Saturday because it was the last day of his weekly school routine, which ran from Monday to Saturday. Keeping the library open and serving the customers in this way did not disturb the actual activities of the school when the library was located in its premises. Niemi possibly wanted to keep Sunday as a day of rest from his library activities, too. Moreover, the parishioners who lived further out, tended to travel on a Saturday when they came to church so that they could deal with other business and sign up for Holy Communion, and the library opening hours fitted in well with this.

The loans registers of Kivijärvi library also offer some further explanations for the exceptional opening hours. Using them it is possible to ascertain which was the day of opening before the establishment of the lending library by private persons and which thereafter. From the loans registers, we can deduce that previously Sunday had been the most popular day for borrowing: almost a quarter of the loans were registered on Sundays and other religious holidays. Saturday was almost as popular, and over one fifth of the loans were made then. The rest of the loans were distributed fairly evenly over the other weekdays, of which Wednesday was the most popular.[665]

Although, from 1888 on, the rules of the library stipulated that Saturday was the only official day of opening, Sunday continued to be a prominent time for borrowing books in Kivijärvi as it was in practice the only day of leisure for those who worked in agriculture. Even so it is noteworthy that from the late 1870s on books were borrowed more frequently on weekdays, and in Kivijärvi approximately 75 percent of the loans were made on days other than Sunday, and although the Sabbath was an important day for reading, the books were mainly borrowed on weekdays. However, for practical reasons, many did their borrowing in conjunction with their trips on other business to the church village, and these usually took place at weekends, when people had most time to spare, or they travelled there to go to church. On the other hand, it was possible to borrow books on any day of the week should the need arise.

When attention is focused more closely on particular years in the operation of the library, one can observe that, at the annual level, the most popular days for borrowing remained the same apart from a couple of

---

662 Junnila 1995, 243.
663 Lahtinen 1963, 8.
664 KKA, Minutes of the meeting of the board of governors of Kivijärvi lending library, 9/4/1888.
665 Table 13.

Table 13. Days of opening of Kivijärvi lending library 1877–1897.

Day of the week	N	%
Monday	145	11.6
Tuesday	111	8.9
Wednesday	166	13.2
Thursday	116	9.3
Friday	99	7.9
Saturday	272	21.7
Sunday	311	24.7
Not known	34	2.7
Total	**1254**	**100.0**

N = Number of the loans registered.
Source: KKA, loans registers 1877–1897; Almanac archive of Helsinki University: nineteenth-century almanacs.

exceptional years. For example, in 1887, when the largest number of books were borrowed from Kivijärvi lending library, the greatest proportion (33.6 percent) were borrowed on Saturdays, while the next most popular day for borrowing was Wednesday (20.9 percent) and the following was Sunday (13.6 percent). The greatest change took place in 1890, after which Saturday clearly became more popular than, or at least as popular as, Sunday for borrowing books. Here, one can see that the regulations of the library were adapted to this practice, which became established at the end of the 1880s, and Saturday afternoon was chosen as the official time of opening. In the years 1893–1897, Thursday became an even more common day for borrowing than Saturday.[666] The reason for the popularity of Thursday cannot be ascertained with any certainty from the available sources.

It was not very common for books to be borrowed on religious holidays or on their eves, although books were borrowed to some extent on Midsummer's Eve, Midsummer's Day, New Year's Eve and New Year's Day, Easter Sunday and even Good Friday. By analyzing the borrowing days by month and season according to the agricultural cycle of work it is possible to ascertain how the daily rhythm of work affected the reading of books, which was a leisure time activity. For example, the heaviest harvesting work took place in the period from August through October, while the period from November to January was the darkest and often the coldest time of the year, and hence less work was done outdoors than in the other seasons. Consequently, on the basis of the evidence provided by the loans registers, winter (November through January) was the busiest time for borrowing books, although spring (February through April) was almost as popular.[667] One might suppose that people had least time for reading during the harvest months, but in fact least books were borrowed in the early summer period from May to July, which was the lightest time of the year. On the other hand, that was the

---

666 Table 14; KKA, loans registers 1877–1897.
667 This trend was quite similar in Kangasala, but there the spring months were more popular time for reading than November. Ojanen 2011, 58.

Table 14. The busiest borrowing days of the week for Kivijärvi library 1877–1897.

Day of the week	1877–1882		1883–1887		1888–1892		1893–1897		Year not known	
	N	%	N	%	N	%	N	%	N	%
Monday	1	1.9	90	11.5	47	13.6	7	10.4	–	–
Tuesday	4	7.4	73	9.3	32	9.3	2	3.0	–	–
Wednesday	2	3.7	116	14.8	41	11.9	7	10.4	–	–
Thursday	6	11.1	68	8.7	23	6.7	19	28.4	–	–
Friday	10	18.5	63	8.0	24	7.0	2	3.0	–	–
Saturday	17	31.4	159	20.2	79	22.9	17	25.4	–	–
Sunday	13	24.1	192	24.3	93	26.9	13	19.4	–	–
Not known	1	1.9	25	3.2	6	1.7	–	–	2	100.0
Total	54	100.0	786	100.0	345	100.0	67	100.0	2	100.0

N = Number of the loans registered.
Source: KKA, loans registers 1877–1897; Almanac archive of Helsinki University: nineteenth-century almanacs.

time when sowing was done, and the cattle were taken out to graze and needed to be herded. The largest number of loans were made in September and December,[668] when there was most time available for reading. The loans registers do not permit us to make any assumptions about what time of the day the library was used, but apparently the opening hours were relatively flexible, and if necessary the parishioners could borrow books whenever the librarian was available.

By comparison, from 1860 on, the people's library in Helsinki was open for one hour on Wednesdays and Sundays between 4 and 5 p.m. The largest number of works borrowed in one day was in 1861 when 185 volumes were taken out, and in the following year 154 volumes were borrowed in a single day. The librarian had to have assistants in order to get through the work. The auxiliary workers were unpaid volunteers. Self-service did not work because the customers were unaccustomed to borrowing, and the works usually had to be found using registers that were difficult to decipher. The most sought-after books were constantly out on loan. Detailed information concerning both the book and the borrower were entered in the loans register. It was not until much later that index numbers were adopted. A fee was charged for some of the loans, and an account was kept of this.[669]

In 1866, the library was open for three hours a week on Wednesday, Saturday and Sunday, but in 1871 it returned to the old practice of opening for two hours on Wednesday and Sunday.[670] The small libraries of the countryside operated in freer way. For example, in her report on Alajärvi library, a library inspector called Olga Risula stated: 'The public has free access to the shelves and can sit and read in the library room throughout the day because the librarian lives in the same house. The municipal assemblies have gladly availed themselves of the same right in connection with their numerous meetings.' This situation was quite good for the countryside. On the other hand, it could happen that

---

668 Table 15; KKA, loans registers 1877–1897.
669 Hirn 1998, 24.
670 Hirn 1998, 27.

Table 15. Seasonal borrowing in Kivijärvi lending library 1877–1897.

Season	1877–1882		1883–1887		1888–1892		1893–1897		Year not known	
	N	%	N	%	N	%	N	%	N	%
spring (February–April)	3	5.6	223	28.3	102	29.6	11	16.4	–	–
summer (May–July)	4	7.4	153	19.5	65	18.8	16	23.9	1	50.0
autumn (August–October)	10	18.5	187	23.8	100	29.0	14	20.9	1	50.0
winter (November–January)	37	68.5	213	27.1	77	22.3	26	38.8	–	–
Not known	–	–	10	1.3	1	0.3	–	–	–	–
Total	54	100.0	786	100.0	345	100.0	67	100.0	2	100.0

N = Number of the loans registered.
The division into seasons follows the agricultural work cycle.
Source: KKA, loans registers 1877–1897; Almanac archive of Helsinki University: nineteenth-century almanacs.

a library might not always be open for the customers, for example, in cases where there was no separate library room, and the librarian who kept the collection at home was away.[671]

The opening times of popular libraries in Finland were very similar to those in France after the middle of the nineteenth century. There the opening times in the countryside were more limited than in the cities, and in some places the library was closed altogether during the busiest weeks of the harvest season. It was considered that the rural libraries could serve their customers best on long winter evenings and at other times when the agricultural workers were unemployed. These libraries were often situated in the municipal offices or the local school, although a library might sometimes be located in the home of a member of the library committee, who also performed the duties of librarian.[672]

All in all, library opening times crucially affected the accessibility of the collections to rural readers. In lending libraries like that of Kivijärvi, however, it was possible to be flexible about opening hours if necessary in order that the customers might be able to avail themselves of the services of the library. My research reveals that opening times in the countryside were not limited to those mentioned in the library's regulations; in practice the library might be open every day of the week if the teacher or a member of his family happened to be at home.

The observant reader may have noticed from the life story of Kivijärvi lending library that has been related so far a small but all the more important contradiction, which upsets the harmonious chronological order of the library's activity: How is it possible that there are entries in the loans registers of the library established by private persons dating back to 1877 when the library was only founded in 1888? By comparing the loans registers and the minutes of the meetings of the board of governors of the library, one can be sure that the registers referred to the same books that were procured for

671 Eskola 1999, 132.
672 Barnett 1973, 328.

the library when it was being run by private persons, and that the registers in question were indisputably those of the latter library.[673] So what about this small discrepancy then? Some of the borrowers seem to have been customers of the library about ten years before it was established.

This is a key question for this whole study, since it shows how small details can affect the continuity of the library's operation and how great was the influence of individual persons on its birth and development. The situation is made even more complicated by the fact that Schadewitz's statistics on the first parish libraries in the Province of Vaasa reveal some new contradictions. Those who collected information for these statistics in 1895 were informed that the lending library in the church village of Kivijärvi had 78 works. In the following year, it was reported that the lending library founded by private persons in Kivijärvi possessed 145 works.[674]

However, the surviving loans registers of this library refer to only 129 works that were borrowed. Although the collections and the libraries were thus in principle separate, the information about loans made from them was entered in the same registers. On the other hand, the information about the books in the different collections may have been reported separately for Schadewitz's statistics because officially it was a question of two different libraries. But why were there two libraries operating in the church village when the old church parish library was supposed to have closed down by that time?

This puzzle can be solved by examining how the duties of librarian were handled. Two pieces of information that were recorded in supplementary statistics published in the calendars of the Society for Popular Enlightenment for 1890 and 1896 are of crucial importance in studying the history of Kivijärvi library. They show that in the early 1890s the librarian of both the lending library established in Kivijärvi in 1872 and the one founded by private persons in 1888 was the same person: the teacher Sakari Niemi.[675] From these scraps of information we can thus deduce that for a number of years there were in fact two libraries operating in the village and that the books in their collections appeared in the same loans registers because they had the same librarian. But how could Niemi have entered the information about the two different libraries that he ran in the same registers? In order to solve this question, we must consider the formation of the collections of the libraries more closely, because there is where the answer lies.

673 KKA, loans registers 1877–1897.
674 Table 7.
675 Society for Popular Enlightenment calendars 1890 and 1896.

The funding and acquisition of the collections

THE FINANCIAL POSITION OF THE LIBRARY

The private founders described the early stages of the formation of the collection of Kivijärvi library as follows:

> Now nearly a year has elapsed since a lottery was held in order to fund the improvement of the lending library of Kivijärvi and its organization so that it might fulfil its purpose. But although such a long time has passed, it [the library] has only come into being, nothing else. A big obstacle to further progress has been the fact that the municipality lingered over approving the rules until June. When the rules were finally ratified by the appropriate authority, the procurement and proper ordering of books was quickly begun. And last Sunday, it was announced to the congregation in church that there were new books in loanable condition available for borrowing by those who wished to do so for a fee of 10 pence. Whether the choice of books has been successful, the future will show; we have done our best, but perhaps we have not obtained all the books that we wanted.[676]

So, what was the financial position of the library like in the longer run? Kivijärvi lending library received its funding from membership and loans fees and fines as well as donations and collections. Some of the actual works were also donated. From the 1850s on, lotteries had been organized to collect funds to subsidize the foundation of popular libraries.[677] The funding of the activities of these libraries was initially dependent on the charitable contributions of private persons. A collection was made to finance the acquisition of books for Saarijärvi Library, and of the 64 roubles that it produced the Chief of Police, Wilhelm von Hertzén, contributed almost a third.[678] The operations of the people's library in Keuruu in Central Finland were supported in the 1860s and 1870s by selling handicraft items produced by the local sewing club and by arranging lotteries.[679]

From the mid-nineteenth century on, and in the countryside particularly in the 1870s, lotteries and other similar entertainments, such as evening galas and theatrical performances, were the most favoured way of collecting money for common projects and events. It was mainly women who were responsible for the practical organization of the lotteries, and they for example made and sold needleworks for promoting the popular education. Often the proceeds from these went to supporting elementary schools, secondary schools and lending libraries. Lotteries always attracted a lot of people and provided a new way for people to spend time together in joint endeavours.[680]

---

676 KKA, Minutes of the annual general meeting of Kivijärvi lending library, 29/1/1889.
677 Närhi 1963, 77.
678 Junnila 1995, 243.
679 Rainio 1988.
680 E. Lehtonen 1994, 165–183, 210–214; Pietilä 2003, 126. See also Ahlstedt 1987, 5–8; Tarikka 2002, 2.

The early stages of popular library activities elsewhere in Finland were very similar to those in Kivijärvi. After the Decree on Municipal Government came into force, the Municipal Board of Laihia in Southern Ostrobothnia assumed responsibility for the administration of the people's library there and began to take charge of it. The library was located in the premises of the elementary school of Isokylä and was run by the teacher. At the same time, the extension and development of the small library became the object of civic attention, and a number of devotees began to organize lotteries to finance these efforts. Involved in this were young students whose fathers were vicars in the area and other representatives of the local gentry. A lottery held in August 1876 yielded a profit of 730 marks. A week later, the lottery committee reported the funds accruing from the lottery to the Municipal Board, and in the autumn of that year the Municipal Board decided to use some of these funds for the purchase of religious literature. The municipal assembly approved the proposal, and the sum of 500 marks was spent on acquiring suitable works from Helsinki. A quarter of this sum (125 marks) was used for buying religious works, mainly books by Luther, Arndt, Kemp and Bunyan and an annotated Bible edited by Wilhelm Carlsson. Generally, two copies were purchased of each of the most valuable works. The library itself had the books hard-bound, and bookcases were procured to house them.[681]

A lottery held in Kivijärvi in 1888 was a public event in which the participants were served coffee and tea and for which an entrance fee was charged. The supplies were obtained from the shops of both Juho Anjelin and Elias Jäsberg. Possibly, some other entertainment apart from the actual lottery was also organized.[682] Elsewhere in Finland, too, it was common for voluntary fund-raising collections to be organized for the benefit of libraries.[683] In spring 1896 it was noted in Kivijärvi: 'Of the funds accruing from an evening gala held last summer, Chief of Police Adrian Svens deposited with the library 55 marks 65 pence, that is half of the accruing profits. The contribution was accepted with great gratitude.'[684]

It was decided at the time of the library's foundation to use the funds acquired from the membership and loan fees and the fines together with the donations and funds accruing from collections and other activities such as lotteries and public entertainments to start up, maintain and expand the operations of the library. According to the rules of the library, members comprised the founders and all persons who contributed a fee of one mark annually over period of ten years or a single payment of five marks.[685] Unfortunately, apart from a few exceptions, neither the minutes nor the accounts reveal the names of all those who paid the membership fee, nor do

681 S. Seppälä 1954, 60.
682 KKA, accounts of Kivijärvi lending library 1888.
683 Karjalainen 1977, 115–116, 119–120.
684 KKA, Minutes of the meeting of the board of governors of Kivijärvi lending library, 14/5/1896.
685 KKA, Minutes of the meeting of the board of governors of Kivijärvi lending library, 9/4/1888.

they show the total number of members or the annual increase in the size of the membership, so it is impossible to form from the sources a clear picture of the membership of the library or to ascertain complete annual statistics of the income obtained from membership fees. For example, the accounts for the years 1889–1891 mention for each year only one annual membership fee of one mark.[686] During 1897 no new members joined the library, and there were no paying members at all.[687] There was no great increase in the membership at any stage.

The loan fee was fixed in the library's rules in 1888 at ten pence per volume for the duration of the loan. The board of governors reserved the right to reduce the fee or remove it altogether if it had a detrimental effect on the borrowing activities. On the other hand, those who were careless enough to exceed the loan time incurred a fine of ten pence per week (with any period exceeding four days being counted as a whole week). It was the task of the board of governors to collect the fines from negligent borrowers. If the return of a book was delayed by more than three months past the due date, the work was considered to have been lost and the borrower had to compensate the library for the price of the work. The library did not accept back books that were torn or stained or otherwise damaged, and the borrower was obliged to recompense the library for them.[688]

In Saarijärvi, for example, borrowing had initially been free, but subsequently the parish administration collected money for the acquisition of works for the library even from the landless classes of the population. In 1863, the parish assembly decided that the Crown Bailiff should collect at the request of the vicar five kopeks from landed farmers and two kopeks from crofters and craftsmen annually. The late return of a book incurred a fine of one kopek for the first week and two for the following one. If a borrower damaged a book, he or she was obliged to pay the price of the book and an additional fine amounting to one quarter of the price. By 1880, the library had accumulated altogether 1500 marks.[689] In Northern Karelia, again, the rules of libraries in the countryside fluctuated considerably with regard to whether a borrowing fee was charged or not and what kind of fines were imposed for the non-return of borrowed books. Some charges were voluntary. In Kitee, it seems that these charitable donations were ostensibly deposited in the poor box of the parish; in other words they were used for poor relief.[690]

The loan fees and fines that accrued in Kivijärvi in the years 1888–1892 did not bring much money into the coffers of the library, and in the early years its capital otherwise remained fairly low. For example, the accounts for

---

686 KKA, Accounts of Kivijärvi lending library, 1889–1892.
687 KKA, Minutes of the annual general meeting of Kivijärvi lending library, 28/1/1898.
688 KKA, Minutes of the meeting of the board of governors of Kivijärvi lending library, 9/4/1888.
689 Junnila 1995, 243.
690 According to the rules, the money was to be placed in the *reikä-niekka laatikko* (slot box). Järvelin 1966, 49–53. Wooden statues representing poor and/or disabled men begging for alms were installed outside Finnish churches. The figures contained boxes and a slot in the chest through which money could be inserted.

1891 showed a debit of 70 pence because the expenditure had exceeded the income in that year. At the end of the year, there was altogether 16 marks 93 pence in the till of the library. After the following year, the funds of the library amounted to 20 marks 13 pence.[691] At that time, the price of the volumes that were purchased varied from approximately one mark or one mark fifty pence to three or four marks. Thus the fees and fines that were collected did not permit many new works to be purchased let alone cover other operational expenses. The monetary values of the books have been ascertained from the few surviving books that were available for borrowing by the people of Kivijärvi at that time and which had the price marked in them. The value does not necessarily indicate the original purchase price but rather a slightly later estimate of the cost of replacing the book if it should be damaged.[692]

Thus the fees and fines did not cover the cost of acquiring many new works for the collection, not to mention the expenses involved in running the library. Similarly, in the later collection catalogues, which extend into the early years of the twentieth century, very few books were priced at over five marks.[693] A loan fee was commonly charged in Finnish lending libraries in the nineteenth century. However, the amounts of money collected from loan fees were without exception extremely small, and in the course of time there was a tendency to get rid of them altogether. They were basically intended to be some kind of surety rather than to cover all the costs of the library.[694] On the other hand, indigent members of the population were commonly allowed to borrow books free of charge.[695]

In a meeting on 24 January 1895, the board of governors of Kivijärvi lending library decided to collect funds for the extension of the library and the acquisition of more recent works by means of 'contribution lists', which several 'persons who had benevolently promoted the affairs of the library' undertook to administer. In the lists, the board of governors requested 'those esteemed citizens who wished to support a good cause to be so kind as to enter [...] their names and a sum of money on the list and to pay the money to the administrator of the list'. The collectors touted their lists around the parish over the course of the spring, and in April the librarian Sakari Niemi received the funds accruing from the contributions. The Chief of Police, Adrian Svens, and a tanner called J. Tamminen had undertaken to administer the collections, and the former deposited with the library the sum of 27 marks 70 pence and the latter 27 marks 25 pence accruing from the collection.[696]

691 KKA, Accounts of Kivijärvi lending library 1888–1892; Minutes of the annual general meetings of Kivijärvi lending library, 15/2/1892 (Annual report for 1891) and 26/1/1893. On the financial position of the library, see also H. Mäkelä 1991, 29.
692 KKA, The collection of old books of Kivijärvi lending library. Cf. H. Mäkelä (1991, 30), who estimates the price of a book in 1880 to have been 1–5 marks.
693 KKA, collection catalogues of Kivijärvi lending library.
694 Karjalainen 1977, 118–119.
695 Järvelin 1966, 50; Karjalainen 1977, 118–119.
696 KKA, Minutes of the annual general meeting of Kivijärvi lending library on 24/1/1895 and of the meeting of the board of governors on 10/4/1895.

Only one of these contribution lists has survived, that administered by Tamminen, who collected money from about seventy persons. Only two of the contributors appeared anonymously ('N.N.') in the list, all the others signed their own names. The donations were not particularly big, but even so there were differences between them. The amounts donated varied from ten pence to one mark fifty pence, which represented the highest single donation, contributed by a landed farmer called Matti Hiitola (real name: Puranen)[697] from the village of Lokakylä. The next largest donations (1 mark 25 pence) were made by a shopkeeper called G. E. Tainio and H. (possibly standing for Heikki) Turpeinen. Matti Holm, a retired landed farmer and church warden from the village of Penttilänkylä, gave a mark, as did his son Heikki Holm, and Matti Hakkarainen, the master of Penttilä Farm, was naturally not to be outdone by his neighbour, so he too contributed a mark to the collection. The same amount was given by H. Hämäläinen, who was possibly the step-father of Matti Hakkarainen.[698]

The majority of the donations, however, varied between 25 and 50 pence, and the contributors included Isak Pölkki, Konstantin Minkkinen, Konstantin Oikkelmus, J. H. Vesterinen, S. Lyytinen, H. Holm (a tailor), Kustaa Kannisto, the Chief of Police Fröjdman, Ida Anjelin, Wille Kainulainen, Jeremias Svedberg, Alma Hämäläinen, Hilma Oinonen, Theodor Flinkman, J. E. Backman, Alfred Backman, Matti Piispanen, Antti Pigg and Antti Niemelä (real surname probably Kotilainen), G. Leppänen, Taavetti Rytkönen and his wife Eva Stina Ahonen, Gideon Kainulainen, a Mrs Holm (probably Anna Kinnunen, the wife of Matti Holm), Sandra Hakkarainen, Pekka Kotilainen, Juho Lindholm, Juho Lyytinen, Joh. Saihoniemi, Johan Kotilainen and Heikki Kannisto. The librarian Sakari Niemi received the whole list of donations on 10 April 1895.[699] The donors thus included both men and women, and the library was supported by the families of tradesmen and by landed farmers, crofters and craftsmen.

As in the loans registers, the forms in which the names were written in this list varied. For example, the forename 'Juho' is sometimes written 'Joh.' although it refers to the same person who was informally called 'Juho' or 'Jussi'. Sometimes the surnames are written out fully, sometimes in an abbreviated form with the omission of the letters 'n' or 'en' for names ending in '-nen'. Some of the names are given in their standard Finnish- or Swedish-language forms, some in their familiar vernacular forms. For example, Oskari Rosenström's Swedish-language family name is given in this form, but Heikki Rosenström's name appears in the vernacular form 'Hente Ruusens'. The forename 'Konstantin' appears for different persons in the forms 'Kostani' or 'Konstantti'. The names were entered in the list by Tamminen or possibly in some cases by the donors themselves.[700] The

---

697 Although the peasants in the countryside had traditional surnames, the names of the farms owned by them were sometimes used in the records as their surnames (as here: Hiitola). S. Kotilainen 2008a, 298–299.
698 List of donations for Kivijärvi lending library in 1895.
699 List of donations to Kivijärvi lending library in 1895.
700 List of donations to Kivijärvi lending library in1895.

different forms show how 'freely' the details of the loans and borrowers were recorded in those days. The identification of individuals was made in relation to the rest of the local community, and instead of a person's surname the name of his or her place of abode, or in the case of a woman, that of her spouse was mentioned after the forename. It was enough for the person who drew up the list that the person in question could be identified locally.[701] As late as 1904, it was decided 'to send round a list in which each person could voluntarily enter an offering' in order to collect funds for the library and (exceptionally) to pay for the salary of the librarian.[702]

Throughout the time of its existence, the privately founded lending library applied for funding from the municipality, but it received very little. In the spring of 1891, it was decided to remind the municipal assembly that it should swiftly implement a decision it had made regarding the library on 24 June 1888. The minutes of the library's board of governors do not reveal just what that decision was, but probably the library was seeking financial or other support from the municipality.[703] Because no municipal minutes for that year are available, the amount of the support that was applied for and the decision of the assembly are veiled in obscurity. In the spring of 1896, the fate of the library was again in the balance, and it was left to the municipal assembly to decide it. The board of governors of the library announced that, if the assembly refused to assist the library, it would be left entirely to its own devices.[704] In the following spring, the chairman of the board of governors Sakari Niemi and the Chief of Police Adrian Svens were chosen to report on the state of the privately founded library to the municipality and to request assistance from it. The funds of the library continued to be low.[705]

There is a really surprising item concerning the library in the minutes of a municipal assembly meeting in February 1898. The members of the assembly had come to the conclusion that the municipality should henceforth support the activities of the library. According to the minutes, it was decided to apply the rules of the privately established library also to the books of the church parish library. However, the loan fees were dispensed with, and only fines continued to be imposed to help finance the library's activities. In addition, the municipality decided to subsidize the maintenance of the library.[706] Thus at that stage it was noticed that the imposition of loan fees at any rate did not increase the number of borrowers. This meant a return to the original idea of free borrowing that had prevailed at the time of the church parish libraries.

---

701 For further details, see S. Kotilainen 2008a, 284–299.
702 KKA, Minutes of the meeting of the board of governors of Kivijärvi lending library, 14/4/1904.
703 KKA, Minutes of the meeting of the board of governors of Kivijärvi lending library, 19/2/1891.
704 KKA, Minutes of the meeting of the board of governors of Kivijärvi lending library, 14/5/1896.
705 KKA, Minutes of the annual general meeting of Kivijärvi lending library, 21/1/1897.
706 Archives of the Municipality of Kivijärvi, Municipal assembly meeting 12/2/1898, 6 §.

The stages in the life of the lending library in the church village become even stranger when we note that the municipal assembly only decided to combine the collections of the libraries in 1898. In the light of the surviving loans registers, however, I had previously arrived at the conclusion that the decision of the municipal assembly to unify the libraries only made official a situation that had prevailed in practice for some time, in which the collections of the libraries constituted one and the same lending library, which was run by the elementary school teacher. In the end, this mystery can only be solved by examining the contents of the libraries' collections more thoroughly.[707] As a result of this decision by the municipal assembly, however, the recording of the registers of loans ceased for some time, and no later registers have been preserved in the library's archive. Part of the reason for this is undoubtedly the fact that the long-serving librarian Sakari Niemi moved away from Kivijärvi to take up a new post as a teacher elsewhere.[708] After his departure, those who replaced him as librarian did not keep such a firm grip on its activities.

The early libraries in the countryside in Finland were usually founded with funds provided by donations. Sometimes a church parish decided to grant common funds for the foundation or support of a library. Generally, after the years of crop failure, money for library activities was no longer available from public funds until the municipal assemblies began to use the money accruing from the taxation of alcohol to support the libraries.[709]

In the 1870s, the municipalities began more generally to take the libraries under their wing and to support them with regular annual subsidies.[710] For example, the activities of the people's library in Helsinki were supported with money collected by the city from the taxation of alcohol.[711] From the end of that decade on, the municipalities in northern Central Finland also began to subsidize local libraries with funds collected from taxes on alcohol and the poll tax. However, these subsidies given by the municipalities were very meagre right up to the early twentieth century.[712] It is known that the Municipality of Kivijärvi supported its library with funds accruing from the taxation of alcohol either side of the turn of the century. For example, in 1898 it decided to divide the funds from the taxation of alcohol that were distributed from the coffers of the province to the municipalities into equal parts between the four elementary schools in the Municipality of Kivijärvi. In addition to the school in the church village, there were elementary schools in the church village of Kinnula and in the villages of Muhola and Pudasjärvi. Exactly the same measure was taken a couple of years later.[713]

---

707 The collections are described in detail in the next chapter. For a similar slow and unclearly defined development from church parish libary to municipal lending library, see Ellä 1994, 12–13.
708 Appendix 1.
709 Järvelin 1966, 40.
710 E. Seppälä 1963, 66.
711 Närhi 1963, 154–156. The same thing happened in Kuopio in 1875. Huttunen 1981, 21–22; Toivanen 2000, 406.
712 Mönkkönen 1988a, 539.
713 Archives of the Municipality of Kivijärvi, minutes of the council meetings on 29/10/1898 and 22/1/1900.

In 1904, the Society for Popular Enlightenment offered the popular libraries the opportunity to apply for donations of books. Heikki Lipponen, the schoolmaster and librarian informed the society that a privately founded lending library was operating in the municipality. According to this information, there was one people's library that had come under the ownership of the municipality by the end of preceding year, i.e. the lending library of Kivijärvi founded by private persons, and the municipality had subsidized its activities over the three previous years as follows: in 1901, no subsidy; in 1902, 61 marks 21 pence; in 1903, 61 marks 32 pence.[714]

In 1904, it was decided to distribute the money accruing from the taxation of alcohol as follows: four fifths was divided equally between the four elementary schools and one fifth equally between those libraries that had ratified sets of rule, with the additional proviso: 'If only one [library] has rules, then let it be given to that one.'[715] In this way, the members of the assembly perhaps strove to ensure that the lending library in the church village would obtain sufficient funds. The clause probably led to Leppälänkylä Library deciding to apply for a ratified set of rules for its activities in 1906. Thus in February 1908, the municipal assembly was obliged to state that out of the money accruing from the alcohol tax, 20 marks would be given to every library that had a set of rules ratified by the provincial governor and the remainder would be divided equally between the four elementary schools of the municipality.[716] The next time when these alcohol tax funds were distributed, it was decided to give each of the municipality's libraries 20 marks for the procurement of an encyclopaedia and to divide the rest equally between the schools to provide clothing assistance for poor pupils.[717]

The municipalities had to use the money given annually to them from the taxation of alcohol for publically beneficial purposes. Most of this money went to funding the operation of elementary schools, but libraries also typically received some share of it.[718] In the early twentieth century, only about a quarter of all popular libraries received regular subsidies from either the municipalities, the parishes or benefactors. For example, in Kivijärvi's neighbouring parish, Perho, a tax of 10 pence was levied on all payers of poll tax to support the library. It was estimated that in 1890 the amounts spent by rural municipalities on libraries accounted for about 0.2 percent of their total expenditure.[719] The financial position of many rural libraries did not improve until the turn of the century or after it.

---

714 KKA, application form for book donations from the Society for Popular Enlightenment 1904.
715 Archives of the Municipality of Kivijärvi, minutes of the council meeting on 5/3/1904.
716 Archives of the Municipality of Kivijärvi, minutes of the council meeting on 22/2/1908.
717 Archives of the Municipality of Kivijärvi, minutes of the council meeting on 21/12/1908.
718 Järvelin 1966, 54–58.
719 Schadewitz 1903, 46, 49–50.

The acquisition of books by Kivijärvi lending library

In Finland, it was generally those persons who had been engaged in the founding of the libraries who were initially responsible for the acquisitions. For example, in the libraries of the countryside in eastern Finland, the acquisitions were taken care of by either the boards of governors, municipal assemblies or separate acquisition committees established by the municipalities.[720]

The resources of Kivijärvi library were initially modest. In 1888 the private persons who founded it managed to collect enough funds to cover all the projected acquisitions in the early years. The proceeds from a lottery organized on 2 February 1888 amounted to altogether 204 marks, while the expenses incurred by the lottery came to 22 marks 65 pence, the expenses involved in creating a set of rules for the library nine marks 60 pence, the purchase of new books and the repairs to old ones, postal shipping and sundry expenses 124 marks 95 pence, making a total expenditure of 157 marks 20 pence, which when deducted from the proceeds left a residual balance of 46 marks 80 pence. At the same time the loan fees and fines had brought in 30 pence, so there was altogether 47 marks 10 pence in the kitty of the library at the time of its founding meeting in April 1888.[721]

The library had its own account in the Postal Savings Bank, in which the funds were lodged.[722] The availability of literature in the surrounding area was meagre, and orders for books to expand the collection had to be made by post or in other ways. Since the distances involved in the delivery of the books were long, this also involved postal and shipping expenses. Apparently, that was why shopkeeper's son Axel Anjelin was asked to bring back books on his trip to Jyväskylä: in order to avoid the extra costs involved in ordering them. Some really active librarians who had the opportunity to do so, like Matti Taipale in Saarijärvi, went all the way to Helsinki to buy books; he had done this in connection with other business in the capital back in the 1850s. Indeed, at that time it was even more difficult to find literature in Finnish than it was a few decades later.[723]

However, the Kivijärvi library did acquire some new works fairly quickly, a year or two after their publication. For example, some works published in 1891 and 1892 were acquired on 11 February 1894. They included Santeri Ingman's *Reservikasarmissa* [In the reserves' barracks], a translation of H. C. Andersen's *New Fairy Tales* and the collected plays of the Jyväskylä writer Robert Kiljander, the total price of which amounted to 15 marks. It was decided to withdraw the money in the Postal Savings Bank account for this purpose.[724] Price catalogues of the newest books were ordered from

---

720 Järvelin 1966, 76.
721 KKA, Minutes of the founding meeting of Kivijärvi lending library, 9/4/1888.
722 KKA, Minutes of the annual general meeting of Kivijärvi lending library, 26/1/1893.
723 S. Kotilainen 2013a.
724 KKA, Minutes of the annual general meeting of Kivijärvi lending library, 29/1/1894.

the Society for Popular Enlightenment, the bookseller G. W. Edlund and Werner Söderström in connection with the acquisition of these works.[725]

During the early decades of Finland's status as an autonomous grand duchy in the Russian Empire, there were very few books published in Finnish that could be acquired for the collections of Finnish-language popular libraries[726]. However, the number grew, and in the 1850s, about 350 works were published in Finnish, in the 1860s 500 and in the 1870s about 940. A considerable number of these were religious works. The diffusion of literature among the common people was also impeded by the fact that the publishing and printing of works in Finnish failed to develop and by the slowness and the expense of delivering books owing to high postal costs. However, from the 1860s on, rail transport reduced the cost of the delivery of books over long distances. In the early nineteenth century, the publication of books had been expensive, but for the writers the situation was eased by the fact that in the 1830s the Finnish Literature Society began to publish books in Finnish. At the end of the century, the amount of literature published in Finnish started to grow.[727] Until the 1830s, there had been very few bookshops in Finland. In that decade and the following one, however, G. O. Wasenius and A. C. Öhman started up bookshops in Helsinki and Porvoo respectively. Around 1830, the reading population of Finland was just over 20,000 persons out of a total population that was approaching a million and a half.[728]

In the mid-nineteenth century, the publication of books was still a very undeveloped activity that bookshops and presses undertook alongside their other business.[729] Moreover, some writers printed, published and distributed both their own and others' books. Even by the beginning of the 1860s, not a single novel had been written in Finnish. The book markets in the country were very localized: for example, books published in Helsinki might be hard to come by in Turku. The towns of the interior were extremely isolated when it came to new books. For example, a book parcel posted from Helsinki to Kuopio in eastern Finland travelled first to the coast of the Gulf of Bothnia, from there across the sea to Stockholm, whence it went up the country to the town of Haparanda on the northern border between Finland and Sweden and then down to the coastal city of Oulu, from where it was eventually delivered by horse and cart (or sleigh in winter) to Kuopio.[730]

Although so little of the published literature was in Finnish, even in the 1850s about 90 percent of all literature printed and disseminated in Finland ended up being read by the common people. Most of these works were bought not from official bookshops but often from the 'book boxes' of itinerant traders who toured round the countryside and the markets. The

---

725 KKA, Minutes of the meeting of the board of governors of Kivijärvi lending library, 10/4/1895.
726 See also Appendix 4.
727 Karjalainen 1977, 39–44; Sulkunen 2004.
728 Mäkinen 1999, 173.
729 Leino-Kaukiainen 1990, 8.
730 Häggman 2008, 12, 24, 26.

bookbinders also sold books wholesale to the itinerant traders for them to sell on. The contemporary intelligentsia tended to forget that most of the literature that spread around Finland in the nineteenth century had been written in the sixteenth and seventeenth centuries. On the other hand, the obsolescence of the language and ideas expressed by it did not worry either the intelligentsia or the ordinary people of the time. Thus there were two different kinds of markets for books in the country, and the larger one was definitely not for new works on contemporary themes.[731]

In the early decades of the nineteenth century in Finland, more Swedish-language works of fiction published and printed in the former mother country of Sweden were sold than works published in Finland itself.[732] In the 1850s around 30 titles of fiction and other forms of imaginative literature were published in Finnish, in the 1860s just under 80, and in the 1870s about 190.[733] Although up to that time, more literature had been published overall in Swedish than in Finnish, in the beginning of the 1870s the numbers evened out, and in the 1880s, the annual number of titles published in Finnish exceeded that of Swedish-language publications. In 1905, about 30 percent of the literature that was published was in Swedish and 70 percent in Finnish. The production of books in Finland gradually grew from the 1860s on, but the 1880s and the turn of the century were periods of particularly vigorous activity. The Finnish language took a strong hold in the schools, and a lot of new schoolbooks in Finnish were needed. Similarly, the amount of fiction and other creative literature in Finnish grew. The printing industry was also rapidly becoming mechanized at that time.[734]

Several new publishing houses and bookshops were established at the end of the nineteenth century: Weilin & Göös and Gummerus in 1872, Werner Söderström (WSOY) in 1878, Otava in 1890, the Swedish-language Söderström & Co in 1891 and Arvi A. Karisto in 1900. The first proper bookshop, that of G. O. Wasenius, was established in Helsinki in 1823, and by 1859 there were 16 bookshops in the city, 39 in 1877, and 56 in 1900.[735] Two lecturers at the Teacher Training Seminary, K. G. Göös and A. G. Weilin, began their business activities in Jyväskylä in 1872, when they established a bookshop, a press and a bindery with the object of publishing Finnish-language textbooks for the elementary schools. However, the company soon concentrated its activities on the production of specialized printed matter like accounts books, and in 1883 it moved to Helsinki in search of a better market.[736] In the period 1874–1918, another important and successful publisher of Finnish-language literature that was understandable by the common people was the Society for Popular Enlightenment.[737] All this activity considerably increased the amount of literature in Finnish that was available, which in turn facilitated the activities of popular libraries.

731 Häggman 2008, 72–74.
732 Mäkinen 1999, 172–176.
733 Järvelin 1966, 6.
734 Häggman 2008, 179, 278–279; K. Laitinen 1997, 154.
735 K. Laitinen 1997, 154.
736 Leino-Kaukiainen 1990, 9–10.
737 Häggman 2008, 216; Karjalainen 1977, 39–44.

The books in the oldest collection of Kivijärvi library came from a wide variety of different publishers (e.g. Edlund, Frenckell, Karsten, Lillja). Later, there was a clear concentration in the acquisition of books, and according to the library's loan registers and book catalogues over a quarter of the works in the library's collection were published by WSOY.[738] A bookshop was established in Saarijärvi in 1880, and bookshops were also opened in Viitasaari and Karstula at the beginning of the nineteenth century.[739] Despite this, the privately founded library in Kivijärvi also acquired books by sending members to Jyväskylä to buy them or ordering them by post.[740]

The average lending library in Central Finland contained 208 volumes, while the average for the whole country was 326.[741] Originally, the people's libraries fitted onto a few shelves; in other words, the medieval tradition of small Finnish libraries continued. At the beginning of 1889, there were 40 books available for borrowing in the library of Kivijärvi, but the number was expected to rise soon to a hundred. The founders of the library, who were responsible for the acquisition of books, wanted to retain the right to decide what they thought would be suitable reading for the local people. The 1889 annual general meeting of the members of the library decided to acquire for the library a batch of books brought by Axel Anjelin in Jyväskylä, although some works were rejected. The minutes of the meeting do not reveal what the rejected books were. New books were loaned unbound to borrowers in order to save costs and thereby accumulate funds for the library. It was also decided to have a bookcase made for the collection.[742] This was to be made by Kalle Rein by March 1889. In the annual general meeting in February 1891, it was decided to have the bookcase painted 'at least with an undercoat'.[743]

The first acquisitions of the library established in 1888 were new books and number labels to be attached to them. The books of the old collection of the library in the church village were also to be repaired with the funds of the new library. A label was affixed to the cover of each book stating the name of the library, the index number and price of the book and the main conditions of lending stipulated by the board of governors in Sections 5 and 7 of the rules of the library.[744] The library tried to make recently acquired books available to the customers as soon as possible once they had been furnished with these labels and given an index number.[745]

---

738 KKA, Loans registers (1877–1897) and collection catalogues of Kivijärvi lending library.
739 Mönkkönen 1988a, 537.
740 KKA, Minutes of the meetings of the board of governors of Kivijärvi lending library, 1888–1912.
741 Mönkkönen 1988a, 539.
742 KKA, Minutes of the Annual General Meeting of Kivijärvi lending library, 27/1/1889. In Nivala, too, the books were kept in a cupboard reserved for the collection. H. Mäkelä 1991, 22.
743 KKA, Minutes of the meeting of the board of governors of Kivijärvi lending library, 19/2/1891; Accounts of Kivijärvi lending library 1889.
744 KKA, Minutes of the meeting of the board of governors of Kivijärvi lending library, 9/4/1888.
745 KKA, Minutes of the meetings of the board of governors of Kivijärvi lending library, 6/6/1895 and 14/5/1896.

The increase in civic associations and social activeness in the late nineteenth century together with a rise in the standard of living and an increase in reading literacy created a readership for new Finnish works. Economically, too, the time was favourable for profitable business activities in publishing. The period of Finland's autonomy under Russia was generally one of very favourable economic growth since the country experienced a time of almost unbroken peace, and Finnish industry, thanks to the prevailing fiscal and customs policy, enjoyed a significant competitive advantage over its Russian counterpart. Furthermore, the enactment of freedom of trade and the liberation of retail trade in the countryside after the mid-century meant that the rural people, who constituted 90 percent of the population, no longer needed to travel to a few distant towns and rarely held markets to buy their wares. A lot of new money came into the countryside with the sale of forests and the development of lumbering and dairy farming. The domestic markets grew as the prices of basic commodities remained almost the same for several decades and the wage levels of the working class rose. Books, often sold in the form of cheap series of booklets, were among the first consumables to be aimed at the masses.[746]

Suomen Kustannusyhdistys (the Finnish Book Publishers Association) was founded in 1857. There was already a bookshop in almost every Finnish town, but the commercial conditions were poor. Generally, the business took place on commission with the publisher sending a large stock of his books to the shopkeeper, who had the right to return unsold copies. This was really the only way for the publisher to distribute large numbers of books, but it was also a risky activity. The accounts were settled once a year, and there was no proper system of guarantees. Many of those who sold books on commission neglected to settle their accounts with the publishers, and many might also go bankrupt during the course of the year. The Book Publishers Association addressed this issue, and commission rights, credit and confirmed sales prices together with accompanying reductions were awarded only to booksellers approved by the association. Later, the book trade rights were acquired by the Finnish Book Publishers Association, which was controlled by large publishing houses, and new rights to sell books were awarded only after strict consideration.[747]

In the nineteenth century, the price of a book was not determined by the daily market: it was always fixed and printed on the cover. Therefore, the publisher had to be able to predict the price and the size of the edition that would enable him to make a profit. Nor did the bookshops operate in a free market environment; rather the field was regulated and governed by attempts to limit the book trade to specialist shops. From the societal perspective, a book was an important instrument of education. Bookshops and publishers were regarded as responsible cultural institutions, which were supported by the state, the university and the press. The Finnish book market was intentionally created to serve the ends of the national awakening. The modern market for books came into being in Finland in the period

746 Häggman 2001, 9–12.
747 Häggman 2001, 14–15.

between 1880 and 1914. It was only then that newspapers, non-fiction literature and domestic *belles lettres* began to reach the whole population as transportation conditions, the book trade, literacy, the publicity received by books and the demand for them all reached levels that permitted publishers to print larger run-offs. The whole concept of reading was also changing radically. The elementary schools had produced a new generation of readers whose literacy skills were noticeably better than those of their forbears and who were constantly in search of new reading material.[748]

The publishers noticed at an early stage the significance of popular libraries for increasing the consumption of literature. As early as 1861 a catalogue of books recommended for people's libraries was published and distributed free of charge. It contained over a thousand works, half of which were religious. It could be ordered from G. L. Söderström's bookshop in Porvoo.[749] Söderström also advertised his books in newspapers,[750] as did other publishers. His son, Werner Söderström, set up a publishing house, with the assistance of his father, who was also a notable publisher. Werner Söderström also exploited the networks he had created during his student days with great acumen. When he was a student, he had become acquainted with several of the leading Fennomans, and he later cooperated with them, publishing their works and receiving literary advice from them. Indeed, the main benefit he reaped from his years of study was the creation of this network, not the master's degree he received. Thirdly Söderström had an excellent network of agents in the provinces of Finland. This network consisted of clergymen and teachers who disseminated Fennoman ideals at the local level and were enthusiastic supporters of popular enlightenment.[751]

In Northern Karelia, for example, the lack of regular funds quickly debilitated the financial position of the rural libraries there. The income accruing from loans soon diminished as the customers became familiar with the contents of the collections, and it was not possible to purchase new works owing to the lack of funds.[752] The Society for Popular Enlightenment assisted rural libraries in obtaining books. It published and disseminated literature about contemporary popular libraries, and it provided financial support for struggling libraries. The publications of the society were non-fiction informative works written in easily comprehensible language or guides and handbooks giving practical advice in different areas of life. From the 1870s on, the Society for Popular Enlightenment acted as an agent in procuring books for the people's libraries. At the same time, it recommended to them particular works that it considered suitable. Werkko had proposed a list of works annotated with critical notes in his work that appeared back in 1879. From 1882 on, the society began to sell its books to libraries at half price, and some were even distributed free of charge. In the 1880s, the lists of works that the society recommended to the people's libraries were drawn

748 Häggman 2001, 15–16.
749 E. Seppälä 1963, 62.
750 *Keski-Suomi*, annual volume 1887.
751 Häggman 2008, 247–249.
752 Järvelin 1966, 60.

up by experts and included in the calendars published by the society.[753] Since the number of titles of works in Finnish was still rather meagre, it was easier to evaluate them with regard to their contents.

The society strove constantly to improve the variety and quality of the collections of the popular libraries. It began to publish a list of books containing a critical assessment of each work and guidelines for running a library. Dr. Valfrid Vasenius' booklet *Neuvoja kansankirjastojen hoidosta* [Advice on running popular libraries] together with a list of 486 books that were suitable for people's libraries appeared in 1891. The list was checked and approved by a committee of the Society for Popular Enlightenment before it was published. Realist literature was not readily accepted, since the chairman of the society did not consider it to be appropriate.[754] Both the lists of works published in the calendars of the Society for Popular Enlightenment and those that were issued separately with critical assessments intended for the people's libraries had a strong influence on the contents of the collections of the parish libraries.[755] They represented the upper class's conception of what was suitable and acceptable reading material for the common people.

The enlightenment work of the local enthusiasts in Kivijärvi received further support from an expert source when it was decided in the annual general meeting of Kivijärvi library to apply for (corporate) membership of the Society for Popular Enlightenment.[756] The founding meeting of the Society for Popular Enlightenment had been held in Jyväskylä in 1874, and it immediately attracted numerous members in Central Finland. In its first year of operation, as many as 12 percent of its members were from this region, most of them from the town of Jyväskylä. Later, too, the activities of the society were well supported in the region. Twelve persons from Kivijärvi immediately joined the Society for Popular Enlightenment, including the shopkeeper Juho Anjelin, vicar V. A. Konsin, the chiefs of police Julius Colliander and Nils Holmström, the teachers Daniel Liukkonen and Antti Räsänen and three landed farmers called Gabriel Orava, Antti Kotilainen and Matti Rytkönen (who was later to be the chairman of the Municipal Executive Board).[757] Of these, Konsin and Holmström were chairmen of the board of governors of Kivijärvi Elementary School.

In May 1892 Kivijärvi library's acquisition of books was facilitated when it received a list of works sold through and published by the Society for Popular Enlightenment.[758] In 1902, the society began to publish a critical list of works in Finnish for librarians, which appeared from 1902 to 1907. In 1905, Aksel August Granfelt's *Opas kansankirjastojen hoidossa* [A guidebook for the running of people's libraries] came out.[759] Similar lists

---

753 Inkilä 1960, 74–75, 150, 168–169; S. Kuusi 1946, 347–348; Werkko 1879, 240–241.
754 S. Kuusi 1946, 350–351.
755 Meriranta 1984, 132.
756 KKA, Minutes of the annual general meeting of Kivijärvi lending, 19/2/1891.
757 Inkilä 1960, 38; Mönkkönen 1986, 438; Mönkkönen 1988a, 537.
758 KKA, 'Kivijärven lainakirjastoon v. 1892 Toukok. 15. P.'. List of works recommended by the Society for Popular Enlightenment (books sold through the society and supplied by it).
759 Granfelt 1905; Inkilä 1960, 175; S. Kuusi 1946, 398, 405.

of works suitable for popular libraries were also published in Sweden. In fact, the Swedish lists went so far as to select the literature according to the gender and age of the readers. For example, older men were recommended to read history, travel accounts, biographies and agriculture, while for women religious literature was suggested. Behind these recommendations lay the contemporary idea that the customers of a popular library should not read and educate themselves so much that they would rise above their social station, and the popular enlighteners sought to ensure that this did not happen by controlling what they read.[760]

However, the library of Kivijärvi did not need to buy all its new works as it also received donations of books, usually from persons closely connected with its administration or from other parishioners who took an active interest in popular enlightenment. For example, a landed farmer called Lauri Vesterinen donated the fifth volume of the Finnish translation of Topelius' *Fältskärns berättelser* [Tales of a Barber Surgeon], apparently in 1885, and a couple of years later a member of the municipal assembly called Matti Rytkönen gave a work titled *Runoelmia* [Poesies].[761]

The educated inhabitants of the church village and other members of the highest stratum of its society actively checked the contents of the works in the library's collection when they served on the board of governors. Thus the books that were acquired for the collection always underwent a form of 'pre-censorship' by the board of governors. A joint meeting of the members of the library and the board of governors in 1890 discussed the acquisition of new books, but it was decided to give up the idea apparently for financial reasons and to limit the acquisitions to immediately ordering 10 volumes of the calendar published by the Society for Popular Enlightenment.[762]

In 1895, four works were purchased for the library, and one work was donated to it (*Risuja* [Scraps], a collection of writings compiled by pupils of Tampere Teacher Training Lyceum; it was donated by Toivo Anjelin, who had attended this school himself).[763] The desire of the board of governors to control the contents of the library's works is indicated by the following statement: "The list of works of donated to the library by the Society for Popular Enlightenment was approved with a number of reservations. It was decided to express pure gratitude to the donators for this precious gift.[764] Thus not even all the literature sent by the Society for Popular Enlightenment seems to have been suitable reading for the commons in the opinion of some members of the board of governors.

For a small library like that of Kivijärvi, the advice and support offered by the Society for Popular Enlightenment were particularly important, and so every effort was made to ensure that it should continue to receive them. For

---

760 Jarlbrink 2010, 51.
761 KKA, loans registers of Kivijärvi lending library 1877–1897.
762 KKA, Minutes of a joint meeting of the members and the board of governors of Kivijärvi lending library, 29/1/1890.
763 KKA, Minutes of the annual general meeting of Kivijärvi lending library, 24/1/1895.
764 KKA, Minutes of the meeting of the board of governors of Kivijärvi lending library, 14/5/1896.

example, in 1897 it was decided to pay the membership fee to the Society for Popular Enlightenment in arrears as it had not been paid on time owing to a lack of sufficient funds.[765] In the 1890s, more than 750 new people's libraries were established in Finland, over three times more than in the previous decade. This development was influenced above all by the regular annual support provided by the Society for Popular Enlightenment for popular libraries from 1896 onwards. The society distributed a collection of books to the value of 50 marks to 20 poor people's libraries on the condition that each library spent an equivalent sum of its own on the purchase of books in the same year. The Werner Söderström publishing company also donated 20 collections worth 50 marks each for the society to use. Altogether 120 applications for assistance were received. Gradually the society accumulated more assistance funds so that in 1903, for example, it was able to provide subsidies amounting to 9555 marks for altogether 141 libraries.[766]

The majority of Finnish rural lending libraries at the turn of the century had fewer than 200 works available for borrowing. There were few libraries (less than 10 percent of the total number) that contained over 500 books. The value of the stock of most libraries was estimated to be at most 500 marks in the mid-1870s. Most of the people's libraries in towns at that time contained over 1000 works and had a monetary value of over 1000 marks.[767] Kivijärvi lending library was typical in that its stock of books was very small, and there certainly was not always sufficient new reading material to serve the needs of fast readers. The selection of works for the collection was determined by the personal tastes of the board of governors, and donations of books were perhaps often a way for them to get rid of 'unnecessary' or surplus works that had collected on their own bookshelves; in any case, it was to a great extent a matter of charity.

If we think of the 21st century, the fundamental purpose of a library is to offer its customers whatever important or necessary information they happen to need at any particular time. In Central Finland in the nineteenth century, a library offered whatever its resources permitted, and the importance and necessity of the information offered was determined by those who decided about the acquisitions. However, at least on the basis of the minutes of the meetings of the members and the board of governors of the library, nobody seems to have complained about the contents of the collection of Kivijärvi lending library. That was not the custom in those days. The customers of the rural libraries did not have the same opportunities to decide for themselves what they could read as the customers of libraries in towns, where more literature was available. In the countryside, the decisions were made by others, who had had more schooling or were of a higher social station; in other words, a person's ability to write often meant that he or she had power

---

765 KKA, Minutes of the meeting of the board of governors of Kivijärvi lending library, 21/1/1897. In the following year, the library decided to pay the a and b series fees, amounting to six marks. KKA, Minutes of the meeting of the board of governors of Kivijärvi lending library, 28/1/1898.
766 S. Kuusi 1946, 401–403.
767 Schadewitz 1903, 32–33, 35.

over what was read in the parish.[768] However, the minutes of the meetings of the board of governors of Kivijärvi library did not record precisely who decided which works should be acquired. Apparently, the decisions were eventually reached by a consensus.

When one considers the development of publishing in the nineteenth century, it is no wonder that for example the collection of Kivijärvi library was not particularly extensive, especially since it was also necessary to travel long distances to obtain the books. Certainly, the acquisition of books became brisker towards the end of the century, but from the point of view of the borrowers a significant proportion (just under 40 percent) of the works that were acquired before 1897 were published prior to the 1880s, while about 35 percent of the collection had been published in the 1880s.[769] Even so, the collection contained not only works of Finnish-language Fennoman literature but also some important classics of world literature that were read all over Europe, albeit perhaps not to the same extent any longer in the 1880s.

The organization of the library and practical lending activities

THE IDEAL OF PRECISE ORDER AND REGULATED OPERATIONS

The library of Kivijärvi has already been examined above as a spatial entity. A rural library shared the space in which it operated with other activities, so that the library only existed in the space reserved for it during its opening hours, concretely in the form of bookshelves in a bookcase. However, the library can also be regarded as an entity of order, defined by the provisions of its rules and its board of governors, and from these we can ascertain the reasons for, and the principles of, its activities. A library can also be seen an opportunity, as a contributory factor defining the identity of the reader and as an imagined ideal (in the same way as an 'imagined nation') or as an instrument for the exercise of power.[770]

For example, the people's libraries of the nineteenth century were a manifestation of the exercise of power by the higher social groups and their need to educate the peasants. When the books of a library were loaned to the parishioners, the rules of the library as an organization and the power of the librarian extended indirectly into the homes of the borrowers. However, it was in the selection of works for the library's collection that the board of governors exercised its power to the greatest extent. Since the library constituted a concentration of the use of power at the local level, its organization also reveals something about the values and mentalities that influenced its operation. That is why I study in detail how the books were loaned and borrowed, because these practices indicate where the borrower was located in this power system.

---

768 Jarlbrink 2010, 45. I examine people's informational needs and the reception of the collection by them in Chapter 5.
769 KKA, Collection catalogues of Kivijärvi library.
770 Anderson 2006 [1983]; Manguel 2006. I examine these other dimensions of the library in the following chapters.

Since the customers of public libraries were not yet permitted direct access to the shelves to choose their books for borrowing, detailed catalogues (which were published generally in town libraries in Finland as well as in the United States, for example) were indispensible for the customers to be able to find the reading matter they were looking for. It was thought that self-service would not only disturb the order of books on the shelves but would also lead to 'random' reading, which was less desirable than having the customer make his or her choice from a catalogue and not have the book in his or her hands. The compilation of catalogues was complicated by the fact that in the United States, for example, it was very common before the 1870s for the books to be catalogued and arranged on the shelves according to their date of acquisition. Consequently, works on the same subject were generally located far apart from one another on the shelves. Moreover, this practice meant that catalogues and classifications had to be constantly renewed as new acquisitions were made.[771] The preserved archive sources allow us to conclude that this was very typical of the early Finnish lending libraries, too, and the same problems were to be found in the lending library of Kivijärvi.

One of the tasks of the popular libraries was to inculcate a sense of order and responsibility in the people.[772] The new 'proper' way to read in the nineteenth century was to sit immobile and upright with one's arms on the table and to read silently without disturbing others or taking up too much space. One should read in a systematic way, following the order of the book and being careful not to damage it. Reading was considered to be a demanding exercise that required attention and effort. The place for a book at home, too, was in a library or on a special bookshelf.[773] The practice of reading silently was a part the new practice of reading in which the lending libraries aimed to train the people. Borrowed library books were to be handled with care. Initially there were about 500 volumes in Helsinki City Library, and a year later over 800. In the course of a year, the number of loans could exceed 7000, and each volume was borrowed ten times a year on average. The heavy use of the books caused them to become dilapidated. For example, at that time in Norway it was reported that many persons who read library books in bed used the covers of the books to snuff out candles before the advent of oil lamps and electric lights, which resulted in the books getting dirty and smeared with wax.[774]

As late as the 1920s, attempts were made to advise the customers of Finnish libraries about how to act in case an infectious disease broke out at home. Evidently, the fear that books spread infections and the fact that they were dirty put off many of the 'better classes' from using public libraries, and sometimes children, too, were prohibited from borrowing books from libraries.[775] The fear was not altogether unjustified. While in Kivijärvi, for

---

771 Garrison 1979, 4.
772 Jarlbrink 2010, 57.
773 Heikkinen 2013, 229.
774 Hirn 1998, 25.
775 Eskola 1999, 134.

example, on average 65 people died every year in the 1870s, in 1885 the mortality rate had risen sharply as a result of outbreaks of scarlet fever and measles. Of the 162 persons who died in that year, 60 children under 15 years of age died of those diseases.[776] However, there is no mention of anything about contagious diseases or the measures taken to prevent them from spreading in the documents connected with the library.

In the libraries of the nineteenth century, order was the ideal. The greater the number of works in the collection, the more important it became to be able to find the information one needed swiftly. So as to preserve order, the whole library organization was divided into ever smaller parts. For example, in his guidebook for popular libraries in 1905, Granfelt recommended that rural libraries should be organized in such a way that in each municipal centre there would be a main library owned by the municipality and in each elementary school district a privately-owned district library that was subsidized by the municipality. [777]

The systems of classification used by Finnish libraries in the nineteenth century were not generally particularly uniform: each library devised its own method of organizing its collection. Some systems were more detailed than others.[778] Granfelt recommended the American Melvil Dewey's Decimal Classification System, in which the books were divided thematically into ten main categories, and these then subdivided into ten sub-categories designated by Arabic numerals. The books were then arranged in alphabetical order within the sub-categories. It was a simple but efficient system, and it could also be used for ordering larger numbers of books. It also made it possible to locate new acquisitions on the shelves and remove works from the collection more efficiently.[779] However, the thematic classification developed by Dewey himself reflected the world view of his time and place of abode (a phenomenon for which Manguel has used the term 'Anglo-Saxonism'), and therefore was not necessarily applicable all over the world.[780]

It was considered to be indispensible for a library to have a room or premises of its own in order for it to be able to move over to an open shelf system that would allow the customers themselves to pick the books they wanted from the shelves. Although this requirement was considered to be a *sine qua non* for a modern library in Finland, too, at the latest in the 1920s, its implementation had to be postponed. Even in the early 1930s, the libraries of some of the large towns did yet not have a system that permitted the ordering of the books according to their content, and the old system of ordering the books on the shelves according to the time of their acquisition continued to be in use. The first open shelves were used in Porvoo City Library, which was inspired by practices in the United States. At the same time, there was

776 Myllymäki 1986, 100.
777 Granfelt 1905.
778 Järvelin 1966, 80.
779 Garrison 1979, 5. For a further discussion of the development of classification e.g. in France and Germany, see Barnett 1973, 424–430, and Minter 2009.
780 Granfelt 1905; S. Kuusi 1946, 407; Manguel 2006, 57–59.

a shift towards offering the users of the library greater freedom of choice and permitting them to make their own discoveries by sifting through the works. This self-service also made the operation of the library more efficient. A state library committee had already earlier recommended that public libraries should adopt the Dewey decimal classification system for the categorization of books, and its first Finnish adaptation was drawn up in 1913.[781] By 1927, as many as 96 percent of American libraries had adopted Dewey's system of classification.[782]

A Finnish-language guide to Dewey's decimal system was published in 1925, when it was adopted in many libraries. There were no other widely-used categorization systems in use. However, many librarians still did not know how to categorize books or did not see the need to do so, and they considered a division into non-fiction, fiction and worn-out volumes to be sufficient. The most common type of library catalogues in the 1920s were hand-written lists of acquisitions, in which the information was entered directly from the purchased books. The urban libraries published printed catalogues of their collections, which they kept on display in the library premises and sold to their customers. The first catalogues of Helsinki lending library were printed in 1871 using a numerical system indicating the place of the work on the shelves[783]. On the other hand, there were generally no libraries without any kind of catalogue at all. A book was valued as an object and a possession, and the writing of catalogues by hand was part of the process of taking care of this property. The traditional lending system entailed writing down the information about loans by hand in the form of a list ordered according to either the borrowers or the titles of the works. More progressive libraries adopted a card indexing system. In the 1930s, Finnish librarians became acquainted with the Detroit system, which came to be used for several decades.[784]

The categorization and cataloguing of books brought order to small libraries as well. Some of the surviving hand-written catalogues of Kivijärvi library possibly go back to 1889, and the last one dates from 1903–1904. This is clear from the fact that they contain specific dates referring to these periods. Apparently, the catalogues were re-drafted every few years, and the older ones were perhaps destroyed. In Kivijärvi, a subject-ordered cataloguing system was still in use in the early twentieth century. For example, the catalogue of books in the library of Lappeenranta and Lappee was organized from the 1860s on into six thematic categories: religion, history, maps and geography, law, science (i.e. agriculture, mathematics and medicine), and fiction. [785]

The board of governors of Kivijärvi library did not hold regular meetings at three-month intervals, as was recommended by Werkko in his model set of rules, or at least no minutes were taken at them. Nor did the board of

---

781 Eskola 1999, 132; Eskola 2001, 79–80.
782 Garrison 1979, 5.
783 Hirn 1998, 32.
784 Eskola 1999, 133; Eskola 2001, 80.
785 Toivanen 1985, 21.

governors discuss the establishment of village libraries or hold a summer meeting at the turn of May and June to check whether the library's collection was intact and the books undamaged at the beginning of the school's summer holidays.[786] The annual general meetings of Kivijärvi lending library were usually held early in the year, in January or at the latest in February. In other words, the time of the annual general meeting was, typically for associations, at the beginning of the year, when the accounts for the previous year could be examined and an operational plan for the coming year could be drawn up. Thus the choice of the time of the annual general meeting was dictated more by economic and organizational concerns than by the requirements of school work and the schedules of the semesters. However, according to the regulations the meeting had to be convened in January by the board of governors. Usually this was the only meeting held during the year. The annual report for the previous year, the statement of accounts and the library's funds were always examined in the annual general meeting, the board of governors was granted discharge of liability and other decisions concerning the affairs of the library were made.[787]

In exactly the same way, the rules that governed Helsinki people's library up till 1867 stipulated that the annual general meeting should be held in January and that the annual report and a statement of the library's financial situation were to be presented in it. In the same meeting a new board of governors and auditors were elected.[788] In Kivijärvi, the meetings were almost always held in the elementary school, which had become established as the site of the library. Occasionally, meetings were also held at the home of one of the board members, such as that of Elias Jäsberg, the shopkeeper, which was close to the school building.[789]

The convening of the meetings was conducted according to the library's rules. At the turn of the century, most libraries in the countryside did not have any fixed set of rules, although some did have rules ratified by a society, a municipal assembly, the provincial government and even the Senate.[790] There was always some instance that approved the rules, even if it was only the municipality, even though in Kivijärvi, for example, the library was privately owned. Thus in 1888, the proposed set of rules for Kivijärvi library was submitted to the municipal assembly for approval.[791] Just as the municipal assembly was the ratifying body, it was also the library's chief source of support. Even then, the board of governors was already trying to shift the responsibility for the supervision and also the funding of the library to the municipality. The rules drawn up in 1888 remained in force throughout the time Kivijärvi lending library operated. At least the library's

786 Werkko 1879, 255.
787 KKA, Minutes of the meeting of the board of governors of Kivijärvi lending library, 9/4/1888.
788 Hirn 1998, 22.
789 Table 16.
790 Schadewitz 1903, 32.
791 KKA, Minutes of the meeting of the board of governors of Kivijärvi lending library, 9/4/1888.

Table 16. Meetings of the Board of Governors of Kivijärvi lending library 1888–1912.

Year	Number of meetings	Site of meetings
1888	1	Elementary school
1889	1	n/a
1890	1	Pajamäki (Jäsberg)
1891	1	Elementary school
1892	1	Elementary school
1893	1	Elementary school
1894	1	Elementary school
1895	3	Elementary school
1896	2	Elementary school
1897	1	Elementary school
1898	1	Elementary school
1899	0	–
1900	0	–
1901	0	–
1902	0	–
1903	1	Elementary school
1904	1	Elementary school
1905	0	–
1906	0	–
1907	0	–
1908	0	–
1909	0	–
1910	0	–
1911	1	Elementary school
1912	1	Elementary school

n/a = not available
Source: KKA, Minutes of the annual general meetings of Kivijärvi lending library 1888–1912.

records do not show that they were changed at any time. In Central Finland, Hankasalmi library, for example, got its first set of rules in 1881 and then a new set in 1902.[792] The Society for Popular Enlightenment planned model rules for parish and village libraries in the 1890s. They were distributed to all popular libraries, and they were soon generally adopted.[793] Then, at the latest, those libraries that had hitherto functioned in a more informal way began to draw up sets of rules for themselves.

The popular libraries needed constant care and supervision. Books had to be acquired and rendered into a loanable condition: some had to be bound, and all had to be stamped and catalogued.[794] The meetings of the board of governors usually dealt with the acquisition of books, binding, loan times and other matters connected with the operational principles of the library. Librarianship measures were taken to prevent the wear and tear

792 Naumanen 1966, 252.
793 S. Kuusi 1946, 356.
794 Hirn 1998, 22.

of books and to ensure that the library was able to offer the most up-to-date literature despite the fact that the resources available were extremely limited. The minutes of the meetings of the members or of the board of governors contain no mention of the board having insured the collection of books with a fire insurance company. Werkko had also recommended that libraries should reserve 25 marks for book binding, correspondence and other sundry expenses.[795] However, in some other matters the library in Kivijärvi was administered in accordance with Werkko's model rules. For example, the board of governors allowed longer loan times for those works that had more pages. Admittedly, Werkko had pointed out in his instructions that it was not the number of pages alone that determined the reading time involved, but rather the content of the book.

THE LENDING AND CARE OF BOOKS AND THE IMPOSITION OF FINES
In Kivijärvi, it was decided from the very beginning to keep a strict record of the borrowing activities. Borrowing was also restricted in that one borrower could take out at most two volumes at a time for a maximum period of four weeks. However, the rules stated: 'Nevertheless, loans of larger volumes can be renewed once.' Books were not loaned to just anybody, and 'dubious and unknown borrowers' were required to pay a surety for the price of the book.[796] In the same way, in the people's library of Jyväskylä Teacher Training Seminary, the name of every person who borrowed a book was entered beside the title of the book in the loans register. If a borrower was not known to the person registering details of the loan, their address was written after their name.[797]

There were different loaning practices depending on the parish. The oldest loans register of Tampere people's library has been preserved. It was a note book in which the name of the borrower, the title of the borrowed book and in the final column the return date were entered. In practice, the borrowing process took place in such a way that the librarian read out the titles of the works on the shelf, and the first person to raise their hand or call out got to borrow the book they wanted. There was a kind of auctioning of the books, so that people did not need to ask for them in vain. Initially, the customers had got to inspect the contents of the shelves, but because the resulting loss of works was so great, this practice was abandoned in 1862. In Vyborg, the customers got to choose their books directly from the bookshelves.[798] The collection of Kivijärvi fitted into one bookcase, so it is probable that the librarian was able to keep a close check on the contents of the bookcase and recorded the details of the book that was being borrowed as soon as he took it out of the bookcase. No more precise information about the local practice of lending has been preserved.

---

795 Werkko 1879, 253, 255.
796 KKA, Minutes of the meeting of the board of governors of Kivijärvi lending library, 9/4/1888.
797 Lahtinen 1963, 9.
798 Hirn 1998, 28.

Werkko gave the following recommendations on how to handle lending: The librarian should keep two catalogues of the books. In one, they should be entered in the order of their acquisition by the library. The title, author, year and place of publication and the price of the work should be entered in this register. In the other, the books should be categorized according to their subject matter and within each category listed in alphabetical order. The latter catalogue was to be re-drafted every three years, printed by order of the board of governors and sold at a reasonable price to the customers. And if the catalogue was not printed, it should be placed on public view. Information concerning the loan – the year, month and day when the work was borrowed, the name and occupation of the borrower, the name of the village in which he or she resided and, after the book was returned, the date of its return – was to be entered in the loans register. In the case of Kivijärvi, for example, it has been necessary to use a genealogical investigation to ascertain the occupations or social ranks and to a great extent also the places of abode of the borrowers in order to be able to supplement the information in the original register. According to Werkko's instructions, the index number of the book and the name of the library that owned it were to be written on the cover of every book. A paper label with the number of the book was to be pasted on the back cover in order to make it easier for the librarian to find the book.[799]

Werkko presumed that the librarians would keep extremely exact annual records of the numbers of works borrowed from the popular libraries, the gender distribution of the borrowers and the numbers of works borrowed by individual borrowers as well as of the times of the year in which the borrowing activity was concentrated, how the use of the library was distributed between different social groups and what subjects were of most interest to the readers. Moreover, he proposed that the librarian should check for possible causes if there was a falling-off in borrowing and record what books the customers found difficult to read. One can easily understand that it would take decades before rural librarians would have the opportunity to carry out such a detailed analysis. This is particularly obvious when one examines the information that has survived about the lending activities of the libraries. Certainly, in principle, the librarians could have come at least close to carrying out the statistical measures outlined by Werkko if they had wished to, but in Kivijärvi at any rate not even the elementary school teachers who served as librarians on the side undertook the compilation of such extensive statistics.[800]

What is particularly striking about the activities of the lending library established by private persons in Kivijärvi is the fact that, although its proclaimed aim was to expand the use of the library, the numbers of loans[801] would seem to have suffered a decline just when the library was intensifying its activities in 1888. In the previous year, the number of loans had been over 200, but over the next five years ever fewer books were borrowed. The board

---

799 Werkko 1879, 256–257.
800 Werkko 1879, 258, 261.
801 For a further discussion of these, see the following chapter.

of governors commented on the situation in 1890 as follows: 'Borrowing has been appreciably lower than in the previous year, one substantial reason for which is probably the fact that there have not been temporary visitors residing in the area and using the library as in the previous year, and perhaps the fines have also frightened off some thoughtless borrowers.' In February 1891, it was decided to re-invigorate the lending activities of Kivijärvi library by sending out catalogues of the books that were available for borrowing to the larger village communities.[802] Despite the fact that the library offered its customers not only the services of the librarian but also assistance of this kind in finding books that were personally suitable for them, borrowing in that year continued to be less active than it had been before.[803]

The library strove to take the best possible care of its small collection. For example, in the case of an illustrated work about Finland, '… it was decided to lend [it] out only to people who would take good care of the book in every way'.[804] In the early times, libraries were recommended to lend out books not only to permanent inhabitants of the municipality but also to temporary residents against a security. It was not until 1928 that the free loan of books became the general policy of public libraries in Finland. Late returns or damage to a book, on the other hand, were to be subject to fines.[805] The library of Alajärvi in Southern Ostrobothnia initially even sent out reminders by post. In 1872, the librarian, a church warden called Matti Paavola, sent a letter to Pastor Johan Helenius asking him to return a book that his son had borrowed from the library (apparently on behalf of a maidservant at the vicarage). The book in question was *Suomen kansan satuja ja tarinoita* [Fairy stories and tales of the Finnish people]. The pastor answered the letter and stated that the price of the unreturned book would be paid together with a compensation for the weeks when the book had been missing.[806]

Werkko's model rules, too, proposed fines for the failure to return a book on time. They also stipulated that, if a book was damaged when it was out on loan, the borrower should be obliged to recompense the library for the price of the book.[807] The annual reports appended to the minutes of the annual general meetings of Kivijärvi library mention the names of those persons who had failed to pay their fines during the previous year. On the other hand, it was also mentioned if a customer had paid up his or her overdue fines.[808] Admittedly, it would appear that in some years in the 1890s, despite the strict regulations, the officers of the library sometimes intentionally incurred fines for overdue loans themselves in order to subsidize the operation of the

---

802 KKA, Minutes of the annual general meeting of Kivijärvi lending library, 19/2/1891. (Annual report for 1890.)
803 KKA, Minutes of the annual general meeting of Kivijärvi lending library, 15/2/1892. (Annual report for 1891.)
804 KKA, Minutes of the meeting of the board of governors of Kivijärvi lending library, 6/6/1895.
805 Eskola 1999, 134.
806 Kivipelto 1966, 236–237.
807 Werkko 1879, 261.
808 E.g. KKA, minutes of meetings of the board of governors of Kivijärvi lending library, 1890–1891, 1893.

library. One inevitably gets this impression from the fact that persons like the mistress of a farm called Riikka Vesterinen and the son of Chief of Police Ivar Fröjdman received fines for overdue loans in 1893.[809] In 1897, fines were paid by Elis Björnholm (a head pharmacist), Toivo Anjelin (the son of the shopkeeper), Riikka Westerinen, a landed farmer called Juho Puranen and E. Tainio.[810] Of course, it is also always possible that they simply failed to return the books they borrowed on time.

The sums accruing from the fines imposed by the library established in Kivijärvi by private persons amounted to only a few marks. It was decided in 1891 to call in the unpaid overdue fines by announcing them in church.[811] In the following year's annual general meeting, it was stated: 'The previous year's annual report was read and examined item by item, and it was decided that the old fines mentioned in 1 § of the minutes amounting in total to 1 mark 10 pence, which are also mentioned in the annual report of the previous year, should be annulled and cancelled since they have not been paid despite being publically announced and politely requested.'[812] In its early years, the funds of the library in Leppälänkylä accrued mainly from loan fees of 5–10 pence per book. In addition, fines for the overdue return of books were paid, but these amounted to very little.[813] The funding of acquisitions was to a great extent dependent on the payment of fees and loans. Although Kivijärvi municipal assembly decided to get rid of loan fees in 1898, they were soon reinstituted, at least temporarily. In 1904, the loan fee of 10 pence a book in Kivijärvi was restricted to only those works that contained 300 pages or more. For other books, the fee was only 5 pence.[814]

Kaarle Werkko's model rules forbade the binding of several works together. In that way, customers would not be prevented from reading works that had been bound together with others that were on loan to someone else.[815] However, this recommendation had to be circumvented because of the library's lack of resources. Books were usually purchased for rural libraries like the one in Saarijärvi, for example, from the publishers in soft-bound form, and the libraries then had them stitched together under hard covers by book binders. This practice of binding several works together was undertaken for economic reasons, and it causes difficulties in calculating the numbers of works possessed by the libraries.[816] Before the nineteenth century, books were hardbound individually everywhere. Generally, the

---

809 KKA, Minutes of the annual general meeting of Kivijärvi lending library, 29/1/1894.
810 KKA, Minutes of the annual general meeting of Kivijärvi lending library, 21/1/1897.
811 KKA, Minutes of the meeting of the board of governors of Kivijärvi lending library, 19/2/1891.
812 KKA, Minutes of the meeting of the board of governors of Kivijärvi lending library, 15/2/1892.
813 Names and loans register of Leppälänkylä lending library. A. Kotilainen 1979, 5.
814 KKA, Minutes of the meeting of the board of governors of Kivijärvi lending library, 14/4/1904.
815 Werkko 1879, 262.
816 Suomela 1963, 657–658.

books were sewn by hand, and the binding of each copy of the book was carried out separately, even in the case of so-called trade bindings (i.e. commercial bindings of multiple copies of the same book prior to sale).[817]

In 1890 in Kivijärvi, it was decided 'for the time being to lend out soft-bound books and to have only those that were in most need of repair hard-bound'.[818] In 1892, a decision was taken to have the "'disintegrating' books of Kivijärvi library hard-bound in Saarijärvi as before. The transportation of the books back and forth was agreed with the postman.[819] The same procedure continued in the following year.[820] Right up to 1894, Sakari Niemi was entrusted with the task of having several books hard-bound.[821] In 1897, it was noted that there were probably no funds available for this. Nevertheless, it was decided to facilitate borrowing by keeping some works that had been published in serial format hard-bound together for the time being, so that the loan fee for a single volume was charged for them. Such works included an anthology of short stories by folk writers titled *Syvistä riveistä* [From the deep ranks of the people], a translation of Louis Thomas's *Les fabuleuses inventions* [Fabulous inventions], Bergroth's *Suomen kirkon historia pääpiirteissä*än [The main features of the history of the Finnish Church] (for which it was planned to acquire parts 9 and 10), Danielson-Kalmari's *Suomen sota ja sotilaat v. 1808–1809* [The Finnish War and Finnish soldiers, 1808–1809] and a translation of Zachris Topelius' *Läsning för barn* [Reading for children]. It was also decided to extend the loan time as required.[822]

In the following year, it was decided to have the books of the library that were in the worst condition hard-bound 'as far as funds permitted, by the policeman [Pekka] Kotilainen'.[823] From the beginning of 1901 on, the library's new acquisitions were hard bound by a craftsman from Saarijärvi called Sirén and on either side of the turn of 1901 and 1902 by a policeman called Pekka Kotilainen. It is probable that the books had also been bound previously by Sirén, but having the work done by Kotilainen in the same parish was cheaper than sending them to Saarijärvi. Another reason for this new arrangement might have been the fact that Kotilainen was willing to bind some of the books on credit. In 1901, the cost of binding books alone was 27 marks (some of which was paid to Sirén), while at the beginning of 1902 Kotilainen agreed to bind books to the extent of 33 marks

---

817 Dane 2012, 25–26.
818 KKA, Minutes of the annual general meeting of Kivijärvi lending library, 29/1/1890.
819 KKA, Minutes of the annual general meeting of Kivijärvi lending library, 15/2/1892.
820 KKA, Minutes of the annual general meeting of Kivijärvi lending library, 26/1/1893.
821 KKA, Minutes of the annual general meeting of Kivijärvi lending library, 29/1/1894.
822 KKA, Minutes of the annual general meeting of Kivijärvi lending library, 21/1/1897.
823 KKA, Minutes of the annual general meeting of Kivijärvi lending library, 28/1/1898.

on credit.[824] Pekka Kotilainen, who was born on Rasi Farm in the village of Penttilänkylä, himself borrowed books from the library, and he appears to have been good at the job of book-binding or at least interested in it.[825]

A closer analysis of the practical lending activities of Kivijärvi library shows that in the late nineteenth century, the use of power in libraries was hierarchical, and it was strictly governed by such factors as the library's set of rules. Even so, in the countryside it was in many respects possible to exercise some flexibility when practical needs so required. For example, books could be borrowed outside regular opening times, loan times could be extended and the registration of information about the borrowers could be less strict, at least if the borrower was familiar and was otherwise a person who was known to take proper care of his or her affairs and work. Probably the idea behind this was in this way the popular education of at least a small group, the customers of the library, would be furthered. Despite these concessions, however, the authority and position of the librarian and the board of governors were not questioned.

The boards of governors of the local parish libraries thus took responsibility for the small details of running them. The practical work involved, however, was always the responsibility of the librarian. In the early years, the continuity of the membership of the board of governors of Kivijärvi library created greater stability, as did the long term of office of the librarian, Sakari Niemi. Later, financial difficulties impeded the envisioning of future activities and long-term strategic planning. However, the librarian could, if he so wished, strive constantly to direct the development of activities, as for example Matti Taipale, the librarian of Saarijärvi, did in the early days of the library there. The contents of the collection of a library, the choice of which was also the most important goal of the activities of the board of governors, provide further information about the results of the librarian's work.

Summarizing, one can conclude that Fennomania and popular education endeavours had a significant influence on the foundation and development of lending libraries in remote regions as well. The persons who were members of the boards of governors usually belonged to the higher strata of society and were significant figures in the local community. The clergy had a strong influence in promoting the activities of popular libraries, while elementary school teachers took care of the running of the libraries as part of their teaching duties. Elementary schools often provided premises for the libraries and the scene where borrowing took place. The financial position of lending libraries in the countryside remained weak for a long time and various voluntary contributions were needed to make them viable. Despite this, it seems to have been a matter of honour with the promoters of popular enlightenment to ensure that the libraries continued to function despite intermittent difficulties: the existence of the library signified the partial achievement of their goals. In this sense, it was possible to use the people's library to create in the countryside a cradle of written information, which concomitantly made it possible to increase the people's immaterial capital

---

824 KKA, Accounts of Kivijärvi lending library, 1901–1902.
825 Kivijärvi READERS.

and to lower the threshold between the educated classes and the common people. In spite of this, the libraries slightly continued to bear the stamp of institutions where the enlightenment was handed down from above since rarely did ordinary people themselves participate in influencing the practical activities of the library.

4. The Book Collections

The extent and the contents of the collections

THE VALUE OF THE COLLECTIONS AND THE GENRES OF
LITERATURE IN THEM

In 1860, the parish of Kivijärvi had just over 3100 inhabitants, the same number as a decade later. At that time, the collection of the lending library in the church village comprised only a few dozen books. Half-way through the 1870s, the collection in the school in the church village contained 140 works.[826] Thus if each of the works in the library had been out on loan at the same time,[827] under five percent of the population would have been able to read them at any one time. On the other hand, the collections of rural parish libraries generally were not necessarily any bigger. The average number of volumes in libraries in the Province of Vaasa in 1875 was 191, and their monetary value was about 291 marks.[828] However, an assessment of the size of the collection of Kivijärvi library and its expansion at different times is fraught with problems because the information about it varies widely. I shall now examine the contents of the collection in greater detail. Such an examination reveals the founders' plans and goals for the library, while the number of loans is an indication of the views and preferences of the borrowers.

According to the statistics of Schadewitz, in 1895 there were 78 works, amounting in value to 312 marks, in the collection of the library that had been founded in the church village of Kivijärvi in 1862. In the privately

---

826 Berner 1878, 94. While the titles of translated works have generally been given in their original form, in a few cases it has not been possible for me to ascertain the title of the original work with certainty, and thus the title of the Finnish translation is given in the text. In some cases it may be that the Finnish works consist of collected excerpts which do not correspond to single works in the original language.
827 Here it has been assumed that the books were not hard-bound together, but it is very possible that at least some of them were bound together under soft covers, which would mean that the number of volumes available for borrowing would have been even fewer than 140.
828 Werkko 1879, 200.

established library in Kivijärvi, for its part, there were 145 works totalling 399 marks in value in 1896. For the purposes of comparison, one can further note that there were 102 books in the library of Kivijärvi Youth Association in 1903, and their monetary value was 80 marks.[829] What is particularly striking in the collection catalogues of the library that have survived from the 1870s is that a collection of 79 devotional works was continuously catalogued separately from more secular non-fiction and works of *belles lettres*.[830] A closer scrutiny of these works reveals an interesting fact: a considerable number of them had in fact belonged to the older collection of the church parish library and were apparently incorporated in the collection of the privately founded library.

The suggested theory about the 'joint operation' of the parish lending library in the church village and the library founded by private persons in one and the same premises earlier in this book is corroborated by a small side mention attached to the collection catalogues of the library. It states: 'The monetary value of the spiritual works of the library when they were purchased in June 1889 was about 319 marks and the value of the newer library about 265 marks.'[831] In other words, it was decided in 1889 to buy the old collection of religious works of the church parish library for the privately founded library. This small scrap of information proves that in practice the two libraries had already been merged at that time, although the municipality did not make an official decision on this matter until 1898. Moreover, since the minutes of meetings of the board of governors and the annual general meetings of the library between 1888 and 1912 mention the acquisition of the same works that are recorded in the loans registers as having been borrowed, there is reason to assume that the same registers were also used by the privately established library. They contain mentions of some purchases in the 1890s and more exact records of acquisitions in 1903 and 1904.[832] Thus the 'same' library (with whatever remained of the works in its collection) that had been established by members of the clergy decades earlier continued to function under the auspices of the association of private persons.

The ownership of the collections was generally not very clearly recorded anywhere in Finland when the first popular libraries began to be founded. The libraries were often established as a result of the endeavours of active library enthusiasts; in the early days, they received numerous denotations, and funds were also acquired through money collections. When the clergy established many of the first people's libraries, they often took care of the book collections, and therefore the books were generally regarded as the property of the church parish. In practice, over the course of time and an abatement in the activities of the libraries concerned, many of these collections passed into the ownership of the municipalities. Along with

---

829 Schadewitz 1903, 102.
830 KKA, Collection catalogues of Kivijärvi lending library.
831 KKA, Collection catalogues of Kivijärvi lending library.
832 KKA, Minutes of the meetings of the board of governors and annual general meetings of Kivijärvi lending library 1888–1912.

the establishment of elementary schools, the old book collections of the church parish libraries were then transferred to them. In many cases, private associations also took over the care of the old collections received from the church parishes. On the other hand, it was rare for any official decisions to be made regarding changes in the ownership of the libraries, and sometimes the authentication of the ownership of the old book collections continued into the early twentieth century.[833]

According to the minutes of meetings of the annual general meeting of the lending library, at the beginning of 1899 there were 40 books available for borrowing in Kivijärvi library. Apparently, only repaired and hardbound works were included in this number since the figure deviates so much from those mentioned above. However, the number of available works was expected to rise to 100 in the near future.[834] The library founded by private persons loaned out books from the old collection of the church parish library, but it also added new works to this collection. The incorporation of the old collection into that of the library founded by private persons can be verified by comparing information about the works mentioned in the loans registers of the privately established library with marks in the books of the old church parish library because many of the surviving works have index numbers that match those of the works in the catalogue. Thus, in the period from 1870 to 1910, the collection of the library also comprised the works of the two earlier libraries to the extent that they had survived and were in a good enough condition to be borrowed.

Few (under 20 percent) of the works belonging to the oldest church parish collection have survived, which makes it impossible to ascertain the dates of publication of all the works from the books themselves. The dating of the books is partly based on the fact that in the case of older books the purchase price of an individual book in marks is not recorded in the catalogues of the library that was founded by private persons in the 1880s, whereas it is for those that were acquired at the turn of the 1870s and 1880s.[835] Consequently, one can adduce that the unpriced books belonged to the older collection, which was acquired in the 1850s (when the prices were often recorded in kopecks) or at the latest in the 1860s. I have thus concluded that, if a price was not marked in the catalogue at the turn of the 1870s and 1880s, it was a case of an older edition of the book.

About one tenth of the books belonging to the oldest collection were according to the available information about publication dates published before the 1840s, 27 percent certainly before the establishment of the library and almost half of them anyway before the 1880s. The year of publication of 25 Finnish-language Bibles belonging to the library is unknown, which means that the years of publication of over 30 percent of the works cannot be ascertained.[836]

---

833 Järvelin 1966, 38–39.
834 KKA, Minutes of the annual general meeting of Kivijärvi lending library 29/1/1889. Annual report for 1888.
835 KKA, Collection catalogues of Kivijärvi lending library.
836 KKA, Collection catalogues and loans registers of Kivijärvi lending library 1877–1897; the old collection of the library; Kivijärvi BOOKS.

The majority (over 60 percent) of the altogether 129 works available for borrowing in the years 1877–1897 were religious. Actual non-fiction works accounted for less than 10 percent and fiction and other forms of creative literature for under 30 percent.[837] This was fairly typical of the collections of rural lending libraries that were acquired during the middle years of the nineteenth century and continued to be actively borrowed down to the end of the century. Of the 168 books acquired for the library of Saarijärvi during its first year of operation, one third consisted of religious literature.[838] Of the 166 books in Alajärvi library in 1866, again about a third (49 works) were religious, 21 books were about historical or geographical subjects, 21 dealt with agriculture or animal husbandry, 48 were works of fiction or other forms of *belles lettres*, and there were 27 miscellaneous works. In the early twentieth century, most of the books were works of fiction or other genres of imaginative literature. From 1868 on, the library in Alajärvi was housed in the sacristy of the church, as was the case in many other parishes, and it was possible to borrow books before or after church services.[839] In early-nineteenth-century Norway, too, the lending libraries of the countryside clearly differed from those of the towns in that most of the books in their collections were works of religious literature.[840] According to the collection catalogues, altogether a little under a half of the works in Kivijärvi library represented various genres of *belles lettres*, a quarter were religious and slightly over a quarter non-fiction literature.[841]

At the turn of the 1850s and 1860s, the book stocks of popular libraries tended to be composed mainly of religious works. However, in this respect there were certain exceptions to be found among libraries in Central Finland. About one third of the first books to be acquired for the library in Saarijärvi were religious, which at the time was an indication that the persons in charge of the library were very liberal in their outlook, while the library recently established in Keuruu exceptionally procured only Finnish-language secular literature, this despite the fact that the founders of this library, too, were clergymen and the first librarian was the daughter of the parish curate.[842]

By the beginning of the 1880s, a quarter of the books in Kivijärvi library were works of fiction or other types of *belles lettres*. Of the 129 works listed in the loans registers, 85 were written by men, eight by women, one had more than one author, and 35 (including the Bible) were written anonymously. Of the works of *belles lettres*, over 70 percent were written by men, despite the fact that in the eighteenth and especially the nineteenth century women both wrote novels and above all read them. Men were the authors of over 70 percent of all the books in the collection of Kivijärvi library, while only

---

837 KKA, loans registers of Kivijärvi lending library 1877–1897.
838 Junnila 1995, 243. Similar tendency was visible in the collections of neighbouring lending libraries: see also the Karstula library collection of old books.
839 Kivipelto 1966, 235.
840 Eide 2010, 128.
841 It is impossible to determine the type of four works, which could not be identified owing to deficient information in the catalogues. KKA, Collection catalogues of Kivijärvi lending library; the old collection of the library.
842 Rainio 1988; Suomela 1963, 653.

a little over 10 percent were certainly written by women. About a fifth of the books were edited works or had no specific author, and in a few cases it is impossible to ascertain the identity of the writer.[843]

In interpreting the statistical information about the stocks of the library, one should also take into account the fact that the number of volumes does not in all cases mean the same thing as the number of books. Because the libraries strove to save on the cost of binding books, several thinner works were sometimes bound together into one volume.[844] This was also done in Kivijärvi library, for economic reasons.[845] Of the works borrowed from the collection of Kivijärvi lending library between the years 1877 and 1897, about a fifth were under 100 pages in length, while about 16 percent had from 100 to 200 pages, and over 40 percent had more than 300 pages. Correspondingly, about a quarter of the total number of works in the collection had under 100 pages, another quarter 100 to 200 pages and just under a quarter more than 300 pages. The largest works had 700 or 800 pages or more.[846]

Loans statistics of the Kivijärvi lending library

Research on library history has traditionally exploited sources that compare the number of loans with the total size of the local population.[847] Behind this lies the idea that public libraries were intrinsically at the disposal of everyone. However, this statistical method does not give the number of loans in proportion to the number of borrowers because in no age do all members of the population used the services of the library. Particularly when we examine the end of the nineteenth century, we must take into account the fact that first of all the illiterate members of the population did not borrow books from the library, at least not to read themselves, and secondly that the members of the higher social groups for a long time shunned the popular libraries that were available to the general public because they generally had private book collections of their own.

According to Schadewitz's statistics, in almost a quarter of rural libraries the number of loans did not even equal the number of works they contained. This was to a great extent a result of the fact that the collections of small libraries were not updated to keep pace with the readers' quest for new reading material.[848] In the light of the borrowing statistics, the activities

---

843 KKA, loans registers of Kivijärvi lending library and the old book collection of Kivijärvi lending library.
844 Karjalainen 1977, 5–6.
845 KKA, loans registers of Kivijärvi lending library and the old book collection of Kivijärvi lending library.
846 In about 13 percent of the works in the collection in the period 1877–1897 and in 15 percent of the books in the total collection of the library, the number of pages cannot be ascertained, or then it varied so greatly from one edition to another that it is impossible to place it in any of the above mentioned categories. KKA, loans registers (1877–1897) and collection catalogues of Kivijärvi lending library and the old collection of books.
847 See e.g. Kelly 1977, 517–519; Laakso 2010, 30.
848 Schadewitz 1903, 37–38.

Table 17. Loans made from Kivijärvi library 1877–1897.

Number of loans

Years	N	%
1877–1882	54	4.3
1883–1887	786	62.7
1888–1892	345	27.5
1893–1897	67	5.3
Not known	2	0.2
Total	**1254**	**100.0**

Source: KKA, loans registers 1877–1897.

Table 18. Annual numbers of loans made from Kivijärvi library 1877–1897.

Number of loans

Years	N	%
1877	4	0.3
1878	1	0.1
1879	3	0.2
1880	1	0.1
1881	3	0.2
1882	41	3.3
1883	179	14.3
1884	87	6.9
1885	132	10.5
1886	168	13.4
1887	220	17.5
1888	175	14.0
1889	90	7.2
1890	43	3.4
1891	25	2.0
1892	12	1.0
1893	11	0.9
1894	17	1.4
1895	14	1.1
1896	19	1.5
1897	6	0.5
Not known	3*	0.2
Total	**1254**	**100.0**

* One work was borrowed in either 1881 or 1882.
Source: KKA, loans registers 1877–1897.

Table 19. *The distribution of literary genres in the collection of Kivijärvi lending library*

Numbers of loans	religious		non-fiction		belles lettres		total	
Years	N	%	N	%	N	%	N	%
1877–1882	23	42.6	1	1.9	30	55.5	54	100.0
1883–1887	292	37.2	109	13.9	385	48.9	786	100.0
1888–1892	265	76.8	24	7.0	56	16.2	345	100.0
1893–1897	67	100.0	–	–	–	–	67	100.0
not known	2	100.0	–	–	–	–	2	100.0
Total	649	51.7	134	10.7	471	37.6	**1254**	**100.0**

Source: KKA, loans registers 1877–1897.

of Kivijärvi library were most lively in the 1880s. However, the number of loans actually decreased in the period after the library was re-established by private persons, when its operations were made more efficient and a set of rules was drawn up for it.[849]

An examination of the annual numbers of loans shows even more clearly how rapidly the use of the library grew in the 1880s. This decade was the heyday of Kivijärvi lending library's activities; thereafter borrowing waned and finally died out altogether for decades.[850] From the 1890s on, the responsibility for library services shifted increasingly from the lending libraries to the elementary schools, but these tended to be used solely by the pupils of the schools rather than the adult population.

In Kivijärvi, most books per day of opening were borrowed in the 1880s. On 29 November 1885, which was the first Sunday in Advent, altogether 10 books were borrowed and the same number on Sunday 23 May 1886. The busiest year in the history of Kivijärvi lending library was 1887, and in the summer of that year the parishioners showed particular enthusiasm for using their library. On Saturday 11 June, altogether 11 works were borrowed and on Saturday 9 July 12 books. The record number of loans in a single day was made on Saturday 20 August, when altogether 16 works were borrowed.[851] Nevertheless, the number of loans in Kivijärvi library did not even remotely approach the figures in Saarijärvi, where altogether 97 loans were made on the busiest Sunday in 1897.[852] However, the loans statistics do show that the use of the library in Kivijärvi was particularly brisk in 1887, and this undoubtedly led to the intensification of library activities and the re-establishment of the library by private persons in the following year.

Fiction and others forms of belles lettres overtook religious literature to become the most favoured reading material in Kivijärvi lending library in the 1870s and 1880s. After the establishment of the library by private persons, however, there took place an interesting reverse trend in the borrowing figures that ran contrary to the predominant development in Finland:

849 Table 17.
850 Table 18.
851 KKA, loans registers 1877–1897.
852 Suomela 1963, 658.

Table 20. The distribution of loans from Kivijärvi lending library according to the gender of the borrowers in the years 1877–1897.

Years	Male N	%	Female N	%	Units* N	%	Total N	%
1877–1882	29	5.7	23	42.6	2	3.7	54	100.0
1883–1887	376	47.8	394	50.1	16	2.1	786	100.0
1888–1892	209	60.6	135	39.1	1	0.3	345	100.0
1893–1897	51	76.1	16	23.9	-	-	67	100.0
not known	1	50.0	1	50.0	-	-	2	100.0
Total	**666**	**53.1**	**569**	**45.4**	**19**	**1.5**	**1254**	**100.0**

The percentages of the borrowers are calculated according to the numbers of loans and not the numbers of actual borrowers since generally individual borrowers took out several loans during the examined period.
* This refers to entities such as schools, local courts and households that were designated only by the place of residence or the surname of the family.
Source: KKA, loans registers 1877–1897.

although fiction generally became the most popular form of literature in Finnish lending libraries towards the end of the century, in Kivijärvi the reactivation of the library's activities led to an increase in the borrowing of religious literature and to its superseding other genres in popularity. In the last period (1893–1897), the literature that was borrowed was exclusively devotional.[853] Possibly this was a result of the fact that the fiction had by then been 'exhausted' and the plots of the novels become so familiar that there was no fictional reading material left that was of interest to the customers. By contrast, works of religious literature had traditionally been perused over and over again with ever renewed contemplation, offering as they did material for further reflection in repeated readings.

Another perhaps even more significant reason may be the fact that there was another powerful religious revival in the parish. Midway through the century, when the first lending library was established, Evangelism had gained sway in the area, and the core of the library's collection still consisted of works that were important to the Evangelicals, but the revivalist movement in the 1890s was mainly Laestadian. It is naturally not possible to verify this with regard to the borrowers because there is no specific information available about their religious convictions. In any case, there would not seem in the light of the surviving sources to have been any immediate 'modernization' of the library's collection in the late 1880s into one befitting a lending library that sought to provide mainly practical new non-fiction and entertaining literature and to further the reading skills of the members of the parish. On the contrary, the main object of their interest continued to be traditional devotional works.

Men represented a slight majority of the borrowers noted in the loans registers of Kivijärvi lending library. However the numbers of loans made by women were almost as high. In the 1880s they actually briefly exceeded those of men but then declined again with the advent of the 1890s, and in

---

853 Table 19.

Table 21. *The distribution of loans according to the gender of the borrowers and literary genre.*

Genres	religious		non-fiction		belles lettres		total	
	N	%	N	%	N	%	N	%
Male	358	55.2	80	59.7	228	48.4	666	53.1
Female	280	43.1	53	39.6	236	50.1	569	45.4
Units*	11	1.7	1	0.7	7	1.5	19	1.5
Total	**649**	**100.0**	**134**	**100.0**	**471**	**100.0**	**1254**	**100.0**

* This refers to entities such as schools, local courts and households that were designated only by the place of residence or the surname of the family.
Source: KKA, loans registers 1877–1897.

the end men made over three quarters of the total number of loans.[854] In order to obtain a more exact picture of the longer-term distribution of loans according to the gender of the borrowers, it would be necessary to have data about the borrowers from the mid-nineteenth century into the twentieth. On the basis of the information provided by the loans registers covering only a couple of decades, it is not possible to reach any certain conclusions for example about the long-term development of reading among women or to ascertain whether it increased or declined between the establishment of the collection of the first church parish library and the turn of the century.

The figures provided by the loans registers of Kivijärvi library indicate that slightly more men read religious literature than women. They also read considerably more non-fiction works, whereas both sexes read about the same amount of imaginative literature, although women were the main readers of novels. In this respect, the reading habits of the people of Kivijärvi correspond to the universal view that women constituted the majority of readers of *belles lettres* although the differences between men and women were quite small with regard to this particular type of literature. All in all, the gender distribution of the readers of Kivijärvi was fairly even, and there were no significant divergences between men and women.[855] The collection of Kivijärvi lending library was fairly limited. Indeed the popular libraries of the larger towns in Finland also suffered from the same problem at that time.[856] This was to a great extent a consequence not only of their poor financial situation and the particular nature of book publishing in Finland but also, especially in the countryside, of the libraries' dearth of opportunities for acquiring new works.

854 Table 20. See the following chapter for a more detailed discussion of the gender differences between borrowers.
855 Table 21.
856 E.g. E. Seppälä 1963; Hirn 1998.

The oldest collection of the church parish library

THE MOST BORROWED WORKS IN THE PERIOD 1877–1897

In the next section I examine in greater detail the literature contained in the collections of Kivijärvi lending library and the information concerning borrowing. I enquire what kind of literature the most popular works represented and consider possible reasons for the preferences of the customers for certain works.

It was not until the nineteenth century that literature became in Finland a social institution in which writers, critics, printers, book merchants, publishers and the press all had their own roles to play. A national literature, particularly in the Finnish language, was for the most part only created in the nineteenth century.[857] Behind this development lay the influence of the Fennoman movement, popular enlightenment and the improvement in the official position of the Finnish language as well as a complex interaction between the traditional oral and the newer written culture.

The 'second revolution' in book production took place in the nineteenth century. Thanks to new technology, it became possible to exploit the process of printing, which had been developed during the time of the Renaissance, more effectively. The mechanical production of paper made it possible to produce books more rapidly and in greater numbers. Newspapers began to be published, accompanied by yellow journalism and other forms of light reading matter. The channels for the dissemination of literature grew in number and variety. More and more libraries and reading rooms were established, evening reading recitals were organized and literary societies were founded. The network of bookshops became more professionally organized, and cheaper popular editions of books were printed. The road and rail networks were gradually extended into the remote areas, and this was also a key factor in the spread of literature.[858]

In Germany, the publication of books grew considerably during the so-called 'long nineteenth century' (the period from the end of the eighteenth century to the time of the Weimar Republic). It doubled in the late eighteenth century and continued to increase thereafter. Many more book titles were published in the early 1910s in Germany than in other leading industrial countries such as France, Britain or the United States.[859] However, the total number of books printed in Britain, for example, quadrupled between 1846 and 1916, while at the same time the average price of a book halved. In addition, the number of newspapers and periodicals also increased rapidly during that period.[860]

The collection of Kivijärvi lending library in the nineteenth century was fairly typical of its time. For example, the people's library in Vaasa contained works by the German pedagogue August Wilhelm Grube and descriptions of folk life by Per Thomasson, but apart from those there was little other

---

857 Vartiainen 2009, 206; Table 22.
858 Vartiainen 2009, 473.
859 Tatlock 2010, 4.
860 Heikkinen 2013, 227.

Table 22. The publication of first editions in Finnish in the nineteenth century.

Years	First editions (N)
1809–1855	425
1858–1865	481
1866–1875	574
1876–1885	1299

Source: Leino-Kaukiainen 1990, 10; Tommila 1980, 264.

than devotional literature, which the city library neglected to acquire at all. A large number of temperance pamphlets were also acquired for the people's library. In the mid-nineteenth century, books came out presenting new achievements in the natural sciences in an easily comprehensible form: for example, Otto Ule's *Warum und weil* [Why and Because].[861] This, like for example Antero Warelius' work of popular enlightenment *Enon opetuksia* (Part. 1) [Uncle's lessons], which was published in 1845, was sold for 12–15 kopeks a copy. These works, which represented more secular literature, became sales hits in the 1840s (several thousand copies were sold), and reprints were made as soon as one edition sold out. On the other hand, a cheap price or an interesting subject did not alone affect the popularity of works. For example the religious communities supported the distribution and consumption of their own favourite works. The students had chosen the above mentioned works to include in their collection of books for disseminating education and culture to the countryside.[862]

The books that were available for borrowing in Kivijärvi in the years 1877–1897 included A. W. Grube's biography of Abraham Lincoln and the first part of his *Charakterbilder aus der Geschichte und Sage*[863] [Heroes of History and Legend]. This Grube's series of history books was read also in the practice school of Jyväskylä Teacher Training Seminary by the schoolchildren.[864] The character of the people's library in Vaasa was educative, and it contained, like that of the one in Kivijärvi, translations of works by Dickens and Topelius as well as Runeberg's collected works and J. C. Schmid's novel *Genovefa*. It was most actively used by the children of working-class families, servant girls and the apprentices of artisans.[865] According to a catalogue printed in 1873, the collection of the lending library in Kuopio contained many of the same works that were read in Kivijärvi: for example, Grube's *Charakterbilder aus der Geschichte und Sage*, Luther's works, Bunyan's *The Pilgrim's Progress*, Hollatz's *Evangelische Gnadenordnungen* [The Order of Evangelical Grace in the Economy of Salvation[866]], Warelius' *Enon opetuksia* [Uncle's lessons],

---

861 Finnish title: *Mintähden ja sentähden*. Hakapää 2008, 65–66; Lehtikanto 1964, 47. Contrary to what Hakapää states, the work was translated, not written, by Samuel Roos.
862 Hakapää 2008, 65–66.
863 Finnish title: *Kertomuksia ihmiskunnan historiasta*.
864 KKA, Collection catalogues and the old collection of books of Kivijärvi lending library; Haikari 2016, 160.
865 Lehtikanto 1964, 48.
866 Finnish title: *Armon järjestys autuuteen*.

Table 23. The most borrowed works of Kivijärvi lending library 1877–1897.

	Work	Number of Loans N	%
1.	Ernst Eckstein, Besuch im Karzer (Lukon takana)	29	2.3
	Pietari Päivärinta, Elämän havainnoita I–II		
2.	Martin Luther, Evankeliumi-postilla	27	2.2
3.	Eero Salmelainen, Suomen kansan satuja ja tarinoita 3	27	2.2
4.	Edvard Mau, Fire hundrede fortaellinger for skolen og hjemmet (Kristillinen lukukirja kotia ja koulua varten)	26	2.1
5. – 8.; a)	Karl Listner & Friedrich Gerstäcker, Erlebnisse in Australien: Reiseerinnerungen and Nach dem Schiffbruch (Siirtolaisen elämänvaiheet & Haaksirikon jälkeen)	25	2.0
	Wilhelm Herchenbach, Der Sklavenhändler von Benguela (Orjakauppias Benguelassa)		
b)	Gustaf Henrik Mellin, Paavo Nissinen	25	2.0
	Johan Olof Åberg, Österbottens perla (Pohjanmaan Helmi)		
	Johan Olof Åberg, Aina		
c)	J.C. Schmid, Genovefa (Genoveva)	25	2.0
	Jules Sandeau, La roche aux mouettes (Lokkiluoto)		
	Theodolinda Hahnsson, Kaksois-veljekset		
d)	Novelleja ja kertomuksia 4 (Weilin & Göös)	25	2.0
9.	Martin Luther, Epistola-postilla	24	1.9
10.	Emil Reinbeck, Wir sind unsterblich! (Ihmisen oleminen kuoleman jälkeen)	23	1.8
Total		1254	100.0

The numbers of loans refer to the individual copies borrowed not the works. Works under the same ordinal numbers were bound under the same hard covers. The last column indicates the percentage of loans out of the total number of loans made in the years 1877–1897. Source: KKA, loans registers of Kivijärvi lending library 1877–1897.

Suomen kansan sadut ja tarinat [Tales and legends of the Finnish people], and translated literature like Defoe's *Robinson Crusoe*, Schmid's *Genovefa*, Beecher-Stowe's *Uncle Tom's Cabin* and Scott's *Ivanhoe* and *The Bride of Lammermoor*.[867] Thus at that time the collection of the library in Kivijärvi would appear to have been comparable in quality with the collections of libraries in larger towns.

In order to ascertain the reading needs of the section of the population who used the library, one can examine the list of the most borrowed works. *Pyhä Raamattu* [The Holy Bible], of which there were 25 copies in the collection, was the most borrowed work (161 loans). The Bible was the only work of which the library possessed such a large number of copies, and hence it was by far the most borrowed work. However, it is not included in this and the following sections among the most popular works in terms of volumes borrowed because the number of loans per volume were fewer. Many of these volumes contained different titles bound together under the same cover, so it is not possible to be certain which of the titles in the

867 Huttunen 1981, 19. See also the Karstula library collection of old books.

volumes were the most read. After all, it was not necessary to read the whole volume, and the reader could choose which of the titles he or she most fancied. In terms of the numbers of loans, most of the books borrowed from Kivijärvi lending library in the years between 1877 and 1897 were devotional works. The most frequently borrowed literature included both Finnish and translated literature. The most popular of the religious works was Luther's *Evankeliumi-Postilla* [Gospel postil].[868] The least read books in the library were mainly the religious works from the oldest collection.[869]

When the country was separated from Sweden in 1809, there were two presses in Finland. One was in Vaasa, and the other was Frenckell's press in Turku, which shared the privileges granted to the Academy of Turku. At the beginning of the ensuing period of autonomy under Russia, more printing presses were established in Turku and Vyborg. The first printing press in Helsinki was established in 1818. From the early decades of the nineteenth century on, several new printing presses, which also engaged in publishing activities, were established in the larger cities (Helsinki, Turku, Porvoo, Kuopio and Vaasa). In 1830 there were altogether nine printing presses operating in Finland.[870] In the mid-nineteenth century, a book merchant called G. W. Edlund became the leading publisher of books in the country. He published about 50 works annually, most of which, however, were in Swedish, although he also had a strong interest in publishing works in Finnish. Publishing was mostly concentrated in Helsinki, but the Finnish Literature Society in Vyborg and J. W. Lillja in Turku were also important operators in the field. The latter's business was taken over in 1862 by G. W. Wilén, who became well-known mainly as a publisher of newspapers and religious literature at the end of the century.[871]

There was also a lending library attached to Lillja's publishing house in Turku that opened in 1851. It operated as a side business of his bookshop, and it was used to market the books produced by the publishing house. The aim of the library seems to have been mainly to serve the functionaries and burghers of the city, since its customers needed to have a reasonably wide knowledge of languages. The library contained an extensive collection of *belles lettres* in Swedish as well as non-fiction works mainly in German and French and to a lesser extent in English, Italian, Spanish and Portuguese. The stock of the bookshop and the lending library together formed one big collection, from which customers could either borrow or buy books according to their needs.[872]

---

868 I have not been able to ascertain whether this work was a translation of Luther's *Hauspostille* or his *Kirchenpostille*, or possibly a collection of excerpts from either or both of these original works. The same holds true for the Finnish titles *Lyhyt evankeliumi-postilla* and *(Lyhyt) Epistola-postilla*, in which the word 'Lyhyt' means 'Short'.
869 KKA, Loans registers of Kivijärvi lending library 1877–1897; Table 23.
870 Autero 1993, 38–39; Kulha 1972, 5.
871 Leino-Kaukiainen 1990, 9: Paloposki 2013, 57–58.
872 Autero 1993, 66–68.

Table 24. The most borrowed works in Kivijärvi lending library 1877–1887.

	Work	Number of Loans	
		N	%
1.	Eero Salmelainen, *Suomen kansan satuja ja tarinoita 3*	27	3.2
2.	Ernst Eckstein, *Besuch im Karzer (Lukon takana)*	25	3.0
	Pietari Päivärinta, *Elämän havainnoita I–II*		
3.	J. C. Schmid, *Genovefa (Genoveva)*	24	2.9
	Jules Sandeau, *La roche aux mouettes (Lokkiluoto)*		
	Theodolinda Hahnsson, *Kaksois-veljekset*		
4.	*Novelleja ja kertomuksia* 4 (Weilin & Göös)	24	2.9
5.	Karl Listner & Friedrich Gerstäcker, *Erlebnisse in Australien: Reiseerinnerungen and Nach dem Schiffbruch (Siirtolaisen elämänvaiheet & Haaksirikon jälkeen)*	23	2.7
	Wilhelm Herchenbach, *Der Sklavenhändler von Benguela (Orjakauppias Benguelassa)*		
6.	Alexander Friedrich Franz Hoffman, *Leo (Jäämerellä)*	22	2.6
7. – 10.; a)	Gustaf Henrik Mellin, *Paavo Nissinen*	20	2.4
	Johan Olof Åberg, *Österbottens perla (Pohjanmaan Helmi)*		
	Åberg, Johan Olof, *Aina*		
b)	Walter Scott, *The Talisman (Talismani)*	20	2.4
c)	Pietari Hannikainen, *Pitäjään kirjasto*	20	2.4
d)	Eero Salmelainen, *Suomen kansan satuja ja tarinoita 1–2*	20	2.4
Total		840	100.0

The numbers of loans indicate the individual copies borrowed not the works. Books designated by the same ordinal numbers were bound under the same hard covers. The last column indicates the percentage of loans out of the total number of loans made in the years 1877–1887. Source: KKA, loans registers of Kivijärvi lending library 1877–1897.

1852, J. W. Lillja began to publish reading matter in language that was understandable by the common people in a publication called *Lukemisia Kansalle* [Reading for the people]. It consisted of small booklets (8 or 16 pages in length), which were commonly called *penninkirjallisuus* (penny literature). The content was initially made up of religious or enlightening material. Soon the subjects also came to include social education, economic information, practical instructions and the natural sciences. The publication of this reading material turned out to be extremely profitable for Lillja.[873] Kivijärvi library contained ten or so of these booklets, which were published at the turn of the 1850s and 1860s.[874] The collections of other rural libraries in the 1870s also mainly consisted of religious and other literature that was considered to be morally acceptable and which avoided political and religious contradictions.[875]

The first work published by the Finnish Literature Society was a translation of Heinrich Zschokke's *Das Goldmacherdorf* [The Goldmakers' Village][876] by

873 Autero 1993, 106–107.
874 Kivijärvi BOOKS.
875 H. Mäkelä 1991, 17.
876 Finnish title: *Kultala*.

C. N. Keckman in 1834. The original work, which was first published in 1823, had been translated into several languages and was an international success. The book was regarded as a suitably instructive work in terms of its content for the common people. A similar didactic tendency was visible in the translation of literature for children and young persons. The works of Christoph von Schmid, a Catholic priest, were also translated into Finnish. Schmid was very popular in Germany, and translations of his works spread around Europe. In them a didactic and moralizing element was woven into an entertaining and exciting story. *Genovefa* [Genoveva of Brabant][877] (translated into Finnish by Antti Räty in 1847) is an adaptation of a much-used medieval German legend. It was an extraordinary success in Finland. A fifth impression of it was taken in 1888, and the total edition amounted to nearly 12,000 copies, which was probably a record for translated fiction in Finland at that time.[878] Kivijärvi lending library contained translations of both *Das Goldmacherdorf* and *Genovefa*, but only the latter was in the loans registers for 1877–1897, so possibly the former was not acquired until later when the privately established library was functioning (i.e. after 1897).[879] Both works also belonged to the collection of Saarijärvi library, but in the case of *Das Goldmacherdorf* not until the 1898 edition appeared.[880]

The selection of fiction in Kivijärvi lending library consisted mainly of historical novels. After the mid-nineteenth century, the view that literature in Finnish had a formative nation-building purpose became established among the promoters of a Finnish national culture. Concomitant with this view was the creation of a chair in literature at the Imperial Alexander University of Finland in Helsinki and the establishment of literature as a regular subject of instruction.[881] The most popular works of fiction in Kivijärvi were the recently published translation of Ernst Eckstein's *Besuch im Karzer* [The Visit to the Cells][882] and Pietari Päivärinta's *Elämän havainnoita* [Observations of life] I–II, which were bound together into one volume. Almost as popular in Kivijärvi was Part 4 of *Suomen kansan satuja ja tarinoita* [Finnish fairy tales and stories], edited by Erik Rudbeck. Other favourites included translations of Sandeau's *La Roche aux mouettes* [Gull Rock][883] (one of the books, and the only work of fiction, recommended by the Society for Popular Enlightenment in its first catalogue in 1874),[884] von Schmid's *Genovefa*, Hoffman's *Leo* [Leo Bertram, or the Brave Heart][885] and Walter Scott's *The Talisman*[886].[887]

877 Finnish title: *Genoveva tahi kertomus yhen jumalisen rouan viattomasta kärsimisestä*.
878 Lassila 2007, 91. See also Pääkkönen 2007.
879 KKA, Loans registers (1877–1897) and collection catalogues of Kivijärvi lending library.
880 Collection catalogues of Saarijärvi lending library; Saarijärvi BOOKS.
881 Lehtinen 1999, 201–202.
882 Finnish title: *Lukon takana*.
883 Finnish title: *Lokkiluoto*.
884 Inkilä 1960, 168.
885 Finnish title: *Jäämerellä*.
886 Finnish title: *Talismani*.
887 KKA, Loans registers of Kivijärvi lending library 1877–1897; Table 23.

Of these works, *Genovefa*, for one, maintained its popularity with Finnish readers for decades. Although, in the opinion of the promoters of popular enlightenment, the book was not of an especially high quality, educative or conducive to furthering the national revival, particularly for many young readers in the late nineteenth century it represented their first initiation into reading a new kind of secular fiction, escapist literature. The first Finnish-language edition of *Genovefa* came out in 1847, and it was still among the most borrowed books of some libraries in the 1920s.[888] Elsewhere in Finland,[889] Scott's *The Talisman* was one of the great favourites in the 1880s, while Eckstein's *Besuch im Karzer* became one of the most sought-after books in the 1890s.[890] There were no readers in Kivijärvi of the work *Lutheruksen Bibliallinen lauseisto ja tawarasto* [this was a collection of writings by Martin Luther] or of Pietari Päivärinta's work *Minä ja muut* [I and others].[891]

The influence of traditional Pietist literature on the Evangelical revival

The collection of the oldest lending library in Kivijärvi would not have come into being without the existence of a strong local Evangelical movement. The Finnish revivalist movements took their main inspiration from Continental European and Anglo-Saxon religious literature, which spread into Finland mainly by way of Sweden. This literature included numerous spiritual works inspired by Pietism, Herrnhutism and Puritanism, such as the postils of Johann Arndt, David Hollatz, Christian Scriver, Anders Nohrborg, Johann Philipp Fresenius, Thomas Gouge, Johan Wegelius and Anders Björkqvist. These works were read in the revivalist movements and disseminated by them in new editions. They were complemented by several other devotional works and hymnbooks such as *Sionin Wirret* [Songs of Zion] and *Halullisten sielujen hengelliset laulut* [Spiritual hymns of yearning souls]. However, the books were based on dogmatically very different premises, which in turn led to different emphases in the dogmas of the various sects.[892]

The early collection of Kivijärvi library included such works as Hedberg's *Uskon oppi autuuteen* [Faith as a way to salvation] (1844), Thomas Gouge's *A Word to Sinners, and a Word to Saints* (1861),[893] as well as works by Dent and Bunyan and several by Luther.[894] For example, Bunyan's *The Pilgrim's Progress*[895] was a work that was ideologically close to the Evangelical

---

888 Mäkinen 2003, 326.
889 Eskola (1991) has studied the acquisition of translated literature for Finnish libraries from the 1880s on. However, her research does not include a single library from Central Finland in the 1880s and 1890s, nor does it anyway comprehensively cover popular libraries all over the country, although it does provide material for comparing data.
890 Eskola 1991, 125.
891 KKA, Loans registers of Kivijärvi lending library 1877–1897.
892 Murtorinne 1992, 101.
893 Finnish title: *Sana syntisille ja sana pyhille*. Thomas Gouge's work was published in London in 1668 and appeared in a Finnish translation in 1800. T. Laine 2000, 234.
894 KKA, Collection catalogues of Kivijärvi lending library 1877–1897.
895 Finnish title: *Kristityn vaellus*.

movement. It was widely disseminated particularly among American Evangelicals since the concept of a pilgrimage served well as a metaphor for the mobile colonial American society of the nineteenth century, which seemed to be in a continuous state of movement (colonization, the settlement of the West, the building of the railroads, and so on).[896] Also in Finland Bunyan's book was one of the most popular religious books of the time in the popular libraries.

A woman from Kannonkoski recalls how her father still used to read a book by Carl Olof Rosenius, the Bible and Hedberg's *Uskon oppi autuuteen* in the early decades of the twentieth century. If the family did not go to church on Sunday morning, the whole household had to be there 'at nine o'clock listening as Father or Seve [Oikarinen] read and sang. You had to listen'.[897] Another woman from Kannonkoski recalled how, in the early years of the twentieth century, either she as a child or her grandfather used to read a whole long sermon from a postil on a Sunday morning. The servants were not present. Her grandmother and grandfather were devout people, and it was forbidden to talk aloud at home during a church service. No work of any kind was permitted on the Sabbath: the hay was not brought in, and nobody was allowed to go out to work in the fields or to pick berries. In addition to the Bible, the books that were read in homes were postils, hymnbooks, the Gospels, Svebilius' *Catechism*, *Siionin Kannel* [The harp of Zion] and *Harpun Säveliä* [Strains of the harp].[898]

Pietism came into being within the sphere of Continental Protestantism in the seventeenth century and reached its full florescence in the eighteenth century. It became the most significant reformist movement along with Anglo-Saxon Puritanism since the Reformation. Pietism sought to deepen the experience of religious life and to increase the individual's personal involvement in it. It brought about changes not only in personal devotional practice but also in the activities of the church and in theology. It left its mark on the whole of society and culture wherever its influence reached.[899] Pietism spread into Finland at the end of the seventeenth century. The first adherents were students and university graduates in Turku.[900] The spontaneous religious revivals that began in the second half of the eighteenth century show how literacy deeply affected the daily life of ordinary people. Within these movements, it was believed that an independent study of sacred texts was important for conversion. Arthur Dent's book *A Sermon of Repentance*[901] was one of the works read by the revivalists.[902]

Most of the literature of German origin that was read in Finland before the nineteenth century was religious, and it was to a great extent connected with the spread of Pietism. The most important of these writers

---

896 Brown 2004, 8–9.
897 SKSÄ KKA 1. Kannonkoski 13N (transcription of an interview).
898 SKSÄ KKA 1. Kannonkoski 10N (transcription of an interview).
899 Wallmann 1997, 11.
900 E. Laine 1997, 9.
901 Finnish title: *Totisen kääntymisen harjoitus*.
902 Häggman 2008, 48–49.

was Johann Arndt, a minister and author of devotional works who had died centuries earlier in 1621. His major works were *Wahres Christentum* [True Christianity, Books 1–4][903] (1605–1610) and *Paradiesgärtlein aller christlichen Tugenden* [The Garden of Paradise][904] (1612). In Germany, his works were an essential part of the libraries of burghers in the eighteenth century. His main work, *Wahres Christentum*, was published in Swedish in 1647, but the first volume did not come out in Finnish until 1832. Only one of his works was translated into Finnish before Finland came under Russian rule in 1809. *Paradiesgärtlein*, which was translated into Swedish in 1646, appeared in Finnish (*Paratiisin yrttitarha*) in 1732. There were numerous re-prints of it. Despite the delay in their appearance in Finnish-language editions, the influence of Arndt's works in Finland was already considerable immediately after the publication of the Swedish translations, since the clergy and the burghers of the cities were then able to read them.[905] The collection of Kivijärvi lending library contained translations of The Third Book of True Christianity and Catechetical Sermons.[906]

Pietism arrived in Finland, as in the other Nordic countries, at the turn of the seventeenth and eighteenth centuries. It emphasized a deeper experience of religious life and a practical, active observance of devotion. It also strove to reform the church. Finnish Pietism was above all a movement that aimed at bringing about concrete changes within the church and society. This type of Pietism can be regarded as being initiated by Philipp Jakob Spener's work *Pia desideria*, which was published as the foreword to Arndt's *Postil* in 1675.[907] The earliest British 'narrative' that was translated and published in Finland was John Bunyan's religious allegory, *The Pilgrim's Progress*, originally published in 1678. Several Finnish translations came out in the course of the nineteenth century, but they were made from German and Swedish, not directly from English. The translation of works of fiction proper into Finnish began with Daniel Defoe's Robinson Crusoe (originally published in 1719).[908] The edition of *Robinson Crusoe* in Kivijärvi lending library was a Finnish translation by Theodolinda Hahnsson published in 1875.[909]

Arndt was the most popular individual writer of devotional works throughout the whole time of Swedish rule over Finland. Arndt and his successors influenced the theological thinking and the devotional writings of the Finns. Pietist literature proper reached Sweden and Finland in the works of Spener, Francke and the Halle theologians. In the eighteenth century, their publication in Swedish-language editions was prevented by censorship.[910]

903 Finnish title: *Neljä kirjaa totisesta kristillisyydestä*.
904 Finnish title: *Paratiisin yrttitarha*.
905 Laasonen 2003, 106–110; E. Laine, 1999, 79.
906 Finnish title: *Katekismussaarnoja*. KKA, Collection catalogues and the old collection of books of Kivijärvi lending library. See also Saarijärvi BOOKS; Karstula library collection of old books.
907 Dahl 2010, 10; Engelsing 1974, 63; E. Laine 1999, 78.
908 Leppihalme 2007, 154.
909 KKA, Collection catalogues of Kivijärvi lending library 1877–1897.
910 E. Laine 1999, 79.

Johann Arndt's *Paradiesgärtlein* was also disseminated around the country in new Finnish editions in the nineteenth century. It continued to be a sales hit for WSOY right into the beginning of the twentieth century.[911]

The young clerics of The Awakening (*Herännäisyys*] movement were keen to engage in a deeper theoretical consideration of the principles of the movement and also of the functioning of the church. An emphasis on individual religious experience, which was influenced especially by German revivalist pamphlets, was anyway characteristic of the revivalist movements. They were also inspired by the tradition of the Reformation and the confession of the Evangelical Lutheran Church. Consequently, there was an increase in interest among members of The Awakening movement in Luther and his works in the 1830s, when some of them were translated and published in Sweden. As a result, in the early 1840s the clerics of The Awakening became enthusiastic about translating his works into Finnish, too. One of their major achievements was the appearance in 1844 of F. G. Hedberg's programmatic major work *Uskon oppi aututeen* [The Doctrine of Faith unto Salvation].[912]

Pastor Henrik Renqvist (originally Kukkonen) experienced a powerful religious awakening when he was still a student in the early nineteenth century after reading Arthur Dent's work *A Sermon of Repentance*. It strongly moulded his conception of faith, which later became part of the basic ideology of The Awakening movement. Renqvist translated tracts of the Stockholm Evangelical Society into Finnish. For example, *Yxi sangen merkillinen historia* [One very strange story] was published in 1815. Abraham Achrenius and his son Antti were leaders of an ecstatic revivalist movement which appeared in the second half of the eighteenth century in south-west Finland. Anders Björkqvist (1741–1809), a clergyman who was a member of the revival, published a postil in 1801 entitled *Uskon harjoitus autuuteen* [The practice of faith unto salvation].[913] The Awakening movement in the area around Mikkeli in Savonia was characterized by an assiduous reading of the Bible and other religious literature. Especially the leading members of the movement read a lot, including literature that was not exclusively religious. It is likely that this was the reason why a lending library was founded in Mikkeli as early as in 1856.[914]

Measured in terms of titles, number of pages and editions, Martin Luther was clearly the most read and purchased writer in Finland in 1858. He was in a completely different league from national literary giants like Johan Ludvig Runeberg, Topelius and other secular writers.[915] Available for borrowing in the lending library of Kivijärvi were 25 copies of the Bible, and translations

---

911 Häggman 2001, 53.
912 Murtorinne 1992, 148–149.
913 Murtorinne 1992, 110–111, 118–119.
914 Three years later, the composition of its collection was as follows: 108 works of religious literature, 33 historical works, 54 works of *belles lettres*, 74 works described as 'reading for the commons' and 17 volumes dealing with agriculture. Rosendal 1915, 120.
915 Häggman 2008, 115.

of Luther's commentary on the Sermon on the Mount, Bunyan's *The Pilgrim's Progress*, Hedberg's *Den enda Salighetens Wäg* [The only road to salvation][916], a biography of Luther, *Uskon oppi autuuteen* [Faith as a way to salvation] and *Kristillinen kirkkohistoria* [A Christian church history], a translation of a work by Kristian Gottlieb Barth. Other Christian literature that was read were included *Kuinka on lapsi kasvatettava j.n.e.* [How to bring up a child, etc.], *Turmiolan Tommin elämäkerta* [The biography of 'Tommy of Perditionville'], *Kääntymisen harjoitus* [The practice of conversion], and translations of Luther's *Lyhyt epistola-postilla*, Johann Qvirsfeld's *Neuvermehrte himmlische Garden-Gesellschaft*[917] and Johan Gerhard's *Mediationes sacrae*.[918]

When one examines the most borrowed works in Kivijärvi lending library even more closely, i.e. in the 1870s and again in the period just before the establishment of the library by private persons, one notes that the list of the ten most borrowed works closely resembles the corresponding list for the whole period under examination. This is a result of the fact that borrowing was most brisk in the 1880s, i.e. the period immediately preceding the establishment of the privately founded library. The bibles in the collection were borrowed altogether 87 times. Pietari Hannikainen's work *Pitäjään kirjasto* [A library for the parish] and Salmelainen's *Suomen kansan satuja ja tarinoita 1–2* [Fairytales and stories of the Finnish people, 1–2] were also very popular works. The collection of religious literature (apart from the Bible) attracted the readers' interest least in these years.[919] What then changed when the new library was established by private persons?

The collection of the privately founded library

THE RISE OF THE NOVEL

The Bible remained the most borrowed work (altogether 64 loans) in the collection during the first five years of operation of the privately founded library. Contrary to what one might expect, the most borrowed works represented old religious literature although the reading of fiction and other forms of *belles lettres* had increased in the period immediately preceding 1888. The works of Martin Luther were particularly popular. The least read volumes were non-fiction and a few devotional works.[920] Here it is worth remembering that the library functioned for a long time under the auspices of the church parish. Frans Petter Krank, who assumed the post of vicar in 1883, was very active on the board of governors of the elementary school in that decade and at the end of it he himself experienced a Laestadian

---

916 Finnish title: *Ainoa autuuden tie*.
917 Finnish title: *Taivaallinen Yrttitarhan seura*.
918 KKA, collection catalogues of Kivijärvi lending library. Luther was popular also elsewhere in Central Finland, see Saarijärvi BOOKS; Karstula library collection of old books.
919 See Table 24.
920 See Table 25.

Table 25. The most borrowed works in Kivijärvi lending library 1888–1892.

	Work	Number of Loans	
		N	%
1.	Martin Luther, *Epistola-postilla*	16	4.6
2.- 3.; a)	Martin Luther, *Tohtori Martti Luteeruksen hengellinen aarre-aitta* [This was a collection of spiritual writings by Martin Luther]	15	4.3
b)	Martin Luther, *Evankeliumi-Postilla*	15	4.3
4. – 5.; a)	Martin Luther, *Lyhyt evankeliumipostilla*	12	3.5
b)	Otto Funcke, *Verwandlungen, oder, Wie ein Sehender blind und ein Blinder sehend wird (Muutokset eli miten näkevä tulee sokeaksi ja sokea näkeväksi)*	12	3.5
6. – 7.; a)	Jean Frédéric Lobstein, *L'année Chrétienne Ou Une Parole Sainte Méditée Pour Chaque Jour (Kristillinen vuosi eli yksi Jumalan sana joka päivä mietitty)*	9	2.6
b)	Edvard Mau, *Fire hundrede fortaellinger for skolen og hjemmet (Kristillinen lukukirja kotia ja koulua varten)*	9	2.6
8.	Martin Luther, *Lyhyt epistola-postilla*	8	2.3
9. – 11.; a)	Emil Reinbeck, *Wir Sind Unsterblich! (Ihmisen oleminen kuoleman jälkeen)*	7	2.0
b)	*The Holy Bible* (one of 25 copies available for borrowing)	7	2.0
c)	Johan Gerhard, *Meditationes sacrae*	7	2.0
Total		**345**	**100.0**

The numbers of loans indicate the individual copies borrowed not the works. Books under the same ordinal numbers were bound under the same hard covers. The last column indicates the percentage of loans out of the total number of loans made in the years 1888–1892. Source: KKA, loans registers of Kivijärvi lending library 1877–1897.

awakening. Since his family played an active part in the administration of the library, one can deduce that the members of the church parish and of the revivalist movements were encouraged to use the library, and this very probably also explains the great popularity of religious literature.

The American War of Independence and the French Revolution had led to the spread of liberty and ideals of freedom, and at the same time the paramount positions of the nobility and the church were questioned. Literary traditions were overturned, and romanticism became the dominant movement in literature. The pre-eminence of the romantic movement in European culture lasted for only a very short period, from about 1790 to 1830. Romanticism came into being in Germany and Britain, from where it spread to Scandinavia, France and other parts of western and eastern Europe to become a pan-European movement. German romanticism was characterized by the imitation and idealization of the Middle Ages and particularly of the literature that described medieval folk culture. The interest in folk culture led to extensive activities in collecting traditional oral folklore. Folk poetry was also recorded by numerous poets, and there was considerable interest in folk tales as well.[921] In Finland collecting traditional oral folklore was strongly connected with the national revival.

Kivijärvi library also contained a copy of *Suomen kansan satuja ja tarinoita* [Finnish fairy tales and stories] (four volumes) published by the Society for Popular Enlightenment. During his student years, Erik (aka Eero) Rudbeck (1830–1867), who later Finnicized his surname to Salmelainen, received a grant from the Finnish Literature Society to study folk poetry in northern Central Finland. In the summer of 1850, together with Albin Rothman he toured round the regions of Saarijärvi and Viitasaari, and he also visited Kivijärvi. Saarijärvi, in particular, interested him since J. L. Runeberg, the national poet of Finland, had spent time there in his own student days 30 years earlier, working as a home tutor to the children of members of the local gentry. It was decided to compile the material collected by Rudbeck and Rothman into a publication, which was then published by the Finnish Literature Society. Rudbeck was given the task of editing the work. The first two volumes in the series were published in the early 1850s, the third in 1863 and the fourth in 1866.[922] *Suomen kansan satuja ja tarinoita* Vol. 2 contained a story titled *Taivaase[e]n menijä. Kivijärveltä Hämeestä* [The traveller to heaven. From Kivijärvi in Tavastia].[923] The copies in Kivijärvi library were acquired either during the time of the church parish library or at the latest when the library was functioning in the school because they were available for borrowing before 1888. They were very popular locally.[924]

The novels in the collection of Kivijärvi lending library were to a great extent national romantic in tone, while realism, which was the fashionable literary movement of the time, was largely ignored. Descriptions of the life of the common people and works of folk authors were represented among the most borrowed books by Paavo Korhonen's *Viisikymmentä runoa ja kuusi laulua* [Fifty poems and six songs] – 'Vihta-Paavo' [Birch Whisk Paavo], as Korhonen was known, was one of the early-nineteenth-century peasant poets from Rautalampi[925] – and Pietari Päivärinta's *Elämän havainnoita* [Observations of life]. They can be regarded as representing what in the opinion of the intelligentsia was suitable reading for the poor population of the countryside and as writing about subjects with which ordinary people could identify. For example, Päivärinta's works can be located somewhere between national romanticism and proto-realism. His work was characterized by a didactic and moralizing tone. His picture of the ordinary people was patriotic and romantic but at the same time its folksy quality appealed to the readers of the rural population.[926]

In Pietari Päivärinta's series *Elämän havainnoita* [Observations of life], which appeared in ten parts between 1880 and 1889, the narrative technique largely follows the same pattern from one story to the next. The first-person

---

921 Vartiainen 2009, 351, 353, 378–379.
922 Haltsonen 1931, 7, 15–25, 27–29, 65–77; Suomela 1963, 333.
923 Salmelainen 1873, 113–122.
924 KKA, the loans registers of Kivijärvi lending library 1877–1897.
925 Hallikainen 1964, 96.
926 Kohtamäki 1964, 433–439.

narrator stops at a place where he hears the life story of a local inhabitant; in other words, there are two first-person narrators: the actual narrator relates a story told by the main character in the first person.[927] In works like the romantic melodramas of Jaakko Gummerus and Theodolinda Hahnsson, sentiment had not really been regarded as intrinsic in the way of life of the common people. Thus descriptions of the common people such as those found in the works of writers like Päivärinta – for example, in his autobiographical work *Elämäni* [My life], in which he depicts decent family life – were considered to be more suitable and educative reading for the commons. Admittedly, Päivärinta not only employed autobiographical material in writing this work but also used his imagination, so it was not a pure autobiography.[928] Kivijärvi library contained altogether six copies of Päivärinta's works, all published in the 1880s.[929]

Another writer who was popular in Kivijärvi was Kalle Kajander (1862–1926), one of the most productive and best-known depictors of the life of the common people.[930] In 1896 the literature acquired for the people's library in Tohmajärvi in eastern Finland was vetted, and it was noted that works of 'the present realist trend' contained depictions of vices and sins without any condemnation of them at all. This kind of literature was regarded as injurious for the reading public of the countryside. The messages contained in the works of writers like Juhani Aho, Minna Canth and Teuvo Pakkala were considered to be un-Christian, because in accordance with the principles of realism they dealt very frankly with contemporary societal problems like poverty, social inequality, illegitimate pregnancies, and infanticide. In their works, these writers thus sought to draw the readers' attention to issues like the position of women and the improvement of social conditions.[931]

There was also a local element in evidence in the library in that the collection contained the works of authors from Central Finland. In addition to the works of the writer and publisher, Jaakko Gummerus, there were two by Karl (or Kaarle) Heino (originally Lindroos, 1848–1921), who wrote under the pen name K. Heino. He had received a doctorate from the University of Leipzig in 1891 and was a teacher of Latin at Jyväskylä Lyceum from 1892 to 1916.[932] Two of his works were included in the collection of 129 books mentioned in the loans registers of Kivijärvi lending library.[933]

The concepts '*kansankirjailija*' (folk writer) and '*kansankirjallisuus*' (folk literature) were created by the Fennomans at the end of the nineteenth century. The word *kansa* (the people, folk) in Finnish literature meant the common people of the countryside, including both the landed peasants and

---

927 Lappalainen 1999a, 37.
928 Lassila 2008, 112, 121.
929 KKA, Collection catalogues of Kivijärvi library; the old book collection of Kivijärvi lending library.
930 K. Laitinen 1997, 344.
931 Järvelin 1966, 84–85.
932 Kotivuori 2005. Ylioppilasmatrikkeli 1853–1899: Karl Heino. Web publication 2005. Accessed 7/7/2012; SKS database of authors, http://dbgw.finlit.fi/matr/tiedot.php?id=5274, Accessed 7/7/2012.
933 KKA, loans registers of Kivijärvi lending library 1877–1897.

the landless population. A folk writer was thus one who wrote original, new Finnish literature and whose works dealt with the living conditions of the common people and were written specifically for them. Since there were few established Swedish-speaking writers who knew Finnish, the Fennomans considered that the common people could best be reached by Finnish native-speaker writers who were themselves of humble origins. Their work would reveal the ways of thinking and experiences of the common people themselves.[934]

Folk writers were thus considered to be those persons who had risen from the ranks of the common people to be writers despite having little formal education. However, the concept is somewhat problematic in that the educational backgrounds of those authors who were considered to be folk writers were diverse, and not all of them were of lowly origin. In their works, they depicted the kind of life that they were familiar with, which was usually rural. Their activities were connected with the rise of realism and the strengthening of the nationalist movement in the late nineteenth century. They were the inheritors of the tradition of the *rahvaan runoniekat* (bards of the common people) of the turn of the eighteenth and nineteenth centuries, but their medium was prose not poetry. In composing their works, folk writers used stock models, taken for example from the oral narrative tradition and the works of Pietari Päivärinta. Like him, many of them were initially employed as assistant reporters on newspapers. They were mostly men, the one exception being Mathilda Roslin-Kalliola, who began writing in the 1890s.[935]

One example of these works in the collection of Kivijärvi library was *Kruunun metsissä* [In the Crown forests], written in 1891 by Juhana Kokko under the *nom-de-plume* of Kyösti.[936] Other folk writers who were read in Kivijärvi were Kauppis-Heikki, and Santeri Alkio.[937] In Kauppis-Heikki's novels *Kirottua työtä* [Damned work] (1891) and *Aliina* (1896), the acquisition of reading and writing skills by ordinary people is not seen as an altogether positive thing, as the contemporary endeavours to promote popular education assumed. In these novels, it was claimed, women learnt to express themselves in writing, but they 'misused' the skill that they had acquired either in writing love letters or by giving public expression to their deepest sentiments and moral views. By contrast, in the works of Santeri Alkio, education brings ordinary people nothing but good. In his first work, *Teerelän perhe* [The Teerelä family] (1886), a decent young man who has married into a farming family learns to read and write, and this educational capital turns out to be a blessing for him. *Eeva* (1888) again emphasizes the importance of training and education for women too. Alkio's *Puukkojunkkarit* [The knife fighters] (1894) also describes the importance of education for social law and order.[938]

---

934 Lassila 2008, 5, 9, 15–17; Liikanen 2003, 259–266, 295–302.
935 Lappalainen 1999b, 64.
936 Lappalainen 1999b, 68.
937 KKA, Collection catalogues of Kivijärvi lending library.
938 Lappalainen 1999b, 69.

One of the most important German writers of the nineteenth century was Fritz Reuter, a social critic and realist, who was also a satirical depictor of his times. Kivijärvi lending library contained his verse epic *Kein Hüsung* [Homeless][939], which described class conflict in the countryside, a subject that possibly appealed to many Finns as well. The landless population in Germany, who have no prospects for the future, escaped their predicament by emigrating to America. Reuter, who wrote in *Plattdeutsch*, was the best-known German writer of his time who used dialect. This was certainly a significant factor in Finland, too, where the language of early literature was based to a great extent on the vernacular of the common people. For Reuter, dialect was a means of creating a picture of the age and of giving a voice to the common people. His works remained on the market for a considerable time (14 titles were published in Finland between 1870 and 1939).[940]

The novel was the main literary genre of the romantic period. Many of the novels had protagonists who were unable to adapt to the bourgeois world and fled to convents or monasteries or to remote corners of the world, where they became hermits. The historical novel has often been regarded as coming into being with the publication of *Waverley* by the Scottish writer Walter Scott (1771–1832) in 1814. Walter Scott was one of the most productive British romantics and one of the most popular authors of his time. Although he wrote adventure stories that contained many of the elements of literature for young people, in his own time (before the growth in the amount of literature produced for children and young people), he was regarded as a writer of exciting historical novels. Scott began to create a new type of historical novel. In his texts, the depiction of nature and an often melancholy and nostalgic narrative are combined with imaginative subjects. Scott was born in Edinburgh and grew up in the countryside, where he became interested in the early history of Scotland and its traditional legends. Early on in his career, he had edited a collection of folk ballads. He wrote a new series of historical novels situated in the English past. They included *Ivanhoe* (1820), a story set in the time of the Crusades, which was translated into Finnish in 1870.[941] The collection of Kivijärvi library contained altogether four of Scott's works: in addition to *Waverley* (Finnish translation 1904) and *The Talisman* (trans. 1880), there was *The Bride of Lammermoor*[942] (trans. 1871 or 1883) and the previously mentioned *The Fair Maid of Perth* (trans. 1878).[943]

The breakthrough of the historical novel took place at a time of great upheavals and revolutions in Europe (c.1789–1814). All this reinforced people's awareness of the past, a realization that history is a continuous stream of changes, that processes of change are going on all the time and also that history affects the course of every person's life. Scott transformed the art of the novel. In his works he used the voice of the omniscient narrator, and although the events of the novels are situated in real settings, he attributed only minor roles to well-known historical characters such as monarchs and

---

939 Finnish title: *Koditon*.
940 Lassila 2007, 95–96.
941 Heikkinen 2013, 219–220; Vartiainen 379, 406–407, 410.
942 Finnish title: *Lammermoorin morsian*.
943 Kivijärvi BOOKS.

created imaginary characters for his protagonists. His works also contained precise depictions of nature. His language was slightly antiquated, which had the effect of lending verisimilitude to his stories.[944]

From the early nineteenth century on, the political climate in Europe began to be influenced by nationalist ideologies. The emphasis on national unity and the discovery of a national identity[945] were part of this political programme for a nation state. The history of the nation and its own language came to occupy a central position in this development. In the field of literature, the idea of national unity and a kind of cultural 'original state' that defined the identity of the whole nation was linked to this political programme. In literature, the most important themes came to be history, a national literature and the language of the people. These were combined with mysticism, an interest in the human mind and an excessive emphasis on the self. The rise of nationalist sentiment inspired people to become aware of the significance of their own national culture.[946]

In Finland, Zacharias Topelius' *Fältskärns berättelser* [Tales of a Barber Surgeon][947] (translated into Finnish between 1878 and 1882) is the title of a series offering a Finnish a view of Swedish history from the Battle of Breitenfeld to the coup d'état of Gustav III.[948] There were a score or so of titles by Topelius available for reading in Kivijärvi library. They were mainly translations from the series *Fältskärns berättelser*, *Vinterqväller* [Winter evenings][949] and *Läsning för Barn* [Reading for children][950].[951]

A cultural awakening took place in Scandinavia at the beginning of the nineteenth century. For example, German literature had a strong influence on Danish cultural life, and the Danish poet and playwright Adam Oehlenschläger (1779–1850) introduced a new kind of romantic poetry into Denmark. His plays and poetry were influenced by German romanticism and were linked with the national historical trend.[952] Literature from the rest of Europe and beyond often reached Finland through Sweden in Swedish translations, and in the first half of the nineteenth century, Scandinavian works occupied an important position in translated literature into Finnish. For example, Adam Oehlenschläger's tragedy *Fostbrødrene* [The blood brothers, Luostariveljekset] was published in Finnish in 1847.[953] None of his works was to be found in the collections of Kivijärvi library, but there was one in Saarijärvi library.[954]

944 Heikkinen 2013, 220.
945 About it's continuity, see e.g. Ihalainen 2005.
946 Vartiainen 2009, 455.
947 Finnish title: *Välskäärin kertomuksia*.
948 Vartiainen 2009, 456.
949 Finnish title: *Talvi-iltain tarinoita*.
950 Finnish title: *Lukemisia lapsille*.
951 KKA, Collection catalogues of Kivijarvi lending library; the old book collection of Kivijärvi lending library.
952 Vartiainen 2009, 456.
953 Kantola 2007, 54.
954 KKA, Collection catalogues of Kivijärvi lending library; the old book collection of Kivijärvi lending library; Collection catalogues of Saarijärvi lending library; Saarijärvi BOOKS.

The works of James Fenimore Cooper (1789–1851) were central in the development of the American novel in the romantic age. It has been claimed that he resembled Walter Scott. Both their oeuvres successfully combine adventure stories with skilful story-telling.[955] Later, both acquired a reputation as writers for young people. Cooper's novels described life in the American West and the encounter between the native American Indians and the foreigners who arrived on the continent. *The Last of the Mohicans* (1826)[956], which was translated into Finnish in 1882, 1914 and 1945, is the best-known of the five novels in the *Leatherstocking* series. In it, Cooper examines another conflict, that between civilization and the natural state.[957] Early on, only Cooper's American Indian books were known in Finland, and his sea adventures were not translated into Finnish at all.[958] The first Finnish translation of *The Last of the Mohicans* and the 1872 translation of *The Pathfinder*[959] were acquired by Kivijärvi library.[960] Transnational comparison shows that in addition to Cooper's works, translations of novels by writers like Dickens, Scott and Harriet Beecher-Stowe were at the time among the most popular works in the people's libraries in Finland and also in France, for example.[961]

Literature in the nineteenth century was characteristically international. Numerous translations in different languages were published, and some genres of the novel became international. For example, the Gothic, historical, adventure and social novel all became common. In the course of the nineteenth century, genres of literature intended for women, children and young people also developed. Particularly novels and serial narratives became important forms of mass culture. The traditional oral folk culture was moulded into a popular literary form, and thereby the whole nation became acquainted with it. At the same time, it was possible to supervise and censure this escapist literature more strictly than before.[962]

Particularly for women, fiction opened up a new opportunity to write about history at a time when they could not yet pursue careers as academic historians. For example, women wrote two thirds of all the historical narratives and novels that were published in Sweden between 1856 and 1866, whereas in Germany the proportion of women writers of historical fiction was lower, below a third. In Finland, the first historical novel of Fredrika Runeberg (the wife of the national poet Johan Ludvig Runeberg), *Fru Catharina Boije och hennes döttrar* [Mrs Catharina Boije and her

---

955 Vartiainen 2009, 463.
956 Finnish title: *Viimeinen mohikaani*.
957 Vartiainen 2009, 464.
958 Nyman & Kovala 2007, 169.
959 Finnish title: *Kuvauksia metsänelämästä sivistyksen äärimmäisillä rajoilla*.
960 KKA, Collection catalogues of Kivijärvi lending library; the old book collection of Kivijärvi lending library.
961 Barnett 1973, 324.
962 Vartiainen 2009, 474–475.

daughters][963] was set in the period of the Great Wrath. The book was written in the 1840s although it was not published until 1858.[964]

Some of the literature written in Swedish in Finland was translated into Finnish in the nineteenth century, Among the early Finnish women prose authors writing in Swedish were Sara Wacklin, whose work *Hudrade minnen från Österbotten* [A hundred memories from Ostrobothnia] was translated into Finnish in the years 1872–1876 and again in 1898–1900, and the above mentioned Fredrika Runeberg, whose novel *Fru Catharina Boije och hennes döttrar* first appeared in Finnish in 1881.[965] The first Finnish translation of this work was part of the collection of Kivijärvi library. The gap in time between the publication of original works and their translations into Finnish decreased towards the end of the century.[966]

Also in Kivijärvi lending library's collection included Harriet Beecher-Stowe's work *Uncle Tom's Cabin* (1852), which was translated into Finnish under the title *Setä Tuomon tupa* in an abbreviated adaptation for children fairly soon after the publication of the original in 1856. In 1893, two different versions of the work were published in Finnish by different publishers. Both were adaptations. An unabbreviated version appeared in the B Series of the magazine *Kyläkirjasto* in 1899 and 1900. Another two adaptations for children were published in 1905 and 1923. The other works of the author that were translated into Finnish did not achieve the same popularity.[967]

The first Finnish translations of mystery and crime stories appeared in the late nineteenth century. Two novels by the English author Wilkie Collins (1824–1889) were published in 1880.[968] He created the first model for crime stories and who-done-its with his novels *The Woman in White* (1860), which was translated into Finnish in 1880, and *The Moonstone* (1868), translated into Finnish [*Kuun kivi*] in 1949. The detective in the latter book was the prototype of the protagonists of later who-done-its. Before Collins, Edgar Allan Poe had created the character of the detective Auguste Dupin, who became better known in the United States. Later, the best-known protagonist of this genre came to be Arthur Conan Doyle's Sherlock Holmes, with whose adventures the crime novel really began.[969] The books available for borrowing in Kivijärvi library in the period 1877–1897 contained a translation of Collins's *The Woman in White* [Finnish title: *Naisen haamu*].[970]

WORKS OF POPULAR ENLIGHTENMENT

The literature of the 1880s and 1890s exhibits an optimistic belief in the importance of work to promote popular education. Linked to this was the dream of a union between the common people and the educated classes,

---

963 Finnish title: *Rouva Katariina Boije ja hänen tyttärensä: kertomus ison vihan ajoilta*.
964 Heikkinen 2013, 225.
965 Heikkinen 2013, 225.
966 Katajamäki 2007, 68.
967 Nyman & Kovala 2007, 168–169.
968 Lappalainen 1999a, 40.
969 Vartiainen 2009, 518.
970 KKA, Collection catalogues of Kivijärvi lending library.

although such ideals were also regarded with suspicion by some. The subject of popular education came to the fore especially in the 1870s, when the Society for Popular Enlightenment was founded and began to support the activities of people's libraries and folk high schools. Such writers as Pietari Päivärinta and Theodolinda Hahnsson, in particular, emphasized the importance of educating the people. The reading of literature was considered important especially in the works of the folk writers; on the other hand, the texts of some members of the intelligentsia spoke of the dangers inherent in reading literature.[971] In the 1880s, WSOY distinguished itself by publishing the works of numerous folk writers, including Pietari Päivärinta and strove to aim part of its production at 'the people'.[972]

Sometimes the lives of the active supporters of the libraries and contemporary works of popular literature intersected in surprising ways. The people's library of Kivijärvi also contained some works by Theodolinda Hahnsson (1838–1919), the wife of a secondary school teacher from Hämeenlinna. She was the first woman who wrote novels and short stories in Finnish. She published her first novel, *Haapakallio*, in 1869. While her first husband J. A. Hahnsson (d. 1888) was still alive, Theodolinda had kept a boarding house and obtained extra income by writing and translating. In 1896 she re-married and took the surname of her new husband, Baron Yrjö Sakari Yrjö-Koskinen, who was a senator and a central figure in the Fennoman movement. The works that Hahnsson translated into Finnish were almost all written in Swedish. They included, for instance, descriptions of everyday life by Zacharias Topelius and Fredrika Bremer. Theodolinda, Y. S. Yrjö-Koskinen and Hilja Haahti, her daughter by her first husband, were founding members of the Union of Finnish Writers.[973]

Theodolinda Hanhsson's first husband, J. A. Hahnsson, taught Finnish in Kokkola Middle School. The family began consciously to change their home language from Swedish to Finnish in the late nineteenth century, and their children's surname was correspondingly changed to Haahti. Theodolinda's husband read her first short story in Finnish to a certain Dr. Blomstedt[974], who was of the view that they should be published in the Finnish Literature Society's series *Novellikirjasto* [The short story library]. Theodolinda Hahnsson said that she had wanted to write her story for 'the deep ranks of the people'.[975] Hahnsson's short stories, novels, poems and plays were inspired by Fennoman ideology and were written in an idealistic and national romantic style. The subjects were generally connected with the common people, whom the Fennoman ideology considered to constitute a font of talent, which by means of education and upbringing could be guided into working for the benefit of their mother country. The same themes and

---

971 Lappalainen 1999b, 70–71.
972 Häggman 2001, 70, 74–75.
973 Hirvonen 1993, 208–209; Lilius 2007, 179; Tuulio 1979, 239.
974 Very likely he was Oskar Blomstedt, a Latin teacher and translator and Docent in Finnish and Hungarian at Helsinki University. Also a journalist.
975 Haahti 1945, 165; Yrjö-Koskinen 1916, 145–146. On the change of language, see Lindgren & Lindgren 2006, 355.

settings are repeated throughout her works, but it was probably the very lack of surprise and the familiarity that this created that was the reason for their popularity.[976] There were also religious undertones in her works, although at that time literature was tending to adopt a more rationalist approach to the depiction of humankind.

Theodolinda Hansson was the daughter of a clergyman, and in her childhood household there had been five maid servants to whom she related in her own words in Finnish the stories she had read in Swedish. The servant girls regretted that such stories had not been published in Finnish. Later, in her memoirs, Hahnsson said that this gave her the idea of writing about events in the lives of people like the maids, which she thought they would be interested in reading about.[977] She was the youngest daughter of Carl Limón, the curate of Kiikka in the chapelry of Tyrvää in south-west Finland, and his second wife, Maria Christina Mollin; she was named Sofia Theodolinda, but as a child she was called Fia. The forefather of the Limón family is considered to have been Jakob Limonius, who was ordained in 1704 and became a minister in Siuntio (Sjundeå) in southern Finland. His youngest son, who worked as an independent provincial surveyor, shortened the family surname to Limón. His son Johan Magnus and his grandson, Carl Magnus Limón, chose a career in the ministry.[978]

Limón, the curate of Kiikka, is related to have been a lettered person who was keen on literary activities. The children in the Kiikka chapelry were taught at home by a tutor before the boys were sent away to school. The oldest of the sons, Werner, graduated from school and entered the university after passing his student matriculation examination in 1846. In Helsinki, he, like many other young men, became fervently inspired by the ideals of the national awakening that Snellman had initiated, and he took them back to his home chapelry. The curate subscribed to the newspaper *Suometar*. Limón and his family moved into the vicarage in Pälkäne in central southern Finland in 1848, after which Fia began to be called Theodolinda. Her brother Werner later married Maria Hällfors, the daughter of the previous vicar of Pälkäne, Dean Isak Emanuel Hällfors.[979]

Dean Carl Limón succeeded in getting six schools established in different parts of the parish of Pälkäne. In each of the schools there was teaching for six weeks a year. His son Werner was also interested in developing popular education. When he was ordained as a minister in 1850 and appointed to be his father's assistant, he was at home all year round and had the opportunity to disseminate the nationalist ideals in practice. To begin with, the schools in the parish were only temporary, but the parish assembly was considering establishing them on a permanent basis. Werner Limón volunteered to teach religion in them free of charge for as long as he continued to be his father's assistant in the village and to contribute to the funding of the schools.

---

976 Launis 2005,10; Sainio 2004.
977 Yrjö-Koskinen 1916, 145; Tuulio 1979, 240.
978 Haahti 134–138; Kotivuori 2005. Ylioppilasmatrikkeli 1640–1852: Johan Limonius. Web publication 2005. Accessed 9/1/2012.
979 Haahti 1945, 138–140, 152; Haahti 1956, 74–75.

Werner Limón became the vicar of Kivijärvi in 1867 and died there of typhoid fever the following year. Theodolinda was also interested in popular enlightenment endeavours and wanted to write more Finnish-language reading material for the common people.[980] As mentioned above, several of her works were contained in the collection of Kivijärvi library. It is difficult to estimate in retrospect whether the officers of the library were aware when they procuring new works in the period from the 1870s to the 1890s that the writer was the sister of the former vicar of the parish.

Many of the early narratives written in Finnish were intended principally for members of the upper classes who were native speakers of Finnish or who had learned Finnish. For example, the early works of Pietari Hannikainen, K. J. Gummerus and Theodolinda Hahnsson were sometimes read aloud while the members of the family sat around, and the lessons that they taught were discussed. According to literary scholars, early Finnish prose writers such as Niljs Aejmelaeus,[981] Theodolinda Hansson, K. J. Gummerus and Pietari Hannikainen wrote primarily for the educated classes in order that they might learn to use the Finnish language. Later, in her memoirs, Hahnsson emphasized the popular enlightenment aspect of her works, but they also came to be an important vehicle for educating the upper classes, who spoke Swedish as their mother tongue and wished for reasons of national(ist) politics to learn to use Finnish in their daily interaction. At the same time, these writers were able to show that it was possible to write original literature in Finnish. At that stage, members of the educated classes did not have complete confidence in the common people's desire and ability to read fiction. Other genres of literature were considered to be more useful for the commons. For the intelligentsia, on the other hand, literature in Finnish was no more interesting in terms of its artistic merits than other literature, and therefore reading it had to be justified in terms of nationalist endeavours and language policy.[982]

Even in the 1860s, members of the upper classes both in Finland and elsewhere in Europe were broadly of the opinion that the manners and language of the common people were 'coarse', just as their emotional life and their ability to express themselves were primitive compared with those of the educated classes.[983] However, the common people constituted a foundation stone of the Fennomans' programme, and they legitimated the movement's aim to raise the Finnish language into a position in which it would be the dominant language of culture in Finland. Not only was literature the most important instrument for achieving this goal, but it also provided the intelligentsia with a way of acquainting themselves with the life of the common people. The folk element thus became a part of culture during the romantic age, but it was not adopted wholesale; only certain elements, refined to comply with the aesthetic ideals of the age so that they

---

980 Haahti 1945, 145–146.
981 Pastor Aejmelaeus published the first Finnish short story (or novelette), which he wrote in 1838. Jokipii 1971.
982 Lassila 2008, 10, 44.
983 Lassila 2008, 63–64.

might provide suitable reading for the members of the educated classes, were selected. A prime example of this promotion of the folk element is *The Kalevala*, the national epic compiled from oral bardic poetry by Elias Lönnrot.[984] The collection in Kivijärvi library included Lönnrot's *Kalevala* and *Kanteletar*.[985]

In the nineteenth-century Finnish nationalist conception, 'the people' meant mainly a Herderesque concept of a cultural nation. This was combined with the ideas of J. V. Snellman and Yrjö Sakari Yrjö-Koskinen, in which the people and nationality were united. Particularly Snellman and his disciples politicized the concepts of 'the people' and 'the nation' into a real ideal of nationhood. Every nation had its own historical destiny. The spirit of the nation was expressed in its language and its national literature. In Finland, the educated class was mainly Swedish-speaking, and thus Finnish was still predominantly the language of the common people in the mid-nineteenth century.[986] In the mind of the intelligentsia, 'the people' was equated with the land-owning peasants, who, being an official estate with representation at the Diet, also possessed some political power – unlike the landless population, who continued to grow in numbers in the course of the nineteenth century.[987]

Baron Yrjö Koskinen (1830–1903) was an historian, statesman and journalist, and an ideologist of Finnish nationalism. Koskinen published several textbooks and historical studies, some works of fiction and a few poems.[988] Some of his works were also to be found in Kivijärvi library.[989] He was a member of the administrative organs of a number of nationally significant societies and associations such as the Society for Popular Enlightenment and the Finnish Literature Society. Yrjö Koskinen believed that the task of the elementary schools was to awaken in the pupils the desire to pursue real, i.e. independent, studies, and he linked this with the idea of self-improvement. By independent study, Koskinen meant reading at home without external prompting. He was also of the opinion that a sufficient number of parish and village libraries should be established in addition to promoting independent reading,[990] and to this end in the late 1850s he proposed that public funds should be provided for the purpose. Ever since his early years as a student, he had worked to promote the library movement. He adopted the principle that support and the acquisition of funds for libraries should be as closely connected with the common people as possible, and therefore in 1853 he proposed that libraries should charge loan fees in the belief that books would be regarded as cheap and worthless if they were available for borrowing free of charge. Already in the end of

---

984 Lassila 2008, 11, 13.
985 KKA, Collection catalogues of Kivijärvi lending library; Kivijärvi BOOKS.
986 Lassila 2008, 66.
987 Häggman 2001, 8: Liikanen 2003, 274–292.
988 Kemppinen 2001, 8.
989 E.g. *Suomen kansan historia* [A history of the Finnish people]. KKA, Collection catalogues of Kivijärvi library.
990 Kemppinen 2001, 230; Mäkinen 2009e, 160–161.

the 1850s Yrjö-Koskinen proposed, that new popular libraries should be established with the help of public funding.[991]

Already from the 17th century on non-fiction for children and younger people had been translated in Finnish. Secular Finnish-language literature for young people began to be produced in the mid-nineteenth century, at the same time as the same kind of literature for adults. This process was promoted by Fennoman ideology, popular education, the development of elementary schools and libraries and the expanding activities of civic associations. In the second half of the nineteenth century, more than a thousand works of literature for children and young people came out in Finland. Over 80 percent of them were translations. Many of the classics, like the works of Defoe, Beecher-Stowe, Swift and Cervantes (which were also to be found in the collection of Kivijärvi library), were first translated in adaptations for young people. The most important writer for children and young people at that time was the Swedish-speaking Finnish writer Zacharias Topelius. A four-volume collection of Finnish fairy tales and stories, *Suomen kansan satuja ja tarinoita* (1852–1866) edited by Eero Salmelainen also provided an important stimulus for Finnish-language literature for the young.[992]

The works of two teachers, Alli Nissinen and Immi Hellén, were the most important examples of contemporary poetry for children. Nissinen's anthologies *Pikkupalleroisille* [For tiny tots] (1888) and *Palleroisille iloksi* [For the pleasure of toddlers] (published in five volumes between 1892 and 1902) contained not only poems, but also fairy tales and stories. These works were acquired by Kivijärvi library. Hellén's corresponding anthologies were entitled *Lasten runoja* [Poems for children] (1898) and *Lasten lauluja* [Songs for children] (1899).[993] Kivijärvi library contained Hellén's work *Eeva Aarnio: kertomus nuorille* [Eeva Aarnio: a story for young persons].[994]

The earliest magazines for light reading in Finland were published for Swedish-speaking readers, and they contained a lot of translated material. The first Finnish-language magazine was *Kyläkirjasto* [The village library], which appeared from 1873 to 1914. It was a copy of the British *Penny Magazine*, and it was edited by K. J. Gummerus, a teacher from Jyväskylä. Most of the material in it consisted of prose fiction and religious narratives. Its character changed in 1877, when Gummerus founded an affiliated magazine called *Kyläkirjaston kuvalehti* [The village library illustrated magazine], which achieved great popularity. *Kyläkirjasto* functioned rather like a book club, for its subscribers received a work of either non-fiction or fiction three or four times a year. Usually, Gummerus published the same work as an independent book. Gummerus' principles and values were characterized by an enlightening outlook and Christian decency, and this determined the contents of the magazines.[995]

---

991 Kemppinen 2001, 231; Mäkinen 2009e, 159.
992 Bengtsson 2012; Kuivasmäki 1999, 313.
993 Lappalainen 1999a, 31–32.
994 KKA, Collection catalogues of Kivijärvi lending library; the old book collection of Kivijärvi Lending library; Lappalainen 1999a, 31–32.
995 Leino-Kaukiainen 2007b, 156.

Kaarle Werkko, an elementary school teacher, came up with the idea for the calendar of the Society for Popular Enlightenment because he was dissatisfied with the subjects of the articles accompanying the existing almanacs. On the other hand, he realized what important works the almanacs were for the people of the countryside. The models for the calendars of the Society for Popular Enlightenment came from Estonia and Sweden, but despite this they were original Finnish publications, works that promoted Fennoman ideology and Finnish literature.[996] There were 11 copies of the society's calendars in the collection of Kivijärvi library, most of them published in the 1880s.[997]

There was still extremely little Finnish literature dealing with health care earlier in the 1880s, and the common people had hardly any way of finding out how to deal with various kinds of diseases. However, the newspapers did begin to publish the first articles on this subject in those days. *Terveydenhoitolehti* [The health care paper] began to appear at the beginning of 1889; it was one sheet in size, and it came out every two months.[998] The first four (1889–1892) annuals were acquired by Kivijärvi Library.[999]

In the statistics compiled by Schadewitz about rural lending libraries, the works of the following writers were the most popular: Jaakko Gummerus, Harriet Beecher-Stowe, Aina (the *nom de plume* of Edith Forssman), Theodolinda Hahnsson, J. L. Runeberg, Minna Canth and Walter Scott.[1000] All these authors apart from Canth were also read in Kivijärvi. The collections of the rural libraries in eastern Finland, like that of Kivijärvi library, contained translations of *Genovefa, Uncle Tom's Cabin, Eräkäs*[1001] works, and works by Dickens, Scott, Gogol, Verne and Lagerlöf.[1002] The collections of the people's libraries were very similar in different parts of the country although the decisions on acquisitions were made locally.

The historical literature in the library of Kivijärvi in the second half of the nineteenth century was represented by works of national history. They included Danielson-Kalmari's *Suomen sota ja sotilaat* [The Finnish War and soldiers] I–II and *Suomen yhdistäminen Venäjän waltakuntaan* [Finland's annexation into the Russian Empire], Yrjö-Koskinen's *Suomen kansan historia* [A history of the Finnish people] and *Johtavat aatteet ihmiskunnan historiassa* [Leading ideals in the history of humanity]. Also available for borrowing were translations of Axel Bergholm's *Historisk läsebok för skolan och hemmet* [A historical reading book for school and home][1003] and Louis Thomas's *Les*

---

996 Häggman 2008, 223; Inkilä 1960, 158.
997 Kivijärvi BOOKS.
998 Kulha 1972, 109.
999 KKA, Collection catalogues of Kivijärvi lending library; the old book collection of Kivijärvi lending library.
1000 Schadewitz 1903, 41.
1001 The word *erakäs* is old Finnish and means 'hermit'. Here it is probably a matter of works whose titles contained this by different authors.
1002 Järvelin 1966, 83.
1003 Finnish title: *Historiallinen lukukirja*.

fabuleuses inventions [Fabulous inventions[1004]].[1005] All in all, the collection of the privately founded library contained a fairly varied selection of literature, both Finnish and foreign, although it was a very modest collection of a rural library. The needs of children and young people had been taken into account in the acquisitions, and the number of works of fiction grew considerably.

New acquisitions at the turn of the century

REALIST LITERATURE IN PEOPLE'S LIBRARIES

It is not until the beginning of the twentieth century that Finland can be considered to have been a country that possessed a real national literary tradition of its own. By that time, publishers had begun to operate on a professional basis, and a network of bookshops was being created. The readings skills of the population were also improving all the time. The works of Topelius, Päivärinta, Aho, Åberg, Starbäck and Aleksis Kivi continued to be the most read books in people's libraries in the countryside. Also popular were books of sermons and the works of Martin Luther.[1006]

The most borrowed works in Kivijärvi lending library in the years 1893–1897 were all examples of traditional religious literature. There were 67 loans in all, amounting to fewer than ten per volume for the most popular books.[1007] Ignoring the loans registers, however, one can note from the library's collection and the acquisitions at the turn of the century that more modern works of fiction and other types of *belles lettres* were acquired for the lending library at that time. Probably they were borrowed in greater numbers than the works of the old collection, but because no records of the numbers of books that were borrowed have survived, it is impossible to estimate from the available sources the extent to which more modern works of fiction and non-fiction works were borrowed in relation to the books in the old collection.[1008]

The late romantic movement was located between romanticism and realism. Among the major works of romantic fiction in Russia were those of Nikolai Gogol (1809–1852). His short novel *Taras Bulba* (1835), which was translated into Finnish under the same title in 1878, 1913, 1946, 1959 and 1986, was written in a romantic vein and used patriotic rhetoric to describe a Cossack community.[1009] The first Finnish translation was acquired for the library in Kivijärvi.[1010] The first Finnish translation of this work also belonged to the collection of for example Nivala library.[1011] The realist novel

---

1004 Finnish title: *Suuret keksinnöt*.
1005 KKA, Loans registers of Kivijärvi lending library 1877–1897.
1006 Schadewitz 1903, 40–41.
1007 KKA, Loans registers of Kivijärvi lending library 1877–1897.
1008 KKA, Collection catalogues of Kivijärvi lending library; the old book collection of Kivijärvi lending library.
1009 Vartiainen 2009, 494, 497.
1010 KKA, Collection catalogues of Kivijärvi lending library.
1011 In Nivala the book was acquired already in the same year when it was published. H. Mäkelä 1991, 33.

of the nineteenth century sought to simulate reality with the greatest possible verisimilitude. As a literary movement, realism was at its height in the early 1870s. It was characterized by an interest in moral and ethical questions. Biography was a popular form of realist literature.[1012]

Realism was a major movement particularly in the fiction of Victorian Britain. Its main setting was the urban culture of the industrial age. One symbol of the fairly uniform and stable literary culture that prevailed there was the three-decker novel, which continued to dominate the book market down to the end of the nineteenth century. It was a novel published in three parts, of which the number of pages and sales price were fixed. It originally arose from the libraries' need to allow the works of an individual writer to circulate as efficiently as possible from one reader to another. Novels that appeared in serial form also affected the development of the genre. The most successful and best-known English novelist of the Victorian age was Charles Dickens (1812–1870), whose works dealt with many of the sore points of industrial society. He employed the techniques of both the serial novel and the three-decker novel in a natural way. His ability to moderate his own objectives to the demands of his readers increased his popularity, as did his skill as a public presenter. In his works, the struggle between good and evil was a dominant theme. Dickens's only historical novel proper, *A Tale of Two Cities* (1859),[1013] was translated into Finnish under the title *Kaksi kaupunkia* in 1903 and again in 1928–1929.[1014] The earlier translation was available in Finnish to the customers of Kivijärvi library from the early years of the twentieth century on.[1015]

The realist period was short-lived in Finnish literature.[1016] One finds hardly any works by representatives of Finnish realism in the people's library of Kivijärvi, although the realist movement flourished in world literature, especially French and Russian, in the period between 1830 and 1880. Realism reached the Nordic countries in the 1870s, and in Finland it was characteristically a phenomenon of the 1880s. The movement examined the societal and cultural effects of contemporary phenomena, and the main themes of literature came to be modernization, secularization, positivism, liberalism, urbanization and industrialization together with the ills caused by these.[1017]

No works by the most important representative of Nordic realism, Henrik Ibsen (1828–1906), were to be found in the lending library of Kivijärvi, but there were works such as *Mary* and *På guds veje* [On God's way][1018] by the Norwegian social critic and playwright Bjørnstjerne Bjørnson

1012 Vartiainen 2009, 477.
1013 Heikkinen 2013, 224; Law & Patten 2009, 162.
1014 Vartiainen 2009, 499–501, 505.
1015 KKA, Collection catalogues of Kivijärvi lending library.
1016 Lappalainen 1999a, 11.
1017 Lappalainen 1999a, 8–10.
1018 Finnish title: *Jumalan teillä*.

(1832–1910),[1019] who was awarded the Nobel Prize for Literature in 1903.[1020] In addition to other social issues, a major theme of Nordic realist literature was the societal and communal role of women. By this time writing had also become a profession for some women. Selma Lagerlöf (1858–1940) was the first Nordic female author to receive general recognition and acclaim. She received the Nobel Prize for Literature in 1909. Her two-volume work *Jerusalem* [The Holy City] (1901–1902], which was translated into Finnish in 1902, describes the birth of a religious community and deals with questions relating to people's ability and failure to adapt. She was made the first female member of the Royal Swedish Academy.[1021] In Kivijärvi, people were able to read not only *Jerusalem* but also translations of her works *Antikrists mirakler* [The Miracles of Antichrist][1022] and *Herr Arnes penningar* [Herr Arne's Hoard/ The Treasure[1023]].[1024]

The development of the Russian realist novel was influenced by the French and British realists. Leo Tolstoy (1828–1910) began his literary career by publishing his autobiography in three parts: *Detstvo* [Childhood] (1852), which was translated into Finnish in 1904, 1952 and 1983, *Otrochestvo* [Boyhood] (1854), translated in 1904, 1952 and 1983, and *Yunost'* [Youth] (1857), translated in 1905, 1952 and 1983.[1025] Tolstoy wrote these works, which combined fact and fiction, when he was serving as an army officer in the Caucasus. *Anna Karenina* (1875–1877) was translated into Finnish in 1910–1911, 1961 and 1978). In his last novel, *Voskresenie* [Resurrection][1026] (1899), which was translated into Finnish in 1899–1900, 1952 and 1984, he criticized social conventions as well as the church and the state.[1027] Kivijärvi library's collection contained translations of Tolstoy's collected stories and a work titled *Kuolema*[1028].[1029]

The first breakthrough of modernist literature in Finland took place in the 1880s, when realist influences began to enter the country from Russia, the Nordic countries and France. At the same time, folk writers lost favour, and their works soon began to appear antiquated. The difference between them and the realists was that, although both wrote about poverty, misery, drunkenness, crime and insecurity, in the opinion of the folk writers these evils were formative: they had a higher purpose which was ordained by God and which people themselves could not understand. Modernist realism, on the other hand, did not accept the view that the significance of these wrongs

---

1019 Vartiainen 2009, 585; KKA, Collection catalogues and the old book collection of Kivijärvi lending library.
1020 Kantola 2007, 56.
1021 Vartiainen 2009, 581–583.
1022 Finnish title: *Antikristuksen ihmetyöt*.
1023 Finnish title: *Aarne Herran Rahat*.
1024 KKA, Collection catalogues and the old book collection of Kivijärvi lending library.
1025 Finnish title: *Lapsuus, Poikaikä ja Nuoruus*.
1026 Finnish title: *Ylösnousemus*.
1027 Vartiainen 2009, 557–558, 562.
1028 This was possibly a translation of *Smert' Ivana Iljiča* [The Death of Ivan Ilyich].
1029 KKA, Collection catalogues of Kivijärvi lending library.

was determined by a force outside the lived reality of society. The realists considered that the problems arose out of the structures of society and the relationships and conflicts that existed between the individual and social power.[1030]

A large number of important social changes took place in the age of realism. The so-called 'society of the estates' in Finland gradually broke down and was replaced by the 'class society', while the process of modernization accelerated and caused a conflict between the old and the new. The Finnish Party split into the Old Finns and the Young Finns; for the latter, social issues were more important that the status of the Finnish language, the pet hobbyhorse of the former. The Estates of the Clergy and the Peasants opposed the ideology of the Young Finns and formed a bastion of conservatism.[1031] Young, educated Finnish-speakers greeted the realist works of writers like Minna Canth with interest and admiration. By contrast, readers with national romantic and Christian ideals abhorred realist literature and were horrified by the effects that it might have.[1032]

Over half of the Finnish literature of the realist period was narrative in character. About a fifth consisted of novels, and over a quarter of all literature was written by women. Other forms of fiction such as (collections of) tales and short stories were more typical of the age than were broad social novels. One reason for this was that newspapers and magazines favoured small-scale prose works. Moreover, many writers preferred to call their works stories rather than novels.[1033]

A large number of historical novels, many of them written by women, were published in Finland in the 1880s. The first historical novel written in Finnish in the realist period was E. F. Jahnsson's *Hatanpään Heikki ja hänen morsiamensa* [Heikki of Hatanpää and his bride] (1884). There was a second wave of historical novels in the 1890s, which on the one hand was a result of the oppressive rule of Russia and on the other of Karelianism, a movement in art in the early 1890s that sought its inspiration from Karelia. The main theme of Santeri Ivalo's novel *Juho Vesainen* (1894), which is set in the late sixteenth century, is revenge and its futility.[1034]

In realist literature, the narrator was required to be objective, but even so the texts of Pietari Päivärinta, for example, address the reader directly with didactic observations. The narrator is not completely absent from the text, and characteristically realist literature is strongly narrator-centric. The narrator connects the destinies of individuals with the broader social and historical situation. This happens, for example, in novels of student life like Arvid Järnefelt's *Isänmaa* [Fatherland] (1893) as well as in historical novels like Santeri Ivalo's *Juho Vesainen*, in which the narrator describes the course of events in the past almost like an historian.[1035] These aforementioned works were acquired also by Kivijärvi library.

1030 Lassila 2008, 97, 99.
1031 Lappalainen 1999a, 13.
1032 Tiirakari 1999, 17.
1033 Lappalainen 1999a, 36.
1034 Lappalainen 1999a, 39.
1035 Lappalainen 1999a, 41.

At the beginning of their careers, realist writers like Juhani Aho, Kauppis-Heikki, Kaarlo Kramsu, K. A. Järvi and Teuvo Pakkala occupied important positions as journalists, particularly in the provincial newspapers that had been taken over by the Young Finns party, one of which was the Jyväskylä newspaper *Keski-Suomi*. These papers published translations of realist and naturalist foreign works and presented realist Finnish literature in a positive light.[1036]

Like the realist novels, the other genre of literature that was dominant at the time, dramaturgy, also sought to address social problems. Many of the realist novelists started out by writing folk plays. Teuvo Pakkala's play *Tukkijoella* [On the logging river] (1899) can be regarded as one example of this. Like the folk plays of Minna Canth, for example, his works continued to be popular in summer theatre presentations throughout the twentieth century.[1037] Pakkala's *Tukkijoella* was acquired by Kivijärvi library in 1904.[1038]

Amateur dramatics were an import part of the activities of civic associations in Kivijärvi at the turn of the century, they put on new Finnish plays as well as classical national dramas. The presentation of plays became part of the endeavours to promote popular enlightenment from the mid-nineteenth century on. Robert Kiljander, a post master from Jyväskylä, was a friend of one of the best known playwrights of the age, Minna Canth, who had attended the Teacher Training Seminary, and he supported her early on in her career. In his own works, he was not as sharply critical of society as Canth; rather he examined the life style of the small-town bourgeoisie and petty officials in a humorous light. His plays included *Amalia Ystävämme* [Our friend Amalia] (1881), *Postikonttorissa* [In the post office] (1887) and *Pahassa pulassa* [In a bad fix] (1889).[1039] Kivijärvi library contained these works as well as some other plays by him. Another interesting thing is that in one of scripts the cast of characters has been listed, showing which of the parishioners played which character.[1040]

Translated and Finnish literature

The commercialization of publishing increased the amount of escapist literature translated into Finnish that was published in the twentieth century.[1041] Most of the literature that was translated into Finnish in the 1880s was from the Scandinavian languages and German, followed by English; it was not until the following decade that translations of works in the last mentioned language began to reach the same level as those of literature in the other two language groups. Indeed, relatively little English-language literature was translated into Finnish before 1890. Of all the literature

---

1036 Lappalainen 1999a, 18.
1037 Lappalainen 1999a, 14, 29–30.
1038 KKA, Collection catalogues of Kivijärvi lending library; the old book collection of Kivijärvi lending library.
1039 Lappalainen 1999a, 29; Pietilä 2003, 103–104, 166–171.
1040 KKA, Collection catalogues of Kivijärvi lending library; the old book collection of Kivijärvi lending library.
1041 Sevänen 2007, 14.

translated into Finnish, 29 percent was from the Scandinavian languages, 29 percent from German, 14 percent from English, nine percent from French and seven percent from Russian. It was mostly the works of John Bunyan and early classics like Defoe's *Robinson Crusoe* and Beecher-Stowe's *Uncle Tom's Cabin* (which were also read in Kivijärvi) that were translated from English.[1042] In the early twentieth century, *Uncle Tom's Cabin* was still considered among the common people to provide worthwhile, uplifting and educative reading for young people.[1043] Its message was also very close to the teachings of the Evangelical movement.[1044]

Cultural links between Finland and the British Isles were consolidated fairly late. In the Early Modern Age, the cultural currents travelled from France to Germany and from there via Sweden to Finland. During the period of Russian rule, written and other influences were also absorbed from Russia. In the early twentieth century, North America began to assume an increasingly important position concomitantly with the wave of emigration there. Cultural life in Finland had long been oriented towards Scandinavia and Germany rather than the sphere of Anglophone culture. After the Reformation, ecclesiastical connections with Germany became more important, and the church was an agent that exerted a central influence on the development of cultural life, especially at the local level. Finland's connections with Great Britain were mainly commercial. They increased after Finland became a major producer of sawn timber in the 1870s and later also of pulp and paper. Indeed, the main buyer of these products was Great Britain, and a significant proportion of Finnish exports went there.[1045]

In nineteenth-century Finland, the most important institution for the creation and maintenance of cultural links was the Imperial Alexander University (today the University of Helsinki). It strongly influenced the teachers and corps of civil and ecclesiastical office holders that it educated. The position of German scholarship was strong all over Europe in the nineteenth century, and German philosophy occupied a special position because of the influence it had exerted on the national awakening in Finland as well as in other countries.[1046] On the other hand, the growth in emigration from Finland to the United States from the 1870s on created a basis for the later positive attitude to American culture especially among the less educated sections of the population. Nearly 330,000 emigrants left Finland for North America between 1870 and 1914.[1047]

For practical reasons, English began to be taught at an early stage in commercial and naval colleges, but a large proportion of the population remained unfamiliar with it. Although Britain was an important trading partner of Finland and bought Finnish exports in the nineteenth century, the translation of British authors apart from Shakespeare and a few other

---

1042 Kovala 1992, 32–35; Sevänen 2007, 17.
1043 Häggman 2008, 225.
1044 Brown 2004, 7.
1045 Kovala 1992, 21.
1046 Klinge 1989, 906–909; Kovala 1992, 22.
1047 Kovala 1992, 24; Kero 1986, 22–27.

major writers did not increase until the end of that century. To a great extent, this was a result of the fact that a command of English only became common among Finns later on, after the Second World War. Thus in the nineteenth century, the number of potential translators from English who were available was rather low. From the Finnish point of view, English was above all the language of commerce and maritime navigation. In secondary schools, the English language occupied a weak position for a long time. Because of Finland's special geopolitical situation, Finnish pupils were required to learn first Swedish and Russian (which were considered to be domestic languages) before they could study foreign languages proper such as German, French and, of course, the classical languages.[1048]

Jules Verne (1828-1905), Émile Zola and Alexandre Dumas were among the most popular French writers in Finland. The customers of the library in Kivijärvi could read Verne's work *Les Enfants du capitaine Grant* [In Search of the Castaways][1049] (1867-1868), Part I of which was translated into Finnish in 1910, 1923 and 1957, Part II in 1922, 1937 and 1957 and Part III in 1923. Verne's works were adventure stories in which a belief in the power of technology and in man's boundless curiosity were given pride of place.[1050]

The *Bildungsroman* is a type of novel that describes the maturation of the protagonist, his or her growing self-awareness and relationship with the surrounding world. It involves a comprehensive development of the character's whole personality, in which various conflicts mark stages in the journey towards maturity. The *Bildungsroman* was a characteristic type of novel of the realist period in particular. In Finland numerous works describing student life were written. In late-nineteenth-century France, Germany and especially the Nordic countries, the realists favoured descriptions of the growth to maturity of young women. The contemporary debate about women's rights and the discussion on inequality between men and women and the lack of educational opportunities for women is evident in novels written in Finland and the other Nordic countries. One example is Minna Canth's *Hanna* (1886). Juhani Aho's *Papin tytär* [The minister's daughter] (1885) describes the life of a girl from childhood to adulthood.[1051] Often these novels were set in the countryside. Among the works that can be regarded as *Bildungsromane* in Kivijärvi library were Maila Talvio's *Haapaniemen keinu* [The swing at Haapaniemi], *Aili* and *Kansan seassa* [Among the people] (all of them novels about a woman's search for her identity) as well as Arvid Järnefelt's *Isänmaa* [Fatherland].[1052]

Works of the realist period dealing with female emancipation (the works of Minna Canth and Maria Jotuni, for example) are conspicuous by their absence from the collections of the people's libraries in rural Finland, and the same is true of proletarian literature. The contents of the collections were

---

1048 Kovala 1992, 25, 32-35; Leppihalme 2007, 153.
1049 Finnish title: *Kapteeni Grantia etsimässä*.
1050 Vartiainen 2009, 544.
1051 Aalto 2000, 7-8.
1052 KKA, Collection catalogues of Kivijärvi lending library; the old book collection of Kivijärvi lending library.

carefully selected by the boards of governors, whose outlook was extremely traditional. Moreover, in Kivijärvi, for example, the religious climate created by the revivalist movements further increased the conservatism. Of the realists, Maila Talvio (1871–1951) is of local interest in northern Central Finland because her brother Hugo Winter served for a long time as the vicar of the parish of Saarijärvi, and her works were to be found in the collection of Saarijärvi library.[1053] She began her career as a writer in 1895. Her early works juxtaposed different conceptions of morality: the simple traditional way of life of the countryside against the rootless urban lifestyle. Talvio herself was a notable public figure, and she maintained a literary salon. She took an active interest in local heritage work and in numerous other endeavours for the public good. Partly under the influence of her husband, Jooseppi Julius Mikkola, who was Professor of Slavonic Philology at Alexander University in Helsinki, and partly out of her own interest, she acquainted herself with Polish and Lithuanian literature. The couple helped to make various Slavonic cultures known in Finland in many different ways. Talvio translated into Finnish *Quo vadis?*, a historical novel by the Polish Nobel-Prize-winner, Henryk Sienkiewicz.[1054]

The acquisition policy of the popular libraries significantly determined what works were never made available for the common people to read. Locally, it is interesting to note that although the translation of J. L. Runeberg's works into Finnish already began in the 1830s, the collections of Kivijärvi library contained very few of his works, and even in Saarijärvi, where he had lived and was thus a writer of considerable local importance, a translation of his major work *Fänrik Ståls sägner* [The Tales of Ensign Stål] [1055] was only added to the library in a 1910 edition.[1056] It was not always the total oeuvre of a writer that was shunned, only the most suspect works. For example, *Ikuinen taistelu* [The eternal struggle] (1903) by Johannes Linnankoski (the *nom de plume* of Vihtori Peltonen, 1869–1913) belonged to the collection Kivijärvi lending library. It was a Byronic problem play on a Biblical theme: based on the story of Cain and Abel, it saw the conflict between them as an example of the eternal struggle between good and evil. A couple of years later, Linnankoski wrote a completely different kind of novel, *Laulu tulipunaisesta kukasta* [The Song of the Blood-Red Flower], which is a Finnish adaptation of the Don Juan story. The novel caused a great stir in its day. Numerous boy children were baptized 'Olavi' and girl children 'Kyllikki' after its main characters.[1057] However, for understandable reasons, this work was not included in the collections of Kivijärvi lending library.

At the turn of the century, the collection of Kivijärvi lending library expanded to include more recent Finnish literature and more new publications began to be acquired. If the operations of the library had continued to flourish in the early twentieth century, it would have been

---

1053 Collection catalogues of Saarijärvi lending library; Saarijärvi BOOKS.
1054 K. Laitinen 1997, 314–315; Paloposki 2007, 208, 215.
1055 Finnish title: *Vänrikki Stoolin tarinat*.
1056 Katajamäki 2007, 70.
1057 K. Laitinen 1997, 312.

interesting to investigate at what stage literature with more modern content would have been approved for the collection. Despite its limited resources, the board of governors of the library did try to continuously acquire new books and to refurbish the old works, and as a result at the turn of the century the state of the library was not quite as poor as that of many of the collections of early Finnish people's libraries several decades previously. The operations of many of these libraries then collapsed because of a failure to update their collections quickly enough. However, while it is interesting to examine the individual works in a library's collection, it is even more pertinent to inquire who read these works, to study their reading habits and to ascertain what kind of literature local people were interested in.

All in all, the contents of the collection of Kivijärvi lending library indicate first of all the great influence of traditional Pietist literature also for Finnish revivalist movements in the latter half of the nineteenth century. The works of Luther were particularly well represented in the library's old collection. Although the collection contained mainly old-fashioned literature, it was relatively varied for the collection of a small library, and it contained a diverse range of works in different fields. At the same time, the acquisitions of the library took account of not only Finnish and but also translated foreign works so that these new works were acquired if at all possible. Mostly the formation of the collections was regulated by the lack of funds both in the 1860s and 1870s and even still at the end of the century, which prevented the provision of a frequently renewed collection. At the same time as the acquisition of new works dried up, the number of loans decreased. The constant renewal of the collection would have been a guarantee of the library's continued survival, but apparently the local people were not so enthusiastic about the library's activities that they were willing to participate in the raising of funds for the library as they were for other publically beneficial institutions. Obviously, at that stage written culture was a more foreign phenomenon in their daily lives than some more practical activity such as membership of a youth or farmers' association.

5. The Rural People as Readers

The rural population's opportunities for reading

THE WEAK READING AND WRITING SKILLS OF THE PEOPLE
OF KIVIJÄRVI

On the back page of one of the books belonging to the collection of Kivijärvi people's library there is a comment written in pencil: 'This really is a nice book.'[1058] It was a devotional work. Although the regulations of the library did not permit the readers to make any marks in the books, the historian can only secretly wish that more of the customers of the library had written about their reading experiences in the margins so that these reactions might be studied later. In the age of the Internet it would be possible, and perfectly legal, for readers to make their own annotations in the texts of electronic library books. This would then make it possible at the same time to obtain other information about the readers and their backgrounds. But the historian has to make do with more traditional sources to ascertain who the customers of the early popular libraries were. Who then had the opportunity or the desire to use the people's library? How was the use of the library affected by the distance of people's homes from the church village, for example, or their time of life, family ties and education? And what kind of books were read or even bought, and where were they bought? Which members of the population could read and write, and how had they acquired these skills?

The adoption of functional reading and writing skills took place in southern Europe some centuries before it did in the north. Just as in Finland in the nineteenth century, in Italy the common people's view of the world, which was coloured by an oral tradition, overlapped with the newer written culture in the early modern era. Ginzburg's miller, Menocchio, did not only read, but was also able to actively interpret the books that he read in the sixteenth century.[1059] By contrast, the poor reading skills of the ordinary people of Kivijärvi even in the late nineteenth century prevented them from reading any literature that was at all demanding. The definition of good reading literacy in historical research is highly problematic. A person's

---

1058 In Finnish: *'Kyll' tämä kirja on mukava'*.
1059 Ginzburg 2007, 87.

subjective experience of reading skills can be very different from the authorities' view of the matter. Moreover, the information in sources about the level of reading skills can vary considerably at different times. According to the Official Statistics of Finland, 87.4 percent of the adult population of the country could not write in 1880. On the other hand, the same source claims that only 2.4 percent of children over ten years of age could not read. However, a more precise study of the situation at that time revealed that in reality only 2-5 percent of the whole population possessed good practical reading skills.[1060]

As an object of research, the parish of Kivijärvi is an extremely interesting area because in the last decades of the nineteenth century the functional reading and especially writing skills of the population were still very weak there. For example, in 1880 only 4.6 percent of the adult population could both read and write, while the percentage for the whole country was 10.8. At that time, approx. 2.4 percent of all Finnish people over ten years of age were illiterate, but in this parish the proportion was 10.6 percent. Up to the 1920s, i.e. before the Compulsory Education Act, especially the number of people who could write in Kivijärvi was very low compared with the whole Finnish population: only 36 percent as opposed to approx. 65 percent of the population of the whole country.[1061] In 1907 and 1908 the proportion of elementary school pupils of all school-aged children in Finland was, after eastern Lapland, lowest in northern Central Finland.[1062]

The conflict between the statistical and the actual ability to read is explained by the fact that the traditional idea of literacy of the clergy and the common people in the mid-nineteenth century differed from the more modern conceptions of the Fennomans and other groups that sought to promote popular education. For the former, reading was connected with devotional practice. They considered that the literature that people read should be primarily religious, and that reading consisted in going through the same passages again and again. In the same way, it was thought in Lutheran Germany, for example, that the catechism was 'the people's Bible', and that it was not even necessary to have practical reading skills in order to know it. According to the traditional view, the only literature that people needed was religious. The ability to write was considered to be unnecessary and even dangerous. Even in the second half of the nineteenth century, people who could both read and write were sometimes regarded as deviant individuals who could be led astray by reading secular literature. The same kind of thinking about the dangers attached to the common people's active literacy skills was prevalent all over Europe.[1063]

To judge from the entries concerning reading skills in the confirmation records, there were considerable regional and local differences. Partly these

1060 Häggman 2008, 32-33.
1061 Official Statistics of Finland VI:11. Population of Finland 31/12/1880, SVT VI: 56:2, Population of Finland 31/12/1920; Archive of the Parish of Kivijärvi, demographic tables 1880 and 1920.
1062 Haapala 2007, 270.
1063 Häggman 2008, 33-34; Mikkola 2009, 186-189.

arose from the fact that different clergymen employed different criteria in examining people's ability to read. According to the confirmation records, in the 1760s about 60–80 percent of the adult population of southern and western Finland could read, and in some coastal towns the proportion was even higher. This 'Christian literacy' of the Finnish-speaking population, which in practice meant a command of the principles of Christian doctrine, was particularly high around the harbour towns of Rauma and Pori on the west coast, where the Finnish-language merchant class was prosperous and revivalist movements were strong. By contrast, in the east and north, literacy was lower, and people owned fewer books. The confirmation records also indicate that people's reading skills were weak in these parts of the country.[1064] The village communities in the parish of Kivijärvi were situated in the hinterland behind vast stretches of forest. The progress of a written culture was very slow there compared with more densely settled areas.

In the eighteenth century, the ownership of books became more common particularly on the coast, in the towns and among the higher social groups. Often the works owned were hymn books, catechisms or other devotional writings. Secular literature, on the other hand, was still not to be found even in the homes of the prosperous city burghers.[1065] And in the early eighteenth century, particularly in the Finnish countryside, the possession of a Bible was regarded as a kind of luxury and an indication of the wealth of the household. In the nineteenth century, the number of readers increased as the production of books became less expensive along with technical advances in printing and the growth in the market for books, which meant that ever more people could afford to buy literature. Moreover, reading was often harnessed to the promotion of nationalist aspirations and popular enlightenment. The notion of a 'reading nation' has been attributed to this period. This concept referred not only to people who regularly read literature that was written and published in the vernacular tongue but also to the fact that through their reading they were helping to create a national culture.[1066] The social rise of the rural population at that time was furthered by the mere fact that the amount of literature written in Finnish increased, which made it possible also for the common people, who did not know Swedish, to read and study by themselves.

The change-over to new reading habits was, nevertheless, slow in rural areas like Kivijärvi. Religious literature maintained its dominant position well into the nineteenth century, and the habit of reading to oneself *sotto voce*[1067] continued into the twentieth century. People were accustomed to receiving the written word aurally.[1068] Schadewitz analyzed the situation at the beginning of the twentieth century thus: 'The reason for the deficient use of our rural libraries lies partly in the fact that the desire of the common people to read is not as keen as we are sometimes inclined to think when we

---

1064 Häggman 2008, 46–47.
1065 Häggman 2008, 46–47.
1066 Tatlock 2010, 3, 5.
1067 In English: under one's breath.
1068 Häggman 2008, 37.

praise the high standard of our popular education. A great deal still needs to be done in order to make the practice of [reading] literature among the people as general as would be desirable.'[1069] For example, in the town of Mikkeli in eastern Finland at the end of the nineteenth century, those who used the library most were religious masters of households who borrowed devotional literature.[1070] In Central Finland, even at the end of the nineteenth century, the older population still considered the reading of other literature than religious works to be a sin. There was a saying in Karstula that went: 'It's better to lie asleep at home even when it's time to go to church than it is to read worldly books[1071]'. Gradually, a few more enlightened persons came to accept the fact that people might read handbooks related to agriculture as well as religious postils, and the variety of literature read by people in the countryside increased.[1072]

The rise of revivalist movements in the late eighteenth and particularly the nineteenth century also encouraged the agrarian population to read and study religious texts independently. The rise of revivalist movements caused a considerable upheaval in literary culture. They disseminated to their members literature that they considered to be important. Religious popular literature was circulated in large editions that were of modest material quality and whose price was consequently low; in the 1840s, religious pamphlets might cost only a few kopeks. Religious literature was often disseminated more for ideological reasons than to make a profit. For example, much of the printed matter distributed by Henrik Renqvist and the publishing company of the Finnish Evangelical Society was free.[1073]

Even in the mid-nineteenth century, the reading skills of the Finnish rural population were limited to the mechanical mastery of the religious texts taught by the church, and people would not necessarily have been able to understand the contents of more secular texts even though they were nominally classified as 'able to read'. Moreover, there was still very little literature written in easily intelligible Finnish available to the rural commons.[1074] This was especially so because at the time the vocabulary of the Finnish language was expanding strongly with the attachment of new uses to dialect words and the creation of neologisms. There exists no comprehensive research information concerning the reading skills of the population of Kivijärvi in the nineteenth century, but for example in 1828 in the village of Pääjärvi in the neighbouring parish of Karstula, about 70 percent of the villagers were reported in the church records to be good readers and just over six percent poor readers, while 24 percent, i.e. almost, a quarter, reportedly could not read at all.[1075] As mentioned above, in his episcopal visitation in 1875, Bishop Frans Ludvig Schauman noted that while the people of Kivijärvi had a knowledge of the scriptures, their functional

1069 Schadewitz 1903, 41.
1070 Mantovaara 2001, 6.
1071 SKS KRA. Rautiainen, Albert. E 15 1: 247. Karstula.
1072 Mönkkönen 1988a, 537–538.
1073 Häggman 2008, 74; Nuorteva 1988, 92–93.
1074 Karjalainen 1977, 21–22.
1075 Alamäki 1996, 85.

reading skills were hopelessly poor.[1076] It is probable that even in the late nineteenth century the deficient reading skills of the ordinary inhabitants of Kivijärvi prevented them from reading any more demanding literature since local elementary education had only just got under way. The teaching of writing skills came to have an established place in the curriculum only with the foundation of elementary schools. Handwriting did not become a regular school subject until the 1890s.[1077]

Werkko considered that the main reason for the low interest in libraries in the late 1870s was the inability of the parishioners to read or to understand what they read. At that time, the adult population still regarded reading as laborious and preferred to have a text read out to them. Especially those who did hard physical work often quickly fell asleep over their books in the evenings or in the spare moments available to them for reading unless the text was entertaining or amusing. Rarely did people reading in their spare time do so to obtain information or to learn something new: it was more common to look for 'entertaining books'. However, some people were interested in political and social affairs and read newspapers in order to follow current events. Older people still regarded reading as a waste of time that could be spent doing other more useful work.[1078]

THE ROOTS OF THE FINNISH SCHOOL SYSTEM IN LUTHERAN POPULAR EDUCATION

What actually was the cause of the low literacy level of the people of Kivijärvi? In the Nordic countries, the distinction between reading and writing skills is apparent in the fact that rather than the one word 'literacy', two different words are used to refer to them (Swedish: *läskunnighet* and *skrivkunnighet*; Finnish: *lukutaitoisuus* and *kirjoitustaitoisuus*). This linguistic differentiation has an historical background because the two skills have for a long time been kept distinct from one another. In Finland, school buildings were not built in the countryside until after the mid-nineteenth century.[1079] Previously, the church parishes were in charge of education, which was carried out at home and at catechetical meetings arranged in alternate years in different houses, and thus there was not any absolute need for separate school buildings. The late acquisition of writing skills has been explained, among other things, by the fact that there was not much use for the ability to write in Finnish in a society where contacts with the authorities took place through documents written in Swedish, which was the general language of administration. This does not, however, explain why the common people in Sweden likewise acquired writing skills at a fairly late stage since Swedish was their mother tongue. Nor did the slow spread of writing skills result from a lack of means or the low density of settlement. Rather, it was caused by the fact that the teaching of reading skills to the common people was traditionally the task of the clergy, who did not consider it necessary teach them to write as well.

1076 Mönkkönen 1986, 437.
1077 Kotkaheimo 2002, 63.
1078 Werkko 1879, 225–226.
1079 E.g. S. Kotilainen 2013d, 125.

The clergy used this educational prerogative to demonstrate their usefulness to the powers that be. Moreover, for a long time in the Nordic countries, and for longest of all in Finland, the clergy constituted an official estate that was represented in the Diet, and this gave the church an exceptional degree of societal influence.[1080]

Finland was one of the last countries in Europe in which universal compulsory education came into force. In the other peripheral regions of Europe, compulsory education had been enacted by the beginning of the 1870s. The late advent of compulsory education in Finland was partly a result of the church's position as the provider of basic education for children. The education of the people provided by the church was economical for two reasons. The common people were taught 'to read' by having them learn just one text by rote. They were not necessarily taught to read other texts or to write. They were provided with the rudiments of Christian doctrine (which were considered to be enough for the agricultural classes) and reading in classes given by the parish cantors, in village Sunday schools (by often untrained lay parishioners living in the villages) and sometimes also by schoolteachers employed by the church parishes. Dozens of parochial schools were established in Finland in the eighteenth century. Confirmation classes became common in the middle of that century and gradually became compulsory.[1081]

However, it was not until the mid-nineteenth century that parishes all over the country established ambulatory schools for which they employed trained teachers. Before that, basic education had been provided at a fairly low cost. Nor did any expenses occur from the construction of proper school buildings because the classes of the Sunday schools and ambulatory schools were held in private homes in the different villages, as were the annual catechetical meetings, in which the people's reading skills were tested. In the Nordic countries, dedicated school buildings were not built in the countryside until after the mid-nineteenth century. By contrast, in France for example, there was a network of schools even before the enactment of universal compulsory education. In the Nordic countries, the Lutheran parishes were administered by vicars (in other Protestant churches the parishes were governed by elders or vestries), and the activities of the church administration were financed with taxes imposed on the peasants. In Finland, the church parishes remained responsible for educating the common people right up to the beginning of the twentieth century, and in some places even into the following decades.[1082]

The older generations had been taught to fear the clergy, and therefore when they had to read to the ministers they did so with some trepidation. The main purpose of learning to read was to demonstrate to the clergy that one had the required knowledge of the scriptures in order to be confirmed.[1083] In the opinion of Nordic historians, the church and the

---

1080 Matti Peltonen 1992, 93–94.
1081 Häggman 2008, 46; Matti Peltonen 1992, 93–96.
1082 E.g. S. Kotilainen 2013d, 125; Matti Peltonen 1992, 93–95.
1083 Werkko 1879, 227.

state sought to further reading literacy among the people at least from the beginning of the eighteenth century on, which explains why a large majority of the population learned to read with the help of only a very meagre formal schooling. This has been regarded as having come about largely as a result of the clergy's assumption of responsibility for the education and supervision of the people, on the one hand, and, on the other, of the fact that parents took care of teaching their children the rudiments of reading skills themselves. But neither this practice alone nor the long, dark winter, which freed people from other chores and allowed them greater leisure at home, explains the high level of reading and writing literacy among the people of Iceland, for example.[1084]

The dramatic growth in literacy in Iceland at the turn of the eighteenth and nineteenth centuries was a result of the work practices on Icelandic farms, especially the fact that the work rather hindered people from going to school than encouraged them to do so. On long winter evenings the domestic chores were divided into two kinds. The cattle had to be fed and milked, which generally took up two to four hours in the day. The rest of the time was spent working with wool, a task in which all the members of the household participated. As this work went on for hours on end, it could become monotonous and boring, so some kind of entertainment was needed in order to maintain the workers' diligence and keep them awake, and so one of the members of the family used to read aloud to them. There are numerous mentions of this practice in autobiographies and diaries.[1085]

The level of reading skills depends to a great extent on how a reader and his or her skills are defined. The dissemination and consumption of literature among the common people have always been accompanied by a background debate about who has the right to write, read and interpret texts.[1086] The ability to write and the reading of literature in Finland began to increase slowly after the Roman Catholic Church and its written culture extended its influence into Sweden and concomitantly into Finland. The development of writing and of books (as objects) is perhaps the best reflection of the progress of a society, its customs and its culture.[1087] Thus a study of the collection of a rural lending library, for example, can tell about the values and activities of the people of the time. Finnish-language literature in the nineteenth century was created to serve the national awakening. According to the Fennoman ideology, the ordinary people also had to be integrated into a common national culture. The development of reading and writing skills made them part of the united nation that the Fennomans dreamt of, and not just members of a local community. The task of literature was to enlighten and educate the people and to teach them to be 'true' Finns. But what about the interest in literature of the peasants and the other members of the rural population themselves?

1084 Magnússon 2010, 92.
1085 Magnússon 2010, 92–93.
1086 Vartiainen 2009, 21.
1087 Tuomas Heikkilä 2009, 7.

The ownership of books and private collections

THE CLERGY AND REVIVALIST MOVEMENTS AS DISSEMINATORS
OF FINNISH-LANGUAGE LITERATURE

> A local person said to a book merchant: 'You surely have books that lead people astray. I have a Bible and Luther's Postil, and there's enough reading in them.'[1088]

Thus the vicar Lauri Hyvärinen described the attitude of the people of Kivijärvi to the need for new reading matter in the late 1920s. Possibly, the utterer of these words was a parishioner who belonged to some revivalist movement and probably a fairly old person because compulsory education, which strove to arouse people's curiosity about temporal matters as well and to encourage them to read more widely, had already been in force for some years. This quotation certainly does not reflect the way of thinking of the whole congregation, but the vicar chose to tell it as a kind of extreme example. Even so, it is possible that there were many parishioners of this kind. Those who had lived and survived the terrors and tribulations of the bad years of famine were beginning to be in their seventies or more. The youngest of them had probably gone to an elementary school, but many not been able to devote much attention to schooling and learning to read when they were young. Who then owned and read books in the countryside, and what were their motives for doing so?

The procurement and reading of literature was crucially connected with people's estate and social group.[1089] As an educated estate, the Clergy had played a significant part in creating and maintaining the written culture, and they continued to write, read and disseminate literature in the countryside in the eighteenth and nineteenth centuries. The collections of books of the urban clergy in the eighteenth century contained religious manuals and works of German theology. The amount of literature owned by individual clerics, however, varied greatly depending on their position and personal wealth. For example, for financial reasons and thanks to their social networks, vicars usually had more extensive libraries than members of the lower clergy.[1090]

The second half of the eighteenth century saw a significant development in the written culture in Finnish towns. In the eighteenth century, devotional literature constituted the largest individual literary genre in the book collections of the people of Helsinki. However, the proportion of secular literature grew towards the end of the century. In the countryside, religious literature continued to predominate among the common people. Many of the inhabitants of Helsinki had the opportunity to read, either in their original languages or in Swedish translations, contemporary works of literature that the peasants of Sweden and Finland, or peasants in for example France, had

---

1088 KSA, Report on the state of the Parish of Kivijärvi in 1927–1931 made for the 1932 Synodal Meeting and the 1933 General Synod.
1089 af Forselles & Laine 2011, 6.
1090 Ahokas 2011a, 131–139.

never even held in their hands. The bibliographic culture of the cities was even then quite international.[1091] The ownership of books became common only very slowly in rural areas of the other Nordic countries as well. Even at the end of the nineteenth century, most Icelandic families owned only a few works of secular literature or possessed a few book or papers. Owing to the lack of funds there was only a limited amount of literature available, but at the same time reading societies all over Iceland offered the public the opportunity to borrow literature.[1092]

There was no professional group of book merchants proper in the seventeenth century in the realm of Sweden, to which Finland then belonged; rather the right to sell books was granted through privileges. After 1630 a printer could sell the books he printed only in soft-bound form because the sale of hard-bound books was the monopoly of the book binders, a privilege which they gradually had to give up in the course of the eighteenth century. The merchants and the clergy also purveyed and sold books. Before the expansion of the monetary economy in the eighteenth century, books were often acquired by barter.[1093] There were hardly any book merchants in Finland in the last decades of the seventeenth century because the book binders monopolized the sale of books, and consequently until the second half of the eighteenth century determined the selection of literature that was available.[1094]

During the nineteenth century, the sale and distribution of books in Finland was carried out variously by colporteurs (itinerant peddlers of books), bookbinders, printers and agents of Swedish book merchants in addition to their other business. As late as the eighteenth century, the main ways by which books were acquired were through advance orders, the free distribution of printed matter and barter. However, ever since the Middle Ages, Finland had had working trade relations abroad, especially in the Baltic area, and in terms of its bibliographic culture and the distribution of books it had been a part of the rest of Europe ever since those times. Organized trade in books began gradually in the eighteenth century.[1095] They were not always obtained new from book merchants or itinerant colporteurs, and particularly in the towns they were often bought second-hand in book auctions.[1096] Books were also sometimes sold at markets, and this offered an important opportunity for country people to buy them.[1097]

The purveyance of literature to the commons was not just a matter of course everywhere in Europe. For example, in Finland, situated as it was in the remote north, the available literature was mainly in Swedish right up to the nineteenth century, and in rural parishes like Kivijärvi there were hardly

---

1091 af Forselles & Laine 2011, 6–7.
1092 Magnússon 2010, 94.
1093 Burman 1999, 149; T. Laine 2006, 21. On bookbinders as sellers of books in Norway, see Dahl 2010, 19.
1094 Häkli 1991, 38.
1095 T. Laine 2006.
1096 Merisalo, Mäkinen & Laine 1999, 139.
1097 T. Laine 2006, 23.

any readers of Swedish. Because they were relatively expensive, members of the rural population possessed few books. Moreover, books were difficult to obtain because of the poor communications. Thus the kind of literature that was available for them to read, in addition to devotional works, was fairly modest in terms of its content: various kinds of small booklets and almanacs.[1098] Because they were expensive and difficult to obtain, it was common for individuals to lend books to one another even in the nineteenth century.[1099] Consequently, one can wonder what kind of books the people of the remote countryside possessed and ask whether these few works provided sufficient reading matter for them to consider that they did not need the services of a lending library.

The routes by which literature reached the remote countryside were complicated. Johannes Gezelius the Elder, the Bishop of Turku, who sought to advance popular education, reminded the clergy in a ministerial convention in 1667 of the obligation to procure for their congregations the kind of books that the King had urged them to acquire. He also reminded them of the need to procure hymnbooks and Gospels. At the end of that decade, the bishop supplied literature to the parishes of his diocese, and his agents in Ostrobothnia, for example, sold the books that he sent there. The books he distributed were meant mainly for the clergy or then for the parishes' stores of supplies (hymnbooks and Gospels). In his episcopal visitations, too, Gezelius recommended or commanded the parishes to buy books, which they paid for out of their church funds. He further reported about available books in his encyclical letters.[1100]

Bishop Gezelius the Elder had ordered all churches and chapels to procure Bibles, handbooks (i.e. manuals of ecclesiastical offices and rituals), of which there were to be two copies in the larger parishes in case of simultaneous services, two or three hymnbooks, prayer books and the books that the King had ordered the parishes to acquire (for example, *Anatomia Papae* and Luther's *Large Catechism*). According to Gezelius, a parish could stock tracts and other small booklets for sale, and especially new works should be made available for the parishioners to buy. For example, in the ministerial convention of 1688, Gezelius urged the parishes to use church funds to acquire a store of books for sale to the parishioners. If Gezelius' injunctions were followed, a parish would have a kind of small bookstore of its own.[1101] In practice, however, the situation was not quite so ideal in the poor parishes of the interior, where the people could not afford to spend their meagre means on reading matter.

Of the printed matter published in Finnish between 1544 and 1808, 80 percent is estimated to have consisted of works dealing either with religion or with temperance matters. The literature owned by the lower social groups, in particular, was mainly devotional.[1102] So-called 'popular literature',

---

1098 Matti Peltonen 1992, 90.
1099 Karjalainen 1977, 19–20.
1100 Laasonen 1977, 175–176.
1101 Laasonen 1977, 176–177.
1102 Matti Peltonen 1992, 70.

consisting of small printed works which for centuries had enjoyed success among the less affluent and less lettered sections of the population, can be divided into popular prose booklets and song sheets in verse.[1103]

For traditional reasons, the small amount of literature that was consumed on an everyday basis was religious. Secular books were little favoured among the peasant population even as late as the mid-nineteenth century; indeed, they were considered harmful, and reading them was thought to be a waste of time. Home libraries still consisted of a Bible, a hymn book, a few other devotional works such as a catechism and possibly also an ABC primer. Some people might also possess hymn sheets.[1104] The above-mentioned religious works represented practical literature that was needed by everyone for the simple reason that the church checked on people's attendance at services and tested their knowledge of the catechism. If a person wanted to become officially 'an adult' and a full member of the community, he or she had to know the principles of faith. Moreover, there was ever-increasing personal interest in spiritual literature especially among those members of the rural population who belonged to revivalist movements.

The works favoured by the revivalist movements were international, and they transcended the borders between the different religious orders. For example, Finnish revivalists read a lot of traditional German Pietist works, the classics of English devotional literature and more modern Nordic spiritual works. Usually these had been translated from Swedish versions by revivalist clerics. For example, Henrik Renqvist distinguished himself as a translator, publisher and disseminator of religious literature. Compared with Sweden, however, the interest in Luther's works in Finland arose quite late and was at its height in the mid-nineteenth century. For example, Luther's great *Kirchenpostille* [Church Postil[1105]] was not printed in Finnish until 1848–1851. Likewise Johan Arndt's *Wahres Christentum* [True Christianity] only came out in Finnish between 1832 and 1850. On the other hand, Swedish versions of Arndt's works had been read in Finland ever since the seventeenth century.[1106]

The leaders of the revivalist movements wished to disseminate literature among the people in a more organized way than before. The Finnish Evangelical movement decided in the late nineteenth century to establish an association to publish devotional literature. It was called Evankeliumiyhdistys (the Evangelical Association). The pioneer in this endeavour was Anders Silfvas from Helsinki. He was originally a veterinary surgeon employed by the Board of Medicine who had experienced a religious awakening and converted to the Evangelical faith after reading the works of the Swedish writer and revivalist preacher, Carl Olof Rosenius. From the end of the 1860s if not earlier, he began to distribute the works of Luther on his own initiative. He ordered these and other Evangelical printed works from

---

1103 Enges 1985, 21.
1104 K. Laitinen 1997, 155.
1105 Finnish title: *Kirkkopostilla*.
1106 Nuorteva 1988, 97–98.

Sweden. From 1870 at the latest, he began disseminating these to different Swedish-speaking parts of the Province of Uusimaa (Nyland) through the agency of lay preachers.[1107]

At the beginning of the 1870s, the Evangelical Lutheran Association made plans to expand these activities. The task of the association was defined as the dissemination of the Bible, the works of Luther and other spiritual books and magazines whose content was in line with the teachings of the church. The books would be sold by colporteurs, who would also operate as lay preachers. It was originally planned to include in the rules of order of the association a cause stipulating that male colporteurs who had received the right to preach after passing an examination set by the Cathedral Chapter would be issued with a permit to act as authorized colporteurs. Women, too, were accepted as colporteurs, although they had no right to preach. The rules were, however, made less strict with regard to the association's authorization of persons to act as its colporteurs when the Senate removed the condition referring to the surveillance of the Cathedral Chapter.[1108]

The Finnish Lutheran Evangelical Association, which convened for the first time in 1873, procured books both from Sweden and from Finnish publishers. Luther's *Evankeliumi-Postilla*[1109] was ordered from a bookseller called G. W. Edlund and the Bible from the Bible Society. Other spiritual literature in both Finnish and Swedish, including works by Luther, Hedberg, Emil Litzell, Stephan Praetorius, Palearius and Leiner, was also ordered from various sources. In the following year, the association began to recruit so-called 'book sellers', who did not have a permit to preach. Generally, the Finnish domestic missionaries in the 1860s had considered the duties of the colporteurs to be limited to the sale of books and their recommendation by word of mouth to the customers. However, in the Evangelical movement, the sale of books was often accompanied by religious speeches.[1110]

One model for the Evangelical Association was the Anglo-Saxon home mission societies, which used colporteurs to disseminate their literature. This movement had already spread to Sweden in the early nineteenth century, and in Finland these influences grew in strength in the 1830s and 1840s. The founders of the Evangelical Association were apparently also influenced by revivalist activities in Denmark, where, for example, Vilhelm Beck's home mission organization likewise used colporteurs. There was also another Danish association that employed colporteurs, Luthersk Missionsforening (the Lutheran Mission Society), which was Evangelical and opposed Beck's Pietist-oriented organization. It was the latter, a lay movement which

---

1107 Koskenniemi 1967, 36.
1108 Koskenniemi 1967, 37, 41, 43.
1109 As was noted in Chapter 4, I have not been able to ascertain whether this work was a translation of Luther's *Hauspostille* or his *Kirchenpostille*, or possibly a collection of excerpts from either or both of these original works. The same holds true for the Finnish titles *Lyhyt Epistola-postilla* and *(Lyhyt) Evankeliumipostilla*, in which the word 'Lyhyt' means 'Short'.
1110 Koskenniemi 1967, 44, 46, 51.

originated on the island of Bornholm, that more probably served as the model for the Finnish Evangelicals.[1111]

The Evangelical Association mainly published and disseminated the works of Martin Luther, and its efficient sales network furthered their dissemination. In the years 1874 and 1875, the association bought 4200 copies of A. W. Ingman's Finnish translation of Luther's *Evankeliumi-Postilla* from the book merchant G. W. Edlund, and over a thousand copies were sold in 1875. In 1878, the association published translations of Luther's *Hauspostille* [House Postil][1112], *Das apostolische Glaubensbekenntnis* (the Book of Concord)[1113], and the Large Catechism in separate editions. Between 1876 and 1882, the association published Luther's *Lyhyt evankeliumi- ja epistola-postilla* [Short gospel postil], which had appeared in a translation by J. E. Ahlgrén in 1880.[1114] Luther's *Evankeliumi-Postilla*, the *Lyhyt evankeliumi- and epistola-postilla*, and several other works by him also formed part of the collection of Kivijärvi lending library. These works had mainly been inherited from the first library, and most of them were published before the 1860s.[1115]

THE ACQUISITION OF BOOKS ON TRIPS TO TOWN

It was only after the level of education rose, the economy revived and publishing and library activities became more effective that the practice of reading spread to the lower social groups.[1116] When going to town and market, the people of Kivijärvi had traditionally headed for the Ostrobothnian coast in winter. Even after the road to Lohtaja was built in 1858, it was impossible to transport freight overland in summer. Therefore, goods were often brought from the coast in winter along 'ice roads' over the frozen waterways, which easily supported horse-drawn sleighs with loads of over a hundred kilos. Most commonly the people went to Kokkola, where they took tar, butter and sawn planks. From there they brought back iron, salt, flour, tobacco and coffee. Sometimes they made longer journeys if the price of the goods to be sold covered the expenses of the journey and they were sufficiently light to transport over such distances. They took fish to the towns of Tavastia (Häme), where they exchanged it for linen and hemp. They even took furs, forest game and butter to Helsinki and Saint Petersburg. In 1842, an imperial decree made it legal to conduct trade in the countryside.[1117]

Everyone had the right to sell agricultural and dairy products as well as homemade handicraft goods to his or her neighbours. Because this kind of trade was difficult to supervise, the Senate ratified a decree in 1859 which made it legal to establish shops in the countryside. A shopkeeper had to be able to read and write, be a competent bookkeeper and a citizen of good

---

1111 Koskenniemi 1967, 47–48, 50.
1112 Finnish title: *Huonepostilla*.
1113 Finnish title: *Tunnustuskirjat*.
1114 Koskenniemi 1967, 75–77.
1115 Kivijärvi BOOKS.
1116 K. Laitinen 1997, 155.
1117 Lampinen 1986, 269.

repute who had received holy confirmation. Shops in the countryside could not be closer than 50 kilometres to the nearest town. However, no shops were established in Kivijärvi until the 1870s,[1118] and even then they did not prosper and many a shopkeeper ended up bankrupt after a couple of years of operation. Trade was difficult because of the long freight journeys involved, the low density of settlement and also because the people of the countryside did not have much money to spend in those days.[1119]

It has been claimed that by the end of the nineteenth century literature had become more equally accessible to broader sections of the population. The spread of electric lighting and the improvement in the living conditions of the working people promoted a wider consumption of literature.[1120] However, this levelling development took place only after some delay in the remoter countryside. For example, the first electricity company began functioning in the church village of Kivijärvi in the early 1920s, but only for a short time. Electric lighting only became available to the whole population of the municipality and in the outlying villages on a larger scale after the Second World War. There was no railway connection before the mid-twentieth century, and even then it only reached as far as Kannonkoski. The road network did not fully cover the outlying villages for a long time. In the famine years of the 1860s, a road connecting the church village with Karstula was built, but roads in the direction of Kannonkoski did not come into being until later. The old Lohtaja road had run in the direction of Kinnula since the eighteenth century.[1121]

The most important traffic hub at the turn of the nineteenth and twentieth centuries was Myllymäki railway station in Ähtäri. It was the closest station, and people reached it by horse and cart or sleighs and later by a regular bus connection. The post was carried through Karstula, and the first telephone cooperative society installed a connection in that direction at the turn of the century. The journey from Myllymäki to the capital was a long one. When, for example, the sons of the district doctor, Eliel Warén, attended the Finnish Normal Lyceum or Teacher Training Lyceum[1122] in Helsinki in the early years of the twentieth century, they made the 58-kilometre journey from Saarijärvi, where they lived, to Myllymäki in a horse-drawn cart or sleigh, which took about ten hours. After that they travelled all night to Helsinki by train in a third-class carriage with seats, which in winter tended to fill up with drunken market-goers at Haapamäki Station.[1123]

In order to purchase books, the people who tilled the land in northern Central Finland had to be extremely active because ordinary people did not make trips to town for pleasure in the nineteenth century, and any possible book purchases were made in conjunction with other business such as the transportation of goods or the sale of agricultural products. The active selling

1118 Freedom of trade in Finland was enacted in a decree ratified in 1879.
1119 Lampinen 1986, 269–270.
1120 Vartiainen 2009, 473.
1121 Lampinen 1986, 251, 261–262, 280.
1122 A teacher training lyceum or school is one in which training teachers taught.
1123 Ylioja 2003, 36.

of books and the activities of the colporteurs of the revivalist movements did not really begin until the last decades of the nineteenth century. The journey for the people of Kivijärvi to the nearest town (Jyväskylä) to buy books was much longer than it was from Saarijärvi, for example, and the distance to the Ostrobothnian coast, where they had previously travelled, was even greater.[1124]

At the beginning of the 1860s, Jyväskylä was a small inland town of less than a thousand inhabitants.[1125] Despite this, it was rapidly developing into the most important centre of Finnish-language education. There had been a junior school in Jyväskylä ever since 1840, and the first Finnish-language middle school was established alongside it in 1858. A three-form upper secondary school was added in 1862, which from 1873 on was called Jyväskylä Lyceum. In addition to this school, Jyväskylä Teacher Training Seminary with separate units for men and women began to operate in 1863, and a private school for girls was established in the town in 1864.[1126]

Karl Jakob Gummerus, who was born the eldest son of a curate in Kokkola in 1840, greatly influenced the development of the bibliographic culture of Jyväskylä. He came from a family of clerics going back eight generations. When he was a student in the 1860s, he became influenced by the national revival ideology. He himself wrote serial stories in Finnish, at first in newspapers before he entered the publishing business himself. He was a romantic and one of the most productive Finnish-language short story writers of the 1860s and 1870s. Gummerus worked as a teacher of Finnish and Swedish in Jyväskylä Lyceum in the 1870s. At that time, the population of Jyväskylä was 1500, and it increased to 2800 by the turn of the century.[1127]

The town was experiencing a period of lively construction work. The telephone came there in 1885, electric lighting in 1902, and water mains in 1912. Business life in the small town was invigorated by the booming trade in timber in Central Finland. In 1879, the Act on Freedom of Trade further increased the opportunities for development, and the number of shops began to grow rapidly. Books had been sold in some of the town's shops for a long time. The first privilege rights for a bookshop in Jyväskylä were granted in 1849. The establishment of schools further increased the demand for books, and two teachers called Alexander Georg Weilin and Karl Gustaf Göös set up a second bookshop in the town in 1871. It received another competitor in 1877 when H. F. Helminen established a bookshop called Kansalliskirjakauppa (the National Bookshop). Although this went bankrupt, K. J. Gummerus established a new book store in 1888. The town's first printing press was established by F. M. Huhtin in 1864, mainly for the printing of textbooks and newspapers. In 1867 the press was transferred to the ownerships of a district doctor called Wolmar Schildt, and then in 1872 to the Weilin & Göös company.[1128] A bookbindery operated in conjunction

1124 Lahtinen 1963, 7.
1125 Lahtinen 1963, 7.
1126 Leino-Kaukiainen 1990, 18; Tommila 1972, 122–144.
1127 Leino-Kaukiainen 1990, 13–15, 17.
1128 Hakapää 2008, 352; Leino-Kaukiainen 1990, 17.

with the printing shop. Weilin & Göös moved its business activities, apart from the bookshop, to Helsinki in 1883. The company's printing shop had received a competitor in the form of Jyväskylän kirjapaino, a press established by the above-mentioned merchant H. F. Helminen together with K. J. Gummerus and another teacher called Jaakko Länkelä in 1877, and this establishment was left to command the market in the town after the departure of Weilin & Göös. As a result of the so-called 'division of fronts' (the competition between the organs of the Young Finns and Old Finns political parties) in newspaper publishing, another printing press called Keski-Suomen Kirjapaino Oy was established in 1888.[1129]

The first periodical to come out in the town was *Koti ja Koulu. Sanomia lasten kasvattajille* [Home and school. News for child-rearers], which was edited by the lecturers of Jyväskylä Teacher Training Seminary. It appeared from 1864 to 1866. Jyväskylä got its first newspaper in 1868, when Wolmar Schildt (who used the Finnish pen name Wolmari Kilpinen) began to publish the nationalist-oriented *Kansan Lehti* once a week. In 1871 it was joined by *Keski-Suomi*, which became the organ of the Young Finns party in Central Finland in the late 1880s. Its competitor, the organ of the Old Finns, *Suomalainen*, began to appear in 1888, and among its supporters was K. J. Gummerus. He, himself, also edited a periodical called *Kyläkirjasto* [The village library]. Because Jyväskylä was emblematically a city of educational institutions and most of the school pupils came from other parts of Finland, the town became an important centre for the purveyance of newspapers, periodicals and books, and they were disseminated from there all around the country. The town was anyway located in the centre of the country and surrounded by a large Finnish-speaking area, and this created a significant readership for the publications.[1130]

Gummerus also established his own bookbindery, a facility that had been lacking in Jyväskylä after Weilin & Göös moved to Helsinki. The bindery received a licence to operate in 1884. Gummerus also established a bookshop that bore his name in Jyväskylä in 1888. In 1893, he sold his share in the Jyväskylän Kirjapaino printing press to Jaakko Länkelä, and it became exclusively a newspaper press. In its stead, Gummerus established a new press, which bore his name and which concentrated on the publication of books published by him. Jyväskylä continued to be regarded as a town of educational institutions in the early years of the twentieth century, and in 1906 the establishment there of a second university in Finland began to be discussed. Although this project was not actually realized then, supplementary university courses in the summer began to be held there in 1912. Jyväskylä also gradually began to develop into a centre of commerce and industry. The building of the railway made it in 1897 into a traffic hub, and at the same time the town became the most important centre of the Region of Central Finland.[1131]

1129 Leino-Kaukiainen 1990, 18.
1130 Leino-Kaukiainen 1990, 18.
1131 Leino-Kaukiainen 1990, 33–34, 64–65.

The book trade was closely associated with printing and publishing activities in Finland in the late nineteenth century. Up to the 1850s, all bookshops had been situated in the towns, and even in 1912 there were only 32 bookshops operating in the Finnish countryside.[1132] At the turn of the nineteenth and twentieth centuries, one of the biggest challenges for the field of publishing was the extension of a network of bookshops into the countryside. Functional literacy skills had always been weaker in rural areas than in towns. The promoters of popular education maintained the myth of the enlightened peasant who read books, but, according to census statistics, in 1900 over 67 percent of the population above ten years of age could not write. By 1910 writing literacy had become more common, but even then over half of the rural population still could not write. Nor, in practice, did they possess active reading skills either. The cities were about 40 years ahead of the countryside in the advance of literacy since at that time only 15 percent of the urban population were unable to write.[1133]

The disregard for literature in the countryside was still apparent in the use of libraries throughout the period between the two world wars. Although the library institution had spread to cover the whole country, only a few percent of the inhabitants of the rural municipalities of northern and eastern Finland used libraries in the late 1930s, while about one fifth of the inhabitants of towns and cities were customers of libraries at that time. The urban libraries were used above all by members of the working class, since the middle class and the intelligentsia regarded the books in public libraries as dirty, and rumours had it that tuberculosis was spread through library books, although numerous experts strove to deny this misconception. However, about 85 percent of the population of Finland still lived in the countryside at the beginning of the twentieth century. Thus they constituted a huge potential clientele that the bookshop business aimed to reach. Many bookshops in the towns extended their activities into the surrounding countryside and acquired customers from there.[1134]

In Helsinki, the Society for Popular Enlightenment had issued publications that disseminated very useful information and nationalist ideals to the people, and the calendar published by the society was the first general informative work in many rural homes. The society also took the initiative in improving the conditions for bookshops to operate in the countryside by employing more agents to sell books both on a part-time and on a full-time basis and by establishing permanent bookshops in rural areas. For a long time, the agents were typically elementary school teachers with a sympathetic attitude to popular enlightenment, and they purveyed textbooks to the schools in the surrounding localities. Some countryside shopkeepers also extended their range of goods to include literature.[1135]

1132 Tommila 1980, 266.
1133 Häggman 2008, 318.
1134 Häggman 2008, 319.
1135 Häggman 2001, 8; Häggman 2008, 319–320.

At the turn of the century, there was still no actual bookshop in Kivijärvi or its immediate environs. In Karstula, Adiel Kaipomäki, worked there as an agent of Maalaiskirjakauppaliitto (the Rural Bookshop Federation) in the years 1904–1909 and then transferred his stock of books into Karstula Cooperative Store, but this business ended in bankruptcy after two years. Thereafter, the bookshop was maintained by a farmer called J. V. Kinnunen until 1915, and then by a baker, Julius Viljanen, for one year and after him by Eero Palonen until his death in 1926.[1136] In the church village of Kivijärvi, J. V. Salmi, the head teacher of the elementary school, also operated as an agent for books in addition to his regular job, did not take up this activity until the 1910s at the earliest. Clearly, he or some other teacher was also the librarian of the school library in the church village, which was in a way the successor of the municipal lending library. After Salmi, a bookshop was maintained in the church village for several decades by Helmi Tainio, an elementary school teacher who was the daughter of a shopkeeper called Gustaf (Kustaa) Tainio.[1137]

THE OWNERSHIP OF BOOKS ON THE BASIS OF THE EVIDENCE OF DEEDS OF ESTATE

The ownership of books reveals the extent of written culture. The mention of books in the inventories of deeds of estate has been regarded as an indication of the diffusion and appreciation of literature in Finland.[1138] However, it is by no means certain that all the books that people owned actually appear in the inventories. Because they were rare and precious, books could well have been passed down beforehand to younger members of the family. Moreover, the Bible and hymn books may well have been regarded as the common property of the family, or a family Bible, for example may have often been considered to be so essentially a part of the property of the farm that it was not catalogued in the inventory of an individual's estate.[1139] A person might have a lot of other valuable property, but books were not necessarily mentioned at all. Again some of the books owned by a person might have been on loan to someone else when his or her estate inventory was drawn up. On the other hand, some people could not afford to buy books at all. Moreover, estate inventories were not drawn up after everybody died,

---

1136 A teacher called Paavo Meriläinen then kept the shop open for two years before handing the task over to Mrs Jenny Piispanen. After her death in 1950, the bookshop was run by Miikka Piispanen. The bookshop is still functioning in 2016 under the ownership of Mrs Piispanen's descendants. Virtanen 1958, 356. The farmer J. V. Kinnunen who kept a bookshop was very probably Juho Vihtori Kinnunen, i.e. the same person who served as the cantor of Kivijärvi from 1915 on and who had lived in the early years of the century in Karstula, where he had held positions of responsibility in the municipality. It was due to his significant efforts that a municipal old folks (senior citizens) home was built in Karstula with state support. Karjalainen, interview with Cantor J. V. Kinnunen, 1964. For further details, see also S. Kotilainen 2015b.
1137 S. Kotilainen 2005, 15.
1138 af Forselles & Laine 2008, 10.
1139 Kallio 1972, 661.

and commonly not after the deaths of members of the poorest members of the population of Central Finland, or elsewhere in the country for that matter.[1140] However, the most important thing to note in connection with the relationship between estate inventories and the ownership of books is that the owner of books did not always necessarily read them, or at least not all of them. On the other hand, the fewer books there were in a household, the more likely it is that they were read.

The more books a person owned, the more cursorily they were catalogued in the estate inventories. For example, in the estate inventories of clergymen in the eighteenth century, only the total value of the books they owned was entered without any mention of the titles of the individual works.[1141] According to the HENRIK database, one third of the books listed as property in estate inventories in towns consisted of religious literature, while the proportion of such works that were sold in auctions was about a fifth.[1142] In the more prosperous parts of the countryside, the consumption of literature grew slowly but steadily. Before 1750, books had appeared in about seven percent of the estates of deceased landed farmers in the coastal areas of Northern Ostrobothnia, in the period 1750–1769 in about a fifth, in 1770–1779 in approximately 40 percent, in 1780–1789 around 60 percent and in the decade 1790–1799 in as many as 73 percent of cases. The large majority of the books were hymnbooks, and there were also some other devotional works. The wealthiest peasant farms of south-western Finland possessed the largest collections of books. However, they included few secular works and hardly any fiction or poetry before the 1840s.[1143]

According to the evidence of the estate inventories, the number and variety of books possessed by the peasants in the area of Ilmajoki in Southern Ostrobothnia, which was anyway an economically more prosperous region, were much greater than in northern Central Finland. At the turn of the eighteenth and nineteenth centuries, their collections already included works that were purchased by Kivijärvi people's library for the common use of the parishioners only 50–90 years later (for example, translations of Arthur Dent's *A Sermon on Repentance*, David Hollatz's *Evangelische Gnadenordnungen* [The Order of Evangelical Grace in the Economy of Salvation[1144]], and Johann Philipp Fresenius' *Beicht- und Communionbuch* [Confession and Communion Book[1145]]).[1146] The net capital of the peasants of the Central Finland landed peasantry just about quadrupled in the 1870s and 1880s, while the wealth of the rest of the agricultural population did not start to grow until the 1890s. Although the average differentials grew

---

1140 Markkanen 1977, 202.
1141 T. Laine 2011b, 37, 42. Books were generally catalogued more precisely in estate inventories in the eighteenth century. In the nineteenth century generally only the total monetary value of the books was mentioned in estate inventories.
1142 Parland-von Essen 2011, 21.
1143 Mäkinen 1999, 169.
1144 Finnish title: *Armon järjestys autuuteen*.
1145 Finnish title: *Rippi- ja Herran ehtoollisen kirja*.
1146 Vuorela 1957, 45–46. See also Ylitalo 2012, 18.

Table 26. The average net wealth (in marks) in the Judicial Circuit of Saarijärvi in the period 1870–1910, based on estate inventories.

Social group*	1850–1851 EI	marks	1870–1871 EI	marks	1890–1891 EI	marks	1910–1911 EI	marks
Upper classes	2	7 015	1	700	2	34 800	5	6 118
Craftsmen**	–	40	–	520	–	800	–	460
Landed farmers	3	700	17	2 410	20	8 260	33	15 000
Crofters	4	100	9	750	12	860	30	1 130
Cottars**	–	25	–	20	–	70	–	530
Casual labourers	1	30	3	790	6	250	7	380

* Because the number of estate inventories was rather small in some years, the fluctuation in capital between the years is considerable. Therefore the table is only roughly indicative of the average wealth.
** Covering the whole of Central Finland.

The abbreviation EI refers to the number of estate inventories. In the period studied, the Judicial Circuit of Saarijärvi included the parishes of Saarijärvi, Karstula, Kivijärvi and Uurainen. Source: Markkanen 1977, 85, 93, 117, 133, 139, 151.

between the groups, there were still poor, debt-ridden landed peasants in the country (many lost their land to the timber companies as a result either of rash sales of their forests or outstanding debts) and, on the other hand, relatively affluent crofters and casual labourers. The size of the poorest section of the population also increased during the strongest period of population growth from the 1870s to the 1890s. On the other hand, the majority of the landed farmers, functionaries and tradesmen at that time certainly did not need to use all their earnings for living, far from it. Along with the change in economic conditions that began in the 1870s, the landed peasants came to constitute a kind of middle class between the functionaries and the landless population in the countryside of Central Finland.[1147]

However, not everywhere in the countryside did people necessarily have the means to buy many books before the turn of the century, and even the rare home collections that did exist contained few works. In the light of the inventory deeds, the amount of books owned by the people of Kivijärvi was still fairly meagre in the second half of the nineteenth century. There are only a few mentions of books being possessed by members of the agrarian population. Mostly they were hymnbooks, Bibles and other religious works.[1148] The inventory of the estate of Eeva Kautto, the wife of a farmhand called Matts Hakkarainen, in 1858 mentions among his chattels a hymnbook and a New Testament.[1149] In 1886 the estate inventory of Antti Kotilainen, the master of Purala Farm in Kivijärvi, was drawn up. The farm was fairly large by local standards, so there were a few more books than was usually the case. In addition to an account book and other documents

1147 Markkanen 1977, 203; Table 26.
1148 Viitasaari Judicial Circuit, Viitasaari Rural Court District, estate inventories 1838–1853, 1858–1869; Saarijärvi Judicial Circuit, Kivijärvi Rural Court District, estate inventories 1870–1918; KSA, Estate inventory deeds and attachments to marriage banns 1783–1914.
1149 Viitasaari Judicial Circuit, Viitasaari Rural Court District, estate inventories 1858.

related to the household, Kotilainen owned a hymnbook, two copies of the New Testament, an arithmetic book, two copies of Luther's postils and one unspecified book.[1150]

One of the few parishioners whose estate inventory contained books was a farmer called Gustaf Orava. The inventory was drawn up in 1878. Orava owned a farm called Kangas, which was valued at the time at about 10,000 marks. The sparse information in the inventory does not permit us to ascertain exactly the extent of his collection of books, but probably it comprised fewer than ten volumes. It contained a Bible (valued at five marks), various other religious works (four marks) and a legal manual (four marks) written by Johan Kristian Svanljung, a lawyer from Vaasa.[1151] This was most probably the first 1874 edition (the second edition came out in 1882) of the Finnish version of Svanljung's book titled *Uusi käsikirja lainopissa kaikille kansaluokille Suomessa* [A new handbook of law for all classes of people in Finland]. Books on the law were often owned by functionaries and merchants.[1152] Before 1809, a book on the law was the third most commonly owned type of work after a hymnbook and the Bible in the homes of the town burghers. Of the ten most commonly possessed books, it was the only secular one, and it was a very useful and practical aid to merchants in conducting their business.[1153] Orava, too, had a clear need for a legal handbook because he was involved in numerous civic duties; for example, he sat on the bench of jurors, and he drew up deeds of estate for his fellow parishioners.[1154]

For the sake of comparison, we can examine the home collections of books of the inhabitants of Saarijärvi. They, too, were fairly small. To the extent that people owned any books at all, the most common works were again Finnish-language hymnbooks and Bibles. According to the estate inventories, it was still rare for a household to possess a Bible in the mid-nineteenth century. However, books were listed in the inventories made in Saarijärvi more carefully than in Kivijärvi. The estate inventories in Saarijärvi for the years 1809, 1858 and 1866 generally give the titles of the books that constituted part of a deceased person's estate.[1155] Even fewer titles of other religious literature than the basic works were mentioned in them. In some households, there might be a catechism, a prayer book, a New Testament or some other more modest spiritual work. The only work that was not religious was a Finnish-language law book belonging to a landed peasant called Markus Ruuska in the eighteenth century. He was an extremely enlightened person for his time, and he sent his son, Elias, to study at the trivial school in Pori.[1156]

1150 Saarijärvi Judicial Circuit, Kivijärvi Rural Court District, estate inventories 1870–1918.
1151 Saarijärvi Judicial Circuit, Kivijärvi Rural Court District, estate inventories 1878.
1152 Parland-von Essen 2011, 26.
1153 Nuorteva 1988, 96–97.
1154 Saarijärvi Judicial Circuit, Kivijärvi Rural Court District, estate inventories 1870–1918.
1155 Markkanen 1989, 151, 153, 155.
1156 Kallio 1972, 661. A trivial school was a middle school.

Upper-class families probably did not possess much more in the way of books than the peasants. For example, Georg Wallgrén, a vicar who died in 1752, left his heirs only religious literature such as an old Swedish Bible, Svebilius' *Lexikon* and Gyttner's *Postilla*, Wegelius' *Postilla* in Finnish, a few small religious tracts and Kellingius' commentaries on the Psalms. He had given his Bible to his eldest son while he was still alive, but apparently he possessed another Bible and a hymnbook, although they were not separately listed in the inventory. There were three Bibles in Saarijärvi church: one dated from 1642,[1157] another was Bishop Gezelius' Bible (1685),[1158] while the third was a Bible printed in Turku in 1752. There was also an ecclesiastical law book and a register of the Diocese of Porvoo dating from 1742. Books remained just as scarce well into the nineteenth century. However, the devotional literature of the common people did become a little more varied, and the estate inventories mention Finnish translations of such works as Lars Levi Laestadius' *Ens Ropandes röst i öknen* [The Voice of One Crying in the Wilderness][1159], Thomas Gouge's *A Word to the Wicked* and (probably) Niels Hamner's *Vägvisare till det eviga livet* [A signpost to eternal life][1160] together with works about Paradise, attendance at Holy Communion and the creation of the world.[1161]

Only three of the altogether 163 estate inventories made in 1809 in Saarijärvi mention books: five hymnbooks, one copy of Svebilius' *Catechism* and one prayer book. The owners of the books were all farmers, one of whom tilled Crown land. At that time, the parish pastors also had their own libraries. In 1858, altogether 56 estate inventories were drawn up, of which a score (i.e. about a third) mention a book or books. A quarter of the owners of the books were farmers tilling taxed land, just over a third farmers who worked Crown land or crofters, and there was also one surveyor, one casual labourer and two craftsmen.[1162]

Mid-way through the century, secular literature continued to be rare, and the only such books that were read at home were a few handbooks on the law. The librarian of Saarijärvi, Matti Taipale, possessed a large and varied personal collection of books.[1163] During his lifetime in Saarijärvi, there was only one reader who possessed more secular literature than him: a crofter called Emanuel Parkatti, who lived on the land of the vicarage of Kolkanniemi. According to the inventory of his estate in 1863, he possessed a library of 16 works, most of which were religious. It included the following

---

1157 This was the year when the first Finnish-language translation of the whole Bible was published.
1158 The second Bible published in Finnish. It contained corrections of translation mistakes in the first version, and the language was made more faithful to the original. The editing work was carried out by Bishop Gezelius the Elder. This Bible was smaller than its predecessor, and because a man could take it with him on a military campaign, it was also called the 'War Bible' (*Sotaraamattu*).
1159 Finnish title: *Huutavan ääni erämaassa*.
1160 Finnish title: *Tienosoittaja*.
1161 Kallio 1972, 661.
1162 Markkanen 1989, 153.
1163 For further details, see S. Kotilainen 2013a.

works: Nohrborg's *Postilla* [Postils], *Sapatin lepo* [The Sabbath day of rest], Jean de Bernières-Louvigny's *La vie cachée en Dieu avec Jésus-Christ* [The Hidden Life of Christ in God][1164], *Sionin Wirret* [Songs of Zion], *Hengelliset virret* [Spiritual hymns], *Historia pakanain kääntymisestä* [A history of the conversion of the pagans], Arndt's Catechetical Sermons, *Ihmisen sydän* [The heart of man], *Ensimmäinen kansanpuhe* [The first people's speech], *Kuvapiplia* [An illustrated Bible], *Viinan kauhistus* [The horror of Liquor], *Yhteinen historia* [A common history], *Opetuskirja maanviljelyyn* [A guide to agriculture], *Hyödyllisiä ajankuluja* [Useful diversions], *Lyhyt tieto Mittauksesta* [A short handbook of surveying] and *Osotus kettuin ja susiin pyytöön* [A guide to hunting foxes and wolves]. The estate of a crofter called Juhani Kuittu was valued at 50 marks, of which two hymnbooks, a prayer book and a translation of Johan Arndt's *Paradiesgärtlein aller christlichen Tugenden* [The Garden of Paradise] represented one hundredth part of his estate.[1165]

Thus in Saarijärvi, the farmers and the crofters also owned more religious literature apart from just the Bible than in Kivijärvi.[1166] And the collections of the upper classes and the functionaries were considerably larger.[1167] Pastor Benjamin Canthén, who died in Saarijärvi in 1809, owned 30 books, David Roschier, the vicar, left behind 21 works when he died in 1851, while the Crown Bailiff Daniel Philip Danielson, who died in the same year, and a surveyor called Stenbäck, who passed away in 1859, both left 10–15 works. The collections still contained almost uniquely religious or professional literature. Pastor Canthén seems to have been an enthusiastic linguist because he possessed Greek, Hebrew, Latin, German and Swedish dictionaries or grammars and even a work of Virgil. Crown Bailiff Danielson owned a few accounts books and legal works as well as religious literature, and Stenbäck possessed legal works. In addition to his collection of religious books, Vicar David Roschier possessed a copy of Johan Haartman's medical handbook in addition to his collection of religious works. His father, Eric Johan Roschier (1745–1825), also a vicar of Saarijärvi, handed over most of his book collection to his sons while he was still alive.[1168] Thus the examples from Saarijärvi corroborate the claim that valuable books might be passed on to descendants as a kind of advance bequest.

Altogether 81 books are mentioned in the estate inventories of 1858. Usually the more prosperous members of the community owned most books, but excerpts from the estate inventories indicate that in Saarijärvi it was the crofters who possessed most books (about 38 percent of all the books mentioned in the inventories). A third of the books were owned by landed farmers and a fifth by those who were tilling Crown land. Since at that time an inventory was drawn up for only about one third of the persons who died, and the estates of the poorest persons were not inventoried at all,

---

1164 Finnish title: *Salattu elämä Christuxen kanssa Jumalasa*.
1165 Kallio 1972, 661; Markkanen 1989, 156–157.
1166 For further details, see S. Kotilainen 2013a.
1167 Markkanen 1989, 156.
1168 Kallio 1972, 661–662.

the sample covers only that section of the population who, in addition to ensuring their livelihoods, were able to acquire the kind of property that was of particular significance for them in order to show their social position or otherwise as an object of consumption on which they wished to spend their money. Nevertheless, the estate inventory material allows us to conclude that possibly one in six or seven homes in Saarijärvi possessed books in the mid-nineteenth century. Of the total of 111 estate inventories in Saarijärvi in 1866, 25 mention books as property. Relatively there were fewer books than a decade previously. The number of casual labourers had increased and the estate inventories had become less specific. At that time the keenest readers were the farmers, who owned 65 percent of the books mentioned in the inventories. Books were also mentioned in the estate inventories of a shopkeeper, a couple of craftsmen and a Crown official. All of the books mentioned in the estate inventories of 1809 were religious works. In 1858, the proportion of religious literature was 83 percent, but in 1886 only 32 percent.[1169]

On the evidence of the estate inventories, the people of Saarijärvi would seem to have been much more active readers than the inhabitants of Kivijärvi. This may simply have been because there were more upper-class families living in the former parish. But also the peasant population there were more active readers. Because books were expensive, they were procured in the mid-nineteenth century only by those who could afford them and who were also truly interested in reading. On the other hand, the findings of a study of the estate inventories may also be influenced by the possibility that more inventories than usual may have been drawn up because of high mortality rates resulting from factors like epidemics and famine.[1170] For example, in 1808 and 1809, the ravages of war[1171] and the level of mortality in Central Finland were higher in Saarijärvi, through which ran the highway between Kuopio and Vaasa (a strategically important artery), than they were in Kivijärvi, and in consequence people's property and its destruction were documented more specifically there.[1172]

Before the severe famine years of the 1860s, the world view of the agrarian population of Saarijärvi was based on the Bible, postils and hymnbooks. However, the variety of religious literature had increased to a certain extent by the middle of the century, and it included translations of such works as Anders Björkqvist's *Uskon harjoitus autuuteen* [The practice of faith as a way to salvation], Book 1 of Arndt's *Wahres Christentum* [True Christianity], Thomas Gouge's *A Word to the Wicked*, John Bunyan's *The Pilgrim's Progress* (1678) and Lars Levi Laestadius' *Ens Ropandes röst i öknen* [The Voice of One Crying in the Wilderness]. The proportion of books in the property of the departed varied from a hundredth to a tenth. The revivalist movements influenced the acquisition of books earlier in Saarijärvi than in Kivijärvi.

1169 Markkanen 1989, 154.
1170 Markkanen 1989, 151.
1171 The Finnish War (1808–1809) was part of the Napoleonic wars. As a result of it, Finland was annexed from the realm of Sweden into the Russian Empire.
1172 Jääskeläinen 2011, 117.

A Central Finnish Pietist-inspired movement called The Awakening (*herännäisyys* or *körttiläisyys*) flourished in Pihlajavesi, and it is known that some of the people of Saarijärvi also went there to listen to the word of God in the 1840s. Evangelism spread over a wide area in the 1860s. In the early nineteenth century, over three quarters of the books owned by the inhabitants of Saarijärvi represented a seventeenth-century Pietist view of the world.[1173] People still owned very little contemporary literature. The Finnish revivalist movements used traditional Pietist devotional works. There was very little domestic literature in Finnish available in the 1860s. The lack of bookshops and the paucity of reading skills slowed down the dissemination of the most recent religious literature in the countryside. However, the estate inventories do not include many small booklets. And naturally the oral information and forms of the oral tradition that resembled literature (such as folk tales, riddles, poetry and other types of knowledge that were passed on by word of mouth between people) were not recorded in any documents.[1174]

In places like Pylkönmäki in northern Central Finland, home libraries mainly contained religious literature, and from the 1920s and 1930s on also an increasing number of factual works on agriculture and even a little fiction.[1175] Johan Wegelius' *Postilla* [Postil] was available in Krank's vicarage at the turn of the century. At that time, the Conservative Laestadians in Kivijärvi, too, read the 'old translation' of the Bible, dating back to 1776. Luther's *Hauspostille* [House Postil] and *Kirchenpostille* [Church Postil] were also read and *the Lutheran Confessions*. Some people also possessed Johan Fredrik Bergh's *Postilla*. And a few homes subscribed to the Laestadian paper *Sanomia Siionista*.[1176]

Before the establishment of the people's library, the literature available to the inhabitants of Kivijärvi was mainly religious: the Bible, hymnbooks, catechisms and, from the 1870s on, books that were read in school. Very few persons owned a larger number of books, so in that sense the library considerably increased the selection of books that were available for people to read. At the end of the nineteenth century, the book-reading culture of the peasants underwent a big change, which was connected with other upheavals in religious and economic life. At the same time, the intellectual capital acquired from reading books also came to be more appreciated. A book was accorded a value beyond just its worth as a utilitarian object. For example, in Finland in the first half of the twentieth century in particular, a large number of books in a home was regarded as a sign that the inhabitants were educated and cultured.[1177] At the turn of the century, the literature in homes had still been according to my reasearch very practical. The literature acquired by private persons was chosen first on religious grounds and then on the basis of the practical information it offered, or then simply because it was available. The acquisition of books presupposed mobility because

---

1173 Markkanen 1989, 157. Cf. also Karstula library collection of old books.
1174 Hakapää 2008; Markkanen 1989, 158.
1175 Sinisalo 1984, 101–102.
1176 Viljanen 1931, 17, 37.
1177 M. Lehtonen 2001, 42.

they were mainly on sale only in in larger population centres, unless special purveyors of books brought them to local communities. Access to the reading of books required not only the ability to read but also a certain level of affluence and the willingness to take the trouble to obtain them. Who then had the time or the opportunities to use the collections of the people's library if there was not enough reading matter at home?

The customers of Kivijärvi lending library

THE AGE AND GENDER OF THE BORROWERS

A library can make many things possible for people:[1178] for example, it can enable them to develop their reading skills, to learn new things and thereby to improve their position in society, or it can allow them to spend their leisure time in reading books for entertainment and giving free rein to their imagination. The registers of borrowers of books from Kivijärvi lending library reveal who had the time and the opportunities to read, and how the books acquired for the collection of the people's library increased the opportunities for the rural population to acquaint themselves with a new type of literature. It is possible that the lending library of the church parish of Kivijärvi had possibly kept records of the book loans and borrowers earlier, but information about the lending of books has only been preserved from 1877 on, after the task of running the library was assumed by the elementary school teachers, who, having received appropriate training and experience at the Teacher Training Seminary, had the competence to keep more exact records of the borrowers. The customers were mainly members of the local community, but there were also some borrowers from outside the parish. In two cases, members of the latter group are mentioned as coming from Karstula, but for the rest it is impossible to know exactly where they lived as this has not been entered in the loans records.[1179] All in all, the place of abode of 38 (about ten percent) of the borrowers is unknown. However, to judge from their names, most of them would appear to have been locals.[1180]

A collation of the information in the library registers with collective biographical material reveals what kind of reception the parishioners accorded to the library that was established for them and how they used it. It has been assumed in connection with the collective biographical data that the borrower of a book was also its primary reader, but of course there is always the possibility that it was also read by other members of his or her family. The rules of the library established by private persons listed the responsibilities of borrowers according to the contemporary view that the borrower was individually responsible for a book that he or she borrowed. However, the lending library in Kivijärvi did not have any set of rules before 1888, so that before this date books may have been borrowed on a more collective basis and by families as a whole. In any case, the collective

---

1178 Manguel 2006.
1179 KKA, Loans registers of Kivijärvi lending library 1877–1897.
1180 KKA, Loans registers of Kivijärvi lending library 1877–1897; Kivijärvi READERS.

Table 27. The gender of borrowers in Kivijärvi 1877–1897.

Borrowers	N	%
Men	182	50
Women	172	48
Not known	6	2
Total	**360**	**100**

Source: KKA, Loans registers of Kivijärvi lending library 1877–1897.

biographical material shows that among the borrowers there were usually several members of the same family: spouses, children or parents, brothers or sisters.[1181]

The gender distribution of borrowers from Kivijärvi lending library was fairly even, and men formed only a slight majority, just about a half. It is impossible to identify those borrowers whose first names were abbreviated to initials in the loan registers, and thus their gender cannot be known with certainly in all cases. Five of the borrowers were so-called 'unit borrowers': for example, Kinnula elementary school borrowed a Bible for four years. It was borrowed in September, and the loan was renewed annually for the following school year until it was finally returned in the spring of 1889.[1182] Most probably, it was used as a teaching aid. Again, Matti Rytkönen, a shopkeeper who was the chairman of the municipal assembly at the time, borrowed a Bible to use at the autumn session of the local district court in 1889.[1183] In the early days, the libraries also had customers who borrowed books for other purposes than reading. For example, at the court sessions, nobody actually read the Bible, but it was needed for the swearing of oaths. In a case concerning the maintenance of an illegitimate child, a man might swear a special so-called 'purification oath' that he was not the father of the child in question. This was done by uttering the words 'by God and His Holy Gospels' and placing two fingers on the Bible. The swearing of such an oath settled the matter.[1184]

The comparability of the information about lending with that relating to other popular libraries of the time is weak because of its paucity. A score or so years earlier, most of the customers of Alajärvi library during the first four years of its operation in the late 1860s were adult males, with only about eight percent women. Later the proportion of female and child borrowers grew, and before long there were more women than men borrowing books.[1185] Thus, after the middle of the century, reading became just as important an activity for women as it had been for men. However, the men's superiority in functional reading skills becomes emphasized in sources relating to municipal administration, for example; since women did

---

1181 KKA, Kivijärvi library loans registers 1877–1897; Kivijärvi READERS.
1182 Table 27.
1183 KKA, Loans registers of Kivijärvi lending library 1877–1897; Martti Peltonen 1986, 382.
1184 Saarijärvi Judicial Circuit, Kivijärvi Rural Court District, records of proceedings, autumn court sessions 1885, 16§ and 54§.
1185 Kivipelto 1966, 236.

not participate in the conduct of communal affairs in the same way as men, the sources do not record their reading skills as often.

In the 1860s and 1870s, the ladies of Stockholm were able to visit reading salons reserved for women alone, where they could peruse not only books but also newspapers and magazines.[1186] The reading activities of rural women were not segregated like those of the educated upper-class ladies of the towns, and they borrowed the same works as men. Only a few of the least borrowed religious works in Kivijärvi library were borrowed exclusively by men or women, but this was rather a result of the rareness of the occasions on which they were borrowed than the fact that their contents were oriented particularly towards one sex or the other.[1187]

The age of the borrowers tells a lot about how the library was received by the local community. From the 1870s on, school libraries were established in ever-increasing numbers. The foundation of the lending library in the church village of Kivijärvi was closely connected with the establishment of the elementary school, but the oldest part of its collection was religious and not necessarily primarily suitable as reading matter for children. The ages of the borrowers can be ascertained by using the collective biological material to find out their ages when they first borrowed a book from the lending library and their ages at the time of their last loans.

The ages of a significant number (about one third) of the borrowers under examination cannot be ascertained. These include cases where it is not possible to discover whether a parent or a namesake child was involved. Other cases where the ages of the borrowers cannot be identified include those persons whose first names are not known and unit loans, i.e. those taken out under the surname of a family or a place of residence, which cannot therefore be associated with any particular individual. Most of the borrowers whose age can be ascertained (about 40 percent) were between 20 and 49 years old. The proportion of children and young persons (0–19 years old) among the borrowers was over a fifth. There were no really elderly borrowers (over 70 years of age), since none of the borrowers was over 70 when they used the library for the last time. The oldest borrowers were born in the late 1810s.[1188]

The proportion of men among the borrowers was greater than that of women in all age groups apart from the 10–29-year-olds. The youngest customers of the library mainly lived in the church village. At least under-10-year-olds did not borrow books themselves if they lived outside the church village. There were altogether six borrowers who were under ten years of age. Of these, Toivo Anjelin, the son of the shopkeeper, and Kaarlo Fröjdman, the son of the local police chief, later departed to pursue their education in the city, where they went to secondary school and studied at Alexander University in Helsinki to become civil servants. Other young readers included Nestori Piispanen, Silja and Markku Jämbäck and Alma Kotilainen, who all belonged to the landed peasantry or the crofter class.

1186 Jarlbrink 2010, 49.
1187 KKA, Loans registers of Kivijärvi lending library 1877–1897.
1188 Table 28.

Table 28. The age distribution of borrowers in Kivijärvi 1877–1897.

Age	N	%
0–9	6	1.7
10–19	68	18.7
20–29	54	14.8
30–39	43	11.8
40–49	41	11.3
50–59	22	6.0
60–69	13	3.6
not known	117	32.1
Total	364	100.0

The ages of the borrowers have been calculated by comparing their dates of birth with the date of their first loan. If either of these dates is not known, the borrowers' age has been calculated to the nearest year if this is possible on the basis of other biographical information. Source: KKA, loans registers 1877–1897.

Table 29. The age and gender distribution of borrowers in Kivijärvi 1877–1897.

Age	Male		Female		Not known		Total	
	N	%	N	%	N	%	N	%
0–9	4	66.7	2	33.3	–	–	6	100.0
10–19	29	42.6	39	57.4	–	–	68	100.0
20–29	25	46.3	29	53.7	–	–	54	100.0
30–39	26	60.5	17	39.5	–	–	43	100.0
40–49	23	56.1	18	43.9	–	–	41	100.0
50–59	13	59.1	9	40.9	–	–	22	100.0
60–69	10	76.9	3	23.1	–	–	13	100.0
not known	52	44.4	54	46.2	11	9.4	117	100.0
Total	182	100.0	171	100.0	11	100.0	364	100.0

The ages of the borrowers have been calculated by comparing their dates of birth with the date of their first loan. If either of these dates is not known, the borrowers' age has been calculated to the nearest year if this is possible on the basis of other biographical information.
Source: KKA, loans registers 1877–1897.

The Jämbäcks were descendants of Anders (or Antti) Kahelin, who had been the cantor of Viitasaari in his time. Another of their ancestors was Michel Jämbäck, who had worked as a tailor in Kivijärvi in the late eighteenth century.[1189]

The greater number of female borrowers among 10–29-year-olds is probably partly explained by the fact that many of them were unmarried and thus as yet had no family to take care of. On the other hand, there were also some women with families among the borrowers. The largest gender difference was in the 30–39-year-old age group (particularly in farming families, mothers in this age group had the largest flocks of children to take care of and the management of the household took most of their time),

1189 Table 29; KKA, Loans registers of Kivijärvi lending library 1877–1897; Kivijärvi READERS.

Table 30. The customers of Kivijärvi lending library by social group 1877–1897.

Social group	N	%
Functionaries	19	5
Shopkeepers	8	2
Students	1	1
Craftsmen	15	4
Landed farmers	73	20
Crofters	65	18
Cottars	35	10
Casual labourers	27	8
Servants	13	4
Not known	104	28
Total	**360**	**100**

Source: KKA, Loans registers of Kivijärvi lending library 1877–1897.

and among persons over 60 years of age. In the case of older women, it is possible that they did handicrafts at the same time as men of the same age (for example their husbands) read aloud to them. Conversely, men sometimes did craft work while the women read aloud to them, so reading was not necessarily the man's job. One must also take into account the change in reading practices created by the advent of the elementary school in the countryside in just those decades (the 1870s–1890s) when the use of the library was most brisk. Women of the younger generation were very probably more enthusiastic readers than their mothers and grandmothers. However, the number of customers of the people's library examined in this research is so small that is does not permit any more sweeping deductions to be made concerning differences in reading literacy between the sexes.[1190]

THE SOCIAL GROUPS AND PLACES OF ABODE OF THE BORROWERS
Up the 1910s, the customers of the people's library in Turku, for example, comprised mostly Finnish-speaking workers, servants and their children.[1191] In the towns, the upper-classes and the more prosperous sections of the population either purchased their own books or used commercial libraries. In the countryside, the borders between the estates were not so strict, and the social elite of the church village sometimes borrowed books from the parish library just like the landless population. The founders of the people's library that was established in Kivijärvi in 1888 used the library themselves and were clearly interested in reading.[1192]

However, the families of functionaries and tradesmen constituted a small minority of all the borrowers. Because of the deficient nature of the lending data, the largest group of borrowers come under the category 'Not known'. They make up about one third of all the borrowers. Because, to judge from their surnames, not many of them were members of the families of

1190 Table 29.
1191 E. Seppälä 1963, 151.
1192 KKA, Loans registers of Kivijärvi lending library 1877–1897.

Table 31. *Customers of Kivijärvi lending library by social group and gender 1877–1897.*

Social group	Men N	Men %	Women N	Women %	Not known N	Not known %	Total N	Total %
Functionaries	9	47.0	9	47.0	1	6.0	19	100.0
Shopkeepers	5	62.0	2	25.0	1	13.0	8	100.0
Students	–	–	–	–	1	100.0	1	100.0
Craftsmen	12	80.0	2	13.0	1	7.0	15	100.0
Landed farmers	46	63.0	27	37.0	–	–	73	100.0
Crofters	29	45.0	36	55.0	–	–	65	100.0
Cottars	19	54.0	16	46.0	–	–	35	100.0
Casual labourers	16	59.0	11	41.0	–	–	27	100.0
Servants	4	31.0	9	69.0	–	–	13	100.0
Not known	42	40.0	60	58.0	2	2.0	104	100.0
Total	**182**	**50.0**	**172**	**48.0**	**6**	**2.0**	**360**	**100.0**

Source: KKA, Loans registers of Kivijärvi lending library 1877–1897.

functionaries or other upper-class groups, they were at best landed farmers, but the great majority of them are likely to have belonged to the landless population. Of those borrowers whose social station can be ascertained, the farmers and the crofters were among the major groups of borrowers. On the other hand, the proportion of all the landless classes was about 40 percent of the total number of customers; in other words, the library targeted the poorest members of the community. However, it was not just a question of charitable work since many of the local persons of standing, such as landed farmers, functionaries and tradesmen, used the library actively, and some of them very actively.[1193] In the late 1960s, 54 percent of the first customers of the library in Alajärvi were landed farmers, while 18 percent were crofters and another 18 percent were maids and farm hands.[1194]

When one compares the gender differences between the borrowers with their social groups, the differences are greatest in the families of shopkeepers and craftsmen, among whom the number of male borrowers clearly exceeded that of women. Since there were very few such families in relation to the total population of the village, the results are slightly biased by the fact that in some families the members of one sex outnumbered those of the other. For example, in the Anjelin family, only the sons used the library. In crofter families, a slightly higher proportion of women used the library than men, and the difference was even clearer among the servant class. In a few groups, however, the populations are so small that the figures are only roughly indicative.[1195]

The location of Kivijärvi library had an effect on who it was used by. The first lending libraries in the parish were established in the church village

1193 Table 30.
1194 Kivipelto 1966, 236.
1195 Table 31.

Table 32. *The distances of customers' homes from the church village of Kivijärvi 1877–1897.*

Distance

Kilometres	N	%
0–3	84	23
4–13	53	15
14–19	37	10
20–33	57	16
over 33	20	5
10–50*	71	20
Not known	38	11
Total	**360**	**100**

* The distance from the church village to the remotest villages depended to a great extent on whether the journey was made over the lake by boat (or across the ice in winter) or overland by skirting the lake along roads that were partly almost impassable. The villages concerned here are Lokakylä and Talviainen.
Source: KKA, Loans registers of Kivijärvi lending library 1877–1897.

and in Kannonkoski (in conjunction with the sawmill). As a result, the inhabitants of these areas continued to be enthusiastic borrowers in the decades to come. The loans registers permit us to ascertain the distances that the customers had to travel in order to get themselves something to read. The distances to the lending library in the church village from the villages where the borrowers lived have been estimated in the table below. Since the farms were located in sparsely populated areas, their actual location might have been slightly different, and, for example, no information about the location of cots has been preserved in the sources, so their location has been approximated to within a radius of five kilometres. The length of the journey also strongly depended on whether it was made overland by skirting the lake or across the water by boat or over the ice in winter. It was not possible to go over the lake when the ice was breaking up or thin.[1196] The predominance of borrowers from the church village was very typical elsewhere, too, and the majority of the first libraries in Central Finland were located in church villages.[1197] By contrast, during the first four years of its operation, of the total of 151 works borrowed from Alajärvi library, only 12 (8 percent) were taken out by people living in the church village and most of these by the inhabitants of the vicarage.[1198]

As one might expect, most of the borrowers lived in or near the church village, and people from the remotest villages did not set off to borrow books so often. However, the library did have a significant number of borrowers from the most distant villages 'across the lake' such as Talviainen and particularly Lokakylä. Juho Puranen, who later became a member of the board of governors of the library, was a son of the family which lived at Hiitola, the biggest farm in the village of Lokakylä. Many of the landless

1196 Table 32.
1197 Table 33.
1198 Kivipelto 1966, 236.

Table 33. *The distances of customer's homes from the church village of Kivijärvi 1877–1897 according to the gender of the borrowers.*

Distance Kilometres	Men N	Men %	Women N	Women %	Not known N	Not known %	Total N	Total %
0–3	39	46	41	49	4	5	84	100
4–13	21	40	31	58	1	2	53	100
14–19	25	68	12	32	-	-	37	100
20–33	37	65	20	35	-	-	57	100
over 33	10	50	10	50	-	-	20	100
10–50*	35	49	36	51	-	-	71	100
Not known	15	39	22	58	1	3	38	100
Total	182	50	172	48	6	2	360	100

* The distance from the church village to the remotest villages depended to a great extent on whether the journey was made over the lake by boat (or across the ice in winter) or overland by skirting the lake along roads that were partly almost impassable. The villages concerned here are Lokakylä and Talviainen. Source: KKA, Loans registers of Kivijärvi lending library 1877–1897.

members of the population of Lokakylä lived on the estate of this farm, and it is very possible that the owners of Hiitola Farm and their children inspired the villagers of Lokakylä to take up reading. Those who made longer journeys to borrow books were both men and women. Thus, at least on the evidence of the material used in this study, women do not seem to have been prevented by their household chores from reading or travelling to the church village to borrow books. The places of abode of about one tenth of the borrowers cannot be ascertained.[1199]

Although at the end of the nineteenth century the library activities were concentrated in the church village, at the turn of the century they were also revived in the Kannonkoski area. Books were donated to a library established in Leppälänkylä in 1895 by, among others, the Lyytinen and Vesterinen families, the chief of police Adrian Svens, the teacher Sakari Niemi, Kalle Rein and Ida Anjelin (the shopkeeper's wife). Kivijärvi Youth Association, among whose members were Alma Hämäläinen, Hilda Herranen (the daughter of the cantor), Alma Kinnunen, K. Herranen (most probably the son of the cantor), and the chairman of the association Juho Puranen (who had been educated at a folk College of Central Finland) procured new books for the Leppälänkylä library in 1902.[1200] They also ensured that the circulating library of the central organization of youth associations with its collection of about 600 volumes was located in the village of Haapajärvi for four months in 1903.[1201] In this way, the same active supporters of the library, such as Alma Hämäläinen, the Herranen and Anjelin families, Svens and Juho Puranen, tried to extend the practice of reading to the inhabitants of the outlying villages by means of donations and organizational activities.

1199 Table 33.
1200 Names and loans register of Leppäläkylä lending library.
1201 Mönkkönen 1986, 451.

Map 3. The villages of Kivijärvi.

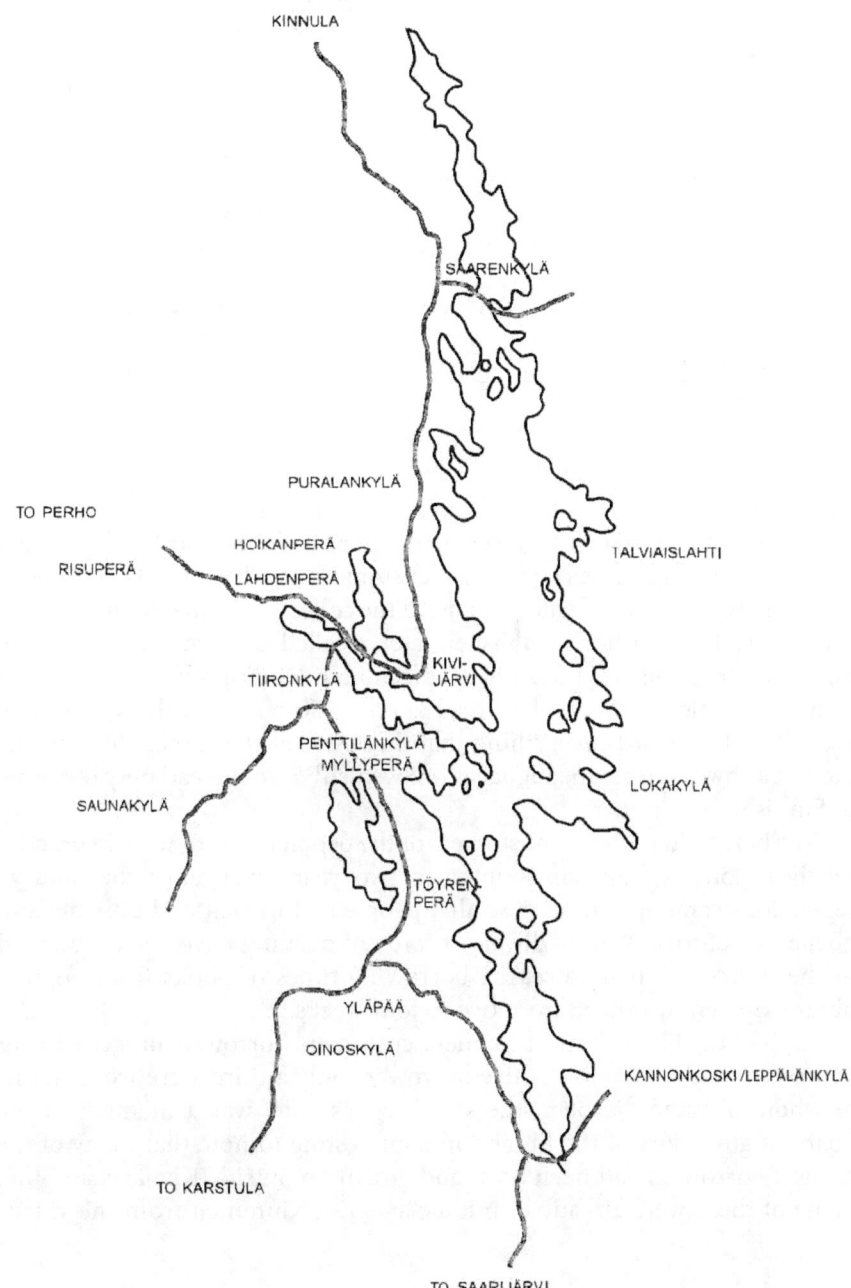

Table 34. The most active customers of Kivijärvi lending library 1877–1897.

	Name	Born	Place of birth	Number of loans	Social group	Sex	Years of customership
1	Elias Honkonen	1860	Karstula	30	Cottar	Male	2
2–3	Hilda Hänninen	1870	Kivijärvi	27	Landed peasant	Female	5
	Kalle Rein (Rehn)	1835	Kerimäki	27	Day labourer (sawmill worker)	Male	5
4	Heikki Leppänen	1846	Kivijärvi	21	Crofter	Male	13
5	Esa(jas) Kinnunen	1864	Kivijärvi	20	Landed peasant	Male	5
6	Kaisa Paajanen	1854		19	Crofter	Female	13
7	Karl August Rosvall	1850	Kuopio	18	Craftsman	Male	14
8–10	Amanda Jäsberg	1855		17	Shopkeeper	Female	3
	Edvard Olsoni	1832	Pelkjärvi	17	Elementary school teacher	Male	9
	Juho Puranen	1864	Kivijärvi	17	Landed peasant	Male	3

Source: KKA, loans registers 1877–1897.

The most assiduous users of the library

There were already keen borrowers in the early days of library activities. For example, Keuruu people's library had customers who borrowed books every week. These borrowers finally exhausted the collection of the library.[1202] Arvi Karisto (b. 1879), a book publisher, later recalled that from the age of 10 on he had read all the books in Hämeenlinna lending library. According to his own calculations he had read about 4000 books in the space of 10 years, 'in other words everything that there was at that time'. However, he did not know any foreign languages or Swedish[1203], so he read only literature in Finnish.

The borrowing times of customers of the people's library were in practice relatively long – from six months to two years even after the library's regulations came into force – so that people had to wait and possibly also queue for returns. Admittedly, no records of queuing have been preserved in the sources.[1204] In France, the borrowing times of books from popular libraries generally ranged from two to four weeks.[1205]

Each of the library's most frequent customers borrowed altogether over 15 books. Of the ten most active borrowers only a third were women, one of whom, Amanda Jäsberg, the shopkeeper's wife, was a member of the board of governors of the library. It is interesting to note that many of the keenest borrowers had been born and grown up outside Kivijärvi and that many of them were already of middle age. Esa Kinnunen from the village

---

1202 Rainio 1988.
1203 J. Niemi 2008, 53.
1204 KKA, collection catalogues of Kivijärvi lending library and the old collection of the library. For a further discussion of the reading speeds of the borrowers and the loan times, see S. Kotilainen 2015d.
1205 Barnett 1973, 328.

Table 35. *The duration (in years) of membership of Kivijärvi lending library 1877–1897.*

Years	N	%
0–1	151	41.5
2–5	75	20.6
6–10	14	3.8
11–14	10	2.8
not known	114	31.3
Total	**364**	**100.0**

The duration of membership has been calculated to the nearest year. Source: KKA, loans registers 1877–1897.

of Tiironkylä, Juho Puranen, the son of the master of Hiitola Farm in the village of Lokakylä, and Hilda Hänninen, who began using the library when the early age of 13, were all young people from the local landed peasant class. Also among the most frequent customers of the library were some craftsmen and workers from Kannonsaha Sawmill. All the local occupational groups were in any case fairly evenly represented. The teacher, Edvard Olsoni, used the library partly for professional reasons. It is striking that many of the most enthusiastic customers only used the library for a few years but managed to read more than many other parishioners during the whole 20 years of its operation. Correspondingly, of the library's 364 customers 151 (over 40 percent) borrowed only one book during these 20 years.[1206]

The decision to borrow a book was influenced by what was available rather than the borrower being able to choose whatever work he or she wished to borrow. However, the archive of the lending library does not reveal whether there was some kind of reservation system in use. When customers came to the library from some distant hamlets, they certainly settled for borrowing whatever books were available at that particular time. The existing sources do not permit us to conduct any more extensive examination of the extent to which borrowers recommended works from the library to one another, but at least in the case of married couples or members of the same family it is evident that one might sometimes recommend a particular book that he or she had read to another person. For example, in late 1889 one Kaisa Paajanen (aka Jauhiainen) borrowed Luther's *Evankeliumi-Postilla* and thereafter her husband, Antti Jauhiainen, borrowed the same work and renewed the loan a couple of times in succession and also took it out again later. Thus they did not necessarily read the book at the same time since each of them borrowed it at different times. On the other hand, it is also possible that whoever of them happened to be visiting the church village took out the book. In the opinion of Kaarle Werkko, the customer of a people's library should not lend a library book on to someone outside his or her own family.[1207] This left open the possibility for a person who wished to do so to read a book borrowed by another member of the same family, and undoubtedly this happened in

1206 Table 34; Table 35.
1207 Werkko 1879, 261.

practice extremely frequently all over the country since Werkko did not consider that he could legislate any further on this practice.

Kaarle Werkko also suggested that a borrower should not be permitted to take out the same book twice in succession in order that the books might circulate more rapidly.[1208] In Kivijärvi lending library, however, books were sometimes borrowed several times in succession by the same customer if he or she had need of them, as we have seen above. For example, in 1883 a certain Anna Loviisa (Abraham's dotter), who was born in Karstula and was the wife of Johan Hänninen (aka Aittolahti), took out Luther's *Lyhyt evankeliumi-postilla* and renewed this loan three times. She did so either because she did not have time to read it all the first time or because she wanted to read it again. In Kivijärvi, the borrowing times were sometimes very long – occasionally even years in length – which is an indication either of slow reading habits or then of intensive re-reading, which would be fitting particularly in the case of devotional works.[1209] However, the loans records indicate that the practice of extensive reading was most common among the people of Kivijärvi since there were no readers who took out only repeat loans; rather a book was most commonly read just once and returned to the library relatively swiftly.[1210]

For the sake of comparison, one can compare the numbers of loans made by Leppälänkylä lending library. The figures are, however, comparable with those for Kivijärvi lending library only for the first three years (1895–1897). During these years, the annual number of loans dropped to under 10 in both libraries, but in Leppälänkylä, the fall was more dramatic since in Kivijärvi the numbers of loans had been waning ever since the end of the previous decade. The loans records for Kivijärvi end in 1897, and there was also a break of several years in the operation of Leppälänkylä library. The turn of the century saw the advent of the 'Ground Frost Years' (Fin. *routavuodet*), when Russia tightened its policy of Russification on Finland and Finnish society experienced a period of uncertainty.[1211]

THE READING AND WRITING ABILITIES OF THE LIBRARY'S CUSTOMERS

The entries for parishioners' reading ability in Finnish church records differed in terms of their notation. For example, an explanation of the marks for the parishioners' reading ability, which ran on a scale from ':' to a full 'XX' indicating excellent reading skills, (see Table 37) was appended to the confirmation registers of the parish of Tenhola in the 1820s.[1212] In the confirmation records of the parish of Kivijärvi for the 1880s and 1890s, reading ability was assessed on a scale reaching only a single 'x' mark without any further explanations appended to the records.[1213]

1208 Werkko 1879, 261.
1209 Mäkinen 1997.
1210 KKA, Kivijärvi library loans registers 1877–1897.
1211 Tables 17–18; Table 36.
1212 Table 37.
1213 KSA, confirmation registers 1880–1899.

Table 36. Numbers of loans and borrowers in Leppälänkylä lending library 1895–1910.

Year	Number of loans	Borrowers
1895	168	46
1896	28	13
1897	9	8
1898	–	–
1899	–	–
1900	–	–
1901	–	–
1902	70	18
1903	71	22
1904	48	17
1905	27	18
1906	125	38
1907	258	54
1908	208	65
1909	227	72
1910	146	36

Source: 'Names and loans registers of Leppälänkylä lending library; A. Kotilainen 1979, 4.

Table 37. Marks for reading ability used in the parish of Tenhola.

Mark	Explanation
:	only spelling syllabes
/	with great difficulty
'/.	unclear
/.	laborious
X	passable
X :	almost satisfactory
X /	satisfactory
X Y	good
X X	very good or excellent

Source: *Vanhat käsialat ja asiakirjat*, 97.

However, it is possible to interpret the five marks used to indicate the reading skills of parishioners who had been confirmed in the parish of Kivijärvi by applying the explanations of the marks used in other parishes to them. For the purposes of this research, the following scale has been constructed: very good or excellent, good, passable, laborious, with great difficulty. It can be regarded as representing the assessment of the parishioners' reading ability by the clergy of the time tolerably well. In assessing the reading skills of the people of Kivijärvi, one must take into account the fact that children under 15 years of age had not yet attended confirmation classes. It was therefore only at that age that a person was regarded by the records of the parish as able to read. However, some children younger than this had already attended elementary school and thus

Table 38. Marks for reading ability used in the parish of Kivijärvi.

Mark	Explanation
/	with great difficulty
' /	laborious
Y	passable
Y .	good
X	very good or excellent

Source: KSA, confirmation registers 1880–1899.

Table 39. The reading ability of the customers of Kivijärvi lending library 1877–1897.

Mark	N	%
/	4	1.2
' /	7	1.9
Y	101	27.7
Y .	40	11.0
X	59	16.2
in child registers	12	3.3
not known	141	38.7
Total	**364**	**100.0**

Source: KSA, confirmation registers 1880–1899.

possessed reading skills. In Kivijärvi, too, a scale of marks with a double 'XX' was used in the children's registers for those who had not been confirmed. For the children and young persons who used the library, the marks for reading skills were generally at least 'satisfactory' and mostly 'good'.[1214] Those children and young persons who were interested in using the library were without exception able readers, and certainly more able than the majority of local members of the same age group.

All in all, the great majority of the customers of Kivijärvi lending library possessed at least passable reading skills in the assessment of the clergy. Only a few had very poor reading ability. The results are vitiated by the fact that the reading ability of almost 40 percent of the customers cannot be assessed in this research from the confirmation records. Nevertheless, it can be concluded that the customers of the library liked reading; it was for them an interesting pastime or a skill that they otherwise felt to be useful.[1215] If reading had been awkward and time-consuming, people would hardly have bothered to travel to the church village to get books from the library.

According to the confirmation records, only two of the 10 most active customers of Kivijärvi lending library knew how to write. The elementary school teacher Edvard Olsoni was naturally an able writer, and the writing ability of the shopkeeper's wife, Amanda Jäsberg, was also assessed as quite good. In addition, the clergy adjudged the writing skills of one Esa Kinnunen,

1214 Table 38.
1215 Table 39.

the son of a landed peasant, to be passable, while those of a sawmill hired labourer called Kalle Rein were assessed differently in different records. All in all, to judge from the church records, about 45 of the identified customers of the library would seem to have possessed some kind of writing skills. Of the ten most active customers of the lending library, the reading ability of eight was excellent, that of one good and of one passable.[1216]

Although in this context it is possible to examine only briefly the use of the library by the most active borrowers, this survey in itself reveals a number of interesting matters. One is that the most enthusiastic borrowers, who were probably also the most able readers, came from outside the local community that is studied in this book, i.e. from places where the teaching of reading skills had been more active for one reason or another: different local school conditions or the fact that the borrowers had been taught to read and write by their families at home. Another important factor is that the most active borrowers had good functional reading skills and they also knew how to write. This shows that their good reading and writing abilities encouraged them to use the library more. Since particularly the older generations lacked these skills, they were not very active users of the library.

'Borrower profiles', short biographies of readers

DIFFERENT RURAL READERS

The function of a library is only fulfilled if it has active customers who are interested in the works it contains. Scrutinizing the works borrowed and read by a number of the inhabitants of the countryside more closely and using them as typical examples of the readers and their reading habits make it possible to obtain a more thorough idea of the differences that existed between the customers of the people's libraries. However, every reader's understanding of what he or she reads is based on his or her personal experiences, and in this sense reading is a very personal activity. Therefore, it is not possible to ascertain the reactions of the readers to what they read purely on the basis of the loans registers, although these can yield some clues. However, a prosopographical approach does show many of the features of the borrowing behaviour of the community.

On the evidence of the loans registers, the library of Kivijärvi was used by several dozens of persons annually during the 1880s. The fall in the number of users began at the same time as the library was re-established by private persons. Because the records of the privately established lending library in Kivijärvi do not specify who were paid-up members of the library apart from the members of the board of governors, it is not possible to draw up any list of them. However, one member is mentioned in the accounts of the library. They state that the membership subscription of one Miss Sylvia Jurva was received in 1889. A year later, her name appears as Sylvia Anjelin after she married Axel Anjelin.[1217] The paid-up members of

---

1216 Kivijärvi READERS.
1217 KKA, accounts of Kivijärvi lending library 1889 and 1890; Table 40.

Table 40. *The annual numbers of customers of Kivijärvi lending library 1877–1897.*

Year	Library customers N	%
1877	4	1.1
1878	1	0.3
1879	3	0.8
1880	1	0.3
1881	3	0.8
1882	22	6.0
1883	74	20.3
1884	53	14.6
1885	72	19.8
1886	89	24.5
1887	101–102	27.7–28.0
1888	80–81	22.9–22.3
1889	45–46	12.4–12.6
1890	28	7.7
1891	15	4.1
1892	9	2.5
1893	5	1.4
1894	14	3.8
1895	11	3.0
1896	9	2.5
1897	5	1.4
not known	3	0.8
Total*	364	100.0

* The total number of users here means the sum of borrowers for the whole period when the library was in operation. The annual number of users has been compared with this to calculate the annual proportion of users.
Source: KKA, loans registers 1877–1897.

a library that functioned as an association in Äspö in Sweden at the same time were sometimes mentioned by name in the records, but no separate list of members was drawn up, nor were the occupations of the borrowers always mentioned in the loans registers. However, they included carpenters, cobblers and landed farmers.[1218] In terms of both their clientele and their collections, rural libraries in Finland were more egalitarian than the more segregated libraries of the towns. The paucity of resources made it necessary to concentrate on a single library which offered reading material (usually in Finnish) at least in principle for all the parishioners.

In 1896, Pastor Hjalmar Kyyniö, Elis Björnholm (a senior pharmacist) and Toivo Anjelin (an upper-secondary-school student) subscribed to the library for one year.[1219] Toivo Anjelin (1874–1934) was a pupil first in Jyväskylä Lyceum and then in Tampere Teacher Training Lyceum, from

1218 Jarlbrink 2010, 50.
1219 KKA, Minutes of the meeting of the board of governors of Kivijärvi lending library, 14/5/1896.

where he graduated in 1896. In the early 1880s, while still under the age of ten, Anjelin borrowed a religious book and some works of fiction such as a translation of Hoffman's *Leo* [Leo Bertram, or the Brave Heart] and *Suomen Kansan Satuja ja Tarinoita* [Fairy tales and stories of the Finnish people] Parts 1–2. He completed a degree in law in 1905 and then worked as a lawyer and the chief of police of Kivijärvi between 1906 and 1911. While he was still a student he had been the acting chief of police of Kivijärvi, and he had served in this capacity in the autumn sessions of Kivijärvi District Court in 1899. Subsequently, he pursued his career as a lawyer and finally ended up as a bank manager in Jyväskylä in the 1920s. Anjelin changed his surname to Anjala, and in the 1930s he donated the church's first altar painting, a work by Carl Bengts, to the church of his native parish of Kivijärvi to replace the wooden cross that had previously hung over the altar there.[1220] Some of the works owned by Anjelin have been donated to the Fennica collection in the library of the University of Jyväskylä.[1221] Toivo Anjelin had what at that time was a rare opportunity to continue his studies in the city and to take up a career as a professional. He inherited from his family an interest in promoting popular education, and he also contributed to the funding and development of local libraries.

Among the enthusiastic borrowers in Kivijärvi were a house painter called Karl August Rosvall (who lived in the house of the shopkeeper Elias Jäsberg and his wife Amanda, who was a member of the board of governors of the library), a joiner called Abraham Lindberg and his family from the church village, Riikka Vesterinen from the Kivikko Farm in Pudasjärvi, Juho Haksander from Kuivaniemi and Anna Liisa Niskanen. Karl Edvard Olsoni[1222], an elementary school teacher from Kinnula, also borrowed a lot of religious books. There were borrowers who came all the way from Karstula, although one of these, the mistress of Takkala Farm, was originally from Kivijärvi. The inhabitants of the Kannonsaha Sawmill community also came to borrow books from the library in the church village of Kivijärvi in the period extending from the 1870s to the 1890s. Evidently, they had got the bug for reading during the time when Tichanoff's library was in operation.[1223]

Edvard Olsoni was born in 1832, the son of a lawyer and estate owner called Johan Fredrik Olsoni, who died in the year following his son's birth. Edvard's mother, Agatha Benedikta, was the daughter of Henrik Johan Lyra, the curate of Pielavesi, and there were also clerics on his father's side. Edvard's elder brother had studied in Kuopio Middle School (formerly Kuopio Trivial School) and Lyceum. After graduating in 1849, he matriculated in the Faculty of Law of Alexander University in Helsinki, and after graduating

---

1220 Appendix 1.
1221 I once happened to notice in a book that I had ordered from the stockroom of this library the stamp of the owner: J. Anjelin. In other words, the book originally came from the collection of Toivo Anjelin's father, Johan Anjelin.
1222 Olsoni was usually known by his second name.
1223 KKA, Loans registers of Kivijärvi lending library 1877–1897.

he worked as a government and district registrar.[1224] There was a printing press, a book shop, and a reading society lending library in Kuopio in 1848, in other words, at the time when Olsoni was attending the lyceum there. In addition, later the bookshops in Kuopio loaned out books for a fee. However the oldest and largest library in terms of its collection was that of Kuopio Lyceum, which was established in the 1840s and already in 1847 contained nearly 3000 volumes. The students of the lyceum also had their own Swedish-language library.[1225]

Edvard Olsoni also graduated as a student from the middle and upper secondary school in Kuopio in 1857 and went on to study theology at the university. However, he became more oriented towards teaching than university studies. After passing his practical teaching demonstration, which qualified him for the posts of teacher and head teacher in primary schools in March 1869, he worked initially as an assistant teacher in Kuopio Primary School from 1864 to 1875, then as a teacher of divinity in Kuopio Teacher Training School in 1874 and 1875 and after that as a teacher in elementary schools in the same city from 1875 onwards.[1226] Olsoni took up his post as an elementary school teacher in the Chapelry of Kinnula in Kivijärvi in October 1878, and he officially moved to Kivijärvi in May 1879. He also served as the chapelry preacher in Kinnula. According to the recollections of local people, he had studied so much theology that he only needed to pass a few more exams in order to qualify for ordination as a minister.[1227] He married Anna Sofia Klemettinen in Kinnula in the summer of 1882. She was the daughter of a farmer from Kaavi. Olsoni was the teacher in the school in the church village of Kinnula from 1878 to 1900. He died in Kinnula on 24 January 1910.[1228]

Olsoni had begun his teaching career in his home town of Kuopio in 1865, and from 1873 on he worked as an elementary school teacher. During that time, he actively strove to further popular education and acquainted himself with the activity of lending libraries. In 1865, the local people donated books to Olsoni for the library of Kuopio Municipal Sunday School for Artisans, which had been founded in 1860. In the following decade, Olsoni served as the librarian of this Sunday school and probably also of another Sunday school. The library of Kuopio Municipal Sunday School for Artisans was intended mainly for craftsmen, their journeymen and apprentices, but it also served other 'known' (i.e. trustworthy) townsfolk after midday on Saturdays and in the morning on other weekdays. The library was located in Olsoni's flat in the house of Gustaf Hakkarainen. It operated until 1892,

---

1224 Kotivuori 2005. Ylioppilasmatrikkeli 1640–1852 and 1853–1899. Web publication 2005. Accessed 10/8/2012. Bergholm 1901, 974; Talvisto 1999, 180; Wanne 1959, 11–12, 20.
1225 Toivanen 2000, 402.
1226 Berner 1878, 157–158.
1227 Leskelä 1967, 29–30.
1228 Kotivuori 2005. Ylioppilasmatrikkeli 1640–1852 and 1853–1899. Web publication 2005. Accessed 10/8/2012. Bergholm, 1901, 974; Talvisto 1999, 180; Wanne 1959, 11–12, 20.

when it was amalgamated with the library of the so-called 'bourgeois' Workers' Association.[1229]

Very few of the founders of the library or the members of the first boards of governors were enthusiastic borrowers. Here it has been assumed that borrowing a book meant the same as reading it. In actual fact, the borrowers did not necessarily read everything they borrowed from cover to cover, and books could also be read communally even though only one person was entered as the borrower.[1230] In 1885, the elementary school teacher Sakari Niemi borrowed the *Children's Postil* and in 1888 a couple of other religious works. At least the first loan can be assumed to have been 'professional literature', but the teacher does not appear to have been an active customer of the library. This could be explained by the fact that he possibly had a library of his own, or then in his capacity as librarian he did not enter all the books he borrowed in the loans register. This is especially likely as the library was housed in the school building, where Niemi himself lived. His wife did not use the library at all. Not did Miss Hemmer, Miss Snellman,[1231] Mrs Anjelin or Mrs Krank borrow books from the lending library. Both of Helga Hemmer's parents had been born in Stockholm, so it may have been that literature in other languages than Finnish was read in her home. On the other hand, Anjelin's sons, Axel and particularly Toivo, did use the lending library. The family of the rural police chief Fröjdman were also active customers of the library. Amanda Jäsberg read quite a lot, and the Jäsbergs' maid Miina also used the library.[1232]

The fact that the members of the families of the functionaries and shopkeepers who founded the library did not actually use it themselves does not necessarily mean that they were not interested in reading. Of course, for some of them engagement in the activities of the library was a form of charitable work since most of the borrowers came from the more indigent sections of the population. However, some members of the local 'intelligentsia' were very enthusiastic borrowers of fiction, and members of the Fröjdman, Jäsberg and Vesterinen families were avid readers of novels and other forms of fictional literature.[1233]

For example, Mathilda Fröjdman, the wife of the district police chief, was the member of her family who borrowed most books from Kivijärvi lending library. She began using the library in 1884. The books she read included Finnish translations of Elizabeth Rundle Charles' *Helena's Household*, Édouard Layboulay's *Abdallah; ou le Trèfle à Quatre Feuilles* [Abdallah, or the Four-leafed Shamrock], Karl Listner and and Friedrich Gerstäcker's *Erlebnisse in Australien: Reiseerinnerungen* [Experiences in Australia: travel memoirs][1234] and Wilhelm Herchenbach's *Der Sklavenhändler von Benguela*

1229 Huttunen 1981, 12; S. Kotilainen 2013d, 130–131; Toivanen 2000, 402.
1230 Matti Peltonen 1992, 78.
1231 In 1885 a person named as 'Snellman' borrowed three works, but it is not possible to say with certainly whether it was Miss Snellman or some other member of the family.
1232 KKA, Loans registers of Kivijärvi lending library 1877–1897.
1233 KKA, Loans registers of Kivijärvi lending library 1877–1897.
1234 Finnish title: *Siirtolaisen elämänvaiheet*.

(The slave trader from Benguela]¹²³⁵. Between the years 1888 and 1894, she read only devotional literature. In 1883, her 11-year-old son, Karl (later Finnicized to Kaarlo) read the Finnish works *Elämän havainnoita* by Pietari Päivärinta, *Paavo Nissinen* by G. H. Mellin and *Novelleja ja kertomuksia* [Short stories and tales] (vols 2 and 4) and the Finnish translations of the novels Ernst Eckstein's *Besuch im Karzer* [The Visit to the Cells], Österbottens perla [The pearl of Ostrobothnia]¹²³⁶ and *Aina* by J. O. Åberg. He also borrowed Volume 2 of *Novelleja ja kertomuksia* a second time in the last part of the year. He visited the library altogether four times in the same year: twice in January, again in March and finally in October. In January 1887 the 12-year-old Betty read the 1884 edition of *Ilmarinen*, an illustrated almanac. According to the loans register, her younger brother, Ivar Fröjdman, visited the library for the only time in his life in May of the same year. He borrowed two books at the same time: Volume 4 of *Novelleja ja kertomuksia* (like his brother Karl before him) and the Finnish translation of Johan Wildt's Danish novel *Oluf Axelsøn og hans Familie, eller Inqvisitions-faengslerne under Sorøe Kloster* [Oluf Axelsøn and his family, or Inquisition prisons under Sorøe Monestary¹²³⁷]. Of the Fröjdman children the most enthusiastic user of the library was Anna, who borrowed most of her books in 1886, when she was 10 years of age. She read the Finnish translations of Volume 1 of Topelius' *Fältskärns berättelser* (Tales of a Barber Surgeon], *Erlebnisse in Australien: Reiseerinnerungen* and *Der Sklavenhändler von Benguela,* von Schmid's *Genovefa,* Jules Sandau's *La roche aux mouettes* [Gull Rock] and the Finnish works *Kaksoisveljekset* [The twin brothers] by Theodolinda Hahnsson, Pietari Hännikainen's *Pitäjään kirjasto* [A library for the parish] and Eero Salmelainen's *Suomen Kansan satuja ja tarinoita* [Finnish fairy tales and stories]. When she was of age to take confirmation, she also borrowed Edvard Mau's work *Kristillinen lukukirja* [A Christian reader].¹²³⁸

As mentioned above, among the most active readers in Kivijärvi were the house painter Karl August Fredrik Rosvall¹²³⁹ and the carpenter Abraham Lindberg¹²⁴⁰ and his family from the church village. Admittedly, Rosvall also lived for some periods of time in the village of Tiironkylä, from where the journey to the church village was several kilometres.¹²⁴¹ Both were working-aged craftsmen. Lindberg's father was Abraham Lindberg, a smith and saw setter, who had come to work in Kannonsaha sawmill. Later, in the early 1850s, among other things he made a pair of wafer irons (for making communion hosts) for Kivijärvi church.¹²⁴² Apparently, the family's interest in reading had begun during the time the father was working in the sawmill. Rosvall's enthusiasm for reading may have been influenced by the fact that

---

1235 Finnish title: *Orjakauppias Benguelassa*.
1236 Finnish title: *Pohjanmaan Helmi*.
1237 Finnish title: *Olli Akselinpoika ja hänen perheensä*.
1238 KKA, Loans registers of Kivijärvi lending library 1877–1897.
1239 Rosvall was born in 1850 in Kuopio.
1240 Lindberg was born in 1845 in Kivijärvi.
1241 KSA, confirmation registers 1875–1879, 388 and confirmation registers 1880–1889, landless persons R nro 26.
1242 2004 inventory of the oldest artifacts belonging to the Church Parish of Kivijärvi.

he had moved to Kivijärvi in 1882 from Vaasa,[1243] in the urban environment of which he might have got used to using a lending library.[1244] The literary taste of both men seems to have been much the same: the Bible, Luther's writings, the Finnish translation of Topelius' *Fältskärns berättelser* [Tales of a Barber Surgeon] and other works of fiction. However, the loan records do reveal one interesting fact: throughout the 1880s Lindberg read works of religious literature and fiction in turn. His children, too, borrowed different kinds of literature from the lending library. By contrast, in the early 1880s Rosvall read only fiction and in the 1890s only devotional works.[1245] One is strongly tempted to suspect that the painter must have experienced some kind of religious awakening in the meantime.

In the early days, craftsmen often constituted a group whose reading ability was superior to that of other sections of the population. One example of this in Kivijärvi was August Kaihlanen, a tailor who was involved in the activities of the board of governors of the lending library. The descendants of the smith Lindberg and the family of the house painter Rosvall were also active users of the library. Another keen user was Karl Johan (aka Kalle) Rein (Rehn, b. 1835), who was employed as a casual labourer at Kannonsaha Sawmill and lived there. He came from Kerimäki, where there was another sawmill owned by Tichanoff. Possibly under the influence of the literature that he had read, he gave his daughters rather unusual forenames: Wilhelmina Serafia and Saima Saali Siveä.[1246]

Johan Krook, the paternal uncle of Selma Saima Silja Krook, another customer of the library, was a Sunday school teacher at Kannonsaha. According to legend, he was referred to as 'Niiles-Juhani there at Kannonsaha'. The forename of the father of Krook was Nils, i.e. Niiles.[1247] The Krooks were descendants of a clerical family who held offices in Saarijärvi and Karstula. This was true also of Heikki Krook, who had helped to re-establish the library in Karstula in the 1870s.[1248] Alpinus Immonen was born in the great famine year of 1868, the son of Petter Immonen, a saw filer, and he was already borrowing books from the library when he was only nine years old.[1249] In this respect, the popular enlightenment endeavours of Michail Tichanoff, the owner of the sawmill, continued to bear fruit into the last decades of the century as the interest in reading aroused among the workers was passed on to their children. The parents, who regarded reading as a worthwhile pastime, had obviously served as an example for their children.

Women also used the lending library. Even the mothers of small children found time to read in the 1880s, despite the fact that it was quite a long journey from the outlying villages to the church village. Ebba Liisa

---

1243 The city had long traditions in popular library activities, for a reading society had already been established there in 1794. Mäkinen 1997, 161–162.
1244 Lehtikanto 1964.
1245 KKA, Loans registers of Kivijärvi lending library 1877–1897.
1246 Kivijärvi READERS.
1247 SKSÄ, KKA 1, Kivijärvi 9N.
1248 Bergholm 1901, 733–736; Roiko-Jokela 1998, 351.
1249 KKA, Kivijärvi library loans registers 1877–1897.

Savelainen (b. 1844), the wife of a crofter called Heikki Leppänen from the Purontaus croft on the Taasila estate in the village of Saarenkylä[1250] read uniquely religious literature. She borrowed altogether seven books over a period of 11 years, including three books in April 1884. Ebba Liisa borrowed the Bible from the library, as did her husband Heikki (a different copy at a different time), which leads us to conclude that they possessed no Bible of their own at home. Heikki was perhaps an even more avid peruser of the Bible and other religious works than his wife. Both of them read the Finnish translation of Johann Baudewin's work *Eltern und Kinder Seelen-Rettung* [The salvation of the souls of parents and children[1251]], and both also borrowed Luther's *Evankeliumi-Postilla*, Heikki several times.[1252]

Riikka Vesterinen,[1253] the mistress of Hiekka Farm in the village of Pudasjärvi and later of Kivikko Farm, for her part, mainly read the fiction that was available in the lending library, despite the fact that she is known to have been a devout woman. Riikka Vesterinen (née Liukko) was born the daughter of a crofter in Keuruu in 1852. As a young girl, she had worked as a maid in vicarages in Keuruu and Alavus and also in Helsinki. She studied for one year at Jyväskylä Teacher Training Seminary, and she was appointed the teacher of the Kivijärvi southern ambulatory school district in 1880. In the following year she married Lauri Vesterinen and became the mistress of a prosperous farm and the mother of a large flock of children. Riikka Vesterinen took an interest in social issues. She was one of the founders of the neighbouring Leppälänkylä elementary school in the early 1890s and a member of its first board of governors. In the parliamentary elections of 1907 she stood as a candidate of the Young Finns party. This was exceptional among women of the peasant estate at that time. Riikka seems to have been particularly devoted to the Finnish translation of Topelius' Tales of a Barber Surgeon, but she also read Pietari Hannikainen's work *Pitäjään kirjasto* [A library for the parish]. Her husband Lauri Vesterinen also read a couple of novels as well as Yrjö Koskinen's *Johtavat aatteet ihmiskunnan historiassa* [Leading ideas in the history of mankind]. It seems that Riikka Vesterinen particularly liked to read the new books that the library acquired since she was often the first borrower. Lauri Vesterinen converted to Laestadianism, but Riikka Vesterinen's faith was not as intransigent as that of her husband, and she had a more tolerant attitude to life. Her husband was accustomed to read from Luther's postils to the members of the household on Sundays.[1254]

Gideon and Alma Orava were the children of a landed farmer called Gustaf Orava. The father had died when they were under ten years of age, so in the 1880s they lived with relatives in the Aho farm in the church village. Gideon and Alma were fairly enthusiastic users of the library. At the age of thirteen, Gideon (b. 1869) read a volume of popular fiction in which

---

1250 Ebba Liisa was born in 1844. KSA, confirmation registers 1875–1879, 1110.
1251 Finnish title: *Wanhempain ja lasten sielun pelastus*.
1252 KKA, Loans registers of Kivijärvi lending library 1877–1897; Kivijärvi READERS.
1253 Kangas 1998, 17–20, 23, 25. See also S. Kotilainen 2013d.
1254 KKA, Loans registers of Kivijärvi lending library 1877–1897; Kangas 1998, 17, 22. 17–19, 21–25. See also S. Kotilainen 2013d.

Genovefa, La Roche aux mouettes [Gull Rock] and *Kaksoisveljekset* [The twin brothers] were bound together. The book was on loan only for four weeks either side of Christmas. After returning the book in January 1883, Gideon, who had now turned 14, borrowed the third part of *Suomen kansan satuja ja tarinoita* [Fairy tales and stories of the Finnish people] from the library. He had it out only for a couple of days. In March Gideon borrowed the first and second volumes of the same work, and again he kept them only for a few days. Either he was a quick reader, or then fairy tales did not interest him anymore. Then in the summer Gideon borrowed Walter Scott's novel, *The Talisman*, which he kept on loan till the following March. He read it once again in late winter 1886 after he had turned 17. It is difficult to say whether it was these works that inspired a longing for faraway places in Gideon or the harsh fact that there were few decent possibilities for a fatherless boy in his home parish, where the landless population had begun to grow excessively. In any case, in the following spring Gideon obtained a passport and emigrated to North America.[1255]

The enthusiasm of the Orava children for reading probably sprang from the situation at home. If the father had not died, Gideon, too, would probably have gone off to study at a senior secondary school, like his cousin Matti Rytkönen (b. 1866), the son of a shopkeeper also called Matti Rytkönen. The fathers' writing skills and the interests had given them a significant position in society, and the ability to read also became an important source of cultural and social capital for their sons. Gideon's younger sister, Alma, only used the library in the summer of 1887, when she was a girl of 14 years of age. She read mostly fiction, including the novels G. H. Mellin's *Paavo Nissinen*, J. O. Årberg's *Österbottens perla* and *Aina* and Edouard Laboulay's *Abdallah* as well as the first volume of the series *Novelleja ja kertomuksia* [Short stories and tales]. She was also attracted by *Järjestävä käsi taloudessa* [An ordering hand in the household] translated by Samuel Roos from Amelie de Frese's Swedish original, which gave practical advice for housewives. Alma always borrowed two books at a time, in other words the largest number allowed.[1256] Thus in the 1880s, the young people of Kivijärvi not only borrowed entertaining literature from the library but also sought to augment their knowledge with useful advice about practical everyday matters.

A PORTRAIT OF THE KIVIJÄRVI READER

The biographical data about the customers of Kivijärvi lending library constitute a collective biographical database that permits one to conclude what kind of person a typical reader in Kivijärvi and more broadly in the remote countryside was. His or her use of the library was subject to a number of central conditions.

The use of the library was impeded and even prevented not only by the existence of loan fees (not many of which accrued in Kivijärvi, as can

---

1255 KKA, Loans registers of Kivijärvi lending library 1877–1897; KSA, confirmation registers 1880–1889, 163.
1256 KKA, Loans registers of Kivijärvi lending library 1877–1897; Kivijärvi READERS.

be deduced from the fact that many customers were not charged at all for borrowing books in the years 1877–1897) but also the limited opening hours, the people's lack of spare time and above all their poor reading skills. The main customers of the library were the common people of the countryside. The families of the local elite also possessed books of their own, and so they used the people's lending library less. In the 1880s and 1890s, young people clearly read more fiction and more secular literature in general than earlier generations had. This was a common trend all over Finland at that time.

The practices for measuring the reading skills of the common people of the Finnish countryside varied not only temporally from the seventeenth century to the nineteenth but also locally, and thus it is not easy to compare reading ability in different parishes. The clergy's definitions of reading ability are better indicators of a mastery of the principles of Christian doctrine than they are of true functional reading literacy. The sources concerning the activities of Kivijärvi lending library that have survived offer a more accurate picture of the common people's personal reading interests and of the kind of literature that they preferred to read in their spare time when they were not studying or cramming the principles of Christian doctrine for the annual catechetical meetings.

A person's chances of using the library improved considerably if he or she lived near the church village. Children and young people visited the library only if they lived nearby. Otherwise, the age of the user did not particularly affect his or her opportunities for using the library; it was more his or her personal situation in life. Landed peasants used the library more than crofters or cotters, but even so there was a considerable number of members of the landless population among the borrowers.

The ability to write would seem to have increased people's interest in using Kivijärvi lending library, or at least to have encouraged them to read more and to seek out more challenging reading matter. Generally, the level of education and reading ability, which gradually improved as the parishioners began to attend the elementary school did not have time to take effect and lead to a significant increase in the use of the library by the beginning of the twentieth century. This does not necessarily indicate that there was not a greater interest in reading than before; rather, the mainly old-fashioned collection of the library might have reduced the people's interest in it. The parishioners' activation of library activities in 1888 did not lead to a successful conclusion in terms of popular enlightenment, since it was just at that time when the use of the library began to wane.

Most of the customers of the people's library consumed the kind of literature that they had traditionally been accustomed to reading. However, since the customers of the library constituted only a minority of the population of the parish, one can conclude that the majority would surely have been interested in slightly more modern reading matter. The library's lack of success in terms of customer numbers is an indication that the improvement in reading literacy did not necessary lead to large numbers of the parishioners becoming customers of the library, and, for example, the establishment of elementary schools did not produce a significant increase in the number of young customers of the lending library at least in the last decades of the nineteenth century. The decrease in the use of the library in the early years of the twentieth century may also be an indication of the development of reading literacy. Persons who had acquired more versatile and functional reading skills were no longer interested in reading traditional popular educational literature and may well have looked elsewhere for their reading matter, or else sought other pastimes than reading. For example, at the turn of the century, the activities offered by associations and clubs became ever more important for those persons who were interested in participating in the current social or political debate and influencing the course of affairs.

Even though individuals actively developed their reading and writing skills, it was still no guarantee that their informational capital increased; it only gave them the opportunity to enhance it. One can ask why the ability to read did not always lead to social advancement. In the case of a few users of the library, men in particular, one can note that their use of the library in their childhood and youth did herald learning and a professional career later in life. However, they were generally members of the families of tradesmen and functionaries, i.e. social groups whose children were expected to take up studies.

By contrast, the children of landed peasants who were encouraged to use the library did not always take advantage of the immaterial capital that they had acquired to seek social advancement. This did happen in some cases but generally only when their parents, and their fathers in particular, had previously exploited their own ability to read and write in their communal activities. Women usually read exclusively 'for their own pleasure', but even so they played an important role in their families in transmitting reading and writing skills since they participated in the early education of their children at home. In the last decades of the nineteenth century, the church and the early elementary schools assumed that children would be taught rudimentary reading skills at home.

Nevertheless, it would seem from my collective-biographical analysis that the use of the library did play its part in advancing reading and writing literacy at a time when not everyone had the opportunity to go to school. The younger generations had more varied reading matter available to them: not only that offered by the library but also schoolbooks and newspapers. The ability to read and write constituted a form of immaterial capital that could be utilized locally, for example in drawing up various documents for the common people and participating in communal decision-making. At that time, it was not very often possible for persons, particularly those members of generations of agricultural families who were born in the early years of the nineteenth century, to obtain a proper formal education, and consequently an independent acquisition of reading skills assumed considerable importance. Therefore, the family background of the borrower and an atmosphere that was favourable to literature in his or her home had a significant influence on the development of his or her reading skills since responsibility for elementary education lay for a long time with the home, and use of the library often took place as a family. The ability to read and write constituted an immaterial resource that enabled those who mastered these skills well to use them to their advantage in various social activities. In practice, these abilities were exploited to the greatest extent by middle-aged and older men who held positions of trust and otherwise wielded power in municipal posts.

6. Readership and Reader Response: Why the library failed to attract readers and ensure its survival

The end of Kivijärvi lending library

Ideas can be transferred and recorded in books, and in them they can travel hundreds of years and thousands of miles.[1257] Books unite different cultural milieus and writers and readers from different ages with one another. But this only happens if the readers are sufficiently literate and have books available for reading. Libraries have throughout the ages functioned as centres for the distribution of books and concomitantly the dissemination of new ideas, as a result of which cultural influences have spread far and wide, even to remote areas. But why did the libraries sometimes fail in these endeavours?

It is not possible to bring the story of the people's library of Kivijärvi to a conclusion without taking it down to the 1920s and 1930s, because the new age in popular education that began then significantly affected the development of the library institution in Finland. At the same time, its history shows just how slow the modernization process was in the case of libraries and the fact that the requirements established for public libraries were not achieved until the 1960s. Universal compulsory education came into force in Finland in 1921. The first Library Act was ratified in 1928. In enacting it, the state undertook among other things to provide financial support for municipalities that maintained libraries. A basic idea behind the law was that the responsibility for the provision and maintenance of libraries would henceforth be primarily the responsibility of the municipalities.[1258] By that time, the reading skills of the people had improved considerably since the 1860s. Regular elementary schooling for at least some of the population during the past half century had changed the significance of education as informational capital and shifted some of the traditional tasks of popular enlightenment from the libraries to the elementary schools.

Between 1904 and 1911, there would seem to have been a quieter period in the activities of Kivijärvi library since no minutes of meetings of the board of governors or records of the member's activities were made. There are accounts records until 1907 and also for 1909. When the collection of the library was checked against the library catalogue in January 1911, it was

---

1257 Tuomas Heikkilä 2009, 7.
1258 Eskola 2009, 293–294.

noticed that numerous works were missing. It was therefore decided to ask borrowers to return the missing books as soon as possible by making an announcement at the church service and through other notices. In other words, an attempt was made to revive the library's activities. It was also noticed that the library's rules had become obsolete, and it was proposed that new ones, preferably based on the model suggested by the Society for Popular Enlightenment, be obtained. Consequently, it was decided to obtain this model set of rules and other guidelines for running a library from the society as soon as possible.[1259]

It was also decided in connection with the stock-taking in 1911 to apply to the municipal assembly for the acquisition of a new bookcase. Its price was estimated to be 20 marks. It was further decided that books that were in poor condition or unbound should be repaired and bound. In addition, it was proposed that the old Bibles in the collection should be donated to poor families or sold off cheaply to desirous buyers at a price of three marks a volume.[1260] It seems that by that time the Bible was so common a possession in the majority of homes, albeit not in the poorest ones, that it was no longer necessary for most people to borrow it from a library. The reorganization of the library in 1911 was prepared by a committee, which proposed that a board of governors comprising five persons should be elected to continue the work of the committee. This board of governors was elected, but the only record of its activities is a single set of minutes from 1912.[1261]

In the spring of 1912, the collection was arranged in its new bookcase, and at the same time all the old religious works that were no longer borrowed were removed, and it was decided to 'hand [them] over on a suitable occasion to private persons for a small consideration'. The old illustrated Bibles had already been sold, and Mrs Annikki Hänninen, the wife of the elementary school teacher, was given the task of collecting the money accruing from their sale in her capacity as treasurer. Elis Karhusaari, a fishery adviser by occupation, was authorized to find out how much of the municipality's unlevied tax on alcohol could be used to subsidize the library. Karhusaari was accustomed to carrying out local duties of this kind, and he was later elected chairman of the municipal assembly, in which post he served from 1916 to 1918.[1262] If there remained enough funds for the library, Mrs Hänninen and Mr and Mrs Karhusaari were authorized to choose and order new works for the library from Werner Söderström and other publishing houses, possibly in the form of a joint order in cooperation with other libraries or private persons.[1263] Since the records end with this set of minutes, there is no way of finding out whether the new books were acquired or how long the library

1259 KKA, minutes of the meeting of the committee of Kivijärvi lending library, 20/1/1911.
1260 KKA, minutes of the meeting of the committee of Kivijärvi lending library, 20/1/1911.
1261 KKA, minutes of the meeting of the committee of Kivijärvi lending library on 20/1/1911 and the meeting of the board of governors on 12/3/1912.
1262 Martti Peltonen 1986, 382.
1263 KKA, minutes of the meeting of the board of governors of Kivijärvi lending library, 12/3/1912.

continued to function after this. Anyway, it is interesting to note that the rural libraries made bulk orders together, presumably in order to save on costs.

In the 1910s and 1920s, the situation of many public libraries was unstable and their activities languished. Some of them had been closed for a long time, and they had no staff. Gradually, efforts were made to improve the condition of public libraries in different municipalities. New works were acquired for them, a new decimal system of classification was introduced and the works were displayed in a new way. The librarians took part in librarianship courses and other types of training. In Central Finland, the shift from the old popular lending libraries to public libraries maintained by the municipalities took place at the latest around the turn of the century. For example, in Keuruu the municipal assembly decided to establish a main lending library in the church village and it ratified its set of rules in 1912.[1264] At the same time, the people's library was taken over by the municipality.

There was a corresponding shift from parochial to municipal libraries elsewhere in the countryside, too. For example, in Nivala in Northern Ostrobothnia, the church parish handed over its library to the municipality in 1912 on condition that the municipality would provide annual support for it and that it should continue to be the main library of the administrative parish.[1265] A State Library Office and a Library Committee were established in 1921. Regional library inspectors began touring the country and reporting on the activities of the public libraries. The financial aid and expert assistance provided for public libraries by the state also grew at that time. Even so, the term *kansankirjasto* (people's library) continued to be used, and the term *yleinen kirjasto* (a calque from the English 'public library') was not yet in general use in the inter-war period. In the countryside, the main library of the municipality was called *kantakirjasto* (the 'base library') and the branch libraries of the villages *piirikirjastot* ('district libraries'). In the towns, libraries were called *kaupunginkirjastot* ('town or city libraries').[1266]

In 1928, it was calculated on the basis of compiled statistics that there were 1650 public libraries operating in the countryside and 55 in towns in Finland. Of these, 62 percent were owned by municipalities. The owners of the others were youth associations, workers' associations and other such organizations. The statistics for 1928 are the only ones for the interwar period in which information about all the public libraries functioning in Finland at the time was collected. The number of libraries appears to have dropped to almost a half of the figure for 1912. However, the number had not really decreased so drastically, and the difference can be explained by the fact that the statistics for 1928 were compiled more precisely. They also took into account those libraries that did not come within the sphere of state assistance. At that time about half of all the public libraries functioning in Finland were subsidized by the state.[1267]

1264 Rainio 1988.
1265 H. Mäkelä 1991, 38.
1266 Eskola 1999, 117–119; Eskola 2001, 73–74.
1267 Eskola 2009, 291.

For example, there was a municipal library in Kinnula, which had become independent from the parish of Kivijärvi in 1914. In 1919, pupils' libraries were established in each of the three elementary schools there. In 1923, the running of the municipal lending library was entrusted to the youth association. Although the Libraries Act of 1928 made it possible for libraries to obtain state subsidies, the Great Depression slowed down the expansion of Kinnula library. The Municipality of Kinnula established a new main library in late 1937. It began to function the following year on a fairly modest scale, in very much the same way as the old popular lending libraries had operated: it consisted of a bookcase located in a corner of a classroom of the elementary school in the church village. It was open twice a week, on Sundays and Wednesdays from 5 to 6 pm.[1268] The same procedure had obtained for the lending library when the first elementary school was established in Kivijärvi 60 years earlier.

In the early years of the twentieth century, the Society for Popular Enlightenment, the Finnish Library Association and the municipalities still disagreed about whether it would be best to establish support associations for the libraries or to transfer them to the ownership of the local authorities. In the opinion of the Society for Popular Enlightenment, a municipal library system would be the most sensible solution.[1269] At the turn of the century, the attitude of the Municipality of Kivijärvi to the transference of the library to municipal ownership would by all appearances seem to have been rather reluctant. The reasons for this were probably financial. At any rate, the old collection of books was conserved (at least in part). There would seem to have been a plan in the late 1920s to establish a municipal lending library in the parish, or at least the municipality was encouraged to do so by the state, since Olga Risula, a state library inspector, wrote in December 1930 that she was sending a bundle of papers about the library project and a printed model set of rules to the municipality. To judge from her letter, Risula had visited Kivijärvi and then continued on to Kinnula, from where she sent the letter to the municipal officials. It seems that action had been taken after the enactment of the Libraries Act in 1928. A number of circular letters sent by the State Library Committee in the years 1928–1933 concerning, among other things, the official qualifications for the post of librarian have been preserved in the archives of the library of Kivijärvi. In addition, the district library inspector of the Province of Vaasa sent information about courses on librarianship organized by the state.[1270]

A budget was drafted for the main library of Kivijärvi for the year 1931. According to it, the annual expenditure would be about 4500 marks. This sum was made up of the remuneration of the librarian (500 marks), the cost of purchasing the library's requisites, fire insurance and sundry expenditures. The biggest outlay (3800 marks) was reserved for the purchase and binding of books. The library's income was estimated to be a state subsidy of 2200 marks plus the amount accruing from fines (25 marks). The outstanding

---

1268 Talvisto 1999, 184.
1269 Järvelin 1966, 40.
1270 KKA, Other documents concerning the lending library.

2275 marks would be covered by the municipality. As one might well expect at the beginning of the Great Depression, the note appended in the budget by the representatives of the municipality officials was: 'Proposal rejected pro tem.'[1271]

From the 1910s on, the activities of the public library in Kivijärvi languished for several decades since no-one could be found to run it. The libraries and book collections of elementary schools supported the work of the teachers and offered the pupils reading matter. However, in the summer of 1951, the municipal council decided to establish a main library in the municipality. Initially, it consisted of a small cupboard located in a conference room of the Municipal Offices, and the job of running it was carried out by the Municipal Secretary in addition to his other duties. Even in the mid-1960s, the library still did not have premises of its own, and it functioned in three rooms reserved for its use in the Municipal Offices. The library was still not used very actively at that time. For example, in 1960 the number of borrowers was only 151 and the number of loans a little over 6000. The population of the parish at the time amounted to just over 3100 persons.[1272] The library possessed slightly more than 1200 volumes. In 1971 there were just over 500 customers and in 1980 about 700.[1273] The spirit of the Library Act of 1928, according to which public libraries were only for people who possessed an elementary education and the provision of library facilities was a form of enlightenment of the people directed from above, continued to prevail.[1274] It was not until the Library Act of 1961[1275] that there was any significant economic improvement over the situation in 1928 with regard to the accessibility and quality of library services in the countryside. Thereafter there was considerable progress into the 1970s.[1276]

The history of the lending libraries in Kivijärvi during the period examined in this book can be condensed into a few crucial junctures.[1277] Probably most of the religious literature (and particularly that which was closely associated with the Evangelical movement) that was later preserved in its collection was first acquired during the early years of the library that was established in 1862. The library that operated in conjunction with Kannonsaha Sawmill was established at the same time. The establishment of both these libraries was influenced by the Evangelical movement, which had spread into the Kivijärvi area, and the activities of its leaders, the vicar Karl Gustav Dahlgrén and the cantor Ferdinand Konstantin Kjellman. The endeavours to promote popular education, which had got off to a good start,

1271 KKA, Other documents concerning the lending library.
1272 S. Kotilainen 2008a, 363.
1273 Mönkkönen 1986, 461.
1274 Mäkinen 2009f, 387.
1275 The act came into force at the beginning of 1962 and was thus commonly also known as 'The Library Act of 1962', although it had been ratified the previous year. With the enactment of this law, the libraries received considerable state subsidies, and public policy on libraries became more effective. Mäkinen 2009f, 388–389, 401.
1276 Vatanen 2002, 11.
1277 Table 41.

Table 41. The life history of Kivijärvi's libraries.

Year	The lending libraries of Kivijärvi	The Grand Duchy of Finland
1857	First library in Central Finland established in Saarijärvi	The Finnish Book Publishers Association founded
1858	Kivijärvi seceeds from Viitasaari as an independent parish	The first Finnish-language secondary school established in Jyväskylä
1859	The Evangelical preacher Kjellman appointed cantor	Recording of minutes of Finnish-speaking parish councils in Finnish begins
1860	Population of Kivijärvi over 3100	Finland gets it own currency unit, the mark (markka)
1861	Libraries established in Karstula and Viitasaari	Deputation of Peasants to the Czar regarding the status of the Finnish language
1862	The first library established; Kannonsaha Sawmill library also founded	Rail traffic begins (Helsinki – Hämeenlinna)
1863	The first people's library in Jyväskylä established	The Language Decree (on the official use of Finnish). The Diet meets
		Jyväskylä teacher training seminary and Girls' secondary school founded
1864	The first vicar appointed to Kivijärvi	
1865		The Municipal Decree: separation of the municipalities and church parishes
1866	Vicar K. G. Dahlgrén moves out of the parish	Elementary School Decree
1867–1868	Epidemics and high mortality	The worst years of famine
1869	Antti Herranen appointed cantor of Kivijärvi	The Church Law of 1869
1872	The library re-established	Weilin & Göös and Gummerus publishing houses founded
1873	The first elementary school established	
1874	Teacher Daniel Liukkonen made librarian	The Society for Popular Englightenment founded in Jyväskylä
1877	First entries in the library's loans register	1877–1878 war in the Balkans; Werner Söderström publishing house founded
1878	Cantor Herranen continues as librarian	Conscription Act (Finns have their own units)
1879		Complete freedom of trade in the countryside enacted
1880	Antti Tokkola appointed librarian	
1881		Alexander III takes the throne
1882		Appointees to official posts required to know both Swedish and Finnish
1883	Vicar F. P. Krank takes up his post	Decree establishing Finnish as a language of administration alongside Swedish
1885	Teacher Sakari Niemi made librarian	
1886		The Language Decree takes effect
1887	Numbers of loans reach their peak	The metric system adopted
1888	A lending library established by private persons	"The Father of the Finnish elementary school" Uno Cygnaeus dies at the age of 77
1890	A. L. Heideman dismissed from his clerical post	Otava publishing house founded; The Postal Manifesto marks the beginning of Russification
1891	The library joins the Society for Popular Enlightenment	
1894	Leppälänkylä elementary school established	Nicholas II takes the throne
1897	Last entries in the loans register	The Union of Finnish Writers founded
1898	The library subsidized by the municipality	Zacharias Topelius dies at the age of 80

1899	Teacher Heikki Lipponen made librarian	The February Manifesto; beginning of the first "Period of Oppression"
1900	Leppälänkylä post stop established	Karisto publishing house founded
1901	Emigration to the USA increases	Finns conscripted for the Russian Army
1902	Escape from conscription to America	Conscription strikes
1903	Library activities revive	
1904	Library activities languish	E. Schauman assinates Gov. Gen. N. Bobrikov
1905	Local political party activities burgeon	General Strike. End of the first "Period of Oppression"
1906	Finnicization of Swedish surnames all over Finland	Equal universal suffrage in national elections enacted A unicameral Parliamentent established
1907	Riikka Vesterinen stands as a parliamentary candidate	The first parliamentary elections
1909	Teacher Kalle Hänninen made librarian	The second "Period of Oppression" begins
1911	Attempts to revive library activities	
1912	The operation of the library ends	The Equality Act (for Russian citizens in Finland)
1914	Impressment, requisitions, etc. in wartime	Outbreak of the First World War
1917	The Civil Guard established	Finland gains independence

were interrupted by the years of severe crop failure and famine. After the demise of the first library, a second one was founded thanks to the efforts of the new vicar, Viktor Konsin, in 1872, and in the following year he also managed to get the first elementary school established in the parish. In 1877, the collections of the library, which were located in the elementary school, contained about 140 works. Although the initiative for the library had originally come from the church parish, it had been re-established with an eye to the needs of the school, and it primarily aimed to cater for the pupils. Although its purpose was to support the work of the school, in practice the majority of its users were adults. However, the activities of the library languished in the early years of the following decade because of the rapid turn-over of teachers, who acted as its librarians.

In 1888 some private persons took up the task, and an association established to develop the library revived its activities for a second time. New books were acquired, and the works of the old collection were repaired. However, it was soon noticed that running the library as an enterprise of a civic association did not bring in enough income to maintain it, and proposals were made to have it transferred to the ownership of the municipality. Finally, in 1898, the old parish collection was officially integrated into the library founded by private persons and became subject to its regulations, and thenceforth the library was subsidized by the municipality; thus an unofficial practice that had been going on for about ten years was officially approved by the municipality. New works still continued to be acquired for the library, although its activities finally declined under municipal ownership. It was replaced in the following decades by school libraries along with the enactment of compulsory education in Finland. It was assumed that the adult population would get their reading matter elsewhere, or at least that developing of the literacy skills of children was the most important goal in those days.

Achieving the founders' goals and satisfying the readers' needs

However well-intentioned and useful the purpose of an activity may be, it does not always reach those whose benefit it seeks to promote. Naturally, a lot depends on whether those who are the objects of charitable and educational endeavours are willing to receive the help and guidance that is offered to them. Those who sought to bring enlightenment to the common people by founding lending libraries in the late nineteenth century ran up against this practical problem in Kivijärvi, too, when they tried to improve the reading skills of the people of the local countryside, and as a result, the organization of the local lending library, which in itself would appear to have been perfectly functional, repeatedly found itself failing.

Why did the activities of the people's library in Kivijärvi languish repeatedly and fail to establish themselves on a permanent basis? Was it a consequence of the paucity of available funds, a lack of interest among the readers, the library's dependence on certain individuals, or something else? The locality was predominantly agricultural and politically a stronghold of the Old Finns party. The reading skills of the parishioners were low, and the severe famine of the 1860s had paralyzed the region both economically and demographically. However, towards the end of the century the population revived and grew strongly. The social and intellectual change at the turn of the century was so rapid that traditional popular education no longer sufficed to maintain the interest of the majority of the population. When the first popular libraries were established, the low rate of school attendance, which was affected indirectly by economic factors, meant that reading skills expanded slowly. Poor parishes did not have the resources to establish schools, and indigent families could not afford to send their children to schools further away.

According to my research, it was characteristic of Finnish libraries that were established in the mid-nineteenth century that they flourished and declined by turns. Their activities were by no means always marked by continuity, and from time to time attempts were made to revive them or to establish new libraries alongside old ones[1278]. The historical study of literacy helps us to understand the change that took place in education and the school system and its significance in different ages. Reading skills were important for acquiring new information and achieving both economic and intellectual growth. The slow and uncertain progress in learning to read shows how complex a matter the acquisition of education and other informational capital was in the rural areas. However, the people of Kivijärvi in the late nineteenth century did not greet the activities of the popular library with unreserved enthusiasm.

The special position of Finland as part of the Russian Empire necessarily influenced the development of people's libraries in the latter half of the nineteenth century. Many social reforms, such as the shifting of responsibility for elementary education from the church parishes to the municipalities, were implemented later than they were, for example in Sweden and the

---

1278 See also Karjalainen 1977, 4.

other Nordic countries. The years after the Crimean War marked a period of radical change in which numerous other social reforms were embarked upon. Legislation that reformed the status of the Finnish language and the interest in improving it for political reasons saw an increase in the significance of local libraries, and was also part of the Fennoman national(ist) policy after the mid-nineteenth century, which saw their function as being more than just the bringing of enlightenment to the people: the realization of the goals of the Fennomans' policy required the support of the people, and consequently the active development of reading literacy and its expansion among the people were key factors ensuring that the commons might be reached and crucial ideological ideas inculcated in them. The changes in society at the end of the nineteenth century and the beginning of the twentieth meant that the church and religious services, and even newspapers, ceased to be the most important channels for the dissemination of information among the people. Social and political activities and participation in them particularly through civic associations and organizations and other charitable endeavours made it possible for the common people themselves to influence the course of events, at least at the local level.

Since the reform in elementary education was tardy in the remote countryside, the acquisition of functional literacy among the people was slow. The life story of Kivijärvi lending library shows, that the libraries did promote its expansion, but not any great extent. The local clergy also took an active part in establishing the first lending libraries, but their reason for doing so was not just the enlightenment of the people; rather, they were significantly motivated by a desire to defend the traditional prerogative of the church to educate the people and the fear that this task might fall into the hands of the lay authorities. Religion also intimately influenced the early libraries in that the revivalist movements – in the area studied here above all Evangelism and to some extent also Laestadianism – created a demand for religious literature.

Compared with the rest of Central Finland, Evangelism burgeoned at a fairly early stage in Kivijärvi. In this movement, reading vernacular religious literature held a central position in the practice of devotion. The powerful early influence of Evangelism in the area is an interesting and very significant phenomenon, which has rarely been taken into account in previous historical research as a factor that promoted the activities of local lending libraries. Moreover, an important preacher in the early Evangelical movement, Cantor Kjellman, worked in the Kannonsaha Sawmill community, which was a strong centre of popular education and from which the revival spread to the surrounding areas. The community had its own school and library, which were supported by the owner of the sawmill, and these increased its significance as a local centre of informational and immaterial capital. It is important to note that the teaching of reading skills, the dissemination of literature and the preaching of religious doctrine coalesced still in the latter half of the nineteenth century. It was only later that the neighbouring parishes of Karstula and Saarijärvi became significant centres of Evangelism. In Kivijärvi, on the other hand, where Evangelism had come earlier, a change of vicar caused a partial abatement in the earlier revivalism and allowed Laestadianism to obtain a stronger foothold at the turn of the century. Despite this, Evangelical revivalist literature still formed the basis of the collection of Kivijärvi library.

My research shows that the libraries of the Finnish countryside worked to a great extent according to the operational principles of German and Central European reading societies and thereby adhered to this tradition. It was only with the advent of the public library movement that they developed in to modern people's libraries. The task of the library in the late nineteenth century was to offer its customers meaningful and necessary information, but at least the library in Kivijärvi could only offer information to the extent that its funds permitted it to acquire. The acquisition of literature in the countryside was limited not only by the scarcity of available resources but also by the fact that the few bookshops that did exist were located far away. Thus numerous publishers, including the Society for Popular Enlightenment, marketed what they considered to be suitable reading matter to the people's libraries by means of catalogues of different kinds. In this way, the acquisition was generally regulated by a more general opinion about what was suitable literature for the commons. The borrowing times were also sometimes relatively long for example in Kivijärvi, and this impeded others than the person who had the book out on loan from obtaining information that they needed. In the light of this research, the possibilities of the rural commons for acquiring information from the lending library were affected not only by their interest in reading but also by such mundane factors as the time available for reading, the distance a person lived from the church village, the conditions for travelling there and the amount of usefulness or entertainment a work was thought to provide in relation to the effort it required to obtain it.

The examination of the opening times of the libraries presented above, which is more detailed than any conducted in previous research, shows that at least in theory the opportunities for using them were strictly limited by the regulations of the libraries. Much in the same way as the collections and the leisure time reserved for reading were limited, the loan period for a book and the opening hours of the library were defined relatively strictly. The libraries operated according to the order created by their rules, on the one hand, and defined by their premises on the other. Although the operations of the libraries were strictly organized and regulated according to national (and international) models, some flexibility and pragmatism was also practised in the countryside to ensure that borrowers might be tempted to participate. For example, the opening times stipulated in the rules were not strictly adhered to if the borrowers wished to use the library at a time that suited them. This research indicates that in principle the libraries were open daily and in practice whenever the librarian or a member of his family was at home if the library was located there, as was often the custom.

At the time when the library was established, the communication of information still took place in a rather traditional way among the people of Kivijärvi. The most important local announcements were made from the pulpit. To some extent, newspapers and other written matter were read both in the parish and elsewhere in the countryside, but information was most effectively passed on by word of mouth. It came from those who had made trips to town or other travellers, and it was disseminated in larger gatherings such as church services, parish assemblies, rural court sessions, weddings and work bees. Thus the oral and written cultures co-existed side-by-side, although the latter was continuously growing in strength. In the middle and later decades of the nineteenth century, folklorists gathered information about the traditional folk culture of the common people, which they thought reflected the mentality of the Finnish people generally.[1279] The reading of library books was still not a natural part of the local culture of Kivijärvi in the nineteenth century, and only a minority of the people were interested in it. The norms and customs of communication changed slowly, and the low level of literacy certainly did not promote this change.

One could also consider that the goal of increasing the reading skills and enthusiasm for reading of the people set by the promoters of popular enlightenment gave them a tool for inculcating the rural population with the 'right' kind of ideas about the world and its ways: in other words, instilling in them a way of thinking that the popular enlighteners considered to be appropriate for them. In this way they to a certain extent obtained the power to decide what the lower orders should think about affairs since the apparent informational needs of the rural population were mainly determined by members of the educated class. What is most interesting about the people's library dealt with here is the fact that from 1888 on it functioned as a civic association (with an annual membership fee) and that it was established by members of the educated classes who had moved to the locality from elsewhere – as indeed were the previous people's libraries established in the 1860s and 1870s. Because the vicars, elementary school teachers (apart from Sakari Niemi) and other office-holders changed fairly rapidly and the library ideal and popular education were confined to a few persons, when they moved away, the running of the library was occasionally left unattended. On the other hand, the members of some families like the Anjelins and the Kranks continued to support the activities of the library for decades. Those who worked in connection with the library formed their own networks or inner circles, whose children, servants and even tenant crofters were the principle customers of the library.

The fact that it was very often elementary school teachers who functioned as librarians in the countryside was very much in accordance with the popular educational principles of the Fennomans. The results of my research indicate that the librarian's work became professionalized only very slowly. In the period studied here librarianship was a part-time job in the countryside, for which the librarian had not necessarily received any training. The professional training of librarians did not generally begin to be developed anywhere in the Western world until the late nineteenth century. In this sense, the training in librarianship that male elementary schoolteachers acquired while studying at the first Finnish Teacher Training Seminary in Jyväskylä and the practice they obtained in looking after the

1279 A. Niemi 1904, 93.

people's library there was a very modern and practical solution for furthering the professional competence of rural librarians.

In the nineteenth century, libraries tended to be located in the same premises as schools in continental Europe and also in the United States as well. In Finland, for about a hundred years rural libraries functioned mainly in other public premises than their own dedicated buildings and very often together with the elementary schools in the church villages. In the same way, early elementary education in the remote villages was organized in the form of ambulatory schools without permanent school buildings. Generally a rather small group of members of the boards of governors had the power to decide about the libraries' rules, acquisitions and lending activities.

An analysis of the stages in the lives of Kivijärvi lending libraries shows that the endeavour of the promoters of popular education to instil what they considered to be a proper way of thinking in the common people by selecting suitable literature for them to read meant that, in this respect, popular enlightenment was superimposed on the people's local culture. The decrease in the use of the library soon after its establishment by private persons suggests that a library aiming at popular enlightenment that was externally imported into the local community did not arouse much interest among the agrarian population, apart from a small minority. At least in the beginning, the selection of books in the privately founded library did not provide reading material in a form that was considered necessary and useful by a broader section of the population. Although the sources do not reveal this, it is clear that the founders of the library did not make much of an effort to satisfy the customers' informational needs by listening to them or asking them to express their wishes about books that would interest them. Rather, they thought that a board of governors appointed for the purpose would on the basis of its members' authority be qualified to decide these matters on behalf of the customers. Thus the objectives of the founders of the library and those of persons who sought new reading material did not completely coincide during the first decades of its operation.

Initially, the activities of Finnish libraries typically took the form of charity work performed by the upper classes for the benefit of the commons. This was what principally distinguished them from the public libraries that were established in the twentieth century with taxpayers' money. Typically, the popular libraries were to a great extent organized by women, although at that time, at least in the countryside, the librarians were predominantly men, usually elementary school teachers. Among the more interesting findings of this research is the fact that the library activities in Kivijärvi were in principle dominated specifically by the wives of long-serving local officials and shopkeepers from two clerical families: the Cheilan(us) family from Keuruu and the Durchman family from northern Finland[1280]. The use of a research method employing a thorough analysis of genealogical data show how the networks of these two families had become woven into the life of the local community. In the countryside there might be more than one member of a nuclear or extended family involved in a library's activities, which

---

1280 Bergholm 1901, 380–382.

meant that the power was concentrated within a very small group. Another interesting observation is that, thanks to the popular educational efforts and the early establishment of a school and library in the Kannonsaha sawmill, many of the young boys who learned to read there later became cantors in the parishes of the region. Popular education provided an opportunity for social advancement, albeit generally only for men. This result of the research can be applied more generally in comparative research on literacy skills.

In Kivijärvi, the activities of the early lending library were continued in the 1880s with the support of an association founded by private persons. The operation of the people's library was for quite a long time dependent on voluntary donations of money and the willingness of private individuals to help. It was not until the very last years of the nineteenth century that the municipality took responsibility for running the library. However, its activities had been more organized when it was a privately founded association, and when it became a municipal library its activities waned, and the emphasis shifted more towards school libraries. By contrast, library activities aimed at the adult population were left to organizations like the libraries of youth associations.

In the Nordic countries, the influence of revivalist movements in promoting people's libraries was considerable. The local expansion of revivalist movements played an important role in disseminating literature and encouraging people to read. However, one should note the 'double-edged' influence of the revivalist movements: on the one hand, they inspired people to study religious texts independently, which may have helped to increase people's reading skills and their desire to read, but on the other hand, the fact that they exclusively favoured religious literature meant that people did not necessarily take to reading more secular and modern works very rapidly. For example, even at the end of the nineteenth century Pietist works from the seventeenth and eighteenth centuries that were highly appreciated within the circles of the revivalist movements constituted a significant part of the collection of Kivijärvi library.

In the case of the people's library studied here, the literature that it made available to its customers was not anyway particularly revolutionary, despite the fact that the ideology of socialism was growing elsewhere[1281]; rather the selection of books made by the board of governors tended to preserve a traditional way of thinking. By selecting the books for the people of the countryside, it was also possible to control what kind of information they obtained. The collections mainly comprised contemporary Finnish popular novels, folk literature, educative works, plays and children's books. Nevertheless, foreign classics were also surprisingly well represented in even this small collection. On the other hand, at the turn of the century realist literature had not obtained a foothold in the library of Kivijärvi, since those

---

1281 The area studied here was a stronghold of support for the Old Finns (Fennomans) at the turn of the century, and the persons who wielded an influence over the activities of the library, such as clergymen and elementary school teachers, would not have approved of socialist-oriented literature. Even the realist movement in literature was regarded as harmful.

who sought to educate the people favoured literature that represented more traditional values. Although in principle, the popular libraries aimed to enlighten the people, the results of my research show that it was possible through them to regulate the extent of the new information that people obtained and to select the kind of information that would help them to advance in their path to learning. Readership took on different forms in different social groups depending on the books that were available to the readers.

In addition to light reading, some of the people of Kivijärvi also clearly sought information, which is indicated by the heavy demand for religious literature. Of course, religion, too, can be a form of entertainment or a leisure-time 'hobby', and one that perhaps better fulfilled the contemporary norms of suitability than the reading of fiction without any higher aims. However, the paucity of non-religious literature in the collection led to a situation in which, thanks to the library, readers who represented a minority of the population and were probably members of revivalist movements were able to read the religious literature they sought while the majority either did not have sufficient reading skills to use the library or were not themselves sufficiently religious to be interested in older literature of this kind. Because the oldest spiritual literature in the collection of the library consisted of reading favoured by the Evangelical movement, one might think that, after Laestadianism gained support in the area, this literature, which was no longer considered to be of central importance in the latter movement, was therefore no longer consumed in the early twentieth century to the extent it had previously been. On the other hand, there were many religious works that could have been of interest to the members of both revivalist sects.

The revivalist movements and religiosity in general abhorred the reading of what it regarded as frivolous, secular literature.[1282] Gradually, however, useful literature, such as works on agriculture, came to be regarded as acceptable, and the range of literature consumed by the ordinary people expanded.[1283] Even so, the annual loans statistics indicate that religious works were still more popular than secular ones in Kivijärvi lending library in the 1880s.[1284] While the religious climate of the area demanded religious literature, those who sought more secular enlightenment perhaps felt that the library did not offer them sufficient reading matter. The number of non-fiction works that were not religious was still low at the beginning of the 1890s, and of these only two dealt with practical matters, while the rest were more works of 'general information'. The educational level of the library's customers affected the kind of reading matter that they sought: if a person had not read much apart from religious literature (for example, in confirmation classes), then he or she tended to choose this kind of reading matter later in life as well, especially as it was regarded as appropriate in the general opinion of the community.

1282 Karjalainen 1977, 113.
1283 Mönkkönen 1988a, 537–538.
1284 Table 25.

All in all, on the basis of a local and international comparison, one can state that a wide variety of economic, political and geographical factors affected the culture of books and reading in the countryside. Reading skills and ways of acquiring information were extremely significant factors in the economic and intellectual transition of the Finnish people into a modern civil society. The culture of the local community also influenced the extent to which the library was used as a source of information. For example, the people of Kivijärvi generally possessed very few books of their own, and their educational level was low. One might then imagine that, at the turn of the century, a people's library would have played a significant role in enhancing people's reading skills in just such a parish, but in fact reading literacy did not improve significantly thanks to the library and only increased when compulsory education came into force and school attendance became more common. The results of my research reveal, that the popular enlightenment endeavours did not necessarily yield positive results everywhere. The activities of popular libraries in Finland continued to flourish in parishes where they had the support of a large section of the population and where they were directed by local enthusiasts. However, these activities were easily threatened if the major actors involved moved away.

Finally, we should consider especially from the viewpoint of the users of the library, what the people of the past did with their reading and writing skills and how they were affected by reading[1285]. For example, this research indicates that the acquisition of information was of great economic importance for the community and society in general. However, what was of supreme importance is the fact that the development of reading skills brought into being a new kind of human immaterial capital. This capital is characterized by the fact that it does not wear out or dwindle with use but is rather enriched by it. The people's libraries gave every reader the chance to develop his or her own reading ability independently, which is why they offered a significant source of information compared with schools, for example. Studying at school has always been attended by coercion to some extent and the teacher's authority over what is learned and how it is learned. By reading independently it was possible to choose how and in what order information was absorbed, although it was not always possible for the reader to choose the books that were available as these were selected when the library's collection of books was acquired. In this sense, the people's libraries really were libraries of the people – important 'liberators of learning', and they made it possible for people to acquire information on their own terms.

In the earlier Finnish research has not very often been analysed, how the communal status of the peasant reader and his or her personal networks in the local community affected the quality of his or her reading habits. In this book we have noticed, that the location of the library in its local community and on the other hand the status and position of its customers in their networks, had a great significance on the use of the library and thus to the improvement of reading skills. My analysis shows that those who borrowed books from people's libraries were persons who possibly could not afford

---

1285 M. Lehtonen 2001, 40.

to buy their own books, or then those who could best afford to do so but wished to participate in the activities of the library as users. The library was most used by those who lived nearby, and the revivalist movements also increased people's interest in using it. The books for the library could mainly be acquired when people made trips to town. Jyväskylä was an important Finnish cultural centre, and the town possessed bookshops, publishing houses, a teacher training seminary and a local press.

The few (under 10 percent) of the population, who used the library mostly read religious literature. Those who sought practical information about more mundane matters probably felt that the library did not offer them enough new information. The low level of education of the population and their accustomization to reading mainly religious literature (in school and at the latest in confirmation classes) determined their reading habits as adults, too. The beginning of elementary education and popular enlightenment improved the reading skills of the local population and at the same time increased their interest in using the library. At the same time, the amount of secular literature written in Finnish grew. The activities of lending libraries continued to flourish in localities where they had a broad base of popular support and where a local enthusiast directed their activities.[1286] On the other hand, these activities often depended on the efforts of a few persons, and they were threatened if, for example, these persons and their families moved away.

The library studied here was most used by children and young persons, while among the middle-aged borrowing was less common. This finding may be a result not only of the fact that it is possible to examine the loans only over a relatively short period but also of the fact that this period coincides with the breakthrough of elementary education. The younger generations had learnt to read and had become used to reading in the elementary school, which had not previously existed in the locality. Generally, the few young parishioners who went on to continue their studies had used the library in their youth. But even if a person did not acquire any further education, the reading of literature brought him or her a considerable amount of immaterial capital, at least by comparison with the literacy skills of the rest of the local community. Those who were most used to using the library were artisans, workers from the sawmill and those who were adjudged by the clergy to possess good reading ability. It would appear that these research findings of my research can be generalized to local communities in the remote countryside.

The keenest readers were generally also able to write. This study of a local library shows that the improvement of the reading skills of the common people and their use of the lending library inevitably increased their immaterial and informational capital. Since the level of reading and writing literacy in the community was low, the possession of these skills opened up opportunities also for those members of the population who had not been to school to take up new posts (including various municipal and parochial positions of trust) despite the fact that participation in local government at

1286 Karjalainen 1977, 117.

the turn of the century demanded much more fluent reading and writing skills than had been required of officials in previous centuries.

However, the distribution of immaterial capital was extremely uneven with regard to age, gender and social rank. In the early twentieth century, women in rural communities still had very few opportunities to utilize their reading skills in practice compared with men. As mothers of families, on the other hand, they played an important role in taking care of the basic education of their children right up to the end of the nineteenth century. For peasant men, on the other hand, good reading skills could open up career opportunities as a cantor, for example, although this also naturally required the possession of musical talent and a good singing voice[1287]. The opportunities for social advancement were limited for those who did not have the opportunity to pursue further studies in the cities. The young men of the families of shopkeepers and functionaries who belonged to family members on the board of governors and its immediate circle benefited in their later careers not only from the actual use of the library when they were young but also from the fact that taking part in the activities of an association that had maintained the activities of a rural library had familiarized them at the practical level with association activities and popular education.

For others, too, the use of the library would certainly seem to have brought the kind of intellectual capital that was not possessed by everyone in the local community. They could discuss and argue about literature and compare their reading experiences in the local context, and possibly these experiences encouraged other members of the community to use the library. The use of the library brought informational capital mainly through the reading of non-fiction, but religious literature also played an important role in the practice of devotional life. The arrival of the revivalist movements brought numerous changes in ways of thinking and a spiritual upheaval to the parish, and in connection with this devotional literature whose origins went back to earlier centuries provided those who experienced a religious revival fresh food for thought. For the majority of the parishioners new informational capital based on reading the books and enthusiasm for reading only came to a significant extent with the advent of school education. Even so, the library offered the adult population an important tool for self-education, especially if they used it for a longer period of time, from one decade to the next.

My study represents a methodological experiment in describing the life history of a people's library. The life stories of the users of the library and their behaviour as customers of the library together reflect the attitudes towards, and ideas about, libraries that prevailed among a section of the population that was to a great extent unable to write. In connection with popular libraries, one cannot literally speak of the people's own libraries because that would imply that they themselves were active in choosing the literature available for reading and sought to promote the vitality of the library through their own endeavours. Rather it was a question of libraries aimed by others at the people, the majority of whom were, however, unwilling

---

1287 See also S. Kotilainen 2015b.

to use them. Probably, in the countryside at any rate, the libraries failed to provide sufficiently for the people's informational needs. It appears that most of the people were not interested in Kivijärvi library's religious literature, nor indeed in its secular works, either because the information that they offered were of no interest to them or, perhaps more justifiably, because they did not possess the reading skills, the time or the opportunities to devote themselves to reading. Thus a library of this kind significantly increased the informational capital of only a few members of the parish. However, the spread of functional literacy as a social practice did change communal relations as it opened up new avenues for the most able individuals to be active in the local community.

The findings of this study can be applied more generally in comparative research on popular libraries. They offer a more comprehensive description of the relationship of different groups of the population to the functional use of the library and show how small details could affect its success. In the future, it would be interesting to conduct (also on the basis of primary sources) wider-ranging comparisons between popular libraries in the Nordic countries and elsewhere in Europe in order to ascertain whether their activities were more commonly beset by interruptions and a lack of continuity than has generally been thought. Although it must be admitted the comparative method cannot be fully implemented within the confines of a single study, the comparison carried out within this single work shows how the practices and implementation of endeavours to promote popular education through libraries were to a great extent influenced by local conditions. The advantage of the comparison is that it reveals the attitudes to libraries that were characteristic of each of the cultures involved. For the people of the Finnish countryside in the late nineteenth century, libraries represented a way of acquiring new information that was still strange and unwelcome. The general applicability and usability of the study still requires further research on the local development of reading literacy and the social and cultural changes that were linked with it. The effects and significance of reading and writing literacy varied according to the age and the culture. Nevertheless, the fact that popular libraries opened the way to a change in education and thinking was a common feature of the culture of the nineteenth century almost everywhere in Europe and also among the poorest section of the population who tilled the land.

The history of Kivijärvi lending library tells of the important time of change when the people of the countryside, who only began to read books independently relatively late, become acculturated to the written word, became acquainted with the activities of the library and received the opportunity to read a wider range of world literature than they had previously had access to. For the majority, the library was simply a harmless, albeit useful, form of diversion. Although the number of users was small, for a few it constituted an important tool for learning and developing their minds. From the point of view of developing people's ability to read and write, the use of even the early library brought about significant changes in the world outlook of the common people: above all a realization that the libraries had made the new ideas engendered by literature available to all. In that sense, the people's libraries were an important early harbinger of equality because they gave all the opportunity to acquaint themselves with a new kind of literature and to benefit from the communication of information. It was then up to each individual to make the effort to learn and to apply or exploit what he or she had learnt.

Appendix 1: Index of persons involved with the libraries of Kivijärvi and members of their families

Anjelin, Johan Wilhelm **Axel** (b. 19/5/1866 in Kivijärvi), an office clerk. Parents: Johan Anjelin (rural tradesman) and Ida Anjelin, née Cheilàn. He married Sylvia Jurva in 1890. He and his family moved from Kivijärvi to Vaasa in 1891. A member of the board of governors of Kivijärvi library (1888–1892), auditor (1889) and treasurer (1890–1891).

Anjelin, Ida Sofia, née Cheilàn (b. 1847 in Viitasaari), the daughter of Michael Cheilàn (tenant farmer, deputy district chief of police of Viitasaari) and Kristina Maria Petrelius, who remarried the vicar of Viitasaari, Dean Aleksander Dahlström in 1858. After the dean died, Kristina Maria lived with the Anjelin family in Kivijärvi. She died in 1890. She was the daughter of David Petrelius, the curate of Kiihtelysvaara, and Margareta Kiljander. Dean Dahlström's first wife was Katarina Sofia Cheilàn. Ida Anjelin moved to the Kannonsaha Sawmill community in the parish of Kivijärvi in 1865 from Viitasaari after she married **Johan Anjelin** (b. 1834 in Anjala), who had been employed as an accountant at the sawmill in Kannonkoski at least from the beginning of the 1860s. Anjelin was originally from the village of Ummeljoki in the parish of Anjala, where there was a hydro-powered sawmill and later a paper mill. Apparently, Anjelin moved to Kannonkoski from Kerimäki at the end of the 1850s. Anjelin, who was employed by the Tichanoffs, met his first wife, Wilhelmina Ruuth (b. 28/3/1844 in Askola) in their Enonkoski sawmill in Kerimäki. His future wife moved to Kivijärvi, where they were married on 17/7/1861. They had a son, Johan Oskar Anjelin (b. 1862, d. 1862). Wilhelmiina Anjelin died during her confinement in 1862 at the age of only 18. In 1871 Johan and Ida Anjelin moved into the church village of Kivijärvi, where he opened a shop. In 1872 the Vyborg merchant house that owned the Kannonsaha Sawmill gave it up and sold it to Johan Anjelin. Sawmilling ceased in 1885. In addition to his shop, Anjelin owned a tannery in the church village. Anjelin was the chairman of the municipal board of Kivijärvi in the years 1877–1879 and 1892–1894 and the chairman of the municipal assembly in 1877–1879. Ida Anjelin died in 1900 in Kivijärvi. She served as a member of the board of governors of Kivijärvi lending library (1888–1898) and was vice chairperson (1890–1898) and treasurer (1892–1893) of the board.

Anjelin, Toivo Theodor Alvian, surname after 1906: **Anjala** (b. 12/6/1874 in Kivijärvi). Parents: Johan Anjelin (rural tradesman) and Ida Anjelin, née Cheilàn. Anjelin attended Jyväskylä Lyceum and graduated from Tampere Teacher Training Lyceum in 1896. He took a degree in Law and was a trainee lawyer at Vaasa Court of Appeal (1902), Master of Laws (1905). He worked as a lawyer and local police chief in his native parish of Kivijärvi in the years 1906–1911. He was a prosecuting counsel at Vyborg Court of Appeal (1915–1917) and judge of Jyväskylä Municipal Court (1919–1922). Later Anjelin was a bank manager in Jyväskylä, where he died on 19/12/1934. He donated Carl Bengts's painting "Pietari kieltää Jeesuksen" (Peter denies Jesus) as an altarpiece for Kivijärvi Church in 1930. He was an auditor for the board of governors of Kivijärvi lending library (1897).

Björnholm, Otto **Elis** Edward, surname after 1906: **Karhusaari** (b. 1874 in Sortavala), a pharmacist and fishing consultant. He moved to Kivijärvi from Helsinki in 1896. Wife: **Alma** Maria **Karhusaari**, née Hämäläinen (b. 1872 in Kivijärvi). Alma Hämäläinen probably served on the first board of governors of Kivijärvi youth association. The family moved to Jyväskylä in 1921. Elis Karhusaari was a member of the board of governors of Kivijärvi lending library, vice-chairman (1904 and 1911–1912 and an auditor (1895 and 1904). His wife, Alma Karhusaari, was a member of the board of governors (1911–1912).

Dahlgrén, Karl Gustaf (b. 9/2/1821 in Hollola). Parents: Sgt. Johan Dahlgrén from Hollola and *Maria (Abrahams dotter) Söyrilä*. He attended Loviisa Trivial School in 1831 and Porvoo Upper Secondary School 1838–1841. He passed the Matriculation Examination in Helsinki in 1842 with the highest grade (laudatur). He was a member of the Tavastia Student Nation. He was ordained in the Diocese of Porvoo in October 1845. Dahlgrén served as a minister in Nastola (a chapelry of the parish of Hollola) in his capacity as assistant to the vicar of Hollola (1845–1849), and as a curate in Hirvensalmi (1849–1852). In Kivijärvi, he began as a curate in 1852, became the vice-pastor in 1856 and the first vicar of the parish in 1864. Wife: Gustava Charlotta Edla Kristina Krogerus (b. 1825 in Orimattila, d. 1914). He moved from Kivijärvi to Jääski (today Lesogorsky in Russia) in 1866. He was appointed Provincial Dean in 1873. He took up the post of vicar of Rautalampi in 1881. Dahlgrén was an important representative of the Evangelical revivalist movement. He died in Rautalampi on 22/1/1896. He founded the first lending library in Kivijärvi in 1862 and served as its librarian.

Ekholm, Bertha Magdalena (b. 1857 in Uusikaarlepyy). Single. Post mistress in the church village of Kivijärvi for nearly 30 years from the end of the nineteenth century to the early 1920s. Her mother tongue was Swedish. She moved from Kivijärvi to Ristiina in 1924. She was a member of the board of governors of Kivijärvi lending library (1894–1898 and 1903) and an auditor (1894, 1897).

Fröjdman, Mathilda, Thilda, née Wilskman (b. 30/5/1844 in Kurikka), wife of the district police chief. Parents: curate of Kurikka Carl Magnus Wilskman and Helena Sophia Alcenius, daughter of the curate of Ilmajoki. Mathilda's brother, Professor Ivar Wilskman (1854–1932), who was known as "the Father of Finnish Sports Culture", was a university PE instructor and wrote books on the subject. Mathilda Fröjdman moved to Kivijärvi from Laukaa in 1879. Her husband, Herman Leonard Fröjdman (b. 1842 in Orisberg), was the chief of police of the Kivijärvi police district in the years 1878–1894. Children: Karl Georg Herman (b. 1872 in Vaasa), Helena Elisabet (b. 1874 in Vaasa) and Anna Matilda (b. 1876 in Laukaa) as well as four other children all born in Kivijärvi: Ivar Waldemar (b. 1880), Minchen Lovisa (b. 1882), Allan Adolf (b. 1886) and Harry Leonard (b. 1888). The family moved to Ilmajoki in 1897. Mathilda Fröjdman served as a member of the board of governors of Kivijärvi lending library (1894–1895).

Heideman, Lempi Oihonna, née Krank (b. 1872). Parents: Frans Petter Krank, the vicar of Kivijärvi, and Maria Elisabet **Betty**, née Durchman. In 1888 she married in Kivijärvi **Arthur** Leopold **Heideman** (b. 8/3/1862 in Oulu), who had moved there in the same year to serve as his father's assistant. Heideman's parents were Henrik Heideman (a master dyer) and Maria Susanna Åhlberg. Heideman graduated from Oulu Swedish-Language Lyceum. He had originally planned to take a degree in some other subject at the university, but when working as a home tutor in a family in Sodankylä, he came into contact with Laestadianism and experienced a powerful religious awakening. Heideman began to study theology in Helsinki, and he was ordained on 28/10/1885. At first he served as a cleric in different parts of Finland, until he was appointed to the post of assistant to the vicar of Kivijärvi on 1/1/1888. In 1890, he was dismissed from his post for alleged heresy. Together with his family, Heideman emigrated to Michigan in the United States to become the pastor of the Apostolic Lutheran Parish of Calumet, and he died there on 7/11/1928. Lempi Heideman served as a member of the board of governors of Kivijärvi lending library and as an auditor (1896).

Hemmer, Helga Katariina (b. 26/2/1856 in Halikko). Parents: Erik Erland Hemmer, a forestry officer on Salamajärvi Forestry Reserve, and Albertina Matilda Zengerlein. She moved to Kivijärvi from Perho in 1887 and from Kivijärvi to Reisjärvi in 1898. There she married Juho Eemil Wierimaa (b. 25/9/1869 in Reisjärvi, d. 3/9/1936), a forestry officer. She died in 1921. A member of the board of governors of Kivijärvi library and vice-chairperson (1888–1889).

Herranen, Antti (b. 14/8/1840 in Kivijärvi). Parents: Matti (Jakob's son) Herranen (a casual agricultural labourer) and Kaisa (Isak's daughter) Mård. He attended the Kannonsaha Sawmill school and pursued further studies for four weeks in Vaasa to qualify as a cantor. He lived with the cantor Ferdinand Kjellman in the sawmill community and served as his assistant. He was appointed a temporary cantor in the parish of Kivijärvi in 1866. Wife: Leena Kaisa Kemppainen. The family moved to Seppälä Farm in the village of Tiironkylä in 1867, from there to Sydänmaa in Tiiro in 1869, and thence into the Lähde farmhouse in the church village in 1874. Herranen was the official cantor of the parish of Kivijärvi from 1869 till his death on 5/2/1913. He had altogether nine children, one of whom, Kalle Herranen, was the cantor of the parish of Kinnula in the years 1917–1951. Antti Herranen was the teacher of Kivijärvi elementary school and concomitantly probably the librarian of Kivijärvi lending library in the years 1873–1874, 1877–1880 and 1884.

Hänninen, Kaarle Wilhelm, Kalle (b. 1878 in Leppävirta), an elementary school teacher. He moved to Kivijärvi from Leppävirta in 1910. He served as the teacher of the elementary school in the church village of Kivijärvi during the years 1909–1912. He died in Kivijärvi in summer 1912. Wife: **Annikki** (Anna Lyytia) **Hänninen**, née Wasama (b. 1883 in Tampere), also an elementary school teacher. She moved from Kivijärvi to Raisio in 1919. Hänninen served as the librarian of Kivijärvi lending library and as chairman of the board of governors (1911–1912). His wife was the treasurer of the board in 1912.

Kjellman, Ferdinand Konstantin (b. 1822 in Sumiainen), the youngest child of Magnus Kjellman, an independent surveyor working under the Provincial Surveyor of the Province of Vaasa. In practice, his field of operation was Central Finland. The family's children were born in the chapelry of Sumiainen. The father-in-law of Magnus Kjellman was Carl Gustaf Schöneman, a sergeant-major and later an ensign in the Rautalampi Company of the Tavastia Province Foot Regiment, which was stationed in Viitasaari. The eldest of the sons, Carl Magnus, was the vicar of Savitaipale. Ferdinand Kjellman was the cantor of Kivijärvi parish during the years 1859–1869. He brought the Evangelical revival to Kivijärvi and was the first representative of Evangelism in the locality. Kjellman also served as a schoolmaster at the sawmill school in Kannonkoski and a lay preacher. Kjellman lived in the sawmill community, and during his spare time he performed the duties of librarian at the library that was established in connection with the sawmill in 1862. In 1867 the Kjellman family moved to Seppälä Farm in the village of Tiironkylä, which was closer to the church village. He was elected the vice-chairman of the first municipal assembly in 1868. However, the famine years and the associated burdens took their toll, and he died the same year in Kivijärvi. He married Anna Susanna Salin (b. 1822) in Sumiainen in 1847. From the 1860s on, the Kjellman family owned part of Lauttamäki Farm in the village of Pääjärvi in Karstula and part of Ahola Farm in the village of Hännilänkylä in Saarijärvi (later part of Pylkönmäki). Kjellman's widow subsequently lived together with her children on Lauttamäki Farm.

Konsin, Viktor August (b. 24/12/1836 in Somero). Parents: Dean Henrik Konsin, the Vicar of Somero and Ebba Wilhelmina Wanochius. Konsin attended an upper secondary school in Turku, studied theology and was ordained in 1859. He served initially as a supplementary cleric in the Åland Islands and other places until he was appointed the curate of Vanaja in 1863. He married Ida Emilia Sulin in 1861. Konsin served as the first agent in Central Finland of the Hunting Company of the Province of Vaasa (founded in 1865), and he was praised as having "practised this commission in an altogether excellent fashion, with enthusiasm and skill". Konsin was vicar of Kivijärvi in the years 1872–1882. He was instrumental in re-establishing the lending library in the church village in 1872 and in establishing the first elementary school in the parish the following year. He was also the chairman of the municipal board of Kivijärvi (1874–1876). He moved from Kivijärvi to Orimattila in 1882, and he was granted the title "Dean" in 1886. He was a delegate at the Diet. Konsin died on 28/1/1904 in Orimattila.

Krank, Maria Elisabet, **Betty**, née Durchman (b. 1843 in Inari), the daughter of Josef Wilhelm Durchman, the Dean of Ruovesi. During his student years, the dean had made friends with supporters of Finnish nationhood like Elias Lönnrot, and the ideal of Finnish nationhood was apparent in the daily life of the vicarage in Ruovesi, for example in the fact that that the language used by the family at home was Finnish. In 1869, she married her cousin, **Frans Petter Krank** (b. 10/9/1844 in Oulu), who was the vicar of Kivijärvi during the years 1883–1910. He was the son of Simon Petter Krank (a sea captain and merchant shipper) and Maria Josefina Durchman. The father died while the boy was still young. His father's brother, the vicar of Kuusamo, assisted him with his schooling. Krank attended an upper secondary school in Vaasa and studied theology in Helsinki. He was ordained on 31/7/1867. Even as a child, the fatherless Frans Petter had spent a lot of time at his uncle's home in the vicarage in Ruovesi, where he became familiar with the ideals of Finnish nationhood. Krank worked as an assistant to his uncle, Josef Wilhelm Durchman in Ruovesi, and he later married the latter's daughter. In 1882 Krank was appointed vicar of Kivijärvi. Vicar Krank was very much a man of the people who involved himself actively in social affairs, played and composed music, hunted and fished and was interested in developing agriculture. The Laestadian revival reached the Kivijärvi area in the 1870s, but it did not start to flourish there until the beginning of the following decade, when Krank was the vicar. He was converted to Laestadianism by his son-in-law, A. L. Heideman. He was awarded the honorific title "Dean" in 1899. He died while still the vicar of Kivijärvi on 28/8/1910. Betty Krank served as a member of the board of governors of Kivijärvi lending library (1891–1898), was the treasurer of the board (1894) and an auditor (1891).

Lipponen, Heikki (b. 1868 in Kaavi), an elementary schoolteacher. He moved to Kivijärvi from Teuva in 1899. Heikki Lipponen was the teacher in the elementary school in the church village in the years 1899–1905. He was appointed to the post through the influence of Vicar Krank, who was the chairman of the board of governors of the elementary school, although the people of Kivijärvi considered him to be too strict a disciplinarian. He married **Maana (Maria) Lipponen**, née Durchman (b. 1866 in Ii), the daughter of Jakob August Durchman, the district police chief of Ii. Mrs Maria Lipponen was the cousin of Betty Krank, the vicar's wife. Heikki Lipponen served as the librarian of Kivijärvi lending library and as chairman of the board of governors and treasurer (1903–1904). His wife, Maana Lipponen, was a member of the board of governors (1903).

Liukkonen, Daniel (b. 2/5/1850 in Hirvensalmi), the son of a freeholder Adam Liukkonen. He attended a lower secondary school in Mikkeli, although he apparently did not complete his education there. He subsequently studied at the Teacher Training Seminary in Jyväskylä (1872–1873). He worked as an elementary school teacher in Sammatti during the spring semester of 1874, and in Kivijärvi during the years 1874–

1877. At the same time he served as the librarian of Kivijärvi school library. He was subsequently a teacher at Uskila elementary school (1881–1884).

Lyytinen, Juho (b. 9/8/1867 in Kivijärvi), a freeholder. Lyytinen was most probably one of the founders of Leppälänkylä lending library and he became its first librarian in 1895. The library was located in one of the rooms of Leppälä Farmhouse, which was Lyytinen's home. The books were kept in a bookcase with glass doors, and the master of the household encouraged his workers to read the books actively. Lyytinen's brother, **Evert Lyytinen** (19/12/1881), attended the College of Central Finland from 1902 to 1903. He participated keenly in many kinds of social activities: for example, he was the chairman of Kivijärvi Municipal Council, and he was present at a meeting of the Constitutionalists in Leppälänkylä elementary school in 1905, which among other things demanded the establishment of more elementary schools in the parish. He succeeded his brother as the librarian of Leppälänkylä lending library until the 1920s. In his spare time, he practiced photography and took many pictures of Kivijärvi and its inhabitants.

Niemi, Sakari, originally Ervastin-Niemi (b. 5/1/1862 in Revonlahti), the son of a land-owning farmer. An elementary school teacher, he graduated from Jyväskylä Teacher Training Seminary in 1885. Niemi was the teacher of the elementary school in the church village of Kivijärvi in the years 1885–1898, the first to have graduated from the teacher training seminary. During the 1880s, Niemi sent numerous folkloristic descriptions of Kivijärvi to the Finnish Literature Society. Together with his wife, **Aina Sofia Niemi**, née Westerlund (b. 1860), he moved to Kivijärvi in 1886 and from there in 1898 to Karunki, where he worked as an elementary school teacher until 1925. In these parishes, Niemi also served as a member of the municipal council and the church council and as the chairman of the guardianship board. He was also active in agricultural and co-operative organizations and in working for temperance and peace. He was a member of the board of governors of Kivijärvi lending library (1888–1898) and treasurer (1895–1898). His wife, Aina Niemi, was a member of the board of governors (1889–1898).

Puranen, Juho (b. 6/12/1864 in Kivijärvi), the son of a family that owned the large and prosperous Hiitola Farm in the village of Lokakylä. Parents: farmer Matti Puranen and Maria Kahelin. He was the first person from Kivijärvi to attend the College of Central Finland (1894–1895). He was elected the first chairman of Kivijärvi Youth Association in 1897. In the early years of twentieth century, he lived in the Aho farmhouse in the church village. Puranen was the chairman of the municipal board of Kivijärvi (1898–1903) and the chairman of the Municipal Council (1907–1909). He was also chairman of the board of governors of the church village elementary school (1906–1915). When Puranen was living there, the Aho house also served as an inn. A member of the board of governors of Kivijärvi lending library 1903. Puranen died in Kivijärvi in 1915.

Räsänen, Andreas (Antti) (b. 1/6/1848 in Tuusniemi), the son of a land-owning farmer. He attended the Finnish Mission School from 1864 to 1870, where he completed his education. He served as a preacher in Tuusniemi (1870–1871), in Jyväskylä (1871), in Viitasaari (1871–1873), in Kuopio prison (1873–1874) and again in Viitasaari (1874). He began working as a teacher and chapel preacher in Kinnula in 1874, and together with these duties he served as the librarian of Kinnula school library. He worked in the 1870s also as a teacher in Karstula, where he often preached on Sundays in the church invited by the local clergy.

Salmi, Juho Vihtori (previously Sund, b. 21/3/1879 in Saarijärvi). The son of a farmer called Matti Sund and his wife Anna, he was an elementary school teacher. He received his teaching diploma at the Jyväskylä Teacher Training Seminary in 1904.

He initially worked as a teacher in Karstula and then, from 1912 on, in the church village of Kivijärvi. While he was living in Kivijärvi, Salmi served as the chairman of the municipal assembly and the municipal council. He was also a member of the church council, a parish auditor and an acting cantor. J. V. Salmis interests included work in support of other Finnic peoples, the Estonian language and music. He had seven children by his first wife, Maria, née Jäntti. Salmi died in 1940.

Seppänen, Jaakko Leonard (b. 1881 in Oulu), a pastor. He moved to Kivijärvi from Vilppula. He served as assistant to the vicar of Kivijärvi during the years 1910–1912. His wife, **Laina** Maria **Seppänen**, née Krank (b. 1881 in Kuopio), was the daughter of Frans Petter Krank, the vicar of Kivijärvi. Seppänen was a member of the board of governors of Kivijärvi lending library (1911–1912), as was his wife (1912). Seppänen and his family moved to Haapajärvi in 1912.

Svens, Adrian (b. 21/8/1864 in Närpiö). Parents: Anders Henrik Svens (a farmer) and Katarina Böling. Graduated from Vaasa Lyceum and took a degree in economic and administrative law in 1890. He moved to Kivijärvi from Närpiö in 1894. Chief of police of Kivijärvi police district (1894–1905). He was a member of the first board of governors of Kivijärvi Youth Association. Svens married **Le(e)ni** (Lempi Helena Maria) **Durchman** (b. 21/1/1876 in Viitasaari), the daughter of Josef Oskar Durchman, the district chief of police of Viitasaari in September 1899. Leeni Svens was the niece of the vicar's wife, Mrs Betty Krank. The mother tongue of both Svens and his wife was Swedish. They were members of the board of governors of Kivijärvi lending library (1903). In 1906 Svens was appointed the Crown Bailiff of the Jurisdictional District of Pietarsaari in Kokkola, where the whole family moved in 1907. From 1910 on, Svens was the branch bank manager of Vasa aktiebank in Kokkola. He died there on 29/1/1916.

Ulén, Wiivi (b. 3/7/1871), the daughter of Gustav Ulén (a surveyor). She came from Laukaa in Central Finland 1893. She took up a position as the post mistress in Kivijärvi in the 1890s. She had attended Vaasa Girls School and Porvoo Ladies College, and after marrying a shopkeeper called Juho Heikki Vesterinen (b. 21/7/1862), she became the elementary school teacher in the Leppälänkylä. Wiivi Vesterinen subsequently served as a self-taught midwife in Kannonkoski. She served as an auditor for the board of governors of Kivijärvi lending library (1892).

Sources: JyMA, KSA, migration certificates[1] 1879–1924, confirmation records 1853–1874, 1880–1930; VSA, registers of marriages 1899; KKA, Minutes of the annual general meetings and meetings of the board of governors of Kivijärvi library 1888–1912; Yrjö Kotivuori, *Matriculation records 1640–1852*: Web publication 2005, http://www.helsinki.fi/Matriculation records, accessed 7/8/2012; *Matriculation records 1853–1899*, http://www.helsinki.fi/Matriculation records/1853-1899/; http://hiski.genealogia.fi/seurakunnat; Bergholm 1901; Berner 1878; Jokipii 1988; Kanervainen 1878; Kokkinen 1994; Koski 1998; A. Kotilainen 1979; Lampinen 1986; Mikkola – Leinonen – Rekola 1937; Mönkkönen 1986; Martti Peltonen 1986; Repo 1990; Sinisalo 1986; Talvisto 1999; Tuomaala 1986; Viljanen 1931; Wanne et al. 1943–1946, 356–357; Wanne 1958; Werkko 1879.

---

[1] A migration certificate (Finnish: *muuttokirja*) was issued by a minister of the church to a person intending to move to another locality. It testified to his or her literacy and knowledge of the scriptures. It could also be used as a testimony of the person's good standing.

Appendix 2: The populations of the church and civic parishes of Kivijärvi, Kinnula and Kannonkoski by decade 1730–1960

KIVIJÄRVI

Year	Population	Increase/decrease Number of persons	Percent
1730*	–	–	–
1740*	–	–	–
1750	395	–	–
1760	514	+ 119	+ 30%
1769**	552	+ 38	+ 7%
1780	730	+ 178	+ 32%
1790	884	+ 154	+ 21%
1800	1061	+ 177	+ 20%
1810	1097	+ 36	+ 3%
1820	1354	+ 257	+ 23%
1830	1753	+ 399	+ 29%
1840	2064	+ 311	+ 18%
1850	2722	+ 658	+ 32%
1860	3167	+ 445	+ 16%
1870	3143	- 24	- 1%
1880	3984	+ 841	+ 27%
1890	4874	+ 890	+ 22%
1900	5458	+ 584	+ 12%
1910	5963	+ 505	+ 9%

1913 The parish of Kinnula became independent of Kivijärvi and the population of Kivijärvi went down:

1913	4219	–	–
1920	4334	- 1629	- 27%
1930	4694	+ 360	+ 8%

1/1/1931 The parish of Kannonkoski became independent of Kivijärvi and the population of Kivijärvi went down:

Year	Population	Number of persons	Percent
1931	2749	–	–
1940	2821	- 1873	- 40%
1950	2791	- 30	- 1%
1960	3121	+ 330	+ 12%

Sources: KSA, population tables 1749–1790, 1793–1950; STV 1915, p. 23 and 1951, p. 19; SVT VI: 1 pp. XLVIII–XLIX, 5 pp. 46–47, 9 pp. 8–9, 22 pp. 14, 37 pp. 75, 45 pp. 274–275, 56:1 pp. 50–51, 73 pp. 27, 74 pp. 28, 98:1 pp. 20–21, A 119 pp. 30–31.
* The population of the whole parish of Viitasaari was 1500 in 1730 and 1600 in 1740.
** No data for 1770 available.

KINNULA

Year	Population	Increase/decrease Number of persons	Percent
1913	1954	–	–
1920	2105	+ 151	+ 8%
1930	2386	+ 281	+ 13%
1940	2610	+ 224	+ 9%
1950	2925	+ 315	+ 12%
1960	3227	+ 302	+ 10%

Sources: STV 1915, p. 23 and 1951, p. 19; SVT VI: 56:1 pp. 50–51, 73 pp. 27, 98:1 pp. 20–21, A 119 pp. 30–31.

KANNONKOSKI

Year	Population	Increase/decrease Number of persons	Percent
1931	2998	–	–
1940	3226	+ 228	+ 8%
1950	3453	+ 227	+ 7%
1960	3480	+ 27	+ 1%

Sources: STV 1951, p. 19; SVT VI: 74 pp. 28, 98:1 pp. 20–21, A119 pp. 30–31.

Appendix 3: The ministers of Kivijärvi up till 1959

Ministers of the parish of Kivijärvi[1]

Before the chapelry of Kivijärvi — *Years of service*

Bartholdi, Matthias	around 1639
Paulinus, Paulus Laurentii	1664–1691 (lived in Viitasaari)
Strannius, Matthias	1697–1732 (from Strannius on the ministers lived in Kivijärvi)
Calonius, Christian Henric	1735–1746

(Intervening period without ministers)

The period of the chapelry of Kivijärvi
Curates

Wikman, Wilhelm Detloff	1750–1778 (first curate)
Lucander, Eric	1778–1784
Tuderus, Johan	1785

(Intervening period without ministers)

Lehen, Johan	1797
Kekoni, Johan Fredrik	1800–1816
Kiljander, Mårten	1816–1822
Dahlström, Alexander	1823–1832
Ruth, Anders	1832–1848
Dahlgrén, Karl Gustaf	1852–1864

Supplementary ministers

Lindblad, Clas Anders	1822–1823
Oleander, Aleksander Magnus	1842–?
Höök, Gustaf Adolf	1848–1852

The period of the independent parish of Kivijärvi
Vicars

Dahlgrén, Karl Gustaf	1864–1866
Limon, Johan Werner	1868
Konsin, Viktor August	1872–1882
Krank, Frans Petter	1883–1910
Räsänen, Pekka	1913–1925
Lehmusvirta, Yrjö Armas	1925–1929
Hyvärinen, Lauri	1930–1934
Havas, Väinö Rafael	1935–1941
Savolainen, Aarne Aulis	1945–1948
Linnansaari, Pauli	1948–1955
Tammiala, Niilo Edvin	1955–1963

1 KSA, Records of baptisms, marriages and funerals 1800–1939; Markkanen 1983, 292; S. Tuomaala 1986, 319–320. Excluding the ministers of the parishes of Kinnula and Kannonkoski, which seceded from Kivijärvi to become independent parishes, Kinnula got its own vicar in 1913 and Kannonkoski in 1931.

Supplementary ministers

Tötterman, Carl Gustaf	1864
Silfvenius, Karl Vilhelm	1866–1872
Wikman, Gustaf Adolf	1882–1883
Jacklin, Anton	1885–1887
Heideman, Arthur Leopold	1888–1890
Helin, Henrik Johan	1890–1892
Hukkanen, Albin	1892–1893
Kyyniö, August Hjalmar	1893–1896
Kuhlman, Anders Kristofer	1896–1897
Antell, Karl Anton Emerik	1897–1898
Lindell, Johan Gabriel	1899
Aalto, Kaarle Konstantin	1901–1902 and 1905–1910
Andelin, Johan Emil	1902–1903 and 1903–1904
Lappalainen, Pekka Fredrik	1909 and 1912–1913
Seppänen, Jaakko Leonard	1910–1912
Lehmusvirta, Yrjö Armas	1924–1925
Viljanen, Paavo Julius	1929–1930
Salonen, Martti Eemil	1934–1935
Kauppinen, Tauno Ilmari	1938
Hakala, Veikko Ilmari	1939–1940
Toivonen, Olavi Leo	1940–1943
Linnansaari, Pauli	1943–1945

Ministers of the mother parish of Viitasaari[2]

Vicars

Porthan, Henrik	1705–1729
Porthan, Sigfrid	1730–(1744)1792
Porthan, Johan	1744–1794 (deputy for his brother)
Boxström, Johan	1795–1823
Kiljander, Mårten	1827–1836
Dahlström, Alexander	1838–1862

Curates

Ignatius, Benedikt	1713–1732
Strannius, Matthias	1732–1735
Castelius, Johan	1735–1743
Alander, Johan	1744–1781
(Porthan, Johan)	(1784–1797)
Ahlgren, Elias	1800–1831
Kjellstrand, Johan Fredrik	1837–1865

Supplementary ministers

Roschier, Jakob	1811–1822
Roschier, David	1823–1825
Romell, Lars	1825–1834
Kiljander, Anders	1828–1834
Svahn, Gustaf Adolf	1831–1832
Polén, Johan Immanuel	1834–1837
Cedervaller, Karl Reinhold	1834–1840
Dahlström, Karl Axel	1841–1857
Kekoni, Henrik	1857–1860

2   Markkanen 1983, 530. The list extends back to the period when Kivijärvi was a chapelry in the parish of Viitasaari.

Appendix 4: History of the Finnish-Language Publishing Business

Few books intended for Finnish readers were published during the six and a half centuries when it belonged to Sweden. It is estimated that only about 1950 works were printed in Finnish during that time, of which books accounted for around 1500. If we include only works that were over 16 pages in length as books, the number was only 174.[1] Of the literature published in the 1720s, about 20 percent was in Finnish, 40 percent in Swedish and 40 percent in Latin. Of this literature, 80 percent was religious, which meant that there was very little fiction or other forms of creative literature.[2]

During the early decades of Finland's status as an autonomous grand duchy in the Russian Empire, from 1809 to 1855, 425 titles in Finnish were published; in other words, almost four times more than during the whole period of Swedish rule. The proportion of works of *belles lettres* in Finnish-language literature grew significantly during the nineteenth century.[3] The publication of books in Finnish reached its first peak in 1865, but the following bad years of famine rapidly paralyzed book production. A new burgeoning began in the 1870s, and in the early 1880s the number of books that appeared in Finnish surpassed that of Swedish-language publications.[4]

The production of books on a large scale got under way in Finland considerably later than in the other Nordic countries. The publication of books in Finnish grew very slowly in the nineteenth century, and the growth in production is explained mainly by an increase in the number of works translated into Finnish. However the amount of indigenous Finnish literature did begin to increase in the 1880s, and it surpassed the number of translations in the early 1910s.[5] For example, in 1895 altogether 670 books were published in Finland, of which 400 were in Finnish and 250 in Swedish, while 530 of the 880 works that came out in 1900 were in Finnish. In the 1850s, the vast majority of the published works were still religious, but by the mid-1870s the proportion of other types of literature had begun to grow. Fiction and other forms of *belles lettres* came onto the market particularly during the following decade, and in the period 1876–1885 they constituted about 30 percent of all the literature that was published.[6]

The first printing press in Finland[7] was established in conjunction with the Academy of Turku in 1642. In Sweden, printing presses were established in the

---

1 Finnish literature in the Middle and Modern Ages has been studied more extensively by Tuomas Heikkilä (2009, 2010) and K. Laitinen (1997, 103–113), among others. For some recent detailed studies of literature in the seventeenth and eighteenth centuries, see Ahokas 2011b; Hakapää 2011; T. Laine 2011b. For a general see Hakapää 2008; K. Laitinen 1997, 114–140.
2 Of this literature, 80 percent was religious, which meant that there was very little fiction or other forms of creative literature.
3 Tommila 1980, 264. Cf. K. Laitinen, 1997, 153.
4 Häkli 1991, 39.
5 Kovala 1992, 28–29.
6 Leino-Kaukiainen 1990, 10.
7 On printing presses, see also Zweygbergk 1958.

seventeenth and eighteenth centuries mainly to serve local needs or to print literature of a particular kind. The principal function of the press of the Academy of Turku was to print dissertations and other academic publications. In the 1660s, Bishop Johannes Gezelius the Elder established in Turku a press to print material for the church, with the aim of promoting literacy and reinforcing the Lutheran faith. His press also printed a considerable number of schoolbooks. Gezelius considered the publication of literature to be important for developing the education of the common people, and so he took up publishing himself, for which purpose he acquired a paper mill in addition to the printing press.[8] Most of the printed works at that time were of pocket size and booklets rather than full-blown books. Vyborg Gymnasium (upper secondary school) got its own press in 1689, and it was also used by the clergy of the Diocese of Vyborg. In 1713, Bishop Gezelius took his printing press and fled to Sweden[9] out of the way of the depredations of the occupying Russian forces during the Great Wrath.[10]

The press was not replaced until 1817, when one was established in Turku by the Bible Society. The Academy together with its library and printing press had also moved out of the way of the war. A family called Frenckell, who had come to Finland from Germany, maintained a printing press in the city from the end of the eighteenth century until the Fire of Turku in 1827. As a result of the damage caused by the fire, the family, along with the university, transferred the bulk of their activities to Helsinki, leaving behind only a smallish branch printing business. In 1856, this branch business ceased to function under the name of Frenckell, and the press was bought by Johan Fredrik Granlund in 1858. In 1877, the press was transferred to the ownership of Gustaf Wilhelm Wilén, a printer. Wilén had already bought the press of J.W. Lillja in 1863, and from it he began to print the newspapers *Åbo Underrättelser* and *Sanomia Turusta* in the following year.[11]

The traditional German typographical rules and practices of the seventeenth century required a strict relationship between language and typeface. Texts written in the vernacular languages of northern Europe (Finnish, Swedish, German, Sámi and others) were to be printed using Gothic type, and particularly the Fraktur typeface, the use of which had become common for body text. Although the use of Antiqua began to increase in the eighteenth century for printing scientific literature and works intended for the educated and middle-classes, Fraktur continued to be used up to the twentieth century as the typeface in publications for the common people. It was particularly used in Swedish- and Finnish-language religious works and hymnbooks as well as in many newspapers and periodicals. The ordinary people shunned Antiqua and required their reading matter to be printed in "Finnish letters" or "church letters", as they called the Fraktur typeface.[12]

During the era of Swedish rule, Finnish literature had, as we have seen, been rather meagre and limited in range. The first written instructions on health care and the treatment of illness intended for the common people were given in almanacs. In Sweden, until the early seventeenth century, these almanacs were translations of German calendrical writings. The early almanacs served as handbooks for health care, and they were originally written by doctors. The Finnish almanacs of the seventeenth century, which were written in Swedish, also regularly contained predictions concerning the outbreak of contagions, which were claimed to be influenced by the positions of the heavenly bodies.[13] Many publications had a long life and continued to be used over

---

8   Laasonen 1977, 412.
9   Perälä 1999, 68–69; E. Seppälä 1963, 2–3.
10 The Great Wrath (Finnish: *Isoviha*) is the term used to describe the oppressive Russian occupation of Finland between 1713 and 1721 at the end of the Great Northern War (1700–1721).
11 E. Seppälä 1963, 3.
12 Perälä 1999, 72–73.
13 T. Laine 2001, 187–188.

several generations. For example, a new Finnish-language hymnbook which came out in 1701 was still in use in 1886.[14]

For about three hundred years, the oldest Finnish literature was not only sparse, it was also narrow in scope. Literary activity did not begin in earnest until the eighteenth century, and the first true literary classics were published in the nineteenth century. Before this, professional writers had not really existed in Finland. In the twentieth century, Finnish literature was less closely connected with the literature of the era of Swedish rule (mainly the eighteenth century) than were the works of contemporary French or British writers, for instance, with corresponding older literature. This was partly a result of the fact that little other than religious literature or non-fiction was published in Finnish. There was a closer connection with Finnish folk poetry, on the other hand, because of the influence of national ideals. Finnish literature was also characterized by the fact that most of it was written in two different languages, Swedish and Finnish. The Finnish language had developed more slowly than Swedish, which being the language of Finland's former ruling country was used by the educated classes and the authorities, and Finnish only came to be used in literature relatively late. Finnish literature absorbed influences from many sources, and it was characterized by the reconciliation and interaction of these foreign traits with its own indigenous features.[15]

Finnish national historiography has generally ignored the fact that the secular and religious literature and newspapers that spread among the common people also had an important place in Finnish literature alongside Finnish-language novels and other forms of *belles lettres*. In fact, the most popular printed matter in the nineteenth century consisted of devotional handbooks, small songsheet booklets and newspapers. Moreover, a large number of works of creative literature first appeared on the pages of newspapers or in the form of bundles of sheets sold by itinerant traders in markets.[16] Just as in Finland, in the eighteenth and even the nineteenth century, a family Bible in England, for example, had not only a religious function but also an educative one, and it occupied an important position as part of the informational capital of the family. In the Victorian age, the Bible came to be a consumable in Britain and America particularly among groups of the higher classes, an object that belonged to every home and was chosen to blend in with the other furnishings.[17]

In 1800, when Finland still belonged to Sweden, the population of the country was about 833,000. The towns were small and at the turn of the century only the population of the capital Turku exceeded 10,000 persons.[18] In the early 1830s, almanacs, newspapers, folk poetry, secular and religious song sheets, a large amount of other devotional literature and some translations of foreign books were published in Finnish. In addition, official printed matter such as decrees and proclamations were published in Finnish. At that time, the literature that came to Finland in translation was mostly Swedish, French, German and English. Among the most popular writers of the time were Walter Scott, Victor Hugo and the Finnish poet Frans Mikael Franzén.[19]

The newspaper *Suometar* began to appear in 1847. It was in terms of both its content and its editorial practice the first Finnish-language newspaper that satisfied more demanding standards. The first paper in Finnish, *Suomenkieliset Tieto-Sanomat*, had appeared in 1776, and it was followed by others in the early decades of the nineteenth century.[20] *Suometar* ceased to appear in 1866.[21] It had been targeted not

14 K. Laitinen 1997, 641.
15 K. Laitinen 1997, 99–100.
16 Häggman 2008, 19.
17 Ferrell 2008, 195–199.
18 K. Laitinen 1997, 98.
19 af Forselles-Riska 2006, 9.
20 K. Laitinen 1997, 151; Nurmio 1947, 10.
21 Kulha 1972, 80.

only at the common people but also at the educated classes, and thus from the outset attention was given to ensuring that its content was of a high quality. It can justifiably be regarded as the best paper of the late 1850s in Finland, including those published in Swedish. In its early years, an important feature of its reporting was news about the Crimean War, the publication of which was permitted because the authorities thought that it would assuage Finnish concerns, since naval and military actions connected with the war were taking place also in the Åland Islands and other places off the coasts of Finland.[22]

During the time when Finland was an autonomous grand duchy within the Russian Empire, the Finnish press readily used articles published in Swedish and German newspapers as sources for its reporting, and there were also frequent references to British and French papers. However, the bulk of the content of Finnish papers consisted of letters and other contributions sent in by readers, although no organized network of agents had at that time been set up. Generally, these writings consisted of letters from a few active persons in the countryside who sent in their contributions on their own initiative.[23]

A decree in 1829 enacted complete preventive censorship in Finland on the Russian model. It stipulated that nothing offensive towards Christianity, the Tsar, the government, the constitution or public decency could be published. The decree also protected the honour of private individuals.[24] In 1850, a language decree issued by Tsar Nicholas I prohibited the publication of any literature in Finnish other than works dealing with religious or economic subjects. The publication of novels both in translation and in their original languages was also forbidden, but it was permitted under special permits to print works that had previously been published in Finnish as well as new Finnish dictionaries and grammars and works of Finnish folk poetry and legends. The aim of the decree was to prevent the spread of revolutionary ideas among the commons. It was in force for a relatively short time, from spring 1850 to 1860. The decree was amended in 1854 and 1857.[25] The Crimean War in the 1850s liberated conditions for publishing in Finland, alleviated censorship and encouraged the common people to active take up reading.[26]

Of the slightly over 2000 Finnish-language works that were published in the period 1830–1879, almost a third (just under 650 titles) were works of religious literature. The proportion of devotional works in the total volume of publications declined steadily: in 1880 it was 26 percent, sinking to 16 percent in 1890 and 14 percent in 1904. The proportion of fiction rose from 16 to over 25 percent in the years 1876–1885. It was 26 percent in 1880, 30 percent in 1890 and 31 percent in 1904. The numbers of titles published indicate that fiction established its position in the field of literature in Finland from the 1880s on.[27]

Publishing in Finland did not develop into an independent line of business until later in the century. Publishing houses remained small concerns, and there was considerable turnover in the field. The position of Finnish-language general publishers became established particularly in the 1890s, when it became possible to engage in continuous book production on a larger scale. This development was significantly influenced by the growth in the size of the reading public.[28]

The conditions for the establishment of modern publishing activities in Finland were a sufficiently large potential buyer market, the economic and technical prerequisites for continuous large-scale production and favourable ideological and cultural conditions

22 Kulha 1972, 41–42.
23 Kulha 1972, 8.
24 Kulha 1972, 14.
25 E. Seppälä 1963, 27.
26 Häggman 2008, 18.
27 Kovala 1992, 16.
28 Kovala 1992, 16.

Table 42. The growth in the number of Finnish-language titles published in the period 1880–1939.

Year	Titles
1880	133
1885	191
1890	314
1895	400
1900	530
1905	690
1910	935
1915	710
1920	1073
1925	1216
1930	1294
1935	1256
1939	1268

Source: Kovala 1992, 15.

both for these and for the actual creation of literature. Consequently, the publication of books in Finland only began on a large scale in the 1880s. The economic boom at the end of that decade was followed by a recession, as a result of which the relative growth in book production slowed down somewhat. The economic depression of 1912 and 1913 and the early years of the First World War led to a clear decline in production, but towards the end of the war and immediately following it, the production of books rose again, levelling out in the 1920s and declining somewhat with the depression of the 1930s.[29]

The golden age of literature in Western Europe is regarded as beginning when the first generation of persons with functional reading skills had grown up and lasting until other media challenged its dominant position. In France and Britain, this period has been placed in the 1890s. The corresponding era in Finland was located between 1905 and 1914, when the sales of books increased annually. In the early twentieth century, the proportion of the combined annual book production of the WSOY and Otava publishing houses was about 20 percent, and by the beginning of the 1930s it had risen to almost a half.[30]

In the late nineteenth century, the paucity of available literature in Finnish was compensated for with translations, which created a foundation for nascent original literature in Finnish.[31] The copyright legislation which was in force in Finland in the late nineteenth century concerned only writers and translators who were Finnish or foreigners domiciled in Finland. It was not always observed in the publication of foreign literature, although an international agreement was signed in Bern in 1886 to protect the copyright of written and artistic works, and most countries on the main continent of Europe signed it. Of the Nordic countries, Norway, Denmark and Sweden signed the agreement at the turn of the century, but Russia, and thus also Finland, remained outside it. Publishing activities in Finland at the end of the nineteenth century were impeded by preventive censorship. This was based on a decree on printing

29 Kovala 1992, 14–15; Table 42.
30 Häggman 2008, 288–289.
31 Sevänen 2007, 16.

issued in 1867 and amended a couple of times in the 1870s and more thoroughly in 1891. The decree stipulated the conditions of the licences and responsibilities of publishers and printers.[32]

The number of published Finnish translations of fiction exceeded the amount of domestic works after the 1850s, and this remained the case right up to the 1930s. However, the foreign fiction served as the model to the domestic in fact only to the end of the nineteenth century. At that time, the amount of domestic prose fiction had established its position with an annual 20 titles published every year, which constituted a considerable proportion of the Finnish-language literature of that time. The large share of translated works of the fiction published in Finland was due to the fact that the domestic production of prose and especially escapist novels was not able to answer the demand. For example in Denmark and Sweden, domestic production surpassed the number of translations earlier than in Finland. Domestic production began to grow faster than the number of translations in Denmark in the 1880s and overtook them at the turn of the century, while in Sweden the golden age of domestic prose literature was the 1910s. Furthermore, during the latter half of the nineteenth century the relative proportion of novels in Sweden was much more significant than in Denmark before the similar domination of original literature.[33]

The preventive censorship of printed matter was completely abolished in 1905, and in the following year an important law on freedom of speech, assembly and association was enacted.[34] In 1905 in Finland, there were 96 presses, 17 bookbinderies and 13 chemigraphic or lithographic facilities, together employing about 3300 persons, of whom a third were women.[35] In 1928 Finland joined the Bern Convention for the Protection of Literary and Artistic Works, which forbade the translation of the work of a foreign author without permission or recompense. Thereafter the publication of translated literature plummeted.[36]

32 Leino-Kaukiainen 1990, 11.
33 Kovala 1992, 29.
34 Häggman 2001, 16.
35 Häggman 2008, 278.
36 Kovala 1992, 28.

Bibliography

Archive sources

Archive of the Church Parish of Kivijärvi (Kivijärven seurakunnan arkisto, KSA), JyMA and the Church Parish of Saarijärvi
    Records of baptisms, marriages and funerals 1800–1939
    Confirmation registers 1772–1939
    Migration records 1853–1924
    Demographic tables tables 1749–1950
    Estate inventory deeds and attachments to marriage banns 1783–1914
    Minutes of meetings of the church and parish councils 1816–1913
    Report on the state of the Parish of Kivijärvi in 1927–1931 made for the 1932 Synodal Meeting and the 1933 General Synod
    Church announcements 1860–1920
    2004 inventory of the oldest artifacts belonging to the Church Parish of Kivijärvi (Museum of Central Finland)

The Provincial Archives of Jyväskylä (Jyväskylän maakunta-arkisto, JyMA), Jyväskylä

Archive of the Parish of Viitasaari (Viitasaaren seurakunnan arkisto, VSA)
    Confirmation records 1781–1855
    Registers of marriages 1711–1899

Judicial district archives:
    Archive of Saarijärvi juridical district (Saarijärven tuomiokunnan arkisto, STK)
        Kivijärvi rural court district, minutes of regular business 1869–1905
        Kivijärvi rural court district, estate inventory deeds 1870–1918
        Kivijärvi rural court district, records of proceedings, autumn and spring court sessions 1870–1900
    Archive of Viitasaari judicial district (Viitasaaren tuomiokunnan arkisto, VTK)
        Viitasaari rural court district, minutes of regular business 1781–1786, 1793–1869
        Viitasaari rural court district, estate inventory deeds 1838–1853, 1858–1869

Kivijärvi library archive (Kivijärven kirjaston arkisto, KKA)
    Minutes of the annual general meetings and meetings of the board of governors 1888–1912
    Accounts 1888–1907, 1909, 1911–1912
    Collection catalogues
    Loans registers 1877–1897
    Other documents concerning Kivijärvi lending library
    The collection of old books of Kivijärvi lending library

Archives of the lending library of Saarijärvi
   Collection catalogues of Saarijärvi lending library

Archives of the lending library of Karstula
   Karstula library collection of old books

Archives of the lending library of Leppälänkylä village (Kannonkoski)
   Leppälänkylä lending library "Names and loans register"

The local heritage archive of the Municipality of Kannonkoski
   The ecclesiastical folklore (oral history) of Kannonkoski]

Archives of the Municipality of Kivijärvi (Kivijärven kunnan arkisto, KA)
   Minutes of meeting of the municipal assembly & the council meeting 1895–1908

Finnish Literature Society, Folklore Archives, Helsinki (Suomalaisen Kirjallisuuden Seura, Kansanrunousarkisto, SKS KRA):
   Kotilainen, Elsa PK 15: 2739. 1938.
   Rautiainen, Albert 4016. 1960.
   Rautiainen, Albert. E 15 1: 247. Karstula.

Recorded Archives of the Finnish Literature Society's Folklore Archives (äänitearkisto, SKSÄ)
   The Archives of Ecclesiastical Folklore (Kirkollisen kansanperinteen arkisto),
   General survey of ecclesiastical folklore (Survey no. 1):
   Kannonkoski (interviewer: Esa Tuomaala 1975)
      10N woman, b. 1910 (interviewer's transcription)
      13N woman, b. 1892 (interviewer's transcription)
   Kivijärvi (interviewer: Esa Tuomaala 1975)
      3N man, b. 1895 (interviewer's transcription).
      9N man, b 1884 (interviewer's transcription).
      Karjalainen, interview with Cantor J. V. Kinnunen, 1964.

Institute for the Languages of Finland (Kotimaisten kielten keskus, Kotus)
   Place Name Archive
      Kivijärvi: Pohjanmäki 1970, Hosia, 1971

Data bases compiled on the basis of original sources (by Sofia Kotilainen)
Kivijärvi BOOKS: a bibliographic database. The bibliographic database combines information about the works in the collection of old books in the library of Kivijärvi up to 1915 with the information contained in the catalogues of the library's collections up to 1915 and lists of borrowers of the library in the years 1877–1897.

Kivijärvi READERS: a collective biographical or prosopographical database of the borrowers of the library has been compiled mainly from documents in the archives of the parishes of Kannonkoski, Kinnula, Kivijärvi and Viitasaari. These comprise records of baptisms, marriages and funerals; confirmation records, records of unconfirmed children, migration records and demographic statistics. The oldest archives of the parishes of Viitasaari and Kivijärvi are stored in the Provincial Archives of Jyväskylä. The lists of borrowers of Kivijärvi library for the period 1877–1897 in the archive of Kivijärvi lending library have also been used as a source. The biographical information thus extends from c. 1800 to 1940. The database includes information about the approximately 365 borrowers and the books that each of them borrowed.

Saarijärvi BOOKS: a bibliographic database. The bibliographic database combines information about the works in the collection of old books in the library of Saarijärvi up to 1915 with the information contained in the catalogues of the library's collections.

Leppälänkylä BOOKS: a bibliographic database. The bibliographic database combines information about the works in the collection of old books in the library of Leppälänkylä up to 1915 with the information contained in the catalogues of the library's collections.

Unpublished sources

Kinnunen, Aino 1951: *Tutkielma Kannonkosken seurakunnan vaiheista*. Keski-Suomen Opiston kansankorkeakoulu.
Kotilainen, Aino 1979: *Kannonkosken kunnan kirjastolaitoksen historiikki*. Tampereen yliopiston täydennyskoulutuskeskus, Proseminar theses 8/10/1979.
Nokkala, Sointu & Niskanen, Liisa [undated text, 1981 or later]: *Kannonkosken seurakunnan historiikki*.

Newspapers

Keski-Suomi 1873–1896.
Kanervainen, Jussi [J. Kr. Svanljung]. Vaasalaisen mietteitä. 12 p. Elokuuta 1878. *Keski-Suomi* 17/8/1878.
Kotilainen, Sofia 2005: Liiketoimintaa Kivijärven kirkonkylällä III osa 1/2. *Viiden Kunnan Sanomat* 19/5/2005, 15.
Kotilainen, Sofia 2008b: Kylmä kirkko ja vähäiset sanankuulijat. *Viiden Kunnan Sanomat* 10–11/2008, 6–13/3/2008, 10, 20.
W. L., Kivijärveltä. Maaliskuulla. [W. L., from Kivijärvi, in March] *Suomalainen* No 24, 24. March 1890.

Printed sources

Almanac archive of Helsinki University: nineteenth-century almanacs http://almanakka.helsinki.fi/fi/arkisto/yliopiston-almanakka-1608-1999/1800-luvun-almanakat.html.
Bergholm, Axel (ed.) 1901: *Sukukirja: Suomen aatelittomia sukuja I–II*. Suomen muinaismuistoyhdistys. Helsinki: Otava.
Berner, Aksel 1878: *Suomen kansakoulut ja niiden opettajat lukuvuonna 1876–77. Tilastollisia ja elämäkerta-tietoja*. Viipuri: "Östra Finland'in" kirjapaino.
Granfelt, A[ksel]. A[ugust]. 1905: *Opas kansankirjastojen hoidossa*. Helsinki: Kansanvalistusseura.
Hellemaa, Lahja-Irene, Jussila, Anja & Parvio, Martti (eds.) 1986[1686]: *Kircko-Laki ja Ordningi 1686* (The Swedish Church Law of 1686). Näköispainos ja uudelleen ladottu laitos vuoden 1686 kirkkolain suomennoksesta. Suomalaisen Kirjallisuuden Seuran Toimituksia 444. Helsinki: Suomalaisen Kirjallisuuden Seura.
Henrik Database, Books and their owners in Finland up to 1809, http://dbgw.finlit.fi/henrik/henrik_english.php.
Konsin, Anita 2000: *Rovasti Viktor Konsin, Orimattilan kirkkoherra v. 1882–1904*. Self-published.
Kotivuori 2005: Kotivuori, Yrjö, *Ylioppilasmatrikkeli 1640–1852 ja 1853–1899*. [*Helsinki University registers of students 1640–1852 and 1853–1899*]. Web Publication 2005, www.helsinki.fi/ylioppilasmatrikkeli.

Laine, Tuija 2000b: *Englantilaisperäinen hartauskirjallisuus Suomessa. Bibliografia*. Suomalaisen Kirjallisuuden Seuran toimituksia 778. Helsinki: Suomalaisen Kirjallisuuden Seura.

Lyytinen, Em. 1904: *Kotimatkalla: evankelinen kalenteri vuodelle 1904*. Helsinki: Suomen Lutherilainen Evankeliumi-Yhdistys, 77–86.

Mikkola, J. M., Leinonen, Artturi & Rekola, Sulo 1937: *Jyväskylän seminaari 1863–1937: muistojulkaisu*. Helsinki: Valistus.

Murtorinne, Eino 1986: *Kirkollisen kansanperinteen yleiskysely*. Helsingin yliopiston Suomen kirkkohistorian laitoksen julkaisuja 1. 3. muuttamaton painos. Helsinki: Helsingin yliopiston Suomen kirkkohistorian laitos.

Official Statistics of Finland (SVT) VI:11. Population of Finland 31/12/1880, SVT VI: 56:2, Population of Finland 31/12/1920; 1915, 1951, VI: 1, 5, 9, 22, 37, 45, 56:1, 73, 74, 98:1, A 119.

Pipping, Fredrik Wilhelm 1856–1857: *Luettelo suomeksi präntätyistä kirjoista: kuin myös muutamista muista teoksista joissa löytyy joku kirjoitus suomen kielellä, tahi joku johdatus sitä tuntemaan*. Suomalaisen Kirjallisuuden Seuran toimituksia 20. Helsinki: Suomalaisen Kirjallisuuden Seura.

Repo, Ville 1990: *Punainen kirstu*. Porvoo – Helsinki – Juva: WSOY.

Salmelainen, Eero (ed.) 1873: *Suomen kansan satuja ja tarinoita. 2. osa*. Toinen painos. Helsinki: Suomalaisen Kirjallisuuden Seura.

Sarlin, Konstantin 1911: *Lepolan vanhuksen muistiinpanoja, piirretyt vaihtelevista aineista pitkän elämän taipaleella: 2 osa*. Kuopio: Kuopion uusi kirjapaino.

Suomalainen kirjallisuus: aakkosellinen ja aineenmukainen luettelo 1878–1938. Helsinki 1880–1940. Suomalaisen Kirjallisuuden Seuran toimituksia 57, lisävihko 1–15. Helsinki: Suomalaisen Kirjallisuuden Seura.

Vasenius, Valfrid 1878: *Suomalainen kirjallisuus 1544–1877: aakkosellinen ja aineenmukainen luettelo. La littérature finnoise 1544–1877: catalogue alphabétique et systématique*. Suomalaisen Kirjallisuuden Seuran toimituksia 57. Helsinki: Suomalaisen Kirjallisuuden Seura.

Vattula, Kaarina (ed.) 1983: *Suomen taloushistoria 3. Historiallinen tilasto. The Economic History of Finland 3. Historical Statistics*. Helsinki: Tammi.

Wanne, Olavi et al. (eds.) 1943–1946: *Uusi sukukirja I*. Suomen Sukututkimusseuran julkaisuja XVI. Helsinki.

Wanne, Olavi 1958: *Jyväskylän lyseon satavuotismatrikkelit*. Jyväskylä: Jyväskylän lyseon entisten oppilaiden yhdistys.

Wanne, Olavi 1959: *Kuopion lukio. Lukiolaiselämäkerrat 1844–72*. Suomen Sukututkimusseuran julkaisuja XXII. Helsinki: Suomen Sukututkimusseura.

Werkko, Kaarle (ed.) 1893: *Matrikkeli Suomen kansakouluista ja kansanopistoista kevätlukukautena 1893. Ensimmäinen osa*. Pori: Satakunnan kirjakaupan kustannustoimisto.

Yrjö-Koskinen [née Hahnsson], Theodolinda 1916: Miten tulin kirjailijaksi. In *Kuinka meistä tuli kirjailijoita. Suomalaisten kirjailijoiden nuoruudenmuistelmia*. Suomen kirjailijaliiton julkaisu. Helsinki: Otava, 145–146.

Literature

Aalto, Minna 2000: *Vapauden ja velvollisuuden ristiriita. Kehitysromaanin mahdollisuudet 1890-luvun ja 1900-luvun alun naiskirjallisuudessa*. Helsinki: Suomalaisen Kirjallisuuden Seura.

Adams, Thomas R. & Barker, Nicolas 2001: A New model for the study of the book. In *A Potencie of life. Books in Society. The Clark Lectures 1986–1987*. Ed. Nicolas

Barker. The British Library studies in the history of the book. London and New Castle: The British Library and Oak Knoll Press, 5-43.

Ahlstedt, Hannu 1987: *Koskenpään kirjastotoimi 1887-1987. 100-vuotishistoriikki.* [Jämsänkoski: Jämsänkosken kaupunki.]

Ahokas, Minna 2011a: *Valistus suomalaisessa kirjakulttuurissa 1700-luvulla.* Bidrag till kännedom av Finlands natur och folk 188. Helsinki: Suomen Tiedeseura.

Ahokas, Minna 2011b: Works of Enlightenment Philosophy in Finnish Cities during the 1700s. In *The Emergence of Finnish Book and Reading Culture in the 1700s.* Eds. Cecilia af Forcelles & Tuija Laine. Studia Fennica Litteraria 5. Helsinki: Finnish Literature Society, 70-94.

Ahonen, Sirkka 2003: *Yhteinen koulu – tasa-arvoa vai tasapäisyyttä? Koulutuksellinen tasa-arvo Suomessa Snellmanista tähän päivään.* Tampere: Vastapaino.

Ahtiainen, Pekka & Tervonen, Jukka & Teräs, Kari 2010: Johdanto: Perinteen paino ja muutoksen paine paikallishistoriassa. In *Kaikella on paikkansa. Uuden paikallishistorian suuntaviivoja.* Eds. Pekka Ahtiainen, Jukka Tervonen & Kari Teräs. Tampere: Vastapaino, 7-25.

Ahvenainen, Jorma 1984: *Suomen sahateollisuuden historia.* Porvoo-Helsinki-Juva: WSOY.

Alamäki, Päivi 1996: Rippikirjat lukutaitotutkimuksessa. Esimerkkinä Karstulan kappeliseurakunta. In *Kirkonkirjat paikallisyhteisön kuvaajina.* Eds. Heikki Roiko-Jokela & Timo Pitkänen. Jyväskylän historiallinen arkisto 2. Jyväskylä: Jyväskylän yliopiston historian laitos, Jyväskylän maakunta-arkisto ja Jyväskylän historiallinen yhdistys, 76-87.

Alamäki, Päivi 1998: Seurakuntaelämä Karstulassa. In *Karstulan kirja.* Ed. Heikki Roiko-Jokela. Jyväskylän yliopiston ylioppilaskunnan julkaisusarja nro 36. Karstula: Karstulan kunta ja seurakunta, 437-482.

Alanen, Yrjö 1937: *Muistelmia Jyväskylän lyseosta 60 vuotta ajassa taaksepäin.* Ylipainos Sisä-Suomessa julkaistusta kirjoitussarjasta. Jyväskylä.

Alapuro, Risto 2004: Historiallisia vertailuja. In *Vertailevan tutkimuksen ulottuvuuksia. Professori Matti Alestalolle 28. 8. 2004.* Eds. Risto Alapuro & Ilkka Arminen. Porvoo: WSOY, 53-66.

Alapuro, Risto 2012: Revisiting Microhistory from the Perspective of Comparisons. In *Historical Knowledge. In Quest of Theory, Method and Evidence.* Eds. Susanna Fellman & Marjatta Rahikainen. Newcastle upon Tyne: Cambridge Scholars Publishing, 133-154.

Alapuro, Risto & Stenius, Henrik 1989[1987]: Kansanliikkeet loivat kansakunnan. In *Kansa liikkeessä.* Eds. Risto Alapuro & al. 2. painos. Helsinki: Kirjayhtymä, 7-52.

Allan, David 2008: *A Nation of Readers. The Lending Library in Georgian England.* London: The British Library.

Altick, Richard D. 1967[1957]: *The English Common Reader. A Social History of the Mass Reading Public, 1800-1900.* Chicago – London: The University of Chicago Press, Phoenix Books.

Anderson, Benedict 2006[1983]: *Imagined communities: reflections on the origin and spread of nationalism.* Rev. ed. London: Verso.

Annala, Vilho 1948: *Suomen lasiteollisuus vuodesta 1681 nykyaikaan. II osa, kehitys 1809 jälkeen.* Ensimmäinen nide. Helsinki.

Appel, Charlotte & Fink-Jensen, Morten 2011: Introduction: Books, Literacy, and Religious Reading in the Lutheran North. In *Religious Reading in the Lutheran North: Studies in Early Modern Scandinavian Book Culture.* Eds. Charlotte Appel & Morten Fink-Jensen. Newcastle upon Tyne: Cambridge Scholars Publishing, 1-14.

Armstrong, Gordon B. 2003: Libraries in Burnley, 1900, and the Absence of a Public Library. *Library History* 19(3) 2003, 211-225.

Aurola, Eelis 1961: *Suomen tehtaankoulut 1636-1881.* Historiallisia Tutkimuksia LXI. Helsinki: Suomen Historiallinen Seura.

Autero, Olavi 1993: *J. W. Lillja 1817–1878. Kirjamiehestä poliittiseksi taistelijaksi.* Historiallisia tutkimuksia 172. Helsinki: Suomen Historiallinen Seura.

Barnett, Graham Keith 1973: *The History of Public Libraries in France from the Revolution to 1939. Part 1–2.* Thesis submitted for Fellowship of the Library Association.

Barton, David 2007: *Literacy, Lives and Learning.* With R. Ivanic, Y. Appleby, R. Hodge & K. Tusting. London – New York: Routledge.

Barton, David & Hamilton, Mary 1998: *Local Literacies. Reading and writing in one community.* London – New York: Routledge.

Barton, David, Hamilton, Mary & Ivanic, Roz 2000: *Situated Literacies.* London: Routledge.

Barton, David & Papen, Uta (eds.) 2010: *The Anthropology of Writing: Understanding Textually Mediated Worlds.* New York, N.Y.: Continuum International Publishing Group.

Bengtsson, Niklas 2012: *Elävät aakkoset. Lasten ja nuorten käännöstietokirjallisuus 1600–1800-luvuilla.* Nuorisotutkimusverkosto/Nuorisotutkimusseura, julkaisuja 135. Helsinki: Avain.

Berndtson, Nils 1983: *Laukaan historia I. Vanhan Laukaan vaiheita esihistoriallisesta ajasta vuoteen 1776.* 2. painos. Laukaa: Laukaan kunta ja Laukaan seurakunta.

Berndtson, Nils 1986: *Laukaan historia II, 1776–1868.* Toimittanut Pertti Torikka. Laukaa: Laukaan kunta ja Laukaan seurakunta.

Black, Alistair 1996: *A New History of the English Public Library. Social and Intellectual Contexts, 1850–1914.* London & New York: Leicester University Press.

Black, Alistair 2000: *The Public Library in Britain 1914–2000.* London: The British Library.

Black, Alistair 2006a: Introduction: the public library in concept and reality. In *Cambridge history of libraries in Britain and Ireland. Volume 3: 1850–2000.* Eds. Alistair Black & Peter Hoare. Cambridge: Cambridge University Press, 21–23.

Black, Alistair 2006b: The people's university: models of public library history. In *The Cambridge History of Libraries in Britain and Ireland, Volume III: 1850–2000.* Eds. Alistair Black & Peter Hoare. Cambridge: Cambridge University Press, 24–39.

Black, Alistair & Hoare, Peter (eds.) 2006a: *The Cambridge History of Libraries in Britain and Ireland, Volume III: 1850–2000.* Cambridge: Cambridge University Press.

Black, Alistair & Hoare, Peter 2006b: Libraries and the modern world. In *Cambridge history of libraries in Britain and Ireland Vol 3, 1850–2000.* Eds. Alistair Black & Peter Hoare. Cambridge: Cambridge University Press, 7–18.

Bloch, Marc 1928: Pour une histoire compare des sociétés européennes. *Revue de synthèse historique* 46 1928, 15–50.

Blommaert, Jan 2004: Writing as a problem: African grassroots writing, economies of literacy, and globalization. *Language in Society* 33 2004, 643–671.

Book History Journal, The Johns Hopkins University Press 1998–.

Bourdieu, Pierre 1985b: *Sosiologian kysymyksiä.* Tampere: Vastapaino.

Bourdieu, Pierre 1986[1983]: The Forms of Capital. In *Handbook of Theory and Research for the Sociology of Education.* Ed. J. G. Richardson. Westport, CT: Greenwood Press, 241–258.

Brown, Candy Gunther 2004: *The Word in the World. Evangelical Writing, Publishing, and Reading in America, 1789–1880.* Chapel Hill and London: The University of North Carolina Press.

Burch, Brian 2006: Libraries and literacy in popular education. In *Cambridge History of Libraries in Britain and Ireland, Vol. 2: 1640–1850.* Eds. Giles Mandelbrote & K. A. Manley. Cambridge: Cambridge University Press, 371–387.

Burman, Carina 1999: Kirjojen kauppa. In *Suomen kirjallisuushistoria 1. Hurskaista lauluista ilostelevaan romaaniin.* Eds. Yrjö Varpio & Liisi Huhtala. Suomalaisen Kirjallisuuden Seuran Toimituksia 724: 1. Helsinki: Suomalaisen Kirjallisuuden Seura, 149.

Byberg, Lis 1993: Public Library Development in Norway in the Early Twentieth Century: American Influences and State Action. *Libraries and Culture* 28(1) 1993, 22–34.

Byberg, Lis 2009: A Short History of Norwegian Public Libraries and 'How They Got That Way'. In *Library spirit in the Nordic and Baltic countries: historical perspectives*. Eds. Martin Dyrbye et al. Tampere: Hibolire, 42–48.

Caine, Barbara 2010: *Biography and History*. Theory and History. Basingstoke, Hampshire: Palgrave Macmillan.

Casper, Scott, E., Chaison, Joanne D. & Groves, Jeffrey D. (eds.) 2002: *Perspectives on American Book History. Studies in Print Culture and the History of the Book*. Amherst and Boston: University of Massachusetts Press (in association with American Antiquarian Society, Worcester, Massachusetts, and The Center for the Book, Library of Congress, Washington, D. C.).

Casson, Lionel 2002: *Libraries in the Ancient World*. New Haven and London: Yale University Press.

Chartier, Roger 1987: *The Cultural Uses of Print in Early Modern France*. Princeton, New Jersey: Princeton University Press.

Colclough, Stephen 2011: Representing Reading Spaces. In *The History of Reading. Volume 3. Methods, Strategies, Tactics*. Eds. Rosalind Crone & Shafquat Towheed. Basingstoke: Palgrave Macmillan, 99–114.

Coleman, James S. 1988: Social Capital in the Creation of Human Capital. *The American Journal of Sociology* 94 1988, S95–S120.

Crawford, John 2007: Recovering the Lost Scottish Community Library: the example of Fenwick. *Library History* 23(3) 2007, 201–212.

Cressy, David 1980: *Literacy and the Social Order. Reading and writing in Tudor and Stuart England*. Cambridge: Cambridge University Press.

Cullen, Clara 2007: 'Dublin is also in great need of a library which shall be at once accessible to the public and contain a good supply of modern and foreign books': Dublin's nineteenth-century 'public' libraries. *Library History* 23(1) 2007, 49–61.

Dahl, Gina 2010: *Book Collections of Clerics in Norway, 1650–1750*. Studies in the History of Christian Traditions, Volume 148. Leiden: Brill.

Dain, Phyllis 2000: *The New York Public Library: a universe of knowledge*. New York: New York Public Library in association with Scala Publishers, London.

Dane, Joseph A. 2012: *What Is a Book? The Study of Early Printed Books*. Notre Dame, Indiana: University of Notre Dame Press.

Darnton, Robert 1982a: What is the history of books? *Daedalus* 111(3) 1982, 65–83.

Darnton, Robert 1982b: *The Literary Underground of the Old Regime*. Cambridge, MA: Harvard University Press.

Darnton, Robert 1984: *The great cat massacre and other episodes in French cultural history*. New York: Basic Books.

Darnton, Robert 1997[1996]: *The Forbidden Best-Sellers of Pre-Revolutionary France*. London: Fontana Press.

Darnton, Robert 2000: An Early Information Society: News and the Media in Eighteenth-Century Paris. *The American Historical Review* 105(1) 2000, 1–35.

Darnton, Robert 2005: Discourse and Diffusion. *Contributions to the history of concepts* 1(1) 2005, 21–28.

Darnton, Robert 2009: *The Case for Books. Past, Present, and Future*. New York: PublicAffairs.

Darnton, Robert 2010: *Poetry and the police: communication networks in eighteenth-century Paris*. Cambridge, Mass.: Belknap Press of Harvard University Press.

Davis, Natalie Zemon 2001: *Martin Guerren paluu* (The Return of Martin Guerre, 1983). Helsinki: Gaudeamus.

Degerman, Henrik 2008: Malmgårds bibliotek. In *När jag får lite pengar så köper jag böcker*. Eds. Tage Jarolf et al. Bokvännens bok 9. [Helsingfors]: Sällskapet Bokvännerna i Finland, 11–36.

Dolatkhah, Mats 2008: The Rules of Reading: Examples of Reading and Library Use in Early Twentieth-Century Swedish Families. *Library History* 24(3) 2008, 220–229.
Duckett, Bob 2003: From Village Hall to Global Village: Community libraries in England's largest county. *Library History* 19(3) 2003, 195–209.
Dyrbye, Martin et al. 2009: *Library spirit in the Nordic and Baltic countries: historical perspectives*. Hibolire, Tampere.
Dyrbye, Martin 2009: From Vocation to Profession – Innovation and Change in the Focus of Librarianship 1905–1959. In *Library spirit in the Nordic and Baltic countries: historical perspectives*. Eds. Martin Dyrbye et al. Tampere: Hibolire, 49–57.
Dyrbye, Martin et al. eds. 2009: *Library spirit in the Nordic and Baltic countries: historical perspectives*. Tampere: Hibolire.
Edlund, Ann-Catrine 2012: *Att läsa och att skriva: Två vågor av vardagligt skriftbruk i Norden 1800–2000*. Nordliga studier 3; Vardagligt skriftbruk 1. Umeå: Umeå universitet & Kungl. Skytteanska Samfundet.
Edlund, Ann-Catrine & Haugen, Susanne (eds.) 2013: *Människor som skriver. Perspektiv på vardagligt skriftbruk och identitet*. Nordliga studier 4, Vardagligt skriftbruk 2. Umeå: Umeå universitet & Kungl. Skytteanska Samfundet.
Edlund, Ann-Catrine, Edlund, Lars-Erik & Haugen, Susanne (eds.) 2014: *Vernacular Literacies – Past, Present and Future*. Northern Studies Monographs 3, Vardagligt skriftbruk 3. Umeå: Umeå University & Royal Skyttean Society.
Eide, Elisabeth S. 2010: Reading Societies and Lending Libraries in Nineteenth-Century Norway. *Library & Information History* 26(2) 2010, 121–138.
Ekko, P. O. 2002: *Länsi-Suomen puumerkkien historia*. Ed.Timo Ekko. [Pori]: [Timo Ekko].
Eliot, Simon 2006: Circulating libraries in the Victorian Age and after. In *Cambridge history of libraries in Britain and Ireland. Volume 3: 1850–2000*. Eds. Alistair Black & Peter Hoare. Cambridge: Cambridge University Press, 125–146.
Elonheimo, Rispa 1996: Seinäjoen kirjaston vaiheita 1865–1995. In *Seinäjoki: Seinäjoen kaupunginkirjasto-maakuntakirjasto*. Eds. Ari Hovila & Anna Silvonen. (Updated 8/12/2009.) www.seinajoki.fi/kirjasto/historia/elonheimo.html, 15/6/2012.
Ellä, Liisa 1994: *Kirjastotoimintaa 125 vuotta Kuortaneella*. Kuortane: Kuortaneen kunta.
Elspaβ, Stephan 2007: 'Everyday language' in emigrant letters and its implications for language historiography – the German case. *Multilingua* 26(2/3) 2007, 151–165.
Elspaβ, Stephan 2012: Between linguistic creativity and formulaic restriction: cross-linguistic perspectives on nineteenth-century lower class writers' private letters. In *Letter Writing in Late Modern Europe*. Eds. Marina Dossena & Gabriella Del Lungo Camiciotti. Amsterdam – Philadelphia: John Benjamins, 45–64.
Engelsing, Rolf 1970: *Die Perioden der Lesergeschichte in der Neuzeit. Das statistische Ausmaß und die soziokulturelle Bedeutung der Lektüre*. Archiv für Geschichte des Buchwesens X, 945–1002.
Engelsing, Rolf 1974: *Der Bürger als Leser. Lesergeschichte in Deutschland 1500–1800*. Stuttgart: J. B. Metzlersche Verlagsbuchhandlung.
Engelsing, Rolf 1976: *Der literarische Arbeiter Band I: Arbeit, Zeit und Werk im literarischen Beruf*. Göttingen: Vanderhoeck & Ruprecht.
Enges, Pasi 1985: Arkkiveisut – kirjallisuutta ja folklorea. *Etiäinen* 1 1985, 21–46.
Epple, Angelika 2012: The Global, the Transnational and the Subaltern. In *Beyond Methodological Nationalism. Research Methodologies for Cross-Border Studies*. Eds. Anna Amelina, Devrimsel D. Nergiz, Thomas Faist & Nina Glick Schiller. New York – London: Routledge, 155–175.
Eskola, Eija 1999: Kirjastotoiminta vakiintuu – kirjasto harrastuksena. In *Kirjastojen vuosisata: yleiset kirjastot Suomessa 1900-luvulla*. Ed. Ilkka Mäkinen. Helsinki: BTJ Kirjastopalvelu, 115–146.

Eskola, Eija 2001: Finnish Public Libraries between the World Wars. In *Finnish Public Libraries in the 20th Century*. Ed. Ilkka Mäkinen. Tampere: Tampere University Press, 73–85.

Eskola, Eija 2009: Yleisten kirjastojen toiminta maailmansotien välisenä aikana. In *Suomen yleisten kirjastojen historia*. Ed. Ilkka Mäkinen. Helsinki: BTJ Kustannus, 290–310.

Fairman, Tony 2007: Writing and 'the Standard': England, 1795–1834. *Multilingua* 26(2–3) 2007, 167–201.

Febvre, Lucien & Martin, Henri-Jean 1998[1958]: *The Coming of the Book. The impact of printing 1450–1800*. The Verso Classics 10. London – New York: Verso.

Ferrell, Lori Anne 2008: *The Bible and the people*. New Haven & London: Yale University Press.

Forssell, Pia 2010: Biblioteket på Sarvlax till 1917. In *Sarvlax. herrgårdshistoria under 600 år*. Ed. Henrika Tandefelt. Helsingfors: Svenska litteratursällskapet i Finland, 51–62.

af Forselles-Riska, Cecilia 2006: Painettu sana Suomessa 1831. Suomalaisen Kirjallisuuden Seuran kirjaston julkaisuja 19. Helsinki: Suomalaisen Kirjallisuuden Seura.

af Forselles, Cecilia & Laine, Tuija (eds.) 2008: *Kirjakulttuuri kaupungissa 1700-luvulla*. Suomalaisen Kirjallisuuden Seuran kirjaston julkaisuja 20. Helsinki: Suomalaisen Kirjallisuuden Seura.

af Forselles, Cecilia & Laine, Tuija 2011: Introduction. In *The Emergence of Finnish Book and Reading Culture in the 1700s*. Eds. Cecilia af Forselles & Tuija Laine. Studia Fennica Litteraria 5. Helsinki: Finnish Literature Society, 6–8.

Forster, Geoffrey & Bell, Alan 2006: The subscription libraries and their members. In *Cambridge history of libraries in Britain and Ireland. Volume 3: 1850–2000*. Eds. Alistair Black & Peter Hoare. Cambridge: Cambridge University Press, 147–168.

Garðarsdóttir, Ólöf 2013: Teaching on the eve of public schooling: Demographic and social features of Icelandic schoolteachers in the beginning of the 20th century. In *Education, state and citizenship*. Eds. Mette Buchardt, Pirjo Markkola & Heli Valtonen. NordWel Studies in Historical Welfare State Research 4. Helsinki: The Nordic Centre of Excellence NordWel, 138–159.

Garrison, Dee 1979: *Apostoles of Culture. The Public Librarian and American Society, 1876–1920*. New York: The Free Press. A Division of Macmillan Publishing.

Ginzburg, Carlo 1996: *Johtolankoja. Kirjoituksia mikrohistoriasta ja historiallisesta metodista*. Helsinki: Gaudeamus.

Ginzburg, Carlo 2007: *Juusto ja madot. 1500-luvun myllärin maailmankuva*. Helsinki: Gaudeamus.

Goody, Jack 1987: *The interface between the written and the oral*. Cambridge: Cambridge University Press.

Goody, Jack 2010: *Renaissances: the one or the many?* Cambridge: Cambridge University Press.

Granfelt, A[ksel]. A[ugust]. 1905: *Opas kansankirjastojen hoidossa*. Helsinki: Kansanvalistusseura.

Graff, Harvey J. et al. (eds.) 2009: *Understanding Literacy in its Historical Contexts: Socio-Cultural History and the Legacy of Egil Johansson*. Lund: Nordic Academic Press.

Grönroos, Henrik & Nyman, Ann-Charlotte (eds.) 1996: *Boken i Finland. Bokbeståndet hos borgerskap, hantverkare och lägre sociala grupper i Finlands städer enligt städernas bouppteckningar 1656–1809*. Skrifter utgivna av Svenska litteratursällskapet i Finland 596. Helsingfors: Svenska litteratursällskapet i Finland.

Haahti, Hilja 1945: Pyhiinvaellusmatkoja äitini muistojen maille. In *Muistikuvia I. Suomalaisia kulttuurimuistelmia*. Ed. Eino E. Suolahti. Helsinki: Otava, 134–168.

Haahti, Hilja 1956: *Kaukaisten aikojen takaa. Sukuni, lapsuuteni ja varhaisnuoruuteni muistoja*. Helsinki: Otava.

Haapala, Pertti 1997[1995]: *Kun yhteiskunta hajosi: Suomi 1914–1920*. Helsinki: Painatuskeskus.
Haapala, Pertti (ed.) 2007: *Suomen historian kartasto*. Helsinki: Karttakeskus.
Haasio, Ari 2010: *Suomen kirjastoseura 1985–2010. Tietoyhteiskunnan tekijä*. Helsinki: Suomen kirjastoseura–Finlands biblioteksförening, Avain–BTJ Finland.
Haavio, Heikki 1952: Matti Taipale 1825–1868. In *Suomen talonpoikia Lallista Kyösti Kallioon. 74 elämäkertaa*. Eds. by Esko Aaltonen et al. Porvoo–Helsinki: WSOY, 397–407.
Haikari, Janne 2016: Mallia näyttämässä: Seminaarin mallikoulut 1869–1900. In Janne Haikari & Sofia Kotilainen, *Opettajuuden mallia – Jyväskylän Normaalikoulun historia 1864–2015*. Jyväskylä: Jyväskylän Normaalikoulu, 93–207.
Hakapää, Jyrki 2008: *Kirjan tie lukijalle. Kirjakauppojen vakiintuminen Suomessa 1740–1860*. Suomalaisen Kirjallisuuden Seuran Toimituksia 1166, Tiede. Helsinki: Suomalaisen Kirjallisuuden Seura.
Hakapää, Jyrki 2011: From Popular Law Books to Rarities of Economics. Merchants' Professional Literature in the Latter Half of the 1700s in Helsinki. In *The Emergence of Finnish Book and Reading Culture in the 1700s*. Eds. Cecilia af Forcelles & Tuija Laine. Studia Fennica Litteraria 5. Helsinki: Finnish Literature Society, 55–69.
Halila, Aimo 1963: *Jyväskylän seminaarin historia*. Porvoo: WSOY.
Hallikainen, Pertti 1964: Rahvaanrunoilijat. In *Suomen kirjallisuus III. Turun romantikoista Aleksis Kiveen*. Ed. Lauri Viljanen. Helsinki, 74–106.
Haltsonen, Sulo 1931: Eero Salmelainen. elämäkerrallisia piirteitä. Eripainos *Suomi V*, 11:stä. Helsinki: Suomalaisen Kirjallisuuden Seura.
Hannesdóttir, Sigrún Klara 1993: Books and Reading in Iceland in a Historical Perspective. *Libraries and Culture* 28(1) 1993, 13–21.
Hanska, Jussi & Vainio-Korhonen, Kirsi (eds.) 2010: *Huoneentaulun maailma. Kasvatus ja koulutus Suomessa keskiajalta 1860-luvulle*. Suomen kasvatuksen ja koulutuksen historia 1. Suomalaisen Kirjallisuuden Seuran Toimituksia 1266: 1, Tiede. Helsinki: Suomalaisen Kirjallisuuden Seura.
Haupt, Heinz-Gerhard 2007: Comparative history – a contested method. *Historisk Tidskrift* 127(4) 2007, 697–716.
Havu, Sirkka 2008: Monrepos'n kartanon kirjasto. In Knapas, Rainer, *Monrepos. Ranskalaisen kulttuurin pohjoinen keidas*. Suomalaisen Kirjallisuuden Seuran Toimituksia 1157, Tieto. Helsinki: Suomalaisen Kirjallisuuden Seura, 87–108.
Heikkilä, Markku 2001: Schauman, Frans Ludvig (1810–1877), Porvoon piispa, käytännöllisen teologian professori, yliopiston vararehtori. In *Kansallisbiografia*. Biografiakeskus, www.kansallisbiografia.fi/kb/artikkeli/3620/, 20/8/2012.
Heikkilä Tuomas 2009: *Piirtoja ja kirjaimia. Kirjoittamisen kulttuurihistoriaa keskiajalla*. Suomalaisen Kirjallisuuden Seuran Toimituksia 1208, Tieto. Helsinki: Suomalaisen Kirjallisuuden Seura.
Heikkilä, Teuvo 1987: *Katsaus kirjastotoimintaan Forssassa 1866–1986*. Forssa: Forssan kaupunki.
Heikkinen, Anja & Leino-Kaukiainen, Pirkko (eds.) 2011: *Valistus ja koulunpenkki: kasvatus ja koulutus Suomessa 1860-luvulta 1960-luvulle*. Suomen kasvatuksen ja koulutuksen historia 2. Suomalaisen Kirjallisuuden Seuran toimituksia 1266:2. Helsinki: Suomalaisen Kirjallisuuden Seura.
Heikkinen, Antero 2013: *Historiallisen ajattelun historia. Eurooppalainen perinne antiikista nykypäivään*. Kirjokansi 1. Helsinki: Suomalaisen Kirjallisuuden Seura.
Heininen, Simo 1999: Painettu suomen sana. In *Suomen kirjallisuushistoria 1. Hurskaista lauluista ilostelevaan romaaniin*. Eds. Yrjö Varpio & Liisi Huhtala. Suomalaisen Kirjallisuuden Seuran Toimituksia 724: 1. Helsinki: Suomalaisen Kirjallisuuden Seura, 36–45.
Held, Ray E. 1963: *Public Libraries in California 1849–1878*. University of California Publications in Librarianship Volume IV. Berkeley and Los Angeles: University of California Press.

Heuru, Kauko, Mennola, Erkki & Ryynänen, Aimo 2011: *Kunta. Kunnallisen itsehallinnon perusteet*. Tampere: Tampere University Press.

Hietala, Marjatta 2001: Foundation of Libraries in the Historical Context. In *Finnish Public Libraries in the 20th Century*. Ed. Ilkka Mäkinen. Tampere: Tampere University Press, 7–19.

Hirn, Sven 1998: *Kansankirjastosta kaupunginkirjastoksi. Helsingin kaupunginkirjasto 1860–1940*. Helsinki: Helsingin kaupunginkirjasto.

Hirvonen, Maija 1993: *Suomen kirjailijat, Finlands författare, Writers in Finland 1809–1916*. Suomalaisen Kirjallisuuden Seuran toimituksia 570. Helsinki: Suomalaisen Kirjallisuuden Seura.

Hoare, Peter (ed.) 2006: *Cambridge history of libraries in Britain and Ireland Vols 1–3*. Cambridge: Cambridge University Press.

Huttunen, Kaarina 1981: Kuopion kaupunginkirjasto v. 1872–1929. In *Kuopion kaupunginkirjasto 1872–1972*. Eds. Kaarina Huttunen & Seppo Hannula. Kuopio: Kuopion kaupunki, 9–74.

Huuhka, Kosti 1955: *Talonpoikaisnuorison koulutie. Tutkimus talonpoikaisnuorison koulunkäynnistä ja siihen vaikuttaneista sosiaalisista tekijöistä Suomessa 1910–1950*. Helsinki: Suomen Historiallinen Seura.

Hypén, Kaisa, Koivunen, Leila & Tunturi, Janne (eds.) 2015: *Kirjoista kokoelmaksi. Kansansivistystä ja kansainvälisyyttä Turun kaupunginkirjastossa 1800–1900-luvuilla*. Helsinki: Avain.

Hyyrö, Tuula 2011: Alkuopetus kiertokoulusta alakansakouluun. In *Valistus ja koulunpenkki. Kasvatus ja koulutus Suomessa 1860-luvulta 1960-luvulle*. Eds. Anja Heikkinen & Pirkko Leino-Kaukiainen. Suomen kasvatuksen ja koulutuksen historia 2. Suomalaisen Kirjallisuuden Seuran toimituksia 1266:2. Helsinki: Suomalaisen Kirjallisuuden Seura, 327–351.

Hyytiäinen, Veijo 1968: Keski-Suomen sahateollisuus vuoteen 1879. In *Keski-Suomi 8*. Jyväskylä: Keski-Suomen museoyhdistys, 123–226.

Häggman, Kai 2001: *Piispankadulta Bulevardille. Werner Söderström Osakeyhtiö 1878–1939*. Helsinki: WSOY.

Häggman, Kai 2008: *Paras tawara maailmassa. Suomalainen kustannustoiminta 1800-luvulta 2000-luvulle*. Helsinki: Otava.

Häkkinen, Kaisa 1994: *Agricolasta nykykieleen. Suomen kirjakielen historia*. Porvoo–Helsinki–Juva: WSOY.

Häkkinen, Kaisa 2002: *Suomalaisen oppikirjan vaiheita*. Helsinki: Suomen tietokirjailijat.

Häkkinen, Kaisa 2015: *Spreading the written word. Mikael Agricola and the birth of literary Finnish*. Studia Fennica Linguistica 19. Helsinki: Finnish Literature Society.

Häkli, Esko 1991: Suomalaiset – kirjan kansa? In *Kirja Suomessa 500 vuotta*. Ed. Marjut Kivelä. Helsinki: VAPK-kustannus, 33–41.

Hämynen, Tapio 1986: Heinäveden historia vuoteen 1865. In Hämynen, Tapio, *Heinäveden historia 1*. [Heinävesi: Heinäveden kunta], 51–378.

Hämynen, Tapio 2009: Kauppaneuvos Michail Tichanoff (1816–1891). In *Suomen Talouselämän vaikuttajat*, Biografiakeskus, http://www.kansallisbiografia.fi/talousvaikuttajat.../, 20/8/2012. Helsinki: Suomalaisen Kirjallisuuden Seura.

Hämäläinen, Albert 1930: *Keski-Suomen kansanrakennukset*. Asutushistoriallinen tutkimus. Helsinki.

Iisalo, Taimo 1992: *Merimies piirsi nimensä. Havaintoja Uudenkaupungin seudun merimiesväestön kirjoitustaidosta 1800-luvulla*. Turun yliopiston kasvatustieteiden tiedekunta, julkaisusarja A: 152. Turku: Turun yliopisto.

Ihalainen, Pasi 2005: *Protestant nations redefined: changing perceptions of national identity in the rhetoric of the English, Dutch, and Swedish public churches, 1685–1772*. Studies in medieval and Reformation traditions 109. Leiden: Brill.

Ihalainen, Pasi, Ilie, Cornelia & Palonen, Kari 2016: Parliament as a Conceptual Nexus. In *Parliament and Parliamentarism. A Comparative History of a European Concept.* Eds. Pasi Ihalainen, Cornelia Ilie & Kari Palonen. European Conceptual History. New York–Oxford: Berghahn, 1–16.

Jakobsen, Uffe & Kurunmäki, Jussi, 2016: The Formation of Parliamentarism in the Nordic Countries from the Napoleonic Wars to the First World War. In *Parliament and Parliamentarism. A Comparative History of a European Concept.* Eds. Pasi Ihalainen, Cornelia Ilie & Kari Palonen. European Conceptual History. New York–Oxford: Berghahn, 97–114.

Inkilä, Arvo 1960: *Kansanvalistusseura Suomen vapaassa kansansivistystyössä 1874–1959.* Helsinki: Otava.

Ivendorff, Adam 2006: *Kirkonvartijan päiväkirja 1846–1897.* Ed. Mikko Kylliäinen. Suomalaisen Kirjallisuuden Seuran Toimituksia 1080. Helsinki: Suomalaisen Kirjallisuuden Seura.

Jalava, Marja 2006: *J. V. Snellman. Mies ja suurmies.* Helsinki: Tammi.

Jalava, Marja 2011: Kansanopetuksen suuri murros ja 1860-luvun väittely kansakoulusta. In *Valistus ja koulunpenkki. Kasvatus ja koulutus Suomessa 1860-luvulta 1960-luvulle.* Eds. Anja Heikkinen & Pirkko Leino-Kaukiainen. Suomalaisen Kirjallisuuden Seuran Toimituksia 1266: 2, Tiede. Suomen kasvatuksen ja koulutuksen historia II. Helsinki: Suomalaisen Kirjallisuuden Seura, 74–94.

Jalkanen, Kaarlo 1976: *Lukkarin- ja urkurinvirka Suomessa 1809–1870.* Suomen Kirkkohistoriallisen Seuran Toimituksia 101. Helsinki: Suomen Kirkkohistoriallinen Seura.

Jalkanen, Kaarlo 1986: *Lukkarin- ja urkurinvirka Suomessa 1721–1809.* Suomen Kirkkohistoriallisen Seuran toimituksia 138. Helsinki: Suomen Kirkkohistoriallinen Seura.

Jarlbink, Johan 2010: Lässcener: Publik och medier på kafé och sockenbibliotek. In *1800-talets mediesystem.* Eds. Jonas Harvard & Patrik Lundell. Mediehistoriskt arkiv 16. Stockholm: Kungliga Biblioteket, 43–64.

Johansson, Egil 1972: *En studie med kvantitativa metoder av folkundervisningen i Bygdeå socken 1845–1873.* Umeå: Umeå universitet.

Johansson, Egil 1977: *The history of literacy in Sweden in comparison with some other countries.* Umeå: Umeå University and Umeå School of Education.

Johansson, Egil 2002: Kyrkan och undervisningen. In *Sveriges kyrkohistoria 4.* Ed. Lennart Tegborg. Stockholm: Verbum, 248–258.

Jokipii, Mauno 1971: *Nils Aejmelaeus. Piirteitä suomalaisen novellin uranuurtajasta.* Suomi 116: 1. Helsinki: Suomalaisen Kirjallisuuden Seura.

Jokipii, Mauno 1988: Keski-Suomen synty. In *Keski-Suomen historia 2. Keski-Suomi maakunta-ajatuksen synnystä itsenäisyyden aikaan.* Ed. Mauno Jokipii. Jyväskylä: Keski-Suomen maakuntaliitto, 12–62.

Jonsson, Pernilla & Neusinger, Silke 2007: Comparison and transfer – a fruitful approach to national history? *Scandinavian Journal of History* 32(3) 2007, 258–280.

Junnila, Heikki 1995: *Saarijärven historia 1865–1985.* Saarijärvi: Saarijärven kaupunki.

Jussila, Osmo 1999: Finland as a Grand Duchy, 1809–1917. In Jussila, Osmo, Hentilä, Seppo & Nevakivi, Jukka, *From Grand Duchy to a Modern State. A Political History of Finland since 1809.* Hurst & Company, London, 3–98.

Järvelin, Ilmi 1966: *Kirjastoliikkeen vaiheita Pohjois-Karjalassa vv. 1850–1930.* Joensuu.

Jääskeläinen, Jussi 2011: *Paikallisyhteisö resurssina ja tuhojen kohteena. Venäjän armeijan logististen ratkaisujen seuraukset Suomen sodassa 1808–1809.* Doktorsavhandling i Nordisk Historia. Åbo: Åbo Akademi.

Kallio, Reino 1972: *Vanhan Saarijärven historia.* [Karstula]; [Uurainen]: Karstulan, Konginkankaan, Kyyjärven, Pylkönmäen, Saarijärven ja Uuraisten kunnat ja seurakunnat.

Kanerva, Unto & Peltonen, Maija-Liisa 1961: *Tampereen kaupunginkirjasto 1861–1961*. Tampere.

Kangas, Lasse 1998: *Vihtori Vesterinen: Paasikiven ministeri*. Jyväskylä: Gummerus.

Kantola, Jaana 2007: Pohjoismainen kirjallisuus. In *Suomennoskirjallisuuden historia 2*. Eds. H. K. Riikonen et al. Suomalaisen Kirjallisuuden Seuran toimituksia 1112. Helsinki: Suomalaisen Kirjallisuuden Seura, 54–65.

Karjalainen, Marjaana 1977: *Kansankirjastojen kehitys Suomessa vuosina 1802–1906*. [Helsinki]: Kirjastopalvelu.

Katajamäki, Sakari 2007: Suomen ruotsinkielinen kirjallisuus suomeksi. In *Suomennoskirjallisuuden historia 2*. Eds. H. K. Riikonen et al. Suomalaisen Kirjallisuuden Seuran toimituksia 1112. Helsinki: Suomalaisen Kirjallisuuden Seura, 66–80.

Kaukiainen, Yrjö 2005: *Rantarosvojen saaristo. Itäinen Suomenlahti 1700-luvulla*. Historiallisia Tutkimuksia 225. Helsinki: Suomalaisen Kirjallisuuden Seura.

Kauranen, Kaisa 2007: Did Writing Lead to Social Mobility? Case Studies of Ordinary Writers in Nineteenth-Century Finland. In *Ordinary Writings, Personal Narratives: Writing Practics in 19th and early 20th-century Europe*. Ed. Martyn Lyons. Bern: Peter Lang, 51–68.

Kauranen, Kaisa 2009: *Työtä ja rakkautta. Kansanmiesten päiväkirjoja 1834–1937*. Helsinki: Suomalaisen Kirjallisuuden Seura.

Kauranen, Kaisa 2013a: Odd Man Out? The Self-Educated Philosopher and his Social Analyses of 19th-Century Finland. In *White Field, Black Seeds. Nordic Literacy Practices in the Long Nineteenth Century*. Eds. Anna Kuismin & M. J. Driscoll. Studia Fennica Litteraria 7. Helsinki: Finnish Literature Society, 120–133.

Kauranen, Kaisa 2013b: Mitä ja miksi kansa kirjoitti? In *Kynällä kyntäjät. Kansan kirjallistuminen 1800-luvun Suomessa*. Eds. Lea Laitinen & Kati Mikkola. Suomalaisen Kirjallisuuden Seuran Toimituksia 1370. Helsinki: Suomalaisen Kirjallisuuden Seura, 19–54.

Keats-Rohan, K. S. B. 2007: Biography, Identity and Names: Understanding the Pursuit of the Individual in Prosopography. In *Prosopography Approaches and Applications. A Handbook*. Ed. K. S. B. Keats-Rohan. Prosopographica et Genealogica Vol. 13. Oxford: Unit for Prosopographical Research, 139–181.

Kelly, Thomas 1977: *History of Public Libraries in Great Britain 1845–1975*. Second edition (revised). London: The Library Association.

Kemppinen, Lauri 2001: *Sivistys on Suomen elinehto. Yrjö Sakari Yrjö-Koskisen kasvatusajattelu ja koulutuspolitiikka vuosina 1850–1882*. Turun yliopiston julkaisuja Sarja C, osa 168. Scripta Lingua Fennica Edita. Turku: Turun yliopisto.

Kero, Reino 1974: *Migration from Finland to North America in the years between the United States Civil War and the First World War*. Migration Studies 1. Turun yliopiston julkaisuja 130. Turku: Institute for Migration.

Kero, Reino 1986: *Suomen siirtolaisuuden historia, osa 1. Pohjois-Amerikkaan suuntautuneen siirtolaisuuden tausta, määrä, rakenne, kuljetusorganisaatio ja sijoittuminen päämääräalueelle*. Turun yliopisto, Julkaisuja nro 10. Turku: Turun yliopiston historian laitos.

Keskinen, Jarkko 2012: *Oma ja yhteinen etu. Kauppiaiden keskinäinen kilpailu ja yhteistyö Porin paikallisyhteisössä 1765–1845*. Turun yliopiston julkaisuja sarja C osa 345. Scripta Lingua Fennica Edita. Turku: Turun yliopisto.

Kettunen, Pauli & Simola, Hannu (eds.) 2012: *Tiedon ja osaamisen Suomi: kasvatus ja koulutus Suomessa 1960-luvulta 2000-luvulle*. Suomen kasvatuksen ja koulutuksen historia 3. Suomalaisen Kirjallisuuden Seuran toimituksia 1266:3. Helsinki: Suomalaisen Kirjallisuuden Seura.

Kivipelto, Toivo 1966: Alajärven kirjaston satavuotisvaiheet. In *Alajärven elämää*. Helsinki: Etelä-pohjalainen osakunta, 231–238.

Klinge, Matti 1989: Saksalaismielinen yliopisto. In *Kuninkaallinen Turun akatemia 1640–1808. Helsingin yliopisto 1640–1990, toinen osa*. Klinge, Matti et al. Helsinki: Otava, 888–931.

Klinge, Matti 1997: Topelius, Zachris (1818–1898), kirjailija, toimittaja, historian professori, valtioneuvos. In *Kansallisbiografia*. Biografiakeskus, http://www.kansallisbiografia.fi/kb/artikkeli/2854/, 20/8/2012.

Knapas, Rainer 2012: *Tiedon valtakunnassa. Helsingin yliopiston kirjasto – Kansalliskirjasto 1640–2010*. Suomalaisen Kirjallisuuden Seuran Toimituksia 1347, Tiede. Kansalliskirjaston julkaisuja 78. Helsinki: Suomalaisen Kirjallisuuden Seura.

Kohtamäki, Ilmari 1964: Suomenkielisen kirjallisuuden elpyminen. In *Suomen kirjallisuus III. Turun romantikoista Aleksis Kiveen*. Ed. Lauri Viljanen. Helsinki, 375–452.

Kokkinen, Marja (ed.) 1994: Kipin kapin koulutietä. Kannonkosken koululaitoksen historiaa vv. 1894–1994. [Kannonkoski]: Kannonkosken kunta.

Korhonen, Teppo 2003: Perinne hallitsee maataloustekniikkaa. In *Suomen maatalouden historia I. Perinteisen maatalouden aika. Esihistoriasta 1870-luvulle*. Eds. Viljo Rasila, Eino Jutikkala & Anneli Mäkelä-Alitalo. Suomalaisen Kirjallisuuden Seuran Toimituksia 914:1. Helsinki: Suomalaisen Kirjallisuuden Seura, 405–432.

Koskenniemi, Lauri 1964: *Sanansaattajia. Suomen Luterilainen Evankeliumiyhdistys kolportööritoimensa valossa 1873–1900*. Helsinki: Suomen Luterilainen Evankeliumiyhdistys.

Koskenniemi, Lauri 1967: *Suomen evankelinen liike 1870–1895*. Helsinki: Suomen Luterilainen Evankeliumiyhdistys.

Koski, Pekka 1998: Sivistystä, valistusta, virkistystä. In *Karstulan kirja*. Ed. Heikki Roiko-Jokela. Jyväskylän yliopiston ylioppilaskunnan julkaisusarja nro 36. Karstula: Karstulan kunta ja seurakunta, 567–590.

Koskinen, Seppo et al. (eds.) 2007: *Suomen väestö*. Helsinki: Gaudeamus, Helsinki University Press.

Kotilainen, Sofia 2001: Het pikkusevverran paljo Kivijärven Perinnepiirin tallentamaa muistitietoa. Kivijärvi: Kivijärven kunta.

Kotilainen, Sofia 2008a: *Suvun nimissä. Nimenannon käytännöt Sisä-Suomessa 1700-luvun alusta 1950-luvulle*. Helsinki: Suomalaisen Kirjallisuuden Seura. (English summary: http://kirjat.finlit.fi/kuvat/978-952-222-048-6_3summ.pdf)

Kotilainen, Sofia 2011: The Genealogy of Personal Names: towards a more productive method in historical onomastics. *Scandinavian Journal of History* 36(1) 2011, 44–64.

Kotilainen, Sofia 2013a: An early spokesman for a vernacular literature: Matti Taipale, farmer, librarian and a promoter of Finnish culture in nineteenth-century Finland. *Scandinavica* 51(2) 2012, 225–243.

Kotilainen, Sofia 2013b: Several names, several identities? The orthography of Finnish country people's names from the 18th to 20th centuries. In *Människor som skriver. Perspektiv på vardagligt skriftbruk och identitet*. Eds. Ann-Catrine Edlund & Susanne Haugen. Nordliga studier 4, Vardagligt skriftbruk 2. Umeå: Umeå universitet och Kungl. Skytteanska Samfundet, 61–74.

Kotilainen, Sofia 2013c: Rural people's literacy skills in the remembrance of the departed: the writing of personal names on sepulchral monuments at the turn of the nineteenth and twentieth centuries. *Mortality* 18(2) 2013, 173–194.

Kotilainen, Sofia 2013d: From religious instruction to school education: elementary education and the significance of ambulatory schools in rural Finland at the end of the 19th century. In *Education, state and citizenship*. Eds. Mette Buchardt, Pirjo Markkola & Heli Valtonen. NordWel Studies in Historical Welfare State Research 4. Helsinki: The Nordic Centre of Excellence NordWel, 114–137.

Kotilainen, Sofia 2015a: National Language Policy at the Local Level: The Realisation of Language Legislation in Late-19th-Century Finland In *Language Policies in Finland and Sweden. Interdisciplinary and multi-sited comparisons*. Eds. Pasi Ihalainen, Mia Halonen & Taina Saarinen. Bristol–Buffalo–Toronto: Multilingual Matters 2015, 147–170.

Kotilainen, Sofia 2015b: Literacy and Social Advancement in Nineteenth-Century Rural Finland: Training to be a Cantor as a Path to a Professional Occupation for a Peasant. *Journal of Social History* 49(2) 2015, 300–316. (Special Issue: The Functions and Purpose of Vernacular Literacy.)

Kotilainen, Sofia 2015c: The significance of the education provided in the sawmill community in the 19th century rural Finland. (*Manuscript for a peer-reviewed journal.*)

Kotilainen 2015d: Kotilainen, Sofia, The reading speeds of borrowers and the loaning and borrowing times in Kivijärvi lending library 1877–1897. (*Manuscript for a peer-reviewed journal.*)

Kotilainen, Sofia 2016: Seminaarin mallikoulun idea ja suomenkielisen harjoittelukoulun synty. In Janne Haikari & Sofia Kotilainen, *Opettajuuden mallia – Jyväskylän Normaalikoulun historia 1864–2015*. Jyväskylä: Jyväskylän Normaalikoulu, 1–86.

Kotkaheimo, Liisa 2002: Lukemaan oppiminen – aapinen. Katsaus kehitystrendeihin ja funktioihin 1500–1950. In *ABC Lukeminen esivallan palveluksessa*. Ed. Inkeri Pitkäranta. Kansalliskirjaston Gallerian julkaisuja nro 2. Helsinki: Helsingin yliopiston kirjasto, Suomen kansalliskirjasto, 33–77.

Kovala, Urpo 1992: *Väliin lankeaa varjo. Angloamerikkalaisen kaunokirjallisuuden välittyminen Suomeen 1890–1939*. Nykykulttuurin tutkimusyksikön julkaisuja 29. Jyväskylä: Jyväskylän yliopisto, nykykulttuurin tutkimusyksikkö.

Kovala, Urpo 1997: Teksti elämänhistorian kehyksessä. In *Aina uusi muisto. Kirjoituksia menneen elämisestä meissä*. Eds. Katariina Eskola & Eeva Peltonen. Nykykulttuurin tutkimusyksikön julkaisuja 54. Jyväskylä: Jyväskylän yliopisto, Nykykulttuurin tutkimusyksikkö, 145–170.

Kovala, Urpo 2013: Tietokirjallisuuden suomennosten taustoja ja kehityslinjoja 1800-luvulla. In *Suomennetun tietokirjallisuuden historia 1800-luvulta 2000-luvulle*. Eds. Outi Paloposki & H. K. Riikonen Suomalaisen Kirjallisuuden Seuran toimituksia 1289. Helsinki: Suomalaisen Kirjallisuuden Seura, 40–50.

Kuisma, Markku 2006: *Metsäteollisuuden maa. Suomi, metsät ja kansainvälinen järjestelmä 1620–1920*. Metsäteollisuuden maa 1. Suomalaisen Kirjallisuuden Seuran Toimituksia 1055:1. 2. korjattu painos. Helsinki: Suomalaisen Kirjallisuuden Seura.

Kuisma, Markku 2011: *Saha. Tarina Suomen modernisaatiosta ja ihmisistä jotka sen tekivät*. Helsinki: Siltala.

Kuivasmäki, Riitta 1999: Suomalaisen lastenkirjallisuuden synty. In *Suomen kirjallisuushistoria 1. Hurskaista lauluista ilostelevaan romaaniin*. Eds. Yrjö Varpio & Liisi Huhtala. Suomalaisen Kirjallisuuden Seuran Toimituksia 724: 1. Helsinki: Suomalaisen Kirjallisuuden Seura, 313–315.

Kulha, Keijo 1972: *Suomen autonomianajan lehdistö. Kehityksen päälinjoja*. Monistesarja 8. Tampere: Tampereen yliopiston tiedotustutkimuksen laitos.

Kuusi, Hanna 2011: *Lainatut, viivatut, tentityt: Ylioppilaskunnan kirjasto/Helsingin yliopiston opiskelijakirjasto 1858–2009*. Suomalaisen Kirjallisuuden Seuran Toimituksia 1321. Helsinki: Suomalaisen Kirjallisuuden Seura.

Kuusi, Sakari 1946: *Aksel August Granfelt. Elämä ja toiminta*. Helsinki: Otava.

Laakso, Mikko 2010: *Kansanvalistajasta kansalaisten olohuoneeksi. Helsingin kaupunginkirjasto 1940–2005*. Helsinki: Helsingin kaupunginkirjasto.

Laasonen, Pentti 1977: *Johannes Gezelius vanhempi ja suomalainen täysortodoksia*. Suomen kirkkohistoriallisen seuran toimituksia 103. Helsinki: Suomen kirkkohistoriallinen seura.

Laasonen, Pentti 2003: Katsaus saksalaisperäiseen kirjallisuuteen Suomessa 1600- ja 1700-luvuilla. In *Vieraskielinen kirjallisuus Suomessa Ruotsin vallan aikana*. Ed. Tuija Laine. Tietolipas 159. Helsinki: Suomalaisen Kirjallisuuden Seura, 104–113.

Lahti, Markku 1991: Vanhan Korpilahden seurakunta. Aika seurakunnan itsenäistymisestä sen lopulliseen jakaantumiseen (1861–1923). Eripainos *Vanhan Korpilahden historiasta*. Ed. Mauno Jokipii. Korpilahti: Vanhan Korpilahden historiatoimikunta Korpilahden kunnan ja seurakunnan tuella.

Lahtinen, Veikko 1963: Jyväskylän kansankirjasto-olot vuosina 1863–1915. In *Jyväskylän kaupunginkirjaston juhlakirja 1863–1963*. Jyväskylä: Jyväskylän kaupungin kirjastolautakunta, 7–35.

Laine, Esko M. 1997: Esipuhe. In Wallmann, Johannes, *Totinen kääntymys ja maailmanparannus. Pietismi kirkkohistoriallisena ilmiönä*. Suomennos Esko M. Laine. Helsinki: Kirjaneliö, 1997, 9–10.

Laine, Esko M. 1999: Pietistinen kirjallisuus ja uuden ajan minä. In *Suomen kirjallisuushistoria 1. Hurskaista lauluista ilostelevaan romaaniin*. Eds. Yrjö Varpio & Liisi Huhtala. Suomalaisen Kirjallisuuden Seuran Toimituksia 724: 1. Helsinki: Suomalaisen Kirjallisuuden Seura, 78–83.

Laine, Tuija 2000: *Ylösherätys suruttomille. Englantilaisperäinen hartauskirjallisuus Suomessa Ruotsin vallan aikana*. Suomalaisen Kirjallisuuden Seuran Toimituksia 775. Helsinki: Suomalaisen Kirjallisuuden Seura.

Laine, Tuija 2001: Kateederilta kansan pariin. Suomalainen lääketieteellinen kirjallisuus 1600- ja 1700-luvuilla. In *Tieto ja kirja*. Helsinki: Suomen tietokirjailijat, 187–210.

Laine, Tuija (ed.) 2003: *Vieraskielinen kirjallisuus Suomessa Ruotsin vallan aikana*. Tietolipas 159. Helsinki: Suomalaisen Kirjallisuuden Seura.

Laine, Tuija 2006: *Kolportöörejä ja kirjakauppiaita. Kirjojen hankinta ja levitys Suomessa vuoteen 1800*. Suomalaisen Kirjallisuuden Seuran Toimituksia 1098. Helsinki: Suomalaisen Kirjallisuuden Seura.

Laine, Tuija 2011a: *Yleisen kirkkohistorian lähteet ja tutkimus*. Suomen Kirkkohistoriallisen Seuran toimituksia 215. Helsinki: Suomen kirkkohistoriallinen seura, 340–350.

Laine, Tuija 2011b: The Clergyman as a Book Owner and Distributor in the Provinces of Uusimaa and Häme During the 1700s. In *The Emergence of Finnish Book and Reading Culture in the 1700s*. Eds. Cecilia af Forcelles & Tuija Laine. Studia Fennica Litteraria 5. Helsinki: Finnish Literature Society, 31–54.

Laine, Tuija 2013: Tietokirjallisuuden suomentaminen ennen 1800-lukua. In *Suomennetun tietokirjallisuuden historia 1800-luvulta 2000-luvulle*. Eds. Outi Paloposki & H. K. Riikonen. Suomalaisen Kirjallisuuden Seuran toimituksia 1289. Helsinki: Suomalaisen Kirjallisuuden Seura, 25–39.

Laine, Esko M. & Laine, Tuija 2010: Kirkollinen kansanopetus. In *Huoneentaulun maailma. Kasvatus ja koulutus Suomessa keskiajalta 1860-luvulle*. Eds. Jussi Hanska & Kirsi Vainio-Korhonen. Suomalaisen Kirjallisuuden Seuran Toimituksia 1266: 1, Tiede. Helsinki: Suomalaisen Kirjallisuuden Seura, 258–306.

Laitinen, Erkki 1988: Väestö ja yhteiskunta. In *Keski-Suomen historia 2. Keski-Suomi maakunta-ajatuksen synnystä itsenäisyyden aikaan*. Ed. Mauno Jokipii. Jyväskylä: Keski-Suomen maakuntaliitto, 63–138.

Laitinen, Erkki 2004: Itsenäisen pitäjän alkutaival vuoteen 1918. In Erkki Laitinen & Janne Vilkuna, *Hankasalmen historia. 1, Esihistoriasta vuoteen 1918*. [Hankasalmi]: Hankasalmen kunta, 231–529.

Laitinen, Kai 1997: *Suomen kirjallisuuden historia*. 4. painos. Helsinki: Otava.

Laitinen, Lea & Mikkola, Kati (eds.) 2013: *Kynällä kyntäjät. Kansan kirjallistuminen 1800-luvun Suomessa*. Suomalaisen Kirjallisuuden Seuran Toimituksia 1370. Helsinki: Suomalaisen Kirjallisuuden Seura.

Laitinen, Lea & Nordlund, Taru 2012: Performing identitites and interaction through epistolary formulae. In *Letter Writing in Late Modern Europe*. Eds. Marina Dossena & Gabriella Del Lungo Camiciotti. Amsterdam – Philadelphia: John Benjamins, 65–88.

Laitinen, Lea & Nordlund, Taru 2013: Language from below? Indexing Identities in the Writings of Common People in 19th-Century. In *White Field, Black Seeds. Nordic*

Literacy Practices in the Long Nineteenth Century. Eds. Anna Kuismin & M. J. Driscoll. Studia Fennica Litteraria 7. Helsinki: Finnish Literature Society, 169–189.

Lakio, Matti 1981: Talouselämä. In *Viipurin kaupungin historia IV osa*. Helsinki: Torkkelin säätiö, 363–422.

Lampinen, Olli 1986: Liikenne, kauppa ja teollisuus. In *Kivijärven kirja*. Ed. Martti Peltonen. Jyväskylän yliopiston ylioppilaskunnan kotiseutusarja N:o 23. Kivijärvi: Kivijärven kunta ja seurakunta, 248–284.

Landgren, Lars 1988: Kieli ja aate – politisoituva sanomalehdistö 1860–1889. In *Suomen lehdistön historia 1, Sanomalehdistön vaiheet vuoteen 1905*. Ed. Päiviö Tommila. Kuopio: Kustannuskiila, 267–420.

Lappalainen, Päivi 1999a: Epäkohdat esiin! – Realistit maailmaa parantamassa. In *Suomen kirjallisuushistoria 2. Järkiuskosta vaistojen kapinaan*. Ed. Lea Rojola. Suomalaisen Kirjallisuuden Seuran Toimituksia 724: 2. Helsinki: Suomalaisen Kirjallisuuden Seura, 8–42.

Lappalainen, Päivi 1999b: Perhe, koti, kansa, isänmaa – kiista yhteiskunnan tukipylväistä. In *Suomen kirjallisuushistoria 2. Järkiuskosta vaistojen kapinaan*. Ed. Lea Rojola. Suomalaisen Kirjallisuuden Seuran Toimituksia 724: 2. Helsinki: Suomalaisen Kirjallisuuden Seura, 43–73.

Lassila, Pertti 2007: Saksankielinen kirjallisuus. In *Suomennoskirjallisuuden historia 2*. Eds. H. K. Riikonen et al. Suomalaisen Kirjallisuuden Seuran toimituksia 1112. Helsinki: Suomalaisen Kirjallisuuden Seura, 91–103.

Lassila, Pertti 2008: *Syvistä riveistä. Kansankirjailija, sivistyneistö ja kirjallisuus 1800-luvulla*. Helsinki: Gaudeamus, Helsinki University Press.

Lauerma, Petri 2013: Finnish Revivalist Movements and the Development of Literary Finnish. In *White Field, Black Seeds. Nordic Literacy Practices in the Long Nineteenth Century*. Eds. Anna Kuismin & M. J. Driscoll. Studia Fennica Litteraria 7. Finnish Literature Society, Helsinki, 158–168.

Launis, Kati 2005: *Kerrotut naiset. Suomen ensimmäiset naisten kirjoittamat romaanit naiseuden määrittelijöinä*. Suomalaisen Kirjallisuuden Seuran toimituksia 1029. Helsinki: Suomalaisen Kirjallisuuden Seura.

Law, Graham & Patten, Robert L. 2009: The serial revolution. In *The Cambridge History of the Book in Britain. Volume VI, 1830–1914*. Ed. David McKitterick. Cambridge: Cambridge University Press, 144–171.

Leapman, Michael 2012: *The Book of the British Library*. London: The British Library.

Leedham-Green, Elisabeth & Webber, Teresa 2006: *The Cambridge History of Libraries in Britain and Ireland. Volume I: To 1640*. Cambridge: Cambridge University Press.

Leffler, Marion 1999: *Böcker, bildning, makt. Arbetare, borgare och bildningens roll i klassformeringen i Lund och Helsingborg 1860–1901*. Bibliotheca Historica Lundensis 91. Lund: Lund University Press.

Lehtikanto, Mirjam 1964: *Vaasa kirjastokaupunkina*. Vaasa: Vaasan kaupunki.

Lehtinen, Marja 1988: Yhteisen kansan valoksi. Käsityksen kansankirjastojen ja lukemisen tavoitteista suomalaisissa sanomalehdissä vuosina 1841–1890. *Kirjastotiede ja informatiikka* 7(2) 1988, 41–55.

Lehtinen, Marja 1999: Kirjallisuuden käsite ja kirjallisuusinstituution eriytyminen. In *Suomen kirjallisuushistoria 1. Hurskaista lauluista ilostelevaan romaaniin*. Eds. Yrjö Varpio & Liisi Huhtala. Suomalaisen Kirjallisuuden Seuran Toimituksia 724: 1. Helsinki: Suomalaisen Kirjallisuuden Seura, 196–203.

Lehtonen, Eeva-Liisa 1994: *Säätyläishuveista kansanhuveiksi, kansanhuveista kansalaishuveiksi. Maaseudun yleishyödyllinen huvitoiminta 1800-luvun alusta 1870-luvun alkuun*. Historiallisia Tutkimuksia 184. Helsinki: Suomalaisen Kirjallisuuden Seura.

Lehtonen, Mikko 2001: *Post scriptum. Kirja medioitumisen aikakaudella*. Tampere: Vastapaino.

Leino-Kaukiainen, Pirkko 1990: *Kirja koko elämä. Gummeruksen kustannustoiminnan historia.* Jyväskylä: Gummerus.
Leino-Kaukiainen, Pirkko 2007a: Suomalaisten kirjalliset taidot autonomian kaudella. *Historiallinen aikakauskirja* 105(4) 2007, 420–438.
Leino-Kaukiainen, Pirkko 2007b: Lehdistö suomennoskirjallisuuden julkaisijana. In *Suomennoskirjallisuuden historia 1.* Eds. H. K. Riikonen et al. Suomalaisen Kirjallisuuden Seuran toimituksia 1084. Helsinki: Suomalaisen Kirjallisuuden Seura, 150–157.
Leppihalme, Ritva 2007: Britteinsaarten kertomakirjallisuus. In *Suomennoskirjallisuuden historia 2.* Eds. H. K. Riikonen et al. Suomalaisen Kirjallisuuden Seuran toimituksia 1112. Helsinki: Suomalaisen Kirjallisuuden Seura, 152–166.
Leskelä, Simo 1967: *Kinnulan seurakunnan vaiheita.* Kinnula.
Levi, Giovanni 1992: *Aineeton perintö. Manaajapappi ja talonpoikaisyhteisö 1600-luvun Italiassa.* (L'eredità immateriale, 1985.) Tutkijaliiton julkaisusarja 73. Helsinki: Tutkijaliitto.
Liikanen, Ilkka 1995: *Fennomania ja kansa: joukkojärjestäytymisen läpimurto ja Suomalaisen puolueen synty.* Historiallisia tutkimuksia 191. Helsinki: Suomen historiallinen seura.
Liikanen, Ilkka 2003: Kansa. In *Käsitteet liikkeessä. Suomen poliittisen kulttuurin käsitehistoria.* Eds. Matti Hyvärinen et al. Tampere: Vastapaino, 257–307.
Lilius, Pirkko 2007: Naiset kääntäjinä 1800-luvun Suomessa. In *Suomennoskirjallisuuden historia 2.* Eds. H. K. Riikonen et al. Suomalaisen Kirjallisuuden Seuran toimituksia 1112. Helsinki: Suomalaisen Kirjallisuuden Seura, 176–180.
Lin, Nan 2003[2001]: *Social Capital. A Theory of Social Structure and Action.* Structural Analysis in the Social Sciences 19. Cambridge: Cambridge University Press.
Lindgren, Klaus & Lindgren, Anna-Riitta 2006: Suomen suuriruhtinaanmaan säätyläisten kielenvaihto. In *Kahden puolen Pohjanlahtea I. Ihmisiä, yhteisöjä ja aatteita Ruotsissa ja Suomessa 1500-luvulta 1900-luvulle.* Historiallinen Arkisto 123:1. Eds. Gabriel Bladh & Christer Kuvaja. Helsinki: Suomalaisen Kirjallisuuden Seura, 326–396.
Lindmark, Daniel 2003: Literacy, Text, Practice, and Culture: Major Trends in the Umeå History of Education Research Group, 1972–2002. *Interchange* 34(2–3) 2003, 153–178.
Lindmark, Daniel 2004: *Reading, Writing and Schooling. Swedish Practices of Education and Literacy, 1650–1880.* Umeå: Umeå universitet.
Linnakylä, Pirjo & Arffman, Inga (eds.) 2007: *Finnish Reading Literacy. When quality and equity meet.* Jyväskylä: University of Jyväskylä, Institute for Educational Research.
Littau, Karin 2006: *Theories of Reading. Books, Bodies, and Bibliomania.* Cambridge: Polity Press.
Lorenzen-Schmidt, Klaus-Joachim & Poulsen, Bjørn 2002: *Writing Peasants. Studies on Peasant Literacy in Early Modern Northern Europe.* Odense: Landbohistorisk Selskab.
Luukkanen, Tarja-Liisa 2013: Lutherilainen Evankeliumi-Yhtiö ja lainakirjastot Lutherin teosten sekä luterilaisen identiteetin levittäjinä 1800-luvulla. *Gladiolus* 2/2013, 31–46.
Lyons, Martyn 2010: *A History of Reading and Writing in the Western World.* Basingstoke: Palgrave Macmillan.
Lyons, Martyn 2012: New Directions in the History of Written Culture. *Culture and History Digital Journal* 1(2) 2012, 1–9.
Lyons, Martyn 2013: *The Writing Culture of Ordinary People in Europe, c. 1860–1920.* Cambridge: Cambridge University Press.
Lyons, Martyn 2015: Writing Upwards. How the Weak Wrote to the Powerful. *Journal of Social History* 49(2) 2015, 317–330. (Special Issue: The Functions and Purpose of Vernacular Literacy.)

Lyons, Martyn, Kotilainen, Sofia & Mäkinen, Ilkka, The Functions and Purpose of Vernacular Literacy: An Introduction. *Journal of Social History* 49(2) 2015, 283–286. (Special Issue: The Functions and Purpose of Vernacular Literacy.)

Magnússon, Sigurður Gylfi 2010: *Wasteland with Words: a social history of Iceland.* London: Reaktion Books.

Makkonen, Anna 2005: *Kadonnut kangas. Retkiä Ida Digertin päiväkirjaan.* Helsinki: Suomalaisen Kirjallisuuden Seura.

Manguel, Alberto 2006: *The Library at Night.* New Haven & London: Yale University Press.

Manley, K. A. 2003: Scottish Circulating and Subscription Libraries as Community Libraries. *Library History* 19(3) 2003, 185–194.

Manninen, Ari 1986: Sotien aika. In *Kivijärven kirja.* Ed. Martti Peltonen. Jyväskylän yliopiston ylioppilaskunnan kotiseutusarja N:o 23. Kivijärvi: Kivijärven kunta ja seurakunta, 473–510.

Mantovaara, Anneli 2001: *Mikkelin pitäjän ensimmäisestä kirjastosta osaksi maakuntakirjastoa. Kirjastolaitos Mikkelin maalaiskunnan alueella 1851–2001.* Julkaisuja. 26. Mikkeli: Mikkelin kaupunginkirjasto – Etelä-Savon maakuntakirjasto.

Markiewicz, André 2000: La bibliothèque dans ses murs: préhistoire et histoire du 43 rue Stanislas. In *La bibliothèque municipal de Nancy 1750–2000.* Ed. André Markiewicz. Nancy: Ville de Nancy, 17–32.

Markkanen, Erkki 1977: *Maaseutuväestön varallisuusolot ja luottosuhteet Sisä-Suomessa elinkeinoelämän murroskaudella v. 1850–1914.* Studia historica Jyväskyläensia 14. Jyväskylä: Jyväskylän yliopisto.

Markkanen, Erkki 1983: *Vanhan Viitasaaren historia.* Viitasaari: Viitasaaren kunta ja seurakunta.

Markkanen, Erkki 1988: Keski-Suomen taloushistoria. In *Keski-Suomen historia 2. Keski-Suomi maakunta-ajatuksen synnystä itsenäisyyden aikaan.* Ed. Mauno Jokipii. Jyväskylä: Keski-Suomen maakuntaliitto, 139–314.

Markkanen, Erkki 1989: Kirjastako kertojaksi. In *Pysy lujana omalla maalla! Erkki Lehtiselle omistettu juhlakirja.* Eds. Erkki Markkanen et al. Studia historica Jyväskyläensia 40. Jyväskylä: Jyväskylän yliopisto, 149–159.

Markkola, Pirjo 2002: *Synti ja siveys: naiset, uskonto ja sosiaalinen työ Suomessa 1860–1920.* Suomalaisen Kirjallisuuden Seuran Toimituksia 888. Helsinki: Suomalaisen Kirjallisuuden Seura.

Martino, Alberto 1990: *Die deutsche Leihbibliothek. Geschichte einer literarischen Institution (1756–1914).* Mit einem zusammen mit Georg Jäger erstellten Verzeichnis der erhaltenen Leihbibliothekskataloge. Beiträge zum Buch- und Bibliothekswesen. Herausgeben von Max Pauer. Band 29. Wiesbaden: Otto Harrassowitz.

McDowell, Kathleen 2009: Toward a History of Children as Readers, 1890–1930. *Book History* 12 2009, 240–265.

Melin, Harri 2005: Vertailevan tutkimuksen monet lähtökohdat. In *Tutkimus menetelmien pyörteissä.* Eds. Pekka Räsänen, Anu-Hanna Anttila & Harri Melin. Jyväskylä: PS-kustannus, 53–65.

Meriranta, Markku 1984: *Valistuksellisen kirjavalintamme juuret: kirjavalintakysymykset Kansanvalistusseuran kansankirjastotoiminnassa 1874–1918.* Helsinki: Kirjastopalvelu.

Merisalo, Outi, Mäkinen, Ilkka & Laine, Tuija 1999: Suomi osana Eurooppaa. In *Suomen kirjallisuushistoria 1. Hurskaista lauluista ilostelevaan romaaniin.* Eds. Yrjö Varpio & Liisi Huhtala. Suomalaisen Kirjallisuuden Seuran Toimituksia 724: 1. Helsinki: Suomalaisen Kirjallisuuden Seura, 126–139.

Merisalo, Outi 2003: *Manu scripta: länsimaisen kirjan historia keskiajalla (500–1500).* Jyväskylän yliopiston ylioppilaskunnan julkaisusarja 69. Jyväskylä: Kampus Kustannus.

Mikkola, Kati 2009: *Tulevaisuutta vastaan. Uutuuksien vastustus, kansantiedon keruu ja kansakunnan rakentaminen.* Suomalaisen Kirjallisuuden Seuran Toimituksia 1251, Tiede. Helsinki: Suomalaisen Kirjallisuuden Seura.

Minter, Catherine J. 2009: The Classification of Libraries and Image of the Librarian in Nineteenth and Early Twentieth-Century Germany. *Library & Information History* 25(1) 2009, 3–19.

Montefiore, Simon Sebag 2012: *Jerusalem. Kaupungin elämäkerta.* Helsinki: WSOY.

Murphy, Sharon 2009: Imperial Reading? The East India Company's Lending Libraries for Soldiers, c. 1819–1834. *Book History* 12(1) 2009, 74–99.

Murtorinne, Eino 1992: *Suomen kirkon historia 3, Autonomian kausi 1809–1899.* Porvoo – Helsinki – Juva: WSOY.

Myllyntaus, Timo 1990: *Education in the Making of Modern Finland.* Helsinki: The Research Institute of the Finnish Economy.

Myllymäki, Seppo 1986: Kivijärven väestö ja yhteiskunta vuoden 1860 jälkeen. In *Kivijärven kirja.* Ed. Martti Peltonen. Jyväskylän yliopiston ylioppilaskunnan kotiseutusarja N:o 23. Kivijärvi: Kivijärven kunta ja seurakunta, 89–147.

Mäkelä, Hanna 1991: *Kirjasto – kylän kunnia. 130 vuotta kirjastotoimintaa Nivalassa.* Nivala: Nivalan kunta.

Mäkelä, Vihtori 1963: Kolanen, Jaakko. In *Eteläpohjalaisia elämäkertoja 1, A–L.* Eds. Reino Ala-Kulju et al. Vaasa: Etelä-Pohjanmaan maakuntaliitto, 306–307.

Mäkinen, Ilkka 1990: Ensimmäinen varusmieskirjasto Suomessa 1849–1860. *Kirjastotiede ja informatiikka* 9(2) 1990, 35–43.

Mäkinen, Ilkka 1997: *"Nödvändighet af LainaKirjasto": Modernin lukuhalun tulo Suomeen ja lukemisen instituutiot.* Suomalaisen Kirjallisuuden Seuran Toimituksia 668. Helsinki: Suomalaisen Kirjallisuuden Seura.

Mäkinen, Ilkka 1999: Lukemisen vallankumous. In *Suomen kirjallisuushistoria 1. Hurskaista lauluista ilostelevaan romaaniin.* Eds. Yrjö Varpio & Liisi Huhtala. Suomalaisen Kirjallisuuden Seuran Toimituksia 724: 1. Helsinki: Suomalaisen Kirjallisuuden Seura, 163–177.

Mäkinen, Ilkka 2000a: Kaarle Werkon rikas elämäntyö kansanvalistuksen, kirjastojen ja raittiuden hyväksi. 15/12/2000. http://www.uwasa.fi/~sukkula/historia/werkko.html.

Mäkinen, Ilkka 2000b: *P. U. F. Sadelin (1788–1858): präst, skribent och biblioteksman.* Finnish information studies 15. Tampere, Åbo, Oulu: Tampereen yliopisto, informaatiotutkimuksen laitos; Åbo Akademi, institutionen för informationsförvaltning; Oulun yliopisto, informaatiotutkimuksen laitos.

Mäkinen, Ilkka 2003: Genoveva, aikansa menestyteos. In *Suomen kulttuurihistoria Osa 3: Oma maa ja maailma.* Ed. Laura Kolbe. Helsinki: Tammi, 326.

Mäkinen, Ilkka 2007: Kirjoitustaidon leviämisen herättämiä epäluuloja 1800-luvun Suomessa. *Historiallinen Aikakauskirja* 105(4) 2007, 402–419.

Mäkinen, Ilkka (ed.) 2009a: *Suomen yleisten kirjastojen historia.* Helsinki: BTJ Kustannus.

Mäkinen, Ilkka 2009b: Kirjastot ennen kansallisuusaatetta: yleisten kirjastojen esihistoria 1800-luvun alkuun. In *Suomen yleisten kirjastojen historia.* Ed. Ilkka Mäkinen. Helsinki: BTJ Kustannus, 13–72.

Mäkinen, Ilkka 2009c: 1800-luvun alkupuoli: kohti kansankirjastoja. In *Suomen yleisten kirjastojen historia.* Ed. Ilkka Mäkinen. Helsinki: BTJ Kustannus, 73–135.

Mäkinen, Ilkka 2009d: Pitäjänkirjastojen läpimurto. In *Suomen yleisten kirjastojen historia.* Ed. Ilkka Mäkinen. Helsinki: BTJ Kustannus, 136–150.

Mäkinen, Ilkka 2009e: Kirjasto fennomaanien kansansivistysohjelmassa. In *Suomen yleisten kirjastojen historia.* Ed. Ilkka Mäkinen. Helsinki: BTJ Kustannus, 151–213.

Mäkinen, Ilkka 2009f: Yleinen kirjasto hyvinvointiyhteiskunnassa 1960-luvun alusta vuosituhannen vaihteeseen. In *Suomen yleisten kirjastojen historia.* Ed. Ilkka Mäkinen. Helsinki: BTJ Kustannus, 384–463.

Mäkinen, Ilkka, 2009g: History of Finnish Public Libraries in a Nutshell. In *Library spirit in the Nordic and Baltic countries: historical perspectives.* Eds. Martin Dyrbye et al. Tampere: Hibolire, 109–133.

Mäkinen, Ilkka 2015: From Literacy to Love of Reading. The Fennomanian Ideology of Reading in the 19th-century Finland. *Journal of Social History* 49(2) 2015, 287-299. (Special Issue: The Functions and Purpose of Vernacular Literacy.)

Määttä, Piia 2014: *Jyväskylän kansakoulunopettajaseminaarin kirjaston kokoelmien muodostuminen 1863-1905.* Suomen historian pro gradu -tutkielma, Jyväskylän yliopiston historian ja etnologian laitos.

Mönkkönen, Mauri 1986: Kansansivistys. In *Kivijärven kirja.* Ed. Martti Peltonen. Jyväskylän yliopiston ylioppilaskunnan kotiseutusarja N:o 23. Kivijärvi: Kivijärven kunta ja seurakunta, 437-472.

Mönkkönen, Mauri 1988a: Sivistyselämä. In *Keski-Suomen historia 2. Keski-Suomi maakunta-ajatuksen synnystä itsenäisyyden aikaan.* Ed. Mauno Jokipii. Jyväskylä: Keski-Suomen maakuntaliitto, 519-610.

Mönkkönen, Mauri, 1988b: Seurakuntaelämä. In *Keski-Suomen historia 2. Keski-Suomi maakunta-ajatuksen synnystä itsenäisyyden aikaan.* Ed. Mauno Jokipii. Jyväskylä: Keski-Suomen maakuntaliitto, 443-492.

Naumanen, Maire 1966: Hankasalmen kansanopetus ja kirjastot. In *Hankasalmen kirja.* Ed. Pertti P. Kuokkanen. Jyväskylän yliopiston ylioppilaskunnan kotiseutusarja N:o 4. Hankasalmi: Hankasalmen kunta ja seurakunta, 237-256.

Navickienė, Aušra, Mäkinen, Ilkka, Torstensson, Magnus, Dyrbye, Martin & Reimo, Tiiu (eds.) 2013: *Good book, good library, good reading: studies in the history of the book, libraries and reading from the network HIBOLIRE and its friends.* Tampere: Tampere University Press.

Niemi, A. R. 1904: *Runonkerääjiemme matkakertomuksia 1830-luvulta 1880-luvulle.* Suomalaisen Kirjallisuuden Seuran toimituksia 109. Helsinki: Suomalaisen Kirjallisuden Seura.

Niemi, Juhani 2008: *Kisällistä kauppaneuvokseksi. Kirjankustantaja Arvi A. Kariston elämäkerta.* Hämeenlinna: Karisto.

Niiranen, Esko 1999: *Juvan lainakirjastojen vaiheita. Juvan kirjastolaitos 1850-1999.* [Juva: Juvan kunta].

Niskala, Kaarina 2007: *Tietoa & tarinoita. Oulun kaupungin kirjastolaitos 130 vuotta.* Oulu: Oulun kaupunginkirjasto.

Nissilä, Viljo 1981: Koulut ja opistot. In J. W. Ruuth & Erkki Kuujo, *Viipurin kaupungin historia IV osa: 1.* Helsinki: Torkkelin säätiö, 439-484.

Nordlund, Taru 2007: Double diglossia – lower class writing in 19th-century Finland. *Multilingua* 26(2-3) 2007, 229-246.

Numminen, Jaakko 2011: *Yhteisön voima: nuorisoseuraliikkeen historia. 1, Synty ja kasvu 1881-1905.* Suomen Nuorisoseurojen Liitto. Helsinki: Edita.

Nuorteva, Jussi 1988: Miten kirjat levisivät kansan käteen? *Opusculum* 8(1-4) 1988, 92-110.

Nurmi, Veli 1964: *Maamme seminaarien varsinaisen opettajakoulutuksen synty ja kehittyminen viime vuosisadalla I.* Jyväskylä Studies in Education, Psychology and Social Research 7. Jyväskylä: Jyväskylän kasvatusopillinen korkeakoulu & Jyväskylän yliopistoyhdistys.

Nurmi, Veli 1988: *Uno Cygnaeus. Suomalainen koulumies ja kasvattaja.* Helsinki: Valtion painatuskeskus-Kouluhallitus.

Nurmio, Yrjö 1947: *Taistelu suomen kielen asemasta 1800-luvun puolivälissä: vuoden 1850 kielisäädöksen syntyhistorian, voimassaolon ja kumoamisen selvittelyä.* Porvoo: WSOY.

Nyman, Jopi & Kovala, Urpo 2007: Yhdysvaltain kirjallisuus. In *Suomennoskirjallisuuden historia 2.* Eds. H. K. Riikonen et al. Suomalaisen Kirjallisuuden Seuran toimituksia 1112. Helsinki: Suomalaisen Kirjallisuuden Seura, 167-183.

Närhi, Mauri K. 1963: *Lukuseurasta kansankirjastoon. Helsingin kirjastotoimintaa 1800-luvulla.* Helsingin kaupungin julkaisuja N:o 18. Helsinki: Helsingin kaupunki.

Ojanen, Outi, 2011: Tapaus lukuharrastuksen heräämisen kartalta. *Kangasalan kir-*

jaston lukijayhteisöt 1870-luvulta 1890-luvulle. http://kangasala-fi-bin.aldone.fi/@Bin/7441f2c00724c006efbe9d2f984a61bc/1415381453/application/pdf/2219974/Tapaus%20lukuharrastuksen%20her%C3%A4%C3%A4misen%20kartalta.pdf.

Ollé, James G. 1971: *Library History. An examination guidebook*. Second Edition. London: Clive Bingley.

Olson, David R. 1985: Introduction. In *Literacy, Language and Learning. The Nature and Consequences of Reading and Writing*. Eds. David R. Olson, Nancy Torrance & Angela Hildyard. Cambridge: Cambridge University Press.

Pajula, Paavo 1960: *Suomalaisen lakikielen historia pääpiirteittäin*. Porvoo–Helsinki: WSOY.

Paloposki, Päivi 2007: Slaavilainen kirjallisuus. In *Suomennoskirjallisuuden historia 2*. Eds. H. K. Riikonen et al. Suomalaisen Kirjallisuuden Seuran toimituksia 1112. Helsinki: Suomalaisen Kirjallisuuden Seura, 206–218.

Paloposki, Outi 2013: Edlundin kustantamo – ensimmäinen suomalainen suurkustantamo. In *Suomennetun tietokirjallisuuden historia 1800-luvulta 2000-luvulle*. Eds. Outi Paloposki & H. K. Riikonen. Suomalaisen Kirjallisuuden Seuran toimituksia 1289. Helsinki: Suomalaisen Kirjallisuuden Seura, 57–65.

Parland-von Essen, Jessica 2011: Book Ownership as a Subject of Cultural-historical Research. Helsinkians and Their Books in the 1700s. In *The Emergence of Finnish Book and Reading Culture in the 1700s*. Eds. Cecilia af Forcelles & Tuija Laine. Studia Fennica Litteraria 5. Helsinki: Finnish Literature Society, 14–30.

Pawley, Christine 2002: Seeking 'Significance'. Actual readers, Specific Reading Communities. *Book History* 5 2002, 143–160.

Peatling, G. K. 2004: Public Libraries and National Identity in Britain, 1850–1919. *Library History* 20(1) 2004, 33–47.

Peltonen, Martti 1986: Kivijärven kunnalliselämä kuntakokouskaudella. In *Kivijärven kirja*. Ed. Martti Peltonen. Jyväskylän yliopiston ylioppilaskunnan kotiseutusarja N:o 23. Kivijärvi: Kivijärven kunta ja seurakunta, 375–402.

Peltonen, Matti 1992: *Matala katse. Kirjoituksia mentaliteettien historiasta*. Helsinki: Hanki ja jää.

Peltonen, Matti 2012: The method of clues and history theory. In *Historical Knowledge. Quest of Theory, Method and Evidence*. Eds. Susanna Fellman & Marjatta Rahikainen. Newcastle upon Tyne: Cambridge Scholars Publishing, 45–76.

Penttilä, Kalevi 1986: *Riihimäen kirjaston historiaa*. Riihimäki: Riihimäen kaupunki.

Perälä, Anna 1999: Kirjan historiaa. In *Suomen kirjallisuushistoria 1. Hurskaista lauluista ilostelevaan romaaniin*. Eds. Yrjö Varpio & Liisi Huhtala. Suomalaisen Kirjallisuuden Seuran Toimituksia 724: 1. Helsinki: Suomalaisen Kirjallisuuden Seura, 68–77.

Pietilä, Elina 2003: *Sivistävä huvi. Suomalainen seuranäytelmä vuoteen 1910*. Suomalaisen Kirjallisuuden Seuran Toimituksia 943. Helsinki: Suomalaisen Kirjallisuuden Seura.

Piilahti, Kari-Matti 2007: *Aineellista ja aineetonta turvaa. Ruokakunnat, ekologis-taloudelliset resurssit ja kontaktinmuodostus Valkealassa 1630–1750*. Bibliotheca Historica 106. Helsinki: Suomalaisen Kirjallisuuden Seura.

Pitkänen, Kari 2007: Suomen väestön historialliset kehityslinjat. In *Suomen väestö*. Eds. Seppo Koskinen et al. Helsinki: Gaudeamus, Helsinki University Press, 41–78.

Prüsener, Marlies 1973: *Lesegesellschaften im achtzehnten Jahrhundert*. Archiv für Geschichte des Buchwesens, Band XIII. Frankfurt am Main: Buchhändler-Vereinigung, 369–594.

Putnam, Robert D. 2000: *Bowling Alone. The Collapse and Revival of American Community*. New York: Simon & Schuster.

Päivärinne, Tiina 2010: *Luonto, tiede ja teknologia. Kansanvalistuksen Suomi-kuva 1870–1920*. Bidrag till kännedom av Finlands natur och folk 183. Helsinki: Suomen tiedeseura.

Pääkkönen, Irmeli 2007: Kultala. *Suomennoskirjallisuuden historia 1.* Eds. H. K. Riikonen et al. Suomalaisen Kirjallisuuden Seuran toimituksia 1084. Helsinki: Suomalaisen Kirjallisuuden Seura, 133–136.

Rainio, Jussi 1988: 130 vuotta lainakirjastoa Keuruulla. Eripainos: *Keuruun Joulu* 1988. Keuruu.

Reuterswärd, Elisabeth 2001: *Ett massmedium för folket: studier i de allmänna kungörelsernas funktion i 1700-talets samhälle.* Studia historia Lundensia 2. Lund: Lunds universitet.

Roiko-Jokela, Heikki 1998: Isänmaan puolesta – karstulalaiset valtakunnanpolitiikan ja kriisien pyörteissä. In *Karstulan kirja.* Ed. Heikki Roiko-Jokela. Jyväskylän yliopiston ylioppilaskunnan julkaisusarja nro 36. Karstula: Karstulan kunta ja seurakunta, 349–387.

Rose, Jonathan 2001: *The intellectual life of the British working classes.* New Haven: Yale University Press.

Rosendal, Mauri 1915: *Suomen herännäisyyden historia XIX:llä vuosisadalla. Neljäs osa 1853–1900.* Oulu: Kustannusosakeyhtiö Herättäjä.

Rubin, Richard E. 2004: *Foundations of Library and Information Science.* 2nd Edition. London–New York: Neil-Schuman Publishers.

Ruoho, Olga 2013: *Nakkilan kunnankirjasto 150 vuotta.* Nakkila: Nakkilan kunta.

Ruuth, J. W. & Kuujo, Erkki 1981: Vuodet 1812–1840. In J. W. Ruuth & Erkki Kuujo, *Viipurin kaupungin historia IV osa: 1.* Helsinki: Torkkelin säätiö, 5–130.

Saari, Mirja 2012: The Development of Finnish into a National Language. In *Standard Languages and Multilingualism in European History.* Eds. Matthias Hüning, Ulrike Vogl & Olivier Moliner. Amsterdam–Philadelphia: John Benjamins, 179–204.

Sabean, David Warren 1998: *Kinship in Neckarhausen, 1700–1870.* Cambridge Studies in Social and Cultural Anthropology. Cambridge: Cambridge University Press.

Sahlberg, Pasi 2011: *Finnish lessons: what can the world learn from educational change in Finland.* New York: Teachers College Press.

Sainio, Venla 2004: Hahnsson, Theodolinda (1838–1919). In *Kansallisbiografia.* Biografiakeskus, www.kansallisbiografia.fi/kb/artikkeli/2818/, 20/8/2012. Helsinki: Suomalaisen Kirjallisuuden Seura.

Salminen, Johannes 1955: *Jarl Hemmer: en studie i liv och diktning 1893–1931.* [Svenska litteratursällskapet i Finland.]

Salomies, Olli 2001: Names and identities. Onomastics and prosopography. In *Epigraphic Evidence. Ancient history from inscriptions.* Ed. John Bodel. London and New York: Routledge, 73–94.

Samppala, Päivi 2010: *Jalasjärven kirjasto 150 vuotta 1860–2010.* Jalasjärvi: Jalasjärven kunta.

Sandersen, Vibeke 2007: Writing ability and the written language of Danish private soldiers in the Tree Year's War (1848–50). *Multilingua* 26(2–3) 2007, 247–278.

Shadewitz, L. 1903: *Suomen kansankirjastot. Tilastollinen katsaus maamme kansankirjasto-oloihin 1900-luvun alussa.* Kansanvalistusseuran toimituksia n:o 129. Helsinki: Kansanvalistusseura.

Seppälä, Eila 1963: *Turun kaupunginkirjasto 1863–1963. Esivaiheita ja myöhempi kehitys.* Turku: Turun kaupunki.

Seppälä, Santeri 1954: Laihian ensimmäinen lainakirjasto. *Bibliophilos* 4/1954, 57–61.

Sevänen, Erkki 2007: Suomennoskirjallisuuden määrällisestä kehityksestä. In *Suomennoskirjallisuuden historia 2.* Eds. H. K. Riikonen et al. Suomalaisen Kirjallisuuden Seuran toimituksia 1112. Helsinki: Suomalaisen Kirjallisuuden Seura, 12–22.

Shera, Jesse H. 1949: *Foundations of the Public Library. The Origins of the Public Library Movement in New England 1629–1855.* The University of Chicago Studies in Library Science. Chicago–Illinois: The University of Chicago Press.

Sinisalo, Hannu 1984: *Pylkönmäki: yhteisön synty ja kehitys.* Pylkönmäki: Pylkönmäen kunta.

Skouvig, Laura 2007: The Construction of the Working-Class User: Danish free public libraries and the working classes. *Library History* 23(3) 2007, 223–238.

Smith-Peter, Susan J. 2005: Provincial Public Libraries and the Law in Nicholas I's Russia. *Library History* 21(2) 2005, 103–119.

Stark, Laura 2011: *The Limits of Patriarchy. How Female Networks of Pilfering and Gossip Sparked the First Debates on Rural Gender Rights in the 19th-Century Finnish-Language Press.* Studia Fennica Ethnologica 13. Helsinki: Finnish Literature Society.

Stark, Laura 2013: Itseilmaisun into ja lehdistön portinvartijat. In *Kynällä kyntäjät. Kansan kirjallistuminen 1800-luvun Suomessa.* Eds. Lea Laitinen & Kati Mikkola. Suomalaisen Kirjallisuuden Seuran Toimituksia 1370. Suomalaisen Kirjallisuuden Seura, Helsinki, 145–177.

Stenquist, Bjarne, 2004: Kirjastot poliittisella agendalla: esimerkkejä Euroopasta. Helsinki: BTJ Kirjastopalvelu.

Stone, Lawrence 1971: Prosopography. *Daedalus* 100(1) 1971, 46–71.

Street, Brian 1984: *Literacy in theory and practice.* Cambridge: Cambridge University Press.

Sulkunen, Irma 1999: *Liisa Eerikintytär ja hurmosliikkeet 1700–1800-luvulla.* Hanki ja jää. Helsinki: Gaudeamus.

Sulkunen, Irma 2004: *Suomalaisen Kirjallisuuden Seura 1831–1892.* Suomalaisen Kirjallisuuden Seuran toimituksia 952. Helsinki: Suomalaisen Kirjallisuuden Seura.

Suomela, Hilkka 1963: Saarijärven kirjastolaitoksen vaiheita. *In Saarijärven kirja.* Ed. Mauno Jokipii. Jyväskylän kasvatusopillisen korkeakoulun ylioppilaskunnan kotiseutusarja N:o 1. Saarijärvi: Saarijärven kunta ja seurakunta, 651–670.

Talvisto, Jari 1999: *Kinnulan historia. Osana Suomenselkää: Pitäjä Kivijärven pohjoispäässä.* Kinnula: Kinnulan kunta ja seurakunta.

Tarikka, Ulla 2002: *Pitäjäntuvalta lähikirjastoksi. Anttolan kunnan kirjastolaitos 1873–2000.* Julkaisuja. 30. Mikkeli: Mikkelin kaupunginkirjasto–Etelä-Savon maakuntakirjasto.

Tatlock, Lynne 2010: Introduction: The Book Trade and "Reading Nation" in the Long Nineteenth Century. *Publishing Culture and the "Reading Nation". German Book History in the Long Nineteenth Century.* Ed. Lynne Tatlock. Studies in German Literature, Linguistics, and Culture. Rochester, New York: Camden House, 1–24.

Tigerstedt, Örnulf 1952: *Kauppahuone Hackman. Erään vanhan Viipurin kauppiassuvun vaiheet 1790–1879.* Toinen osa. Helsinki: Otava.

Tiirakari, Leeni 1999: Miten Minna Canthia luettiin? In *Suomen kirjallisuushistoria 2. Järkiuskosta vaistojen kapinaan.* Ed. Lea Rojola. Suomalaisen Kirjallisuuden Seuran toimituksia 724:2. Helsinki: Suomalaisen Kirjallisuuden Seura, 17.

Toivanen, Pekka 1985: *Lappeenrannan kaupungin kirjasto 1883–1983.* [Lappeenranta]: [Lappeenrannan kaupunki].

Toivanen, Pekka 2000: *Kuopion historia 2. Savon residenssistä valtuusmiesten aikaan.* Kuopio: Kuopion kaupunki.

Toivola, Lasse 1995: *Simeliuksesta Kajanteriin: 'täll tapaa kirjoja lainattii' Hausjärvellä vuodesta 1861.* [Hausjärvi: Hausjärven kunta.]

Tommila, Päiviö 1970: *Jyväskylän kaupungin historia 1837–1965, 2.* Jyväskylä: [Jyväskylän kaupunki].

Tommila, Päiviö 1972: *Jyväskylän kaupungin historia 1837–1965, 1.* Jyväskylä: [Jyväskylän kaupunki].

Tommila, Päiviö 1973: *Keski-Suomen lehdistön historia 2, 1886–1917.* Jyväskylä: Oy Keskisuomalainen.

Tommila, Päiviö 1980: Tiedon leviäminen. In *Suomen kulttuurihistoria II.* Eds. Päiviö Tommila, Aimo Reitala & Veikko Kallio. Porvoo–Helsinki–Juva: WSOY, 254–293.

Tommila, Päiviö 1986: Lukutaidon yleistyminen Suomessa. In *Album amicorum: kirja- ja kulttuurihistoriallisia tutkielmia Eeva Mäkelä-Henrikssonille 29. 7. 1986,* 175–181.

Tommila, Päiviö 1988: Kirjoitus- ja lukutaito Pohjolassa. *Opusculum* 8(1–4) 1988, 111–116.
Torstensson, Magnus 1996: *Att analysera genombrottet för de moderna folkbiblioteksidéerna. Exemplet Sverige och några jämförelser med USA.* Göteborg: Göteborgs universitet.
Torstensson, Magnus 2009: Library Spirit in Sweden – Two Missionary Phases. In *Library spirit in the Nordic and Baltic countries: historical perspectives.* Ed. Martin Dyrbye et al. Tampere: Hibolire, 75–93.
Towsey, Mark R. M. 2010: *Reading the Scottish Enlightenment: books and their readers in provincial Scotland, 1750–1820.* Leiden–Boston: Brill.
Tuomaala, Saara 1986: Kivijärven seurakunnan elämää. In *Kivijärven kirja.* Ed. Martti Peltonen. Jyväskylän yliopiston ylioppilaskunnan kotiseutusarja N:o 23. Kivijärvi: Kivijärven kunta ja seurakunta, 305–374.
Tuomaala, Saara 2004: *Työtätekevistä käsistä puhtaiksi ja kirjoittaviksi. Suomalaisen oppivelvollisuuskoulun ja maalaislasten kohtaaminen 1921–1939.* Bibliotheca Historica 89. Helsinki: Suomalaisen Kirjallisuuden Seura.
Tuulio, Tyyni 1979: *Fredrikan Suomi. Esseitä viime vuosisadan naisista.* Porvoo–Helsinki–Juva: WSOY.
Vandenbussche, Wim 2007: 'Lower class language' in 19th century Flanders. *Multilingua* 26(2–3) 2007, 279–290.
Vansina, Jan 1985: *Oral tradition as history.* London: James Currey.
Vartiainen, Pekka 2009: *Länsimaisen kirjallisuuden historia.* Helsinki: BTJ Kustannus.
Vatanen, Pirjo 2002: *Sääty-yhteiskunnan kirjastosta kansalaisyhteiskunnan kirjastoksi. Yleisten kirjastojemme murroskausi 1890-luvulta 1920-luvulle.* Bibliotheca Historica 74. Helsinki: Suomalaisen Kirjallisuuden Seura.
Vatanen, Pirjo 2009: Kirjastoalan koulutuksen murroksia: kurssit, kirjeopistot ja korkeakoulut … In *Suomen yleisten kirjastojen historia.* Ed. Ilkka Mäkinen. Helsinki: BTJ Finland, 758–778.
Vauhkonen, Ville 2016: *Kohti kirjan oppia. Vanhan Suomen talonpoikien kirjallistuminen Ruotsin kuningaskunnan ja Venäjän keisarikunnan luterilaisuuden risteymässä 1721–1811.* Helsingin yliopisto, teologian väitöskirja.
Vesisenaho, Virpi 1970: Keski-Suomen uskonnolliset liikkeet 1850–1911. In *Keski-Suomi 11.* Keski-Suomen museoyhdistyksen julkaisuja 11. Jyväskylä: Keski-Suomen museoyhdistys, 85–220.
Viljanen, Paavo 1931: *Piirteitä laestadiolaisesta herätysliikkeestä Kivijärven seurakunnassa.* Pastoraalikirjoitus. Helsinki.
Villstrand, Nils Erik 2008: Skriftlighet med förhinder. Den svenska statsmaktens kungörelser i finskspråkiga församlingar under 1700-talet. In *Maktens mosaik. Enhet, särart och självbild i det svenska riket.* Eds. Max Engman & Nils Erik Villstrand. Helsingfors & Stockholm: Svenska litteratursällskapet i Finland & Atlantis, 315–360.
Villstrand, Nils Erik 2011: Kungen, bonden och skriften 1500–1800. Särtryck ur *Kungl. Vitterhets Historie och Antikvitets Akademiens årsbok 2011.* Stockholm: Kungl. Vitterhets Historie och Antikvitetsakademien (the Royal Swedish Academy of Letters, History and Antiquities, KVHAA), 215–223.
Vuontisjärvi, Kati 2010: Vaatimattomasta kirjakokoelmasta ajanmukaiseksi kulttuurikeskukseksi – Rovaniemen kaupungin kirjastolaitos 150 vuotta. In *Pappien harrastuksesta moderniksi kirjastoksi: Rovaniemen kaupunginkirjasto 150 vuotta.* [Rovaniemi: Rovaniemen kaupunginkirjasto - Lapin maakuntakirjasto], 11–66.
Vuorela, Toivo 1957: Mitä kirjallisuutta oli Ilmajoen seudun talonpoikaistaloissa 1700–1800-luvun vaihteessa. *Bibliophilos* 64(4) 1957, 45–46.
Wacklin, Matti 2011: *Kaikkien sielujen apteekki. Tampereen kaupunginkirjasto 150 vuotta.* Tampere: Tampereen kaupunginkirjasto – Pirkanmaan maakuntakirjasto.
Wallmann, Johannes 1997: *Totinen kääntymys ja maailmanparannus. Pietismi kirkkohistoriallisena ilmiönä.* Suomennos Esko M. Laine. Helsinki: Kirjaneliö.

Werkko, K. (ed.) 1879: *Tietoja ja mietteitä Suomen kansa- ja lasten-kirjastoista ynnä luku-yhdistyksistä ja luennoista Vuoteen 1875*. Jyväskylä: Toimittaja.

Westberg, Johannes 2014: *Att bygga ett skolväsende. Folkskolans förutsättningar och framväxt 1840–1900*. Lund: Nordic Academic Press.

Ylikangas, Heikki 1998: *The knife fighters: violent crime in Southern Ostrobothnia 1790–1825*. Suomalaisen tiedeakatemian toimituksia 293. Helsinki: Finnish Academy of Science and Letters.

Ylioja, Merja 2003: Piirilääkäri Warenin perhe Saarijärvellä. *Saarijärven joulu* 27 2003, 34–36.

Ylitalo, Teppo 2012: *Lapuan kirjallinen historia*. Lapua: Lapuan kaupunginkirjasto, Lapuan Sanomat ja Lapuan tuomiokirkkoseurakunta.

Zweygbergk, Ola (ed.) 1958: *Om bokförlag och bokförläggare i Finland. En översikt*. Helsingfors: Finlands Förlagsförening.

Åström, Anna-Maria 2012: Skrivdon och böcker – exempel ur bouppteckningar från Savolax herrgårdar 1780–1850. In *Svärdet, ordet och pennan – kring människa, makt och rum i nordisk historia. Festskrift till Nils Erik Villstrand den 24 maj 2012*. Eds. Christer Kuvaja & Ann-Catrin Östman. Åbo, 279–306.

Abstract

Sofia Kotilainen

Literacy Skills as Local Intangible Capital
The History of a Rural Lending Library c. 1860–1920

This book studies the "grey area" of the success story of rural lending libraries in the Nordic countries through the activities of people's libraries in one area of Central Finland. The study explores the influence of social, cultural, geographical and economic phenomena, such as the spread of revivalist movements, on the reading habits of the local population and reveals interesting reasons why the establishment of elementary schools and popular libraries and the growth of functional literacy did not automatically increase the informational capital of the common people of remote regions or lead to their social advancement.

This study represents a methodological experiment in describing the life history of a people's library. The combination of collective biographical and transnational comparative methods with rarely utilized original sources in this study is innovative and has not been used before in Finnish historical research on functional literacy and popular libraries. The advantage of the comparison is that it reveals the attitudes to libraries that were characteristic of each of the cultures involved.

For the people of the Finnish countryside in the late nineteenth century, libraries represented a way of acquiring new information that was still strange and unwelcome. The distribution of immaterial capital was extremely uneven with regard to age, gender and social rank. In the earlier Finnish research has not very often been analysed, how the communal status of the peasant reader and his or her personal networks in the local community affected the quality of his or her reading habits. This book shows, that the location of the library in its local community and on the other hand the status and position of its customers in their networks, had a great significance on the use of the library and thus to the improvement of reading skills.

Index of Names

Achrenius, Abraham 215
Achrenius, Antti 215
Aejmelaeus, Johan 85
Aejmelaeus, Nils 227, 227n
Agricola, Michael 23
Ahlgrén, J. E. 252
Aho, Juhani 219, 231, 235, 237
Ahonen, Eva Stina 171
Alcenius, Helena Sophia 311
Alexander II, Emperor of all the Russians 72, 96
Alexander III, Emperor of all the Russians 296
Alkio, Santeri 220
Altick, Richard D. 22
Andelin, (Johan) Emil 143, 319
Andersen, H. C. 175
Anjala, Toivo see Anjelin, Toivo
Anjelin (family) 270, 272, 301
Anjelin, (Johan Wilhelm) *Axel* 136–137, 139, 142–144, 146, 175, 178, 279, 283, 310
Anjelin (née Cheilàn), Ida Sofia 136, 139, 142–145, 171, 272, 283, 310
Anjelin, Johan 71, 122–123, 139, 142, 145, 168, 181, 281n, 310
Anjelin, Johan Oskar 310
Anjelin, Sylvia 279, 310
Anjelin, Toivo Theodor Alvian 124, 145, 182, 193, 267, 280–281, 281n, 283, 310
Anjelin, Wilhelmina 310
Anna Loviisa (Abraham's dotter) 276
Armfelt (family) 133
Arndt, Johann 168, 212, 214–215, 250, 262–263
Arvelin, Kaarle 102

Backman, Alfred 171
Backman, J. E. 101, 171
Barth, Kristian Gottlieb 216
Barton, David 24
Baudewin, Johann 286
Beck, Vilhelm 251
Beecher-Stowe, Harriet 208, 223–224, 229–230, 236
Bengts, Carl 281, 310
Bergenheim, Edvard 96, 103
Bergh, Johan Fredrik 264
Bergholm, Axel 230
de Bernières-Louvigny, Jean 262
von Bismarck, Otto 59
Björnholm, Alma Maria see Karhusaari, Alma
Björnholm, (Otto) Elis Edward 143, 145, 193, 280, 292, 311
Bjørnson, Bjørnstjerne 232
Björkqvist, Anders 212, 215, 263
Blomstedt (Dr.) 225
Blomstedt, Oskar 225n
Bobrikov, Nikolai 297
Boxström, Anders 110–111n
Boxström (née Krogius), Eva 110
Boxström, Johan 110–111, 319
Bray, Thomas 93
Bremer, Fredrika 225
de Broen (family) 133
Bunyan, John 168, 207, 212, 214, 216, 236, 263
Bäck, Johannes 128
Böling, Katarina 315

Canth, Minna 219, 230, 234–235, 237
Canthen, Benjamin 262
von Caprivi, Leo 59
Carlsson, Wilhelm 168

353

de Cervantes, Miguel 229
Charles, Elizabeth Rundle 283
de Chateaubriand, François-René 134
Cheilàn(us) (family) 302
Cheilàn, Ida Sofia see Anjelin, Ida Sofia
Cheilán, Ingrid 111
Cheilàn, Katarina Sofia 310
Cheilàn, Kristina Maria 310
Cheilàn, Michael 145, 310
Cheilanus, Mikael 111
Colliander, Julius 181
Collins, Wilkie 224
Cooper, James Fenimore 223
Cygnaeus, Uno 74, 148, 296

Dahlgrén, Johan 311
Dahlgrén, Karl Gustaf 70, 99–100, 107, 110–113, 121, 127–128, 130, 295–296, 311, 318
Dahlström, Alexander 111, 145, 310, 318–319
Dahlström, Kristina Maria see Cheilàn, Kristina Maria 310
Dalin (clerk) 123
Danielson, Daniel Philip 114, 262
Danielson-Kalmari, Johan Richard 114n, 194, 230
Darnton, Robert 22, 24, 26–27, 64
Defoe, Daniel 208, 214, 229, 236
Deichman, Carl 97
Dent, Arthur 212–213, 215, 258
Dewey, Melvil 10, 186–187
Dickens, Charles 207, 223, 230, 232
Doyle, Arthur Conan 224
Dumas, Alexandre 237
Durchman (family) 302
Durchman, Jakob August 313
Durchman, Josef Oskar 315
Durchman, Josef Wilhelm 313
Durchman, Leeni see Svens, Leeni
Durchman, Maria, Maana see Lipponen, Maana 313
Durchman, Maria Elisabet see Krank, Maria Elisabet
Durchman, Maria Josefina 313

Eckstein, Ernst 208, 210–212, 284
Edlund, G. W. 176, 209, 251–252
Ekholm, Bertha Magdalena 142–143, 311
Enqvist, Juho 101
Erasmus of Rotterdam 23

Favorin, Carl Gustaf 114–116

Febvre, Lucien 26
Fernelius, Helena 142
Finne, Jalmari 45
Flinkman, Theodor 171
Forssman, Edith 230
Francke, August Hermann 214
Franklin, Benjamin 84
Franzén, Frans Mikael 322
Frenckell (family) 209, 321
de Frese, Amelie 287
Fresenius, Johann Philipp 212, 258
de Freycinet, Charles 59
Fröjdman (family) 283
Fröjdman, Allan Adolf 311
Fröjdman, Anna Matilda 284, 311
Fröjdman, Harry Leonard 311
Fröjdman, Helena Elisabet (Betty) 284, 311
Fröjdman, Herman Leonard 142, 144, 171, 283, 311
Fröjdman, Ivar Waldemar 193, 284, 311
Fröjdman, Karl (Kaarlo) Georg Herman 144–145, 267, 284, 311
Fröjdman, Mathilda (Thilda) 143–144, 283, 311
Fröjdman, Minchen Lovisa 311
Funcke, Otto 217

Genetz, Arvid 144
Genetz, Emil 144
Gerhard, Johan 111, 216–217
Gerstäcker, Friedrich 208, 210, 283
Gezelius, Johannes (the Elder) 65, 83, 249, 261, 261n, 321
Ginzburg, Carlo 22–24, 240
Gogol, Nikolai 230–231
Gouge, Thomas 212, 212n, 261, 263
Granfelt, Aksel August 181, 186
Granfelt, August Edward 107
Granlund, Johan 105
Granlund, Johan Fredrik 321
Grube, August Wilhelm 206–207
Grönroos, Henrik 28
Gummerus, Kaarle Jaakko (Karl Jakob) 219, 227, 229–230, 254–255
Gustav III 111n, 222
Gustav IV Adolf 133
Gyttner 261
Göös, Karl Gustaf 147, 177, 254

Haahti, Hilja 225
Haartman, Johan 262
Hackman, Johan Friedrich 118
Hackman, Woldemar 118

Hahnsson, J. A. 225
Hahnsson, Theodolinda 208, 210, 214, 219, 225–227, 230, 284
Hakkarainen, Gustaf 282
Hakkarainen, Matti 171
Hakkarainen, Matts 259
Hakkarainen, Sandra 171
Haksander, Johan 281
Hamner, Niels 261
Hannikainen, Pietari 210, 216, 227, 284, 286
Hedberg, Fredrik Gabriel 112, 212–213, 215–216, 251
Heideman, Arthur Leopold 71–72, 145, 296, 311–313, 319
Heideman, Henrik 311
Heideman (née Krank), Lempi Oihonna 143, 145, 311–312
Heikel, Gustav 142
Heino (Lindroos), Kaarle (Karl) 219
Helenius, Johan 192
Hellén, Immi 229
Hellsten, Tobias 70
Helminen, H. F. 254–255
Hemmer, Balder 133
Hemmer, Birger (Börje) 133
Hemmer, Emmy 133
Hemmer, Eric Erland 133–134, 139, 142, 312
Hemmer, Fjalar 133
Hemmer, Helga Katariina 132, 134, 136, 139, 142–143, 145, 283, 312
Hemmer, Jarl 133–134
Hemmer, Johan Abraham 133
Hemmer, Ragnar 133
Hemming (the Bishop of Finland) 82
Herchenbach, Wilhelm 208, 210, 283
Herranen (family) 272
Herranen, Antti 107, 119–121, 149–151, 296, 312
Herranen, Hilda 272
Herranen, Kalle 272, 312
Herranen, Matti 312
Hertz, Johannes 88
von Hertzén, Wilhelm Gotthard 100, 167
Hiitola, Matti see Puranen, Matti 171
Hirvainen, Pauliina 123
Hirvinen, Salomon 154
Hoffman, Alexander Friedrich Franz 210–211, 281
Hollatz, David 207, 212, 258
Holm, H. (tailor) 171
Holm, Heikki 171

Holm, Karl Otto 71
Holm, Matti 171
Holmgren, Otto Wilhelm 70
Holmström, Nils Gustav 149, 181
Honkonen, Elias 274
Hugo, Victor 322
Huhtin, F. M. 254
Hultin, V. K. 60, 60n
Hyvärinen, Lauri 247, 318
Hällfors, Isak Emanuel 226
Hällfors, Maria 226
Hämäläinen, Alma Maria see Karhusaari, Alma 145, 171, 272, 311
Hämäläinen, H. 171
Hänninen (née Wasama), Anna Lyytia, Annikki 143, 292, 312
Hänninen, Hilda 274–275
Hänninen (Aittolahti), Johan 276
Hänninen, Juho 50
Hänninen, Kaarle Vilhelm, Kalle 143–145, 150, 297, 312

Ibsen, Henrik 232
Immonen, Alpinus 285
Immonen, Petter 285
Ingman, A. W. 252
Ingman, Santeri 175 see Ivalo, Santeri
Ivalo, Santeri 234

Jahnsson, E. F. 234
Jauhiainen, Antti 275
Johansson, Egil 24
Johansson, Juho 71–72
Jotuni, Maria 237
Jurva, Sylvia see Anjelin, Sylvia 279, 310
Jämbäck, Markku 267
Jämbäck, Michel 268
Jämbäck, Silja 267
Jäntti, Maria see Salmi, Maria
Järnefelt, Arvid 234, 237
Järvi, K. A. 235
Järvinen, Karl 150
Jäsberg (family) 283
Jäsberg, Amanda 142–143, 274, 278, 281, 283
Jäsberg, Elias 142, 144, 168, 188–189, 281

Kahelin, Anders (Antti) 268
Kahelin, Maria 314
Kaihlanen, August 143, 285
Kainulainen, Gideon 171
Kainulainen, Wille 171
Kaipomäki, Adiel 257

Kajander, Kalle 219
Kannisto, Heikki 171
Kannisto, Kustaa 171
Karhusaari (née Hämäläinen), Alma Maria 143, 145–146, 292, 311
Karhusaari, Elis see Björnholm, Elis 145, 292, 311
Karisto, Arvi 274
Katajamäki, Antti 72
Kauppis-Heikki (Kauppinen, Heikki) 220, 235
Kautto, Eeva 259
Keckman, C. N. 211
Kellingius 261
Kempas, K. 102
Kemppainen, Antti 120
Kemppainen, Leena Kaisa 312
Kemppainen, Maija Brita 120
Kiljander, Margareta 310
Kiljander, Robert 175, 235
Kinnunen, Alma 272
Kinnunen, Anna 171
Kinnunen, Esa(jas) 274, 278
Kinnunen, Juho Vihtori 142n, 257, 257n
Kinnunen, Matti 150
Kirkwood, James 93
Kivi, Aleksis 231
Kjellman (family) 120
Kjellman, Carl Magnus 120, 312
Kjellman, Ferdinand Konstantin 70, 76, 99, 107, 110–113, 117, 119–121, 127, 130, 295–296, 299, 312
Kjellman, Magnus 120, 312
Kjellman, Pehr 120
Kjellman, Rafael Aleksander 121
Klemettinen, Anna Sofia 282
Kokko, Juhana 220
Kolanen, Jaakko 128–129
Konsin, Henrik 313
Konsin, Ida Emilia, 313
Konsin, Viktor 71, 107–108, 128, 142, 149–151, 181, 297, 313, 318
Korhonen, Paavo 100, 218
Kotilainen, Alma 267
Kotilainen, Antti (Niemelä) 171
Kotilainen, Antti (Purala) 259–260
Kotilainen, Antti 181
Kotilainen, Heikki (church warden) 150
Kotilainen, Heikki (lay assessor) 150
Kotilainen, Heikki 159
Kotilainen, Johan 171
Kotilainen, Matti 72
Kotilainen, Pekka 171, 194–195
Kramsu, Kaarlo 235

Krank (family) 301
Krank, Frans Petter 71–72, 128, 145, 151, 216, 264, 296, 311, 313, 315, 318
Krank, Laina see Seppänen, Laina
Krank, Lempi Oihonna see Heideman, Lempi Oihonna
Krank (née Durchman), Maria Elisabet, Betty 143–145, 283, 311, 313, 315
Krank, Simon Petter 313
Krogerus, Gustava Charlotta Edla Kristina 311
Krogius, Eva see Boxtröm, Eva
Krogius, Gabriel 110
Krohn, Julius 119
Krook, Elias 102
Krook, Heikki 101, 140, 285
Krook, Johan (Juhani) 285
Krook, Nils (Niiles) 285
Krook, Selma Saima Silja 285
Kuhlman, Anders 70, 319
Kuittu, Juhani 262
Kyyniö, (August) Hjalmar 145, 280, 319

Laestadius, Lars Levi 71, 261, 263
Lagerlöf, Selma 230, 233
Lamennais (author) 134
Layboulay, Edouard 283, 287
Leiner 251
Leppänen, G. 171
Leppänen, Heikki 274, 286
Leppänen, Juho 119
Levi, Giovanni 53n, 64
Lilius, Anton 154
Lillja, Johan Wilhelm 86, 209–210, 321
Limón, Carl 226
Limón, Carl Magnus 226
Limón, Johan Magnus 226
Limón, (Johan) Werner 76, 105–107, 226–227, 318
Limón, Sofia Theodolinda see Hahnsson, Theodolinda 226
Limonius, Jakob 226
Lincoln, Abraham 207
Lindberg, Abraham (the Elder, smith) 284–285
Lindberg, Abraham (carpenter) 281, 284
Lindeqvist, Erik 101
Lindholm 102
Lindholm, Juho 171
Lindmark, Daniel 21, 24
Lindroos, Karl see Heino, Kaarle
Linnankoski, Johannes 238
Lipponen, Heikki 143–145, 150–151, 153, 174, 297, 313

Lipponen, Maria, Maana 143, 145, 313
Listner, Karl 208, 210, 283
Litzell, Emil 251
Liukko, Riikka see Vesterinen, Riikka
Liukkonen, Adam 313
Liukkonen, Daniel 149–150, 160, 181, 296, 313
Lobstein, Jean Frédéric 217
Luther, Martin 23, 168, 207–209, 209n, 212, 215–217, 231, 239, 247, 249–252, 260, 264, 275–276, 285–286
Luukkonen, Elina 142, 145
Lyons, Martyn 21, 24
Lyra, Henrik Johan 281
Lyytinen (family) 272
Lyytinen, Evert 124–125, 314
Lyytinen, Johan (Juho) 123–124, 171, 314
Lyytinen, S. 171
Lyytinen, Wille 59n, 62
Länkelä, Jaak(k)o 59n, 255
Lönnrot, Elias 39, 147, 228, 313

Malm, Peter 115
Manguel, Alberto 186
Martin, Henri-Jean 26
Mau, Edvard 208, 217, 284
Medici (dynasty) 81
Melancthon, Philip 23
Mellin, Gustaf Henrik 208, 210, 284, 287
Menocchio, the miller 22, 240
Meriläinen, Paavo 257n
Meurman, Agathon 45, 134
Miina, the Jäsbergs' maid 283
Mikkola, Jooseppi Julius 238
Minkkinen, Konstantin 171
Moliis, Henrik 85
Mollin, Maria Christina 226
Mård, Kaisa 312

Napoleon I, Emperor of the French 15, 89, 263n
Nicholas I, Emperor of all the Russias 90, 323
Nicholas II, Emperor of all the Russias 296
Niemi (née Westerlund), Aina Sofia 143–144, 314
Niemi (Ervastin-Niemi), Sakari 136–137, 139, 143–144, 148, 150–153, 162, 166, 170–173, 194–195, 272, 283, 296, 301, 314

Niskanen, Anna Liisa 281
Nissinen, Aili 229
Nohrborg, Anders 212, 262
Nykänen, Matti 119–120
Nyman, Ann-Charlotte 28

Oehlenschläger, Adam 222
Oikari(nen), Sehvanias Heikki (Zefanias Henrik, Seve) 70, 127, 213
Oikkelmus, Konstantin 171
Oinonen, Hilma 171
Ollila, Jaakko 101
Olsoni, Agatha Benedikta (née Lyra) 281
Olsoni, Johan Fredrik 281
Olsoni, (Karl) Edvard 274–275, 278, 281, 281n, 282
Orava, Alma 286–287
Orava, Gabriel 181
Orava, Gideon 286–287
Orava, Gustaf, Kustaa 120, 149–150, 260, 286

Paajanen (Jauhiainen), Kaisa 274–275
Paavola, Matti 192
Pakkala, Teuvo 219, 235
Palearius 251
Palonen, Eero 257
Parkatti, Emanuel 261
Pawley, Christine 50
Peltonen, Matti 53
Petrelius, David 310
Petrelius, Kristina Maria see Cheilàn, Kristina Maria 310
Pigg, Antti 171
Piispanen, Jenny 257n
Piispanen, Matti 171
Piispanen, Miikka 257n
Piispanen, Nestori 267
Poe, Edgar Allan 224
Pohto, Matti 83
Porthan, Henrik Gabriel 83
Praetorius, Stephan 251
Puranen, Heikki 128
Puranen, Juho 142–143, 146, 193, 271–272, 274–275, 314
Puranen, Matti 171, 314
Pynninen, Johan (Juho) 88–89, 118
Päivärinta, Pietari 208, 210–212, 218, 220, 225, 231, 234, 284
Pölkki, Isak 171

Qvirsfeld, Johann 216

Rahikainen, Kaarlo Johannes 109, 128–129, 158
Raitanen, Kustaa 102
Rein (Rehn), Karl Johan, Kalle 178, 272, 274, 279, 285
Rein, Saima Saali Siveä 285
Rein, Wilhelmina Serafia 285
Reinbeck, Emil 208, 217
Reinius, Israel (the Eldest) 85
Reinius, Israel (the Youngest) 85
Reinius, Johan Fredrik 85
Renfors, O. 145
Renqvist (Kukkonen), Henrik 215, 243, 250
Reuter, Fritz 220
Risula, Olga 164, 294
Roine, Reinhold 144
Roos, Samuel 207n, 287
Roschier, David 262, 319
Roschier, Eric Johan 262
Rosenius, Carl Olof 213, 250
Rosenlund, Johan 60
Rosenström, Heikki 171
Rosenström, Oskari 171
Roslin-Kalliola, Mathilda 220
Rosvall, Karl August Fredrik 274, 281, 284–285
Rosvall, Otto 87
Rothman, Albin 218
Rothovius, Isaac 65
Rudbeck (Salmelainen), Erik (Eero) 208, 210–211, 218
Runeberg, Fredrika 223–224
Runeberg, Johan Ludvig 114n, 207, 215, 218, 230, 238
Ruuska, Elias 260
Ruuska, Markus 260
Ruuth, Wilhelmina see Anjelin, Wilhelmina
Rytkönen, Matti (the Elder) 120, 142, 150, 181–182, 266, 287
Rytkönen, Matti 287
Rytkönen Taavetti 171
Räsänen, Andreas (Antti) 149, 181, 314
Räty, Antti 211

Saihoniemi, Joh. 171
Sadelin, Pehr Ulrik Ferdinand 88
Salin, Anna Susanna 120, 312
Salmelainen, Eero see Rudbeck, Erik 208, 210, 216, 218, 229, 284
Salmi (Sund), Juho Vihtori 150, 257, 314–315
Salmi (née Jäntti), Maria 315
Salo, K. F. see Steenroos, K. F.
Sandeau, Jules 208, 210–211, 284
Sarlin, Konstantin 102, 111, 113, 128
Savelainen, Ebba Liisa 285–286
Schadewitz, Leo 30, 92, 97–98, 106, 136, 147, 166, 197, 201, 230, 242
Schauman, Eugen 297
Schauman, Frans Ludvig 77, 92, 92n, 243
Schildt, Wolmar 254–255
von Schmid, (Johann) Cristoph Friedrich 207–208, 210–211, 284
Schöneman, Carl Gustaf 120, 312
Schöneman, Johanna (Jeanne) 120
Scott, Walter 49, 208, 210–212, 220, 223, 230, 287, 322
Scriver, Christian 212
Sederholm 102
Seppänen, Jaakko Leonard 143, 145, 315, 319
Seppänen (née Krank), Laina Maria 143, 145, 315
Shakespeare, William 134, 236
Sienkiewicz, Henryk 238
Silfvas, Anders 250
Simelius, Helene 92
Simelius, Jakob 92
Sirén (craftsman) 194
Snellman, Johan Vilhelm 72–73, 78, 88–89, 93, 100, 134, 136, 226, 228
Snellman, Maria 142
Snellman, Sofia 142–143, 283
Spener, Philipp Jakob 214
Starbäck, Carl Georg 231
Steenroos (Salo), K. F. 150
Stenbäck (surveyor) 262
Stenius, Karl 61n, 100, 109
Sulin, Ida Emilia see Konsin 313
Sund, Anna 314
Sund, Matti 314
Svanljung, Johan Kristian 260
Svebilius, Olov 213, 261
Svedberg, Jeremias 171
Svens, Adrian 143–145, 168, 170, 172, 272, 315
Svens, Anders Henrik 315
Svens (née Durchman), Lempi Helena Maria, *Leeni* 143, 145, 315
Swift, Jonathan 229
Söderström, Gustav Leopold 86, 180
Söderström, Werner 86, 180
Söyrilä, Maria 311

Tainio, E. 193
Tainio, Gustaf (Kustaa) Emil 144, 171, 257
Tainio, Helmi 257
Taipale, Matti 100–102, 104, 140, 153–154, 157, 175, 195, 261
Talvio, Maila 237–238
Tamminen, J. (tanner) 170–171
Thomas (the Bishop of Finland) 82
Thomas à Kempis 111, 168
Thomas, Louis 194, 230
Thomasson, Per 206
Tichanoff (family, merchant house) 115–119, 121–122, 285, 310
Tichanoff, Alexander 118
Tichanoff, Michael 117–119, 123, 281, 285
Tichanoff, Timofei 117
Tichanoff, Wasili 118
Tichanova, Paraskovia 117
Tokkola, Antti 150, 296
Tolstoy, Leo 233
Topelius, Zacharias 69, 92, 182, 194, 207, 215, 222, 225, 229, 231, 284–286, 296
Tuomaala, Saara 48
Turpeinen, H. 171
Tötterman, Karl Gustaf 70, 102, 111, 113, 319

Ule, Otto 207
Ulén, Gustav 315
Ulén, Wiivi 145–146, 315 see Vesterinen, Wiivi

Varvikko, Onni Edvard 144
Vasenius, Valfrid 181
Verne, Jules 230, 237
Vesterinen (family) 272, 283
Vesterinen, Juho Heikki 171, 315
Vesterinen, Lauri 123, 127, 182, 286
Vesterinen (née Liukko), Riikka 193, 281, 286, 297
Vesterinen, Wiivi 315
Viljanen, Julius 257

Villstrand, Nils Erik 37n

Wacklin, Sara 224
Wallgrén, Georg 261
Wanochius, Ebba Wilhelmina 313
Warelius, Antero 207
Warén, Eliel 253
Wasenius, G. O. 176–177
Wegelius, Johan 212, 261, 264
Weilin, Alexander Georg 177, 254
Wierimaa, Juho Eemil 311
Wildt, Johan 284
Wilén, Gustaf Wilhelm 209, 321
Wilskman, Carl Magnus 311
Wilskman, Ivar 311
Wilskman, Mathilda see Fröjdman, Mathilda 311
Winter, Frans Karl Otto Vilhelm 101
Winter, Hugo 238
Weckström, Mathias 87
Werkko, Kaarle 29–30, 80, 84n, 100, 103–105, 107, 139–141, 146–147, 152–153, 156, 161, 180, 187, 190–191, 193, 230, 244, 275–276
Wilén, G. W. 209, 321
Wilke, Adam 89, 118
Willgren, Maria 112
Wrede, Rabbe Gottlieb 87

Ylänkö, O. A. 150
Yrjö-Koskinen (Koskinen), Yrjö Sakari 134, 225, 228–230, 286

Zengerlein, Albertina Mathilda 132–134, 312
Zengerlein, Jakob 133
Zola, Emil 237
Zschokke, Heinrich 210

Åberg, Johan Olof 208, 210, 231, 284, 287
Åhlberg, Maria Susanna 311

Öhman, A. C. 176

Index of Place Names

Aho Farm (Kivijärvi) 286, 314
Ahola Farm (Pylkönmäki) 120, 312
Alajärvi 57, 105–106, 128, 153, 164, 192, 200, 266, 270–271
Alavus 104, 286
Alexandria 81, 83
Anjala 87, 310
Asia Minor 81
Askola 310

Balkan 296
Baltic countries 17, 248
Bern 324–325
Bornholm 252
Boston 10
Breitenfeld 222
Britain 9, 17, 66, 68, 74–75, 85–86, 90–91, 93–94, 155, 157, 206, 217, 232, 236, 322, 324

Calumet 312
Caucasus 233
Central Finland 34–35, 43–44, 47, 58, 60, 69–71, 76–77, 79, 83, 99–102, 104–106, 108–110, 113–116, 119–120, 126–129, 150, 152, 154, 156, 158–159, 167, 178, 181, 183, 189, 200, 218–219, 243, 254–255, 258, 263, 271, 293, 296, 299, 313, 315
Central Ostrobothnia 57, 71, 105, 129
Copenhagen 85, 97
Crimea 299, 323

Denmark 9, 18, 75, 82, 85, 93, 97, 222, 251, 324–325
Dover 133

Eastern Bailiwick of Mustasaari (Korsholm) 114
Eckerö 88
Edinburgh 221
Egypt 81
England 74–75, 84, 86, 93, 97, 322
Enonkoski 117, 119, 310
Estonia 230
Europe 9, 12, 14, 17, 19–20, 24, 31, 54–55, 58, 60, 62, 68, 77, 79, 81, 83, 85, 89, 91, 98, 112, 134, 211, 221–222, 227, 240, 245, 248, 302, 308, 324
Evijärvi 105–106, 153

France 9, 16, 59, 63, 81, 84–85, 90, 134–135, 138, 155, 165, 206, 217, 233, 236–237, 245, 247, 274, 324

Germany 59, 66, 83–86, 90–91, 206, 211, 214, 217, 221, 223, 236–237, 241, 321
Great Britain 123, 236
Gulf of Bothnia 113–115, 122, 176

Haapajärvi 272, 315
Haapamäki 253
Haapaniemi 109
Halikko 133, 312
Halle 214
Hammarland 88
Hankasalmi 110, 154, 189
Haparanda 176
Harjavalta 107
Heinjoki 88
Heinolahti 121
Heinävesi 122
Helsinki 28, 43, 47, 56, 58, 68, 86, 88, 90–92, 98–99, 112, 119, 121, 140,

144, 157, 164, 168, 173, 175–177, 185, 187–188, 209, 211, 226, 236, 238, 247, 250, 252–253, 255–256, 281, 286, 296, 311, 313, 321
Hiekka Farm (Kannonkoski) 286
Hiitola Farm (Kivijärvi) 171, 171n, 271–272, 275, 314
Hilmonkoski 127
Hirvensalmi 111, 311, 313
Hoikanperä 273
Hollola 311
Huopana 109, 127
Hämeenlinna 68, 225, 274, 296
Hännilä(nkylä) 100, 120, 312

Iceland 9, 18, 246, 248
Ii 313
Ilmajoki 104, 258, 311
Ilmolahti 109
Inari 313
Inha Sawmill 115
Ireland 9, 74
Isojoki 104
Isokylä 168
Isokyrö 85, 104
Italy 81, 240

Jalasjärvi 104, 161n
Japan 80
Jauhoniemi 106, 123
Joutsa 110
Jyväskylä 29, 43, 49, 56, 58, 60, 68, 70, 92, 99, 108–110, 112, 122, 129, 144, 147–150, 162, 175, 177–178, 181, 190, 207, 219, 235, 254–255, 280–281, 286, 296, 301, 306, 310–311, 313–314
Jämsä 76, 102, 109–110, 113
Jääski 311

Kaavi 282, 313
Kangas Farm (Kivijärvi) 260
Kangasala 45, 161n, 163n
Kannonkoski 56–57, 57n, 70, 113–117, 119–123, 125–127, 130, 153, 213, 253, 271–273, 310, 312, 315–317
Kannonsaha 57, 57n, 103, 105, 110, 113, 115, 119–120, 122, 124, 126–127, 130–131, 142, 145, 159, 275, 281, 284–285, 295–296, 299, 303, 310, 312
Karelia 88, 119, 234
Karlstad 95
Karstula 43–44, 46–47, 57–58, 60, 77, 79, 101–103, 105–106, 109–110, 114–

115, 120, 127–128, 140, 152–153, 159, 161, 178, 200n, 243, 253, 257, 259, 265, 273–274, 276, 281, 285, 296, 299, 312, 314–315
Karunki 314
Kauhajoki 104
Kauhajärvi 129
Keiteleenpohja 109
Kerimäki 119, 274, 285, 310
Keuruu 101, 104, 109–111, 167, 200, 274, 286, 293, 302
Kiihtelysvaara 310
Kiikka 226
Kiminki 109, 115
Kinnula 56–58, 61, 77, 122, 149, 152, 159, 173, 253, 266, 273, 281–282, 294, 312, 314
Kinnulanlahti Bay 115
Kivijärvi (lake) 61, 73, 113, 115, 127
Kivijärvi (village, in Soini) 106
Kivikko Farm (Kannonkoski) 281, 286
Kokemäki 107
Kokkila (Viitasaari) 128
Kokkola 57, 85, 114, 225, 252, 254, 315
Kolkanniemi 261
Konginkangas 109–110
Kontiolahti 119
Korpilahti 71, 108–110
Korsnäs 104
Kortesjärvi 106
Koskenpää 110
Kotila Farm (Kivijärvi) 142
Kruunupyy 104
Kuhakoski 117
Kuhmoinen 109–110
Kuivaniemi 281
Kungsbacka 133
Kuopio 58, 89, 120, 149, 176, 207, 209, 263, 274, 281–282, 314–315
Kuoppala 126
Kurikka 311
Kuusamo 313
Kymijoki (river) 116
Kyyjärvi 57, 106, 109–110, 159

Lahdenperä 273
Laihia 85, 104, 168
Lake District of Ostrobothnia 104–105
Lapland 241
Lappajärvi 105–106, 129, 153
Lappee 89, 158, 187
Lappeenranta 158, 187
Lapväärtti 104
Laukaa 110–112, 116, 120, 311, 315

Lauttamäki Farm (Karstula) 120, 312
Lehtimäki 105–106, 153
Leipzig 219
Leivonmäki 110
Leppälä Farm (Kannonkoski) 125, 314
Leppälänkylä 44, 47, 49, 57, 57n, 106, 123–126, 138, 151, 174, 193, 272–273, 276–277, 286, 296–297, 314–315
Leppävirta 312
Lesogorsky 311
Lestijokivarsi 115
Liperi 119
Lohtaja 122, 252–253
Lokakylä 171, 271–273, 275, 314
London 83, 155
Louisiana 60
Loviisa 311
Luhanka 110
Lähde Farm (Kivijärvi) 312

Michigan 311
Middle East 81
Mikkeli 154, 215, 243, 313
Mississippi River 59
Muhola 173
Mulikka 109
Mulikka Farm (Pylkönmäki) 126
Multia 102, 110
Munsala 104
Mustasaari 104
Muurame 110
Myllykoski 115
Myllymäki 58, 129, 253
Myllyperä 273
Mänttä 110
Mötönkylä 109

Naantali 82
Nastola 311
Nivala 178n, 231, 293
Nordic countries 9–10, 12, 15–21, 24–25n, 36, 42, 54–55, 58, 69, 75, 82, 91, 93, 97–98, 160, 214, 232–233, 237, 244–245, 248, 299, 303, 308, 320, 324
North America 9–10, 14, 20, 33, 77, 79, 84, 156, 220, 236, 287, 322
Northern Central Finland 25, 32, 42, 57, 76, 114–116, 126–128, 148, 158, 173, 238, 241, 253, 258, 264
Northern Europe 12, 16, 31, 58, 321
Northern Karelia 152, 169, 180
Northern Ostrobothnia 71, 258, 293
Norway 9, 17–18, 85, 93, 97, 154, 185, 200, 324

Nurmes 154
Närpiö 85, 315

Ockelbo 133
Oinoskylä 273
Orisberg 311
Orimattila 108, 311–313
Oslo 97
Ostrobothnia 57, 71, 79, 93, 114–115, 249, 252, 254
Oulu 89, 161, 176, 311, 313, 315

Pajamäki (Kivijärvi) 71, 144, 189
Paris 82–83
Patama Farm (Pylkönmäki) 129, 158
Pelkjärvi 274
Penttilä Farm (Kivijärvi) 145, 171
Penttilänkylä 145, 171, 195, 273
Perho 103, 105–106, 114, 133–134, 139, 153, 174, 273, 312
Petäjävesi 110
Philadelphia 84
Pielavesi 281
Pietarsaari 113–115, 315
Pihlajavesi 110, 264
Pihtipudas 57, 105–106, 110, 120, 127, 159
Pohja 87
Poland 90
Pori 89, 92, 161, 242, 260
Porvoo 108, 110, 146, 176, 180, 186, 209, 261, 311, 315
Province of Uusimaa 251
Province of Vaasa 57, 104–106, 115, 120, 122, 133, 166, 197, 294, 313
Province of Vyborg 89
Pudasjärvi 70, 122, 173, 281, 286
Purala Farm (Kivijärvi) 259
Puralankylä 273
Purontaus (Saarenkylä, Kinnula) 286
Pylkönmäki 57, 61n, 105–106, 109–110, 120, 126–129, 158–159, 264, 312
Päijänne (lake) 116
Pälkäne 76, 226
Pääjärvi 120, 243, 312

Raahe 89
Raisio 312
Raja-aho 109
Rasi Farm (Kivijärvi) 195
Rauhala (Kivijärvi) 132
Rauma 89, 92, 242
Rautalampi 110, 112, 120, 128, 218, 311–312

Reisjärvi 311
Revonlahti 314
Ristiina 311
Risuperä 273
Rome 81
Rovaniemi 45n, 161n
Ruovesi 313
Russia 15–16, 31, 33, 68, 75, 78, 80–81, 122, 176, 179, 209, 231, 233–234, 236, 276, 298, 311, 320, 323–324

Saarenkylä 273, 286
Saarijärvi 43–44, 46, 49, 57–58, 60, 71, 100–106, 109–110, 114, 116, 120–122, 127–129, 140, 149–150, 153–154, 157, 159, 161, 167, 169, 175, 178, 193–195, 200, 203, 211, 218, 222, 238, 253–254, 259–264, 273, 285, 296, 299, 312, 314
Saimaa Canal 118
Saint Petersburg 68, 118, 252
Salamajärvi 77, 114, 133, 133n, 139, 312
Sammatti 313
Saramäki 50
Saunakylä 273
Saunamäki (Kyyjärvi) 109
Savitaipale 120, 312
Savonia 57, 117, 119, 215
Scandinavia 217, 222, 236
Scotland 74, 93, 221
Seinäjoki 146, 154, 157
Seppälä Farm (Kivijärvi) 121, 159–160, 312
Siuntio 226
Skaraborg 120
Sodankylä 311
Soini 105–106, 128, 153
Somero 313
Sortavala 145, 311
Southern Ostrobothnia 58, 85, 94n, 104–106, 120, 125, 129, 146, 154, 168, 192, 258
Southern Ostrobothnian Lake District 57, 105, 127
Stockholm 97, 111n, 132–134, 176, 215, 267, 283
Sumiainen 99, 110, 112, 120, 312
Suovanlahti 109
Sweden 9, 15–18, 22, 24, 28–29, 54, 62, 64, 68, 73, 75, 82–85, 87–88, 90–91, 93, 95, 97, 103, 112, 120, 129, 133–134, 136n, 154, 157, 160, 176–177, 182, 209, 212, 214–215, 222–223, 230, 236, 244, 246–248, 250–251, 280, 298, 320–322, 324–325
Sydänmaa Farm, Tiiro (Kivijärvi) 312
Sysmä 120
Säynetkoski 117–118, 123
Sörnäinen 144

Taasila Farm (Kinnula) 286
Taipale Farm (Saarijärvi) 100
Takkala Farm (Karstula) 281
Talviainen 271–272
Talviaislahti 273
Tarvaala 101, 157
Tampere 45, 58, 92, 182, 190, 280, 310, 312
Taulumäki 60
Tavastia 120, 252
Tenhola (parish) 276–277
Tenhola Farm (Kivijärvi) 159
Teuva 104, 313
Tiironkylä 159–160, 275, 284, 312
Tohmajärvi 219
Toholampi 128
Tornio 89
Turku 23, 58, 65, 68, 70, 82–83, 85–86, 88, 92, 98, 107, 110–111n, 161, 176, 209, 213, 249, 261, 269, 313, 320–322
Tuusniemi 314
Tyrvää 226
Töyrenperä 273

Umeå 24
Ummeljoki 310
United Kingdom 156
United States 9, 16–17, 39n, 60, 66, 80, 86, 91, 93–94, 134–135, 148–149, 155, 185–186, 206, 224, 236, 302, 312
Uskela 133
Uskila 314
Utra 119
Uurainen 110, 259
Uusikaarlepyy 311

Vaasa 43, 56, 58, 60, 84–86, 92, 119, 133, 146, 206–207, 209, 260, 263, 285, 310–313, 315
Vadstena 82
Vanaja 313
Vilppula 315
Vimpeli 104–106, 129, 153
Viitasaari 43, 57, 70, 72–73, 76, 83, 99, 102–106, 109–111, 113–114, 116, 120, 122, 125, 127–129, 145, 149,

152–153, 159, 178, 218, 268, 296, 310, 312, 314–315, 319
Vuoskoski 127
Vyborg 23n, 87–89, 88n, 98, 115–119, 122, 190, 209, 310, 321
Värmland 95

Wales 74–75
Western Europe 14, 16, 20, 31, 39, 58, 122, 324

Wittenberg 23

Ylihärmä 129
Yläpää 273

Åland Islands 88, 313, 323

Ähtäri 58, 115, 253
Äspö 160, 280
Äänekoski 110

Studia Fennica Ethnologica

Memories of My Town
The Identities of Town Dwellers and Their Places in Three Finnish Towns
Edited by Anna-Maria Åström, Pirjo Korkiakangas & Pia Olsson
Studia Fennica Ethnologica 8
2004

Passages Westward
Edited by Maria Lähteenmäki & Hanna Snellman
Studia Fennica Ethnologica 9
2006

Defining Self
Essays on emergent identities in Russia Seventeenth to Nineteenth Centuries
Edited by Michael Branch
Studia Fennica Ethnologica 10
2009

Touching Things
Ethnological Aspects of Modern Material Culture
Edited by Pirjo Korkiakangas, Tiina-Riitta Lappi & Heli Niskanen
Studia Fennica Ethnologica 11
2008

Gendered Rural Spaces
Edited by Pia Olsson & Helena Ruotsala
Studia Fennica Ethnologica 12
2009

LAURA STARK
The Limits of Patriarchy
How Female Networks of Pilfering and Gossip Sparked the First Debates on Rural Gender Rights in the 19th-century Finnish-Language Press
Studia Fennica Ethnologica 13
2011

Where is the Field?
The Experience of Migration Viewed through the Prism of Ethnographic Fieldwork
Edited by Laura Hirvi & Hanna Snellman
Studia Fennica Ethnologica 14
2012

LAURA HIRVI
Identities in Practice
A Trans-Atlantic Ethnography of Sikh Immigrants in Finland and in California
Studia Fennica Ethnologica 15
2013

EERIKA KOSKINEN-KOIVISTO
Her Own Worth
Negotiations of Subjectivity in the Life Narrative of a Female Labourer
Studia Fennica Ethnologica 16
2014

Studia Fennica Folkloristica

PERTTI J. ANTTONEN
Tradition through Modernity
Postmodernism and the Nation-State in Folklore Scholarship
Studia Fennica Folkloristica 15
2005

Narrating, Doing, Experiencing
Nordic Folkloristic Perspectives
Edited by Annikki Kaivola-Bregenhøj, Barbro Klein & Ulf Palmenfelt
Studia Fennica Folkloristica 16
2006

MÍCHEÁL BRIODY
The Irish Folklore Commission 1935–1970
History, ideology, methodology
Studia Fennica Folkloristica 17
2008

VENLA SYKÄRI
Words as Events
Cretan Mantinádes in Performance and Composition
Studia Fennica Folkloristica 18
2011

Hidden Rituals and Public Performances
Traditions and Belonging among the Post-Soviet Khanty, Komi and Udmurts
Edited by Anna-Leena Siikala & Oleg Ulyashev
Studia Fennica Folkloristica 19
2011

Mythic Discourses
Studies in Uralic Traditions
Edited by Frog, Anna-Leena Siikala & Eila Stepanova
Studia Fennica Folkloristica 20
2012

CORNELIUS HASSELBLATT
Kalevipoeg Studies
The Creation and Reception of an Epic
Studia Fennica Folkloristica 21
2016

Studia Fennica Historica

Medieval History Writing and Crusading Ideology
Edited by Tuomas M. S. Lehtonen & Kurt Villads Jensen with Janne Malkki and Katja Ritari
Studia Fennica Historica 9
2005

Moving in the USSR
Western anomalies and Northern wilderness
Edited by Pekka Hakamies
Studia Fennica Historica 10
2005

DEREK FEWSTER
Visions of Past Glory
Nationalism and the Construction of Early Finnish History
Studia Fennica Historica 11
2006

Modernisation in Russia since 1900
Edited by Markku Kangaspuro & Jeremy Smith
Studia Fennica Historica 12
2006

SEIJA-RIITTA LAAKSO
Across the Oceans
Development of Overseas Business Information Transmission 1815–1875
Studia Fennica Historica 13
2007

Industry and Modernism
Companies, Architecture and Identity in the Nordic and Baltic Countries during the High-Industrial Period
Edited by Anja Kervanto Nevanlinna
Studia Fennica Historica 14
2007

CHARLOTTA WOLFF
Noble conceptions of politics in eighteenth-century Sweden (ca 1740–1790)
Studia Fennica Historica 15
2008

Sport, Recreation and Green Space in the European City
Edited by Peter Clark, Marjaana Niemi & Jari Niemelä
Studia Fennica Historica 16
2009

Rhetorics of Nordic Democracy
Edited by Jussi Kurunmäki & Johan Strang
Studia Fennica Historica 17
2010

Fibula, Fabula, Fact
The Viking Age in Finland
Edited by Joonas Ahola & Frog with Clive Tolley
Studia Fennica Historica 18
2014

Novels, Histories, Novel Nations
Historical Fiction and Cultural Memory in Finland and Estonia
Edited by Linda Kaljundi, Eneken Laanes & Ilona Pikkanen
Studia Fennica Historica 19
2015

JUKKA GRONOW & SERGEY ZHURAVLEV
Fashion Meets Socialism
Fashion industry in the Soviet Union after the Second World War
Studia Fennica Historica 20
2015

SOFIA KOTILAINEN
Literacy Skills as Local Intangible Capital
The History of a Rural Lending Library c. 1860–1920
Studia Fennica Historica 21
2016

Studia Fennica Anthropologica

On Foreign Ground
Moving between Countries and Categories
Edited by Marie-Louise Karttunen & Minna Ruckenstein
Studia Fennica Anthropologica 1
2007

Beyond the Horizon
Essays on Myth, History, Travel and Society
Edited by Clifford Sather & Timo Kaartinen
Studia Fennica Anthropologica 2
2008

TIMO KALLINEN
Divine Rulers in a Secular State
Studia Fennica Anthropologica 3
2016

Studia Fennica Linguistica

Minimal reference
The use of pronouns in Finnish and Estonian discourse
Edited by Ritva Laury
Studia Fennica Linguistica 12
2005

ANTTI LEINO
On Toponymic Constructions as an Alternative to Naming Patterns in Describing Finnish Lake Names
Studia Fennica Linguistica 13
2007

Talk in interaction
Comparative dimensions
Edited by Markku Haakana, Minna Laakso & Jan Lindström
Studia Fennica Linguistica 14
2009

Planning a new standard language
Finnic minority languages meet the new millennium
Edited by Helena Sulkala & Harri Mantila
Studia Fennica Linguistica 15
2010

LOTTA WECKSTRÖM
Representations of Finnishness in Sweden
Studia Fennica Linguistica 16
2011

TERHI AINIALA, MINNA SAARELMA & PAULA SJÖBLOM
Names in Focus
An Introduction to Finnish Onomastics
Studia Fennica Linguistica 17
2012

Registers of Communication
Edited by Asif Agha & Frog
Studia Fennica Linguistica 18
2015

KAISA HÄKKINEN
Spreading the Written Word
Mikael Agricola and the Birth of Literary Finnish
Studia Fennica Linguistica 19
2015

Studia Fennica Litteraria

Metaliterary Layers in Finnish Literature
Edited by Samuli Hägg, Erkki Sevänen & Risto Turunen
Studia Fennica Litteraria 3
2008

Aino Kallas
Negotiations with Modernity
Edited by Leena Kurvet-Käosaar & Lea Rojola
Studia Fennica Litteraria 4
2011

The Emergence of Finnish Book and Reading Culture in the 1700s
Edited by Cecilia af Forselles & Tuija Laine
Studia Fennica Litteraria 5
2011

Nodes of Contemporary Finnish Literature
Edited by Leena Kirstinä
Studia Fennica Litteraria 6
2012

White Field, Black Seeds
Nordic Literacy Practices in the Long Nineteenth Century
Edited by Anna Kuismin & M. J. Driscoll
Studia Fennica Litteraria 7
2013

LIEVEN AMEEL
Helsinki in Early Twentieth-Century Literature
Urban Experiences in Finnish Prose Fiction 1890–1940
Studia Fennica Litteraria 8
2014

Novel Districts
Critical Readings of the Works of Monika Fagerholm
Edited by Kristina Malmio & Mia Österlund
Studia Fennica Litteraria 9
2016

www.ingramcontent.com/pod-product-compliance
Lightning Source LLC
Chambersburg PA
CBHW080756300426
44114CB00020B/2739